Strategic Information Systems and Technologies in Modern Organizations

Caroline Howard
HC Consulting, USA

Kathleen Hargiss
Colorado Technical University, USA

A volume in the Advances in Business Information Systems and Analytics (ABISA) Book Series

www.igi-global.com

Published in the United States of America by
IGI Global
Information Science Reference (an imprint of IGI Global)
701 E. Chocolate Avenue
Hershey PA, USA 17033
Tel: 717-533-8845
Fax: 717-533-8661
E-mail: cust@igi-global.com
Web site: http://www.igi-global.com

Library of Congress Cataloging-in-Publication Data

Names: Howard, Caroline, 1953- editor. | Hargiss, Kathleen, 1948- editor.
Title: Strategic information systems and technologies in modern organizations / Caroline Howard and Kathleen Hargiss, editors.
Description: Hershey, PA : Information Science Reference, [2017] | Includes bibliographical references and index.
Identifiers: LCCN 2016045749| ISBN 9781522516804 (hardcover) | ISBN 9781522516811 (ebook)
Subjects: LCSH: Information technology--Management. | Management information systems.
Classification: LCC HD30.2 .S7877 2017 | DDC 658.4/038011--dc23 LC record available at https://lccn.loc.gov/2016045749

This book is published in the IGI Global book series Advances in Business Information Systems and Analytics (ABISA) (ISSN: 2327-3275; eISSN: 2327-3283)

British Cataloguing in Publication Data
A Cataloguing in Publication record for this book is available from the British Library.

All work contributed to this book is new, previously-unpublished material. The views expressed in this book are those of the authors, but not necessarily of the publisher.

For electronic access to this publication, please contact: eresources@igi-global.com.

Table of Contents

Section 2
Strategic Information Applications: Interorganizational Systems

Section 3
Strategic Information Technologies and Applications at the Societal Level: Influences and Ecosystems

Detailed Table of Contents

Social cognitive theory is founded on the belief that learning is shared socially. Triadic reciprocal determinism explains the interrelationship and interaction between environmental cues, behavior, and biological determinants to shape and alter the perception of the self and how individuals assume agentic perspectives in social interactions to approach challenges and pursue goals. Knowing how learners perceived their likelihood to achieve success also provides for a better understanding of the constraints and opportunities of a proposed learning solution. The purpose of this study was to explore the self-efficacy beliefs of adolescents as part of the analysis of the learners in the instructional design system (ISD) model in terms of entry behaviors for the design of a peer tutoring learning environment. The General Self-Efficacy Scale (GSE) was used to interview participants, using the questions as open-ended questions. Observations of the social interactions between participants were collected during focus groups to discuss their responses to the GSE scale. The results of this study suggested that individuals with high self-efficacy not only assume a direct personal agentic perspective when acting alone but that they also assume and motivate others to engage in a collective agentic perspective. Individuals with low self-efficacy assume proxy or surrogate agentic perspectives in social interactions and require prompting to engage and participate. High self-efficacy indicates effective collaboration through the collective agency, which affects success positively in a peer tutoring learning environment. Low self-efficacy affects negatively success in peer tutoring, because individuals with low self-efficacy assume a proxy or surrogate agentic perspective detaching themselves from the interactions. However, individuals with low self-efficacy, through prompting and motivation from peers with high self-efficacy can improve their interactions and as goals are reached, improve self-efficacy.

Advanced persistent threats (APTs) have become a big problem for computer systems. Databases are vulnerable to these threats and can give attackers access to an organizations sensitive data. Oracle databases are at greater risk due to their heavy use as back-ends to corporate applications such as enterprise resource planning software. This chapter will describe a methodology for finding APTs hiding or operating deep within an Oracle database system. Using an understanding of Oracle normal operations provides a baseline to assist in discovering APT behavior. Incorporating these and other techniques such as database activity monitoring, machine learning, neural networks and honeypots/tokens can create a database intrusion detection system capable of finding these threats.

A gravitational motor interact with the locally gravitational field in order to produce a linear and/or rotational thrust able to move in space a given vehicle. The big advantages of such a motor are the facts

Section 3
Strategic Information Technologies and Applications at the Societal Level: Influences and Ecosystems

Information and communication technology (ICT) is continuously setting the pace for a changing, competitive and dynamic global marketplace and representing an enabling platform for business and socioeconomic development. The impact of ICT adoption, diffusion and adoption can go well beyond being a state-of the-art infrastructure; it can have concrete impact on development. ICT strategy development from start to finish, from design to implementation should cater to the different needs of the community whether it is societal, economic, business and political with an aim to realize universal access to optimize the impact in terms of scalability and sustainability. Building the ICT infrastructure and infostructure will not realize quantum leaps in the development process unless it is coupled with concrete projects and initiatives that engage the society at large with its multiple stakeholders from public, private, government and civil society organizations irrespective of their locations whether urban or remote, gender or background. This chapter describes the evolution of the ICT sector in Egypt with an emphasis on national ICT strategy development across its different design and implementation phases as an integral element of Egypt's overall development process within the context of an emerging economy.

One of the main characteristics of the global economy is the creation of oligopolistic markets. The decisions of those industries are characterised by interactivity. The risk arising from the domination of the power of oligopoly is the previous stage of manipulation of the market. This situation is against the concept of competitiveness and causes an entirely new situation to the customer's disadvantage. Mobile industry which is a typical oligopolistic market in Europe leads us to examine this specific market in Greece. Therefore, the present study examines the factors that influence the relationship marketing strategy of the industry. The research was conducted using a sample of 806 users of mobile phones. The method used for the quantitative analysis is chi-square test, discriminant analysis, which is based on Multivariate Analysis of Variance (MANOVA). The study has indicated that intense competition between mobile phone firms in Greece leads to the manipulation of consumers' behaviour. Also, findings of the current research demonstrate that firms create a unified policy in order to restrain their customers' consuming behaviour to a state of inertia, the customer passively re-buys the same service provider without much thought.

Knowledge management system (KMS) is capable of capturing explicit knowledge and tacit knowledge in a systematic manner. As any type of organization scales up, the issue in relation to, how to construct an effective knowledge sharing mechanism in KMS to covert individual knowledge into collective knowledge remains under surveyed. The rising concerns especially focus on the identification of individual knowledge worker, how firms facilitate knowledge sharing and the effectiveness of national knowledge management system. Communities of Practice (CoPs) are well known as effective mechanism to foster knowledge sharing theoretically and practically. This paper aims to explore the journey of CoPs driven KMS from the lens of individuals, firms' business strategies to the perspectives of national interest. On individual level, knowledge nodes are explored in the context of knowledge flow, which often transcend organizational boundaries and are distinct and different than workflow models. Thus, a CoPs centered knowledge flow model in a multinational organization is developed, implemented, and analyzed. On firm level, this model is underpinned in a CoPs framework built around four expected firms' major business strategies including four dimensions and sixteen criteria as a comprehensive mechanism to intensify knowledge sharing effect. Finally, a conceptual model of KMS embedded national innovation system is also addressed.

Statistical modeling, deterministic optimization, heuristic scheduling procedures, and computer simulation enable the strategic design of service systems while considering complex interdependencies in system operations. Performance on multiple dimensions may be investigated under alternative physical configurations and operating procedures while accommodating time-varying mixes of traffic and demands for service. This paper discusses how analytical tools and a conceptual framework developed for inland waterway transportation were extended and applied to the more complex operating environment of commercial airports. Networks of staged queues constitute the conceptual framework and discrete-event simulation provides the integrating modeling platform. Within the simulation model, statistical models represent time-varying behavior, traffic intensity is adjusted, resources are allocated to system users, traffic is controlled according to prevailing conditions, and decision rules are tested in pursuit of optimal performance.

Preface

Strategic Information Systems and Technologies in Modern Organizations contains chapters that reflect organizational use of technologies and applications at all levels of organizations and society as a whole. As reflected in this and our earlier volume, *Strategic Adoption of Technological Innovations*, organizations of all types have used information technology at the firm level for many decades to improve operations, develop innovative processes and organizational forms, create new business models, compete globally, and much more. Both the prior volume and this one contain chapters focused on research and practice on the uses, development, and importance of information technology aimed at achieving organizational performance along with innovative uses of technology for a specific application. Both are comprehensive and collections that can be very useful for practitioners, scholars, academicians, researchers and other industry professionals in providing an understanding of information technology strategy and use in organizations.

Unlike our earlier volume, many of the chapters go beyond the use of technology to achieve organizational performance. The change in contents in this volume reflects the evolution of strategic information systems. Chapters in this volume expand the coverage to include inter-organizational collaboration and societal implementations that can potentially be strategic determinants nationally and internationally.

The first section, "Strategic Information Systems: Organizational Level," focuses on the application of strategic technology at the organizational level. The section begins with Neeta Baporikar's chapter, "IT Strategic Planning through CSF Approach in Modern Organizations," which describes the wide range of interrelated components influencing IT strategy and develops a holistic effective strategic planning process using a CSF approach. Next, Nicolas A. Valcik describes uses for Geospatial Information Systems (GIS), focusing on the use of GIS at a major university for strategic planning in "Using Geospatial Information Systems for Strategic Planning and Institutional Research for Higher Education Institutions." In "Exploring Local Interaction Attributes Affecting Leadership Effectiveness on Assignment in Multinational Companies: A Qualitative Phenomenological Study," Iván Tirado-Cordero and Kathleen M. Hargiss report on research exploring the complex relationships and interactions among environmental cues, biological, and behavioral determinants that influence the way individuals approach challenges and pursue goals.

Other chapters in this section focus on individual standalone applications that can be used by organizations and individuals. In "Detecting Advanced Persistent Threats in Oracle Databases: Methods and Techniques," Lynn Ray and Henry Felch present methods to help detect Advanced Persistent Threats (APT) hiding in Oracle databases. Dan Cuilin focuses on producing a linear and/or rotational thrust engine through the interaction of the local gravitational field and motor to produce movement in "About

Gravitational (Inertial) Motors." The chapters in Section 1 are oriented more towards individual organizations rather than the broader applications in the next two sections.

Strategic technologies and applications among and between are the focus of Section 2, "Strategic Information Applications: Interorganizational Systems." The section begins with "The Role of Knowledge Management Strategies in Cooperation Agreements" in which Mario J. Donate, Jesús D. Sánchez de Pablo, Fátima Guadamillas, and María Isabel González-Ramos use a case study to research the role of knowledge management strategies in alliances. In "Online Real Estate Demand Chain Integration," Emna Cherif describes how strategic information technology can integrate supply chain functions. In "E-Business and Analytics Strategy in Franchising," Ye-Sho Chen, Chuanlan Liu, Qingfeng Zeng, and Renato F. L. Azevedo describe the global growth strategy of a new business model and franchising in emerging markets. Roumen Vragov's chapter, "The Human Behavioral Response to Automated Trading," discusses how computer algorithms are being increasingly used by human traders in markets and can create bias.

In Section 3, "Strategic Information Technologies and Applications at the Societal Level: Influences and Ecosystems," the chapters reflect how strategic use of information technology also has the potential to change society. Specifically, the chapters demonstrate how technology can be used by governments and organizations to affect national and international stakeholders and environments. In "ICT Strategy Development: From Design to Implementation – Case of Egypt," Sherif Kamel and Nagla Rizk describe the information and communication technology (ICT) as an enabling platform for business and socioeconomic development using the case of Egypt to illustrate. Irene Samanta's chapter, "Gaining a Continuous Retaining Relationship with Customers in Mobile Sector," uses the mobile industry in Greece, a typical European oligopolistic market, to illustrate how customers are influenced. In "Knowledge Management System from Individual Firm to National Scale," Mei-Tai Chu describes how a knowledge management system (KMS) is capable of systematically capturing tacit and explicit knowledge, and that Communities of Practice are an effective mechanism for sharing knowledge at all levels.

SECTION 1: STRATEGIC INFORMATION SYSTEMS – ORGANIZATIONAL LEVEL

The chapters in the first chapter are described more fully below:

Neeta Baporikar's chapter, "IT Strategic Planning through CSF Approach in Modern Organizations," describes how the strategic planning efforts can be augmented by the critical success factor (CSF) method and uses the CSF method to provide an integrated framework to enable understanding of the wide range of interrelated influences of IT strategy development. The chapter provides an in-depth synthesis of theory, research, and literature review to develop a holistic and effective strategy planning process using a CSF approach.

In "Using Geospatial Information Systems for Strategic Planning and Institutional Research for Higher Education Institutions," Nicolas A. Valcik describes uses for Geospatial Information Systems (GIS), focusing on the use and implementation of GIS implementation and use of GIS at The University of Texas at Dallas in the Office of Strategic Planning and Analysis (OSPA). GIS add a geospatial component to the statistical and analytical tools typically used to provide data for assessing, developing or modifying institutional policies. Nicolas A. Valcik focuses on a suite of software which compiles and is useful for analyzing demographic data.

The chapter, "Exploring Local Interaction Attributes Affecting Leadership Effectiveness on Assignment in Multinational Companies: A Qualitative Phenomenological Study," by Iván Tirado-Cordero and Kathleen M. Hargiss discusses social cognitive theory as founded on the belief that learning is socially shared. The chapter, reports results of study exploring interactions and relationships among biological, environmental, and behavioral determinants of perceptions of self and agentic perspectives in social interactions to achieve goals and surmount challenges. The authors report a study that suggests individuals with high self-efficacy assume agentic perspectives acting alone and motivate others to engage in collective agentic perspectives.

Lynn Ray and Henry Felch provide a method to detect Advanced Persistent Threats (APT) hiding or operating deep in Oracle databases in "Detecting Advanced Persistent Threats in Oracle Databases: Methods and Techniques." In 21st century organizations, databases are vulnerable and can give attackers access to sensitive data. Heavy use as back-ends to organizational applications, including enterprise resource planning systems, makes Oracle databases at greater risk. Using this method along with machine learning, neural networks, honeypots/tokens, and database activity monitoring can be part of a systems for database intrusion detection.

In "About Gravitational (Inertial) Motors," Dan Cuilin describes how to produce a linear and/or rotational thrust through the interaction of a gravitational motor and the locally gravitational field for a vehicle to move in space. He describes how such a vehicle could be used for almost any kind of vehicle replacing the mechanics with the gravitational fields vehicle. Dan Cuilin describes how in space, a motor must be able to ensure the take-off and/or landing on any planet and carry the load.

SECTION 2: STRATEGIC INFORMATION APPLICATIONS – INTERORGANIZATIONAL SYSTEMS

Section 2 explores relationships among organizations in the following chapters:

In their chapter, "The Role of Knowledge Management Strategies in Cooperation Agreements," Mario J. Donate, Jesús D. Sánchez de Pablo, Fátima Guadamillas, and María Isabel González-Ramos provide a case study to analyze the role of knowledge management strategies (KMS) in alliances. The authors discuss how important designing an appropriate KMS in alliances among technological companies. The case study provides an analysis of KMS linking a Spanish technology-intensive company and innovation intensive businesses and conclude with a discussion of how cooperative agreements for KMS have been managed and implemented to support product diversification and technology development.

In "Online Real Estate Demand Chain Integration," Emna Cherif focuses on developing a simplified implementation architecture for a management system capable of bundling together advanced bundles to differentiate and enhance an online real estate value chain. The authors used an open source Customer Relationship Management system and integrated value-added modules from third-party providers. These along with the architecture that provides integrated demand and supply chain management.

Ye-Sho Chen, Chuanlan Liu, Qingfeng Zeng and Renato F. L. Azevedo focus on the increasingly popular global growth strategy of franchising in emerging markets and the emergence of a new business model in their chapter, "E-Business and Analytics Strategy in Franchising," which utilizes franchising for local responsiveness along with the power of the Internet for global demand-and-supply processes. The authors describe the important role of e-business and analytics strategy in growing and nurturing good relationships between franchisors

Roumen Vragov describes how computer algorithms are being increasingly used by human traders in markets. In the "The Human Behavioral Response to Automated Trading," the author proposes a theoretical model based on the idea that human beings introduce biases in commodity markets when they use automated trading. The chapter presents results of laboratory experiments to test the model predictions and show that human bias reduces the effectives of automated training.

SECTION 3: STRATEGIC INFORMATION TECHNOLOGIES AND APPLICATIONS AT THE SOCIETAL LEVEL – INFLUENCES AND ECOSYSTEMS

Strategic information systems with even broader application are describe in the following Section 3 chapters.

Sherif Kamel and Nagla Rizk's chapter, "ICT Strategy Development: From Design to Implementation – Case of Egypt," describes the *role of in*formation and communication technology (ICT) as an enabling platform for business and socioeconomic development in the competitive and dynamic global marketplace and how it can affect development so should cater to the different needs of the community with an aim of scalability and sustainability. To be effective, ICT must be combined with initiatives and concrete projects engaging society and its multiple stakeholders. The authors describe ICT evolution in Egypt, emphasizing IT strategy as a component of Egypt's development process. integral element of Egypt's overall development process within the context of an emerging economy.

Irene Samanta's chapter, "Gaining a Continuous Retaining Relationship with Customers in Mobile Sector," describes the creation of interactive oligopolistic markets in the global economy. Irene Samanta uses the oligopolistic market, the mobile industry in Greece, to examine influences of the relationship marketing strategy of the industry. Using quantitative analysis of 806 individuals to research how consumer's behaviour is influenced and found that firms create a unified policy so that customers passively re-buy the same service provider without a lot of thought.

The chapter, "Information Technologies and Analytical Models for Strategic Design of Transportation Infrastructure," describe how strategic design of service systems are enabled by deterministic optimization, computer simulation, scheduling procedures, and statistical modeling while allowing for complex interdependencies. L. Douglas Smith, Robert M. Nauss, Liang Xu, Juan Zhang, Jan Fabian Ehmke, and Laura Hellmann present the example of an extension and application to the more complex commercial airport operating environment of a conceptual framework and analytical tools developed for inland waterway transportation

Section 1

Strategic Information Systems:
Organizational Level

Chapter 1
IT Strategic Planning through CSF Approach in Modern Organizations

Neeta Baporikar
Namibia University of Science and Technology, Namibia

ABSTRACT

Although the purpose of strategic planning is straightforward - to outline where an organization wants to go and how it's going to get there - its nature is complex and dynamic. The, critical success factor (CSF) method, can augment strategic planning efforts by illuminating an organization's present situation and potential future. This chapter explores the value of enhancing typical strategic planning techniques with the CSF method and presents an integrated framework for helping modern organizations to understand the broad range of interrelated elements that influence strategy development for Information Technology (IT). The chapter synthesizes documented theory and research in strategic planning and CSFs. It also provides insights and lessons re the pros and cons of integrated strategic planning framework in the context of IT in modern organizations. Through in-depth literature review and contextual analysis, the chapter incorporates suggestions to modern organizations for IT Strategic Planning with CSF Approach for a holistic and effective strategic planning process.

INTRODUCTION

So many important matters can compete for one's attention when framing strategies especially information technology strategies in this ever changing and dynamic ICT world. This makes it often difficult to see the "wood for the trees". What's more, it can be extremely difficult to get everyone in the team pulling in the same direction and focusing on the true essentials. That's where CSFs can help especially in modern organizations which are becoming more and more complex because of networked economies. CSFs are the essential areas of activity that must be performed well if you are to achieve the mission, objectives or goals. By identifying CSFs, one can create a common point of reference to help in directing and measuring the success of any strategy, project or business. As a common point of reference, CSFs

DOI: 10.4018/978-1-5225-1680-4.ch001

help everyone in the team to know exactly what's most important which then helps people perform their own work in the right context and this creates to heave together towards the same overall aims. Thus in simple terms CSFs refer to identifying the things that really matter for success.

The idea of CSFs was first presented by D. Ronald Daniel in the 1960s. It was then built on and popularized a decade later by John F. Rockart, of MIT's Sloan School of Management, and has since been used extensively to help businesses implement their strategies and projects. Inevitably, the CSF concept has evolved, and you may have seen it implemented in different ways. This paper provides a simple definition and approach based on Rockart's original ideas. Rockart defined CSFs as: 'The limited number of areas in which results, if they are satisfactory, will ensure successful competitive performance for the organization'. They are the few key areas where things must go right for the business to flourish. If results in these areas are not adequate, the organization's efforts for the period will be less than desired. They are areas of activity that should receive constant and careful attention from management (Rockart 1979). CSFs are strongly related to the mission and strategic goals of any business or project. Whereas the mission and goals focus on the aims and what is to be achieved, CSFs focus on the most important areas and get to the very heart of both what and how to achieve.

BACKGROUND

Industry executives and analysts often mistakenly talk about strategy as if it were a chess game, but in a game there are just two opponents, each with identical resources, and with luck playing a minimal role. But the real world business and competition is different and certainly it is not a chess game – it is more than that. According to Moschella, D (1999), the real world is much more like a poker game, with multiple players trying to make the best of whatever hand fortune has dealt them. This paper explores the value of enhancing typical strategic planning with the critical success factor (CSF) method. It synthesizes documented theory and research in strategic planning, CSFs and proposes an information framework for enhanced strategic planning. The paper does not advocate or articulate a specific strategic planning approach, though theories are discussed and pointers to published methods are provided. Nor does the paper aim to document the CSF as a method; these are published elsewhere. (Caralli 2004; van der Heijden 1996)

CSF can augment strategic planning efforts by more deeply illuminating an organization's present situation and potential future. Critical success factors represent key performance areas that are essential for an organization to accomplish its mission. In addition, CSFs provide processes that help an organization establish strong ways of thinking, communicating, and making decisions. While future scenario and CSF methods have extensive histories with operational and strategic planning, neither method, on its own, constitutes a strategic planning effort, results in a strategy or strategic plan per se, or even has a direct, explicit interface with strategic planning. However, when used together within a strategic planning process, they noticeably enhance the process and the resulting strategic plan. According to a study by Esteves (2004), the critical success factors (CSF) approach has been established and popularized over the last 30 years by a number of researchers, particularly Rockart (1979). Today, the approach is increasingly used by consultants and IS departments as a means of support to IS strategic planning (Esteves, 2004). Ramaprasad and Williams (1998) underline this position by stating that "there is a great deal of attention devoted to the concept in the IS literature as many argue that the use of CSF can have a major impact on the design, development, and implementation of IS".

In literature, several definitions of CSF exist. Representing one of the most frequently cited definitions, Rockart (1979) uses ideas from Daniel (1961) and Anthony et al. (1972) in defining CSF as "the limited number of areas in which results, if they are satisfactory, will ensure successful competitive performance for the organization" (p. 85). Consequently, Rockart (1979) stresses, that these particular areas of activity should be constantly and carefully managed by a company. In a similar fashion, Bruno and Leidecker (1984) define CSF as "those characteristics, conditions or variables that, when properly sustained, maintained, or managed, can have a significant impact on the success of a firm competing in particular industry", while Pinto and Slevin (1987) regard CSF as "factors which, if addressed, significantly improve project implementation chances" (p. 22). According to Esteves (2004) however, both of these definitions fail to address the comprehensive concept proposed by Rockart (1979), which seeks to identify an ideal match between environmental conditions and business characteristics for a particular company. Within the field of strategic management, the definition of Key Success Factors (KSF) is closely related to the CSF concept. In this context, Ellegard and Grunert (1993) define KSF as a qualification or resource that a company can invest in, which in turn, accounts for a significant part of the observable differences in perceived value and/or relative costs in the companies' relevant markets. In literature, the terms CSF and KSF are often alternately used.

Thus, though the purpose of strategic planning is straightforward - to outline where an organization wants to go and how it's going to get there is complex and dynamic. The, critical success factor (CSF) method, can augment strategic planning efforts by illuminating an organization's present situation and potential future (Baporikar, 2013). This chapter explores the value of enhancing typical strategic planning techniques with the CSF method and presents an integrated framework for helping modern organizations to understand the broad range of interrelated elements that influence strategy development for Information Technology (IT). Critical success factors are defined as the handful of key areas where an organization must perform well on a consistent basis to achieve its mission (Baporikar, 2013). CSFs can be derived through a document review, analysis of the goals, objectives of key management personnel and interviews with individuals about their specific domain and the barriers they encounter in achieving their goals and objectives. The chapter synthesizes documented theory and research in strategic planning and CSFs and provides insights and lessons regarding the value and limitations of the integrated strategic planning framework in the context of IT in modern organizations. Through a method of in-depth literature review and contextual analysis, the chapter incorporates suggestions to modern organizations for IT Strategic Planning with CSF Approach for a holistic and effective strategic planning process.

CSF EVOLUTION

Research on CSF can be traced back to 1961, where Daniel (1961) first discussed "success factors" in management literature. In a broad approach, he focused on industry-related CSF which are relevant for any company in a particular industry. In 1972, Anthony et al. (1972) went a step further by emphasizing the need to tailor CSF to both a company's particular strategic objectives and its particular managers. Here, management planning and control systems are responsible for reporting those CSF that are perceived by the managers as relevant for a particular job and industry. Combining the perspective of both Daniel (1961) and Anthony et al. (1972), Rockart (1979) described a study on three organizations in 1979 which confirmed that organizations in the same industry may exhibit different CSF. The reasons for such a constellation are differences in geographic location and strategies among other factors.

Nevertheless, Rockart was also able to identify analogies between the CSF lists of the three examined organizations: "It is noticeable that the first four factors on the mature clinic's list also appear on the other two lists. (…) These, it can be suggested, are the all-encompassing industry-based factors. The remaining considerations, which are particular to one or the other of the practices but not to all, are generated by differences in environmental situation, temporal factors, geographic location, or strategic situation" (Rockart, 1979, p. 87).

In line with his initial study, Rockart (1982) gathered data in regard to IS executives. This data indicated that executives share a limited number of CSF. "Each executive (…) lists some, but not all, of the CSF gathered from the sample as a whole" (Zahedi, 1988, p. 190). The remaining differences were linked to organizational aspects as well as the time pressure facing the particular manager at the time the data was collected (Rockart, 1982). Furthermore, Rockart (1979) stressed that his approach did not attempt to address information needs related to the field of strategic planning. Instead, his CSF approach concentrates on information needs for management control and seeks to identify data which can be used to monitor and improve existing areas of business. In this context, Rockart (1979) follows Anthony's (1965) categorization of management activities into operational control, management control and strategic planning. However, it must be emphasized that Rockart (1979) limited his approach to management control which was precisely defined by Anthony (1965) as "the process of ensuring that resources are obtained and used effectively toward the attainment of corporate goals". Today, Rockart's (1979) CSF approach is particularly relevant within the limits of project management and IS implementation and therefore often used by IS executives. This is confirmed in a study conducted by Ramaprasad and Williams (1998), in which the results from 263 responses indicate the major areas in which the CSF approach is utilized: project management (63.49%), IS implementation (49.21%), and requirements (47.62%).

Dimensions of CSF

Reflecting the progress in research on CSF, several different CSF dimensions have emerged in literature over the course of the years. In the following, the most common six dimensions according to Esteves (2004) will be reviewed.

1. **Hierarchy vs. Group of CSF:** Rockart (1979) defines a specific hierarchy of CSF which is primarily based upon the organizational level at which the individual strategic issues are discussed. In line with this particular approach, CSF can be addressed on either an industry, corporate or sub-organizational level, thereby forming a certain type of CSF hierarchy within the organization (Rockart & Van Bullen, 1986). While a pre-defined level structure is dominant within the hierarchy suggested by Rockart, Barat (1992) argues that the hierarchy of CSF may also be built upon logical dependencies such as those existent between business aims and the factors influencing these aims. In addition, the hierarchical approach is extended to include groups of CSF. Here, either CSF for a group of organizations belonging to the same particular industry (industry CSF) or CSF for a group of managers in a particular role belonging to different organizations (occupational CSF) is identified. As a result, the idea of generic CSF for these particular groups is addressed (Esteves, 2004).
2. **Temporary vs. Ongoing CSF:** According to Ferguson and Khandewal (1999), CSF can be of either a temporary or ongoing nature. An example of an ongoing CSF is the existence of a project champion in top management, thereby influencing all phases of the project's implementation. On the contrary, the definition of the project scope represents a temporary CSF which is only regarded

critical for a certain period of time. In this context, Ferguson and Khandewal (1999) note that all CSF can be defined in a way that makes them temporary. However the CSF may differ in their individual degree of temporality, some spanning a larger timeframe than others. Consequently, the key is to recognize their individual relevance for different stages within a project's lifecycle.

3. **Internal vs. External CSF:** CSF can further be distinguished by the dimension of which they are internal or external to the particular organization or unit in which they are applied. Arce and Flynn (1997) state that "an internal CSF has related actions taken within the organization; while an external CSF has related actions performed outside the organization" (p. 312). As a result, internal CSF is linked to issues within a manager's range of control, whereas external CSF may not be exclusively controlled by the manager. According to Rockart (1979), the relevance of this CSF dimension is particularly high when determining the proper sources of information within a process of data collection.
4. **Building vs. Monitoring CSF:** Building and monitoring CSF refer, on the one hand, to the amount of control on the part of the management and, on the other hand, to the monitoring or building nature of the actions taken. According to Arce and Flynn (1997), "a monitoring CSF is concerned only with monitoring an existing organizational situation (whereas) a building CSF is concerned with changing the organization or with future planning" (p. 312). For instance, the maintenance of technological leadership would be a CSF which a company could build and control, while changing consumer demographics would represent a CSF which needs to be monitored and not controlled (Esteves, 2004). In a similar approach Rockart and Van Bullen (1986) distinguish between building CSF, used to achieve certain goals or implement a certain degree of change in performance, and monitoring CSF, used to monitor key issues over a larger time frame. Such long term monitoring is often closely related to the strategic and tactical CSF dimension (see below).
5. **Strategic vs. Tactical CSF:** This dimension focuses on the type of planning which takes place within an organization, thereby differentiating between strategic and tactical CSF. According to Esteves (2004), while strategic factors seek to identify which goals are to be achieved, the tactical factors describe possible alternatives in regard to how these goals can be met. Strategic factors, although based on opportunities, often contain a great amount of risk and, therefore, require long term planning primarily executed by senior executives. On the contrary, tactical factors deal with resources required to reach the goals described on the strategic level and only call for a short or medium term planning effort, most often performed by the middle management. According to Ward (1990), "there will normally be a mixture of tactical and strategic CSF. If they are all strategic, the business might founder in the short term while everybody concentrates on the blue skies ahead. Equally, if all CSF are tactical, the business might burn out like a super-nova" (p. 117).
6. **Perceived vs. Actual CSF:** The identified CSF in one organization do not necessarily apply to all other organizations. Rather, each individual company must align their CSF in accordance with their own specific goals and needs. This is where the final dimension comes into play, distinguishing between perceived and actual CSF. Initially proposed by Ellegard and Grunert (1993), the concept of perceived versus actual CSF could bring forth useful implications by shedding light on the knowledge concerning discrepancies between actual and perceived CSF. Experience in this field could, for instance, lead to more stable strategy formulations and implementations. Although the measuring of actual CSF is not possible, Dess and Robinson (1984) suggest a more frequent confrontation of key decision makers with these factors. By doing this, decision makers might win insight on their perceptions in regard to both truly relevant success factors and those which are only perceived as such.

Table 1. Research methods used for CSF identification

Action research Jenkins et al. (1999)
Case studies Gibson et al. (1999), Sumner (1999)
Delphi technique Atthirawong and McCarthy (2001), Brancheau et al. (1996)
Group interviewing Khandewal and Miller (1992)
Literature review Esteves and Pastor (2000), Umble and Umble (2001)
Multivariate analysis Dvir et al. (1996)
Scenario analysis Barat (1992)
Structured interviewing Rockart and Van Bullen (1986)

CSF IDENTIFICATION

In order to identify the relevant CSF, according to Esteves (2004), a wide array of research methods can be used (see Table 1). Among them are for instance the realization of case studies (e.g. Sumner, 1999), group interviews (e.g. Khandewal & Miller, 1992), structured interviews (Rockart & Van Bullen, 1986), as well as the analysis of relevant literature (e.g. Esteves & Pastor, 2000). According to Shah and Siddiqui (2002) the most frequently used method to identify success factors is the realization of a questionnaire.

CSF RELEVANCE

Pinto and Prescott (1988) argued that "the majority of the studies in the critical success factor research stream have been theoretical and have assumed a static view of the importance of various factors over the life of a project. In other words, a critical success factor was assumed to have the same degree of importance, throughout the life of a project" (p. 5). After having examined the criticality of CSF throughout the lifecycle of a project, they came to the conclusion that the degree of criticality of a CSF is subject to change during the different stages of a project lifecycle. Although the number of studies examining the relevance of CSF in regard to the individual phases of the project lifecycle has increased, most studies still remain limited to the sole identification of these CSF, not addressing their individual degree of relevance at all. Out of the more comprehensive studies addressing both the identification and the relevance, two different approaches can be found: The approach implemented by Pinto and Prescott (1988), for instance, is based upon the same set of CSF at all times, while examining their individual degree of criticality along the different project phases. In contrast, other studies have chosen to define different sets for CSF for each project phase. Although differently executed, both concepts generally tend to refer to the same set of CSF. According to Esteves (2004), in order to gain insight on CSF relevance, researchers most frequently use case studies as well as surveys based on interviews. Most of the time, participants are asked to either create a list of the most relevant CSF for each project phase or examine the relevance of individual CSF using a scale which indicates a low, normal or high relevance.

CSF PAYBACK

According to Rockart (1979, p. 87), the following benefits exist for managers when applying the CSF approach:

- "The process helps the manager to determine those factors on which he or she should focus management attention. It also helps to ensure that those significant factors will receive careful and continuous management scrutiny."
- "The process forces the manager to develop good measures for those factors and to seek reports on each of the measures."
- "The identification of CSF allows a clear definition of the amount of information that must be collected by the organization and limits the costly collection of more data than necessary."
- "The identification of CSF moves an organization away from the trap of building its reporting and information system primarily around data that are "easy to collect". Rather, it focuses attention to those data that might otherwise not be collected but are significant for the success of the particular management level involved."
- "The process acknowledges that some factors are temporal and that CSF are manager specific. This suggests that the IS should be in constant flux with the new reports being developed as needed to accommodate changes in the organization's strategy, environment or organization structure. Rather than changes in an IS being looked on as an indication of "inadequate design", they must be viewed as an inevitable and productive part of IS development."

However, according to Esteves (2004), the CSF concept itself can be used for more than only IS design. Current studies, suggesting a number of additional areas of assistance to the management process, reflect this.

STRATEGIC PLANNING

Strategic planning is the process of defining an organization's intentions for achieving its mission. There are many ways to conduct strategic planning, most of which result in a plan or set of plans that articulate organizational goals and a high-level strategy for achieving them. Division-level and organizational unit-level planning should be tied directly to the organization's strategic plan. Strategic planning is not only an important foundation for executing work; it also sets the stage for enterprise architecture, process improvement, risk management, portfolio management, and any other enterprise-wide initiatives. There are many documented approaches to strategic planning (e.g., Fogg 1994).

Strategic planning is the process of defining an organization's plans for achieving its mission. An organizational *strategy* is a derived approach to achieving that mission. The product of a strategic planning effort is typically a document (a *strategic plan*) that elaborates a high-level strategy and articulates the elements that influence it—it is a full description of the organizational environment and intentions. Note that a strategy is directional in nature; although descriptions and analysis of the present situation are included, a strategic plan does not merely endorse the status quo, and it directs change of some kind (Cassidy 2006). Division-level and organizational-unit-level planning should be tied directly to the organization's strategic plan. Strategic planning is not only an important foundation for executing work; it also sets the stage for enterprise architecture, process improvement, risk management, portfolio management, and any other enterprise-wide initiatives. There are many documented approaches to strategic planning (Fogg 1994). Typical strategic planning processes examine an organization's current environment and abilities (the present situation), considerations about how it would like to grow or evolve (the desired future), its aspirations as an organization (what it will strive to do), and its intentions for moving forward (how it will move forward).

These high-level elements are described below:

- **The What:** These are descriptions of what the organization does and what it aspires to achieve - its organizational targets - including its goals, objectives, and quantitative performance measures.
- **The Present:** The present situation, or current environment, is typically described in terms of the organization's mission, guiding principles (or values), organizational strengths (or enablers), and organizational barriers (weaknesses or challenges).
- **The Future:** The desired future is described by the organizational vision and targets.
- **The How:** The preferred route to achieving the organizational goals, objectives, and mission is communicated as a strategy or as strategic goals. Strategic goals typically reflect the primary goals of an organization or enterprise and imply a particular set of strategies.

STRATEGIC PLANNING ELEMENTS

A well-documented strategic plan is critically important for organizing thinking and communicating thoughts. Strategic plans include elements that describe an organization's present state, aspirations, and intentions for the future, and approach for going forward. Table 2 contains the definitions of the terms typically used to describe strategic planning elements.

Understanding these elements and their relationship to one another supports strategic thinking and planning, but also enhances the effective use of CSFs in strategic planning efforts.

Strategic Planning and Organizational Hierarchy

It is important when thinking about strategic planning to think about organizational hierarchy, both in terms of how the strategy will apply to the organization and in terms of the roles and responsibilities for planning. Table 3 presents model of organizational structure, used to organize enterprise architecture concepts. The model identifies three general levels common to most organizations: the institutional (or organizational) level, the managerial level, and the technical level (Thompson 1967, Bernard 2005).

Becoming more common is the organizational network model, where work is carried out by cooperative networks of local and remote individuals and teams. Teams are functionally based and locally managed, removing layers of organizational management. As a result, the teams are flexible and can change function, goals, or make-up as necessitated by internal or external influences (Bernard, 2005). Gunasekaran and Garets articulate some good criteria for strategic planning participation. A well formed strategic planning team should include - executive support and access, a representative microcosm of the organization, with multiple levels of management and an external perspective. (Gunasekaran, 2004) An empowered representative group is the best faction to conduct strategic planning. But strategic thinking must involve personnel at the highest level of an organization. It is not a low-level project or a delegated

Table 2. Strategic planning terms

Term	Definition
Mission	An organization's mission is its primary business or purpose; it describes what an organization does, for whom, and its benefit. The mission of an organization is not a time-bound objective.
Vision	A vision is an ideal that an organization intends to pursue. It links the organization to the future by articulating instantiations of successful execution of the mission. An organization's vision is a source of inspiration and can be broader than the organization's capabilities. It might, in fact, describe what can be achieved in a broader environment if the organization and others are successful in achieving their individual missions.
Goals	Goals are broad, measurable, aims that support the accomplishment of a mission.
Objectives	Objectives are specific, quantifiable, lower-level targets that indicate an accomplishment of a goal.
Guiding Principles	Guiding principles are directive statements that articulate the constraints an organization chooses to place upon the way it achieves its goals. Guiding principles embrace core values and are used to shape an organization's strategy. Guiding principles reflect long-term intentions, but are not necessarily permanent. A guiding principle may seem similar in content to a goal but it lacks measurable aims. A guiding principle can generate a goal when an organization chooses to commit resources to achieving a measurable result regarding its content.
Enablers	Enablers are external conditions or organizational strengths that facilitate an organization's ability to accomplish its goals or objectives.
Barriers	Barriers are external conditions or organizational (internal) weaknesses that hinder an organization's ability to accomplish a goal or objective.
Strategy	A strategy is a derived approach to achieving the mission, goals, and objectives of an organization. It supports the organizational vision, takes into account organizational enablers and barriers, and upholds its guiding principles.
Strategic Plan	A strategic plan is a document that results from a strategic planning activity. It elaborates the organizational strategy and documents the elements that influence it.
Initiative	An initiative is a specific set of actions that implement a strategy.
Actions	Actions are specific steps to achieve a goal or objective and typically have assigned staff and schedule constraints.
Performance Measures	Performance measures describe performance targets relevant to each objective.

Table 3. Model of organizational structure

Level	Organizational/Executive	Managerial	Technical
Purpose	Establish rules and relate to larger society, making possible the implementation of organizational goals.	Mediate between the organization and the task environment; administer internal affairs; provide resources.	Create the organizational product.
Activities	Interface with the external environment to determine the organizational domain and secure legitimacy.	Provide internal political mediation between the organizational levels.	Execute production and/or development functions; protect the production functions from external uncertainties.

Source: *Adapted from Bernard 2005, An Introduction to Enterprise Architecture -Parsons/Thompson Model of Organizational Structure.*

task. Without executive input there is insufficient knowledge and authority to do meaningful strategy setting (Baporikar, 2014a).

IT STRATEGY

Information technology is a resource for organizational and mission-specific requirements (Bernard 2005). In addition to being viewed as a resource for an organization, IT is commonly viewed as an enabler of the nonfunctional requirements, or quality attributes, of a system (e.g., reliability, availability, usability). IT strategy refers to a global level of thinking about IT and its integration with the rest of an organization. The ultimate goal of IT strategic planning is to provide a broad and stable vision of how IT contributes to the long-term success of the organization (Gunasekaran 2004). In today's environment, an organization's existence depends on the effective application of IT. As a result, organizations increasingly look to technology not only to support business opportunities, but also to create competitive advantage (Baporikar, 2014b, 2015 a). IT planning has coincidently been elevated from a tactical management tool to a strategic decision-making vehicle (Ward, 2002). As with organizational strategic planning, there are documented approaches to IT strategic planning (e.g., Cassidy, 2006). Critical success factors are defined as the handful of key areas where an organization must perform well on a consistent basis to achieve its mission. CSFs are typically derived through a documented review of the goals and objectives of key management personnel and interviews with those individuals about their specific domains and the barriers they encounter in achieving their goals and objectives. Levels of management introduce different types of operating environments and thus different levels of CSFs. Commonly identified CSF levels are:

- *Industry,*
- *Organizational,*
- *Division,*
- *Operational-unit* and
- *Individual.*

These labels are general terms that reflect most organizational hierarchies. There is a direct parallel between CSF hierarchy and a typical strategic planning hierarchy.

THE STRATEGY PARADOX

A common criticism of strategic planning is that it is overly involved with extrapolation of the past and present and can create the illusion of certainty regarding the future (Heracleous, 1998). The strategy paradox is the conflict that arises from the need to make operational commitments in the face of unavoidable strategic uncertainty (Raynor, 2007). One solution to the paradox is to separate, and align, the management of commitments from the management of uncertainty so that the work of delivering on organizational commitments is aligned with, but distinct from mitigating the risks associated with future uncertainty and providing exposure to promising opportunities. Because uncertainty increases with the time horizon under consideration, decision making should be allocated to the managerial levels responsible for each approximate time horizon. Executives tend to be well suited for managing strategic planning, scenario planning, and risk, while managers are well equipped for operational planning, the identification of critical success factors, and product or service delivery. With executives focused on managing uncertainty (strategic positioning), operating managers can focus on delivering on commitments (operational effectiveness). Operational effectiveness is akin to efficiency and means performing similar activities better than one's industry peers. Strategic positioning means adopting activities that are different from one's peers or performing similar activities differently (Porter, 1996).

Expanding the breadth and depth of knowledge and thought that are available for making strategic decisions can only strengthen the decisions and strategies themselves. Thus, the CSF method supports strategic thinking and decision making by strengthening perceptions and assumptions that lead to information-based decisions. They also address the strategy paradox by forming a bridge between strategic and operational activities. CSFs identify operational activities that serve the achievement of the mission. Future scenarios help form strategies that lay the groundwork for operational activities.

USING CSFS FOR IT STRATEGY

Organizations often have difficulty developing and implementing IT strategies because they do not maintain an explicit focus on high-level business drivers. As a result, IT strategies often fail to reflect what is important to the organization, the accomplishment of the mission, and long-term resilience. The key to an IT strategy is that it explains how information technology will align with and support an organization's overall business strategy. It should reflect a global level of thinking about IT and its integration with the rest of the organization.

The success of an enabling resource, like IT, relies heavily on aligning IT-strategy with higher level, organizational strategy. Because CSFs can be derived at each level of an organization, they can facilitate alignment. They link organizational strategic interests and the information-planning function. In fact, a good IT strategic plan must include an understanding not only of its own CSFs, but of the CSFs for the divisions of the organization it supports as well as the higher-level organizational CSFs. Organizational CSFs are critical to IT strategic planning because they reflect the business goals of the organization and the field of vision of top management (Caralli, 2004). In addition to supporting strategy development, CSFs also enhance strategic planning to some degree. In particular, CSFs can provide an organizationally tailored filter for identifying driving forces for future development. This method has been piloted in several government strategic planning efforts with positive results. Not only has the integration of these techniques produced robust strategic plans, it has fostered strategic conversation among organizational leadership, inspired data-based decision making, and increased communication across the organizations. This approach can be implemented in stages, at any level, and still realize gradual benefits.

Improving Strategy Execution

Improving strategy execution is at the top of the list of important issues for most corporate executives, followed by concerns about actually having a sound strategy. When strategic planning is done well, with a mature and robust process that guides the effort to ensure completeness - the outcomes can be powerful and position an organization to thrive and sometimes even dominate the competition. Yet only a small percentage of organizations operate with mature planning models that yield complete and comprehensive strategic plans addressing alignment to key dimensions of the business. Not surprisingly, even fewer organizations have mastered the art of fully and successfully executing corporate strategic plans. With successful strategy outcomes continuing to be an elusive prize sought by so many corporate leaders, this part is focused on exploring eight critical success factors related to improving strategy execution. A common mistake organizations make during strategic planning is that over jumping directly into planning for the future. That may not sound like a mistake at first blush, after all...isn't strategic planning all about the future? The current-state analysis phase ofcorporate strategic planning involves gaining a realistic perspective of where the organization is today so that it is possible to plan effectively for moving from the current reality to the desired future. Missing this step puts the strategy and the execution in jeopardy. It helps put everything about the organization into a singular context – with a holistic-360 degree, multi-dimensional view that allows for comparability and planning occurring effectively.

Sometimes organizations feel that they are adequately addressing the current-state by performing a traditional SWOT analysis to provide indications of Strengths, Weakness, Opportunities and Threats. The current-state analysis prescribed here Figure 1, provides far more relevant attribution of the organization and the environment in which it must operate (the business ecosystem) – inclusive of critical aspects, such as: the organization's culture, structure and core values as well as the relationships with customers, partners, employees, suppliers. Likewise, current-state analysis is reflective of the economic fluctuations that occur within that system we refer to as the business ecosystem. The assessment yields a more complete picture of the organization's strengths and weaknesses, and the same is true for the external assessment. Far more is understood and uncovered relative to opportunities and threats using this approach than when using the more traditional SWOT analysis.

A Value Quadrant Analysis (VQA) is an excellent method to truly understand key buyer segments by profitability. Such an understanding allows a business to make informed decisions to drive sales and marketing related strategies - even helping make key decisions related to remaining in one or more quadrants or exiting unprofitable segments. In short, VQA during current-state analysis drives value proposition messaging, strategy development and ultimately should determine strategic investment deci-

Figure 1. Current state analysis

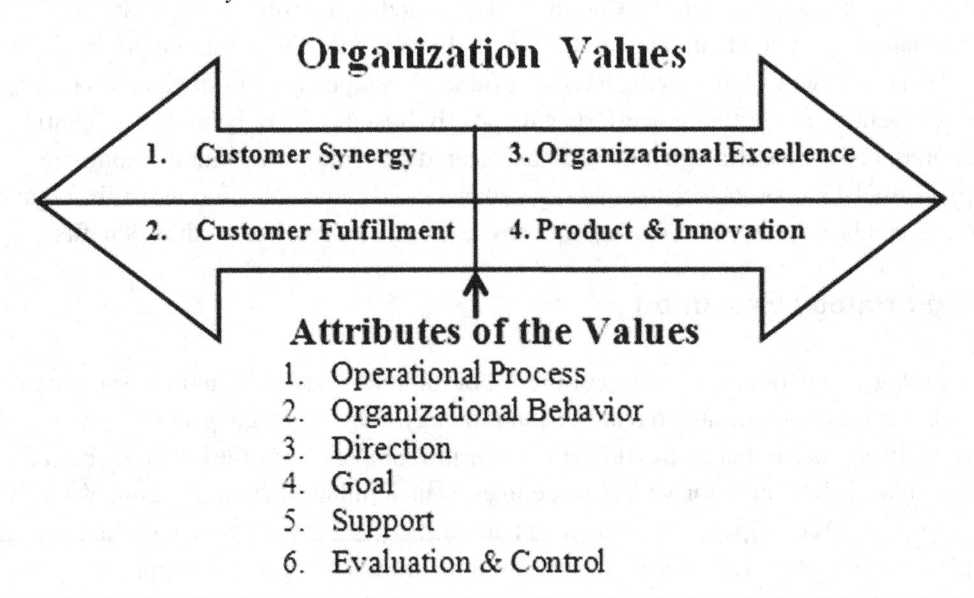

sions. The organizational profile resulting from the current-state analysis, as described, encapsulates key data that will feed the planning process with richer data - broken down into three major components:

1. Operating environment & business processes
2. Business relationships
3. Key performance categories

The holistic understanding of the business ecosystem that comes from having conducted a current-state analysis allows for strategic planning to optimize the shortest path to the future-state, once it has been defined. That path is dependent upon an understanding of the business's core values, culture, value proposition, organizational value quadrants, org structure relative to culture and external competitive environment by line-of-business (including key players like customers, suppliers, partners and channel relationships). The comparison of the organizational profile to the challenges identified during this step result in the gap that serves as the basis for planning.

Requirements of Strategic Planning

Strategic planning requires "real" information related to questions like:

1. What is working well?
2. What is not working so well?
3. What are our organizational vulnerabilities?
4. Where are there untapped opportunities?

To get to this information straight from the source that knows it best, employees must be engaged in the strategic planning process as early as the current-state analysis. This is where most companies make a big mistake. The executive team pulls into a shell to "meet" about the strategic plan and routinely locks out key people from the process that might well have contributed beneficial ideas and information.

This is not done intentionally of course. It is done out of habit and expediency. "*Let's get the executives and their managers into planning sessions and get this done...*" Such sentiments are common and can be heard in companies around the world. It is unfortunate, but closed loop thinking like this often hatches flawed strategies as a result of executive management groupthink. "Happy talk" takes control and the management team convinces themselves that the business is doing relatively well...oblivious to threats and issues awaiting them in the near future. The planning process requires realism to actually produce a valuable result. These realisms are reflected in Table 4.

The Global Factor

Approaches to strategy and planning in multinationals require more effort due to more complex organizational structures and market specific factors global companies face. Corporate strategy must be "localized" to allow the business to respond appropriately to geographic-based opportunities and threats. Likewise, strategy development must include the involvement of the company's foreign business leaders to help the strategy be adapted correctly to local needs. Exactly how this is done is dependent upon the type of structure the company has decided best suits the organization (e.g. matrix, product, geography,

Table 4. Realisms

Serial No.	Type	Interpretation
1	Operational	Businesses need the discipline of a planning process which structures an analysis of operations - allowing the organization's employees to provide input into the planning process. This action engages employees and is especially beneficial in helping executives have a better understanding of today's reality across the business. That dose of operational reality is essential to constructing meaningful strategy and planning realistic execution. Getting to business truth even extends beyond the organization to include engaging key suppliers, distributors, channel partners and customers in aspects of the planning process.
2	Cultural	Business truth includes understanding not only operational issues facing the business, but also more subtle disconnects and problems not so easily detected - yet equally important. Understanding culture is an understanding of "Who are we as a company, really?" Culture is defined by what members of the organization, and the organization as a whole, do to create success. Culture is about an organization's core values and how members define acceptable and unacceptable behavior. In planning, a clear understanding of culture provides a framework for understanding the "What, Why and How" work gets completed.
3	Value Proposition	A value proposition can be thought of as a set of market promises based on capability and credibility, which helps prospective customers understand how the company's offering uniquely addresses specific problems, opportunities and challenges. Testing the internal perception of organization's value proposition at different levels of the organization provides yet another form of business truth. It indicates where there is consistency, where there are disconnects and if value is being communicated to the marketplace effectively.
4	Core Competency	Companies must realistically assess their core competencies because they are the underpinnings of the organization's skills and the cornerstone of successful strategic execution. They represent the fundamental knowledge, abilities and expertise of an organization. True ability to understand and measure organizational core competencies is a critical factor in reaching strategic goals.
5	Industry	Understanding the company's position in the market place is essential. Now more than ever, business leaders must clearly understand the directional flow of their industry and plan for transitions and consolidations that may be occurring now or are on the horizon. Data must be gathered from managers and employees in sales, marketing, customer service, supply-chain and other areas of the business in order to gain true visibility into the organization's industry and market sectors.

etc.). Multinational strategies are shaped by the trade-off between opportunity and risk. Three broad environmental factors determine that trade-off. The first is the prevailing political economy, including the policies of both host and home governments, and the international legal framework. The second is the market and resources of the host country. The third factor is competition from local firms. Given these factors, one challenge multinational companies face is recognizing the need to "localize" strategies. Once that recognition has set in, the next challenge is then determining how best to accomplish localization. Strategy localization is needed in order to allow the business to respond appropriately to geographic-based opportunities and threats. Corporations should expect cultural heuristics to differ from country to country. Likewise, markets operate differently across the world, and there is no "one size fits all" approach to successfully conquering them. Competitor threats must be addressed with locally adapted strategies to be effective, thus the competitive analysis involved with strategic planning is a requirement to successfully navigate the terrain of the region's business ecosystem. Marketing and sales tactics are only part of geographic differentiation, although they are certainly not insignificant in terms of importance. There are also unique supply-chain considerations to factor into local strategies. Resource costs, including labor, vary widely across countries. It doesn't stop there. Legal systems, labor laws and distribution systems also impact local strategy. For this reason, operational considerations related to pricing, production and distribution also cannot be ignored with a cookie cutter corporate strategy that is imposed across countries / geographies. None of this means that the foreign-based division can go rogue and operate business practices that run counter to the strategic goals of the parent. What it does indicate, however, is that parent company's corporate strategy must be operationalized to fit localities.

The People Factor

Implementing corporate strategy is dependent upon the energy, dedication, hard work and faith of the organization's employees. Motivating employees to act decisively in the face of uncertainty is a challenge where many an organization has failed miserably. Simply stated, a considerable amount of energy is required to drive strategies to fruition - and that energy must be generated from within the organization. The more that employees have been involved in the process of creating the strategy, the more they will have already bought into it - helping fuel strategy delivery and thus propelling the momentum of execution to make it both easier and smoother. When it is not possible to broadly involve employees in some way, the communication effort surrounding the strategy needs to be amped up across the organization to compensate for the fact that many if not most employees will be in the dark regarding the strategy and what is expected of them.

CSFS AND GOALS

There can be some confusion between CSFs and goals, which are not the same. Goals are broad, high-level aims that support the accomplishment of the mission. Like goals, CSFs represent things that enable the success of or contribute to the accomplishment of a mission. Goals, however, are often derived from performance management exercises rather than strategic planning, and are set with an eye to achievability rather than organizational success or contribution to accomplishment of the mission. CSFs refer to ongoing operational activities that must be sustained for the organization to function successfully. Where goals help an organization attain success, CSFs ensure an organization's survival. If an organization focuses only on goal-setting, it might, as a result, drop attention from the day-to-day activities that sustain its success.

Goals and CSFs share a many-to-many relationship because organizational goals may rely on the achievement of more than one CSF and a CSF may affect the achievement of several goals. The potential many-to-many relationship between CSFs and goals is indicative of their interdependence and importance for accomplishing a mission (Caralli, 2004). CSFs reflect areas that are important to the organization in the current operating environment and to future success; they remain fairly constant over time, at least in the sense that they are seen as areas critical to the success of the mission in both the present and the future. Rockart writes, "Goals represent the end points that an organization hopes to reach. Critical success factors, however, are the areas in which good performance is necessary to ensure attainment of those goals" (Rockart, 1979).

There is some fluidity among CSFs and goals. As stated earlier, a performance gap in a particular operational area may cause a CSF to be elevated into a fix-oriented goal. Alternately, a goal, once achieved, may migrate to a CSF for sustainment.

FUTURE RESEARCH DIRECTIONS

In an early contribution to the work on critical success factors and management control systems Anthony et al. emphasized that the development of timely, concise measurements was crucial to monitoring identified CSFs (Anthony, 1972). Although not all documented CSF method descriptions include developing CSF measures, measures were also a fundamental part of Rockart's original CSF method. Rockart writes, "Critical success factors are areas of activity that should receive constant and careful attention from management. The current status of performance in each area should be continually measured, and that information should be made available" (Rockart, 1979). Critical success factors can establish a set of performance measures that directly link operational issues to the mission. Further area of research would be to establish this set of performance measures that directly link CSFs especially in the area of IT, Strategic Planning and Modern Organizations. Another interesting research thread would be to see how the dynamic environment of IT convergence with communication and technologies would affect CSFs and counter effect of this on identifying and linking CSFs to strategic planning.

CONCLUSION

Information has emerged as an agent of integration and the enabler of new competitiveness for today's modern organizations in the global marketplace. But the real concern is whether the paradigm of strategic planning changed sufficiently to support the new role of strategic planning, information systems and technology (Baporikar, 2015b). This chapter is an attempt to review the literature in this context and the focus is on CSF as approach for IT strategic planning in modern organizations. Critical success factors and future scenarios are particularly well-suited augmentations to IT strategic-planning efforts. They illuminate an organization's present situation and potential future, respectively, and facilitate the alignment of IT strategy with organizational business drivers. Each technique can be used to strengthen both strategy setting and operational activities. When the CSF method and scenarios are used together and integrated with a strategic-planning method, they also reveal the value of an overarching strategic thinking and strategy development process. They contribute to the strategic thinking and planning process and the development of robust strategic planning information assets.

REFERENCES

Anthony, R. N. (1965). *Planning and Control Systems: A Framework for Analysis*. Cambridge, MA: Harvard University Press.

Anthony, R. N., Dearden, J., & Vancil, R. F. (1972). *Management Control Systems*. Homewood, IL: Irwin.

Arce, E., & Flynn, D. (1997). A CASE Tool to Support Critical Success Factors Analysis in IT Planning and Requirements Determination. *Information and Software Technology*, *39*(5), 311–321. doi:10.1016/S0950-5849(96)01150-0

Atthirawong, W., & McCarthy, B. (2001). *Critical Factors in International Location Decisions: A Delphi Study*. Paper presented at the Twelfth Annual Conference of the Production and Operations Management Society, Orlando, FL.

Baporikar, N. (2013). CSF Approach for IT Strategic Planning. *International Journal of Strategic Information Technology and Applications*, *4*(2), 35–47. doi:10.4018/jsita.2013040103

Baporikar, N. (2014a). Strategic Management Overview and SME in Globalized World. In K. Todorov & D. Smallbone (Eds.), *Handbook of Research on Strategic Management in Small and Medium Enterprises* (pp. 22–39). Hershey, PA: Business Science Reference; doi:10.4018/978-1-4666-5962-9.ch002

Baporikar, N. (2014b). Information Strategy as Enabler of Competitive Advantage. *International Journal of Strategic Information Technology and Applications*, *5*(1), 30–41. doi:10.4018/ijsita.2014010103

Baporikar, N. (2015a). Information Strategy as Enabler of Competitive Advantage. In Economics: Concepts, Methodologies, Tools, and Applications (pp. 599-610). Hershey, PA: Business Science Reference. doi:10.4018/978-1-4666-8468-3.ch032

Baporikar, N. (2015b). Holistic Framework for Evolving Effective Information Systems Strategy. *International Journal of Strategic Information Technology and Applications*, *6*(4), 30–43. doi:10.4018/IJSITA.2015100103

Barat, J. (1992). Scenario Playing for Critical Success Factor Analysis. *Journal of Information Technology*, *7*(1), 12–19. doi:10.1057/jit.1992.3

Bernard, S. A. (2005). *An Introduction to Enterprise Architecture* (2nd ed.). Bloomington, IN: AuthorHouse.

Brancheau, J., Janz, B., & Wetherbe, J. (1996). Key Issues in Information Systems Management: 199495 SIM Delphi Result. *Management Information Systems Quarterly*, *20*(2), 225–242. doi:10.2307/249479

Bruno, A., & Leidecker, J. (1984). Identifying and Using Critical Success Factors. *Long Range Planning*, *17*(1), 23–32. doi:10.1016/0024-6301(84)90163-8

Caralli, R. A. (2004). *The Critical Success Factor Method: Establishing a Foundation for Enterprise Security Management (CMU/SEI-2004-TR-010)*. Software Engineering Institute, Carnegie Mellon University.

Cassidy, A. (2006). *A Practical Guide to Information Systems Strategic Planning* (2nd ed.). Boca Raton, FL: Auerbach Publications.

Daniel, D. R. (1961). Management Information Crisis. *Harvard Business Review*, *39*(5), 111–116.

Dess, G., & Robinson, R. (1984). Measuring Organizational Performance in the Absence of Objective Measures. *Strategic Management Journal*, *5*(3), 265–285. doi:10.1002/smj.4250050306

Dvir, D., Lipovetsky, S., Shenhar, A., & Tishler, A. (1996). Identifying Critical Success Factors in Defense Development Projects: A Multivariate Analysis. *Technological Forecasting and Social Change*, *51*(2), 151–171. doi:10.1016/0040-1625(95)00197-2

Ellegard, C., & Grunert, K. (1993). The Concept of Key Success Factors: Theory and Method. In M. Baker (Ed.), *Perspectives on Marketing Management* (pp. 245–274). Chichester, UK: Wiley.

Esteves, J. (2004). *Definition and Analysis of Critical Success Factors for ERP Implementation Projects* (Doctoral thesis). Universitat Politècnica de Catalunya, Barcelona, Spain.

Esteves, J., & Pastor, J. (1999). *An ERP Lifecycle-based Research Agenda*. Paper presented at the First International Workshop on Enterprise Management Resource and Planning Systems EMRPS, Venice, Italy.

Ferguson, J., & Khandewal, V. (1999). *Critical Success Factors (CSF) and the Growth of IT in Selected Geographic Regions*. Paper presented at the Hawaii International Conference on System Sciences, Hawaii, HI.

Fogg, D. C. (1994). *Team-Based Strategic Planning: A Complete Guide to Structuring, Facilitating, and Implementing the Process*. New York: AMACOM/American Management Association.

Gibson, N., Holland, C., & Light, B. (1999). *A Critical Success Factors Model for Enterprise Resource Planning Implementation*. Paper presented at the European Conference on Information Systems, Copenhagen, Denmark.

Gunasekaran, S., & Garets, D. (2004). Managing the IT Strategic Planning Process. In Healthcare Information Management Systems Cases, Strategies, and Solutions. Springer. doi:10.1007/978-1-4757-4041-7_2

Heracleous, L. (1998). Strategic Thinking or Strategic Planning. *Long Range Planning*, *31*(3), 481–487. doi:10.1016/S0024-6301(98)80015-0

Jenkins, A., Kock, N., & Wellington, R. (1999). A Field Study of Success and Failure Factors in Asynchronous Groupware Supported Process Improvement Groups. *Business Process Management Journal*, *5*(3), 238–253. doi:10.1108/14637159910283010

Khandewal, V., & Miller, J. (1992). Information System Study. In *Opportunity Management Program*. New York: IBM Corporation.

Musashi, M. (2009). *The Book of Five Rings: Classic Treaty on Military Strategy*. Wildside Press.

Pinto, J., & Prescott, J. (1988). Variations in Critical Success Factors over the Stages in the Project Lifecycle. *Journal of Management*, *14*(1), 5–18. doi:10.1177/014920638801400102

Pinto, J., & Slevin, D. (1987). Critical Factors in Successful Project Implementation. *IEEE Transactions on Engineering Management*, *34*(1), 22–27. doi:10.1109/TEM.1987.6498856

Porter, M. E. (1996). What is Strategy? *Harvard Business Review*, (November-December), 61–78.

Ramaprasad, A., & Williams, J. (1998). *The Utilization of Critical Success Factors: A Profile*. Paper presented at the 29th Annual Meeting of the Decision Sciences Institute, Las Vegas, NV.

Raynor, M. E. (2007). *The Strategy Paradox: Why Committing to Success Leads to Failure (and What to Do About It)*. New York: Doubleday.

Rockart, J. (1979, March-April). Chief Executives Define Their Own Information Needs. *Harvard Business Review*, 81–92.

Rockart, J. (1982). The Changing Role of the Information Systems Executive: A Critical Success Factors Perspective. *Sloan Management Review*, *23*(1), 3–13.

Rockart, J., & Van Bullen, C. (1986). A Primer on Critical Success Factors. In J. Rockart & C. Van Bullen (Eds.), *The Rise of Management Computing*. Homewood, IL: Irwin.

Schwartz, P. (1991). *The Art of the Long View: Planning for the Future in an Uncertain World*. Currency Doubleday.

Sumner, M. (1999). *Critical Success Factors in Enterprise Wide Information Management Systems Projects*. Paper presented at the Americas Conference on Information Systems, Milwaukee, WI. doi:10.1145/299513.299722

Umble, E., & Umble, M. (2001). *Enterprise Resource Planning Systems: A Review of Implementation Issues and Critical Success Factors*. Paper presented at the 32nd Decision Sciences Institute Annual Meeting, San Francisco, CA.

van der Heijden. (1996). *Kees. Scenarios: The Art of Strategic Conversation*. John Wiley & Sons Limited.

Ward, B. (1990). Planning for Profit. In T. J. Lincoln (Ed.), *Managing Information Systems for Profit* (pp. 103–146). Chichester, UK: John Wiley & Sons.

Zahedi, F. (1987). Reliability of Information Systems Based on Critical Success Factors Formulation. *Management Information Systems Quarterly*, *11*(2), 187–203. doi:10.2307/249362

KEY TERMS AND DEFINITIONS

Action: A specific step to achieve a goal or objective. An action typically has assigned staff and schedule constraints.

Barrier: An external condition or organizational (internal) weakness that hinders an organization's ability to accomplish a goal or objective.

Critical Success Factors (CSFs): The handful of key areas where an organization must perform well on a consistent basis to achieve its mission.

Enabler: An external condition or organizational strength that facilitates an organization's ability to accomplish its goals or objectives.

Goals: Broad, high-level aims that support the accomplishment of a mission.

Information Systems (IS): The means by which people and organizations gather, process, store, use, and disseminate information.

Information Technology (IT): The hardware, software, and telecommunications that facilitate the acquisition, processing, storage, delivery, and sharing of information and other digital content in an organization. It also is the use of computing, electronics, and telecommunications technology in managing and processing information, especially in large organizations.

Initiative: A specific set of actions that implement a strategy.

IT Strategy: A description of how information technology will support an organization's overall business strategy.

Operational Planning: The process of making decisions about the allocation of organizational resources (capital and staff) to pursue a strategy.

Performance Measure: Performance targets relevant to each objective.

Strategic Goal: A primary goal of an organization or enterprise that implies a particular strategy or set of strategies.

Strategic Plan: A document that results from a strategic planning activity. It elaborates the organizational strategy and documents the elements that influence it.

Strategic Planning: A process for defining an organization's strategy, or direction, and making decisions about how to allocate its resources to pursue this strategy, including its capital and people.

Strategy: A derived approach to achieving the mission, goals, and objectives of an organization. It supports the organizational vision, takes into account organizational enablers and barriers, and upholds guiding principles.

Chapter 2
Using Geospatial Information Systems for Strategic Planning and Institutional Research for Higher Education Institutions

Nicolas A. Valcik
The University of Texas at Dallas, USA

ABSTRACT

This article has been updated since its initial publication in Hansel Burley's Cases on Institutional Research Systems in 2011. There have been additional uses for Geospatial Information Systems, or GIS, at The University of Texas at Dallas since this article originally was published. Many institutional research offices primarily focus on traditional statistical and analytical tools to provide data for assessing, developing or modifying institutional policies. However, Geospatial Information Systems, or GIS, can add a geospatial component to existing data sources to provide in-depth analysis on a wide array of research topics (Ormsby, Napoleon, Burke, Grossl, & Bowden, 2008). A suite of software tools introduced by ESRI in 1997 called ArcGIS has been useful for analytical purposes because it not only compiles and displays large amounts of data but can also plot this data onto maps, which can be particularly useful when analyzing demographic data (ESRI, 2010). This chapter will discuss the implementation and use of GIS at The University of Texas at Dallas in the Office of Strategic Planning and Analysis (OSPA).

GEOSPATIAL INFORMATION SYSTEMS

GIS is a set of tools that can use and layer multiple data sources by geographical location. Developed in the mid-20th century, GIS is primarily used in cartography, urban planning, emergency management, resource management and navigation to name a few. The roots of GIS can be traced back to a graphic developed by John Snow in the 1840's plotting cholera deaths onto a map of London, thus demonstrating to city officials that a contaminated water pump on Broad Street was the source of the outbreak (Crosier & Scott, 2009). GIS uses an object called a GIS layer file (referred to as coverages, shapefiles or geoda-

DOI: 10.4018/978-1-5225-1680-4.ch002

tabases) that provides an overall framework where the analyst can overlay multiple data streams into one massive dataset, often called a geodatabase. B. Grant McCormick of the University of Arizona notes:

A presumption is that key benefits of GIS are to be realized with a system that permeates the enterprise, links divisions, integrates data sources to create new understanding, and creates efficiencies by overcoming territorial boundaries. With this in mind, the term GIS should be seen not solely as the use of GIS software, but rather as a technical framework for integrating disparate datasets, bridging software formats, and responding to a plethora of administrative needs and goals. (McCormick, 2003, p. 63)

A geodatabase can contain several layers of data. For example a geodatabase can utilize a satellite photo that is geo-referenced to a particular location, a data file of addresses or zip codes, and a computer-aided design (CAD) file. All of the images and data would constitute one geodatabase which could then be used to provide a variety of data analysis. The ability to effectively use massive amounts of data (or utilize a database) with imagery is why GIS can provide powerful analytical capability. In addition, GIS can be used to provide campus planning departments with overlays of future construction. Buildings, infrastructure and transportation routes can be "constructed" by a GIS analyst as a layer on top of an existing satellite image. Furthermore, ArcGIS has the ability to render and/or capture landscape features as well as any other object in a three dimensional context.

GIS AT THE UNIVERSITY OF TEXAS AT DALLAS

The University of Texas at Dallas is a research intensive university that became part of the University of Texas System in 1969. The institution emphasizes science, technology, engineering and mathematics fields (STEM) as well as business administration, developmental and cognitive sciences, public affairs and unique and growing programs like Geospatial Information Sciences and Arts and Technology. The university enrolls nearly 20,000 students and is currently undergoing expansion in faculty, staff and facilities (2012). The university's Office of Strategic Planning and Analysis (OSPA) compiles state and federal reports, fulfills external data requests, provides analysis and benchmarking for university administrators and has developed unique software packages like the Logistical Tracking System (LTS). LTS utilizes GIS to accurately account for facility information as well as enable other departments to track assets for operational use, federal reports and state reports.

LTS was originally created to accurately record facility data in the university's mainframe-based space management system (SMS) and to replace an older, interim system based on Microsoft Access called the Space Inventory Database (SID) (Valcik, 2003). University personnel wanted to create highly accurate and detailed campus maps and floor plans from the room and building dimensions already stored in SMS and SID. Existing software products that managed facility information through Computer-Aided Design (CAD) files were evaluated but were neither robust enough nor had the functionality needed to meet the university's requirements because CAD lacks the ability to tie in large amounts of data to the image files. Therefore, the Assistant Director and a team of three individuals developed LTS for the university and have consistently evolved the design since 2001 (Valcik, 2003). The current LTS design utilizes GIS, is developed on a Microsoft SQL.Net Server database and employs Microsoft Visual Studio.Net for the web interface. Originally, the web interfaces were developed with Microsoft Visual Studio and the database was Microsoft SQL Server 2000. (Valcik & Huesca-Dorantes, 2003).

The decision to integrate GIS and LTS was based on several criteria. The university maintains undergraduate and graduate Geospatial Information Sciences degree programs with faculty that possessed extensive knowledge on how to use the ESRI tools ArcGIS and ArcSDE and would provide free support and discounted software to the LTS project team (Valcik, 2007). In contrast, the CAD software resisted successful integration into the LTS programming, was costly to license, and was used by only one person on the entire campus because the university has no architecture department or degree programs. Secondly, OSPA had an employee who had recently earned GIS certification and was capable of using the software to map the floor plans to the facilities. Lastly, OSPA could work with UTD's geosciences department which was using the campus as a "GIS laboratory" for its students. The professors had assigned students to gather Global Positioning System (GPS) data on all university buildings and infrastructure for a class project (Valcik, 2007). Assisting the geosciences department in this endeavor provided OSPA with the data needed for LTS while giving students real-world experience on an active project. Due to institutional licensing agreements and discounted academic price structures, Microsoft products such as Visual Studio 6.0 and SQL Server 2000 were used initially to construct the database and web interface. Finally, there were numerous graduate students in the Erik Jonsson School of Engineering and Computer Science with the skills necessary to perform web interface programming for LTS (Valcik, 2007). Ultimately, the decision to use GIS instead of CAD was influenced by financial constraints, availability of personnel who could use the product and compatibility of the product with an existing facility database.

By integrating GIS with LTS to create floor plans, UTD could more accurately report facility information to the Texas Higher Education Coordinating Board (THECB) and the National Science Foundation survey on research facilities (Valcik, 2007). OSPA has also worked to expand the use of GIS into other aspects of institutional research (Valcik, 2009). OSPA has used GIS to perform data analysis on homeland security issues, benchmarking, and determining operational areas for other departments (i.e. jurisdiction of arrest powers for the university police department). One current project is to link GIS to human resource information to map the proximity of employees' residences to the university. This project has now been expanded to include currently enrolled students and their proximity to the university to answer various inquires from state agencies. GIS is also being used to map the density of courses by building during specific times of the day to demonstrate the potential impact upon parking and traffic patterns on campus.

CHALLENGES ASSOCIATED WITH USING GIS

There were several challenges associated with the adoption and use of GIS. One significant concern at UTD was to determine if GIS was compatible with the LTS application or if the ArcGIS tool would successfully interact with the Microsoft SQL Server tables that comprised LTS. Data was successfully exported from ArcGIS into a .dbf extension. When this was accomplished, the .dbf file was imported into a Microsoft SQL Server table. Once this process was completed, the team experimented with the ArcSDE software on a surplus computer running a Microsoft Server operating system to determine if LTS would interoperate with the ArcGIS geodatabases. The project discovered that ArcSDE was difficult to install and required a Sentinel Key - a hardware SCSI key that plugs into the server SCSI port - to operate the software.

A second challenge was to develop a consistent nomenclature for buildings and spaces. In 2001, the university was still relatively small with an enrollment of 12,455 students (The University of Texas at Dallas, 2010). However, the university was set for rapid enrollment growth to be followed by a series of building projects to accommodate the additional students. By 2009, enrollment had grown to 15,783, a 21% increase in eight years (The University of Texas at Dallas, 2010). Meanwhile, construction projects that included major renovations to existing structures, new construction on five new academic structures, additional student housing, acquisitions of existing buildings from other entities, and the construction of a facilities management complex quickly added square footage to university facilities. The rapid growth strained existing methods for managing facility information, creating business process issues particularly with regard to standardizing naming conventions for rooms and buildings and assigning official building code designations for new and existing buildings for state reporting. For example there were no standardized naming conventions for unassignable spaces (i.e. corridors, stairwells, structure points etc.). The GIS analyst developed a naming convention that would reflect these areas as unassignable on the GIS shapefiles.

A third challenge was the need to import GIS information on a new structure or newly renovated area into LTS without inadvertently including this information on official facility reports prior to the new area becoming operational. It was crucial for the new facility data to be in the system to support operational requirements of various departments (e.g., security). However, if the new building information was reported prior to it becoming operational, it would artificially depress utilization rates, which can have repercussions for plans for new space. By using a batch methodology to upload data from ArcSDE, GIS analysts could utilize new information on buildings that were under construction but were not operational. This would allow for those buildings and floor plans to be used for maps but the data would not be active in LTS for reporting purposes.

All institutions experience turnover, but when the personnel who leave take with them specialized knowledge like GIS training it becomes exceedingly difficult to find a replacement who can both conduct institutional research and use GIS. Three of the original four members of the initial LTS project have since left the university to pursue their careers elsewhere. After the GIS analyst accepted a position with a local government agency, a series of graduate students from the university's GIS program were hired to update floor plans or to create new GIS layers for newly constructed buildings. The benefits to hiring graduate students are that the students gain experience from working on a real-world project and the university is able to acquire highly skilled labor at a lower cost than if a full-time employee were hired to perform the same job. In fact, most of the research assistants who worked on the development of LTS have accepted lucrative full-time positions post-graduation in some part because of the experience they gained from working on LTS. The primary drawback to using graduate students is once again an issue of attrition and the need to train replacements frequently. Furthermore, research assistants require oversight from at least one full-time employee to ensure that proper procedures are being employed. Another drawback is that most graduate students can only work part-time and must schedule their work hours around their classes.

A fourth challenge was convincing other employees to accept the new technology and business processes. Some departments relied upon paper forms and older software and were very hesitant, if not completely resistant, to adopting new technology. When met with resistance, OSPA withdrew from the situation until personnel in the other department were ready to go forward with implementation or until the upper administration required the change. It then became important to demonstrate the value of GIS to administrators who did not understand the technology and the productivity it offered. An accurate, detailed campus map was produced from the new system and provided to administrators in an electronic format which made it simple to update, email and incorporate into presentations. Grounding the esoteric technology with an accessible, easily understood output like a campus map enabled administrators to visualize other uses for this technology.

If a university department wishes to use GIS software to enhance its productivity, there are several key issues to consider. The department must have access to personnel who are expert with this technology or who can provide training to the department's personnel. While it is a viable option to send personnel to formal training classes provided by third-party vendors, this option can be very costly. Approaching faculty for assistance is a way to obtain software, manuals and training without incurring high costs. The department must also determine if GIS software is compatible with their existing databases. GIS is highly compatible with desktop computers as well as servers.

Therefore, a department can make a small financial investment with one license on an existing desktop computer to determine if productivity is improved with the new software. More complex efforts, like the LTS project, will require a modest investment in additional software and a server. Another consideration when using GIS is the need to maintain current shapefiles on cities, regions and the nation. Conducting an analysis of where university employees reside in relation to the university is of little use if the city map being used is ten years out of date.

Finally, the analyst using GIS software must be familiar with the data and be aware of potential errors in the root data. GIS will not correct input errors made by data owners. As seen with both the staff and student map projects, invalid addresses cannot be mapped down to a shapefile. Additionally students and staff members that input post office boxes addresses into the university's information system cannot be mapped down to a particular location, which further reduces accuracy. Furthermore, importing fresh data into GIS can result in errors when joining datasets to incompatible shapefiles or through dissimilar variables, an issue familiar to analysts who write queries in SAS, SPSS or Microsoft Access.

USING GIS FOR EMERGENCY MANAGEMENT

Under the new mandates from the Bioterrorism Preparedness and Response Act of 2002 and the Chemical Facility Anti-Terrorism Standards Act of 2007, higher education institutions must report to the federal government any select agent[2] or chemical deemed to be of interest to Homeland Security that is over a threshold amount (Valcik, 2006; Valcik, November 2009). By using the GIS files, any agent over the legal threshold amount can be tied to the floor plans using LTS's HAZMAT tracking module through a unique identifier which can then be compiled in a report and submitted to the required federal agency. Additionally GIS has the ability to map the security cameras, alarms and other components of the security infrastructure and provide LTS with information about those components (Valcik, Aiken, Xu, & Al Farhan, 2009).

GIS enables LTS to track a wide array of assets that enter, are stored and leave university facilities. For example, a GIS file for a science building can provide a list of valid room numbers to a functional user that is tying research equipment to location and ownership. This improves inventory control and generates more accurate reports to entities that require information for insurance purposes, hazardous materials (HAZMAT) and federal grants (Valcik, 2007).

Not only is an institution able to tie in valid location codes from GIS, but the institution is also able to link a wealth of other characteristics as well (i.e. square footage, coordinates, volume etc.). For emergency

Figure 1. Fictitious research laboratory floor plan

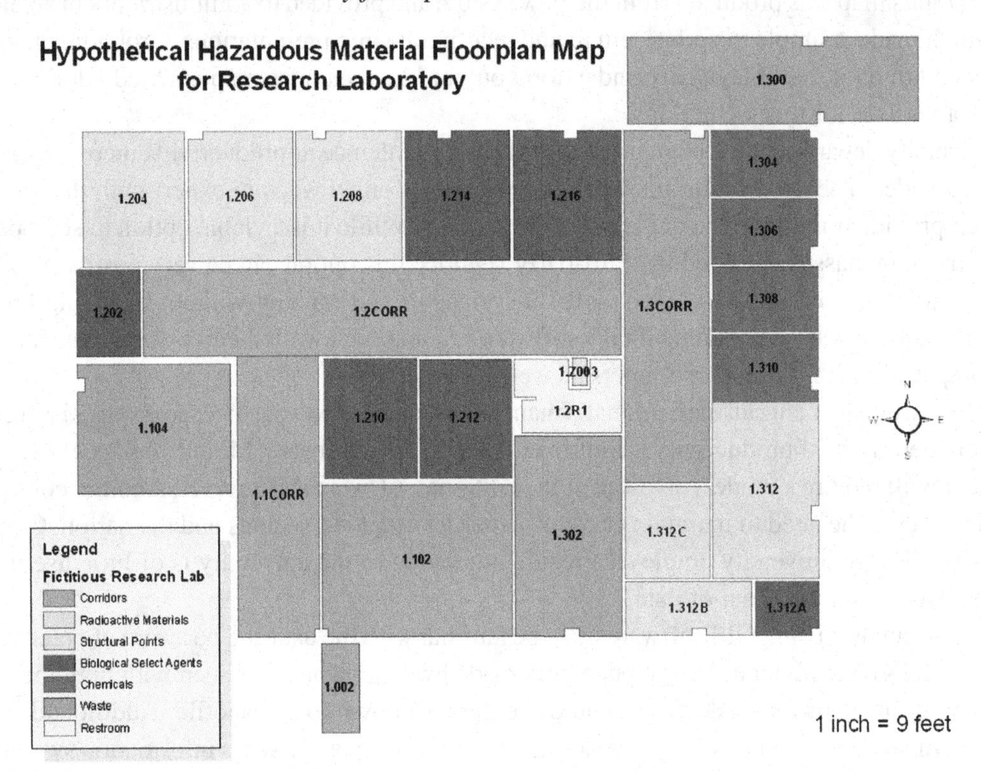

For a more accurate representation of this figure, please see the electronic version.

management purposes GIS can be used to map evacuation paths from facilities and university grounds in the event of an emergency. As described by Stuart Murchison of The University of Texas at Dallas:

At The Pennsylvania State University, a GeoCollaborative Crisis Management System is being built to leverage the current office of physical plant (OPP), the local Council of Governments, campus emergency coordinator and Geography department's geospatial science GeoVista Center. This collaborative creates a process that utilizes GIS base map layers, attribute information and the conversion of OPP allowing for work groups at different locations to manage an incident (MacEachren, et al. 2005). The system architecture is being enhanced with speech and gesture user interfaces that make it easier for decision makers to communicate with the GeoCollaborative Crisis Management system (Brewer, 2002). (Murchison, 2010, p. 81).

Personnel can be mapped through LTS via the GIS floor plans of each university facility. LTS can provide first responders with a list of employees assigned to the building. This same personnel assignment report can be used to enable campus security forces to identify who should be granted access to certain facilities after regular business hours.

USING GIS TO ANSWER GEOGRAPHIC QUESTIONS

Institutional research offices routinely work with databases, charts and graphs. However, GIS offers a way to map down demographic data over a geographic area, such as a campus, city, a county, a region or even the nation. One example that does not lend itself well to the traditional chart or graph is the geographical distribution of employees relative to the university campus. While university administrators can certainly make policy decisions based on other data sources, the use of GIS gives administrators another powerful decision-making tool that can provide information to them to justify or support an action that needs to be taken. However unlike other decision-making tools GIS provides administrators with a graphical representation of the data. This image in turn can provide administrators another conduit that can communicate data to individuals that may not have a background in statistics.

The GIS map in Figure 2 plots the addresses of university employees across the metropolitan area with concentric circles designating distance from the university. This information can be used by university administrators to determine commute times, decide whether to provide staff benefits like daycare or public transportation vouchers, and make informed decisions about when or if to close the school in response to a dangerous weather event. For example, if most employees live north of campus but a dangerous weather event (ice storm, flooding) occurs south of campus, the university can remain open and make special accommodations for those who may live elsewhere. Additionally this type of information can be provided to local transit authorities or city officials where such information may impact policy for entities outside the institution. This same methodology has now been used to construct a map where off-campus students live in relation to the campus for many of the same reasons (Figure 3). Recently, a university executive used these address maps in a presentation to city government officials. The executive wanted to demonstrate how many of the city's residents were enrolled as students at the university and how many residents were employees of the university. GIS information provides a visual component to the presentation that would have been much more difficult to convey with tabular data.

USING GIS FOR COURSE SCHEDULING

By determining which buildings have course loads during certain time frames of certain days, university administrators can plan for future parking lot improvements, roadway construction and ultimately where new buildings should be located (Figure 4).

The example illustrates how administrators can use data on the GIS map to quickly determine which parking lots will be heavily utilized and which buildings are being underutilized during certain days and time frames. This information can then be used to more effectively schedule courses across campus to alleviate parking congestion and better utilize existing campus facilities.

USING GIS FOR INSTITUTIONAL RESEARCH PROJECTS

With GIS, an institutional research office can bring in a wealth of data that can be used in benchmark analyses. Data such as university area in square miles, proximity to major cities, accessibility to major public transportation routes or roadways, population surrounding the institutions and distance to national laboratories are just a few variables that can be used for benchmarking purposes. Figures 1.5 and 1.6 represent a benchmarking

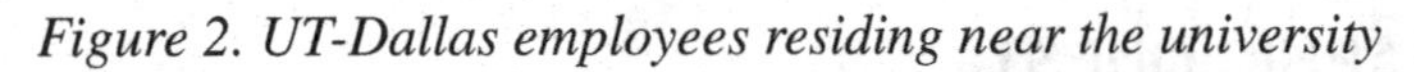

Figure 2. UT-Dallas employees residing near the university

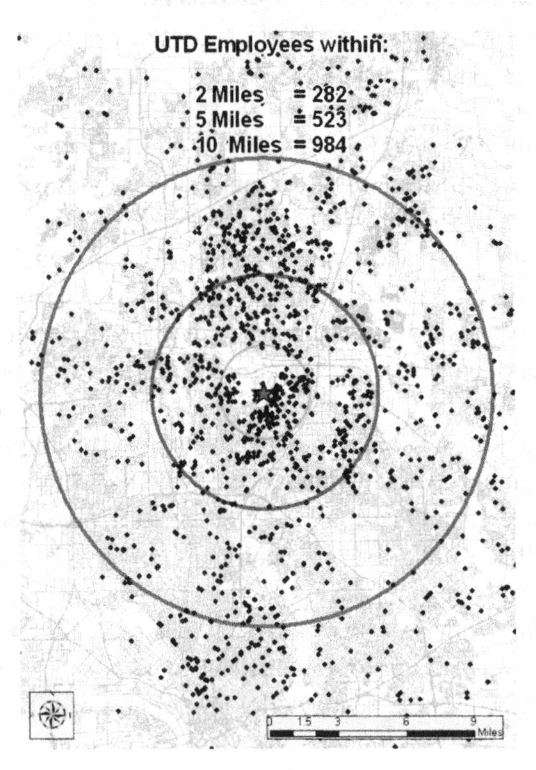

Figure 3. UT-Dallas enrolled students residing near the university – Spring 2012

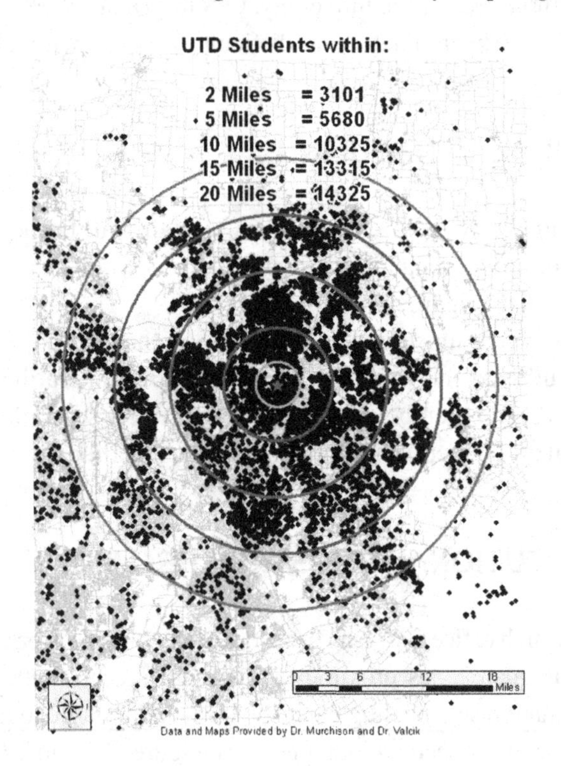

Figure 4. Density of courses located on campus

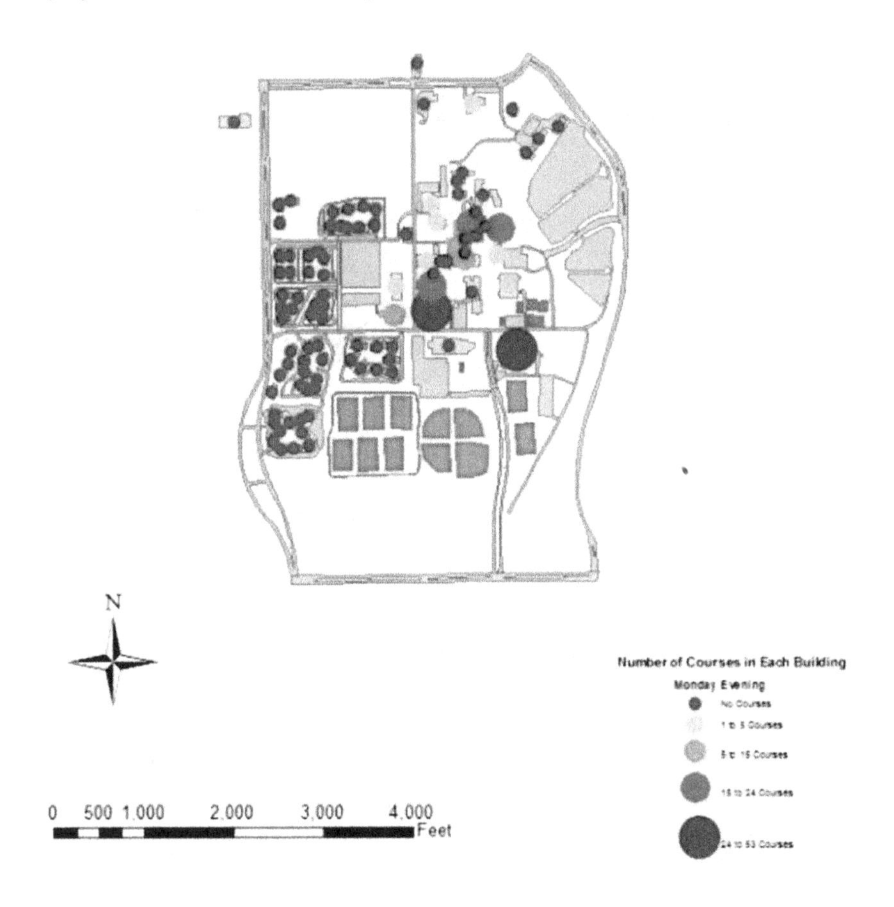

Figure 5.

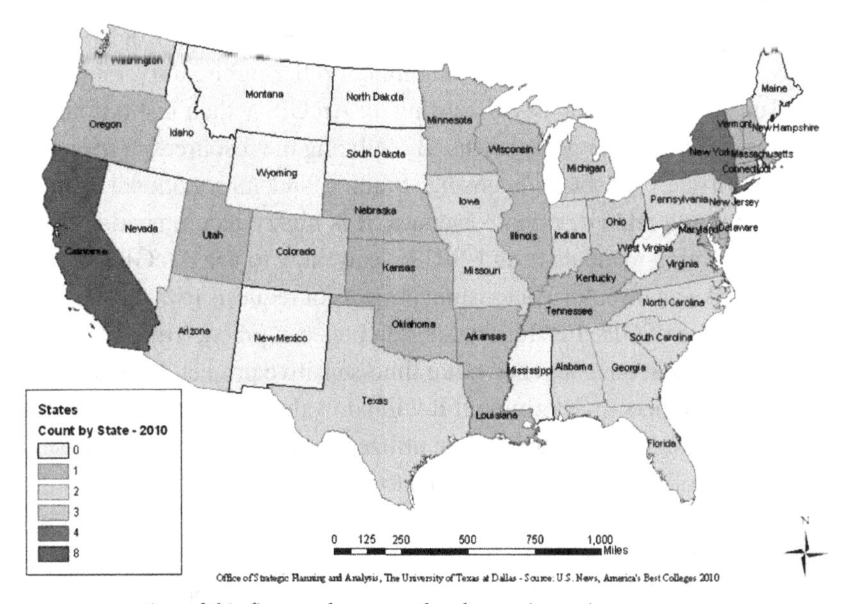

For a more accurate representation of this figure, please see the electronic version.

Figure 6.

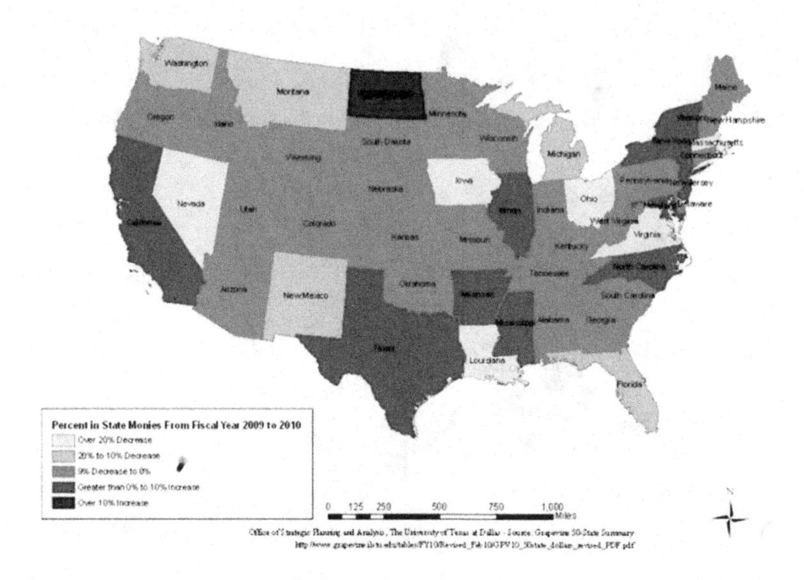

project that compared the number of top tier public universities in each state with state higher education funding data. These GIS maps compile university characteristics and financial data into visualizations that are clear, concise and can be used by college and university administrators to formulate policy.

In 2008 the State of Texas recently designated seven Texas research universities as Emerging Research Universities for the purpose of providing additional financial resources to enable those institutions to obtain top tier status (Daniel, 2008). The institutions designated by the Texas Higher Education Coordinating Board (THECB) were Texas Tech University, the University of Houston, the University of North Texas, The University of Texas at Arlington, The University of Texas at Dallas, The University of Texas at El Paso and The University of Texas at San Antonio (Daniel, 2008). If these institutions use the funding to increase enrollment, improve retention and graduation rates and increase externally funded research, they can propel themselves into top tier status. The State of Texas would surpass California (8 institutions) and New York (4 institutions) by having nine top tier public universities.

Many colleges and universities already have licensing for ArcGIS at their institutions through academic programs in engineering, geography or geosciences. By utilizing the resources in the academic programs, an institutional research office can obtain licensing, training and informational materials more easily and inexpensively than through retail or private avenues. It is highly recommended that the institutional research office purchase training manuals from ESRI to learn how to use ArcGIS. If possible, an institutional research office can take an inventory of existing projects or requests to determine if any can be made more effective through the use of GIS. Institutional researchers can practice using GIS with a small-scale project before attempting to use it on a larger or more time-sensitive project. Experience with the product will enable institutional researchers to determine if it will add value to their research efforts. As with any other data source that an institutional research office utilizes, it is imperative to understand the data used in conjunction with GIS shapefiles or geodatabases and to make sure that the data is accurate. GIS will not compensate for inaccurate data. When using GIS to produce a data map, it is also important to properly reference the data source and make any map clear with concise labeling. If the intended audience cannot understand the output, the output is not useful for any type of analysis or policy making.

USING GIS FOR ADMISSIONS AND RECRUITING

Much as GIS can be used to map where employees and off-campus students live in relation to the institution, GIS can be used to determine where recruiters experience the greatest success in recruiting students. In the past, enrollment managers relied upon applicant addresses or previous high school or community college to determine which regions provided the most prospective students. The enrollment manager would then try to assign personnel and resources to those areas to promote further recruitment. This methodology was reactive to existing data and was unable to provide meaningful information that could enable an enrollment manager to be proactive in successfully promoting new academic programs or moving into new recruiting regions. As stated by David Roy Blough of the University of Wisconsin System:

In higher education, market areas (often called service areas) are the regions from which a college draws most of its students...A college or university may find it difficult, however, to anticipate the size and location of the potential market for new programs or existing programs being extended to non-traditional students. (Blough, 2003, p.47)

If an enrollment manager wants to recruit more students with particular characteristics (standardized test scores, advanced placement preparation) or to recruit from high schools with certain characteristics (geographic location, school size) it is possible to upload datasets obtained from the College Board or the U.S. Department of Education and plot the data on a national map. Where the desired characteristics form clusters represents the most likely new service areas that recruiters can focus their efforts. One drawback to this methodology is that such a study is labor-intensive and requires staff dedicated to conducting the analysis. Also, the recruitment office must obtain current GIS shapefiles from government or non-profit organizations such as the North Texas Central Council of Governments to ensure accurate results.

Recruiting is just one example of how GIS can be used to analyze data as well as assist a higher education institution in effective allocation of resources. As stated by Victor J. Mora of Ohio State University:

There is increased marketing and sophistication in public colleges and more reliance upon technology to conduct computer-based analysis throughout the student recruitment process. One such technology is geographic information systems (GIS). The Ohio State University's Undergraduate Admissions Office began to incorporate the use of GIS into its operations several years ago (Mora, Granados, and Marble, 1997). (Mora, 2003, p. 15)

The same methodology for recruitment can be also used to analyze yield rates for admissions. The patterns could reveal that one recruitment area has a high application rate but a low enrollment yield while another area may have low recruitment but a high yield rate. As stated by Manuel Granados of Ohio State University:

One way to analyze the propensity of enrollment is to look at the geodemographic component; another is by looking at the specific individual characteristics of the student; and a third way is a combination of both. (Granados, 2003, p.31)

If the potential cost savings from a yield rate analysis outweighs the cost of labor and software, it may be worthwhile to consider using GIS to determine financial resource allocation for the next budget year.

USING GIS FOR ALUMNI GIVING

In an era of tight budgets, diminished endowments and decreased state funding, alumni donations take on new importance for higher education budgets. Most development and alumni offices have limited funding and cannot blanket the nation soliciting funds. A directed effort aimed at regions that contain large numbers of alumni would be most effective, particularly if it is determined that alumni happen to congregate in suburbs near a major metropolitan area. For example if there were only three alumni from an institution living in Cheyenne, Wyoming and there were forty alumni living in Baltimore, Maryland, where should an upper administrator go to solicit donations? Conversely, if three alumni had Dallas addresses but a GIS map revealed large clusters of alumni located in Plano, Garland, Desoto, and Irving, it would still be appropriate to hold an alumni event in Dallas because the other four cities are suburbs that encircle Dallas, making Dallas an ideal centralized location with access to major roads and public transportation. As stated by Daniel D. Jardine of Binghamton University:

The Office of Institutional Research at Binghamton University (SUNY) analyzed donating patterns and behaviors of BU alumni from 1992 to 2002...The database used in the analysis includes more than seventy-five thousand records. The vast majority of these records contain address-related data, particularly the zip code of the individual. With the zip code, the alumni data could be geocoded or assigned coordinates to be placed on a digital map in a geographic information system (GIS). Using a GIS can greatly enhance the ability to better visualize alumni data to improve the planning efforts of future campaigns. (Jardine, 2003, p. 77)

There are institutional research offices currently using GIS to plot where the institution receives donations by donor address.. By using GIS they are able to produce a graphical representation of how many donations were given and the dollar amounts of those solicitations. By using this type of data for analysis, the institutional research office can best determine the return on investment for soliciting funds from certain locations and be able to determine from alumni addresses, which regions may be able to be solicited that have not previously been contacted for donations.

EPILOGUE

Including geospatial information systems with standard institutional research practices can supplement and potentially expand an organization's capacity for resource assessment, financial planning, facility expansion, emergency management, and institutional planning. While many institutional research departments do not have responsibilities as broad as those of OSPA at UT-Dallas, institutional researchers can still utilize GIS in ways that can positively impact their institutions. With a modest investment in training, institutional researchers can supplement their standard analytic practices by integrating GIS software with their existing databases. It is important for an institutional research department to carefully evaluate their current practices to determine if any gains can be made by using this type of technology or if GIS can perform or expand upon the kind of analysis the department finds most useful.

The development of LTS allowed for cost savings of $1.68 million (Cost Savings Report FY 2001 – 2003 reported to the State of Texas by UT-Dallas) and has saved even more money since 2003 through automation as well as further expansion of LTS's capabilities (Valcik, 2009). Additionally LTS has won an award from the National Safety Council/Campus, Safety, Health and Environmental Management Association Award of Recognition in the Unique or Innovative Category in 2006. In 2011, The University of Texas at Tyler licensed LTS to track and record data for their facility information and is currently considering using GIS to map down their facilities (2012). The Office of Strategic Planning and Analysis has begun to implement GIS with many of its other institutional research projects, in particular benchmarking projects. The office intends to present this research to university administrators and in regional and national institutional research forums upon conclusion. GIS holds a great deal of potential for graphically displaying traditional demographic data in new, more informative and more accessible ways.

QUESTION AND ANSWERS ON THE CASE STUDY

1. Should every higher education use GIS for analysis?

GIS usage will not be practical for every higher education institution. Some institutions will not have the funds for a GIS license or the personnel to dedicate to such endeavors while other institutions will simply not have the operational needs (i.e. small student enrollment) to justify the investment. Other institutions with operational needs and the available funds and personnel that can be dedicated to perform GIS work should consider using such a tool to enhance their analytically capability as well as answer questions on operational issues.

2. Can GIS be used with other software packages to increase the ability to perform analytical work?

GIS can be interfaced with several different statistical packages that can import or export information to GIS. A prime example would be the use of SAS with GIS. Other software such as the LTS software that The University of Texas at Dallas has developed uses GIS as the main driver to import accurate information into the system. Information from systems such as LTS can also be exported which will allow GIS analysts to produce maps for operational uses. Institutional research offices that are considering using GIS should check software that they currently license to see if there is a possibility to use their existing product with GIS.

3. How hard is it for someone to learn how to use GIS?

Like any other software or programming language, it is possible to learn how to use GIS by oneself. However the author of this chapter highly recommends formal training for new users. GIS applications are complex enough that advanced degree programs, like the ones offered at The University of Texas at Dallas, are necessary to completely master them.

4. Is any special requirements needed to install GIS on a personal computer?

Institutional researchers should always check the ESRI website to see what the latest requirements are to use GIS on their personal computer. For ArcSDE a Sentinel Key is required to be plugged into the USB port of the server where ArcSDE resides. ArcSDE can be used with Microsoft SQL Server,

IBM DB2 and Oracle. It is important for institutional researchers to check their server capabilities as well as ESRI's information to determine whether or not ArcSDE can be used on a departmental server.

5. How should I reference maps that are produced by GIS?

GIS maps (unless they are the fictitious type in Figure 1.1) should include the following information so that the map can be recreated: an arrow indicating North, a scale representing distance on the map (i.e. 1 inch = 1 mile) and a title. Optional items are legends, projection system (i.e. NAD 83) and statistical summary (refer to Figure 1.5). The source data for the map must include a proper citation. A GIS user can accomplish this one of two ways. If there is only one source, then that source can be referenced on the map directly (see Figure 1.6). If the source comes from multiple references, then the user should reference the source in APA format (see Figure 1.2). In this chapter, maps that are referenced in this manner have an asterisk system used to denote the correct source to the map where the source was used.

6. Where might someone find a GIS license in a higher education institution?

An institutional research office can check a variety of academic or administrative offices that may already have a GIS license at their institution. Likely academic departments include Geology, Engineering, Geospatial Information Systems, Political Science, Criminal Justice or Economics. Among administrative departments, Business Affairs may have a GIS license for real estate tracking, architecture or for physical plant uses. For institutions that are in a university or college system, the system office may have a system wide agreement for such a license.

GIS RESOURCES OR INFORMATIONAL WEBSITES

Bruton Center - http://www.utdallas.edu/epps/gis/
ESRI – The developers of ArcGIS - http://www.esri.com/
GIS Department at The University of Texas at Dallas - http://www.utdallas.edu/epps/gis/
North Central Texas Council of Governments - http://www.nctcog.dst.tx.us/
U.S. Geological Survey - http://www.usgs.gov/

REFERENCES

Blough, D. R. (2003). Integrating GIS into the Survey Research Process:Using Geographic Information Systems in Institutional Research. Jossey-Bass.

Crosier, S. (2009). *John Snow: The London Cholera Epidemic of 1854*. Center for Spatially Integrated Social Science, Regents of University of California, Santa Barbara. Retrieved on October 14, 2010. http://www.csiss.org/classics/content/8

Daniel, D. E. (2008). *Executive Summary: Thoughts on Creating More Tier One Universities in Texas*. The University of Texas at Dallas. Retrieved on May 28, 2010. http://www.utdallas.edu/president/documents/executive-summary.pdf

ESRI. (2010). *ESRI Info: Company History*. Retrieved on May 6, 2010. http://www.esri.com/about-esri/about/history.html

Granados, M. (2003). Mapping Data on Enrolled Students. In D. Teodorescu (Ed.), Using Geographic Information Systems in Institutional Research. Jossey-Bass. doi:10.1002/ir.90

Jardine, D. D. (2003). Using GIS in Alumni Giving and Institutional Advancement. In D. Teodorescu (Ed.), Using Geographic Information Systems in Institutional Research. Jossey-Bass. doi:10.1002/ir.94

McCormick, B. G. (2003). Developing Enterprise GIS for University Administration: Organizational and Strategic Considerations. In D. Teodorescu (Ed.), Using Geographic Information Systems in Institutional Research. Jossey-Bass.

Mora, V. J. (2003). Applications of GIS in Admissions and Targeting Recruiting Efforts. In D. Teodorescu (Ed.), Using Geographic Information Systems in Institutional Research. Jossey-Bass. doi:10.1002/ir.89

Murchison, S. B. (2010). Uses of GIS for Homeland Security and Emergency Management at Higher Education Institutions. In N. Valcik (Ed.), *Institutional Research: Homeland Security*. Hoboken, NJ: John Wiley and Sons, Inc. doi:10.1002/ir.344

Ormsby, T., Napoleon, E., Burke, R., Grossl, C., & Bowden, L. (2008). *Getting to Know ArcGIS Desktop*. Redlands, CA: ESRI Press.

The University of Texas at Dallas. (2010). *Enrollment*. Office of Strategic Planning and Analysis. Retrieved on May 17, 2010, from http://www.utdallas.edu/ospa/stats/Enrollment.html

The University of Texas at Dallas. (2012). Student Information Systems. Author.

The University of Texas at Dallas Office of the Registrar. (2012). *Student Information Systems and Logistical Tracking System*. Author.

Valcik, N. (2003). Building a Space Management System. Midwestern Review of Business and Economics,32, 16-21.

Valcik, N. (2006). *Regulating the Use of Biological Hazardous Materials in Universities: Complying with the New Federal Guidelines*. Lewiston, NY: Edwin Mellen Press.

Valcik, N. (2007). The Logistical Tracking System (LTS) Five Years Later: What have we Learned?. In N. Valcik (Ed.), Space: The Final Frontier for Institutional Research. John Wiley and Sons, Inc.

Valcik, N. (2010). New Hazardous Materials (HAZMAT) Federal Regulations for Higher Education Institutions. In N. Valcik (Ed.), *Institutional Research: Homeland Security. New Directions for Institutional Research*. Hoboken, NJ: John Wiley and Sons, Inc.

Valcik, N., Aiken, C. L. V., Xu, X., & Al Farhan, M. S. (2009). Homeland Security in the United States: An analysis of the utilization of novel information and virtual technologies for Homeland Security. In K. Jaishankar (Ed.), *International Perspectives on Criminology and Criminal Justice*. New Castle, UK: Cambridge Scholars Publishing.

Valcik, N., & Huesca-Dorantes, P. (2003). Building a GIS Database for Space and Facilities Management. In D. Teodorescu (Ed.), Using Geographic Information Systems in Institutional Research. Jossey-Bass.

Valcik, N. (2009a). University Enhances Its Logistical Tracking System with GIS. *ESRI ArcNews, 31*(1). Retrieved from http://www.esri.com/news/arcnews/spring09articles/university-enhances.html

Valcik, N. (2009b). *New Homeland Security Concerns Regarding Higher Education Institutions and Chemical Hazardous Materials*. The CIP Report, George Mason University School of Law. Retrieved on May 6, 2010, from http://cip.gmu.edu/archive/cip_report_8.4.pdf

Chapter 3
Exploring Local Interaction Attributes Affecting Leadership Effectiveness on Assignment in Multinational Companies: A Qualitative Phenomenological Study

Iván Tirado-Cordero
Quinnipiac University, USA

Kathleen M. Hargiss
St. Petersburg College, USA

ABSTRACT

Social cognitive theory is founded on the belief that learning is shared socially. Triadic reciprocal determinism explains the interrelationship and interaction between environmental cues, behavior, and biological determinants to shape and alter the perception of the self and how individuals assume agentic perspectives in social interactions to approach challenges and pursue goals. Knowing how learners perceived their likelihood to achieve success also provides for a better understanding of the constraints and opportunities of a proposed learning solution. The purpose of this study was to explore the self-efficacy beliefs of adolescents as part of the analysis of the learners in the instructional design system (ISD) model in terms of entry behaviors for the design of a peer tutoring learning environment. The General Self-Efficacy Scale (GSE) was used to interview participants, using the questions as open-ended questions. Observations of the social interactions between participants were collected during focus groups to discuss their responses to the GSE scale. The results of this study suggested that individuals with high self-efficacy not only assume a direct personal agentic perspective when acting alone but that they also assume and motivate others to engage in a collective agentic perspective. Individuals with low self-efficacy assume proxy or surrogate agentic perspectives in social interactions and require prompting to engage and participate. High self-efficacy indicates effective collaboration through the collective agency, which affects success positively in a peer tutoring learning environment. Low self-efficacy affects negatively success in peer tutoring, because individuals with low self-efficacy assume a proxy or surrogate agentic

DOI: 10.4018/978-1-5225-1680-4.ch003

perspective detaching themselves from the interactions. However, individuals with low self-efficacy, through prompting and motivation from peers with high self-efficacy can improve their interactions and as goals are reached, improve self-efficacy.

INTRODUCTION

Learning is neither a transmissive nor a submissive process. Rather learning is willful, intentional, active, conscious, constructive practice that includes reciprocal intention – action – reflection activities. Humans are different from primates in their abilities to articulate an intention and then to willfully plan to act on it. Actions are integrations of perceptions and conscious thinking. (Jonassen & Land, 2000, p. v)

Learning is for Jonassen and Land a process of meaning making. This process comprises balancing individual perceptions with perceptions of what others know, the responses from the environment, and experiences that lead to action. In other words, an action feeds itself from consciousness and perception. Meaning making also occurs within a social context, and knowledge is shared among the participants within that context.

Knowledge resides in discourse and communication among individuals and their relationships. These relationships also influence how individuals see themselves, perceive their social circle, and assume how their social circle sees them. Social negotiation becomes knowledge negotiation, through which individuals engage in the meaning-making process. This theory shift leads to a focus on the development of student-centered learning theories with special attention to social-mediated communication (Jonassen & Land, 2000). Social interrelationship influences learning and self-perception, also defined as self-efficacy (Ashford & LeCroy, 2010).

Self-efficacy beliefs are domain-specific personal interpretations of capabilities to perform a task or reach a goal (Bandura, 2002; Bruning et al., 2004; Goddard, LoGerfo, & Hoy, 2004; Ormrod, 2006). Confronted by a specific task, individuals would, consciously or unconsciously, evaluate their skills to achieve the domain expectations, leading to how they will approach the task at hand. Bandura (2002) argued that self-efficacy is also modifiable under favorable conditions. According to Bandura (1989a), self-efficacy is influenced by triadic reciprocal determinism, which is the interaction between three factors of causation:

1. Behavior,
2. Environment, and
3. Personal cognitive factors.

According to Bandura:

Human behavior has often been explained in terms of one-sided determinism. In such modes of unidirectional causation, behavior is depicted as being shaped and controlled either by environmental influences or by internal dispositions. Social cognitive theory favors a model of causation involving triadic reciprocal determinism. In this model of reciprocal causation, behavior, cognition and other personal factors, and environmental influences all operate as interacting determinants that influence each other bidirectionally. (p. 2)

Figure 1. Triadic reciprocal determinism

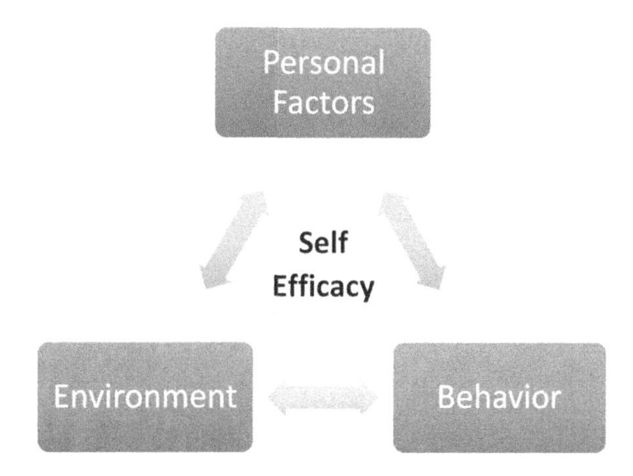

According to Bandura, "because of the bidirectionality of influence between behavior and environmental circumstances, people are both products and producers of their environment" (p. 4), and "seen from the social cognitive perspective, human nature is characterized by a vast potentiality that can be fashioned by direct and vicarious experience into a variety of forms within biological limits" (p. 74). People influence their environments as their environments influence them. People select, create, and perceive their environment according to the interactions between the factors of causation, and they do this while simultaneously creating or perceiving an image of themselves within the specific environment.

People assume models of agency intentionally in social interactions, and according to Bandura (2002), "The determinants and agentic blends of individual, proxy, and collective instrumentally vary cross-culturally" (p. 269)., and These behaviors Bandura (2002) defined as assuming agentic perspectives. An agentic perspective describes the type of interaction or role an individual will assume in a given situation. Bandura (2002) defined three agentic perspectives:

1. Direct personal, exercised individually and independently;
2. Proxy or surrogate, which relies on others to act in behalf of the one who exercises it; and
3. Collective, exercised as a group action.

Self-efficacy changes and develops according to age and developmental stages (Bandura, 2008; Bandura, 2009; & Davis-Kean, Huesmann, Jager, Collins, Bates, & Lansford, 2008). Agency depends not only on environmental influences, but also on the maturity of individuals to interpret events and experiences and intentionally influence life circumstances. Adolescence brings cognitive development of symbolic interpretations and a strong perception of the self is of great importance at this stage of life (Bandura, 2009). Adolescents are also forced to develop new skills as they are trying to understand biological changes and how they fit into a fast-changing society in which technology is transforming how people communicate and relate to each other, learn, and conduct their lives and daily affairs. Adolescence could be a crucial time in the life of any individual, where finding oneself becomes a constant consideration of environmental responses. With the advances of technology, the youth generation receives environmental influences through multimedia communication and away from parental or other authority figures intrusion (Bandura, 2006; Bandura, 2009; Matsushima, & Shiomi, 2003).

Figure 2. Agentic perspectives of human agency

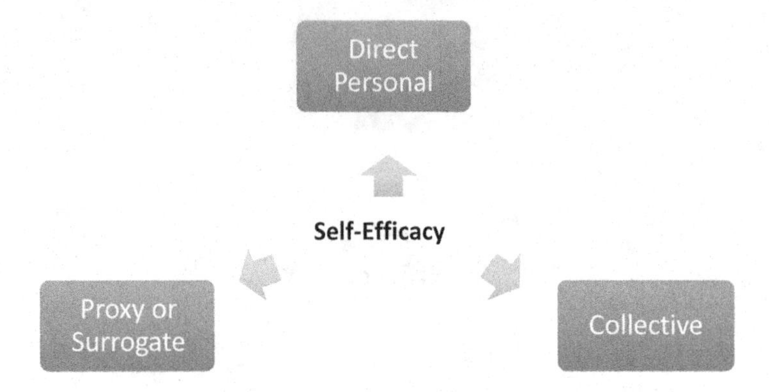

BACKGROUND

Conducting analysis is the first logical step in the instructional system design (ISD) process in order to get a clear understanding of the problem before providing effective instructional solutions (Brown, 2002; Gupta, Sleezer, & Russ-Eft, 2007; O'Brien & Hall, 2004; Phillips, 2000; Smith & Ragan, 2005). The analysis of the learners goes beyond demographic characteristics and pretesting knowledge on the subject matter but identifying entry behaviors for the learning environment. An effective peer tutoring learning environment requires learners to assume collective agency perspective and the negotiation of knowledge among equals (Topping, 2005). According to Topping, peer learning, "is possibly as old as any form of collaborative or community action" (p. 631) and defined peer learning as "the acquisition of knowledge and skill through active helping and supporting among status equals or matched companions" (p. 631). Learners communicate to understand the subject in discussion, deeper stimulating higher order thinking, taking in the knowledge contribution of the participants, and figuratively speaking building greater knowledge than learners on their own.

Individuals assess themselves and measure their capabilities and skills to succeed against those expected or required by the learning environment they ought to experience. These are self-efficacy beliefs, the capacity to recognize skills, or lack thereof, to succeed in a given enterprise. Individuals assume agentic perspectives based on self-efficacy beliefs that determine how they interact socially. Self-efficacy beliefs have a malleable quality that allows individuals to modify their perception of themselves and their skills to achieved desired goals. Assessing self-efficacy beliefs and agentic perspectives to engage in a peer-tutoring learning environment not only serves individuals to evaluate their chances of success, but allows instructional designers to help individuals achieve their goals by designing learning goals and instructional strategies that facilitate modification and transformation of self-efficacy beliefs.

PROBLEM STATEMENT

Instructional designers aim to provide effective learning solutions not only for the acquisition or transference of knowledge but also providing for a transformative learning experience. Knowing how learners perceive their likelihood to achieve success also provides for a better understanding of the constraints and opportunities of a proposed learning solution (Graham, 2011). Bruning, Schraw, Norby, and Ronning

(2004) proposed that individuals will pursue and put more effort and persistence into those activities they consider achievable based on the perception they have of their skills to succeed, and learning is no exception. Behaviors such as task engagement, performance, anxiety, stress, persistence, and coping skills are affected or influenced by those perceptions (Conner & Norman, 2005; Luszczynska & Schwarzer, 2005; Schwarzer, 2008).

People behave in social interactions as they see themselves and pursue goals more actively when they believe these are achievable. For instructional purposes, self-efficacy provides hints of how people would behave in specific situations. Exploring self-efficacy beliefs can lead one to predict the model of agency learners will adopt when engaging in a peer-tutoring learning environment. This prediction is considered an entry behavior, which informs the ISD process. Learning goals and instructional strategies are then directed to improve self-efficacy and collaborative learning.

This is significant for the field of instructional design in the continuous effort to design instruction in which learning becomes a transformative process through helping learners improve self-efficacy beliefs. While this study focused on the analysis of the learners and identification of entry behaviors for an online peer-tutoring system before moving on fully into design and development of such system, the identification of agentic roles in collaborative learning is a task that can be performed by instructors and designers during instruction as formative evaluation, and for summative evaluation as well (Dick, Carey, & Carey, 2008). Learners could have the opportunity to evaluate themselves and their performance, develop awareness of their self-efficacy beliefs (Bruning et al., 2004), and assume responsibility for their self-regulation choices. The same could be used to evaluate their peers and might help to formulate collective goals for helping each other in the transformative process.

PURPOSE OF THE STUDY

The purpose of this interpretive, qualitative study was to explore self-efficacy beliefs for success in a peer-tutoring learning environment, to explore the factors of causation that influence perceptions of the self, and to classify these beliefs as entry behaviors using the models of agency described by Bandura (2002)"

1. Direct personal,
2. Proxy or surrogate, and
3. Collective agency, using an interpretivist approach.

Participation in a peer-tutoring learning environment requires that social interaction and collaborative learning initiatives avoid the conception of lower and higher roles. Peer tutoring requires learners to assume collective agency for effective learning and dynamics, and this agency is influenced by self-efficacy beliefs that are domain specific (Bandura, 2002; Bruning, Schraw, Norby, & Ronning, 2004; Goddard, LoGerfo, & Hoy, 2004), and influenced by factors of causation:

1. Environment,
2. Behavior, and cognitive and biological limitations (Bandura, 1989b).

The plasticity of self-efficacy beliefs allows for improvement under favorable circumstances; therefore, is necessary to identify self-efficacy believes as entry behaviors for such environments in order to design learning goals and instructional strategies. The results could be used to guide the design of an online peer-tutoring learning environment in the selection and development of learning goals and instructional strategies that promote collective agency as a transformative process.

RESEARCH QUESTIONS

Considering the relationship between self-efficacy beliefs, agentic perspectives, and factors of causation in the context of the intended study, if self-efficacy beliefs influence the assumption of agentic perspectives in social interactions (Bandura, 2002), which are simultaneously influenced by factors of causation (behavior, environment, and biological and cognitive limitations) (Bandura, 1989b), then individuals under similar circumstances should assume similar roles when interacting socially. If the factors of causation for different individuals are similar, then their agentic perspective should be similar, then:

- In what ways do self-efficacy beliefs affect success in a peer-tutoring environment?
- What are the similarities and differences in self-efficacy beliefs among participants?

LITERATURE REVIEW

Social Cognitive Theory and Triadic Reciprocal Determinism

In social cognitive theory, learning is shared between individuals and their environments, creating an interaction that allows the environment to influence a person while this person selects, creates, and forms the environment according to the interactions between the two. The environment is influential to individuals as individuals are influential to their environment, neither in total freedom or total submission. Individuals have the power to decide on what stimuli from the environment to receive, categorize, and transform and not to just reside within their environment as mere reactors of external influences imposed upon them (Bandura, 1977). Individuals have limited control over their environment just as the environment has limited control over them.

Social learning theory highlights psychological functioning driven by vicarious, symbolic, and self-regulatory processes (Bandura, 1977). Each one plays an important role for cognitive development, because these are the responses from the individual to the environmental determinants. Bandura described these processes as cognitive control. The influence from the environment comes through external stimuli, which are mostly out of the control of the individual. Individuals not only react to external stimuli, they interpret the external impulses to determine their influence through cognitive control, creating a mutual influence interaction between individual and environment. According to Bandura (1977),

It is largely through their actions that people produce the environmental conditions that affect their behavior in a reciprocal fashion. The experiences generated by behavior also partly determine what a person becomes and can do which, in turn, affects subsequent behavior. (p. 9)

Bandura (1977) conceptualized alternative views of this interaction and how causal processes operate between Behavior (B), Person (P), and Environment (E), which are the elements of triadic reciprocal determination (TRD). The relationship between person and situation can be represented as B = *f* (P,E) where person and environment determine each other but are considered independent entities. When interaction between person and environment is bidirectional, behavior is still considered a result or product of the interaction B = *f* (P <=> E). Behavior is not only a product but an interactive determinant, and interacts reciprocally with personal determinants as it does with environmental determinants, and all three factors operate as "interlocking determinants," which brings back to balance cognitive control with external stimuli, then B <=> P, P <=> E, E <=> B. According to Bandura (2008),

Social cognitive theory conceptualizes the interactional causal structure as triadic reciprocal causation. In this conception, human functioning is a product of a reciprocal interplay of interpersonal, behavioral, and environmental determinants. In the analytic decomposition of triadic determination, different subspecialties of psychology have centered their inquiry on particular segments of the reciprocal interplay. In the reciprocative relation between interpersonal and behavioral determinants, people's biological endowments, conceptions, values, goals, and affective states influence how they behave. The natural and extrinsic effects of their actions, in turn, affect their thought process and affective states. In the reciprocative relation between behavioral and environmental determinants, behavior alters environmental conditions and it is, in turn, altered by the very conditions it creates. In the reciprocative relation between interpersonal and environmental determinants, social influences in the form of social modeling, instructional practices, and various modes of social persuasion alter personal attributes. In the reciprocal impact of this segment, people can affect their environment without saying or doing anything. They elicit reactions from the social environment simply by their physical characteristics, such as their ethnicity, gender, race, age, physical attractiveness, and their socially conferred roles and statuses. The social reactions thus elicited, in turn, affect the recipients' conceptions of themselves and others in ways that either strengthen or reduce the environmental bias. (p. 34-35)

People are exposed to multiple ways for acquiring their conceptions, values, goals, and affective states that influence behavior. According to Bandura (1977),

Psychological theories have traditionally assumed that learning can occur only by performing responses and experiencing their effects. In actuality, virtually all learning phenomena resulting from direct experience occur on a vicarious basis by observing other people's behavior and its consequences for them. The capacity to learn by observation enables people to acquire large, integrated patterns of behavior without having to form them gradually by tedious trial and error. (p. 12).

Humans do not only learn vicariously, since their capacity to utilize symbols and apply meaning to them provides opportunities to guide themselves for future behavior (Bandura, 1977). Individuals interpret experiences in a symbolic fashion to alter their behavior and determine alternative course of action. Symbolic processes allow reflective thought and opportunities to solve problems without attempting all possible solutions. Similarly, individuals can exercise control over their own actions through their self-regulatory capacities, which are supported and regulated by external influence. When facing a specific situation or environmental stimuli, individuals have the capacity to consciously act in a certain fashion or refrain from acting. Each behavior will receive an external response, which leads to learning through response consequences.

The motivational function of response consequences helps anticipate outcomes symbolically to use past experiences to foresee future consequences of behavior (Bandura, 1977). Motivational responses serve as preventive actions to avoid negative consequences or to be prepared if those negative consequences occur. Behaviors that are reinforced produce an increase of that behavior, but when there is awareness of a reward producing more automatic responses to stimuli, "awareness is not an all-or-none phenomenon" (p. 20). The response to a behavior must be interpreted as acceptable by the individual for the behavior to be increased favorably.

Social cognitive theory also describes how individuals anticipate probable consequences and use control capabilities to regulate their behavior based on their expectations (Bandura, 1977). According to Bandura, "environmental events can predict either other environmental occurrences, or serve as predictors of the relation between actions and outcomes" (p. 59). This phenomenon is defined as "antecedent determinants." Antecedent determinants allow individuals to create scenarios and react to them, which leads to anxiety, defensive behavior, aggression, symbolic expectancy, and vicarious expectancy. Bandura stated,

People often behave appropriately without either personal experience or explanation of probable response consequences. This is because information about predictive stimuli is derived vicariously by observing how the behavior of others is reinforced in different situations. Although actions are frequently guided by judgments based on what one has observed or been told, the maintenance of antecedent determinants that have been established verbally or vicariously ordinarily requires periodic confirmation through direct experience. (p. 86)

Antecedent determinants come as a response from the individual to possible environmental cues. It is important to keep in mind that the person is not isolated from the environment that provided the stimuli that influenced the symbols for the creation of possible scenarios. Individuals anticipate environmental stimuli based on interpretation of past experiences or symbols provided by the environment and respond to environmental stimuli that have not yet come to pass.

Actions have consequences, and it is through those consequences that behaviors are regulated, which Bandura (1977) described as "consequent determinants" and "for the most part, response consequences influence behavior antecedently by creating expectations of similar outcomes on future occasions" (p. 96). Consequent determinants include external reinforcement such as incentives, rewards, punishment, vicarious reinforcement, and self-reinforcement. Consequence determinants are responses and potential responses from the environment towards behavior, which acts simultaneously with antecedent determinants and behavior to create reciprocal interactions between behavior, environment, and personal factors. As presented previously, both antecedent determinants and consequence determinants are subject to interpretation by personal factors to regulate behavior based on environmental or self-imposed perceived punishment or rewards.

"From social learning theory, psychological functioning is a continuous reciprocal interaction between personal, behavioral, and environmental determinants" (p.194) and "people's expectations influence how they behave and the outcomes of their behavior change their expectations" (p. 195). The reciprocal interaction does not imply that personal, behavioral, and environmental determinants influence through balanced counter reactions or that all have the same power at the same time, but rather that it is a mutual influence. Bandura stated that,

Thus, behavior partly determine which of the many potential influences will come into play and what forms they will take; environmental influences, in turn, partly determine which behavioral repertoires are develop and activated. In this two-way influence process, the environment is influenceable, as is the behavior it regulates. (p. 195)

Until rewards or punishment from the environment come to pass as a result of activation by behavior, they are only potential. The capacity of individuals to use symbolic interpretations of potential scenarios provides for regulation of behavior, therefore changing the expectations of potential responses from the environment; triadic reciprocal determination can be represented here as B <=> P, P <=> E, and E <=> B simultaneously.

As previously mentioned, determinism does not make individuals surrogate of environmental responses, nor completely free of environmental influences. Bandura (1977) stated,

In philosophical discourses, freedom is often considered antithetical to determinism. When freedom is defined in terms of options and rights, there is no incompatibility between freedom and determinism. From this perspective, freedom is not conceived negatively as the absence of influences or simply the lack of external constraints. Rather, it is defined positively in terms of the skills at one's command and the exercise of self-influence which choice of action requires. (p. 203)

Individuals develop skills and personal controls to influence their environment based on biological and cognitive limitations in conjunction with antecedent and consequent determinants in the mutual reciprocal interaction of these factors. As stated by Bandura (1989), "because of the bidirectionality of influence between behavior and environmental circumstances, people are both products and producers of their environment. They affect the nature of their experienced environment through selection and creation of situations" (p. 4). Individuals select activities based on their skills, competencies, and preferences, and create and select environments through their actions.

It is unconceivable to predict accurately how individuals will react to environmental determinants at any given time; rather, it is a succession of events that influence how personal skills are developed and how behavior and life circumstances will unfold (Bandura, 1989). Influential determinants include social influences based on age, family, education, social groups, and so on, while biological limitations also play an important role in influential factors and how these are interpreted. Through the course of life, unforeseen and unpredictable events like accidents, illness, relocation, broken relationships, career changes, and so forth can also be an influence. Technology is another factor of influence to be considered, since social changes often comes with technological advances, and these are used in customary ways by individuals within their context (Bandura, 1989).

Bandura (2009) explained how mass communication plays a crucial role in how individuals see and interpret environmental cues through new forms of social interaction, vicarious learning, abstract modeling, symbolization, and self-regulatory capabilities without immediate experience. Technology expands immediate social circles and interactions, from which individuals draw new sets of antecedent and consequent determinants that regulate behavior in ways that were not easily possible without technology. Television, Internet, and other forms of mass communication that provides new social constructions of reality, new forms of modeled behavior, and a vast array of possible scenarios beyond the immediate physical environment influence individuals. An example of the extension of the immediate physical environment is the participation in social networks through Internet communication. According to Bandura (2009), "people share information, give meaning by mutual feedback to the information they exchange, gain understanding of each other's views, and influence each other" (p. 118). Also,

Through interactive electronic networking people link together in widely dispersed locals, exchange information, share new ideas, and transact any number of pursuits. Virtual networking provides a flexible means for creating diffusion structures to serve given purposes, expanding their membership, extending them geographically, and disbanding then when they have outlived their usefulness. With increasing interactivity through blogging and pod postings, Internet technology is interconnecting people globally in the virtual social networks of the cyberworld. (p. 119).

Bandura (2006) analyzed the factors developmental changes, technology, and the exercise of control and regulatory skills, also called human agency, focusing on adolescents. Before describing the influence of technology in adolescents in their specific developmental process of change, it is necessary to discuss the concept of human agency in human functioning.

Agentic Perspectives of Human Functioning

Bandura (2008) stated that "to be an agent is to influence intentionally one's functioning and life circumstances" (p. 16). Individuals are not just the result of their environment or life circumstances, but rather individuals consciously contribute to their environment or life circumstances to change their environments and themselves. According to Bandura, "Given that individuals are producers as well as products of their life circumstances, they are partial authors of the past conditions that developed them, as well as the future courses their lives take" (p. 165). In other words, if past circumstances shaped a specific behavior, individuals are capable and responsible for applying personal controls to influence the circumstances and themselves in order to redirect the course of their lives, and this is possible through human agency.

There are four characteristics of human agency:

1. Intentionality,
2. Forethought,
3. Self-reactiveness, and
4. Self-reflectiveness.

Individuals can plan, set goals, act upon their plans and goals, and examine their own actions. According to Bandura (1989b),

Persons are neither autonomous agents nor simply mechanical conveyers of animating environmental influences. Rather, they make causal contribution to their own motivation and action within a system of triadic reciprocal causation. In this model of reciprocal causation, action, cognitive, affective, and other personal factors, and environmental events operate as interactive determinants. Any account of the determinants of human action must, therefore, include self-generated influences as contributing factors. (p. 1175)

Furthermore,

In acting as agents over their environments, people draw on their knowledge and cognitive and behavioral skills to produce desired results. In acting as agents over themselves, people monitor their actions and enlist cognitive guides and self-incentives to produce desired personal changes. They are just as much agents influencing themselves as they are influencing their environment. (p. 1181)

Social cognitive theory presents three models of agency:

1. Individual,
2. Proxy, and
3. Collective (Bandura, 2006).

People use individual agency to influence their self-regulatory processes and exercise intentionality, forethought, self-reactiveness, and self-reflectiveness to bear with environmental cues. Individual agency is the role played to influence antecedents, actions, and responses to make conscious choices in order to influence the environment, seeking well-being regardless of the level of control an individual has over social and institutional conditions (Bandura, 2001). Nevertheless, individual agency is not necessarily exercised egocentrically, but rather can be exercised to the benefit of others. Bandura (2008) stated that, "people's life pursuits, goals, values, and aspirations influence the form their agency takes and the purposes their efficacy beliefs serve. In point of fact, personal efficacy can serve diverse purposes, many of which subordinate self-interest to the benefit of others" (p. 28).

The lack of control over environmental circumstances forces individuals not to exercise individual or direct personal agency in every situation and "everyday functioning requires an agentic blend of these three forms of agency" (Bandura, 2006, p. 165). No model of agency is completely abandoned when it is primarily acting in a given situation, but individuals consciously can shift and exercise the model of agency that better suits the specific situation. Individuals can recognize that they are incapable or unprepared to endure a situation on their own and rely on others to help them achieve specific goals. According to Bandura (2001),

People also turn to proxy control in areas in which they can exert direct influence when they have not developed the means to do so, they believe others can do it better, or they do not want to saddle themselves with the burdensome aspects that direct control entails. (p. 13)

Even under these circumstances, proxy agency requires intentionality, forethought, self-reactiveness, and self-reflectiveness. Bandura also stated that,

In addition to the hard work of continual self-development, the exercise of personal control often carries heavy responsibilities, stressors, and risks. People are not especially eager to shoulder the burdens of responsibility. All too often, they surrender control to intermediaries in activities over which they can command direct influence. They do so to free themselves of the performance demands and onerous responsibilities that personal control entails. (p. 13)

While proxy agency might gain negative connotations, in many areas of life things can only be achieved through social interdependency, which in some cases entails relying on the competency of or working in coordination with others. However, surrendering control for extended periods of time may reflect egocentric behavior or that no self-development has taken place (Bandura, 2006). After some time, individuals who surrender control to the capabilities of others to influence their circumstances should be able to develop the means to do so on their own or collectively.

Social cognitive theory emphasizes in the concept of collective agency (Bandura, 2001). Knowledge, skills, resources, beliefs, practices, and so forth abide collectively in the minds of group members and are exercised to achieve common goals (Bandura, 2006). Working collectively increases the opportunities and probabilities to attain desired goals not only by the sum of efficacy beliefs of individual participants, but through a perceived collective efficacy (Bandura, 2001). With the advances of technology, individuals are not limited to the immediate physical environment, and may increase collective agency traits through a symbolic environment (Bandura, 2008). According to Bandura (2008), "people worldwide are becoming increasingly enmeshed in a cyberworld that transcends time, distance, place, and national borders" (p. 26).

Bandura (2008) argued that the globalization of cultural identity is allowing individuals to increase their observational learning capacities. What is modeled by society is also changing, as well as how people interpret the symbols of environmental cues. Individuals receive a vast array of information through modeled behavior and symbolic environmental cues that are shaping their behavior and the external responses from their immediate physical and extended social context which has become more hybrid and ethnically blended. As a result, new behaviors emerge reshaping cognitive, affective, and other personal factors.

Agentic Perspective of Adolescents

Different periods of life present certain prototypic challenges and competency demands for successful functioning. Changing aspirations, time perspectives, and societal systems over the course of the life span alter how people structure, regulate, and evaluate their lives. (Bandura, 2006, p. 1)

Social learning theory presents the relationship between environmental, behavioral, and individual factors and the reciprocal influence among these factors. According to Bandura (2009), "major sociocultural changes that make life markedly different—such as technological innovations, economic depressions, military conflicts, cultural upheavals, and political changes—modify the character of the society in ways that have strong impact on life courses" (p. 2-3). As societies change and are expanded and globalized through technology, behaviors change, and personal factors change as well. Society is experiencing environmental changes that seem to coexist together in a short period of time, shaping cognitive, affective, and personal factors of the youth generation rapidly.

People change, and their perspectives on life, goals, expectations, symbolic interpretation, affective, and cognitive factors change, as does how they manage their lives, how they perceive their capabilities to manage their lives, and how they conduct themselves through the different developmental stages. Biological changes, age, social roles, and status are influential factors in the process of adoption of an agentic perspective (Bandura, 2009). Circumstances can take different paths as life goes on, and people can be prepared or not to respond to sudden unexpected environmental changes, just as for those changes that come more gradually. Bandura stated that,

People are often inaugurated into new life trajectories through fortuitous circumstances. Fortuity does not mean uncontrollability of its effects. There are ways that people capitalize on the fortuitous character of life. They make chance happen by pursuing an active life that increases the fortuitous encounters they will experience. People also make chance work for them by cultivating their interests, enabling beliefs, and competencies. These personal resources enable them to make the most of opportunities that arise unexpectedly. (p. 2)

Each phase of life presents opportunities, limitations, and challenges and similarly, society offers different chances and life experiences as it evolves. Bandura (2009) argued that,

The adolescents of yesteryear grew up in an environment quite different from that of the youth of today. They are players in an electronic era of rapid social and technological change that is transforming how people communicate, educate, work, relate to each other, and conduct their business and daily affairs. (p. 2)

As life is different, so too are its expectations and demands, specially for adolescents who have to face biological, social, and educational transitions simultaneously, first during pubertal changes and later as they approach adulthood (Bandura, 2009). Many new skills have to be developed, and "social cognitive theory emphasizes personal growth through mastery and other enabling experiences as the more normative developmental process" (p. 7). Moreover,

Adolescents need to commit themselves to goals that give them purpose and a sense of accomplishment. Without personal commitment to something worth doing, they are unmotivated, bored, or cynical. They become dependent on extrinsic sources of stimulation. A vision of a desired future helps to organize their lives, provides meaning to their activities, motivates them, and enables them to tolerate the hassles of getting there. (p. 10)

Adolescents need environmental factors and efficient models and symbols that will allow them to understand their position in the form of agency in order to influence their lives allowing them to transition, according to circumstances, from one model of agency to another. The development of skills will allow them to have more control over external influences and societal cues (Bandura, 2009). How adolescents perceive themselves and their capacities to succeed will play an important role in the primary model of agency they will adopt and how they will shift agency as opportunities are introduced. A strong concept of the self and recognition of skills, also defined as self-efficacy beliefs, are crucial through all ages and life phases, but mostly in such an important stage as that of adolescence.

The concept of the self in social cognitive theory needs to be analyzed from the perspective of human nature, which changes over time or can be different for different social groups or environmental contexts (Bandura, 2008). For example, Bandura distinguishes between theological and evolutionary conceptions of human nature, where the first conceives humans created by divine design and purpose, while the latter is devoid of humans from intentional plans or purpose, but rather shaped by random environmental factors. Humans can influence their environment and the outcomes of their actions to a certain extent. The perception individuals have of their capacities to accomplish success in influencing environmental outcomes is what is defined as self-efficacy beliefs (Bandura, 2008).

Figure 3. The relationship between self-efficacy, commitment, and purpose in adolescents self-efficacy beliefs

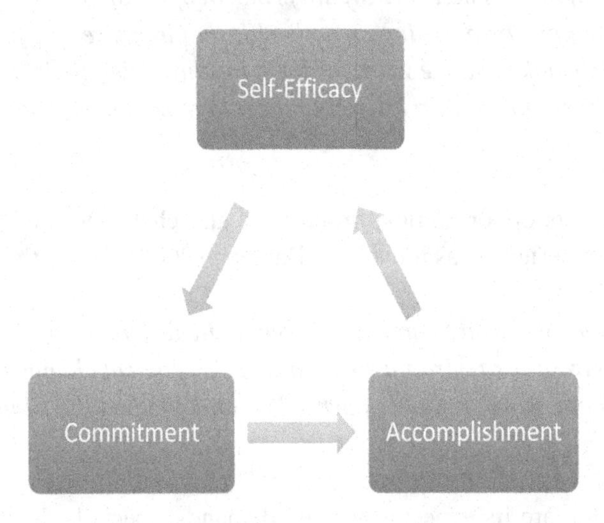

Bandura (2008) stated the duality of self-efficacy beliefs between individualistic and collective perspectives. Various social systems provide interpretations of the self, but social systems themselves are not static, therefore, the perspective between individualism and collectivism shifts based on situational context within the environmental context. For example, members of a team will all perform collectively for the benefit of the team. Specific members of the team with perform better individually while still benefiting the collective outcome. One member of the team cannot achieve individual benefits by performing separately from the team. The self-efficacy of individuals is combined to achieve success collectively. According to Bandura, "personal efficacy is valued, not because of reverence for individualism, but because a resilient sense of efficacy has generalized functional value regardless of whether activities are pursued individually or by people working together for common cause" (p. 28).

Bandura (2008) stated that, "belief in one's efficacy is a key agentic resource in personal development, successful adaptation and change. This core belief operates through its impact on cognitive, motivational, affective, and decisional processes" (p. 38). Optimism and pessimism comes from self-efficacy beliefs, affecting goals, aspirations, motivation, outcome expectations, perseverance, how opportunities and limitations are viewed, the manner in which individuals respond to adversity, and "moreover, efficacy beliefs affect the quality of emotional life and vulnerability to stress and depression" (p. 38). Self-efficacy is also domain-specific. No one can reach mastery of every area of human functioning; rather, people develop skills in different areas of life based on talent and interest, and to suit roles or specific demands of society, depending on their development stage, and physical factors. During life, as society changes its demands, individuals also have to adapt and re-consider their capacities (Bandura, 2008). For Bandura,

Social cognitive theory highlights the forward-looking impact of our biological endowment, rather than backward-looking speculation about adaptation to primitive conditions of prehistoric times. The study of how humans are changing endowed heritages, circumventing biological constraints, and shaping their future through social and technological evolution is more fruitful than spinning fanciful stories about prehistoric mating patterns in drafty caves. (p. 42)

Bruning, Schraw, Norby, and Ronning (2004) define self-efficacy beliefs as "the degree to which an individual possesses confidence in or her ability to achieve a goal" (p. 111), and relate them to behavioral outcomes and outcome expectancy. According to Bruning et al., "self-efficacy should not be confused with general self-esteem" (p. 112). Individuals judge their capabilities to perform a task within a specific domain while understanding their limitations and advantages. For Bruning et al., "High self-efficacy positively affects performance, whereas good performance, in turn, positively affects one's sense of self-efficacy" (p. 112), affecting engagement on challenging tasks and persistence despite failure antecedents. Bruning et al. pointed out that self-efficacy also affects how individuals seek help. Individuals with high self-efficacy will seek help to clarify what path or strategies to follow to achieve a goal, while individuals with low self-efficacy will seek help to intentionally let others answer their questions so they do not have to go through the stress of finding answers on their own.

Another aspect of self-efficacy Bruning et al. (2004) pointed out is the response to failure based on judgment of capabilities and not necessarily capabilities themselves. Individuals may possess the capabilities to efficiently succeed in a specific task, but judge themselves incapable of doing so. Similarly, this judgment may affect how two different individuals with the same capabilities see success or failure as well as how they describe the experience. Here is where feedback comes into play. Individuals may not see what others can see in them, thus through feedback they can improve their self-efficacy by developing awareness of their capabilities. Individuals with high self-efficacy are better at reaching their goals because they set short-term goals rather than unreachable long-term goals, and as short-term goals are reached, self-efficacy improves. Zulkosky (2009) abridged a definition of self-efficacy as follows,

Self-efficacy makes a difference in how people feel, think, behave, and motivate themselves. In terms of feeling, a low sense of self-efficacy is associated with stress, depression, anxiety, and helplessness. Such individuals also have low self-esteem and become pessimistic about their accomplishments and personal development. In terms of thinking, a strong sense of efficacy facilitates cognitive processes and performance in a variety of settings, including quality of decision-making and academic achievement. When it comes to behaving, self-efficacy can influence people's choice of activities. Self-efficacy levels can increase or hamper motivation. People with high self-efficacy approach difficult tasks as challenges and do not try to avoid them. (p. 94)

Zulkosky (2009) pointed out that at times, individuals could overestimate their capabilities and fail for lack of preparation or knowledge in performing specific tasks. This aspect of self-efficacy does not undervalue the capacity of the individual to learn and prepare for a task, but provides insight into the need for correlating perceived capacities with awareness of required capacities in order to reach specific goals. According to Zulkosky, "self-efficacy is not concerned with specific skills one has but rather with the judgments of what a person can do with those specific skills" (p. 98). Individuals work harder when what they perceive of themselves and what is required is balanced. This does not mean they have all it takes, but that individuals have the skills to acquire the lacking knowledge and skills required to achieve the goal.

Paunonen and Hong (2010) studied self-efficacy for the prediction of task-performance on verbal, numerical, spatial, and mechanical cognitive ability domains and found that "self-efficacy beliefs can add unique information to the prediction of task performance" (p. 354) and how individuals approach a task. Paunonen and Hong stated that, "someone high in self-efficacy might do better because that person approaches a task with a different mindset than does someone low in self-efficacy, even though both people might be at the same level of ability" (p. 340). Paunonen and Hong stretched the concept of self-efficacy beliefs to encompass a domain-specific function and not just a homogeneous disposition lacking a context of action. According to Paunonen and Hong, "some studies have shown that very broad self-efficacy measures can predict important behaviors and life outcomes" (p. 341), like the General Self-Efficacy (GSE) scale. They also stated that self-efficacy measures should match the domain of interest; otherwise, the measure will have weak predictive value.

Prat-Sala and Redford (2010) studied the interplay between motivation, self-efficacy, and how individuals approach studying in terms of strategies, skills, and processes for reading and writing in undergraduate learners. Prat-Sala and Redford stated,

From a theoretical point of view, self-efficacy in reading and writing can be understood as being a sub-part of a more general self-efficac7 for learning. However, focusing on these two aspects of self-efficacy should give us a clearer picture on bow students' beliefs about their abilities in reading and writing relate to their approaches to studying and hence identify where interventions may be considered. (p. 287)

The general attitude of an individual towards studying can be measured or characterized by the intentions to understand a text (Prat-Sala & Redford, 2010). Different variables come into consideration when analyzing general attitude, such as self-esteem, gender, age, coping strategies, and personality. Experience on the task and the learning environment were a factor of interest in the study.

Some of the learners in the study were in the university for only two weeks at the time of the study. The lack of experience manifested as limitations in the learners to properly express their approach and strategies to reading and writing and, therefore, to make a connection between their self-efficacy beliefs and the skills required to complete the task at hand (Prat-Sala & Redford, 2010). There is a relationship between the skills required to succeed in a task and self-efficacy beliefs, hence, individuals can perform better judgment of their capabilities to reach a goal through awareness of what is required to reach it.

Webb and Sheeran (2008) also proposed that self-efficacy beliefs are just part of the equation for individuals to reach desired goals, and that planning increases the probability for success, which is consistent with Bruning et al. (2004) when it comes to setting short-term goals leading to the achievement of a main goal, because it develops commitment promoting the behavior change. Is not that planning will change behavior by default; rather it will motivate and promote the behavior more. According to Webb and Sheeran (2008), "forming an if–then plan specifying when, where, and how to achieve a particular goal could make the outcome feel easier to obtain. Research that has investigated the impact of implementation intentions on self-efficacy has also produced equivocal findings" (p. 375). Planning short-term objectives can increase self-efficacy because it makes the goal more attainable. However, it is not a guarantee that the behavior will change.

Davis-Kean, Huesmann, Jager, Collins, Bates, and Lansford (2008) stated that self-efficacy belief constructs and behaviors vary across different stages of life. One subject of interest for research they point out links self-efficacy beliefs with behavior, since the ability to perform is not a determinant to act upon. Davis-Kean et al. argued that children of early age have difficulty with abstract concepts of the relationship between behaviors and their consequences, but that this phenomenon changes over the years, and as consequence, the relationship between self-efficacy and performance also varies. To confirm this relationship, it is necessary to perform research across time to specify at what ages or stages of development it changes. The researchers pointed out that adolescence is a crucial time for abstract development in order to mature towards more reflective activities and behavior.

The relationship between the abstract relationship between self-efficacy and behaviors presented by Davis-Kean et al. (2008) relates to the four characteristics of human agency (intentionality, forethought, self-reactiveness, and self-reflectiveness) allowing planning, setting goals, acting upon plans and goals, and examining behaviors (Bandura, 1989b). As children grow older, these cognitive skills become stronger, and the connection between self-efficacy and behaviors is more evident than in younger years. While Coutinho (2008) agreed with the changes in the relationship between self-efficacy and metacognition across development stages, she stated that the relationship with performance is difficult to study in children, and argued, "this leaves a gap in our understanding of how such variables change and operate as students grow older" (p. 165).

Coutinho (2008) focuses on the relationship between self-efficacy and metacognition, then measuring performance through GPA results. Metacognition refers to a higher-order mental process to plan and use skills and strategies to solve a problem. It regulates the activities that control the learning process, and it shows in academic performance. On the other hand, referring to self-efficacy, Coutinho argues that receiving feedback improves perception of capacities for performance and that the converse is also true. Coutinho also states that the link between self-efficacy and metacognition affects performance, and those individuals with confidence in their abilities tend to perform better and successfully complete a task. However, in the study, Coutinho found that the influence of self-efficacy over performance is independent from metacognition, and individuals with good metacognition tend to perform better.

Wang, Peng, Huang, Hou, and Wang (2008) focused their study on distance learners to examine the relationship between motivation, learning strategies, self-efficacy, attribution and performance as measured by learning scores. They studied motivation in distance learners through three dimensions:

1. Cognitive, or intrinsic interest in learning;
2. Self-improvement, or reasons for participating in a distance learning environment; and
3. Affiliated, which refers to external motivations or expectations.

Their results show a correlation between self-efficacy, learning strategies, and results, as well as a correlation between self-efficacy, internal attribution, motivation, and results. According to Wang et al., higher self-efficacy help produce better learning strategies, and consequently produces better results. They argue that distance learners require training in learning strategies in order to develop awareness of these strategies and that instructors should examine which areas are the weakest in order to provide learning-support services. Furthermore, instructors need to understand the self-efficacy of the learners, in this case in distance learning, because it can determine consequent behaviors while also being affected by past behavior. Wang et al. stated "distance education institutions may help learners to enhance their self-efficacy by allowing them to acquire successful experiences or by allowing them to observe the learning behavior of others having substantial experience" (p. 26).

Poellhuber, Chomienne, and Karsenti (2008) focus on peer collaboration in distance learning as the domain for self-efficacy in response to drop-out rates, and state that helping students remain in a course not only improves achievement but also improves self-efficacy for those that are currently in the course and builds antecedents for those entering the course. Engaging in peer-collaborative activities might improve social integration, sustain motivation, increase involvement in course work, develop persistence, and improve results, leading to higher self-efficacy (Poellhuber et al., 2008). One important aspect in improving self-efficacy for distance learning was feedback along with collaborative learning experiences. Students who experienced difficulties in motivation, comprehension, time-management, and decrease of engagement in the course overcame these issues by turning to their peers, and sometimes their tutor, for support, while those who pushed themselves to isolation ended up dropping out of their course. The low feedback on peer-collaborative activities was attributed to technical and course design factors; the data was taken from interviews, and shows a little-but-positive impact of collaboration on self-efficacy. Knowledge of self-efficacy beliefs of the learners in the specific context can help instructional designers and distance-learning instructors in the selection of learning goals and instructional activities in order to provide a learning environment that provides opportunities for peer interaction to promote success and improve self-efficacy beliefs.

Margolis (2005) presents insights to increase self-efficacy in struggling learners through tutoring, because it provides the opportunity for the learner to receive feedback, develop learning strategies, see better academic results, and as consequence, enhance their perception of skills and capabilities. The success of tutoring depends mostly on the experience and expertise of the tutor. Margolis identifies four sources of self-efficacy beliefs that tutors can focus on to increase and improve self-perception of skills in learners:

1. Mastery experiences, referring to antecedents of success and failure;
2. Vicarious experiences, or observing others succeed, especially those coming from other learners they view as similar;
3. Verbal persuasion, in the form of positive feedback and motivation; and
4. Physiological state, or recognizing, for example, anxiety levels, and encouraging relaxation and control.

According to Margolis, assessing self-efficacy and helping it to increase is an ongoing process when working with struggling learners until they learn to develop learning strategies and intrinsic motivational cues.

Muris (2001) argued that individuals generally consciously know what they need to improve self-efficacy, but lack the confidence to execute those required changes. Muris studied the relationship between social and academic self-efficacy and depression in adolescents, and the results indicated that low self-efficacy is an indicator for long-term depression. Muris used a measure for self-efficacy in children (SEQ-C) that focuses on three areas:

1. Social,
2. Academic, and
3. Personal or self-regulatory.

An updated version of this measure will be used in this study. According to the results of the study (Muris, 2001), academic self-efficacy influences depression more than social self-efficacy. There is a gender difference between self-efficacy and depression, with the relationship being stronger in girls that it is in boys. Muris argues that low self-efficacy could be an indicator of an affective disorder.

Lin and Overbaugh (2009) studied how collaborative online instruction and the selection of asynchronous or synchronous peer interaction affects self-efficacy beliefs based on gender. Asynchronous interaction refers to those communication tools and activities in which learners connect at different times, such as discussion boards and blogs, while synchronous tools allow for learners to connect simultaneously for real time interactions though text or video chat. According to Lin and Overbaugh, gender affects the preference for these options because other factors such as learning styles, delivery format, satisfaction, motivation, and computer technology skills may be connected to gender as well, and as consequence, affect self-efficacy. Lin and Overbaugh argued that female learners focus on relationships and collaborative learning, while male learners focus on information transaction and a sense of competition.

The results of their study show that gender is not of strong influence in preference for asynchronous or synchronous online peer interaction, but it is a factor in self-efficacy beliefs towards such environments (Lin & Overbaugh, 2009). Synchronous interactions require more preparation before the session, the capacity to follow through with conversation and debate, and skills to articulate knowledge in a short period of time. In asynchronous interaction, learners can prepare ahead of time and also take time to respond. Individuals with low self-efficacy may feel threatened by synchronous participation while individuals with higher self-efficacy may feel comfortable in either environment.

Peer Tutoring Environments

In the previous section, the literature provided insight into social cognitive theory, agentic perspectives, self-efficacy beliefs in specific contexts and different age groups, and recommendations on how to help individuals improve their perception of capabilities to achieve a goal. This study aims to explore self-efficacy beliefs for a peer-tutoring learning environment in the analysis for the learners. Therefore, this section provides characteristics of different peer-collaborative activities and learning environments focusing on peer tutoring as a tool for exploring self-efficacy beliefs in social interaction. Differences between tutoring and peer tutoring are also explained.

According to Topping (2005), peer tutoring is as old as any form of community action that requires collaboration and has always taken place, implicitly or explicitly. Sometimes, peer tutoring is mistaken for "mentoring," which states role differentiation between mentor and mentee. Topping defines peer tutoring as "acquisition of knowledge and skill through active helping and supporting among status equals or matched companions. It involves people from similar social groupings who are not professional teachers helping each other to learn and learning themselves by so doing" (p. 631). The difference between tutoring and peer tutoring is that the first has defined tutor/tutee roles and knowledge transmission is unidirectional; while the second has these roles continuously shift to produce bidirectional cognitive challenge among participants. Topping presents types of peer-learning implementation and effects.

Topping (2005) describes peer tutoring and peer collaboration as the oldest form of peer learning, the first, in practice, taking the form of mentoring instead of a bidirectional cognitive transaction. On the other hand, peer collaboration is not simply working together, but developing cognitive interdependence to achieve specific goals. For these interactions to be successful, clear structure and shared accountability are required. Without structure and accountability, students are left stranded in the learning process or having one or just some group members to do all the work. Also, it is important for students to receive assessment and feedback from their instructors in order to monitor and assess their process and improve future endeavors. When peer tutoring is implemented efficiently, it produces good academic results and moreover, it enhances social and communication skills (Topping, 2005). Since positive results are evident for peer-tutoring activities, then it "should enable both researchers and practitioners to design ever more adaptive and effective forms of peer learning" (p. 635).

Other aspect that requires attention in peer tutoring is feedback, monitoring, and assessment, not from teachers and instructors, but rather from students and among themselves (Topping, 2005). When individuals receive positive feedback and encouragement from matching companions, self-efficacy increases because they see each other at the same level. Also, when individuals seek to achieve the same goal, each one becomes a motivator and in the process, individuals monitor themselves and their partners. Results help individuals assess performance and not only willy the individual utilize the experience as an antecedent to succeed in future collaborative learning endeavors, but also skills learned in the social environment transfer when they are learned individually (Topping, 2005).

King-Sears (2001) argued that there is an existing gap between theory and practice and that methods of learning and teaching supported by research to be effective are not used enough in schools, this being the case of peer-mediated learning. Peer-mediated learning improves academic performance, helps develop reading comprehension skills, shifts the roles of learners from passive to active, develops socially acceptable communication, and increases the sense of shared responsibility in the learning process. According to King-Sears, "the purpose of 21st-century education is to develop learning communities within schools that mirror what students' living communities will look like in the future" (p. 100). While proof of efficacy of peer-mediated learning methods exists in research and literature, in practice, students are left on their own, and some teachers do not know how to implement these practices efficiently.

Havnes (2008) states that while peer-mediated learning is used as a pedagogical tool, there are other reasons to increase interaction in the learning process, as it is an effective method that can stimulate development outside the curriculum. As King-Sears (2001) also confirms, this emulates how people learn outside of school. According to Havnes (2008), learning should emulate society and its changes, which expand beyond the classroom and into the workplace and everyday life. Because individuals develop into active members of society during higher education years, there is an interest in peer tutoring to facilitate the development of social interdependency (Havnes, 2008). Havnes emphasizes that peer learning involves individuals in the same social standing interacting without the intervention of teachers, with the main purpose being to encourage collaborative learning.

According to Havnes (2008), participation of the teacher is important for effective implementation and monitoring of peer-learning interactions until individuals are ready to evaluate and assess each other and develop their own initiatives for participation. Not having the participation of the teacher is in other ways an advantage to the learners developing innovative solutions to problems and correcting themselves when wrong. Collaborative learning requires the combination of individual effort and reflection for a common goal. The dynamics of peer-learning activities are embedded in a specific context of learning needs and social practices, which simultaneously creates the motivation and expectations (Havnes, 2008).

Xu, Gelfer, Sileo, Filler, and Perkins (2008) studied the social interactions of children who were not native English speakers and compared it with those who were. Xu et al. states that these children are not just limited by the language barriers, but that they come from communities with low academic expectations, which contribute to a lack of motivation and low self-efficacy beliefs. These issues could lead to cognitive and social-skills-development challenges. According to Xu et al., "social play with peers is one of the most important areas in which children develop positive social skills" (p. 618), and it is through peer interaction that they experience learning in ways not often available in regular classroom settings. The language barrier might make a difference in their interactions.

Xu et al. (2008) present class-wide peer tutoring (CWPT) as an alternative intended to promote peer-mediated learning among children of the same age, with general and special education needs, arguing that it can provide greater learning results than teacher-directed learning alone. In their study, Xu et al. concluded that social interaction behaviors improved with the intervention. With proper encouragement, students engaged in social interaction with their equals more freely than with teachers. Among other factors that may affect the interaction, personality plays an important role in how individuals approach social-interaction activities. Moreover, CWTP was also shown to promote academic achievement.

Hsiao, Brouns, Kester, and Sloep (2009) present another variation of peer-learning, through learning networks where people engage in informal learning experiences, looking for opportunities to improve their knowledge collaboratively. After formal school education, individuals continue seeking knowledge through informal sources of information where they can have control over their learning goals and how learning is achieved. Learning networks allow individuals to get together, share knowledge, and assume responsibility for their learning with no predefined learning activities or expecting someone, like a teacher or instructor, to deliver content knowledge like in formal education settings (Hsiao et al., 2009). Sharing knowledge is a process of negotiation and collaboration in order to achieve mutual understanding and solve learning objectives, which can be individually or collectively, without a formal social structure. Nevertheless, some conditions are necessary for these interactions to effectively occur. Hsiao et al. discussed three:

1. Group composition,
2. Communication media, and
3. Task characteristics.

It is likely, according to Hsiao et al. (2009), that group composition in learning networks is heterogeneous academically, in learning goals, environmental antecedents or experiences, and knowledge about the subject matter, and without social structure, which reflects how people normally learn in community. These characteristics forces individuals to carefully select and analyze the information received, leading to higher-order thinking skills. Communication media and the frequency with which it is used influence the efficacy of knowledge negotiation in a timely manner. There are plenty of Internet technologies for individuals to choose from. Although online, presence is still a requirement for communication to be effective in this setting. The task characteristics are as heterogeneous as the group composition could be, but this should not limit the group to collaborate towards independent goals while achieving collective goals, if communication of goals and intentions occur using the roles of tutor and tutee interchangeably in the process (Hsiao et al., 2009).

Palloff and Pratt (2005) argued that online collaboration promotes the development of critical thinking skills, co-creation of knowledge and meaning, reflection, and transformative learning. Engaging individuals is the most challenging task in the process of online collaboration. For Palloff and Pratt, in order to sustain online collaboration, it is necessary to develop a sense of community, then community and collaboration will sustain each other in a cyclical interaction, allowing individuals to acquire deeper levels of knowledge construction, promoting initiative, creativity, and critical thinking, sharing common goals, and increasing self-regulation. While the benefits of online collaboration are clear and Internet technologies provide for these interactions to take effect, engaging individuals remains the toughest task in the process (Palloff & Pratt, 2005).

There are individual and group considerations for effective engagement in online collaboration. Individuals seek a sense of personal accomplishment, satisfaction with the interactions online, a feeling that they can express themselves, and the ability to work and process information at their own pace (Palloff & Pratt, 2005). As a group, individuals seek a sense of wellbeing and support, as well as the reduction of isolation through teamwork and collaboration. They also seek to join goals, solve problems together, manage conflicts, and connect socially (Palloff & Pratt, 2005). These characteristics are developed through participation and collaboration, building a sense of community in the process, which activates the cyclical reaction: community < = > collaboration. Differences in expectations that are not communicated will cause unwillingness to participate. Online collaboration requires individuals to set the stage through clearly communicating their personal and group goals and expectations, followed by designing and developing the environment for effective interactions.

Instructional System Design Models

The design process includes the activities of analysis, strategy development, evaluation, and revision. Although the instructional design process may often be portrayed as linear, in practice, it is frequently iterative, moving back and forth between activities as the project develops. (Smith & Ragan, 2005, p. 15)

Smith and Ragan presented an instructional system design (ISD) model based on three major steps:

1. Analysis,
2. Strategy development, and
3. Evaluation, as influenced by Dick and Carey (Dick, Carey & Carey, 2008) and the model by Davis,

Alexander and Yelon (1974). For Smith and Ragan (2005), using a systematic process for the design of instruction allows the learner to remain the center focus of the instruction, supports effective instruction that is appealing for the learner, and supports coordination for implementation, facilitates congruence between objectives, activities, and assessment, and an organized framework for solving learning issues. A systematic approach keeps consistency between goals, instructional strategies, and evaluation. For the purpose of this study, each part of the model will be described, but greater attention will be given to the analysis phase, especially the part related to the learners.

The analysis phase in the Smith and Ragan (2005) model consists of the scrutiny of the learning contexts, the learners, and the learning tasks leading to writing test items. Analyzing the learning context involves determining an instructional need and describing the learning environment where instruction will take place. The reason for conducting needs-assessment is to determine that there is an actual instructional need for which instruction is required; otherwise it is unproductive to invest time and resources into something not considered necessary. On the other hand, describing the learning environment comprises an examination of every aspect surrounding the desired instruction: learners, instructional materials, instructors, equipment, facilities, the organizational culture, its dynamics, and the larger system where the organization belongs, among other areas that can affect the learning process.

According to Smith and Ragan (2005), instruction must be appealing to the learners not only because the context analysis reflects that there is an instructional need, but also because they need to be interested in order to engage effectively. Smith and Ragan present a framework for analyzing the learners that includes:

1. Cognitive,
2. Physiological,
3. Affective, and
4. Social characteristics.

Cognitive characteristics include but are not limited to: aptitudes, development, language and reading levels, visual literacy, learning styles, learning strategies, general knowledge, and specific knowledge of the subject content. Physiological characteristics relate to sensory perception: general health, limitations, disabilities, and age, among others.

Affective characteristics comprise a more personal perception of the self:

- Interests,
- Motivations,
- Attitudes,
- Experience,
- Anxiety levels,
- Beliefs,
- Attribution to success, and
- Other self-perceived characteristics that will determine success or failure.

The social characteristics comprise relationships to peers, perceptions towards authority, predisposition to cooperation or competition, ethics, socioeconomic status, and ethnic background (Smith & Ragan, 2005).

The analysis phase of the Smith and Ragan (2005) model continues with the learning task at hand, in which the learning goals, the statements of purpose, and intentions for the instruction are developed. Learning goals combine what is expected of the learners at the end of the instruction related to the specific task along with the acquisition of transferable and transformative skills. At this point, context, learners, and task find their interrelationship. Then, the Smith and Ragan model suggests writing test items, determining organizational, delivery, and management strategies, followed by the production of instruction. Lastly, formative and summative evaluation is conducted.

For the purpose of this study, the framework for analysis of the learners guided the exploration of self-efficacy beliefs of the participants. In the Gerlach and Ely (1980) model, this framework for the analysis of the learners is defined as the assessment of entry behaviors, a term that is going to be used in this study to describe self-efficacy beliefs towards a peer tutoring learning environment. Smith and Ragan (2005) encourage instructional designers to utilize what better fits their needs when designing instructions, providing for the incorporation of other models within theirs. While an old model, designed before the proliferation of Internet technologies for instructional purposes, Gerlach and Ely created a model for peer collaboration guided by the findings in the entry behaviors assessment. With creativity, the model can be upgraded to fit alongside the Internet technology available today. Other parts of the Gerlach and Ely model, like determination of strategy, organization of groups, and allocation of time, space, and resources, followed by evaluation, fit along with the strategy and evaluation phases of the Smith and Ragan model.

Table 1. Age and gender breakdown of participants

Age	Males	Females	Total
13	1	0	1
14	0	0	0
15	7	6	13
16	4	7	11
17	4	1	5
Total	16	14	30

PROCEDURE

Description of the Sample

The participants were 30 adolescents, aged between 13 and 17, who actively participate in sports and other social and group activities through a martial arts and fitness academy. At the time of the study, participants were active members or related to active members of the school. The parents of participants were also invited to participate in the study, and 30 parents agreed to participate. The parents were also interviewed regarding the self-efficacy of their children.

Procedure

Interviews with the participants were conducted using the questions of the General Self-Efficacy Scale (GSE) as open-ended questions. The GSE scale uses a value system for the responses being 5 the highest and 1 the lowest (Appendix A), when used as a quantitative data collection tool. This study was a qualitative study using the questions in the GSE as open-ended questions. Based on the literature description of self-efficacy and agentic perspectives, and being this study of qualitative interpretive nature, the responses were reviewed and value was assigned. Participants who showed the characteristics of self-efficacy described in the literature as well as behaviors that reflect the assumption of agentic perspectives in the presented situations were assigned values from high to low. The responses were then classified in 5 groups by level of self-efficacy:

1. High,
2. Moderate to high,
3. Moderate,
4. Moderate to low, and
5. Low self-efficacy.

Group 1 represents adolescents that show characteristics of high self-efficacy beliefs. According to the literature high self-efficacy beliefs is characterized by a consideration of the situation and its demands in order to compare with possessed kills in order to adapt and achieve a goal (Bandura, 2009). Individuals with higher self-efficacy beliefs can look into the past and consider previous experiences and their results as a platform to face future endeavors. Higher self-efficacy is also characterized by self-regulation and sticking to their aims until a goal is reached. Time and consistency are two important characteristics for this group as well as being able to control their emotions under stressful situations to focus on the problem.

Group 2 represents adolescents with moderate to high self-efficacy. Some characteristics of this group are the positive attitude towards difficulties, and the ability to help a group focus. These are natural leaders and motivators. They also confront situations without fear. The downside characteristic of this group is the lack of perseverance when situations are not solved in a short period of time.

Group 3 represents moderate self-efficacy. Moderate self-efficacy is characterized by recognition of skills to succeed and resourcefulness to face difficulties often clouded by specific situations in which the individual may feel intimidated by others or not interested to show what they are capable of. This may result in complete abandon of the task or goal. Individuals with moderate self-efficacy may show the skills to succeed individually adopting a direct-personal agency (Bandura, 2009) but rarely work in a team or group oriented environment.

Group 4 represents moderate to low self-efficacy. Individuals in this group are good team players but try to maintain a low profile. Self-efficacy is affected in this group by lack of control over emotional outbursts that limit their capacity to consider their resourcefulness and skills to face a challenge. Rather these individuals tend to see the limitations to achieve a goal rather than the possibilities.

Group 5 allocates individuals with low self-efficacy beliefs. In this group, individuals lack the capacity to recognize their skills to face challenges or to endure long-term goals. They quit easily or simply do not engage in endeavors that may represent an uneasy challenge. Low self-efficacy affects and reflects itself in academic pursuits.

Table 2. Self-efficacy group classification by gender

Gender	Group 1	Group 2	Group 3	Group 4	Group 5	Total
Males	9	1	4	1	1	16
Females	7	1	2	3	1	14
Total	16	2	6	4	2	30

Table 3. Self-efficacy group classification by age

Age	Group 1	Group 2	Group 3	Group 4	Group 5	Total
13	0	1	0	0	0	1
14	0	0	0	0	0	0
15	9	0	2	1	1	13
16	3	1	3	1	1	11
17	4	0	1	2	0	5
Total	16	2	6	4	2	30

One adolescent was selected from each group taking in consideration the responses to the interview questions that were more descriptive and comprehensive. The adolescents selected to represent their group were identified as A1, A2, A3, A4, and A5. The responses from the parents of the selected adolescents were then compared with the responses of their children. This was done with the purpose of exploring how the parents see their children on each different situation as presented by each question in the GSE and how they contrast in their views. After the interviews were compared, the adolescents were invited to a focus group to discuss the questions of the GSE scale and their answers with each other. The adolescents and their interactions during the focus group were observed and documented by the researcher. These observations were compared with their interview answers and the answers from their parents to determine if their self-efficacy is accurate with their behavior in real-life situations. A relationship between self-efficacy beliefs and the agentic perspectives of the adolescents was explored to address the research questions.

DISCUSSION

The results of this study suggested that individuals with higher self-efficacy beliefs trust their skills based on results from previous experiences that reinforced confidence to face unexpected challenges or to pursue future goals. This showed that high self-efficacy is reflected in the assumption of a personal agentic perspective when acting alone and a collective agentic perspective when interacting with peers. The results also suggested that individuals with low self-efficacy are more detached from group interactions. Individuals with lower self-efficacy assumed a proxy or surrogate agentic perspective and required prompting to engage in the interactions.

From an ISD perspective and focusing in the analysis of the learners for the design of a peer tutoring learning environment, the results provided insight to instructional designers in the decision-making that follows. Based on the Smith and Ragan (2005) ISD model, the analysis of the learners is followed by the development of instructional strategies. As intended in this study, the analysis of the learners was modified using the concept of "entry behaviors" from the Gerlach and Ely (1980) model. This concept focuses on pre-knowledge and affective skills for group collaboration. The Gerlach and Ely (1980) model also focuses in the development of instructional strategies for group collaboration and peer tutoring is a collaborative endeavor, therefore the model is incorporated in the strategy phase of the Smith and Ragan (2005) model. The results of this study help decide how groups are organized based on differences and similarities in self-efficacy, how much time groups need to communicate to ensure equal participation among participants, where and how groups meet, and the selection of instructional materials based on the learning needs and instructional strategies.

Self-efficacy beliefs can affect success in a peer tutoring learning environment. Peer tutoring requires collaboration. Understanding the differences in self-efficacy beliefs among the participants provided insight in individual and group expectancies and needs. To an individual level, self-efficacy could predict results in goals attainability as well as engagement during learning activities in both personal and group endeavors. Individuals with low self-efficacy detached themselves from the interactions with peers and required prompting to participate. Prompting was provided by participants with higher self-efficacy beliefs who not only trust their skills but motivate others to trust in theirs promoting a collaborative environment.

The results of this study suggest that for promoting for participants of a peer tutoring learning environment to achieve success groups can be organized ensuring that low self-efficacy individuals are alongside with individuals with higher self-efficacy. It is necessary to avoid allocating groups where most participants have low self-efficacy leaving the burden to motivate and prompt peers to one or two people. Equally important is to avoid creating groups where all participants have low self-efficacy beliefs. Good communication or collaboration cannot be expected when individuals are detached from interactions. Self-efficacy and the agentic perspectives assume by individuals also serve to decide how much time is needed for participants to communicate and achieve results. Individuals with higher self-efficacy are more inclined to assume a collective perspective, communicate easily and promptly, and achieve results faster.

The results of this study also support the literature regarding the relationship between adolescents and the pursuing of goals that seem attainable in considerable short time (Bandura, 2009; Davis-Kean, Huesmann, Jager, Collins, Bates, & Lansford, 2008). Adolescents raised in a society where life is fast paced, goals feel attainable when they seem to be reachable. Reaching short-term goals help adolescents increase and improve self-efficacy and how goals are pursued in the future. The results also support the concept of intentionality, forethought, self-reactiveness, and self-reflectiveness based on the level of self-efficacy (Davis-Kean et al., 2008; Bandura, 1989b).

According to Margolis (2005) certain characteristics show, improve, and increase self-efficacy and the results of this study are supported by. Self-efficacy allows individuals to refer to experiences and antecedents of success and failure. Experimenting vicarious experiences, and experiencing and observing the success of other equals help increase confidence. Verbal persuasion, motivation, feedback, and affirmation provide instances for individuals to focus on their skills and increase self-efficacy. Self-efficacy also allows individuals to recognize and cope with anxiety when facing challenging situations. The results supported these statements. Individuals with high self-efficacy beliefs reflect on their skills and coping skills and recognize their flaws and their abilities to learn new skills. These characteristics were observed and documented in this study.

LIMITATIONS

This study presented several limitations. According to Bandura (2002), Bruning et al. (2004), and Godard, LoGerfo, and Hoy (2004), self-efficacy beliefs are domain-specific personal interpretations of capabilities to perform a task or reach a goal. The General Self-Efficacy (GSE) scale is used for evaluating general self-efficacy. The questions of the GSE are not focused for specific domains. Participants could provide examples in any area of their lives and not on a specific one, which could affect the results of the study.

Many participants did not provide enough or comprehensive descriptions in the interviews which limited the selection of examples of each group classification of levels of self-efficacy. The focus group was relatively short and just a one-time occurrence. The focus group was not directed to a specific learning endeavor but to their interactions. Some individuals are not necessarily outgoing or might take a little longer than others to warm up to the interactions specially when the discussion is directed to personal information. The focus group consisted in a participant from each group level of self-efficacy and other group combinations were not attempted in the focus group. Personality traces were not taken in consideration during the study. The participants met only once and there were no follow up after the focus groups to document individual feedback describing their personal experiences during the discussion.

IMPLICATIONS FOR PRACTICE

Instructional designers need to focus on the needs of the learners, wants, motivations, and skills when designing instruction that will effectively achieve the expectations from which it was designed. The analysis of the learners cannot be limited to age, gender, and other demographic information that does not reveal attitudes and aptitudes about learning or personal perceptions of skills to succeed and reach specific learning goals. This study proved the importance to seek an understanding of self-efficacy beliefs especially when it comes to a learning environment that requires collaboration among participants, as it is the case with peer tutoring. Exploring self-efficacy beliefs as entry behaviors provided an idea of how participants ought to interact with their peers and the results proved the expectations accurate. In practice, the instructional designer would have a foundation for making decisions regarding learning goals and instructional strategies.

The exploration of self-efficacy beliefs, as shown by the results of this study, provide a theoretical foundation to allocate people in collaborative groups based on their level of self-efficacy. The results showed that individuals with higher self-efficacy promote and motivate participation from those individuals with low self-efficacy beliefs who do not actively engage in social interactions on their own and need prompting to do so. The allocation of groups by levels of self-efficacy, and size of the group is an important aspect to consider in peer tutoring and other collaborative learning efforts. A participant of a group with low self-efficacy can feel overwhelmed by participating in a group too large or where specific individuals take control of the group not allowing for further interactions or not seeking the participation of others. The results show that individuals with moderate self-efficacy may be this kind of individual. A balanced group can provide the expected success of the learning experience.

Self-efficacy beliefs are also an important consideration when developing learning goals. This study showed that individuals rely on success on previous experiences to judge their skills to succeed in future situations. Individuals, especially adolescents, seek and engage in pursuing of goals that seem attainable in a considerable short time (Bruning et al., 2004). In practice, instructional designers must consider the design of short-term goals that allow learners to improve self-efficacy as each short-term goal is achieved and the learning experience progresses. Peer motivation, prompting, and feedback are important aspects of the learning experience to consider that can be considered as part of the instructional activities.

RECOMMENDATIONS FOR FUTURE RESEARCH

Further research exploring self-efficacy beliefs should focus on domain-specific tasks. While general self-efficacy provide useful information, focusing on specific tasks for specific learning experiences could provide more accurate and purposeful results for the design of instruction. Further studies should explore and compare results on general self-efficacy to domain-specific self-efficacy. Participants can be equally assessed focusing in specific situations evaluating the perception of their skills in that situation instead of trying to evaluate each person in different situations.

In this study, one focus group was conducted selecting one participant from each group representing the level of self-efficacy:

1. High,
2. Moderate to high,

3. Moderate,
4. Moderate to low, and
5. Low self-efficacy.

Recommendations for further research include allocating participants in several focus groups using different combinations of self-efficacy. For example, one focus group can allocate five participants with the same level of self-efficacy, while another focus group can allocate four participants with low self-efficacy and only one with high self-efficacy, and so forth. These interactions can be documented and compared to explore which group combinations interact more effectively.

Further research could also include task oriented and follow up focus groups and interviews. Task oriented focus groups should follow domain-specific self-efficacy beliefs exploration. If domain-specific self-efficacy is explored then focus groups should pursue a domain-specific goal in which observations of the interactions can be compared with learning results. Participants should be allowed to come together more than once to explore the interactions as they convey in the task repeatedly until the goal is reached. Follow up focus groups and interviews should be considered after goal-oriented focus groups to explore the experience of the participants. Data from each focus group can be compared to explore progress and to assess if there is any improvement in self-efficacy. Data from interviews before focus groups can be compared with data from the interviews after the focus groups as well.

CONCLUSION

This study explored self-efficacy beliefs as entry behaviors for participating in a peer tutoring learning environment based on social cognitive theory and triadic reciprocal determinism (TRD). Bandura (2002) explained that self-efficacy beliefs are influenced by TRD, which describes the interactions of environmental cues, behavior, and cognitive limitations to form the perceptions of the self and the skills to succeed and achieve goals. According to Bandura, self-efficacy leads to the assumption of agentic perspectives for social functioning:

1. Direct personal,
2. Proxy or surrogate, and
3. Collective.

The results of this study suggested that individuals with high self-efficacy not only assume a direct personal agentic perspective when acting alone but that they also assume and motivate others to engage in a collective agentic perspective. Individuals with low self-efficacy assume proxy or surrogate agentic perspectives in social interactions and require prompting to engage and participate.

This study answers the question regarding in what ways do self-efficacy beliefs affect success in a peer-tutoring environment. Peer tutoring is a learning experience that requires collaboration among peers (King-Sears, 2001; Topping, 2005); therefore, the level of self-efficacy provides indications of what agentic perspective will be assumed by the learner. High self-efficacy indicates effective collaboration through the collective agency, which affects success positively in a peer tutoring learning environment. Low self-efficacy affects negatively success in peer tutoring, because individuals with low self-efficacy assume a proxy or surrogate agentic perspective detaching themselves from the interactions. However, individuals with low self-efficacy, through prompting and motivation from peers with high self-efficacy can improve their interactions and as goals are reached, improve self-efficacy.

This study also explored the similarities and differences in self-efficacy beliefs among participants. The results of the study showed that participants assess their skills to succeed in future endeavors through previous experiences. Participants who were able to face difficult and challenging situations effectively in the past are more likely to feel confidence in their skills to succeed in the future. Participants who in the past failed to succeed are most likely to disvalue their skills to succeed in the future.

The study provided information for instructional designers to consider when designing a peer tutoring learning environment. The analysis of the learners should include an exploration of self-efficacy beliefs as entry behaviors to decide in the design of learning goals and instructional strategies. Instructional designers can foresee how learners will interact towards a collective goal if they know what are their perceptions of their skills and which agentic perspective they are more likely to assume. This can also provide for designing instruction that not only presents attainable goals but also that at the same time provides for learners to improve their self-efficacy as learning progresses.

REFERENCES

Ashford, J. B., & LeCroy, C. W. (2010). *Human behavior in the social environment: A multidimensional perspective* (4th ed.). Belmont, CA: Wadsworth, Cengage Learning.

Bandura, A. (1977). *Social learning theory*. Englewood Cliffs, NJ: Prentice-Hall.

Bandura, A. (1989a). Social cognitive theory. In R. Vasta (Ed.), Annals of child development. Vol.6. Six theories of child development (pp. 1-60). Greenwich, CT: JAI Press.

Bandura, A. (1989b). Human agency in social cognitive theory. *The American Psychologist*, *44*(9), 1175–1184. doi:10.1037/0003-066X.44.9.1175 PMID:2782727

Bandura, A. (2001). Social cognitive theory: An agentic perspective. *Annual Review of Psychology*, *52*(1), 1–26. doi:10.1146/annurev.psych.52.1.1 PMID:11148297

Bandura, A. (2002). Social cognitive theory in cultural context. *Applied Psychology*, *51*(2), 269–290. doi:10.1111/1464-0597.00092

Bandura, A. (2005). Evolution of social cognitive theory. In K. G. Smith & M. A. Hitt (Eds.), *Great minds in management* (pp. 9–35). Oxford, UK: Oxford University Press.

Bandura, A. (2006). Adolescent development from an agentic perspective. In F. Pajares & T. Urdan (Eds.), *Self-efficacy beliefs of adolescents* (Vol. 5, pp. 1–43). Greenwich, CT: Information Age Publishing.

Bandura, A. (2006a). Toward a psychology of human agency. *Perspectives on Psychological Science*, *1*(2), 164–180. doi:10.1111/j.1745-6916.2006.00011.x PMID:26151469

Bandura, A. (2008). Toward an agentic theory of the self. In H. Marsh, R. G. Craven, & D. M. McInerney (Eds.), Advances in Self Research: Self-processes, learning, and enabling human potential (vol. 3, pp. 15-49). Charlotte, NC: Information Age Publishing.

Bandura, A. (2009). Social cognitive theory of mass communications. In J. Bryant & M. B. Oliver (Eds.), *Media effects: Advances in theory and research* (2nd ed.; pp. 94–124). Mahwah, NJ: Lawrence Erlbaum.

Bogdan, R. C., & Biklen, S. K. (2007). *Qualitative research for education* (5th ed.). Boston: Pearson.

Brown, J. (2002). Training needs assessment: A must for developing an effective training program. *Public Personnel Management*, *31*(4), 569–578. doi:10.1177/009102600203100412

Bruning, R. H., Schraw, G. J., Norby, M. M., & Ronning, R. R. (2004). *Cognitive psychology and instruction*. Upper Saddle River, NJ: Prentice Hall.

Conner, M., & Norman, P. (Eds.). (2005). Predicting health behaviour (2nd ed. rev.). Buckingham, UK: Open University Press.

Coutinho, S. (2008). Self-efficacy, metacognition, and performance. *North American Journal of Psychology*, *10*(1), 165–172.

Creswell, J. W. (2008). *Educational research* (3rd ed.). Upper Saddle River, NJ: Pearson.

Davis, R. H., Alexander, L. T., & Yelon, S. L. (1974). *Learning system design: an approach to the improvement of instruction*. New York: McGraw-Hill.

Davis-Kean, P. E., Huesmann, L. R., Jager, J., Collins, W. E., Bates, J. E., & Lansford, J. E. (2008). Changes in the relation of self-efficacy beliefs and behaviors across development. *Child Development*, *79*(5), 1257–1269. doi:10.1111/j.1467-8624.2008.01187.x PMID:18826524

Dick, W., Carey, L., & Carey, J. O. (2008). *The Systematic Design of Instruction* (7th ed.). Boston, MA: Allyn & Bacon.

Gardner, H. (2004). The Theory of Multiple Intelligences (20th anniversary ed.). New York, NY: Basic Books.

Gardner, R. III, Nobel, M., Hessler, T., Yawn, C. D., & Heron, T. (2007). Tutoring system innovations: Past practice to future prototypes. *Intervention in School and Clinic*, *43*(2), 71–81. doi:10.1177/10534512070430020701

Gelo, O., Braakman, D., & Benetka, G. (2008). Quantitative and qualitative research: Beyond the debate. *Integrative Psychological & Behavioral Science*, *42*(3), 266–290. doi:10.1007/s12124-008-9078-3 PMID:18795385

Gerlach, V. S., & Ely, D. P. (1980). *Teaching & media: a systematic approach* (2nd ed.). Englewood Cliffs, NJ: Prentice-Hall.

Goddard, R. D., LoGerfo, L., & Hoy, W. K. (2004). High school accountability: The role perceived collective efficacy. *Educational Policy*, *18*(3), 403–425. doi:10.1177/0895904804265066

Graham, S. (2011). Self-efficacy and academic listening. *Journal of English for Academic Purposes*, *10*(2), 113–117. doi:10.1016/j.jeap.2011.04.001

Gupta, K., Sleezer, C., & Russ-Eft, D. F. (2006). *A practical guide to needs assessment* (2nd ed.). San Francisco, CA: John Wiley and Sons.

Havnes, A. (2008). Peer-mediated learning beyond the curriculum. *Studies in Higher Education*, *33*(2), 193–204. doi:10.1080/03075070801916344

Hsiao, Y. P., Brouns, F., Kester, L., & Sloep, P. B. (2009). *Using Peer Tutoring to Optimize Knowledge Sharing in Learning Networks: A Cognitive Load Perspective*. Retrieved March 6, 2011 from http://celstec.org/printpdf/1210

Jonassen, D. H., & Land, S. M. (2000). *Theoretical foundations of learning environments*. Mahwah, NJ: Lawrence Erlbaum.

Judge, T. A., Erez, A., Bono, J. E., & Thoresen, J. (2002). Are measures of self-esteem, neuroticism, locus of control, and generalized self-efficacy indicators of a common core construct? *Journal of Personality and Social Psychology*, *83*(3), 693–710. doi:10.1037/0022-3514.83.3.693 PMID:12219863

Kearsley, G. (2004). *Online education: Learning and teaching in cyberspace*. Belmont, CA: Thompson.

Kim, Y., & Baylor, A. L. (2006). A social-cognitive framework for pedagogical agents as learning companions. *ETR&D*, *54*(6), 569–596. doi:10.1007/s11423-006-0637-3

King-Sears, M. E. (2001). Institutionalizing peer-mediated instruction and interventions in school: Beyond Train and Hope. *Remedial and Special Education*, *22*(2), 89–101. doi:10.1177/074193250102200203

Ligorio, M. B., Talamo, A., & Simmons, R. (2002). Synchronic tutoring of a virtual community. *Mentoring & Tutoring*, *10*(2), 137–152. doi:10.1080/1361126022000002455

Lin, S. Y., & Overbaugh, R. C. (2009). Computer-mediated discussion, self-efficacy and gender. *British Journal of Educational Technology*, *40*(6), 999–1013. doi:10.1111/j.1467-8535.2008.00889.x

Luszczynska, A., Scholz, U., & Schwarzer, R. (2005). The general self-efficacy scale: Multicultural validation studies. *The Journal of Psychology*, *139*(5), 439–457. doi:10.3200/JRLP.139.5.439-457 PMID:16285214

Luszczynska, A., & Schwarzer, R. (2005). Social cognitive theory. In M. Conner & P. Norman (Eds.), *Predicting health behavior* (2nd ed.; pp. 127–169). Buckingham, UK: Open University Press.

Margolis, H. (2005). Increasing struggling learners self-efficacy: What tutors can do and say. *Mentoring & Tutoring*, *13*(2), 221–238. doi:10.1080/13611260500105675

Matsushima, R., & Shiomi, K. (2003). Social self-efficacy and interpersonal stress in adolescence. *Social Behavior and Personality*, *31*(4), 323–332. doi:10.2224/sbp.2003.31.4.323

Muris, P. (2001). A Brief Questionnaire for Measuring Self-Efficacy in Youths. *Journal of Psychopathology and Behavioral Assessment*, *23*(3), 145–149. doi:10.1023/A:1010961119608

O'Brien, E., & Hall, T. (2004). Training Needs Analysis: the first step in authoring e-learning content. *Proceedings of the 2004 ACM Symposium on Applied Computing*. Retrieved August 16, 2009 from http://delivery.acm.org.library.capella.edu/10.1145/970000/968090/p935-obrien.pdf?key1=968090&key2=3210411521&coll=portal&dl=ACM&CFID=824734&CFTOKEN=52522302

Ormrod, J. E. (2006). *Educational psychology: Developing learners* (5th ed.). Upper Saddle River, NJ: Pearson/Merrill Prentice Hall.

Pajares, F. (2009). Toward a positive psychology of academic motivation: The role of self-efficacy beliefs. In R. Gilman, E. S. Huebner, & M. J. Furlong (Eds.), *Handbook of positive psychology in schools* (pp. 149–160). New York: Taylor & Francis.

Palloff, R. M., & Pratt, K. (2005). *Collaborating Online: learning together in community*. San Francisco, CA: Jossey-Bass.

Paunonen, S. V., & Hong, R. Y. (2010). Self-efficacy and the prediction of domain-specific cognitive abilities. *Journal of Personality*, *78*(1), 339–360. doi:10.1111/j.1467-6494.2009.00618.x PMID:20433622

Phillips, J. J. (2000). *Performance analysis and consulting*. Alexandria, VA: ASTD.

Poellhuber, B., Chomienne, M., & Karsenti, T. (2008). The effect of peer collaboration and collaborative learning on self-efficacy and persistence in a learner-paced continuous intake model. *Journal of Distance Education*, *22*(3), 41–62.

Poggenpoel, M., & Myburgh, C. P. H. (2005). Obstacles in Qualitative Research: Possible Solutions. *Education*, *126*(2), 304–311.

Prat-Sala, M., & Redford, P. (2010). The interplay between motivation, self-efficacy, and approaches to studying. *The British Journal of Educational Psychology*, *80*(2), 283–305. doi:10.1348/000709909X480563 PMID:20021729

Schmidt, A. M., & DeShon, R. P. (2010). The moderating effects of performance ambiguity on the relationship between self-efficacy and performance. *The Journal of Applied Psychology*, *95*(3), 572–581. doi:10.1037/a0018289 PMID:20476834

Scholz, U., Gutiérrez-Doña, B., Sud, S., & Schwarzer, R. (2002). Is general self-efficacy a universal construct? Psychometric findings from 25 countries. *European Journal of Psychological Assessment*, *18*(3), 242–251. doi:10.1027//1015-5759.18.3.242

Smith, H. M., & Betz, N. E. (2000). Development and validation of a scale of perceived social self-efficacy. *Journal of Career Assessment*, *8*(3), 286. doi:10.1177/106907270000800306

Smith, P. L., & Ragan, T. J. (2005). *Instructional Design* (3rd ed.). Hoboken, NJ: Wiley.

Topping, K. J. (2005). Trends in peer learning. *Educational Psychology*, *25*(6), 631–645. doi:10.1080/01443410500345172

Wang, Y., Peng, H., Huang, R., Hou, Y., & Wang, J. (2008). Characteristics of distance learners: Research on relationships of learning motivation, learning strategy, self-efficacy, attribution and learning results. *Open Learning*, *23*(1), 17–28. doi:10.1080/02680510701815277

Webb, T. L., & Sheeran, P. (2008). Mechanisms of implementation intention effects: The role of goal intentions, self-efficacy, and accessibility of plan components. *The British Journal of Social Psychology*, *47*(3), 373–395. doi:10.1348/014466607X267010 PMID:18096108

Wood, C. L., Mackiewicz, S. M., Van Norman, R. K., & Cooke, N. L. (2007). Tutoring with technology. *Intervention in School and Clinic*, *43*(2), 108–115. doi:10.1177/10534512070430020201

Xu, Y., Gelfer, J. I., Sileo, N., Filler, J., & Perkins, P. G. (2008). Effects of peer tutoring on young childrens social interactions. *Early Child Development and Care*, *178*(6), 617–635. doi:10.1080/03004430600857485

Zulkosky, K. (2009). Self-Efficacy: A Concept Analysis. *Nursing Forum*, *44*(2), 93–102. doi:10.1111/j.1744-6198.2009.00132.x

Chapter 4
Detecting Advanced Persistent Threats in Oracle Databases: Methods and Techniques

Lynn Ray
University of Maryland – University College, USA

Henry Felch
University of Maine – Augusta, USA

ABSTRACT

Advanced persistent threats (APTs) have become a big problem for computer systems. Databases are vulnerable to these threats and can give attackers access to an organizations sensitive data. Oracle databases are at greater risk due to their heavy use as back-ends to corporate applications such as enterprise resource planning software. This chapter will describe a methodology for finding APTs hiding or operating deep within an Oracle database system. Using an understanding of Oracle normal operations provides a baseline to assist in discovering APT behavior. Incorporating these and other techniques such as database activity monitoring, machine learning, neural networks and honeypots/tokens can create a database intrusion detection system capable of finding these threats.

INTRODUCTION

Today's attackers are skilled at using a vast amount of sophisticated tools to gather information and attack their targets (Tankard, 2011). These attackers are using Advanced Persistent Threat (APTs) techniques that are proving hard to detect with todays security appliances. The combination of stealth, zero-day exploits, social engineering and multiple techniques contributes to this problem. Because APTs use a dynamic range of diverse techniques, its impossible to devise a common analysis framework (Casenove & Kowalczewska, 2015). Oracle databases are a prime target for attackers using APTs because of their storage of sensitive data. To combat this threat, one needs to establish a means to detect these activities within the database.

DOI: 10.4018/978-1-5225-1680-4.ch004

This chapter provides some methods that can help in detecting APTs hiding or operating within Oracle databases. The first section briefly describes what APTs are to better understand their purpose and how they operate. The second section describes issues with detecting APTs within databases. The last section introduces possible methods for detecting APTs hiding or operating within an Oracle database. Using a combination of these techniques can greatly improve the possibility of finding APTs. The objectives of this chapter is to introduce some of the issues faced by Oracle databases and recommendations to solve them.

BACKGROUND

Before determining how to detect APTs, one needs to understand just what is an APT. Also the means of how they operate is important to determining how to detect them.

What Are They?

APTs are sophisticated cyber-attacks to get valuable information (Casenove & Kowalczewska, 2015). They use custom malware to gain leverage within a network. They may use a wide variety of tools and techniques to gain access to the target. They can vary their tools and techniques used depending on the target. The attackers are persistent and adjust their tactics to get around any protection mechanism in their way. They perform repetitive and continuous attacks over a long time. APT attacks use long-term campaigns and stealthy techniques (Chen, Desmet, & Huyens, 2014). Attackers use zero-day and and encryption to avoid detection. The attackers also consistently change their tactics as the defensive measures change (Kim, Cho, & Yeo, 2014). This makes them difficult to detect and stop. APTs can last for months to years depending on the attacker. It was believed that the skills needed to integrate an APT attack is too sophisticated for the average hacker. However, the tools available today require only basic skills to use and can be utilized to conduct an APT attack.

How Do They Work?

APT attackers meticulously plan and execute their attacks. Each attack may use unique features and techniques but the six stages are always the same (Chen, Desmet, & Huyens, 2014). These include reconnaissance, delivery, initial intrusion, command and control, lateral movement and data exfiltration. The goal is to extract information constantly from within the organization. An attacker selects a target and acquires information about it that can be exploited. Reconnaissance is used to gather the information by use of data mining or analytics (Chen, Desmet, & Huyens, 2014). Next attackers deliver exploits such as spear phishing or watering hole attacks. This way the attacker gains entry to the organization's network to find vulnerabilities to exploit. The next phase deals with getting unauthorized access to the target's network (Chen, Desmet, & Huyens, 2014). At this point the attacker has established a foothold through installed malware on the database server. To accomplish the exploitation, the attacker may use the Tor network to hide their tracks. Also remote access tools (RAT) may be used to help setup a command and control (C&C) communications channel back to the attacker. Using C&C, RAT and Tor, the APT attacker can move around the server to discover valuable data (Chen, Desmet, & Huyens, 2014). Lastly, the exfiltration phase is where data is downloaded and sent back to the attacker.

Another way is to establish a web site to store their malware and send emails to unsuspecting victims. When a user clicks on a URL they are sent to the attackers site and the malicious software is downloaded. Then the malware establishes a command and control (C&C) communications pathway back to the attacker. From here the attacker can perform actions to gather information, destroy data or deface a system. One of these actions is to update the malware code and infrastructure used in the attack. These C&C paths may be encrypted to prevent easy detection (Chen, Desmet, & Huyens, 2014; Mandiant, 2010). Now the attacker can look around and establish higher privileges or obtain passwords. They would be interested in discovering administrator accounts since they have elevated privileges into many systems. Next the attacker can install various utilities for carrying out their attack. Now they can establish a foothold and begin stealing data and setting up staging servers. They can also create many infected sites to use. If an infected system is found and taken down, the attacker finds out and moves operations to any infected machine on the same network. They may have several infected systems to use to hide their operations. They can also rotate these around to keep from being found. Thus increasing the difficulty in detecting APTs.

ISSUES AND PROBLEMS DETECTING APTs

Finding APTs can be challenging. To reduce damages from APTs, one needs to find the malware-infected computers as soon as possible (Liu, Chen & Hung, 2012). To accomplish this requires the cyber security professional to utilize many different methods and techniques to spot APTs. Lastly, an APT will continue to try to break into their target until it meets its objective. Once in, they disguise and morph themselves to avoid detection. This further complicates detecting them. Because APTs use multiple techniques that are different from normal hackers they leave behind different traces or signs of their presence. These signs include: an increase in privileged logins after hours; discovering widespread Trojan backdoors; unauthorized information flows; finding unauthorized data bundles; and discovery of tools used to capture user accounts. These and other issues are discussed below.

Unauthorized Access/Escalation of Privileges

A significant issue from APTs can come from one attempting to gain access to the database (Whitman & Mattord, 2015). One issue is being able to identify the insider threat which may be a system administrator or database administrator (DBA). So how does one monitor their activity? How does one determine what is and is not the norm? Using role-based access control is one possible idea that has been used for years to control access. Kamra, Terzi, and Bertino (2008) recommended using role-based access control (RBAC) for determining the presence of malicious behavior. The problem with this idea is how to determine what is normal versus abnormal behavior. How does one baseline normal behavior? Kul, Luong, Xie and Coonan (2016) built Ettu to detect abnormal behavior and distinguish it from normal ones. However, the system could only handle small amounts of data.

Another issue is preventing one from gaining elevated privileges. Normally APTs exploit the privileges of users for their gain. Attackers try to obtain trusted user accounts and work to get them elevated to administrator rights for accessing more areas in the database. How to prevent this from happening creates another problem in detecting APTs. Still database systems need to scale well in dynamic environments to ensure confidentiality, integrity and availability of the data being stored (Jaidi & Ayachi, 2015). System privileges and roles SYS and SYSMANAGER are controlled by system administrators and need to be controlled from accidentally granting access to the server or database. Also giving users the privilege of "create any role" or roles "with admin option" can give them admin rights (Jaidi & Ayachi, 2015). This allows them to pass on privileges to others instead of just one user. Unless managed carefully, this can cause a serious security issue.

The use of SQL injection is one of the leading causes of outsider data collection (Chougule, Mukhopadhyay, & Randhe, 2013). In an APT, an attacker can choose to use SQL injection to get unauthorized access to information in the database without having to log in. The attacker enters a URL for their target and adds SQL code to cause the web server to transmit the request to the database. In this way, the attacker bypasses the authentication and use multiple queries and other SQl commands embedded within the URL (Kharche, Patil, Gohad, & Ambetkar, 2015; Chougule, Mukhopadhyay, & Randhe, 2013). APT attacks can use INSERT and SELECT commands within a SQL command to attempt access to a database (Guarniere, Marinovoc, & Basin, 2016). These can be used within SQL injection attacks and modify a database's state affecting its confidentiality and integrity.

Once an APT attacker gets a foot hold in a database or server, they setup a command and control (C&C) communications channel back to them. This is used to control the system and help them gain deeper infiltration of the system. Using the C&C connection, attackers can attempt to get to higher privileges such as root or administrator in order to take over the server. These C&C communication paths use a variety of ports to communicate with (Parunak, Nickels, & Frederiksen, 2014). This makes it difficult to track. With over 65,000 different ports to choose from, it becomes difficult to monitor each one.

Unauthorized Information Collection/Data Sniffing

Unauthorized gathering of information or sniffing is another common issue with attacks (Whitman & Mattord, 2015). A common action of attackers using APTs is to gather intelligence about their target (Binde, McRee, & O'Connor, 2011; Tankard, 2011). They do this by port scans to discover what ports and services are running on the Oracle database (Sood & Enbody, 2012). These scans can also disclose the type of Oracle database, which could be used to find exploitable vulnerabilities. NMap is a readily available tool that can perform these scans. Detecting when these scans occur and alerting appropriate personnel become necessary in order to help recognize initial attempts to inject APTs in the database.

Access to sensitive data is the prime target for attackers using APTs. This checking of any activity that accesses the classified or sensitive data is of prime importance. Any unauthorized extracting of data is a clear sign APTs may be operating in the database. Auditing of any access to this data should be performed (Myalapalli, 2014). Since attackers may not be aware of normal database access procedures, they will display a deviation from the way users normally access the database (Kundu, Sural, & Majumdar, 2010). This is similar to an impersonation attack. Also APT attackers may use the authorized user account to attempt access to unauthorized areas.

It is difficult to determine where APTs originate from due to lack of data flow information from the hacker (Casenove & Kowalczewska, 2015). However, one can determine the source of the malware. APTs use a command and control (C&C) communications channel to control the malware on the targeted system. However, the specific ports or IP addresses used by these C&C is vast (Parunak, Nickels, & Frederiksen, 2014). Also they may use the stealthy Tor network to hide their tracks. A means to discover these C&C channels in Oracle database servers is needed to at least determine if an APT exists.

Loss of Data Confidentiality or Integrity

Attackers may use APTs to defeat the confidentiality or integrity of the data in the database. Being able to capture and identify any changes to the Oracle database will be important. These include changes to users, schemas, stored procedures, triggers and sensitive information stored in the database. Alerts and reports could be established to DBA or system administrator personnel for review. However, this is similar to the fox watching the hen house. How does one monitor the DBAs or system administrators? Because SQL statements may be used to access the database, the reviewer needs to be able to understand SQL. Ettu has the capability to detect SQL injections but lacks the ability to handle large and offline data files (Kul, Luong, Xie, & Coonan, 2016).

Increase Use Big Data and Cloud-Based Data Storage

With the rapid use of cloud-based services from companies like Amazon, Google and Microsoft, there is a security risk in using any of these technologies (Whitman & Mattord, 2015; Wu, Zhu, Wu, & Ding, 2013). Most of these vendors support a database as a service (DBaaS) model which moves an organization's data security responsibility to a third-party cloud service provider (Mehak, Masood, Ghazi, Shibli, & Khan, 2014; Wong, Kao, Cheung, Li, & Yiu, 2014). Storing an organization's information assets on another party system removes one from knowing how the data is protected against insider or outside threats. There has been little research on the security of this model. These concerns include protecting data at rest, in transit or being processed. The use of cloud storage also helps fuel the problem with handling big data. Big data is when companies collect and store mountains of data over time. One of the concerns is the lack of evidence that the cloud service provider complies with federal, state or industry security requirements (Gardner, Cova, & Nagaraja, 2014). This can negatively affect the privacy, confidentiality and integrity of the data being stored. Gardner, Cova, and Nagaraja, (2014) found that it was too expensive to encrypt these databases in order to protect the data. Choi, Choi, and Kim (2014) found that RBAC and Context-aware RBAC (C-RBAC) cannot address the dynamic needs of handling the needs between users and the cloud service provider. Therefore, there is a need to find an effective and practical solution for handling dynamic access control needs.

SOLUTIONS AND RECOMMENDATIONS

The first thing one needs to do to detect APTs is to know what systems you have and any vulnerabilities that exist. To reduce damages from APTs, one needs to find the malware-infected computers as soon as possible (Liu, Chen, & Hung, 2012). This is because attackers target unpatched and misconfigured systems. To accomplish this requires establishing behavior-based pattern detection techniques to help in finding APTs. These techniques need to be different from detecting malicious applications in network or operating systems because of their design (Kamra, Terzi, & Bertina, 2008). This is because APTs are designed for their specific targets. In this case, Oracle databases and files. One also needs to take into account insider threats such as disgruntled employees. Database Administrators (DBAs) are given greater privileges than others and could cause grave damage to organizational data. The methods described will take into account the need to monitor all database activity to include insiders.

Establish Dynamic Profiling

Intrusion detection systems using anomaly-based techniques find malicious behavior from knowing what is normal. Kamra, Terzi, and Bertino (2008) recommend using role-based access control (RBAC) for determining the presence of malicious behavior. Normal user profiles are built using RBAC as a baseline to standardize activities and access. Their method grouped individuals based on their normal behavior. Using this method one should be able to detect anomalies that deviate from the profile (Kamra, Terzi, & Bertina, 2008). A classifier such as a neural network could be trained to identify normal behavior and alert when an abnormal behavior is detected. The use of dynamic profiling of users can have a significant impact on how to analyze and characterize behavior in applications and databases (Lizarraga, Lysecky, & Lysecky, 2013). Lizarraga, Lysecky, and Lysecky (2013) created a dynamic profiling optimizing platform for capturing changes in behavior to create metrics that can be used to detect APTs. However, this research was only a proof of concept so further research is needed before using this technique.

Creating a dynamic profile of how applications and users work helps establish a baseline or whitelist of approved activities (Kamra, Bertino, & Lebanon, 2008). Tankard (2011) recommends that this baseline should be complete and locked down to prevent unauthorized changes. All user activity to include use of SELECTs, CREATE, REVOKE, GRANT, UPDATE and stored procedures would be monitored for unusual activities. This makes it easier to determine abnormal activities that can identify APT malware. Scheduled changes to application or users can be used to update the baseline so that it is current. To create this profile takes time to collect and identify normal activities in the database. The profile needs to consist of information describing users, roles and processes at different levels of granularity based on transactions against the database (Kamra, Bertino, & Lebanon, 2008; Kundu, Sural, & Majumdar, 2010). The benefits out weigh the tasks needed to create the profile. Dynamic profiling monitors both Oracle user and application activity and alerts security and DBA personnel when abnormal behavior is discovered. Using dynamic profiling, users and applications can be quarantined until they have been reviewed. The tasks needed to help establish this are described below.

Monitor User Account Privileges

Normally APTs exploit the privileges of users for their gain. Attackers try to obtain trusted user accounts and work to get them elevated to administrator rights for accessing more areas in the database. Monitoring any changes to user account privileges can lead to finding the presence of APTs within a database. CA Technologies (2012) recommend using privileged identity management for monitoring administration accounts since they can cause the most damage if compromised. User rights management establishes an automated process for reviewing user access rights to determine if excessive rights have been given.

Oracle SYSDBA privileges allow one to control the database from outside normal controls (Oracle 2016b; Oracle, 2012). These should be monitored for any unauthorized access or use in case an attacker is using them. Reviewing the ORA_DBA group for any unusual members can help detect the presence of APTs. Also the dba_role_privs and dba_tab_privs tables should be monitored for unauthorized users. Normal users would include the DBAs, object owners or application administrators (Li, Yang, Ren & Hu, 2009). An APT attacker would want to elevate their privileges to allow them the amount of control as a DBA for establishing themselves.

Control Access to Database

To access an Oracle database, each user must be assigned access by a database administrator (DBA). Oracle uses profiles to help the DBA put specific controls on using or accessing resources (Paci, Mece, & Xhuvani, 2012). In Oracle there are at least 100 privileges a user can be given. There are too many for a DBA to properly track and manage. One example called system privileges gives the user the ability to execute DDL statements that can create and manipulate individual objects (Paci, Mece, & Xhuvani, 2012). Attackers can use APTs to gain access to a database and create an account. They can then elevate their rights by use of a GRANT privileges command. Therefore, the DBA should monitor the use of this specific command. Also one should monitor who has system privileges since they can execute ALTER, CREATE, EXECUTE ANY PROCEDURE or DELETE commands to alter database tables (Paci, Mece, & Xhuvani, 2012).

Users are assigned roles to obtain database privileges. The Oracle Enterprise Security Manager is used for central privilege management. It gathers and stores roles from the Oracle Internet Directory. Groups of individuals are given roles and each role has certain privileges assigned to it. This makes it easier to manage users access to the database. In Oracle, there are specific default roles that need to be monitored. The Connect Role gives users the ability to login and create tables (Paci, Mece, & Xhuvani, 2012). An advanced role called Resource Role gives users advanced rights such as creating triggers and procedures. A DBA should have a baseline of what triggers and procedures are on the database. That way they can compare current activity with that of the baseline. This can help identify intruders or APTs that may be in the database. The last role is only assigned to DBAs and should be easy to find out if any unauthorized users have this role.

The use of access control mechanisms provides a guaranteed way of ensuring that any questionable access to sensitive data is prevented (Ghazinour & Ghayoumi, 2015). It also can restrict legitimate users from accidentally seeing information they are not suppose to see. Ghazinour and Ghayoumi (2015) devised a trusted dynamic user interface (TDUI) for enhancing RBAC. Sitting between the user and database, the TDUI checks all user access against a defined set of roles to make sure they are authorized to access sensitive information. Otherwise they are denied. A data use manager (DUM) is a tool that DBAs can use to administer policies to data stores. It then uses these to monitor user activity to detect unauthorized access. It imposes no access control to data but can be used to detect abnormal activity. The DUM intercepts queries and checks them against the policies to find malicious activity. The power of data use management in action. An Ontology-based access control model (Onto-ACM) that addresses the issue with CSPs was devised using a semantic analysis model (Choi, Choi, & Kim, 2014). This model used context reasoning to analyze requirements of the CSP access control model. The Onto-ACM uses interference processing for access authorization and thus can overcome the needs for handling dynamic access control needs.

There are specific procedures and tables that should be monitored to detect the presence of APTs in Oracle databases. The set_security procedures should be checked to ensure it is enabled. If disabled, it will remove database protection. Another group of procedures define changes to objects or creating objects. These can be important in discovering changes that an attacker may have created a new object in the database. The add_object procedures and remove_object procedures can show changes to protected objects. Grant_permission and revoke_permission procedures changes who can access the object. There are also tables linked to these procedures that should be monitored as well to detect changes from APTs. Security_object table contains information on protected objects while the user_permission table has information who has permission over these objects. The ddl_log would be invaluable to review because it contains information about DDL statements executed by users (Paci, Mece, & Xhuvani, 2012).

Access to sensitive data is the prime target for attackers using APTs. This checking of any activity that accesses the classified or sensitive data is of prime importance. Any unauthorized extracting of data is a clear sign APTs may be operating in the database. Activity logs can be used to prove the existence of APTs by monitoring the export of large amounts of data from a database like Oracle (CA Technologies, 2012). Any failed or successful use of SELECTs or data changes should be monitored. These can help in detecting the presence of an APT and attacker accessing sensitive data on the database. Failed logins and SQL errors can help pinpoint the attempt of attackers trying to use APTs to gain access to the database. Attackers through the malware may try to access sensitive data using user accounts with elevated privileges. Then the data is packaged and sent back to the attacker or to another malicious server under the control of the attacker. Monitoring this activity will be important to discovering APTs operating in the database. Tracking data exfiltration can be done using watermarks. Using watermarks, scanning software can be used to detect when watermark data is being extracted from the database (Brancik & Ghinita, 2011). It can also track when the data is stored on a compromised server for later exfiltration. APTs want to be stealthy and hide their tracks. Using watermarks on the data defeats this purpose. Chougule, Mukhopadhyay and Randhe (2013) used a reverse proxy help counteract SQL injection attackers. In this model a SQLInjectionPreventer was used to detect up to three tries by the same IP address, the IP is blocked and security personnel are alerted. It proved effective in protecting database servers against not only SQL injection attacks but cross-site scripting ones as well. A limitation of this method is that it uses a signature check to validate the URL against extra expressions that may have been added (Chougule, Mukhopadhyay, & Randhe, 2013).

Since attackers may not be aware of normal database access procedures, they will display a deviation from the way users normally access the database (Kundu, Sural, & Majumdar, 2010). This is similar to an impersonation attack. This is when the attacker logs into the database using a stolen account and uses it during unusual times (Wu & Huang, 2009). Also APT attackers may use the authorized user account to attempt access to unauthorized areas. This alerts the security personnel of unauthorized access to database objects (Wu & Huang, 2009). Comparing this activity with baseline information on past normal database access sequences, one should be able to find APT activity in a database. Data leakage and database activity monitoring framework can be used to detect abnormal behavior. Profiles were created by a behavior-based whitelisting. Once created one can detect anomalous database transactions and alert security personnel.

Content-awareness is a method for finding new APT threats. Data intelligence is integrated into any decision on granting access to the database (CA Technologies, 2012). This helps in identifying data access patterns according to CA Technologies (2012). According to CS Technologies (2012), this method looks at changes in data access, use, quality and access frequency to determine abnormalities. An APT having acquired administrator privileges may consistently request access to sensitive data that they may not be authorized to. Also they may read and export large amounts of the same data to a remote storage location. Downloading and requesting hundreds of gigabytes of data consistently can also be a clear sign of an APT operating. Suddenly increasing these actions from monthly to daily processes can also be an indication of an APT.

Monitor Suspicious Communications

Oracle uses very specific ports and services to operate. It is important that no two services use the same port at anytime. It is important to know what ports are running on the database at all times. These ports can be found in the Oracle /etc/services file. Therefore, it is important to monitor communications between the malware and controller using command and control (C&C) traffic. This is because APTs attack patterns may use botnets and rootkits as part of their attack tools for infecting a database (Liu, Chen, & Hung, 2012). Liu, Chen, and Hung (2012) recommend using a mechanism called retrospective detection that finds infected systems using information about the C&C. In some cases botnets may connect to several C&C systems to prevent detection or for failover (Liu, Chen, & Hung, 2012).

Detecting the backdoor communications of APTs is made easy by the fact they usually only do outbound transmissions. That is why it's important to analyze all traffic leaving a database since they may exfiltrate sensitive data from the database (Gardner, Cova, & Nagaraja, 2014; Tankard, 2011). These backdoors are used by the malware to call home periodically to check in. APTs can also utilize remote administration tools (RAT) or rootkits to setup these back doors (CA Technologies, 2012). These usually contain a Trojan horse within the APT. The attacker uses these to manage their exploited systems (Sood & Enbody, 2012). Monitoring ports that are used by RAT can help detect the presence of APTs. These may include file transfer protocol (FTP), simple mail transfer protocol (SMTP) and others (Sood & Enbody, 2012). These are not normally used ports for Oracle database servers.

According to Sood and Enbody (2012), a misconfigured database server can allow these protocols to be used by attackers to launch attacks. One can detect APTs communicating over unusual ports or traveling to unrecognized destinations (Brill, 2010). Oracle databases use TCP ports 1521-1525 to listen for requests. Other TCP ports include 64000-64999 for handling the processing of requests. Checking for other open ports can indicate the presence of C&C channels on the database. Mandiant (2010) found that backdoors might use UDP protocols as well to disguise their communications. It is also known that APTs may also use Secure Shell (port 22) and IRC (port 6667) for C&C. Listening for these beacons back to the control server can quickly identify the presence of the APTs (Parunak, Nickels, & Frederiksen, 2014; Brill, 2010). Szymczyk (2009) supports this and adds that peer-to-peer network (P2P) are also used and should be monitored as well. A known RAT called Poison Ivy uses port 3460 for communicating C&C (Binde, McRee, & O'Connor, 2011). Any of these ports are not normal traffic communicating with an Oracle database and should be suspect of possible APTs. Sood and Enbody (2012) recommend breaking down C&C protocols from where the communications are coming from, patterns of the communications, and domain reputation.

APTs may also use multiple backdoors to hide their C&C channel and provide alternate means to maintain communications (Gardner, Cova, & Nagaraja, 2014). This may add difficulty in determining where the malicious backdoors are. Setting strict communication standards and establishing these in a baseline, one can find these malicious ports and services. One may also want to monitor the table dba_db_links table for unusual links to other databases outside the networks. A normal pattern for APTs is to gather and send captured data to a compromised database for later retrieval.

Also APT malware may encrypt the data file going over the C&C channel to mast what they are doing. It can be difficult and costly to try and decrypt the traffic. An APT may also aggregate data into compressed files protected by a password (Gardner, Cova, & Nagaraja, 2014; Binde, McRee, & O'Connor, 2011). Attackers may compress these files using RAR archive format and transferred using protocols such as FTP (Binde, McRee, & O'Connor, 2011; Mandiant, 2010). However, all one needs to do is detect the presence of this unusual traffic to assume that something suspicious is going on. Mandiant (2010) found that only 10% of these backdoors were using this method. Also it is not a commonly used method. So another means of detecting APTs is looking for the use of encrypted traffic between an Oracle database and some unknown location. From this data, security personal and DBAs can create fingerprint rules as part of the dynamic profile baseline for rapidly detecting APTs in Oracle databases.

Check for Suspicious Files

Hiding APTs can be as simple as putting malware files in unusual places one normally doesn't look for. A good example is putting a cache of files in the recycle bin that can be an indicator of APTs (Brill, 2010). Finding executable programs in this cache should be treated as suspicious and dealt with immediately. APTs may try to access Oracle software libraries to plant executables or alter these libraries. Changes to the Oracle software directory can indicate malicious activity (Oracle 2016b; Oracle, 2012). There may be normal changes to these areas but only by DBAs. Therefore, any unmanaged changes need to be detected before they can compromise the dataset. Any malicious activity within these areas can jeopardize the operation of the database.

Establish Baseline of Normal Processes

The first element to prepare is a baseline on normal activities in the database. The DBA should know what processes and users can access the oracle database. Many use TOAD, a database-monitoring tool, to check the activities in the database. Using this dynamic profiling process, DBA and security personnel should obtain enough information to create a baseline of normal activity on the database. The baseline may take weeks to months to collect and devise what is normal activity in the oracle database. They will also need to filter out any activities that are easily recognized as abnormal operations. Enough time and detail should be taken to collect and define the right activities for the baseline. Otherwise, the baseline could cause a high number of false positives making the detection of APTs difficult for the neural network IDS. False positive occurs when the detection systems can't clearly determine if the data shows an intrusion or not. It passes the decision to the human for sorting it out and making the final determination.

The DBA should have a complete list of all normal Oracle processes and procedures. This is to facilitate auditing anyone accessing sensitive data. Any unusual activity should be investigated for possible APT malware. The attacker's purpose is to find and access this data for possible gain. Finding APTs can be identified when least used applications or external systems are found. Also occasional traffic patterns can be identified in the dynamic profiling baseline as being abnormal. The routine beaconing of APT infected systems is a good example of this occasional traffic. APTs must periodically call back to their controller to check in and receive instructions.

An important part of the dynamic profile is to establish normal transaction activities in order that they can be used to compare current transactions. These transactions contain a sequence of database queries composed of SELECT, INSERT, DELETE and UPDATE commands (Kundu, Sural, & Majumdar, 2010). Kundu, Sural, and Majumdar (2010) suggested using a transaction logger to parse the transactional data to find the specific information needed to compare against the baseline. Using a database ID tag for all transactions to find any dependencies in the data. Then use these against the baseline and log files to find abnormalities (Kamra, Bertino, & Lebanon, 2008). Databases may have standing queries that are installed once and execute continuously. These processes should be addressed in the baseline profile to guard against APTs from disguising their activities as a routine process. Routine monitoring of current standing queries and comparing them to the baseline can detect if an APT is present in the Oracle database.

Other signs of APT activity in Oracle databases include off-hour processes running on the database. APTs like to access sensitive data and extract it late at night. It has been found that most attacks occur between 10 PM to 4 AM ET when most users would not be at work (Binde, McRee, & O'Connor, 2011; Mandiant, 2010). Attackers may decide to extract data over time or all at once. These long sessions or large data transfers can be an indication of APTs in the database. Using the baseline profile can help to identify these processes as APTs. This information is extracted using botnets as part of the APT (Sood & Enbody, 2012). Therefore, detecting the presence or communications being used during non-business hours can help detect an APT operating within an Oracle database.

Oracle has another procedure called extproc that allows someone to use the Oracle process account to execute an application located outside the database (Oracle 2016b; Oracle, 2012). This is a normal operation for APTs after they get into a database. Some versions of Oracle have addressed this issue. Versions lower then 11.1 should be monitored for any activity using this procedure (Oracle 2016b; Oracle, 2012).

Establish Routine Auditing Process

After devising the baseline, one needs to collect information on current activities. This will require Oracle log files to be collected. Auditing involves collecting information on SQL statements, privileges, schema and communications activity. Setting up this auditing is very important to detecting APTs. Auditing is used to account for any actions taken by users (Myalapalli, 2014). This includes setting up an automated means to discover and alert of any suspicious data access by using triggers (Myalapalli, 2014). Gathering this information will help determine whether an activity is legitimate or not. It will also be used to investigate suspicious behavior as well as the one performing the action. A database activity monitoring (DAM) tool can automate the process and reduce the time to discover APT activity. It can also monitor activities and alert security personnel if there is suspicious events happening with the database (Myalapalli, 2014; Kim, Cho, Lee, Kang, Kim, Hwang, & Mun, 2013). Kim, Cho, Lee, Kang, Kim, Hwang, and Mun (2013) induces the *DB-i* that monitors the protocols between users and the database. It analyzes the database sessions and queries to detect unauthorized access to the database. The *DB-i* uses a local outlier factor for capturing and measuring abnormal access in database logs.

One must turn on Oracle logging in order to begin collecting information on possible APT activity. In Oracle, there are two types of audit records: standard and fine-grained. Enabling standard audit records will collect information on all operations. This will have a negative affect on the database performance and can be more harmful than the APT itself. Fine-grained audit records allow one to devise specific policies that are less harmful than standard audit records. These policies are simple and can record queries and SELECT, INSERT, UPDATE, MERGE and DELETE operations within the Oracle database. These policies are managed by the dbms_gfa package. One must set the parameters for the dbma_fga. add_policy to create fine-grained audit policies (Oracle, 2016a; Oracle, 2011). The fine-grained audit reports can detect the abnormal activities that APTs do. These include accessing a table after hours or weekends, using remote IP addresses, making modifications to tables, multiple login failures and attempts to login by non-existent users (Oracle 2016a; Oracle, 2011). Therefore, we want to do finer auditing to capture specific events.

The Oracle database audit information is written to the sys.aud$ and sys.fga_logs$ tables (Oracle 2016a; Oracle, 2011). This makes it important to retrieve this information for determining if non-SYS users are doing unauthorized activity. This is because only SYS users are allowed to perform DML operations. These tables can also be used to collect information on users who connect using SYSDBA and SYSOPER (Oracle 2016a; Oracle, 2011).

One can use a data dictionary view to find information on database activity in Oracle. The dba_fga_audit_train view will show all the audit trail information using fine-grained auditing (Oracle 2016a; Oracle, 2011). Other data dictionary views that are important to detecting APTs include V$PROCESS and V$SESSION_LONGOPS. V$PROCESS has information on current processes running in the Oracle database (Oracle 2016a; Oracle, 2011). This would be good for finding abnormal activity running in the Oracle database. V$SESSION_LONGOPS can be used to detect when an attacker is trying to transfer large amounts of data. These are manual processes and would be time consuming when trying to find APTs quickly.

Automating the collection of this and other log data needs to be done so that a neural network IDS can process it. A simple method is to configure syslog to collect and store the information in a file that can be accessed by the database agent. Configuring syslog is accomplished by adjusting the syslog.conf file in Oracle to identify where to store syslog data (Oracle 2016a; Oracle, 2011). The DBA should set this up and use the SYSLOG() function to log the information.

Organizations need to establish and maintain a routine process for reviewing all security logs and alerts. Their activity or presence can be found if the investigator is as persistent as the threat. APT activity can also be detected using security and activity logs. These should be reviewed daily but automating reports can reduce the workload. Performing timely and routine reviews of the audit logs can help discover APTs before they can cause too much harm (Oracel 2016b; Oracle, 2012). The use of neural networks and database agents can help automate this process. They can collect these logs from multiple databases for correlation and discovery of APT activity. Gartner recommends the use of such database activity monitoring systems for helping detect changes in databases (Kamra, Bertino, & Lebanon, 2008). In Oracle, syslog data can be prepared using the fine-grained audit information from sys.aud$ and sys.fga_logs$. Syslog can collect and store this information then send it to the neural network IDS for processing.

Handling big data attacks can be challenging. To combat this is to monitor abnormal behavior using data analytics. This involved the use of role mining, access logs and model user behavior to detect abnormal behavior. Chari, Habeck, Mollo, Park, and Teiken (2013) devised such a system that used machine learning and profiling. However, it had a high false positive rate. One way to handle this is to aggregate the data for specific time periods and then perform the analytics.

Use Threat Intelligence

A defense strategy needs to leverage what they know about the repeated attacks. Setting up an intelligence feedback loop, one can identify intrusion attempts and better understand the adversaries attack patterns (Chen, Desmet, & Huyens, 2014). The amount of information in logs and other reporting material can be over whelming for any security individual or team. Using a SIEM equipped with an integrated threat intelligence capability can correlate information from multiple sources and provide real time reporting. They also reduce a lot of the noise and false positives current IDSs and other devices produce. These devices can also prioritize the threats so as to only notify you of critical ones.

One should also use the Kill Chain Taxonomy to achieve this prioritization and to help determine the intent of the attacker's efforts. A multi-layer defense system is a way of collecting and analyzing log information from various sources (Moon, Im, Lee, & Park, 2014). It utilized agents to discover APTs in a target system. This system used machine learning to build a white list or normal behavior for detecting malicious behavior. Another improvement is a two-stage database IDS which uses both signature and anomaly-based detection techniques. In this model, anomaly detection is used in the first stage while signature detection in the second (Panigrahi, Sural, & Majumdar, 2013). It tracks transactions as either being normal, abnormal or suspicious. It keeps track of normal transactions history based on past behavior. A generic behavior repository is also built on different past malicious data. Adding data mining to an IDS can improve its capability to detect database activity. The Optimal Data Access Dependency Rule Mining (ODADRM) algorithm extends the k-optimal rule discovery algorithm for detecting abnormal transactions such as those from APTs (Sohrabi, Javidi, & Hashemi, 2014). It extracts dependency from data transactions to find malicious behavior. However, it can't identify malicious read only transactions.

Deploy Database Agents

The use of database software agents can help automate the detection of APTs. They can be installed and configured within Oracle databases to discover abnormal behavior and alerting the security and DBA personnel. Each agent is composed of a filtering agent and detection engine to discover anomalies in a database (Bhatt, Koshti, Agrawal, Malek, & Trivedi, 2011; Szymczyk, 2009). The filter agent collects information from the database logs and passes them to the detection engine. The detection engine compares the information to established rules. For databases, one would use the current profile baseline as the rules to compare against.

Agents can monitor activities such as the use of elevated privileges, changes to the database and access to sensitive tables by users. These are installed by system administrators and can detect when they are tampered with. They can send their information in real time thus allowing for a quicker response by appropriate personnel. These agents run continuously and are adaptive to changes in database behavior. They are also mobile and can be moved to other databases in case of possible infections in multiple locations. Agents help to monitor blind spots such as when someone directly accesses the database. Their mining of large amounts of data and events make it an ideal device to use in detecting APTs in Oracle databases. They communicate directly with the database and monitor changes to the database in places where no one can access. It can also monitor direct connections to the database that DBAs or other privileged users may use.

These database agents are specific to the types of databases. This is because each agent needs to be configured to work with different types of database. One should use Oracle database agents so that they can collect Oracle specific log and audit data. The syslog and other audit information uses a specific format that the database agent needs to pass onto the neural network IDS engine. The database agent can be used to convert the data to a format for our neural network IDS engine to use when comparing the baseline to it. DAMs can use the information from agents to help detect APTs in databases. These can be helpful in monitoring insider threats as well. They also analyze protocols and observe database traffic (Kim, Cho, Lee, Kang, Kim, Hwang, & Mun, 2013).

Utilize Neural Networks and Honeypot Technology

The heart of any IDS is the engine for analyzing all the information collected to detect APT activity. This engine must be able to take different inputs and determine if the activity is malicious. It will compare input data from database agents and baseline configurations to Oracle log information in order to detect APTs. An anomaly-based intrusion detection technique uses this same method to compare different data to determine abnormal behavior. This method is normally used in neural networks and can be used as a means to automate detection of APTs in a database. The neural network can automate many of the aforementioned techniques and methods for detecting APTs. Any deltas detected can mean the presence of APTs.

The neural network would monitor users connection points usually in an application connected to the oracle data. The neural network will collect traffic entering and leaving the database to determine if APT C&C traffic exists. It will also detect if the traffic is encrypted or compressed. This can be a sign of possible APTs communicating with its remote control center. Data about what's going on in the Oracle database needs to be fed to the neural network. This is the job of the database agent. The database agent collects information from the Oracle logs to send to the neural network IDS engine. These logs contain information on current activities going on in the database. Combined with database agents, the neural network can check current database activity against the baseline profile.

Before any detection can be done, the neural network will have to be trained. Training is needed to make sure the neural network can recognize legitimate activity. It can be trained on using the baseline from the dynamic profile as a model of normal behavior. Once trained, the neural network can recognize normal activity against malicious. This way any abnormality in Oracle database activities can be easily detected. Li, Yang, Ren and Hu (2009) support the use of training intrusion detection systems and comparing current behavior against an established model. Another important aspect of the training is that it relies heavily on having a current profile baseline to accurately find APTs.

The use of machine learning algorithm with data mining and anomaly-based behavior detection can enhance the training of neural networks (Siddiqui, Ferens, Khan, & Kinsner, 2016). Yazdani, Panahi, and Poor (2013) proposed an eXtended Classifier System (XCS) intrusion detection classifier based on machine learning. Their system used if-then set of rules to determine the behavior of APTs. The learning came from use of genetic algorithms.

To enhance alerts of possible APTs is to use a database honeypot or honeynet. A honeypot is a cost effective solution against APT attacks. It acts as a decoy to track and alert on intrusions to networks (Mali, Raj, & Gaykar, 2014). Honeypots are considered traps to detect and counteract unauthorized intrusion. They are used to primary with network intrusions but can be adopted for database intrusions. An important attribute of honeypots is that they don't create false positives or negatives (Fronimos, Magkos, & Chrissikopoulous, 2014). Using multiple techniques to detect APTs such as honeypots can significantly increase early detection of intrusions. Honeypots are straight forward, use less resources and can provide a proactive detection of APTs (Saud & Islam, 2015). Some example Honeypots include: Honeyd, Kippo, Spector, Dionaea, Mantrap and KFSensor. A smaller version of a honeypot is called a honeytoken. These are a digital entity used to capture digital intrusions in databases (Kambow & Passi, 2014; Mali, Raj, & Gaykar, 2014). Honeytokens can be fake data that has been inserted into a database to track suspicious and unauthorized activity. They are configured to be of interest to intruders and can't be distinguished from real data entities (Shabtai, Bercovitch, Rokach, Gal, Elovici, & Shmueli, 2016). The HoneyGen system is a method of automatically generating honeytokens from real production data. In this way they become more tempting to intruders. Future research is needed to determine the tradeoffs in detection rate and cost of using honeytokens (Shabtai, Bercovitch, Rokach, Gal, Elovici, & Shmueli, 2016).

FUTURE RESEARCH DIRECTIONS

APTs will continue to evolve and be a threat to databases. Future detection of APTs will rely on use of multiple tools and techniques. Also future research is needed in detecting APTs in big data environments. Big data concerns continue to grow because of its increasing capacity to store data (Wu, Zhu, Wu, & Ding, 2013). Some of the tools and techniques discussed should be investigated in this area to see their potential. This includes analyzing other databases to include IBM DB2 and MS SQL. These other databases are heavily used in organizations. Access control models to deal with dynamic environments especially in cloud-based systems need further research. The use of ontology reasoning proved to help address the difference between users and CSPs. With cloud-based computing becoming the norm, it will be imperative for having a solution for managing privacy and access control in these environments.

The capabilities of honeytokens and neural network can provide insight into detecting new APT attacks. Further research is needed on seeing the capabilities of using honeytokens and neural network capabilities in creating profiles of APT behavior. Because of the current use of zero-day malware, detection techniques will need to seek better ways of using anomaly-based detection. Further research is needed to see how this can be integrated with SIEM technology for creating automated alerts. Devising models of APT activity is needed in order to devise protection methods one can use to prevent damage to databases. To accomplish this requires further research in devising new techniques in data mining. Also anomaly-based detection capabilities using machine learning algorithms and data mining techniques can also enhance the detection of APTs. Including database agents in the mix can also enhance the detection capability as well.

CONCLUSION

APTs can be a security issue and concern for Oracle databases. This becomes more apparent as more databases are used to store sensitive data and accessible globally. Compounding this is the fact that detecting their presence can be difficult and challenging to find. However, using a wide range of detection methods along with neural networks and database agents can help reduce this issue. Thus, its best that the security and DBA personnel be as persistent in their search for APTs as APTs are to attacking a database.

REFERENCES

Bhatt, C., Koshti, A., Agrawal, H., Malek, Z., & Trivedi, B. (2011). Architecture for intrusion detection system with fault tolerance using mobile agent. *International Journal of Network Security & Its Applications*, *3*(5), 167–175. doi:10.5121/ijnsa.2011.3513

Binde, B. E., McRee, R., & O'Connor, T. J. (2011). *Assessing outbound traffic to uncover advanced persistent threat*. Retrieved May 1, 2016, from http://www.sans.edu/student-files/projects/JWP-Binde-McRee-OConnor.pdf

Brancik, K., & Ghinita, G. G. (2011, February). *The optimization of situational awareness for insider threat detection*. Presented at the First ACM Conference on Data and Application Security and Privacy, San Antonio, TX. doi:10.1145/1943513.1943544

Brill, A. E. (2010). From hit and run to invade and stay: How cyberterrorists could be living inside your systems. *Defense Against Terrorism Review*, *3*(2), 23–36.

Casenove, M., & Kowalczewska, K. (2015). APT – The new cyberforce? *The Polish Quarterly of International Affairs*, *3*, 719.

Chari, S., Habeck, T., Molloy, I., Park, Y., & Teiken, W. (2013, June). *A bigdata platform for analytics on access control policies and logs*. Presented at the SACMAT 2013, Amsterdam, The Netherlands. doi:10.1145/2462410.2462433

Chen, P., Desmet, L., & Huyens, C. (2014, September). *A study on advanced persistent threats*. Presented at the 15th Conference in Communications and Multimedia Security, Aveiro, Portugal.

Choi, C., Choi, J., & Kim, P. (2014). Ontology-based access control model for security policy reasoning in cloud computing. *The Journal of Supercomputing*, *67*(3), 711–722. doi:10.1007/s11227-013-0980-1

Chougule, A., Mukhopadhyay, D., & Randhe, V. (2013). *Reverse Proxy Framework using Sanitization Technique for Intrusion Prevention in Database*. CoRR, abs/1311.6578

Fronimos, D., Magkos, E., & Chrissikopoulous, V. (2014, October). *Evaluating low interaction honeypots and on their use against advanced persistent threats*. Presented at the 18th Panhellenic Conference on informatics, Athens, Greece. doi:10.1145/2645791.2645850

Ghazinour, K., & Ghayoumi, M. (2015, November). *A dynamic trust model enforcing security policies*. Presented at the International Conference on Intelligent Information processing, Security and Advanced Communication, Batna, Algeria. doi:10.1145/2816839.2816909

Guarniere, M., Marinovoc, S. & Basin, D. (2016). *Strong and provably secure database access control*. CoRR, abs/1512.01479

Jaidi, F., & Ayachi, F. L. (2015, January). *The problem of integrity in rbac-based policies within relational databases: Synthesis and problem study*. Presented at the 9th International Conference on Ubiquitous Information Management and Communication, Bali, Indonesia. doi:10.1145/2701126.2701196

Kambow, N., & Passi, L. K. (2014). Honeypots: The need of network security. *International Journal of Computer Science and Information Technologies*, *5*(5), 60986101.

Kamra, A., Bertino, E., & Lebanon, G. (2008, June). *Mechanisms for database intrusion detection and response*. Presented at the Second SIGMOD PhD Workshop on Innovative Database Research, Vancouver, Canada. doi:10.1145/1410308.1410318

Kamra, A., Terzi, E., & Bertina, E. (2008). Detecting anomalous access patterns in relational databases. *The VLDB Journal*, *17*(5), 1063–1077. doi:10.1007/s00778-007-0051-4

Kharche, S., Patil, J., Gohad, K., & Ambetkar. (2015). *Preventing sql injection attack using pattern matching algorithm.* CoRR, abs/1504.06920

Kim, S., Cho, N. W., Lee, Y. J., Kang, S., Kim, T., Hwang, H., & Mun, D. (2013). Application of density-based outlier detection to database activity monitoring. *Information Systems Frontiers*, *15*(1), 55–65. doi:10.1007/s10796-010-9266-9

Kim, S. J., Cho, D. E., & Yeo, S. S. (2014). Secure model against apt in m-connected scada network. *International Journal of Distributed Sensor Networks*.

Kul, G., Luong, D., Xie, T., & Coonan, P. (2016, April). *Ettu: Analyzing query intents in corporate databases*. Presented at 2016 World Wide Conference, Montreal, Canada.

Kundu, A., Sural, S., & Majumdar, A. K. (2010). Database intrusion detection using sequence alignment. *International Journal of Information Security*, *9*(3), 179–191. doi:10.1007/s10207-010-0102-5

Li, Y., Yang, D., Ren, J., & Hu, C. (2009, August). *An approach for database intrusion detection based on the event sequence clustering*. Presented at the Fifth International Joint Conference on INC, IMS and IDC, Seoul, South Korea. doi:10.1109/NCM.2009.30

Liu, S. T., Chen, Y. M., & Hung, H. C. (2012, August). *N-victims: An approach to determine N victims for APT investigations*. Presented at the 13th International Workshop on information Security Applications, Jeju Island, South Korea. doi:10.1007/978-3-642-35416-8_16

Lizarraga, A., Lysecky, R. & Lysecky, S. (2013). Dynamic profiling and fuzzy-logic-based optimizing of sensor network platforms. *ACM Transactions on Embedded Computing Systems, 13*(3).

Mali, Y. M., Raj, R. M. J. V., & Gaykar, A. T. (2014, April). Honeypot: A tool to track hackers. *Engineering Science and Technology: An International Journal*, *4*(2), 52–55.

Mandiant. (2010). *M Trends:The advanced persistent threat*. Retrieved May 1, 2016, from www.princeton.edu/~yctwo/files/readings/M-Trends.pdf

Moon, D., Im, H., Lee, J. D., & Park, J. H. (2014). MLDS: Multi-layer defense system for preventing advanced persistent threats. *Symmetry*, *6*(4), 997–1010. doi:10.3390/sym6040997

Myalapalli, V. K. (2014, March). An appraisal to overhaul database security configurations. *International Journal of Scientific and Research Publications*, *4*(3), 1–4.

Oracle. (2011). *Oracle Database Security Guide 11g Release 1 (11.1)*. Retrieved May 1, 2016, from http://docs.oracle.com/cd/B28359_01/network.111/b28531.pdf

Oracle (2012). *DISA oracle 11 database security technical implementation guide Version 8 Release 1.9*. Retrieved May 1, 2016, from http://iase.disa.mil/stigs/app_security/database/

Oracle. (2016a). *Oracle Database Security Guide 12c Release 1 (12.1)*. Retrieved May 1, 2016, from http://docs.oracle.com/database/121/DBSEG/toc.htm

Oracle (2016b). *DISA oracle 12c database security technical implementation guide Version 1 Release 3*. Retrieved May 1, 2016, from http://iase.disa.mil/stigs/app_security/database/

Paci, H., Mece, E. K., & Xhuvani, A. (2012). Protecting Oracle PLP/SQL source code from a DBA user. *International Journal of Database Management Systems*, *4*(4), 43–52. doi:10.5121/ijdms.2012.4404

Panigrahi, S., Sural, S., & Majumdar, A. K. (2013). Two-stage database intrusion detection by combining multiple evidence and belief update. *Information Systems Frontiers*, *15*(1), 35–53. doi:10.1007/s10796-010-9252-2

Parunak, H.V.D., Nickels, A. & Frederiksen, R. (2014, May). *An agent-based framework for dynamical understanding of dns events (DUDE)*. ACySe, Paris, France.

Saud, Z., & Islam, M. H. (2015, September). *Towards proactive detection of advanced persistent threat (apt) attacks using honeypots*. Presented at the 8th International Conference on Security of Information and networks, Sochi, Russian Federation. doi:10.1145/2799979.2800042

Shabtai, A., Bercovitch, M., Rokach, L., Gal, Y., Elovici, Y. & Shmueli, E. (2016). Behavioral study of users when interacting with active honeytokens. *ACM Transactions on Information and Systems Security, 18*(9).

Sohrabi, M., Javisi, M. M., & Hashemi, S. (2014, June). Detecting intrusion transactions in database systems: A novel approach. *Journal of Intelligent Information Systems*, *42*(3), 619–644. doi:10.1007/s10844-013-0286-z

Sood, A. K. & Enbody, R. J. (2012). Targeted cyber attacks: A superset of advanced persistent threats. *IEEE Security & Privacy Magazine, 99*.

Szymczyk, M. (2009, June). *Detecting botnets in computer networks using multi-agent technology*. Presented at the Fourth International Conference on Dependability of Computer Systems, Brunow, Poland. doi:10.1109/DepCoS-RELCOMEX.2009.46

Tankard, C. (2011). Persistent threats and how to monitor and deter them. *Network Security*, *8*(8), 16–19. doi:10.1016/S1353-4858(11)70086-1

Technologies, C. A. (2012). *Advanced persistent threats: Defending from the inside out*. Retrieved May 1, 2016, from http://www.ca.com/us/collateral/white-papers/na/Advanced-Persistent-Threats-Defending-From-The-Inside-Out.aspx

Whitman, M., & Mattord, H. (2015, October). *Ongoing threats to information protection.* Presented at the Information Security Curriculum Development Conference, Kennesaw, GA.

Wong, W. K., Kao, B., Cheung, D. W. L., Li, R., & Yiu, S. M. (2014, June). *Secure query processing with data interoperability in a cloud database environment*. Presented at the ACM SIGMOD International Conference on Management of Data, Snowbird, UT. doi:10.1145/2588555.2588572

Wu, G., & Huang, Y. (2009, May). *Design of a new intrusion detection system based on database*. Presented at the 2009 International Conference on Signal Processing Systems, Singapore.

Wu, X., Zhu, X., Wu, G., & Ding, W. (2013). Data mining with big data. *IEEE Transactions on Knowledge and Data Engineering*, *26*(1), 97–107.

Yazdani, N. M., Panahi, M. S., & Poor, E. S. (2013). Intelligent detection of intrusion into database using extended classier system. *Iranian Journal of Electrical and Computer Engineering*, *3*(5), 708–712.

KEY TERMS AND DEFINITIONS

Advanced Persistent Threat (APT): A collection of techniques used by attackers to gain access to computers and databases.

Anomaly-Based: A technique used to discover abnormal behavior in information systems.

Command & Control Communications (C&C): A communications channel that allows attackers to remotely control malicious software on a server.

Data Mining: A means of extracting information from a data large source.

Database Agent: A piece of software installed on a database that collects user activity.

Honeypot: A copy of a realistic information system used as a decoy to protect real servers from attackers.

Intrusion Detection System: A security system used to detect intruders accessing an information system or network.

Remote Access Trojan (RAT): A malicious program that is used to remotely connect to computers and control them.

Role-Based Access Control (RBAC): A means to control access to databases based on giving users roles and permissions to access information in a database.

Chapter 5
About Gravitational (Inertial) Motors

Dan Ciulin
E-I-A Lausanne, Switzerland

ABSTRACT

A gravitational motor interact with the locally gravitational field in order to produce a linear and/or rotational thrust able to move in space a given vehicle. The big advantages of such a motor are the facts that it can be used for nearly any kind of vehicle, even in free space, and may be placed inside the vehicle as the necessary interactions with the environment are realized through gravitational fields but not by direct mechanical interaction as for actual motors used for vehicles. Generally, in mechanics a physical motor may be considered as a 'transducer' between some input (equivalent) energy existing on a vehicle and the output (equivalent) obtained movement of this vehicle. For space treks, such a motor must be able to ensure the take-off and/or landing of a space vehicle on any given planet and carry the entire load corresponding to this vehicle including also the necessary energy sources and eventually a human crew. By analogy with the Levitron toy the atomic particles, and the maglev such motor may be built. The paper presents some ideas and mathematical models that may help to build such a gravitational motor. It starts by presenting the energy based differential equations that have as solution analytic complex exponential functions, elliptic and ultra-elliptic functions adding also a physical interpretation of their coefficients. Forces and torques in mechanic and electro mechanic are presented and also methods to obtain such forces using only torques. Based on the modified Euler equations of a gyroscope with an added magnet like for the Levitron toy, an electro-mechanical gravitational motor may be built and a mathematical model for the gravitational waves is also deduced. Maybe, by using this kind of waves, a permanent contact between an interplanetary ship and the earth can be kept. Another kind of inertial motor may be based on the direct transfer of the energy of acoustical and/or ultra-acoustical waves that represents the desired 'inertia' of a vehicle to this vehicle. This kind of transfer may be realized using convenient acoustical and/or ultra-acoustical 3-D sources. This last method has the advantage that uses no mechanical component in movement and then may lead to a better reliability. Associated with a good and convenient technology that may be developed on the presented bases, all these tools are of most strategic importance. Applications may be found in interplanetary telecommunications and treks but also for a new, more sure and versatile, telecommunications systems and terrestrial vehicles. The presented tools may be used for mathematically modeling the fields and ensure also a more comprehensive understanding.

DOI: 10.4018/978-1-5225-1680-4.ch005

INTRODUCTION

In nature, any 'change' correspond to an interaction that implies an exchange of energy and/or its equivalent, the mass. Then, any 'change' may lead to a 'transformation'. It is known that the energy (and/or action) based differential equations established relations between the items that interact and have as solution degenerate elliptic (complex exponential), elliptic and/or ultra-elliptic functions. All these functions are periodic having real and imaginary periods. Physically, the real periods may represent the 'time interval of the given transformation' and/or also 'it's dynamic' and the imaginary periods may have other significations too. As an example, for the complex exponential functions, the imaginary period is connected to the 'damping' of a given system. The time integral of the exchanged energy during the (real) period of such function correspond to a '(realized) action'. We remember that Kaluza-Klein theory (Wikipedia, Kaluza-Klein, 2016) in 5 dimensions use the action and the variation principle to unify the Einstein and Maxell theory. It is known that the analytic functions must satisfy the Cauchy-Riemann equations:

$$\begin{cases} \dfrac{\partial u[x,y]}{\partial x} = \dfrac{\partial v[x,y]}{\partial y}; \\ \dfrac{\partial v[x,y]}{\partial x} = -\dfrac{\partial u[x,y]}{\partial y}; \end{cases} \tag{1}$$

which represents the 'condition of analyticity'. These relations are some kind of 'symmetries' of the analytic functions. From Noether's theorem (Wikipedia, Noether theorem, 2016), it results that the waves and/or gravitational fields that may be modeled by these functions conserve their energy. This is in accord to the fact that light may come from very far away stars and also that on earth, the energy used to lift vertically a given mass with 1 meter is equal to the energy obtained when this mass return to its initial position. Similarly, a celestial corps (and/or a human satellite or probe) may inertial move very long time without the need of any motor.

A transformed item may remain inside its initial domain and/or may be transferred to another domain. In this last case the transformation is generally realized through a 'transducer'. Many motors may be considered as 'transducers'. As a well-known example, an electric motor 'transfers' the input electrical energy into the output mechanical rotation energy. Generally, the mass is a good transducer to the gravitational fields and also for the electromagnetic fields as for some structures like aerials. One remark that the atomic particles as electron, positron, proton, may be assimilated to a Levitron toy (Wikipedia, Levitron, 2016), because they have spin and magnetic moment. More, they 'wobble' like a gyroscope through electron spin resonance (Wikipedia, EPR, 2016), and/or nuclear magnetic resonance (Wikipedia, NMR, 2012) effects as example. From here it results that in some cases, the 'action-reaction' Newton principle may not take place always in the 'input' domain of a transducer (Wikipedia, Reactionless drive, 2016). Generally, any 'transformation' needs energy and/or mass transfer and also time. Then, a motor cannot instantly transfer to his vehicle the necessary energy to move in a given desired direction even if it is very powerful. Anyhow, the motor transfer energy to the 'inertia' of the vehicle and in time, these transferred energy must compensate the losses and ensure the necessary energy for the vehicle to follow the desired trajectory. We may observe that the inertia of a given mass may be equivalent to a kind of 'polarization' of the mass of vehicle and that in some conditions as free space and/or on an ideal horizontal way (nearly) without frictions on earth, a vehicle may follow its way without the need of any motor. For these reasons, actual motors are less powerful and, as an example for a car, it needs a system to exchanges the speeds that match the speeds where the motor is efficient with the actual speed of the vehicle. Due to this situation, an equivalent 'soft landing and/or lift up' of a plane is also possible. The fact that same transforms may imply transducers lead to the idea that the electromagnetic fields exist in another space than the gravitational field and then, as a 'space at the output of a transducer'. By a crude analogy, another languish different from English needs to be 'translated to English' to be understood. Mathematical models using complex exponential, elliptic and/or ultra-elliptic functions have the 'complex time' as the independent variable. For higher dimensions, the ultra-elliptic functions may have many 'complex times' as independent variables, probably corresponding to the 'dimensions at the output of a given transducer'. These may be also put in conjunction with the 11 dimension of the string theory where each period of such functions may be considered as generated by a 'string' (Wikipedia, String theory, 2012).

Based on these ideas and to presents more explicitly the subject, I had split the chapter 'Gravitational (inertial) motors' into 6 sections. This will lead the reader to acquire, step by step, the necessary knowledge to follow. The first section presents the energy based differential equations that lead to polynomials, complex exponential functions, elliptical and ultra-elliptical functions. Physically, these functions that results as an exchange of energy, may represents the physics in a different manner and then, leads to a different fruitful point of view. Some physical interpretations are also presented. As any motor generate force and/or torque, these are passed in review in the section 2 'Force and torque for mechanic and electro-mechanic devices'. Section 3 'Gravitational (inertial) systems', presents and compares the possible gravitational inertial systems. This (mainly) leads to the gyroscope who is a 3D mechanical transducer with a good efficiency. By adding a magnet to a gyroscope like for the Levitron top, one obtains an electro-mechanical transducer with a good efficiency. This is shown in the section 4 'Levitron type gyroscope' where a mathematical model of this device is presented. It can be also observed that a Levitron type gyroscope is the main device of a given (future) inertial motor. As a Levitron type gyroscope is also an electro-mechanical transducer, it can exchange electromagnetic waves due to the movement in 3D of its 'built in' magnet. These waves are also 3D and may be considered as gravitational waves. This is presented in the section 5 'Gravitational waves'. The section 6 'About inertia' uses some analogies to physically define inertia as an acoustic and/or ultra-acoustic wave. On these bases, a better inertial motor may be built and a proposed bloc-diagram is presented. The chapter 'Conclusions' passes in review all these and add also some tools that may extend the presented theory.

GRAVITATIONAL (INERTIAL) MOTORS

Energy Based Differential Equations

Mechanically, the energy E is defined by:

$$E = \frac{m.v^2}{2} = \frac{m}{2}.\left(\frac{ds}{dt}\right)^2 \tag{2}$$

where v is the speed, s the space, m the mass and t the time. Then, energy bases differential equations may be generally of the form:

$$\left(\frac{dy}{dt}\right)^2 = \dot{y}^2 = P_k\left[y\right] \tag{3}$$

where $P_k[y]$ is a polynomial of degree k. Differentiating the relation (3) it results:

$$\frac{d}{dt}\left(\dot{y}^2 - P_k\left[y\right]\right) = 2.\ddot{y}.\dot{y} - \frac{dP_k\left[y\right]}{dt} = 2.\ddot{y}.\dot{y} - \dot{y}.Q_{k-1}\left[y\right] = 0 \tag{4}$$

where $.Q_{k-1}\left[y\right]$ is a polynomial of degree k-1. As $\dot{y} \neq 0$, we get:

$$2.\ddot{y} = .Q_{k-1}\left[y\right] \tag{5}$$

Then, for $P_1[y]=a_1y+a_0$ we get:

$$2.\ddot{y} - a_1 = 0; \Rightarrow .\ddot{y} = \frac{a_1}{2}; \Rightarrow y = C_1.\frac{t^2}{2} + C_2.t + C_3 \tag{6}$$

but this is the well known relations between the space, speed and acceleration: $s = a.\frac{t^2}{2} + v.t + s_0$.

For $P_2[y]=a_2y^2+a_1.y+a_0$ we get:

$$\ddot{y} - a_2.y - 0.5.a_1 = 0; \Rightarrow y = C_1.e^{j.\omega.t} + C_2 \tag{7}$$

where $\omega = \sqrt[2]{a_2}$ and C_1, C_2 constants. Physically, the relation (7) may represent a mechanical (mass-spring) resonator where all terms are forces and/or an electrical (coil-condenser) resonator where all terms are voltages. As a possible extension, the differential Equation 7 may become:

$$\ddot{y} + b_1.\dot{y} + .b_2.y = 0 \tag{8}$$

where the term $b_1.\dot{y}$ has physically the signification of 'friction force' in mechanics and/or 'damper voltage' in electricity. The solution of this equation is:

$$y = C_1.e^{\frac{-b_1+\sqrt[2]{b_1^2-4.b_2}}{2}.t} + C_2.e^{\frac{-b_1-\sqrt[2]{b_1^2-4.b_2}}{2}.t} \tag{9}$$

Generally, $b_1^2 - 4.b_2 < 0$ and then the solutions becomes complexes including trigonometric and hyperbolic functions. It may be remarked that 3 forces exists in this case: attraction, revulsion and 'friction' or its equivalent 'damper voltage' and also a magnetic torque may be added.

For $P_3[y] = a^3.y^3 + a_2 y^2 + a_1.y + a_0$ we get, after some transformations, the relation:

$$\dot{y}^2 = 4.y^3 + g_2.y + g_3 \tag{10}$$

which leads to Weierstrass elliptical functions where g_2, g_3 are some coefficients. It may be remarked that a polynomial of degree 4 may be solved based on the polynomials of degree 3 and the Jacobi elliptic functions connected with Weierstrass elliptical functions, are defined by polynomials of degree 4. Mechanically, 5 forces may be considered: attraction, centrifugal, Coriolis, inertia and friction.

Physical interpretations may be found for the coefficients f_{nm-j} of the polynomial:

$$Q_r[y] = f_{mm}.y^r + f_{mm-1}.y^{r-1} + ... + f_0 \tag{11}$$

Mechanically, the term f_0 may represent a force and the term f_1 may be the 'linear elasticity coefficient' defined as:

$$f_1 = \frac{\partial F}{\partial y} \tag{12}$$

Next, the term f_2 may be defined as a 'pressure' (force applied on a surface as 'y^2' may be considered as a surface):

$$f_2 = \frac{\partial F}{\partial (y^2)} \tag{13}$$

and the term f_3 as a 'volume pressure':

$$f_3 = \frac{\partial^2 F}{\partial (y^3)} \tag{14}$$

Further extensions in this way lead to 'hyperspaces' and/or 'spaces at the output of a transducer'.

Remarks

Calculating the energy of a system may leads to a scalar differential equation. Generally, the solutions of these equations are analytical functions and/or parts of it. For 1-D systems, like for sounds signals, all the modeling functions may be considered as analytical because for any real 1-D function $f(t)$, an analytical signal $z(t)$ may be found by:

$$z(t) = f(t) + i.\mathcal{H}\left[f(t)\right] = f(t) + i.\frac{PV}{\pi}.\int_{-\infty}^{\infty}\frac{f(\tau)}{t-\tau}.d\tau; \rightarrow i = \sqrt[2]{-1} \quad (15)$$

where $\mathcal{H}\left[.\right]$ is the Hilbert transform and PV means 'principal value of the integral'. For higher dimensions, the class of analytical functions is less reach (Bruce P-Palca, 1991).

An analytic function that models a physical system and/or an equivalent field, must be non-linear, and must have also an associated algebra. As an example, the most used functions to models the sounds are the trigonometric functions sine and cosine. Remembering that in the complex plane, the sine function is the 'imaginary' projection of the unit position vector and the cosine is the real projection of this vector, it results:

$$e^{i.t} = \mathrm{Cos}(t) + i.\mathcal{H}\left[\mathrm{Cos}(t)\right] = \mathrm{Cos}(t) + i.\mathrm{Sin}(t); i = \sqrt[2]{-1} \quad (16)$$

where the numbers $\{1,i\}$ may be the equivalents to the unit vectors $\left\{\vec{i},\vec{j}\right\}$ as in the relation:

$$\vec{V}_2 = \mathrm{Cos}(\theta).\vec{i} + \mathrm{Sin}(\theta).\vec{j} \quad (17)$$

where $\vec{V}_2$ is a 2-D vector. Trigonometric functions are used into the Fourier series and transform as a 'known functional basis' to represent any physical sound by a number of given coefficients and/or a given 'spectra'. The 'complex plane $e^{i.\omega_0.t}$, may be considered as the 'fundamental plane' and the other planes $e^{i.k.\omega_0.t}$ as equivalent to 'higher dimensions 'k complex planes'. By frequency modulation, it results:

$$\left(e^{i.t}\right)^{\omega} = e^{i.\omega.t} \quad (18)$$

which is the kernel of the Fourier transform and where 'ω' may be considered as a pulsation (frequency) of the Fourier spectra. The kernel of the Fourier transform is also a 'degenerated elliptical function' which has the elliptic modulus $m \equiv 0$. A special type of frequency modulation leads to the hyperbolic functions (Ciulin, 2004):

$$\left(e^{i.\omega.t}\right)^{-\frac{i.\sigma}{\omega}} = e^{\sigma.t} \quad (19)$$

The kernel of the Laplace transform, which is a nice extension of the Fourier transform, is an amplitude modulation (product) between the kernel of the Fourier transform and the hyperbolic function represented in (19). The Laplace transform uses as kernel the analytical complex function $e^{p.t} = e^{(\sigma+i.\omega).t}$ which constitutes the basis of trigonometric and hyperbolic functions. Using Fourier and/or Laplace transforms, a 1-D time function differential equation is 'switched' to a spectral domain, where by simple algebraic rules, a solution may be found. Due to the extension to the hyperbolic functions, Laplace transform that is more 'powerful' than the Fourier transform. Laplace transform is given by:

$$\begin{cases} S(p) = \int_{-0}^{\infty} s(t).e^{-p.t}.dt \\ s(t) = \frac{1}{2.\pi.j}.\int_{a-j.\infty}^{a+j.\infty} S(p).e^{p.t}.dt \end{cases} \left\langle i = \sqrt[2]{-1}; p = \sigma + i.\omega; a > \sigma_0 \right\rangle \tag{20}$$

Mathematically, the 'potentials' are generally represented in the complex where their imaginary part represents the 'orthogonal' part of their real part. The real part of the potentials corresponds to the 'dissipative energy' and their imaginary part to the 'conservative energy'. The kernels of the Laplace transform suggest an intuitive association between the pulsations σ and the 'dissipative energy' but also between the pulsations ω and the 'conservative energy'. If one consider the independent variable time 't', as 'real', the Laplace kernel represents physically a 'complex potential'. The real part of this potential implies 2 frequencies connected with the 2 pulsations σ and ω:

$$\begin{cases} d = \frac{\sigma}{2.\pi} \\ f = \frac{\omega}{2.\pi} \end{cases} \tag{21}$$

The 'd' may be interpreted as a 'damper imaginary frequency' and 'f' as a real frequency. It can be observed that for example, in the case of the filtering problems, there exist filters which lead nearly to the same results using the real and/or the imaginary frequencies (Chen,Wai-Kai, 1995). This may lead to the idea that nearly the same results may be obtained using 'different ways' in the complex frequencies plane. For non-linear differential equations, the Laplace transform is sometimes less helpful because it may lead to equations more difficult to be solved.

The trigonometric functions Sin and Cosine lead sometimes to Fourier series with a very big number of terms. This is, for example, the case of the Fourier series of 1-D rectangular signals. The Haar wavelet series (Wikipedia, Haar wavelet, 2012) uses other 'bricks' but sine and cosine to built this series. Actually, this used bricks group all the Sine and Cosine terms which represent a rectangular signal. This leads to a series which had few terms for rectangular signals but the associated algebra is different. Other types of wavelets exist (Wikipedia, wavelet, 2012) and are useful for a given set of input signals. It may also be observed that for the Fourier transform, a function which had a small time-support have a very big frequency support and also that a big 'time support' correspond to a small frequency support. As an example, the Dirac impulse time-function had nearly a 'zero' 'time support' but an infinite frequency support. The only functions which had practically finite 'time support' and finite frequency support are the Gaussian functions.

An intelligent use of Fourier series and transform leads to the Shannon sampling theorem (Shannon, 1949). Using this theorem, any 1-D frequency bandwidth-limited signal may be easily represented mathematically by a sampling series. A transform similar to the Laplace transform for this 'discreet domain' of samplings is the 'z-transform' (Capellini et al., 1978):

$$\begin{cases} X(z) = \sum_{n=-\infty}^{\infty} x(n).z^{-n} \\ x(n) = \dfrac{1}{2.\pi.j}.\oint_{C} X(z).z^{n-1}.dz \end{cases} \tag{22}$$

where the curve C is a counter-clockwise closed contour in the convergence region of X(n) and encircling the origin of z complex plane.

For a polynomial $P_k[y]$ of order 2 and/or less, the equivalent differential energy equation may correspond to a single differential equation or even to a system of only 2 differential equations which may physically represent 'potentials'. The equivalents tools for 2-D physical systems, as for example the images, are 2-D Fourier series, 2-D sampling theorem and 2-D z- transform. These tools are built as a 2-D Cartesian extension by using the product of their equivalent 1-D and it supposes that the 2 orthogonal dimensions X and Y are independent. The analogies between the complex exponential function as in the relation (15) and the vector representation of the OXY plane may confirm that. This leads, for example for the 2–D sampling theorem, to a very big number of samples. It is known that practically, there exists a same correlation between the pixels of an image in X and Y direction (Ciulin, 2006). It may be observed that the kernel of the Fourier and/or Laplace 1-D transforms is 2-D and the kernel of the 2-D z-transform is 4-D. The images may be represented also by using elliptical Jacobi functions SN, CN and DN which are analytic (Ciulin, 2010). These are complex 4-D functions. The advantage is the fact that here the whole image is considered but not also its X and/or Y scanning.

In 1-D, an analytic function may have a single independent variable as for the kernel of Fourier integral ($e^{i.\omega.t}$) where the complex independent variable contains only the imaginary part. Anyhow, the kernel of the Laplace integral $e^{(\sigma+i.\omega).t}$ contains also a real part but using only a single independent variable, the 'time'. In fact, only the pulsations complex coefficients of time lead to a complex independent variable. Using a scanning procedure, 1-D methods may be extended to 2-D and as results, the 2-D sampling theorem, 2-D Fourier series, etc.

The complex elliptical 2-D coordinates α,β are based on trigonometric functions:

$$\begin{cases} x^2 = \dfrac{\left(A.\text{Cos}(\alpha) - \dfrac{a^2-b^2}{2}\right).\left(A.\text{Cos}(\beta) - \dfrac{a^2-b^2}{2}\right)}{a^2-b^2} \\ y^2 = \dfrac{\left(A.\text{Cos}(\alpha) + \dfrac{a^2-b^2}{2}\right).\left(A.\text{Cos}(\beta) + \dfrac{a^2-b^2}{2}\right)}{a^2-b^2} \end{cases} \tag{23}$$

In this relations, *A,a,b* are coefficients. It can be seen that this relation has not a simple physical interpretation as for the case of the 1-D almost because the independent variables are complex angles. 2-D images may also be processed using Jacobi complex elliptical functions (Ciulin, 2011). It may also be remarked that the surface in 2-D and 3-D are represented in Cartesian coordinates by functions of two independent variables as, for example:

$$z=f(x,y) \tag{24}$$

where 'x, y' represents the 'addresses' of any pixel and 'z' the 'contents' of the image in 2-D and/or the address of the equivalent pixel' in 3-D. That seems to suggest that the vectors may be represented by functions of many independent variables.

For 3 degree of the polynomial $P_k[y]$, this may correspond to a system of 3 differential equations, as for example, for the gyroscope (Lindsay, 1965), (Ciulin, 2008). Physically, these may represent fields which have a vector and/or tensor structure. Then, the equivalent system of 3 differential equations that models the Euler mobile system of coordinates had 3 independent variables, the Euler complex angles. Computing the energy of the system may lead to a single differential equation connected, for example, to the nutation angle of the gyroscope. Solving this equation leads to a Weierstrass elliptical function corresponding to the nutation movements. From here, others Weierstrass elliptical functions corresponding to the precession and spin movements can be computed. It can be observed that if one uses the Jacobian but not the energy of the system, it may result for an about similar system, a differential equation of a higher order than 3 (Kuang et al., 2005) which leads to ultra-elliptic functions. From physical point of view, this is so because one considers also other independent variables. Weierstrass elliptical function $\wp(u)$ may be built in a similar manner as for the function Ctg(u) and its derivative $\frac{1}{\mathrm{Sin}^2(u)}$. One can start from the function $\sigma(u)$ which replaces the function $\mathrm{Cos}(u)$:

$$\sigma(u) = u.\prod_{m_1,m_2}\left(1-\frac{u}{\omega}\right).e^{\frac{u}{\omega}+0.5.(\frac{u}{\omega})^2};\omega = m_1.\omega_1 + m_2.\omega_2 \tag{25}$$

where 'u' is a complex independent variable, and ω_1,ω_2 are 2 (complex) periods. Then:

$$\wp(u) = -\frac{d\left(\frac{\frac{d\sigma(u)}{du}}{\sigma(u)}\right)}{du} \tag{26}$$

The function $\sigma(u)$ introduces the double periods and the relation (26) the double poles in the fundamental lattice. The term $e^{0.5.(\frac{u}{\omega})^2}$ in the relation (25) suggest that the Weierstrass function may have some properties in common with the Gaussian functions. It can be observed that the function Ctg(u) is a (kind of) homographic transformation (Möbius transformation) using the well known trigonometric functions Cos(u), Sin(u). Then, we may build an analytic function of 2 periods by:

$$w(t,\omega_1,\omega_2) = \frac{e^{i.\omega_1.t}+1}{e^{i.\omega_2.t}-1} = \frac{\{\mathrm{Cos}(\omega_1.t)+1+i.\mathrm{Sin}(\omega_1.t)\}.\{\{\mathrm{Cos}(\omega_2.t)-1-i.\mathrm{Sin}(\omega_1.t)\}\}}{\{\mathrm{Cos}(\omega_2.t)-1\}^2+\mathrm{Sin}^2(\omega_1.t)} \tag{27}$$

Some analogies with the analytic Jacobi elliptic functions may be observed.

The relation (27) may suggest a way to build a ultra-elliptic function. To build a hyper- elliptic function defined by 5-th degree polynomial, we may write:

$$f_5(z_1, z_2, g_2, g_3, g_4, g_5) = \frac{\wp_1(z_1, g_2, g_3) + k_1}{\wp_2(z_2, g_4, g_5) + k_2} \tag{28}$$

which have 2 complex arguments z_1,z_2 and only 3 periods because we had choose the coefficients g_2,g_3 so that the function $\wp_1(z_1, g_2, g_3)$ have the periods ω_1,ω_2 and the coefficients g_4,g_5 so that the function $\wp_2(z_1, g_4, g_5)$ have the periods ω_2,ω_3. Here, k_1,k_{21} are (complex) scalars. It can be also observed that this procedure may be used to build even other hyper-elliptic functions.

We observe that the solutions of differential equations based on the energy are analytic functions. These are between polynomial, trigonometric, hyperbolic, elliptic and ultra-elliptic functions. As trigonometric and hyperbolic functions may be considered degenerated elliptic functions and polynomial functions as a (serial) approximation of these functions, we may consider that all these solutions are periodic. Depending on the degree of the polynomial $P_k[y]$, these functions may have one and/or many distinct (complex) periods. Generally, such a function may have as independent variables real and/or complex angles and physically, it may model the gravitational field. One may consider that each frequency associated with a period represent, from a physical point of view, the angular velocity around a given coordinate axis. Then, all these solutions may be represented by spectral means. For a time varying system, an instantaneous sequence (frequency) spectrum may tend, during a long enough time interval when the system tends to a steady-state situation, to a periodic spectrum. The necessary time interval may be shorter if the system is 'resonant'. A resonant system realizes an energy accumulation on the resonant frequency. Then, the amplitude of this frequency becomes bigger until the inherent losses balance the energy accumulation. For many-dimensional systems, a many dimensions resonance may lead to the very big amplitudes on this resonant frequency. An electronic device able to 'copy' a given sequence and/or frequency of another electronic device and/or signal is the well-known Phase Lock Loop. Extension of such systems for meromorphic functions is presented in (Ciulin, 2010a).

It can also be observed that the Kaluza–Klein theory (Wikipedia, Kaluza-Klein, 2012) apply a variation principle to the action (which is the time-integral of the energy) to obtain the Einstein and Maxwell theory starting from a 5-dimensional free space geometry. Then, as elliptic and ultra-elliptic functions are the mathematical solutions of the energy based differential equations and it may represent the electromagnetic and/or gravitational field, these functions may be also solutions for the Kaluza–Klein theory. As elliptic and ultra-elliptic functions are periodic functions, may be their spectral representations put also in conjunction with the string theory? (Wikipedia, String theory, 2012).

FORCE AND TORQUES FOR MECHANIC AND ELECTROMECHANIC DEVICES

Rotations are realized by torques but the translation by forces. It may be observed that a rotation with a very big radius may be locally considered as a translation. On earth, the rotations are generally converted into translation by using the friction force but in the free space, other methods have to be used.

Statically, forces may be created inside a single domain (Wikipedia, force, 2012). As example, the attraction gravitational force $\vec{F}_m$ between two masses m_1,m_2 depends on the gravitational constant G used to describe the relative strength of gravity, the distance r between the centers of mass of these two objects and of the unit vector $\vec{r}$ pointed from the center of the first object toward the center of the second object:

$$\vec{F}_m = \frac{G.m_1.m_2.\vec{r}}{r^3} = m_1.\vec{a} \tag{29}$$

The second part of the relation (29) realize the connection with the Newton (dynamic) relation where $\vec{a}$ is the equivalent acceleration of the mass m_1. On earth, the relation (29) becomes $\vec{F}_e = m_1.\vec{g}$ where $\vec{g}$ is the gravitational acceleration which may also be considered as equivalent to a local gravitational field. Similarly, in electrostatic (Wikipedia, electrostatics, 2012):

$$\vec{F}_e = \frac{q_1.q_2.\vec{r}}{4.\pi.\varepsilon_0.r^2} = q_1.\vec{E} \tag{30}$$

where q_1,$q_2$are two electrostatic charges, ε_0 the electric constant connected to the magnetic constant μ_0 by $\varepsilon_0 = \frac{1}{\mu_0.c^2}$, c is the speed of the light in vacuum and $\vec{E}$ the electrostatic field.

For the static magnetic field $\vec{B}$ only torque $\vec{\tau}_m$ may be observed:

$$\vec{\tau}_m = \vec{m} \times \vec{B} \tag{31}$$

In this relation, $\vec{m}$ is the magnetic dipole of the considered permanent magnet and '×' stay for the 'vector cross product'.

Dynamically, the Lorenz force $\vec{F}_{em}$ made also a connection between the magnetic field $\vec{B}$ and the (mechanically) speed $\vec{v}$ of a charged (q) particle:

$$\vec{F}_{em} = q.\left(\vec{E} - \vec{v} \times \vec{B}\right) \tag{32}$$

This is represented in Figure 1 where the resulted forces are in red. As any translation can be locally considered like a rotation with a big enough radius, we may replace the speed $\vec{v}$ by:

$$\vec{v} = \vec{\Omega} \times \vec{R} \tag{33}$$

where $\vec{\Omega}, \vec{R}$ are respectively the angular speed and the radius of this rotation movement. Then:

$$\vec{F}_{em} = q.\left(\vec{E} - \vec{\Omega} \times \vec{R} \times \vec{B}\right) = q.\left(\vec{E} - \vec{R}.\left(\vec{\Omega} \bullet \vec{B}\right) + \vec{B}.\left(\vec{R} \bullet \vec{\Omega}\right)\right) = q.\left(\vec{E} - \vec{R}.\left(\vec{\Omega} \bullet \vec{B}\right)\right) \tag{34}$$

where '•' stay for the vector dot product and $\vec{R} \bullet \vec{\Omega} \equiv 0$ by considering $\vec{R}$ orthogonal with $\vec{\Omega}$.

The force for the gravitational field is defined by the relation (Lindsay, 1965):

$$\vec{F}_G = m.\left(\vec{g} + 2.\vec{\omega} \times \dot{\vec{r}}_{ma} + \vec{\omega} \times \vec{\omega} \times \vec{r}_m\right) = m.\left(\vec{g} + \vec{a}_{cor} + \vec{a}_c\right) \tag{35}$$

where $\vec{\omega}$ is the angular speed and $\vec{r}_m$ is the position vector of a considered mass m in the moving axis coordinates, $\vec{a}_{cor}$ is the Coriolis acceleration and $\vec{a}_c$ the centripetal acceleration. If an object is only subject to the attraction of the earth we have:

$$\vec{F}_{earth} = m.\left(\vec{g} + \vec{\omega} \times \vec{\omega} \times \vec{r}_m\right) \tag{36}$$

By considering the relations (29) and (30) it results that the apparent acceleration a_m on the earth is:

$$a_m = \vec{g} - 2.\vec{\omega} \times \dot{\vec{r}}_m \tag{37}$$

It can be seen that in gravitation, the only repulsive forces are the centripetal, Coriolis and 'inertial forces'.

Connections between the gravitational and electromagnetic field may be established starting from the Poynting vector which represents the (vector) power of the electromagnetic field:

$$\vec{P}_P = \vec{E} \times \vec{H} = \frac{1}{\mu_0}.\vec{E} \times \vec{B} \tag{38}$$

and observing that the power in mechanics is given by:

$$P_m = \frac{d\left(\vec{F} \bullet \vec{s}\right)}{dt} = \frac{d\,\dfrac{m.\vec{v} \bullet \vec{v}}{2}}{dt} = m.\vec{v} \bullet \vec{a} = \vec{F} \bullet \vec{v} \tag{39}$$

where m is the mass of an equivalent particle, $\vec{v}$ its speed, $\vec{s}$ is space, $\vec{a}$ its acceleration, and $\vec{F}$ the mechanical equivalent force. By considering the acceleration (and then the local gravitational field) as constant we have:

$$m.\vec{v} \bullet \vec{a} = \vec{E} \times \vec{H} \bullet \frac{\vec{v}}{\left|\vec{v}\right|}; \Rightarrow \vec{a} = \frac{\vec{E} \times \vec{H}}{m.\left|\vec{v}\right|}; \Rightarrow \vec{F}_m = \frac{\vec{E} \times \vec{H}}{\left|\vec{v}\right|} \tag{40}$$

because $\vec{v} \neq 0$. This relation represents the equivalence between the gravitational and electromagnetic fields as, by generalization and following the relation (30), we may write:

$$\vec{F}_m = \frac{G.m_1.m_2.\vec{r}}{r^3} = m_1.\vec{a} = m_1.\vec{G}_f \tag{41}$$

where $\vec{G}_f$ may be considered as the local gravitational field. Another relation may be obtained starting from the Lorenz force where for an instant we will neglect the electrical field $\vec{E}$ .Then:

$$\vec{F}_{em} = -q.\vec{v} \times \vec{B} \tag{42}$$

Dot multiplying this relation by the space variable 's' it results in an energy W equation:

$$W = \vec{F}_{em} \bullet \vec{s} = \frac{m}{2}.\vec{v} \bullet \vec{v} = -q.\vec{s} \bullet \vec{v} \times \vec{B} = -q.\vec{v} \bullet \vec{B} \times \vec{s} \tag{43}$$

As $\vec{v} \neq 0$, by considering the Maxwell's equations: it results

$$m.\vec{v} = 2.q.\vec{s} \times \vec{B}; \Rightarrow \vec{a} = 2.q.\left(\vec{v} \times \vec{B} + \vec{s} \times \frac{d\vec{B}}{dt}\right) = 2.q.\left(\vec{v} \times \vec{B} - \vec{s} \times curl\left(\vec{E}\right)\right) \tag{44}$$

where $m.\vec{v}$ represents the momentum of the particle.

GRAVITATIONAL (INERTIAL) SYSTEMS

A (future) gravitational (inertial) motor must be able to develop for the 'lift up' of a vehicle, inertial forces bigger than at least 10 to more than 100 times its own weight. As for a terrestrial motor vehicle, this inertial motor must interact with its environment. Let us consider now, as example, a car. She realizes her translation by the friction between its spinning wheels and the ground. The desired direction is assured generally by the 'direction angle' between the front wheels and the actual direction of the car. Generally, a car motor cannot generate torques able to insure a car translation on a road with a high slope by ensuring also from the beginning a good speed but, by gradually increasing its inertia, she may assure a convenient speed in translation. Formally, the energy transfer between the car motor and the environment is realized by friction between a convenient torque and speed of the wheels of the vehicle and the road but also by 'inertia' of the car. In free space, the friction cannot be used but a system which converts internal mechanical torques/forces into (external) inertial torques/forces. Such system is, for example, a gas-jet engine. Taking into account the Equation (29), it can be seen that to get an inertial force one must accelerate a mass. Then, a part of the mass of the ship is accelerated and thrown out from the ship. It is known that a gyroscope is a special device that has the property to 'separate' the input and the output axis of torques. If one applies conveniently mechanical torques of an input axis, inertial torques may results on the output axis (Sivoukhine, 1982).

Then, a gyroscope may develop inertial torques $\vec{T}_z$:

$$\vec{T}_z \cong I_x.\vec{S}_x \times \vec{\Omega}_y \tag{45}$$

where I_c is its moment of inertia, $\vec{S}_x$ is its angular (spin) speed, $\vec{\Omega}_y$ is its angular precession speed and '×' stand for vector cross product. Following (Ciulin, 2009), one may use a 'gyroscopic doublet' (Granger, 1985), (Caius, 1951) where a mechanical input torque $\vec{\Omega}_y$ is conveniently applied between two gyroscopes. It will result a force $\vec{F}$:

Figure 1. System generating the Lorenz force which is represented in red

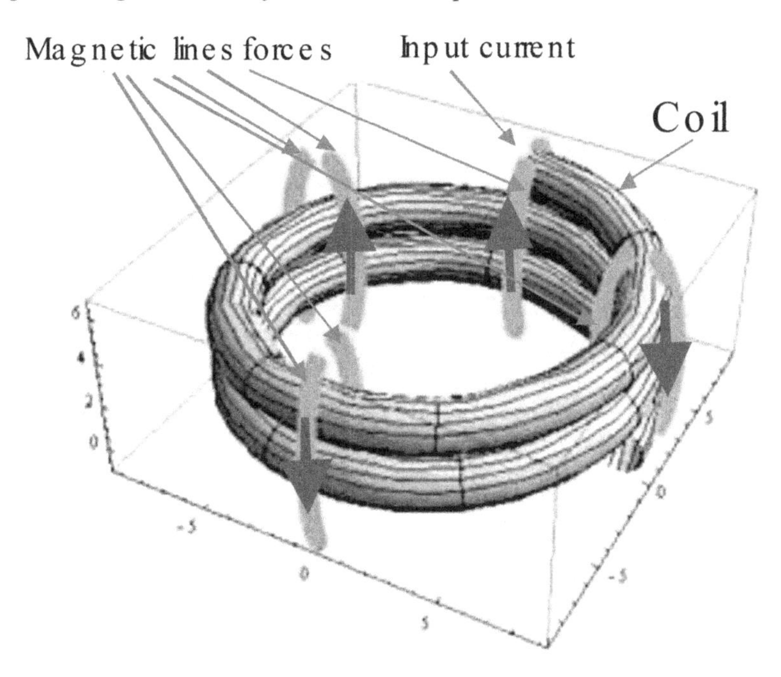

$$\vec{F} \cong \vec{\Omega}_y.I^2.S^2.\cos\left[angle\left(\vec{S}_1,\vec{S}_2\right)\right] - \vec{S}_2.I^2.S.\vec{\Omega}_y.\cos\left[angle\left(\vec{S}_1,\vec{\Omega}_y\right)\right] \tag{46}$$

As for a thermal motor, this system creates two pulses of force during a precession period of the gyroscopes. The mass of the vehicle will integrate these pulses over many periods and will increase then its inertial energy. An intelligent system is necessary to control mechanically the applied input torques and correlate them with the position in space of the gyroscopes. It can be observed that only the nutation movement produces these 'pulses force' and the torques applied to 'Y' axis 'pumped' the necessary energy for this movement (see also the Figure 8). A simulation of the nutation torques and the resulted mean value force over a period of precession of a gyroscope in steady-state is shown in Figure 2. A given analogy may be observed between the figure 1 where a mechanical force results as a mean value of the sum of the magnetic torque inside an electric coil through which an electric current exists and the Figure 2 where a mechanical force results as a mean value of the sum of the nutation pulses of a gyroscope. Evidently, in the second case the mathematical model uses elliptic functions but not complex exponential functions.

Using a gyroscope with an added magnet as for the Levitron (Ciulin, 2010) avoid the necessity to use a 'gyroscopic doublet', as the necessary energy may be pumped by an electromagnetic field. More, the electromagnetic field may pump directly the energy to the nutation movement. The big advantage is the fact that the input 'bending' torques are now produced by a magnetic field but the 'restoring' (gravitational) torques produced by the gyroscope are inertial. Then, a control system using actual technology is relatively simple. This method realizes also a separation between the input (electromagnetic) energy and the output (inertial) energy. Another advantage is the fact that the source of the electromagnetic field can be installed on the ship. In this way, interplanetary travels may be theoretically envisaged if a convenient source of energy is also available on this ship. Compared with the system using a 'gyroscopic doublet'

Figure 2. Simulation of the nutation torques and the resulted mean value force over a period of precession of a Top

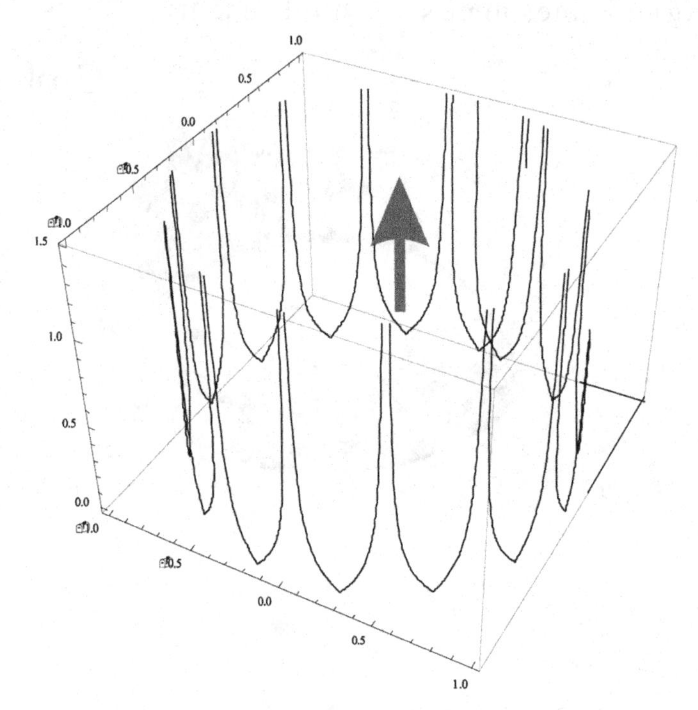

which presents only 2 inertial force pulses by a precession period, the system which uses a 'Leviton' like gyroscope may have many in functions of its parameters This may ensure a better maneuverability of the ships. Of course, many motors of this type may be used on a given ship in order to ensure the necessary 'lift up' force and reliability but also to avoid some internal torques which may even damage the ship during the fast accelerations.

To obtain an inertial force, a gas-jet engine can be used. It has the advantage that it can work continuously for a given time but has a poor energetic efficiency and need to loose masses in the space. Based on the 'gyration' property of gyroscopes, a (pulsate) inertial force (Ciulin, 2008) may be created without the need to thrown out masses but it needs a 'doublet' to have an 'internal strong point'. The use of gyroscopes with an added magnet avoids the necessity of a 'doublet' as this time the 'bending' energy is pumped by an electromagnetic field (Ciulin, 2010b). The big advantage is the fact that the electromagnetic bending torques are separate from the inertial (gravitational) restoring torques of the gyroscope and also, that the control is easiest with the actual technology. More, the source of the electromagnetic field may be 'embarked' on the ship and then, if it includes a source of energy, this ship can theoretically fly anywhere in the space.

LEVITRON TYPE GYROSCOPE

Let suppose a (simple) gyroscope on which a (nearly) vertically polarized magnet (in red) has been fixed like for a Levitron Top. We place the mass center of this gyroscope on the origin of a mobile system of coordinates o, x', y', z'. An absolute system of coordinates O, X, Y, Z like in Figure 3, has the origin of this mobile system of coordinates at the end of the position vector $\vec{R}_0$. The spin $\vec{s}$ of the gyroscope and its magnetic moment $\vec{B}$ make an angle θ with the oz' axis of the mobile system of coordinates o, x', y', z' like in Figure 4. The axis oz' make an angle θ with the axis OZ and the axis ox' and angle ψ with the axis OX.

Without considering the influence of the built-in magnet, we have (Lindsay, 1965):

$$\begin{cases} \vec{R}_f = \vec{R}_0 + \vec{R}_m \\ \dfrac{d\vec{R}_f}{dt} = \dfrac{d\vec{R}_0}{dt} + \dfrac{d\vec{R}_{ma}}{dt} + \vec{\omega} \times \vec{R}_m \\ \dfrac{d^2\vec{R}_f}{dt^2} = \dfrac{d^2\vec{R}_0}{dt^2} + \dfrac{d^2\vec{R}_{ma}}{dt^2} + 2.\vec{\omega} \times \dfrac{d\vec{R}_{ma}}{dt} + \vec{\omega} \times \vec{\omega} \times \vec{R}_m \end{cases} \tag{47}$$

where the term $\dfrac{d\vec{R}_{ma}}{dt}$ represents only the variation in time of the amplitude of $\vec{R}_m$. The term $2.\vec{\omega} \times \dfrac{d\vec{R}_{ma}}{dt}$ corresponds to the Coriolis acceleration and the term $\vec{\omega} \times \vec{\omega} \times \vec{R}_m$ to the centripetal acceleration.

For a Top (and/or gyroscope), the Euler equations on the mobile system o, x', y', z' may be written (Lindsay, R. B, 1965), (Ciulin, 2008, 2010b) as:

$$\begin{cases} \omega_x = \dfrac{\partial \theta}{\partial t} = \dot{\theta}; \Rightarrow \dot{\omega}_x = \ddot{\theta} \\ \omega_y = \dfrac{\partial \psi}{\partial t}.\mathrm{Sin}(\theta) = \dot{\psi}.\mathrm{Sin}(\theta); \Rightarrow \dot{\omega}_y = \ddot{\psi}.\mathrm{Sin}(\theta) + \dot{\psi}.\mathrm{Cos}(\theta).\omega_x \\ \omega_z = \dfrac{\partial \psi}{\partial t}.\mathrm{Cos}(\theta) = \dot{\psi}.\mathrm{Cos}(\theta); \Rightarrow \dot{\omega}_z = \ddot{\psi}.\mathrm{Cos}(\theta) - \dot{\psi}.\mathrm{Sin}(\theta).\omega_x \end{cases} \tag{48}$$

From here it results:

$$\begin{cases} \dot{\theta} = \omega_x; \Rightarrow \ddot{\theta} = \dot{\omega}_x \\ \dot{\psi}_{(y)} = \dfrac{\omega_y}{\mathrm{Sin}(\theta)}; \Rightarrow \ddot{\psi} = \dfrac{\dot{\omega}_y - \omega_y.Cot(\theta).\omega_x}{\mathrm{Sin}(\theta)} \\ \dot{\psi}_{(z)} = \dfrac{\omega_z}{\mathrm{Cos}(\theta)}; \Rightarrow \ddot{\psi} = \dfrac{\dot{\omega}_z - \omega_z.\mathrm{Tan}(\theta).\omega_x}{\mathrm{Cos}(\theta)} \end{cases} \tag{48'}$$

and also:

$$\begin{cases} I_{xx}.\dot{\omega}_x - I_{xx}.\omega_y\omega_z + S.I_{zz}.\omega_y = L_x \\ I_{xx}.\dot{\omega}_y + I_{xx}.\omega_x.\omega_z - S.I_{zz}.\omega_x = 0 \\ I_{zz}.\dot{S} = 0 \end{cases} \tag{49}$$

where L_c is the mechanical torque applied on the ox' axis, $I_{xx'}, I_{yy'}, I_{zx}$ are the moments of inertia, $\omega_z + s = S$ and due to the symmetry, $I_{xx} \equiv I_{yy}$. It can be observed that the angle θ is connected with the nutation movement and the angle ψ with the precession movement. Here we had considered that an external torque is applied only on the ox' axis. For a top example, $L_x = m.g.l.\text{Sin}(\theta)$ where *m* is the mass of the top, *g* the gravitational acceleration and *l* the distance between the end of the top and its mass-center For this simple case, the energy equation leads to a third-degree polynomial and then to Weierstrass elliptic functions (Ciulin, 2010b).

Let now consider a more general case where the externally applied torques is given by:

$$L_x = \sum_{n=1}^{N} K_n.\text{Sin}\left(n.\theta\right) \tag{50}$$

For this case, the energy equation becomes:

$$\frac{1}{2}.\left[I_{xx}.\left(\omega_x^2 + \omega_y^2\right) + I_{zz}.S^2\right] + \sum_{n=1}^{N} \frac{K_n}{n}.\text{Cos}\left(n.\theta\right) = E \tag{51}$$

Even if we consider only 2 terms in the series (50), it results in a polynomial of sixth-degree which leads to ultra-elliptic functions.

In the case of a Levitron type gyroscope, we have to consider also the influence of the added magnet as for a system structure equivalent to the Levitron toy, the starting 'lift-up' force is due to a repelling strong magnetic field $\vec{B}_T$ existing on a magnetic base. If $\vec{B}_g$ is the magnetic field of the added magnet, by considering a simplified model and the relation (49) it results: $L_x = B_g.B_T.\text{Sin}(\theta)$. Due to the fact that the added magnet moves with the gyroscope, we have to consider that $\vec{B}_g = \vec{B}_g(\theta, \psi, t)$ (Berry, M. V., 1996). The change of the magnetic field $\vec{B}_g$ may be also due to other kinds of movements than the changes of angles θ,ψ and then:

Figure 3. Levitron type gyroscope with fixed and mobile systems of coordinates

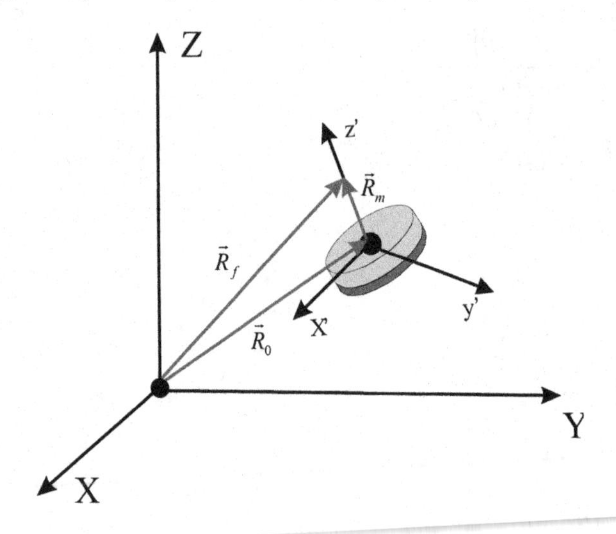

Figure 4. Levitron type gyroscope with fixed and mobile systems of coordinates

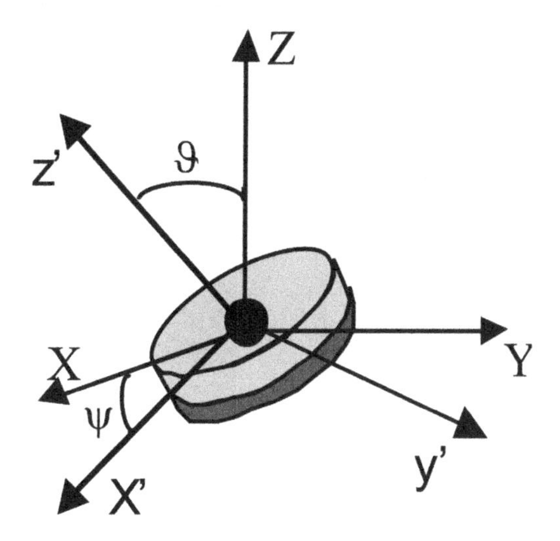

$$\begin{cases} \dfrac{d\vec{B}_g}{dt} = \dfrac{\partial \vec{B}_g}{\partial t} + \dfrac{\partial \vec{B}_g}{\partial \theta}\dot{\theta} + \dfrac{\partial \vec{B}_g}{\partial \psi}.\dot{\psi} \\ \dfrac{d^2\vec{B}_g}{dt^2} = \dfrac{\partial^2 \vec{B}_g}{\partial t^2} + \dfrac{\partial^2 \vec{B}_g}{\partial \theta^2}\dot{\theta}^2 + \dfrac{\partial^2 \vec{B}_g}{\partial \psi^2}\dot{\psi}^2 + \dfrac{\partial \vec{B}_g}{\partial \theta}.\ddot{\theta} + \dfrac{\partial \vec{B}_g}{\partial \psi.}.\ddot{\psi} + 2.\dot{\psi}.\dfrac{\partial^2 \vec{B}_g}{\partial \theta, \partial \psi}.\dot{\theta}. + \dfrac{\partial^2 \vec{B}_g}{\partial t, \partial \psi} + 2.\dot{\theta}.\dfrac{\partial^2 \vec{B}_g}{\partial \theta, \partial t}.\dot{\psi} \end{cases} \tag{52}$$

and taking in account (48’) it results:

$$\begin{cases} \dfrac{d\vec{B}_g}{dt} = \dfrac{\partial \vec{B}_g}{\partial t} + \dfrac{\partial \vec{B}_g}{\partial \theta}.\omega_x + \dfrac{\partial \vec{B}_g}{\partial \psi}.\left(\dfrac{\omega_y}{\mathrm{Sin}(\theta)} + \dfrac{\omega_z}{\mathrm{Cos}(\theta)}\right) \\ \dfrac{d^2\vec{B}_g}{dt^2} = \dfrac{\partial^2 \vec{B}_g}{\partial t^2} + \dfrac{\partial^2 \vec{B}_g}{\partial \theta^2}\omega_x^{\ 2} + \dfrac{\partial^2 \vec{B}_g}{\partial \psi^2}\left(\dfrac{\omega_y}{\mathrm{Sin}(\theta)} + \dfrac{\omega_z}{\mathrm{Cos}(\theta)}\right)^2 + \dfrac{\partial \vec{B}_g}{\partial \theta}.\dot{\omega}_x + \dfrac{\partial \vec{B}_g}{\partial \psi.} \\ .\left(\dfrac{\dot{\omega}_y - \omega_y.Cot(\theta).\omega_x}{\mathrm{Sin}(\theta)} + \dfrac{\dot{\omega}_z - \omega_z.\mathrm{Tan}(\theta).\omega_x}{\mathrm{Cos}(\theta)}\right) + 2.\left(\dfrac{\omega_y}{\mathrm{Sin}(\theta)} + \dfrac{\omega_z}{\mathrm{Cos}(\theta)}\right).\dfrac{\partial^2 \vec{B}_g}{\partial \theta, \partial \psi}.\omega_x. \\ + \dfrac{\partial^2 \vec{B}_g}{\partial t, \partial \psi} + 2.\omega_x.\dfrac{\partial^2 \vec{B}_g}{\partial \theta, \partial t}.\left(\dfrac{\omega_y}{\mathrm{Sin}(\theta)} + \dfrac{\omega_z}{\mathrm{Cos}(\theta)}\right) \end{cases} \tag{52'}$$

On the mobile Cartesian coordinate system we have:

$$\vec{B}_g = B_{xg}.\vec{i} + B_{yg}.\vec{j} + B_{zg}.\vec{k} \tag{53}$$

The relation (52’) and (53) gives the new terms introduced by the added magnet. In these relations, we have considered only the main Euler angles θ,ψ. Then, by adding the terms connected with the magnetic field $\vec{B}_g$, the relation (49) becomes:

$$\begin{cases} \left(I_{xx} + \frac{\partial B_g}{\partial \theta}\right).\dot{\omega}_x - \left(I_{xx} + \left(\frac{\partial B_g}{\partial \psi}\right)^2 . \frac{1}{\mathrm{Sin}(\theta).\mathrm{Cos}(\theta)}\right).\omega_y.\omega_z + I_{zz}.S.\omega_y \\ + \left(\frac{\partial B_g}{\partial \psi}\right)^2 . \left(\frac{\omega_y.\omega_z}{\mathrm{Sin}(\theta).\mathrm{Cos}(\theta)} + \frac{\partial B_g}{\partial \psi}\frac{s.\omega_y}{\mathrm{Sin}(\theta)}\right) = L_x \\ \left(I_{xx} + \frac{\partial B_g}{\partial \psi} . \frac{1}{\mathrm{Sin}(\theta)}\right).\dot{\omega}_y + \left(I_{xx} + .2.\frac{\partial^2 \vec{B}_g}{\partial \theta, \partial \psi} . \frac{1_x}{\mathrm{Cos}(\theta)}\right).\omega_x.\omega_z \\ - \left(I_{zz}.S.\omega_x + 2.\left(\frac{\partial^2 \vec{B}_g}{\partial \theta, \partial t} . \frac{\omega_x.\omega_z}{\mathrm{Cos}(\theta)} + \frac{\partial B_g}{\partial \psi}\frac{s.\omega_x}{\mathrm{Sin}(\theta)}\right)\right) = L_y \\ \left(I_{zz} + \frac{\partial \vec{B}_g}{\partial \psi.} . \frac{1}{\mathrm{Cos}(\theta)}\right).\dot{S}_z = L_z \end{cases} \quad (54)$$

where we had also considered the relations (52) and (53). The terms $\frac{\partial B_g}{\partial(.)}$ and $\frac{\partial^2 B_g}{\partial(.,.)}$ represents the first and second order 'sensitivities' of the variations in time of the magnetic field $\vec{B}$ due to the variation of the angles θ,ψ. The relation (54) supposes that *s* is nearly constant. It can be observed that the relation (54) include the magnetic field $\vec{B}_g$ in the equations of a top and then, its equivalent 'energy'. This allows to the possibility to transfer energy by electromagnetic field and then insure the possibility to realize the necessary bending torques without the necessity of a 'strong point' in a free space.

To control the position in space of a Levitron type top it is interesting to synchronize an external oscillator to its nutation movement (Ciulin, 2008, 2009, 2013). This may be done by using the waves generated by the mechanical movements in space of the associated magnet. The signal corresponding to the nutation movement, proportional to the angle of nutation, will correspond to the electromagnetic projection of these waves. For a given Levitron, this signal is known except for its exact frequency and phase. To separate only this signal, one can maximize the correlation energy between the received signal and a nearly similar signal locally generated by an internal oscillator inside a Phase-Lock-Loop (PLL). The block-diagram of such a system is presented in (Ciulin D., 22013a). At the beginning, based on the presented theory and actual technology, a toy drone equipped with one or many Levitron top placed on two gimbals, activated by electromagnetic waves generated by a transmitter existing on the drone and controlled by un system nearly similar to the systems that actually control the drones toys may be built. This will allow finding out a new technology that 'master' these new gravitational motors. A big advantage of such motor is the fact that it can be placed 'inside the drone shell' without any external mechanical connection and then may be protected for the eventually external interactions. It can be remarked that this is not the case with the helix of actual drones. More, such motors may ensure much bigger accelerations of a drone that actual motors with helix.

GRAVITATIONAL WAVES

It may be observed that starting from a torque $\vec{T}$ we obtain:

$$\begin{cases} \dfrac{d\vec{T}}{dt} = \dfrac{d\left(\vec{F} \times \vec{r}\right)}{dt} = \vec{F} \times \vec{v} \\ \dfrac{d^2\vec{T}}{dt^2} = \vec{F} \times \vec{a}; \Rightarrow m.\vec{a}_1 \times \vec{a} \end{cases} \tag{55}$$

where $\vec{F}$ is a force, $\vec{r}$ the position vector, $\vec{v}$ is the speed and $\vec{a}, \vec{a}_1$ are accelerations. We had kept also the same notations as in the relations (38) to (44) for the vector operations. Of course, in the relation (55) we had considered the force $\vec{F}$ as constant. As in the relation (41), we may consider these accelerations as equivalents to some gravitational fields:

The same procedure may be used for the energy with some equivalents results:

$$\begin{cases} \dfrac{dE}{dt} = \dfrac{d\left(\vec{F} \bullet \vec{r}\right)}{dt} = \vec{F} \bullet \vec{v}; \\ \dfrac{d^2\vec{T}}{dt^2} = \vec{F} \bullet \vec{a}; \Rightarrow m.\vec{a}_1 \bullet \vec{a}; \end{cases} \tag{56}$$

For magnetic fields, using the relation (31), it results:

$$\vec{\tau}_m = \vec{m} \times \vec{B}; \Rightarrow \vec{L} = \vec{B}_g \times \vec{B}_T \tag{57}$$

and also because $\vec{B}_T$ does not change in time:

$$\begin{cases} \dfrac{d\vec{L}}{dt} = \dfrac{\partial \vec{B}_g}{\partial t} \times \vec{B}_T \\ \dfrac{d^2\vec{L}}{dt^2} = \dfrac{\partial^2 \vec{B}_g}{\partial t^2} \times \vec{B}_T \end{cases} \tag{58}$$

In elliptic coordinates, the wave's equation is:

$$\begin{aligned} \frac{\partial^2 \vec{B}_g}{\partial t^2} = \frac{\varepsilon}{c^2}.\Delta_e\left[\vec{B}_g\right] = \frac{\varepsilon}{c^2}.\left(\left(\wp(\varphi)\right) - \wp(\psi)\right).\frac{\partial^2 \vec{B}_g}{\partial \theta^2} \\ +\left(\wp(\theta) - \wp(\varphi)\right).\frac{\partial^2 \vec{B}_g}{\partial \psi^2} \\ +\left(\wp((\psi) - \wp(\theta)\right).\frac{\partial^2 \vec{B}_g}{\partial \varphi^2} \end{aligned} \tag{59}$$

where $\wp(.)$ is the Weierstrass elliptic function (Smirnov, 1955). Then, the torque $\vec{L}$ may be expressed as:

$$\vec{L} = \iint \frac{\varepsilon}{c^2} \cdot \begin{pmatrix} (\wp(\varphi) - \wp(\psi)) \cdot \dfrac{\partial^2 \vec{B}_g}{\partial \theta^2} \\ +(\wp(\theta) - \wp(\varphi)) \cdot \dfrac{\partial^2 \vec{B}_g}{\partial \psi^2} \\ +(\wp(\psi) - \wp(\theta)) \cdot \dfrac{\partial^2 \vec{B}_g}{\partial \varphi^2} \end{pmatrix} \times \vec{B}_T . dt^2 \tag{60}$$

For the case of a Levitron type gyroscope, we had to add also the torques $L_x = B_g B_T . \mathrm{Sin}(\theta)$. Here we had not considered the terms corresponding to the electrical field resulted from the Maxwell equations. In free space and in Cartesian coordinates these equations are:

$$\begin{cases} curl(\vec{B}) = \dfrac{\varepsilon . \mu}{c^2} \cdot \dfrac{\partial \vec{E}}{\partial t} \\ curl(\vec{E}) = -\dfrac{\varepsilon . \mu}{c^2} \cdot \dfrac{\partial \vec{B}}{\partial t} \\ div(\vec{E}) = 0 \\ div(\vec{B}) = 0 \end{cases} \tag{61}$$

A very interesting case supposes that also the external field $\vec{B}_T$ is time-varying (and then not realized by a permanent magnet). In this case, the relation (58) becomes:

$$\begin{cases} \dfrac{d\vec{L}}{dt} = \dfrac{\partial \vec{B}_g}{\partial t} \times \vec{B}_T + \vec{B}_g \times \dfrac{\partial \vec{B}_T}{\partial t} \\ \dfrac{d^2 \vec{L}}{dt^2} = \dfrac{\partial^2 \vec{B}_g}{\partial t^2} \times \vec{B}_T + 2 . \dfrac{\partial \vec{B}_g}{\partial t} \times \dfrac{\partial \vec{B}_T}{\partial t} + \vec{B}_g \times \dfrac{\partial^2 \vec{B}_T}{\partial t^2} \end{cases} \tag{62}$$

If $\dfrac{\partial^2 \vec{B}_T}{\partial t^2}$ have a similar (or even a close) form to $\dfrac{\partial^2 \vec{B}_g}{\partial t^2}$, a resonance effect may arrive which will pump much more energy to the gyroscope. Anyhow, even in this case we can return to the mechanical torques in a same manner as for the relation (60). Taking into account (Ciulin, 2008, 2010b) and the fact that only 2 mechanical angles are enough for the mathematical model of a gyroscope, it results that the external time-varying field $\vec{B}_T$ needs to pump energy only on the spin and on the nutation movements. It may be also observed that the 'rectangular terms' in the relations (54) appears due to the fact that the Euler mobile system is written in a hybrid Cartesian and elliptic coordinates but only elliptic coordinates.

In 3D elliptic coordinates, the gravitational waves are modeled by the relation (59). It differs from ordinary electromagnetic waves because are based on the elliptic functions but trigonometric one. For this reason, these waves may be better compared with the field generated by the electromagnetically sustentation platforms as for example in (Wikipedia, Smaglev, 2016). One observe that the waves generated by sustentation platforms are generally modeled by complex exponential functions where the vertical 'Z' considered dimension is very small compared with the horizontal dimensions 'X' and 'Y'. On 14 September 2015, at 9:50:45 universal time, gravitational waves were detected by the LIGO's automated systems and had emerged at a frequency of 35 Hz and then speed up to 250 Hz before disappearing 0.25 seconds later. (Wikipedia, gravitational waves, 2016). This was the practical proof that gravitational waves exist.

REMARKS

It may be observed that a force and/or torque results by the interaction of 2 fields as in the relations (31), (40). The relations (30) and (41) seem to show that a force results as the interaction between a field and the matter. A more elaborate consideration shows that for the relation (30), any matter with electrical charge generates an electric field around this charge (Ladon, I. F., 1949):

$$\vec{E}_1 = -grad\left(\frac{q}{r}\right) \tag{63}$$

and for the relation (42) that any matter generate around it a gravitational field $\vec{G}_{f_1}$:

$$\vec{F}_m = \frac{G.m_1.m_2.\vec{r}}{r^3} = m_1.\vec{G}_f; \Rightarrow \vec{G}_{f_1} = \frac{G.m_1.\vec{r}}{r^3} \tag{64}$$

Then, by considering the relations (46) and the mechanical definition of a torque, on earth, the inertial torque realised by a gyroscope is given by:

$$\vec{T}_z = \vec{F} \times \vec{r} = m.\vec{g} \times \vec{r} \cong I_x.\vec{S}_x \times \vec{\Omega}_y; \tag{65}$$

The equivalence between these relations shows that an equivalent mass m_e will be:

$$m_e = \frac{\left|I_x.\vec{S}_x \times \vec{\Omega}_y\right|}{\left|\vec{g} \times \vec{r}\right|} \tag{66}$$

which is evidently much bigger than the real (static) mass of the gyroscope but only this increased (equivalent) mass may realize a gravitational field able to interact with the gravitational earth field to produce the given torque $\vec{T}_z$. From a physical point of view, the spin energy of the gyroscope lead to this increased mass as that can be practically observed with a Power Ball toy.

It can be observed that a gyroscope is a physical system with '2 entries' corresponding to the spin and nutation angles (the main Euler angles) and an output, the resulting forces and/or torques. The corresponding mathematical model uses Weierstrass complex elliptical functions with also 2 independent variables. For an ordinary top, the gravitational applied torque is (Lindsay, R. B, 1965):

$$\vec{T}_g = \vec{l} \times \vec{g} = \begin{vmatrix} \vec{i} & \vec{j} & \vec{k} \\ l_x & l_y & l_z \\ 0 & 0 & g \end{vmatrix} = g.\left(\vec{i}.l_y - \vec{j}.l_x\right) = g.\vec{V} \tag{67}$$

The interaction between this torque and the gyroscopic inertial torque $\vec{T}_i$ give a force:

$$\vec{F}_R = \vec{T}_i \times \vec{T}_g = I.\vec{S} \times \vec{\Omega}_y \times g.\vec{V} = \vec{\Omega}_y.\left(I.\vec{S} \bullet g.\vec{V}\right) - g.\vec{V}.\left(I.\vec{S} \bullet \vec{\Omega}_y\right) \tag{68}$$

The force $\vec{F}_R$ is due to the nutation restoring pulses and its mean value over a precession period maintain 'up' the center of the mass of the top. This force cannot overpass the weight of the top because in this case the top will float and its end will be not based on the strong point which assure the gravitational bending torque $\vec{T}_g$. If $\vec{S}$ is very big, the bending torque $\vec{T}_g$ will produce very small restoring pulses and the precession period will be very big too. Then, 'the top sleep' (Lindsay, 1965). For a smaller $\vec{S}$, the bending torque $\vec{T}_g$ will produce very big restoring pulses but a small precession period. As results, the lifting force $\vec{F}_R$ obtained as a mean value of same restoring pulses of different direction over a precession period will change its direction and the top will fall down. We remember that only an external applied torque to a gyroscope that spin may leads to its movements of nutation and precession.

For a Levitron type top, the bending torques are realized by the interactions between two magnetic fields $\vec{B}_T$ and $\vec{B}_g$: the magnetic field of the base and the own magnetic field of the Levitron top. This had the advantage that the need for a strong point is avoided. More, as the two these magnetic fields are in opposition, the top is repulsed and can fly because due to its spin, it cannot change its direction in space. Remembering that a gyroscope may exchange the energy between its spin, precession and nutation movements, we may observe that the Levitron top can float at a higher attitude than that corresponding to the magnetic repulsion but needs a convenient spin frequency. At a lower spin frequency, the top oscillate between 2 attitude levels before landing sideway. Anyhow, the highest possible attitude is given by the level of interaction between the magnetic fields $\vec{B}_T$ and $\vec{B}_g$ which may yet ensure convenient bending torques. At a spin faster than 26 revolutions per second, the bending torque realized by the fields $\vec{B}_T$ and $\vec{B}_g$ begins not to be enough to ensure a good nutation movement and the top begin to be unstable (Levitron instructions).

For a Levitron top, the bending torques are realized by the interactions between two magnets and this torques are applied all the time in a similar way in which a gravitational torques are applied all the time to an ordinary top. Using electromagnetic waves to interact with the magnet $\vec{B}_g$ has the advantage that the wave can be switched off during the restoring time and the source of this wave can be 'embarked' on the top (Simon and all,1997). This will ensure a higher lifting force and the possibility of floating farther in space. If the sender of this electromagnetic waves exists on the board of a vehicle equipped of such Levitron top motor, this vehicle may move anywhere in space.

ABOUT INERTIA

A mass in rotation increases its diameter of rotation. This may lead to the idea that the energy of inertia is stoked inside the equivalent 'elasticity' of this mass. A well known simple physical model of a 'mass-spring' as in figure 5 is modeled by the differential equation:

$$m.\frac{d^2x}{dt^2} + k.x = mg \tag{69}$$

where m is the considered inertial mass, x and k are the 'elongation' and the elasticity of the given spring and g is the earth gravitation acceleration. This differential equation has the solution:

$$x = \frac{mg}{k} + C_1.\mathrm{Cos}\left[\sqrt[2]{\frac{k}{m}}.t\right] + C_2.\mathrm{Sin}\left[\sqrt[2]{\frac{k}{m}}.t\right] \tag{70}$$

where C_1,C_2 are integration constants. Then, the period T of these oscillations is:

$$\omega = \frac{2.\pi}{T} = \sqrt[2]{\frac{m}{k}}; \Rightarrow T = 2.\pi.\sqrt[2]{\frac{m}{k}} \tag{71}$$

Physically, for this system, the dynamical inertial force $m.\frac{d^2x}{dt^2}$ of the mass is equal to the elasticity force of the spring k,x and the static force mg represents the 'weight' of the mass m applied to this system. In other words, the inertial energy of the mass is equal to the energy stored inside the spring. Such a system 'works' only if the spring is attached to a 'strong point' (a ceiling as example) because only in this situation the force mg may be applied to the spring. In steady-state, only the solution $x = \frac{mg}{k}$ exist and then, the spring is longer than its ordinary size due to the weight of the mass m. If a vertical mechanical impulse is applied to the system, ideally in the absence of any losses by friction, such a system may oscillate forever following the Equation (70). A symmetrical system like in Figure 6 has the advantage that it can oscillate in any 3-D space position without the need of any 'strong point'. The equivalent differential equation of this system has the general solution:

$$x = C_1.\mathrm{Cos}\left[\sqrt[2]{\frac{k}{ma+mb}}.t\right] + C_2.\mathrm{Sin}\left[\sqrt[2]{\frac{k}{ma+mb}}.t\right] \tag{72}$$

In free space, such a structure that receive a mechanical impulse on one of its masses will began to oscillate but will follow also the direction of this mechanical impulse. A 3-D lattice of such systems may be like the molecules of a solid matter where the nucleus of each atom may be (mainly) equivalent to the '(inertial) mass' and the atomic and molecular fields forces may be equivalent to the 'spring'. One remembers that such a structure has been envisaged for the interaction between the light and ultra-acoustical waves in matter. It seems that 'inertia' may be assimilated to a special kind of 'dynamic mass polarization' that ensure a non-relativistic movement of this mass due to a 'dynamic exchange between the gravitational field and the (inertial) energy stocked inside it'. Observing that atomic particle like the nucleus and/or electron may be assimilated to a Levitron top, by a movement in space, the electromagnetic fields around them will be modified and then also the 'shape' of the atom and molecule that contains these particles. Inside a mass, the equivalent inertial oscillations propagate as 'acoustic and/or ultra-acoustic waves' but due to the oscillations of the nucleus and/or electrons that are 'polarons' (Wikipedia, Polaron, 2015), gravitational waves also result that interact with the gravitational environmental field. Evidently, the equations of the ultra-acoustic waves in the matter corresponding to the 'inertia' will be more sophisticated that in the relations (70) and (72) mainly due to the 'group effect' and to the fact that a mass may move in many ways.

If two masses are fixed together, the acoustic and/or ultra-acoustic waves will propagate from one mass to the other and, after a time, the ensemble of two masses will have the same 'inertia'. If two masses are 'in physical contact' but may have different speeds, a friction between the surfaces in contact results and the relative movement energy is transformed into 'heat energy'. We remember that the friction force is defined by μ,x where μ is the friction coefficient and the spring force by k,x. As well-known examples, a human placed inside a vehicle that change its speed, even if it is attached to this vehicle, will 'feel' the effects of these gravitational waves and also, that an actual 'car braking system' uses the friction to change the 'inertia' of this car into heat. It is also known that no undesirable health effects were observed on earth and/or on same manned space vehicles due to the (steady-state) inertial waves.

All these suggest another type of 'inertial motor', a system that can directly inject 'ultra-acoustic wave energy' corresponding to a desired 'inertia' into a given mass. In principle, this may be done by 'saser (Sound amplification by stimulated emission of radiation)' (Wikipedia, Saser, 2015) and as these waves are 3-D, a 3-D equivalent ultrasound source has to be used (Ciulin, 'Some forgotten problems', to be published). A system like in Figure 7 may probably ensure the (inertial) move of a vehicle in any desired direction.

The vehicle must be equipped with an inertial 3-D sensor of its position and movements. Another 3-D sensor will be used to detect the acoustic and/or ultra-acoustic waves connected to the 'inertia' of this vehicle. One and/or many 3-D acoustic and/or ultra-acoustic actuators may equip this vehicle and be used to inject the acoustic and/or ultra-acoustic waves energy necessary to ensure the inertial energy that will move the vehicle in the desired direction. A system control compares the actual trajectory of the vehicle with the desired one obtained by an external control and modifies conveniently the energy and shapes and timing of the injected 3-D ultra-acoustic waves. Any modification has to be done starting from the actual sensed 3-D ultra-acoustic waves and trying to keep the new injected ultra-acoustic waves signals nearly 'in phase' with the (actually) existing acoustic and/or ultra-acoustic waves. It is also known that a kind of equivalent technology is actually used for the drones. This kind of 'inertial motor' has the big advantage that by 'scrambling the existing inertia of acoustic and/or ultra-acoustic waves', the inertia' of the vehicle will vanish and probably, the resulting energy will heat the vehicle. By considering that the inertia corresponds to a kind of 'ordered polarization', a parallel may be considered to the 'Curie point' (Wikipedia, Curie temperature, 2016) where the permanent magnetization of a mass is lost when a thermal radiation energy injected at this mass overpass the temperature of this value.

In theory, these 'inertial dynamical polarizations' equivalent to 'inertia' may also be induced into a given mass by energy injected using electromagnetic waves to control the spin and nutation/precession movements of its existing atomic particles. This may be equivalent to a kind of 'tractor ray'. Probably,

Figure 5. Mass-spring system

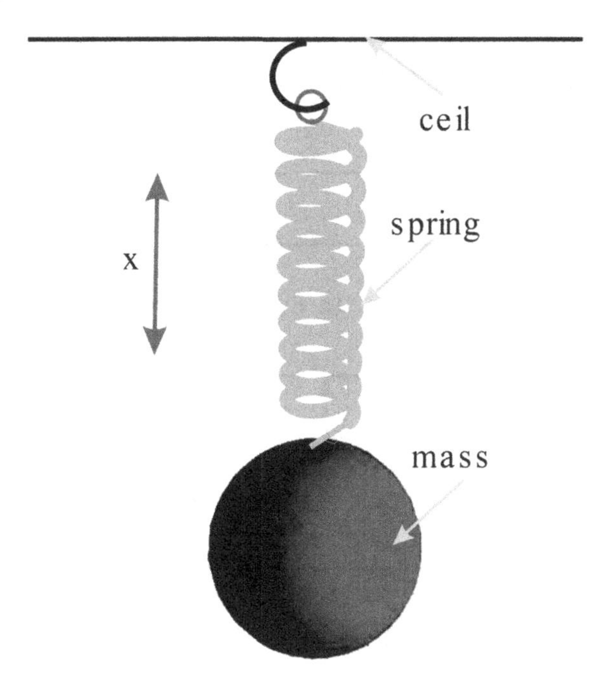

Figure 6. Symmetrical mass-spring system

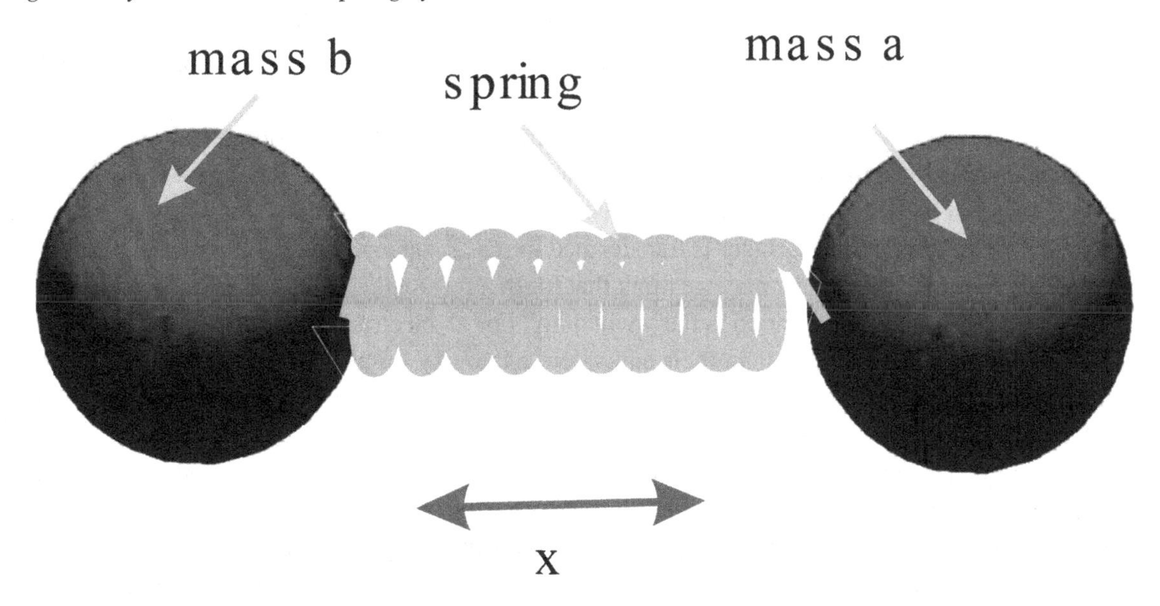

even for a Levitron top like motor and/or for an acoustic and/or ultra-acoustical inertia like motor, it will be not necessary to know exactly the (existing) wave signals: applying some well-synchronized impulses may be enough! As the well-known example, a seesaw needs only some well-synchronized impulses to increase its energy! It is also known that some impulses nearly in 'opposed phase' may quickly stop the seesaw! We remark also that the mathematical model for the seesaw uses elliptic functions.

Figure 7. System control of the inertial movement of a vehicle

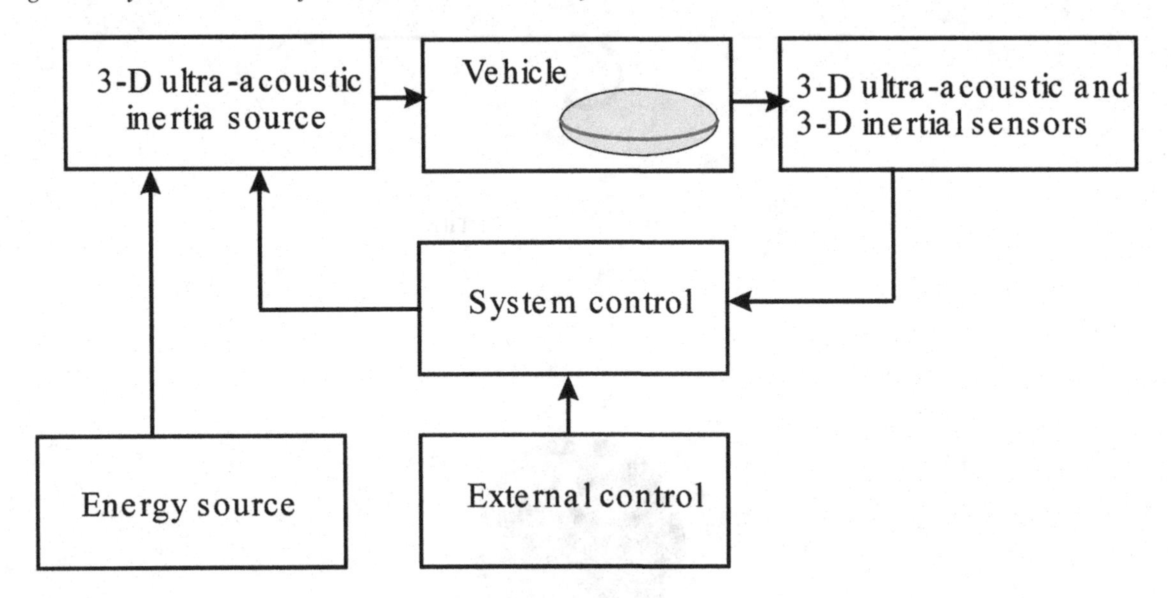

CONCLUSION

Generalized rotation is the main feature of complex-exponential, elliptic and ultra-elliptic functions that represents the variation in time of the (generalized) angles. Rotations lead also to feedback loop tool that maintains the values of some parameters of living beings ensuring their health and, for electronic systems, maintains the values of some parameters ensuring their convenient work. An extension to meromorphic functions for a feedback loop system has been presented in (Ciulin, 2010a). By rotation, a whole voltage-current characteristic of some electronic devices as the tunnel diode and neon tube may be displayed in spite of the fact that they present a negative slope which may lead to instabilities. Similarly, by rotation, a 'hysteresis window' of a Smith trigger is transformed into a 'Z' characteristic without any 'jump.' As rotation need energy to be realized, may we think that for that reason the hysteresis appears for passives systems? A digital form of the rotation is the 'switching'. For an electronic system, this leads to digital systems that are more performing than their equivalent analog systems. This leads also to computers which, between any other important applications, realize a kind of 'bridge' between the physical and mathematical model of a system.

The trigonometric, hyperbolic, elliptic and ultra-elliptic functions are solutions of energy based differential equations. All this function uses the time-variation of (generalized complex) angles as independent variables. Such analytic homogenous functions are then a very good choice to represent systems in the free space. Each independent angle is connected with a period which may be even imaginary and all these functions are periodic. Similarly to the manner to extend the function $e^{(\sigma+i.\omega).t}$ to elliptic functions, an extension to many variables ultra-elliptic functions is presented in (Eilbeck et al., 2016). Functionally, a vector and/or tensor structure is represented by a many variables function and then, a tensor and/or vector model of a gyroscope may be functionally represented by ultra-elliptic functions. An ordinary top (Lindsay, 1965), (Ciulin, 2009, 2010b) leads to a mathematical model that represents the 3 Euler angles by 3 elliptic Weierstrass functions. An ultra-elliptic function may then enclose all these functions. Otherwise, if this top is pumped with energy on its nutation frequencies, the definition poly-

Figure 8. Bending (green) and restoring (red) nutation pulse

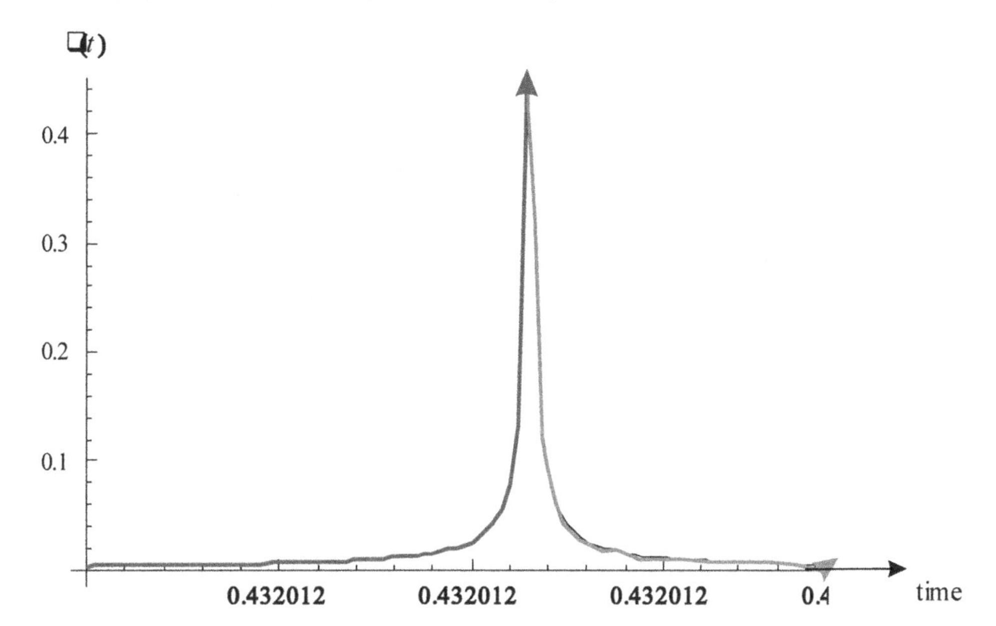

nomial of the equivalent (energy) differential equation becomes of 5 degrees and/or higher and this leads to ultra-elliptic functions as solutions (Kuang et al., 2005). Figure 8 shows a nutation bending and restoring pulse.

For mechanical devices, the rotation brings to some important innovations as the car, clock, mechanical automata and thermo-mechanical motors. To realize a translation movement, a car use wheels in rotation and the 'friction' between these wheels and the ground. A method that is based on inertia (Ciulin, 2009, 2010b) may also convert the rotation into translation. Because this method does not use 'friction' as the well known traditional methods, it may present a better efficiency and can be used even in free space. A Levitron type gyroscope pumped electromagnetic conveniently on its spin and nutation is a good example. By considering that many Levitron type gyroscopes may be used in parallel to increase the 'lift up' force and to ensure the necessary reliability, this kind of inertial motors may be used for terrestrial and even space vehicles.

For a Levitron type top, we had added the terms concerning the magnetic fields into the mathematical model of an ordinary top. Then, it results also a wave equation using elliptic functions having as arguments the time-variation of the angles of Euler mobile system of coordinates (Smirnov, 1955). This wave is gravitational as it is based on elliptic functions that represent the 3D motion of a gyroscope. It may also be used to pump energy to a Levitron type top and/or to control its position in space by changing some parameters. It results an inertial motor that is electro-mechanic and then may have a limited reliability. Now, we remember the analogy between a Leviton type top and, for example, the atomic nucleus. It is known that by the method of the Nuclear Magnetic Resonance, movements of nutation and precession of the nucleus may be induced electromagnetically. Then, a convenient technology may be developed to pump electromagnetically energy into a given matter and control the desired nutation and spin of the nucleus of its atoms in such a manner to obtain statistically a desired inertial force into a desired direction. If successful, this will leads to an electronic and electromagnetic inertial motor with a good reliability because it will have any mechanical component in movement. Such inertial motor will respond more

Figure 9. Ellipse, parabola and hyperbola

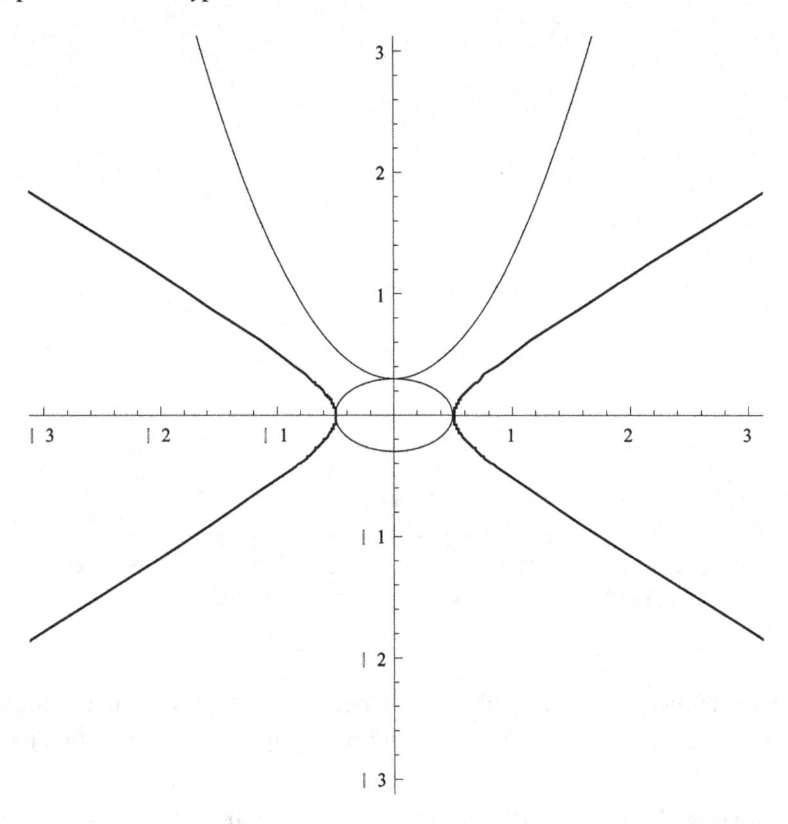

quickly to any desired change of parameters due especially to the higher frequencies of the spin, nutation and precession movements. Remembering that a given Levitron type gyroscope from a group may be pumped separately, with a more advanced technology, one may envisage to change conveniently also the inertia of the embarked crew members (and objects) into an interplanetary ship so to create, inside this ship, an equivalent of the 'earth gravitational environment'. In this way, the effects due to the ship accelerations (and space position) will be diminished or even avoided. Of course, using the frequencies corresponding to the nutation and precession movements of the nucleus may avoid the necessity of a static magnet as it is the case for the Nuclear Magnetic Resonance devices.

An associated gravitational wave is generated directly by a Levitron type top. Its energy depends evidently on the external energy pumped to the top. Another kind of generator for this type of wave may be built, for example, by using 3 electronic oscillators, each generating the real part of a Weierstrass elliptical functions corresponding to the time-variation of the 3 Euler angles. Of course, these oscillators must be correlated and also to have the possibility to change same parameters in order to 'tune correctly' with the Leviton type top which has to be pumped. Sensors may be used in a loop to correlate the parameters of the received waves from the top with the parameters of these generated waves. To increase the sender power, amplifiers may be used. Some 3D aerials may be used to generate the necessary fields which will pump energy into the top and control its parameters. One may observe that these kinds of gravitational waves are connected to an equivalent mechanical system having 3 angles. A system with many angles which correspond to ultra-elliptical functions may leads to a gravitational wave equation of the form:

$$\frac{\partial^2 U}{\partial t^2} = k\sum_{i=1}^{n} L_i.\frac{\partial^2 U}{\partial \theta_i^2} \tag{73}$$

where L_i are the Lamé coefficients, k a parameter, θ_i the considered angles and U the considered field.

Another method to change the 'inertia' of a vehicle is to inject acoustic and/or ultra-acoustic convenient wave signals in it. In theory, this method realizes a direct transfer of the input energy to the inertia of the vehicle but seems more difficult to be used for the crew existing inside the vehicle as it needs some physical direct contacts between many actuators and crew. Our daily experience in the trains and or buses seems to confirm that because we need many physical contacts with the vehicle to keep our position in space.

The (theoretical) tools presented here seem to be a kind of 'bridge' between the classical theory and some modern theories:

- The elliptic and ultra-elliptic functions are a solution of the energy based differential equations. They may also represent the fields. Kaluza-Klein theory (Wikipedia, Kaluza-Klein, 2012) starts from the 'action' which is a 'time integral of the energy' to represents the Einstein and Maxwell theories of fields in 5 dimensions.
- The elliptic and ultra-elliptic functions may be spectrally represented. An extension for the Jacobi elliptic function was presented in (Ciulin, 2011). The string theory (Wikipedia, String theory, 2012) represents the elementary particles by 'vibrating strings'. The M-theory includes also the Super-String theory and needs 11 dimensions.
- The elliptic and ultra-elliptic functions may also represent waves. Electromagnetic waves are well known and may be materially represented by photons. The presented mathematical model for gravitational waves implies 3 correlated inertial-electromagnetic waves that are modulated by the elliptical signals corresponding to the movement of a gyroscope. May we consider that these kinds of waves are materially represented by '3 entangled photons in a special manner' (EuroPhotonics, 2012) now when gravitational waves have been also proved to exists (Wikipedia, gravitational waves, 2016)? May this be extended to elliptic and/or ultra-elliptic gravitational waves? It may also be observed that such a particle composed of '3 entangled photons in a special manner' has no static mass but may rotate (spin) only on two main Euler angles corresponding to the nutation and precession like a (hypothetical) graviton!
- Generally the mass is defined through its interaction with the gravitational field. It is known that the 'weighting mass' may be in some situations, very different from the 'inertial mass'. As presented before, an 'inertial excited mass' may have a different value from the static mass of the same body and in Einstein theory of relativity, the (dynamic) mass depend on its speed for relativistic speeds. May that also be connected with the Higgs boson? (Higgs, 2012).
- An ellipse has the equation:

$$\frac{x^2}{a^2} + \frac{y^2}{b^2} = 1; a, b > 0 \tag{74}$$

With the change of variable in this equation, we get (Wikipedia. Conic sections, 2012):

$$\begin{cases} u = \frac{1}{x}; \\ v = \frac{1}{y}; \end{cases} \Rightarrow \frac{u^2}{a^2} + \frac{v^2}{b^2} = u.v; \Rightarrow \begin{cases} A = \frac{1}{a^2}; \\ C = \frac{1}{b^2}; \\ B = -1; \end{cases} \Rightarrow \begin{cases} hyperbole.if.a.b > 2 \\ parabole.if.a.b \equiv 2 \\ ellipse.if.a.b < 2 \end{cases} \quad (75)$$

and for u,v finite and $ab>2$, the initial ellipse will become hyperbola. This may be put in conjunction with the homographic (Möbius) transformation that generates the elliptic and ultra-elliptic functions. All these functions have 2 (independent) periods for each complex variable. Figure 9 represents the ellipse, parabola and hyperbola curves.

- It is known that each atomic orbit may contain only 2 electrons with opposite spin. As the elliptic and ultra-elliptic functions can represent also the field corresponding to such particles, may we consider that each complex variable of an ultra-elliptic function is associated to a given atomic orbit?
- As the ultra-elliptic functions which models the gravitation have the time as the independent variable for each of its complex variable, may this be connected with the Einstein theory of relativity where the time is different for each observer? More, may we consider that some observer may exist at the output of the same transducer?
- It can be remarked that the conversion between the internal torques and/or and the inertial torques and/or forces need also 'partial rotations' (vibrations) to be realized. The nutation movement is an example (Penrose, 2005). May we consider that conversion like a more sophisticated Carnot cycle? (Wikipedia, Carnot cycle, 2012).
- The relations that converts the Cartesian coordinates to elliptical one, using the Weierstrass $\wp$ functions are (Wikipedia, elliptic functions, 2012):

$$\begin{cases} x^2 = 4.\frac{(\wp(\alpha) - e_1).(\wp(\beta) - e_1).(\wp(\chi) - e_1)}{(e_1 - e_2).(e_1 - e_3)} \\ y^2 = 4.\frac{(\wp(\alpha) - e_2).(\wp(\beta) - e_2).(\wp(\chi) - e_2)}{(e_2 - e_3),(e_2 - e_1)} \\ z^2 = 4.\frac{(\wp(\alpha) - e_3).(\wp(\beta) - e_3).(\wp(\chi) - e_3)}{(e_3 - e_2).(e_3 - e_2)} \end{cases} \quad (76)$$

where g_2,g_3 are some parameters of the $\wp(.)$ function, e_1,e_2,e_3 are the roots of its definition polynomial and m_1 a parameter of Jacobi functions:

$$\begin{cases} g_2 = -4.(e_1.e_2 + e_1.e_3 + e_2.e_3) \\ g_3 = 4.e_1.e_2.e_3 \\ e_1 + e_2 + e_3 = 0 \\ m_1 = \frac{e_2 - e_3}{e_1 - e_3} \end{cases} \quad (77)$$

To obtain relations that converts the elliptical coordinates to Cartesian one it may be useful to use Jacobi elliptical functions:

$$\begin{cases} \sqrt[2]{\wp[u]-e_1} = \dfrac{CN[u]}{SN[u]} \\ \sqrt[2]{\wp[u]-e_2} = \dfrac{DN[u]}{SN[u]} \\ \sqrt[2]{\wp[u]-e_3} = \dfrac{1}{SN[u]} \end{cases} \tag{78}$$

Taking into account the well-known properties of these Jacobi elliptic functions, the desired relations may be found as algebraic solutions of a system of equations. It may be remarked that replacing the Weierstrass $\wp(.)$ function by Jacobi elliptic functions allows the system (76) to be algebraically inverted. It may also be remarked that in the relation (76), the degree of the Cartesian coordinates, by considering also the multiplying constant $(e_1-e_2).(e_1-e_3)$, is 3 then the same as for the real part of the Weierstrass elliptical functions. If we consider also the complex extensions, the degree is 6. May we replace the Weierstrass $\wp(.)$ by the Jacobi elliptic functions in the relation (74) to obtain also ultra-elliptic functions?

- It seems that in some situations, the movement of a top realize a kind of 'knotting trajectory.' This may be observed also for the light. (Photonics.com, 2012). May we consider that this happened for a kind of special kind of 'energy conversion'?
- A gravitational (inertial) motor may be based on a gyroscopic doublet, on a Levitron type gyroscope, on a system that uses the equivalence between the mass and the Levitron type gyroscope and/or on direct transfer of acoustic and/or ultra-acoustic inertial waves to a given vehicle. Practically, convenient technologies will use electrical current as a source of energy. The method based on a gyroscopic doublet is electro-mechanic, implies a (brute) forced movement of gyroscopes and has a low efficiency and reliability. The methods based on the analogy between the Levitron type gyroscope and the matter has no mechanical component in movement and then a good reliability but implies electrical energy sources and higher frequencies technology. Similarly, the methods based on the direct transfer of acoustic and/or ultra-acoustic inertial waves to a given vehicle are more simple and efficient but implies electrical energy sources, (relative) higher frequencies technology and a direct physical contact between the acoustic and/or ultra-acoustic actuators and the vehicle to modify its inertial energy. Generally, the use of an inertial motor avoid the necessity to throw mass outside the vehicle and then, needs less powerful motors for the earth 'take off' as example. More, this kind of motor may be placed inside the shell of the vehicle without the need to have some outside components as, for example, a helix or a jet-nozzle.

I hope that these theoretical tools and also those presented in my papers will be useful for a new necessary technology able to create a good inertial motor and a good telecommunication system based on gravitational waves for the future starships but also for some terrestrial applications. If confirmed in practice, this presented theory may open many opportunities in many fields.

ACKNOWLEDGMENT

The author wishes to thanks to Sir Professor Berry for his encouragement and advice and also to Professor Birkedal Henrik and his wife Victoria for many fruitful discussions. Last but not least, he wishes to thank Doctor Caroline Howard, Doctor Kathleen M. Hargiss and all the IGI Global team for their help and encouragement in writing this paper.

REFERENCES

Blau, S.K. (2003). The Force Need Not Be With You: Curvature Begets Motion.

Capellini, V., Constantinides, A.G., & Emiliani, P. (1978). Digital filters and their applications. London: Academic Press.

Chabat, B. (1959). *Introduction à l'analyse complexe* (Tome 2: fonctions de plusieurs variables). Moscou: MIR.

Ciulin, D. (1979, July). Statistical accumulation in time for distribution of noise in L2. *Proceedings of theInternational Symposium on Circuits and Systems*, Tokyo, Japan.

Ciulin, D., & Longchamp, J.-F. (1995). Verfahren und Vorrichtung zur Reduzierung der Nutzbandbreite eines bandbegrenzten Signals durch Kodieren desselben und Verfahren und Vorrichtung zum Dekodieren des bandbegrenzten SignalsVerfahren und Vorrichtung zur Reduzierung der Nutzbandbreite ein..." European patent: DE58908835D - 1995-02-09.

Ciulin, D. (2006, November 26–December 1). Inverse Problem for a Car Headlight Reflector. *Proceedings of Virtual Concept '06*, Playa Del Carmen, Mexico.

Ciulin, D. (2007, December 3-12). About Sign function and some extensions. *Proceedings of the CISSE '07 Online E-Conference*.

Ciulin, D. (2007a). Motor that assures space displacements of a vehicle by means of inertial forces. Idea for European Project Proposal, Proceedings of ERIMA07' symposium, Biarritz.

Ciulin, D. (2008). System to produce mechanical inertial force and/or torque. *Proceedings of the International Joint Conference on Computer, Information and System Science and engineering (CIS^{2}E '08).*

Ciulin, D. (2009). *System to produce mechanical inertial force and/or torque. In Technological Developments in Education and Automation*. London: Springer.

Ciulin, D., (2010). A Nearly One-to-One Method to Convert Analog Signals into a Small Volume of Data. First Part: 1-D Signals. *International Journal of Strategic Information Technology and Applications*, *1*(4).

Ciulin, D. (2010a). Loops and extensions to meromorphic signals. *Proceedings of theInternational Conference on Advances in Recent Technologies in Communication&Computing, ARTCom '10*, Kottayam, Kerala, India.

Ciulin, D. (2010b, December 3-12). Models for some smart toys and extensions. *Proceedings of CISSE '10 Online E-Conference.*

Ciulin, D. (2011). A Nearly One-to-One Method to Convert Analogue Signals into a Small Volume of Data. Second Part - 2-D Signals and More. *International Journal of Strategic Information Technology and Applications*, *2*(4).

Ciulin, D., (2013). Contribution to a future inertial motor and more. *International Journal of Strategic Information Technology and Applications*, *4*(1).

Ciulin, D., (2013a). About space-time and more. *International Journal of Strategic Information Technology and Applications*, *4*(3).

Devlin, K. (1998). Mathematics: The new golden age (in Romanian). Fundatia Theta, Arta grafica, Bucuresti: Romania.

Du Val, P. (1973). *Elliptic Functions and Elliptic Curves*. Cambridge: University Press.

Earnshaw, E. (1842a). On the nature of the molecular forces which regulate the constitution of the luminiferous ether. *Transaction Cambridge Philosophical Society*, *7*, 87–112.

Eilbeck, J.C., Enolskii, V.Z., Previato, E. (2016). On A Generalized Frobenius - Stickelberger Addition Formula. *Letters in Mathematical Physics*, *63*(1), 5-17.

EuroPhotonics. (2012). Euro Photonics Autumn 2012, "Atoms signal their entanglement. *Science*, *2012*. doi:10.1126/science.1221856

Gell-Mann, M. (1994). *The quark and the jaguar*. New York: W.H. Freeman and Company.

Goursat, E. (1949). *Cours d'Analyse Mathématique* (Vol. II). Paris: Gauthier Villard.

Granger. A.R. (1995). Fluid Mechanics. (1995). New York: Dover Publications, INC.

IFAC. (2012). IFAC Keyword List of Control Terminology.

Ishlinsky, A. (1984). *Orientation, gyroscopes et navigation par inertie* (Vol. 1 & 2). Moscou: MIR.

Kleinsasser, J. (2012, September 21). Physicist explains significance of Higgs boson discovery. *Phys. org*. Retrieved from http://phys.org/news/2012-09-physicist-significance-higgs-boson-discovery.html#_methods=onPlusOne%2C_ready%2C_close%2C_open%2C_resizeMe%2C_renderstart%2Concircled%2Conauth%2Conload&id=I0_1350801851796&parent=http%3A%2F%2Fphys.org

Kuang, J. L., & Leung, A. Y. T. (2005). Homoclinic orbits of the Kovalevskaya top with perturbations. *Journal of Applied Mathematics and Mechanics*, *85*(4).

Ladon, I. F. (1949). Les bases du calcul vectorielle (Vol. 1 & 2). Romania.

Les, C. B. (2012). Laser swarm could swat asteroids away. *Photonics Spectra*, June.

Lian, K.-Y., Wang, L.-S., Fu, L.-C. (1994). Controllability of Spacecraft Systems in a Central Gravitational Field. *IEEE Transaction on Automatic Control, 39*(12).

Lindsay, R.B. (1961). Physical mechanics. London: D.Van Nostrand Company, Inc.

Matthews, R., & Sample, I. (1996). Breakthrough as scientists beat gravity. *The Journal of ideas*, 4.

Misner, C.W. & Thorne, K. (1988). *Gravitation*. W. H. Freeman and Company.

NASA.gov. (2012). NASA. Retrieved from http://www.nasa.gov/mission_pages/station/main/index.html

Palca, B.P. (1991). An introduction to complex function theory. Berlin: Springer Verlag.

Penrose, R. (2005). *The road to reality*. Vintage books.

Photonics Media. (2014). Photon state teleported at 25 km. Retrieved from http://www.photonics.com/Article.aspx?PID=6&AID=56699&refer=weeklyNewsletter&utm_source=weeklyNewsletter_2014_09_25&utm_medium=email&utm_campaign=weeklyNewsletter

Photonics.com. (2012), Knots in light! Retrieved from http://www.photonics.com/Article.aspx?AID=52196&refer=weeklyNewsletter&utm_source=weeklyNewsletter_2012_11_01&utm_medium=email&utm_campaign=weeklyNewsletter

Poole, C.P., Jr. (1967). Electron spin resonance. A comprehensive treatise on experimental techniques. London: Interscience Publishers.

Shannon, C. E. (1949). Communication in the Presence of Noise. *Proceedings of the IRE*, 37.

Sivoukhine, D. (1982). *Cours de physique générale, Mécanique*. Moscou: MIR.

Smirnov, V. I. (1955). *Cours de Mathématiques supérieures* (R. Technica, ed., Vol. 3).

Simon, M. D., Heflinger, L. O., & Ridgway, S. L. (1997, April). Spin stabilized magnetic levitation. *American Journal of Physics*, *65*(4).

Thorne, K. S. (1994). *Black holes & time warp*. London: W.W. Norton & Company.

Wikipedia. (2012). Carnot cycle. Retrieved from https://en.wikipedia.org/wiki/Carnot_cycle

Wikipedia. (2012). elliptic functions. Retrieved from http://en.wikipedia.org/wiki/Elliptic_function

Wikipedia. (2012). electrostatics. Retrieved from http://en.wikipedia.org/wiki/Electrostatics

Wikipedia. (2012). force. Retrieved from http://fr.wikipedia.org/wiki/Force_(physique)

Wikipedia. (2012). Haar wavelet. Retrieved from http://en.wikipedia.org/wiki/Haar_waveletHaar

Wikipedia. (2012). hysteresis. Retrieved from http://fr.wikipedia.org/wiki/Hyst%C3%A9r%C3%A9sis

Wikipedia. (2012). Kaluza-Klein. Retrieved from http://fr.wikipedia.org/wiki/Th%C3%A9orie_de_Kaluza-Klein

Wikipedia. (2012). M-theory. Retrieved from http://en.wikipedia.org/wiki/M-theory

Wikipedia. (2012). Maxwell's equations. Retrieved from http://en.wikipedia.org/wiki/Maxwell's_equations

Wikipedia. (2012). Nuclear magnetic resonance. Retrieved from http://en.wikipedia.org/wiki/Nuclear_magnetic_resonance

Wikipedia. (2012). Rotation. Retrieved from http://fr.wikipedia.org/wiki/Rotation#En_math.C3.A9matiques

Wikipedia. (2012). Spin. Retrieved from http://en.wikipedia.org/wiki/Spin_(physics)

Wikipedia. (2012). String theory. Retrieved from http://en.wikipedia.org/wiki/String_theory

Wikipedia. (2013). Atom. Retrieved from http://en.wikipedia.org/wiki/Atom

Wikipedia. (2013). Atomic Nucleus. Retrieved from http://en.wikipedia.org/wiki/Atomic_nucleus

Wikipedia. (2013). Causality. Retrieved from https://en.wikipedia.org/wiki/Causality

Wikipedia. (2013). Electron. Retrieved from http://en.wikipedia.org/wiki/Electron

Wikipedia. (2013). Magnetic field. Retrieved from http://en.wikipedia.org/wiki/Magnetic_field

Wikipedia. (2013). Magnetic Moment. Retrieved from http://en.wikipedia.org/wiki/Magnetic_moment

Wikipedia. (2013). Neural network. Retrieved from http://en.wikipedia.org/wiki/Neural_network

Wikipedia. (2013). neuron. Retrieved from http://www.scholarpedia.org/article/Neuron

Wikipedia. (2013). Total order. Retrieved from http://en.wikipedia.org/wiki/Total_order

Wikipedia. (2013). Transducer. Retrieved from http://en.wikipedia.org/wiki/Transducer

Wikipedia. (2013). Visible Spectrum. Retrieved from http://en.wikipedia.org/wiki/Visible_spectrum

Wikipedia. (2013). Wave. Retrieved from http://en.wikipedia.org/wiki/Wave

Wikipedia. (2013). Work function. Retrieved from http://en.wikipedia.org/wiki/Work_function

Wikipedia. (2014). Gyroscope. Retrieved from http://en.wikipedia.org/wiki/Gyroscope

Wikipedia. (2014). Soliton. Retrieved from http://fr.wikipedia.org/wiki/Soliton

Wikipedia. (2014). Soundcloud. Retrieved from https://soundcloud.com/esaops/a-singing-comet

Wikipedia. (2014). Standing Wave. Retrieved from http://en.wikipedia.org/wiki/Standing_wave

Wikipedia. (2014). Telecommunications. Retrieved from http://en.wikipedia.org/wiki/Telecommunication

Wikipedia. (2015). Saser. Retrieved from https://en.wikipedia.org/wiki/Sound_amplification_by_stimulated_emission_of_radiation

Wikipedia. (2016). Curie temperature. Retrieved from https://en.wikipedia.org/wiki/Curie_temperature

Wikipedia. (2016). gravitational waves. Retrieved from http://www.sciencemag.org/news/2016/02/gravitational-waves-einstein-s-ripples-spacetime-spotted-first-time

Wikipedia. (2016). Levitron. Retrieved from https://en.wikipedia.org/wiki/Levitron

Wikipedia. (2016). Electron paramagnetic resonance. Retrieved from https://en.wikipedia.org/wiki/Electron_paramagnetic_resonance

Wikipedia. (2016). Noether's theorem. Retrieved from https://en.wikipedia.org/wiki/Noether%27s_theorem

Wikipedia. (2016). Polaron. Retrieved from https://en.wikipedia.org/wiki/Polaron

Wikipedia. (2016). Reactionless drive. Retrieved from https://en.wikipedia.org/wiki/Reactionless_drive

Wikipedia. (2016). Smaglev. Retrieved from https://en.wikipedia.org/wiki/smaglev

Section 2

Strategic Information Applications:

Interorganizational Systems

Chapter 6
The Role of Knowledge Management Strategies in Cooperation Agreements

Mario J. Donate
University of Castilla-La Mancha, Spain

Fátima Guadamillas
University of Castilla-La Mancha, Spain

Jesús D. Sánchez de Pablo
University of Castilla-La Mancha, Spain

María Isabel González-Ramos
University of Castilla-La Mancha, Spain

ABSTRACT

In this chapter, the role of knowledge management strategies (KMS) in cooperation agreements is analyzed in a technology-intensive company. Knowledge management in alliances implies to establish an organizational design to both explore and exploit knowledge for achieving competitive goals (for each partner). The importance of alliances for technological companies and the necessity of designing suitable KMS in alliances—in terms of objectives and goals, knowledge management tools, and support systems—are explained first of all. Moreover, the analysis of a case study on KMS in the alliances of a high-tech Spanish company with businesses in innovation intensive settings is developed by the authors. Finally, this chapter will conclude with a discussion on the way that the implementation aspects concerning KMS in cooperation agreements have been managed by the company in order to support technology development and product diversification.

INTRODUCTION

The interest in alliances and cooperation agreements has grown among strategic management scholars over the past 25 years (Grant & Baden-Fuller, 2004; Meier, 2011; Yang, Zheng, & Zhao, 2014). In particular, the strategic management literature has recognized alliances as a source for firms to acquire and improve their knowledge-based capabilities in current innovation-intensive environments (Oxley & Sampson, 2004). Alliances can thus operate as a mechanism for firms to develop a competitive advantage, outperforming their rivals by means of the company's proven access to economies of scope

DOI: 10.4018/978-1-5225-1680-4.ch006

and scale, complementary capabilities and knowledge, the possibility of competing in new markets, the improvement of their learning capacity, or the sharing of costs and risks of R&D projects, among other reasons (Saxton, 1997; Ireland, Hitt, & Vaidyanath, 2002; Luo, 2008).

A Knowledge Management Strategy (KMS) is considered in this chapter as one of the main factors in order for firms to achieve these objectives and build collaborative advantages through cooperation agreements (or alliances). Managing organizational knowledge in alliances involves working on the best possible strategic design to create, acquire, maintain, transfer and apply organizational knowledge developed or acquired amongst the partners in order to achieve competitive goals (Guadamillas, Donate, & Sánchez de Pablo, 2006).

A clear relationship exists between cooperation agreements and the way KMS are established by firms in order to obtain specific knowledge outcomes. For instance, Lane and Lubatkin (1998) and Stuart (2000) contend that the main objective of partners in a technological alliance is inter-organizational learning, as a consequence of the difficulty faced by each partner in terms of internally solving their competitive challenges. Inter-organizational learning is based on the absorptive capacity of the company, which represents its ability to asses, assimilate and use the external (acquired) knowledge (Cohen & Levinthal, 1990; Lane & Lubatkin, 1998). For that learning to take place, an adequate KMS has to be developed to effectively exploit the flows of knowledge that are produced in the cooperation agreement through absorptive capacity (Grant & Baden-Fuller, 2004). In doing so, the development of innovations will speed up, thus making its implementation over a short period of time possible, ultimately leading to important advantages for the firm whilst encouraging a superior level of learning (Stuart, 2000).

In order to effectively manage a cooperation agreement, organizational and technical aspects have to be taken into account: the use of information technology (IT) and the systems that make the access to knowledge easier, the organizational culture that fosters innovation development and ethical and responsible behavior, and human resources (HR) practices. All of these make the establishment of a coherent structure for knowledge management in cooperation agreements a complicated issue (Schmaltz, Hagenhoff, & Kaspar, 2004; Guadamillas et al., 2006).

Other important problems also arise in cooperation agreements, which make the effective development of collaborative activities and knowledge sharing complex issues. Meier (2011) summarizes all those aspects influencing (intra and inter-organizational) knowledge outcomes such as:

1. The characteristics of knowledge;
2. Those of the alliance partners;
3. Those of their interaction and relationship; and
4. The way knowledge management is developed in the alliance (active knowledge management).

Taking into account these issues, in this chapter we attempt to analyze the KMS of companies involved in cooperation agreements, and in particular, a number of aspects related both to the sharing and transmission of knowledge from the *knowledge-based view of the firm*. The role of technical and organizational factors in these processes will be thus analyzed in relation to culture, HR practices, and the management of IT systems.

This chapter will be structured as follows: Firstly, the importance of KMS for individual companies in alliances in order to develop a collaborative advantage and obtain important returns on their R&D investment will be explained. Secondly, we shall analyze the importance of organizational and strategic aspects that are involved in this process, stressing those factors that make the effective transmission and sharing of knowledge a complex task for a firm. Finally, the role of KMS oriented towards innovation in cooperation agreements will be analyzed in a high-tech Spanish company (Tecnobit). This firm maintains cooperation agreements that are considered as being essential for knowledge creation and innovation development. The manner in which implementation aspects concerning KMS in cooperation agreements have been managed and the way they have contributed to the attainment of their strategic objectives will be explained by the authors.

KNOWLEDGE MANAGEMENT IN COOPERATION AGREEMENTS

As Inkpen (2000) points out, learning in a cooperation agreement consists of gaining access to the partner's knowledge in order to combine it with the particular assets of the firm to be used in business activities. Moreover, Inkpen, and Beamish (1997) contend that while the establishment of an alliance permits access to knowledge between partners, the transfer of knowledge which enables learning will only occur when certain conditions that make this possible are in place. Furthermore, owing to tacit and non-observable knowledge being more valuable in terms of strategic content (Spender, 1996), firms may establish specific mechanisms to acquire this kind of knowledge, all of which is difficult and costly when put into practice.

Among other authors, Hamel (1991), Khanna, Gulati, and Nohria (1998), Lane and Lubatkin (1998) and Stuart (2000) argue that the main objective of partners in cooperation agreements is inter-organizational learning as a consequence of the difficulties faced by firms when attempting to internally resolve problems of differing natures for which specific knowledge is required. Hence, learning can be based on a wide variety of aspects such as market characteristics, operational problems, technological capabilities, management abilities and so on. On the other hand, the alliance structure can be considered as a "laboratory" for the organizational learning of each partner where the firm's knowledge pool is created and developed (Inkpen, 1998). In order to make this possible, learning has to be an important aspect of the strategy of partners, who should also have skills to learn and integrate the new knowledge into their current knowledge base.

In addition to this, certain elements are required to make the advantages that have been gained through learning and knowledge transfer effective for partners. Mesquita, Anand, and Brush (2008) point out the following:

1. Knowledge transfer has to be agreed;
2. Assets and capabilities have to be specifically developed through the alliance;
3. A suitable governance structure has to be developed in order to protect specific assets and coordinate the use of complementary resources and capabilities.

Firms establish different kinds of objectives and try to attain them through the development of diverse types of strategic alternatives. The KMS of a firm is thus based on the best possible strategic design in order to create, maintain, transfer and apply organizational knowledge to achieve competitive goals (Earl, 2001; Maier & Remus, 2002; Choi & Lee, 2003; Garavelli et al., 2004; Donate & Guadamillas, 2007; Donate & Canales, 2012). The development of a KMS includes all the operations related to the creation, acquisition, integration, storage, transmission, protection and application of knowledge (Day & Wendler, 1998). In relation to cooperation agreements, KMS is focus on managing those flows of knowledge which are linked to exploitation and exploration processes, depending on the goals and scope of the established cooperation agreement. Based on the work of Donate and Guadamillas (2007) and Donate and Canales (2012), four dimensions make up the KMS of a company:

1. Knowledge management (KM) conception;
2. KMS objectives;
3. KM practices and tools;
4. KM support systems.

KM Conception

Cooperation agreements enable the firm to acquire and/or exploit the knowledge of one or more partners in order to attain specific objectives and goals. In general terms, the KM concept refers to the company's strategic orientation in respect of knowledge, which is reflected in the way managers understand the potential contribution of KM for the firm. For example, they could understand that KM is just related to the use of information technologies or, conversely, be aware that it is a wider concept that includes both human and technical aspects (Huplic, Pouloudi, & Rzevski, 2002). In relation to cooperation agreements, it would express the main role that KM plays in the inter-organizational system. Obviously, the KM concept should be consistent with the alliance objectives because the more coherent they are, the more effective the final result of the cooperation agreement will be (Sánchez de Pablo, 2009).

KMS Objectives

This dimension could be understood as a company's orientation towards the solution of the knowledge "gap" in different operative and strategic areas within the organization: quality problems, efficiency searching, new product development, solutions to customer service failures, etc. (Zack, 1999; Earl, 2001, p. 229). In general, organizations attach greater importance to the accomplishment of certain objectives over others. Moreover, managers will consider that KS can contribute towards the fulfilment of objectives to a greater or a lesser degree. This fact may influence the way KM tools are designed and used in order to accomplish these objectives (Davenport, DeLong, & Beers, 1998). In relation to alliances, objectives are established to acquire, explore or exploit partner knowledge, thus influencing the KM tools, the governance structure of the alliance and its implementation support systems. Clearly, all these aspects will differ depending on the alliance goals. For instance, pursuing the improvement of technological capabilities as an objective is not the same as trying to improve the level of the efficiency in the manufacturing area.

KM Tools

These are the specific methods or initiatives used by the organization to support the creation, transfer, storage, retrieval and application of knowledge, and they could include technical and human components (Alavi & Leidner, 2001; Alavi & Tiwana, 2003). As Davenport et al. (1998, p. 44-45) point out these KM initiatives specifically seek to create knowledge repositories, to improve knowledge access and transfer or manage knowledge as an asset –including its protection. In addition, the organization could focus on several procedures in a comprehensive manner, or using some of its tools in a specific way. In an alliance, the main method for a partner to generate knowledge is through its acquisition, either on a voluntary basis or through learning by doing. Once the knowledge is created, mechanisms may be established to transfer knowledge from one location to another. Moreover, the storage of explicit knowledge can constitute a necessity, for which IT-based instruments built on a common basis could be very useful. Some initiatives might also be developed to apply the alliance knowledge, such as interdisciplinary teams or specific instruments based on IT, such as expert systems (Alavi & Tiwana, 2003). Finally, knowledge protection in the alliance is an important issue, although in some cases partners can protect their knowledge by establishing clauses in contracts, designing specific mechanisms (e.g. passwords, firewalls) or relying on the establishment of cooperation agreements in the future (Inkpen, 1998).

Implementation Support Systems

These are organizational aspects that should make the development of KM processes easier, such as a "knowledge-focused" culture, HR practices, flexible structures, and technical systems. Culture should promote knowledge exchange and sharing in order to allow for continual innovation and change (Nonaka, 1994).

Moreover, there are a number of essential changes that KM initiatives imply in HR practices to make implementation possible. Thus, those related to the promotion of access to or availability of the knowledge of experts, the development of work teams and communities of practices, or incentive methods for monitoring and controlling process systems, among others, stand out as important elements in accomplishing the strategic –knowledge– objectives of alliance partners. The implementation of a KMS should also be supported by a suitable structure, which encourages the attainment of objectives and the development of knowledge processes in the cooperative agreement. Finally, technical systems refer to IT-based tools used for developing (and making easier) certain knowledge processes, such as data bases, e-learning tools, intranets or other communication instruments among partners. In general, the promotion of inter-dependence among partners is an essential aspect in order to improve the impact of the KMS on the alliance performance. Inter-dependence has thus a key role by promoting cooperation (e.g., Dyer, 1997), generating synergies (e.g., Saxton, 1997), encouraging reciprocity (e.g., Wiklund & Shepherd, 2009), and leveraging commitment to and trust in the alliance (e.g., Kale et al., 2000) (1).

One of the most relevant aspects in the KMS development process is the design of the implementation support systems, which are referred to technical, human and organizational elements of KM in relation to the governance of the alliance. Owing to their importance, all these aspects will be analyzed next.

TECHNICAL AND ORGANIZATIONAL ASPECTS OF KMS IN COOPERATION AGREEMENTS

Culture

Culture may be understood as a collective thinking that identifies members in a group or category (Hofstede, 1991; Rodríguez & Wilson, 2002). For knowledge transfer that is produced among partners to generate learning, it is necessary that differences between knowledge bases of partners in a cooperation agreement exists (Lane & Lubatkin, 1998). At the same time, the relationship has to be close enough for an appropriate transfer of knowledge to take place (Mowery et al., 1998). So a balance concerning both aspects –knowledge base differences and integration– has to be achieved. When cultural distance is high, novelty in terms of knowledge increases albeit communication capacity among partners reduces as well. As learning is being developed among partners, their capacities tend to converge and knowledge transfer is considered to be a critical aspect (Evangelista & Hau, 2009).

As an alliance evolves, a common culture based on shared values is created, which generates trust and supports mutual learning among partners. New knowledge and shared capabilities are thus created, increasing the alliance value (Inkpen, 1998; Hitt et al., 2004). In other words, culture is related to trust, as cultural rules and values influence its development over time. In this sense, it is necessary to understand the partner's culture, by trying to identify which values are more beneficial to the alliance, along with those aspects that require a greater level of control. Moreover, trust and cultural adjustment are both interdependent elements, as poor cultural adjustment may produce suspicions among companies and generate a significant barrier in the way of building up mutual trust (Sampson, 2005; Wittman et al., 2009).

An additional aspect concerning culture in cooperation agreements is the existing link with HR management. In this sense, HR has to contribute in building a shared culture that strengthens the alliance and encourages employees to accept common objectives in addition to mutual identification with a common project, making the coordination and control processes easier in the domain of the cooperative agreement. This common culture reduces uncertainty, promotes the endeavors of partners, creates respect for the basic values of each partner, generates interdependence and facilitates conflict resolution (Guadamillas et al., 2006). In order to make it possible, information sharing, transparency, trust and leadership are necessary (Sampson, 2005).

HR Management

Quinn, Anderson, and Finkelstein (1996) point out a number of changes that KM implies for HR management in a firm. Practices that support the development of knowledge processes stand out, such as the development of teams and communities of practice, control based on the assessment of processes instead of results, or incentives that are designed in order to share knowledge. In a cooperation agreement, HR practices may have a significant influence on success since contribute to make the adjustment between corporate partners' cultures and specific HR practices of the companies easier (the establishment of common objectives and practices). Certain HR practices also offer more effective control mechanisms, promote inter-organizational learning, and encourage the selection and development of teams needed to share knowledge and work in an effective manner.

HR management should be designed to make the knowledge transfer among alliance partners easier, improve communication and promote trust, especially in terms of the reciprocal partners relationship (in which the search and selection processes for a partner are included), partner-alliance relationships (which seeks a coherent and structural integration of knowledge) and the search for an optimal management of the partners asymmetries in relation to culture, vision and values. The main HR practices that promote knowledge transfer and organizational learning are, among others: strategy and procedures training; development of a common culture for the alliance; promotion of the work teams; development of employees' careers; programs that supply for increased work experience at various locations, functions and countries through the transfer of explicit knowledge; development of handbooks for employee training; development of specific databases and electronic systems to gather, share and apply knowledge in the alliance domain.

Effective HR management should therefore contribute to the improvement of learning processes, create and exploit synergies and efficiency, and support the development of knowledge processes. In order to accomplish these objectives, critical aspects and potential HR issues derived from the cooperation agreement that the firm has to consider in relation to its KMS are:

1. Employees are reluctant to changes. In this sense, problems will depend on the alliance type (obviously, some agreements will imply more changes than others) and motives for the companies to establish the cooperation agreement (e.g., exploration vs. exploitation). Motivation systems and information transparency are required in order to make the implementation and acceptance of changes easier.
2. Owing to the independence that each firm maintains, partners should make the HR strategy that is developed in individual companies compatible with the HR strategy which is applied to the alliance, because problems could arise in relation to employees, such as:
   a. Company employees might perceive that the treatment given to employees connected with the alliance is better concerning certain HR practices: incentives, salary, social benefits, etc.
   b. Alliance employees might consider that the HR strategy is better for them than the strategy which is applied in their companies. Thus, when the alliance finishes and the employee returns to the company, a period of adjustment will be necessary to ensure that the employee's performance is not affected by such changes.
   c. Difficulties of adaptation to new work tasks that are developed in the ambit of the alliance, mainly as a consequence of cultural differences in relation to individual companies.
3. In some cases certain situations could arise, in which company executives might perceive their jobs as being threatened if there is a possibility of substituting certain tasks (e.g., outsourcing) by carrying them out in the ambit of the cooperation agreement. Therefore, a feeling of insecurity might appears and motivation could drop, all of which could affect firm performance.
4. Owing to the temporary nature of alliances, HR managers have to make an effort to motivate employees involved with the alliance to ensure they work properly. In this stage, the generation of an atmosphere that encourages innovation and knowledge exchange is an essential aspect; all the employees should know the objectives and meaning of the agreement and the positive and negative effects on their current situation.
5. The assignment of executives to the alliance. The rotation of executives linked to the agreement is a sensible manner in which to operate, not only on the basis of organizational learning but also by way of avoiding excessive dependence of a specific person in certain aspects of the KMS for the cooperation agreement.
6. Recruitment and selection of the rest of employees involved in the alliance. Personal recruitment may be carried out by each of the companies (partners) or jointly, taking into account the alliance features. Sometimes the personnel selected for the alliance is not suitable or some employees might be disappointed by the fact that they have not been selected to form part of the alliance personnel.
7. Controversies over rewards and salary systems. Incentive systems should be the same for the employees who are participating in the alliance, irrespective of what company they come from and whether they are working exclusively on the agreement or not. Nevertheless, certain problems related to rewards and incentives, such as justice and equity, could arise. In an attempt to avoid such issues, the design and establishment of a committee made up of members from all of the partners

is advisable in order to ensure that the incentives are paid as a result of the contribution to the alliance objectives without considering personal aspects (e.g., hierarchical position).

IT Systems

IT may play a critical role as a supportive tool in alliances and they can be said to help to explain the fast growth of networks in the last few years (Gulati et al., 2000). The utility of IT can be considerable in the management of important tasks of the agreement, such as the transmission and storage of knowledge and monitoring of activities.

Cooperation agreements reduce transaction risks as trust is generated among partners. In this sense, IT tools permit the storage of information about partners and thus, diminish organizational asymmetries. Moreover, they reduce the loss of information resources in the network (Clemons & Row, 1992). At the same time, IT tools also contribute to leverage the value created in alliances through the partners' joint use of design, engineering or computer assistance tools in manufacturing.

IT tools are a critical aspect of the activities of organizational knowledge management –knowledge and information access, transfer, sharing and storage. IT tools play a critical role in the management of the organizational knowledge owing to the fact that knowledge, under certain conditions (i.e., codification), can be handled as an object that can be split in modules (structured), gathered and subsequently transferred (Zander & Kogut, 1995; Sanchez & Mahoney, 1996).

IT are critical for enabling and supporting information and knowledge sharing processes among partners, which it allows them to generate specific routines and the obtaining of relational rents (Dyer & Singh, 1998). In most cases, these routines make partners an important source of information and ideas, which result in an innovative stream for the firm. However, organizational differences, and divergences in knowledge bases and IT structure among partners have an important influence on the way knowledge is managed in the alliance (Schmaltz, Hagenhoof, & Kaspar, 2004). Figure 1 shows how IT might support the alliance development and management, within the context of a knowledge management system both at firm and alliance level (considering two firms):

As the Figure 1 shows, alliance advantages can occur on two different levels:

1. Individual, through value creation during the interaction process between alliances management and social capital in each firm;
2. Dyadic, through the creation and improvement of specific inter-firm knowledge-sharing routines, which could be defined as "a regular pattern of inter-firm interactions that permits the transfer, recombination or creation of specialized knowledge, (…) and these are institutionalized inter-firm processes that are purposefully designed to facilitate knowledge exchanges between alliance partners" (Dyer and Singh, 1998: 665).

Two issues arise in relation to knowledge transfer among alliance partners, which affect IT tools and their use and effectiveness in supporting the creation and improvement of inter-firm routines and the potential for obtaining relational rents. First, IT tools are required for knowledge codification processes. In so doing, knowledge can be transferred across firm boundaries and can be understood among partners –including the development of a common code shared by firms in the cooperative relationship (Kogut & Zander, 1992) which could even constitute an advantage for partners (Oliveira, 1999). Moreover, IT

Figure 1. Knowledge management systems (KM systems), IT and alliances
Source: Guadamillas, Donate, and Sánchez de Pablo, 2006

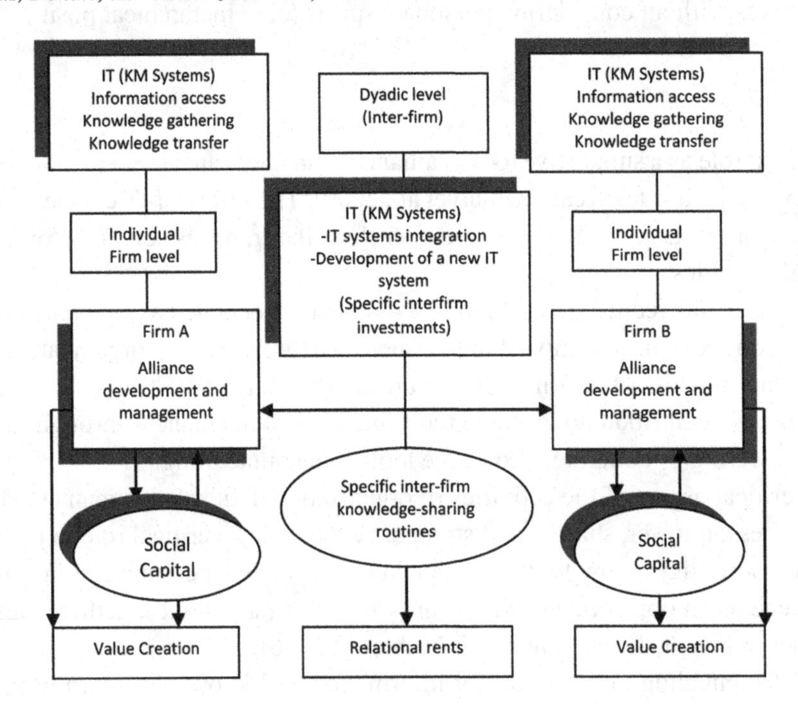

tools can improve the absorptive capacity of each alliance partner, through support for the development of overlapping knowledge bases and interaction among routines.

In general terms, the establishment of a coherent structure for the development of knowledge management in cooperation agreements implies solving some technical problems and taking decisions about what information technologies to use along with the design and implementation of the knowledge management system.

COOPERATION ISSUES RELATED TO KMS

In some cases, alliances fail or their results fall short of what was expected owing to problems in the sharing of knowledge between partners. The main difficulty is to face two potential concerns: to maintain an open knowledge exchange to achieve collaborative advantages; and to control knowledge flows to avoid the unintended leakage of valuable technology (Oxley & Sampson, 2004).

Firms often erect barriers that make the effective development of collaborative activities, knowledge sharing and transmission in alliances difficult. Based on Guadamillas et al. (2006), the main problems discussed in this section will be:

1. The characteristics of knowledge;
2. Distrust between partners;
3. Technological knowledge diversity; and
4. The organizational form or governance structure of alliances.

Characteristics of Knowledge

In order to carry out the alliance objectives successfully, it is essential a certain amount of specific knowledge to be shared between the participating partners. There are some difficulties in relation to knowledge transmission and sharing, especially when knowledge is specific, complex and tacit. This kind of knowledge is difficult to keep and transfer since it depends on the context, experience, language and previously accumulated knowledge (Grant, 1996; Oliveira, 1999). Tacit knowledge is difficult to share and transfer to other people (Nonaka and Takeuchi, 1995). The same problem arises with knowledge that is specific to a context or culture (Zander & Kogut, 1995). Transferring tacit and specific knowledge is a very costly and lengthy process. When knowledge is explicit, it is easier to share and to transfer, but it has less strategic value than tacit knowledge (Zander & Kogut, 1995). Anyway, the acquisition of tacit knowledge can be the main reason to participate in an alliance (Meier, 2011).

Protection of Strategic Knowledge

One of the main risks of cooperation agreements is the difficultly in protecting certain types of essential knowledge (Oxley & Sampson, 2004, p. 727): hints and ideas about strategy orientation, directions and partial results of technological research; competitive benchmarking data; codified knowledge contained in formulas, design and procedures; tacit knowledge involved in skills and routines and the essential competences of key employees that can be hired when the alliance is finished. The risk of the partner developing an opportunistic behaviour in the alliance and appropriating this kind of strategic knowledge is one of the main issues that discourage firms from participating in an alliance. On the other hand, the sharing of strategic knowledge is often necessary to achieve alliance objectives. Trust between participants is required in order to make the exchange of knowledge possible.

Mutual Distrust Among Partners

Firms are especially reluctant to share knowledge with companies that may become competitors in the future. Mechanisms and systems to reduce distrust and opportunism and to improve collaboration between partners are very important. The common space created in an alliance allows partners to share their tacit and explicit knowledge, their abilities and productive processes. Furthermore, if an adequate level of trust is attained it is possible to create and exchange new knowledge, especially of a tacit nature, which afterwards is assimilated by firms, leading them to improve their capabilities (Inkpen, 1998). Therefore, a goal for many cooperation agreements, carried out to access the partner's knowledge, is the internalization of knowledge that is generated in the alliance (Pérez-Nordtvedt et al., 2008). On the other hand, relational capital may arise as a consequence of recurrent relationships among partners that help to overcome mutual distrust (Dyer & Singh, 1998).

Alliance Organizational Structure

The lack of common routines, authority and hierarchical organizational forms may difficult cooperation, knowledge sharing and learning for alliance members. Although all organizational forms have certain disadvantages, partners have to implement the optimal option according to the nature of the agreement (joint ventures, alliances, joint equity ventures, etc.) and objectives. The more hierarchical the organizational forms are, the more they will make the control of processes and performance easier, albeit it also implies higher bureaucracy costs (Oxley and Sampson, 2004).

CASE STUDY ANALYSIS: KMS IN TECNOBIT'S COOPERATION AGREEMENTS

Introduction

In general, a case study aims to examine a "contemporary phenomenon within its real-life context" (Yin, 1994, p. 13). As a research method, it is viewed as improving our knowledge of individual and organizational phenomena (Van Maanen, 1979; Yin, 1994). Case studies primarily involve researchers undertaking an in depth study of a particular organization with a wide variety of information being collected as a result. In our case, we collected multiple data and information from interviews with one of the company's main directors and other company documents. In interviews, questions were kept unrestricted in order to encourage the manager to converse freely (Maykut & Morehouse, 1994). Extracts from internal reports, the company's web page and other relevant documentation were also used to make up the case study.

The analyzed company was chosen by authors for the case study since its growth strategy has been based both on internal development and external knowledge acquisitions from markets (licenses, equipment, employee hiring, purchases of companies) and cooperation agreements. The company was founded in 1976 as *DOI-Associate Engineers*. Located in Madrid (Spain) its main activity centred on the control of industrial processes. In 1981, an industrial plant was created in Valdepeñas (Ciudad Real, Spain) and the company's name was changed to Tecnobit. Over the next decade, the company's development took place: in 1983, an important contract was signed with the Spanish Ministry of Defence; in 1987, the command and control activities began; in 1992, the first EF-2000 contracts (avionics) were obtained; in 2000, the Tecnobit Group was created; and in 2003, companies that made up the Tecnobit Group were melted into a single legal entity. From 2004, a number of changes in shareholding have taken place and finally, the current name for the company is Tecnobit S.L., being its only shareholder Oesia Networks S.L. (formerly known as IT Deusto) from 2008. Nevertheless, Tecnobit has a great autonomy in management and juridical independence, although it is subjected to financial control by Osetia. It is also remarkable that although Tecnobit only represents 10% on total employees in Osetia, it contributes to 50% of the corporation's total sales, which it reflects the high added value of Tecnobit regarding the entire corporation.

Tecnobit is focused on five technological areas:

1. Avionics,
2. Command and control systems;
3. Simulation systems;
4. Optronics; and
5. Radio frequency.

It has three working centres, Alcobendas (Madrid, Spain), Valdepeñas (Ciudad Real, Spain) and Rio de Janeiro (Brasil) and around 400 employees (2014). Table 1 shows the evolution of its main financial figures.

Table 1. Main figures (evolution) in Tecnobit

Concept*	2008	2009	2010	2011	2012 (prov.)
Equity	37.9	43.3	47.5	50.5	52.4
Incomes	65.2	68.1	56.6	51.7	56.5
EBITDA	15.1	11.9	12.0	11.8	N.A
Net profit	6.9	6.0	3.6	1.2	3.0
Clients' portfolio	153.7	150.8	149.8	146.3	147.2
***Million €**					

Tecnobit has devoted, on average, 9% of sales income to R&D in the last few years (4.3 million € in 2011 and around 4million € in 2012). Moreover, in the last few years it has improved its efficiency due to the reduction of commercial and general expenses, achieve through functional and organizational restructuring, all of which is reflected in the financial performance of the company.

What is especially interesting about the evolution of the company is the way it has diversified its business lines, beginning with its main activity of aviation electronics (avionics) spreading to new simulation and training projects within the same industry (2), as well as towards the IT field, through the creation of command and control systems, the development of software, and knowledge management projects. The diversification has been carried out via internal development and knowledge acquisition through cooperation agreements and the purchase of certain companies. With the newly acquired companies, Tecnobit extended its activities beyond the electronics industry, to provide maintenance and technical support to other companies within the industry. During 2006-2010 and 2011-2014 plans, Tecnobit has furthered its expansion strategy, incorporating a computer services company and a radiofrequency company into the business portfolio, and it is currently consolidating its position and growth in related industries. One important point worth mentioning here is the company's effort towards its international expansion, for which the organizational structure has been re-organized (Figure 2).

In the last few years, and in order to face markets stagnation, Tecnobit is betting for product diversification and internationalization. Following this strategic change, the company's organizational structure has changed with the aim to search for new international opportunities and gain flexibility. The company has thus created commercial areas around geographical zones (Asia-Pacific, Middle-East, and North Europe). Moreover, Tecnobit is nowadays holding negotiations in order to enter into an Arab country. This is all reflected in the new Company's plan for 2015-2017.

The Tecnobit's internationalization strategy is strongly dependent of the geographical entry zone. In Asia-Pacific the first step is to get local commercial agents for the firm's representation in order to gain access to new projects. Sometimes, the company has chosen external growth through the acquisition of small firms with knowledge about the local market. This last strategy is difficult to accomplish as the number of potential firms to be acquired is small and legal barriers can be restrictive, especially in the Defence sector, for the direct entry of foreign firms.

From 2010 and in line with its diversification strategy, Tecnobit has also developed projects in the civil ambit, such as technologies embedded in glucometers (sensors to identify glucose levels in blood) for blind people. Moreover, the entry into the Space sector has been one of the most recent landmarks for the company. Specifically, Tecnobit has worked in activities for developing an electronic control

Figure 2. Tecnobit's organizational structure (2014)
**Financial services, administration.*

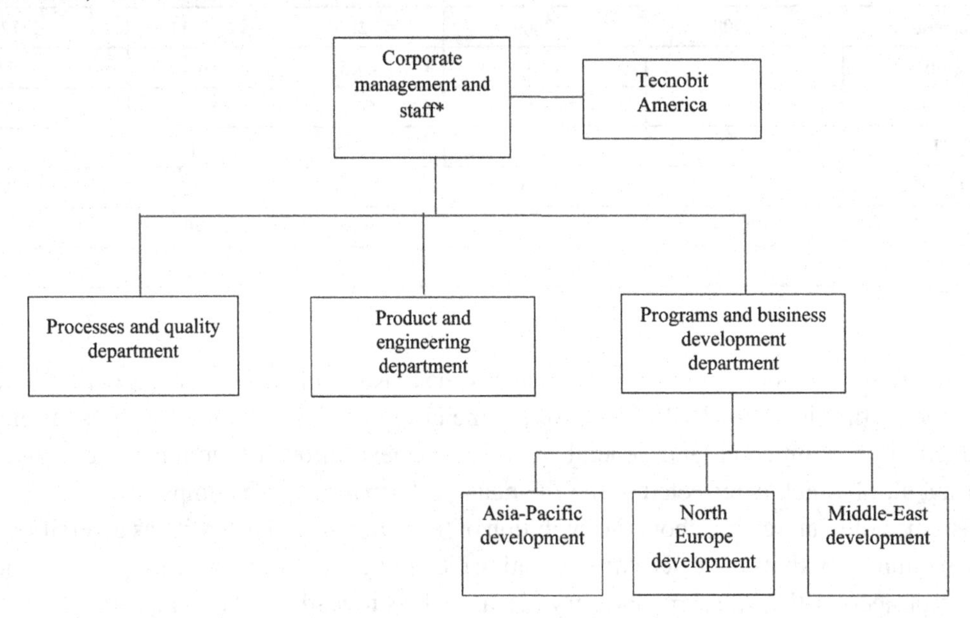

unit (ECU), a power supply unit (PSU) and radiofrequency distribution and control cards for an aerial of electronic sweep REDSAT, equipment that from 2013 are incorporated and currently working in the Hispasat satellite AG1.

Cooperation Agreements in Tecnobit

Cooperation agreements and the purchase of companies have been used by Tecnobit to acquire knowledge that the company did not possess and that would have been difficult and costly to develop internally. Frequently, the acquired knowledge has been complementary to existing knowledge, with which it has been successfully integrated, having in mind that the firm has a good level of absorptive capacity (Cohen & Levinthal, 1990), and occasionally, such knowledge has directly been used to break into new markets. The common characteristic for Tecnobit's cooperation agreements is therefore to take advantage of the complementarity of its partners' resources and capabilities. Moreover, Tecnobit gives priority in its technology agreements to "time to market" strategies since it considers a key point to arrive the first in the market. Time is important because the evolution of technologies is fast and gaining a time advantage implies significant entry barriers for competitors (e.g., contracts; incremental innovation; technology aging for time disadvantage). The firm thus considers essential to contact partners that gives the company the opportunity to lead technological developments in very specialized markets.

Alliances have been developed by Tecnobit to cover different objectives, both to exploit and explore knowledge in different areas (Grant & Baden-Fuller, 2004; Rothaermel & Deeds, 2004; Yang et al., 2014). Alliances frequently present themselves as an option for Tecnobit to grow technologically because involve less financial risk compared to other alternatives, such as company acquisitions. They are also suitable when technological capabilities are too difficult to develop internally and the firm would spend too much time in carrying it out (3). Tecnobit, besides technological alliances, has entered into cooperation agreements with other firms and institutions in financial, commercial, service, manufacturing and industrial domains (4). Sometimes, these firms have important differences to Tecnobit in aspects such as size, sectors or countries, but they are always characterized by complementary knowledge and a compatible culture which have enabled alliance objectives to be accomplished.

Certain Tecnobit's cooperation agreements have particular significance, though they are of a very different nature. On the one hand, in avionics, it has established an exploration alliance with the Israeli company, Rafael DM, on the joint development of a laser indicator (5). It has also been working with the U.S companies Lockheed Martin and Cubic Defence Electronics, in the development of different simulators. It is trying, for example, to adapt Cubic's air simulator (in which this company is the world's technological leader) to the terrestrial domain, such as in combat cars. In this typology of cooperation agreements, Tecnobit recently (2012) manufactured the Audio Management System (AMS), which was incorporated to the A400 M Aircraft for Airbus.

Furthermore, cooperation agreements have been developed with public institutions, such as the University of Castilla-La Mancha, University of Malaga and University of Barcelona for the development of different technological projects. In the civil ambit, from thechnologies developed in the military area, the alliance with Johnson & Johnson and the Medical Service of Castilla-La Mancha in Spain stands out for the development of glucometers.

Moreover, Tecnobit has channeled some of its cooperation agreements projects through its participation in official R&D programs (6), for which it has received financial support. For example, it has participated in the Technological Aeronautic Plan II, which includes important financial support for carrying out these investment projects. It also maintains collaboration projects for technological developments with other government research centers, such as the R&D Army Center of Spain (CIDA).

Tecnobit also has used cooperation agreements for technological development as a means to implement its international expansion. The origin of this strategy arose in 2008 with a specific project to supply two simulation centers for fire operations support (SAFO) which was developed through a contractual agreement with the Brazilian Army. From this agreement the company set up facilities in Rio de Janeiro close to the Brazilian Army School. In the last few years, the company is trying to use this center to gain access to Latin-American countries such as Peru, Chile and Ecuador.

Occasionally, and due to difficulties in incorporating certain capabilities and tacit knowledge into the organization through cooperation agreements or other means (imitation, hiring of technical experts, etc.), technology-intensive firms that had the required capabilities were directly acquired. Essentially, the explanation for these acquisitions is based on the knowledge characteristics to be transferred; that is to say, due to problems of causal ambiguity, high specificity and context-dependency, which would have made the transfer or replication of knowledge and capabilities difficult to carry out otherwise (DeCarolis & Deeds, 1999; Grant, 1996; Reed & DeFillipi, 1990).

KMS for Cooperation Agreements in Tecnobit

In this section, Tecnobit's KMS in cooperation agreements is exposed, distinguishing its objectives and KM conception, KM tools and the most significant aspects of the implementation support systems.

Objectives and KM Conception

As previously commented, objectives for KMS in alliances combine both exploitation and exploration issues. On the one hand, depending on the exact nature of these goals, cooperation agreements have ranged from joint ventures (in the case of exploration objectives in order to pool knowledge and other kinds of resources with the partner company) to contractual agreements and informal structures when the exploitation of the partner's knowledge and resources has been necessary. For Tecnobit, the more exploratory is the alliance, the more innovative will be the final aim of the cooperation agreement. Obviously, the structure of the alliance will be different in relation to tools and systems because the problems that need to be solved are different as well. On the other hand, the perspective of Tecnobit's managers concerning KM conception is clear: the company employees should bear in mind that the human and cultural component is as important as IT tools in the development of projects, and KM should not be only centered on information management but in trying to promote interaction and knowledge sharing among employees, and employees-partners in cooperation agreements.

IT Tools and Systems for KM

Tecnobit's current IT tools for knowledge management, apart from being oriented towards external markets, are widely used both in the internal organization and cooperation agreements. They are based on the use of web technologies in open and multi-platform systems, jointly with the development of applications and content with international standards through the use of document management and content tools. In terms of KM tools based on IT, the following stand out as being the most important: information and control systems, document management tools, storage systems and other data and information archive systems. Overall, these tools have been designed to assist in the creation, storage, retrieval, transfer and application processes of knowledge management, permitting the development of these processes in order to attain the company and alliance objectives in the ambit of KMS.

KMS Support Systems

Tecnobit considers that one of the main success factors in an alliance is trust between partners. For this reason, it considers necessary to develop a shared culture with its alliance partners. An optimal alliance plan is thus necessary, in which the search for a partner and the understanding of the partner´s culture are key issues. Consequently, Tecnobit selects partners that complement its culture in the search for common goals.

With the objective of enhancing efficiency and further integration whilst providing greater flexibility to its innovative activities and change, the organization has been structured around projects. The decision-making process is, therefore, decentralized, on the basis that the closer the decision unit is to the decision to be taken, the better qualified is to do it. This kind of flexible structure is applied in some exploration alliances under which the integration of employees from different companies is required. Tecnobit has developed a policy whereby employees are continuously moving between projects, thus increasing flexibility. In doing so, communication between employees and knowledge transfer becomes easier.

Moreover, it exists a high level of flexibility since the employees are assigned to diverse projects within different lines of activity to cover the alliance needs, thus trying to develop a "concurrent engineering" where employees "can think about everything", as they have a global vision of the company's projects. As a result, the employees move within all lines of activity, which promotes knowledge sharing and stimulates creativity (Nonaka and Takeuchi, 1995). This organizational structure also allows Tecnobit to rapidly respond to changing customer needs and preferences, which ultimately permits its adjustment to the dynamic and complex conditions of the environment.

In addition, the main HR practices of Tecnobit that support KM processes in alliances are:

- The design and implementation of extensive training practices.
- The use of teamwork. The firm considers that teamwork is the best option in order to achieve its alliance goals. The interaction between employees from different firms increases shared knowledge, making the development of learning processes possible. In teamwork it is important to select the most suitable employees to achieve the common objectives. Moreover, a continual negotiation process should be carried out between partners to immediately solve the problems that may arise from the alliance.
- The specific contracting of highly qualified external employees.
- The identification of internal employees with the best abilities, skills and qualifications to work in each activity of the alliance. HR practices may contribute to the alliance success if managers are able to identify employees with the ability to establish better interpersonal relationships, on the basis that they have more highly developed social abilities and are able to learn and transfer knowledge more easily. During the last year, certain exploratory studies have been carried out in Tecnobit in order to identify the most suitable employees from a learning perspective in terms of its intra-organizational learning network. With this perspective in mind, managers could develop reward systems and motivational schemes for their employees and adjust their management style to the existing conditions (Sánchez de Pablo et al., 2008).
- The design and implementation of incentives systems to promote specific aspects in the alliance, such as knowledge sharing or the extensive use of IT.
- The development of a shared culture between partners. The importance of a shared culture has been previously analyzed but it is necessary to emphasize that Tecnobit fosters a shared culture which encourages employees to accept a common alliance vision. Thus, more benefits can be obtained by making the coordination and control of common activities easier; (control must be carried out on two levels: individual and inter-organizational).
- The design of employees' careers. Usually, alliances are of a temporary nature, in other words, their time span is limited. In order to avoid uncertainty among employees working in the alliance, Tecnobit has developed well-established career plans for employees in the company.
- The development of a balanced remuneration plan within the alliance. Its main objective is to avoid situations of unfair compensation on each side of the alliance.
- The use of electronic databases and other specific IT solutions.
- Finally, it is important to note that these practices allow for some degree of individual and group autonomy while ensuring the achievement of the goals of the cooperation agreement. Table 2 summarizes KMS in Tecnobit's cooperation agreements.

CONCLUSION

In this chapter, KMS in alliances has been pointed out as an instrument to achieve the objectives of partners by establishing the company's orientation towards KM, tools and instruments to develop knowledge processes, and systems to support the KMS implementation, amongst which HR practices and flexible structures are included. Organizational problems in alliances concerning knowledge management have

Table 2. KMS in Tecnobit's cooperation agreements

Dimensions	Brief explanation	
KM Concept	To obtain knowledge and integrate it to achieve exploration or exploitation objectives, bearing in mind that KM is not only related to IT management but that cultural and human factors are also very important for alliance success.	
KMS Objectives	Exploitation of partners' technologies and resources to gain in respect of quality, efficiency or service to clients.	
	Exploration of partners' knowledge in order to improve innovation capabilities and learning.	
KM Tools	Knowledge creation	Socialization and sharing of knowledge through formal and informal meetings, teamwork and tools based on IT.
		Interdisciplinary teams with university researchers
	Knowledge storage	Databases for each common project
	Knowledge protection	Confidentiality and non-concurrence agreements in contracts
Implementation support systems	Culture	To establish principles and values based on the transfer and sharing of knowledge among partners in relation to alliance goals
		To develop inter-organizational knowledge networks through cooperative projects
	HR Practices	Promotion of access to databases
		Rewards given to employees who suggest new ideas and share their knowledge
		To assign key employees to the alliance
	Structure	Work teams, joint ventures, contracts or informal structures, depending on the alliance objectives (exploration vs. exploitation)
	Technical Systems	Databases, data-mining, data warehousing
		Collaborative systems based on networking

also been addressed. Finally, the way in which an innovation-intensive company establishes its KMS based on different alternatives of knowledge exploration or exploitation in alliances, has been drawn.

Although each alliance implies the development and implementation of a specific KMS, the analysis of this Company shows how, in order to face strong competitive requirements, the coherence of the KMS in relation to the aim of the cooperation agreement has to be importantly considered by managers. Aspects concerning the exploration or exploitation of knowledge that is generated, shared and applied also have to be analyzed by each partner, such as: the exclusivity and complementary domains of strategic knowledge; the creation of new knowledge; and finally, rent appropriation, mainly by the establishment of mechanisms that allow each partner to protect its knowledge domain while knowledge sharing is maximized and leveraged. Managers should thus ask themselves certain questions concerning the structure and governance of the cooperation agreement, such as: how could new knowledge be developed and what are the factors that have an influence in this process? For each factor considered, what kinds of mechanisms are available for the company and how could they be used to facilitate knowledge management? In this sense, is the flexibility of the existing organizational alliance adequate? How IT tools could be better utilized to manage knowledge in the alliance? What kind of HR practices would facilitate sharing of knowledge among partners, while minimizing the risk of undue appropriation of strategic knowledge?

The response to all these questions implies the design of an adequate KMS for the alliance, wherein objectives, KM conception, KM tools to be used and implementation systems (structure, HR practices, and culture) should be coherent and support the overall strategy of the organization. Particularly, it is especially important to manage cultural elements and deal with human issues (Kale et al., 2000; Bhagat et al., 2002). In so doing, transfer of knowledge is possible to carry out, both to exploit and explore knowledge from other partner(s). As the case study of Tecnobit shows, in dynamic markets, companies have difficulties in order to grow, enter into new markets or be technologically innovative, meaning that alliances are essential to gain access to complementary knowledge (Arend et al., 2014). Firms also have to search for technological solutions in order to store, create and transfer knowledge effectively in the alliance, whilst protecting their most valuable knowledge from imitation. Hence, it is more difficult for a partner to imitate tacit than explicit knowledge, which should be protected from appropriation through some kind of mechanism. Anyhow, for a firm to be able to assimilate and exploit a partner's knowledge, it requires a certain amount of absorptive capacity, which ultimately depends on its capabilities (Cohen & Levinthal, 1990). Trust is also a key factor for a successful cooperation agreement, since it is a link between partners' responsible behavior and knowledge sharing in the alliance. Consequently, in an alliance, KMSs should be oriented to generate trust along with an adequate environment to achieve objectives and goals by all partners.

Tecnobit is nowadays in a situation of changes for its adaptation to a new strategy that from 2012 is betting for product diversification and the entry in new geographical markets. The success of this new strategy depends on commercial aspects (how to entry in new markets) and technological challenges (what aspects of the technologies will be the most appreciated by customers). Cooperation agreements will be necessary in both cases to achieve strategic objectives. The exploitation of current technologies and the exploration of knowledge through new projects of R&D (both individual and collaborating with partners) will be essential aspects to assure the sustainability of the firm's competitive advantage.

The adjustments that Tecnobit has carried out in the last few years in its internal organization (structure) and human resource management are fundamental aspects for the support of the new strategy. The change in the perspective regarding its portfolio of technologies from technological areas to products seems coherent with this new strategic path that is being developed by the firm. Moreover, Tecnobit will continue to make an effort to invest and develop new projects in R&D in order new emergent technologies to be created, giving a proper balance to its technology portfolio in the future.

REFERENCES

Alavi, M., & Leidner, D. (2001). Knowledge management and knowledge management systems: Conceptual foundations and research issues. *Management Information Systems Quarterly*, *25*(1), 107–136. doi:10.2307/3250961

Alavi, M., & Tiwana, A. (2003). Knowledge management: The information technology dimension. In M. Easterby-Smith & M. A. Lyles (Eds.), *Organizational learning and knowledge management* (pp. 104–121). London: Blackwell Publishing.

Arend, R. J., Patel, P. C., & Park, H. D. (2014). Explaining post-IPO venture performance through a knowledge-based view typology. *Strategic Management Journal*, *35*(3), 376–397. doi:10.1002/smj.2095

Bhagat, R. S., Kedia, B. L., Harveston, P. D., & Triandis, H. C. (2002). Cultural variations in the cross-border transfer of organizational knowledge: An integrative framework. *Academy of Management Review*, *27*, 204–221.

Chan, K., & Liebowitz, J. (2006). The synergy of social network analysis and knowledge mapping: A case study. *Int. J. Management and Decision Making*, *7*(1), 19–35. doi:10.1504/IJMDM.2006.008169

Choi, B., & Lee, H. (2003). An empirical investigation of knowledge management styles and their effect on corporate performance. *Information & Management*, *40*, 403–417. doi:10.1016/S0378-7206(02)00060-5

Clemons, E. K., & Row, M. C. (1992). Information technology and industrial cooperation: The changing economics of coordination and ownership. *Journal of Management Information Systems*, *9*(2), 9–28. doi:10.1080/07421222.1992.11517956

Cohen, W. M., & Levinthal, D. A. (1990). Absorptive capacity: A new perspective on learning and innovation. *Administrative Science Quarterly*, *35*(1), 28–152. doi:10.2307/2393553

Davenport, T., DeLong, D., & Beers, M. (1998). Successful knowledge management projects. *Sloan Management Review*, *39*(2), 43–57.

Day, J. D., & Wendler, J. C. (1998). Best practices and beyond: Knowledge strategies. *The McKinsey Quarterly*, *1*, 19–25.

Donate, M. J., & Canales, J. I. (2012). A new approach to the concept of knowledge strategy. *Journal of Knowledge Management*, *16*(1), 22–44. doi:10.1108/13673271211198927

Donate, M. J., & Guadamillas, F. (2007). The relationship between innovation and knowledge strategies: Its impacts on business performance. *International Journal of Knowledge Management Studies*, *1*(3/4), 388–422. doi:10.1504/IJKMS.2007.012532

Dyer, J. H. (1997). Effective interfirm collaboration: How transactors minimize transaction costs and maximize transaction value. *Strategic Management Journal*, *18*(7), 535–556. doi:10.1002/(SICI)1097-0266(199708)18:7<535::AID-SMJ885>3.0.CO;2-Z

Dyer, J. H., & Singh, H. (1998). The relational view: Cooperative strategies and sources of interorganizational competitive advantage. *Academy of Management Review*, *23*(4), 660–679.

Earl, M. (2001). Knowledge management strategies: Toward a taxonomy. *Journal of Management Information Systems*, *18*(1), 215–233.

Evangelista, F., & Hau, L. N. (2009). Organizational context and knowledge acquisition in IJVs: An empirical study. *Journal of World Business*, *44*(1), 63–73. doi:10.1016/j.jwb.2008.03.016

Garavelli, C., Gorgoglione, M., & Scozzi, B. (2004). Knowledge management strategy and organization: A perspective of analysis. *Knowledge and Process Management*, *11*(4), 273–282. doi:10.1002/kpm.209

Grant, R. M. (2002). *Contemporary strategy analysis. Concepts, techniques, and applications* (4th ed.). Boston: Blackwell Publishers.

Grant, R. M., & Baden-Fuller, C. (2004). A knowledge accessing theory of cooperation agreements. *Journal of Management Studies*, *41*(1), 61–79. doi:10.1111/j.1467-6486.2004.00421.x

Guadamillas, F., Donate, M. J., & Sánchez de Pablo, J. D. (2006). Sharing knowledge in cooperation agreements to build collaborative advantage. In S. Martínez-Fierro, J. A. Medina-Garrido, & J. Ruiz-Navarro (Eds.), *Utilizing information technology in developing cooperation agreements among organizations* (pp. 99–122). Hershey, PA: IGI Global.

Gulati, R., Nohria, N., & Zaheer, L. (2000). Strategic networks. *Strategic Management Journal, 21*(3), 203–215. doi:10.1002/(SICI)1097-0266(200003)21:3<203::AID-SMJ102>3.0.CO;2-K

Hamel, G. (1991). Competition for competence and interpartner learning within international cooperation agreements. *Strategic Management Journal, 12*, 83–103. doi:10.1002/smj.4250120908

Hitt, M. A., Ireland, R. D., & Santoro, M. D. (2004). Developing and managing cooperation agreements, building social capital and creating value. In A. Ghobadian et al. (Eds.), *Strategy and performance: Achieving competitive advantage in the global marketplace*. New York: Palgrave. doi:10.1057/9780230523135_2

Hofstede, G. (1991). *Cultures and organizations: Software of the mind*. New York: McGraw-Hill.

Huplic, V., Pouloudi, A., & Rzevski, G. (2002). Towards an integrated approach to knowledge management: Hard, soft, and abstract issues. *Knowledge and Process Management, 9*(2), 90–102. doi:10.1002/kpm.134

Inkpen, A. C. (1998). Learning, knowledge acquisitions, and cooperation agreements. *European Management Journal, 16*(2), 223–229. doi:10.1016/S0263-2373(97)00090-X

Inkpen, A. C. (2000). A note on the dynamics of learning alliances: Competition, cooperation, and relative scope. *Strategic Management Journal, 21*(7), 775–779. doi:10.1002/1097-0266(200007)21:7<775::AID-SMJ111>3.0.CO;2-F

Inkpen, A. C., & Beamish, P. W. (1997). Knowledge, bargaining power, and the instability of international. *Joint Ventures Academy of Management Review, 22*(1), 177–202.

Ireland, R. D., Hitt, M. A., & Vaidyanath, D. (2002). Alliance management as a source of competitive advantage. *Journal of Management, 28*(3), 413–446. doi:10.1177/014920630202800308

Kale, P., Singh, H., & Perlmutter, H. (2000). Learning and protection of proprietary assets in cooperation agreements: Building relational capital. *Strategic Management Journal, 21*, 217–237. doi:10.1002/(SICI)1097-0266(200003)21:3<217::AID-SMJ95>3.0.CO;2-Y

Khanna, T., Gulati, R., & Nohria, N. (1998). The dynamics of learning alliances: Competition, cooperation, and relative scope. *Strategic Management Journal, 19*(3), 193–210. doi:10.1002/(SICI)1097-0266(199803)19:3<193::AID-SMJ949>3.0.CO;2-C

Kogut, B., & Zander, U. (1992). Knowledge of the firms, combinative capabilities, and the replication of technology. *Organization Science, 3*(3), 383–397. doi:10.1287/orsc.3.3.383

Lane, P. J., & Lubatkin, M. (1998). Relative absorptive capacity and interorganizational learning. *Strategic Management Journal, 19*(5), 461–477. doi:10.1002/(SICI)1097-0266(199805)19:5<461::AID-SMJ953>3.0.CO;2-L

Liebowitz, J. (2007). Developing knowledge and learning strategies in mobile organisations. *International Journal Mobile Learning and Organizations*, *1*(1), 5–14. doi:10.1504/IJMLO.2007.011186

Luo, Y. (2008). Structuring interorganizational cooperation: The role of economic integration in cooperation agreements. *Strategic Management Journal*, *29*(6), 617–637. doi:10.1002/smj.677

Maier, R., & Remus, U. (2002). Defining process-oriented knowledge management strategies. *Knowledge and Process Management*, *9*(2), 103–118. doi:10.1002/kpm.136

Meier, M. (2011). Knowledge management in cooperation agreements: A review of empirical evidence. *International Journal of Management Reviews*, *13*, 1–23. doi:10.1111/j.1468-2370.2010.00287.x

Mesquita, L. F., Anand, J., & Brush, T. H. (2008). Comparing the resource-based and relational views: Knowledge transfer and spillover in vertical alliances. *Strategic Management Journal*, *29*(9), 913–941. doi:10.1002/smj.699

Mowery, D. C., Oxley, J. E., & Silverman, B. S. (1998). Technological overlap and interfirm cooperation: Implications for the resource-based view of the firm. *Research Policy*, *27*(5), 507–523. doi:10.1016/S0048-7333(98)00066-3

Nonaka, I. (1994). A dynamic theory of organizational knowledge creation. *Organization Science*, *5*(1), 14–37. doi:10.1287/orsc.5.1.14

Nonaka, I., & Takeuchi, H. (1995). *The knowledge-creating company*. New York: Oxford University Press.

Oliveira, M. (1999). Core competencies and the knowledge of the firm. In M. A. Hitt, (Eds.), *Dynamic strategic resources: Development, diffusion, and integration* (pp. 17–41). New York: John Wiley and Sons.

Oxley, J. E., & Sampson, R. C. (2004). The scope and gobernance of international R&D alliances. *Strategic Management Journal*, *25*(89), 723–749. doi:10.1002/smj.391

Pérez-Nordtvedt, L., Kedia, B. L., Datta, D. K., & Rasheed, A. A. (2008). Effectiveness and efficiency of cross-border knowledge transfer: An empirical examination. *Journal of Management Studies*, *45*(4), 714–744. doi:10.1111/j.1467-6486.2008.00767.x

Rodríguez, C. M., & Wilson, D. T. (2002). Relationship bonding and trust as a foundation for commitment in U.S.-Mexican cooperation agreements: A structural equation modeling approach. *Journal of International Marketing*, *10*(4), 53–76. doi:10.1509/jimk.10.4.53.19553

Sampson, R. C. (2005). Experience effects and collaborative returns in R&D alliances. *Strategic Management Journal*, *26*(11), 1009–1031. doi:10.1002/smj.483

Sanchez, R., & Mahoney, J. T. (1996). Modularity, flexibility, and knowledge management in product and organization design. *Strategic Management Journal*, *17*(S2), 63–76. doi:10.1002/smj.4250171107

Sánchez de Pablo, J. D. (2009). Influencia de la estrategia genérica de la empresa en la estrategia empresarial. *Revista Europea de Dirección y Economía de la Empresa*, *18*(4), 155–174.

Sánchez de Pablo, J. D., Guadamillas, F., Dimovski, V., & Škerlavaj, M. (2008). Exploratory study of organizational learning network within a Spanish high-tech company. *Proceedings of Rijeka Faculty of Economics Journal of Economics and Business*, *26*(2), 257–277.

Saxton, T. (1997). The effects of partner and relationship characteristics on alliances outcomes. *Academy of Management Journal*, *40*(2), 443–461. doi:10.2307/256890

Schmaltz, R., Hagenhoff, S., & Kaspar, C. (2004). *Information technology support for knowledge management in cooperation.* Paper presented at the Fifth European Conference on Organizational Knowledge, Learning, and Capabilities, Innsbruck, Austria.

Spender, J. C. (1996). Making knowledge the basis of a dynamic theory of the firm. *Strategic Management Journal*, *17*(S2), 45–62. doi:10.1002/smj.4250171106

Stuart, T. E. (2000). Interorganizational alliances and the performance of firms: A study of growth and innovation rates in a high-technology industry. *Strategic Management Journal*, *21*(8), 791–811. doi:10.1002/1097-0266(200008)21:8<791::AID-SMJ121>3.0.CO;2-K

Wiklund, J., & Shepherd, D. A. (2009). The Effectiveness of Alliances and Acquisitions: The Role of Resource Combination Activities. *Entrepreneurship Theory and Practice*, *33*(1), 193–212. doi:10.1111/j.1540-6520.2008.00286.x

Wittmann, C. M., Hunt, S. D., & Arnett, D. B. (2009). Explaining alliance success: Competences, resources, relational factors, and resource-advantage theory. *Industrial Marketing Management*, *38*(7), 743–756. doi:10.1016/j.indmarman.2008.02.007

Yang, H., Zheng, Y., & Zhao, X. (2014). Exploration or exploitation? Small firms alliance strategies with large firms. *Strategic Management Journal*, *35*(1), 146–157. doi:10.1002/smj.2082

Zack, M. (1999). Developing a knowledge strategy. *California Management Review*, *41*(3), 125–145. doi:10.2307/41166000

Zander, U., & Kogut, B. (1995). Knowledge and the speed of transfer and imitation of organizational capabilities: An empirical test. *Organization Science*, *6*(1), 76–92. doi:10.1287/orsc.6.1.76

ENDNOTES

[1] Luo (2008) points out that inter-dependence is based on resource interdependence, strategic links and relational and structural aspects. Luo (2008) also stresses the importance of economic integration, defined as the interdependence which is created by partners in relation to resources that have been jointly generated and their future use.

[2] Some examples are: electro-optical sensors, command systems, and naval and aviation control systems.

[3] Joint ventures have been occasionally used by Tecnobit in order to reduce risks and generate new technologies.

[4] In order to develop these alliances, the firm should have abilities for alliance government, as the success of the alliance, in terms of objectives achievement, strongly depends on them (Ireland, Hitt and Vaidyanath, 2002).

[5] In this sense, the enlargement of Tecnobit's facilities has actually been carried out to appropriately face cooperative projects with this company.

[6] Among these programs, ATICA, PATI, CEDETI and PROFIT are the most important ones.

Chapter 7
Online Real Estate Demand Chain Integration

Emna Cherif
DePaul University, USA

ABSTRACT

In this paper, we propose a solution for demand chain management using APIs (application programming interfaces) integration in the online real estate. We propose online real estate management system that includes advanced modules that can be bundled together, creating differentiation and enhancing the value chain. We propose a simplified implementation architecture for an integrated demand and supply chain management system for online real estate services. We use a formal specification language for specifying the functional components of the demand chain management system and interaction with real estate entities and actors. We choose an open source Customer Relationship Management system as a platform to manage some of the online real estate modules. Other value-added modules are integrated from third-party providers using their open interfaces.

INTRODUCTION

Real estate is an information-intensive business. Agents connect buyers to sellers through control and dissemination of information (e.g., via the Multiple Listing Service, MLS). Agents have valued information skills that they bring to make both listing and sales. Since houses are expensive, not easily describable and infrequently bought or sold, most people still feel the need for assistance with this transaction from a professional. As well, these are all factors that tend to keep the transactions costs high

Nowadays, buyers and sellers can use the Internet to list and search for houses, potentially by-passing traditional real-estate agents. Thus, the mediating role of real estate agents have been reduced or eliminated because the Internet permits the buyer and seller to manage their relationship directly.

The growth of real estate commerce on the internet and the number of new sites providing real estate tools and information has also affected both real estate practices and the roles of industry players. As a result, changes in this industry will have significant impact on the interaction between the real estate system and the real estate entities.

DOI: 10.4018/978-1-5225-1680-4.ch007

Also, the rapid development of the internet, especially web-based information transfer between companies, their suppliers, their customers, and various service providers, has improved information management in supply chains (Johnson & Whang, 2002).

Supply management has focused on moving products and services downstream towards the customer. Demand chain management changes the emphasis towards 'customization', responding to product and service opportunities offered by specific customers or customer groups sharing particular characteristics.

The markets have become much more volatile, and under such conditions the old assumptions are not always valid. Gattorna (2010), Christopher and Holweg (2011)Harrington et al. (2011), and Ericsson (2011a) argue for a critical review and reinvention of current supply chain models.

Madhani (2015) presents various frameworks and models for understanding DCM and its key drivers.

Through a DCM approach, firms could enhance the overall efficiency by interlinking the marketing and SCM operations, and at the same time meet the long-term strategic goals and maximize CLV.

Soosay and Hyland (2015) aims to review the literature and address how well the body of knowledge on supply chain collaboration corresponds with our contemporary society pertaining to some key themes, and also to provide a discussion on areas for future research.

Donovan and Manuj (2015) explains the complex process of strategic demand management by developing a comprehensive theoretical framework that integrates research focused on diverse aspects of demand management such as product characteristics, environmental uncertainties, operational strategies, integration between supply and demand processes, and performance outcomes.

Ceren (2015) builds up a conceptual framework for sustainable demand chain management (SDCM) and calls for further research on the integration between marketing and SSCM both at the theoretical and empirical levels.

Santosa and D'Antone (2014) presents a comprehensive framework of intra-firm departmental integration and reconnect the framework to related contributions in marketing and supply chain management literature to improve the DCM approach. It outcomes refine and show the complexity of the idea of alignment (integration) between the demand and supply chains proposed by the DCM approach.

Agrawal (2012) explore various factors of DCM that would help firms in enhancing their market responsiveness capabilities in a dynamic business scenario.

Bustinza et al. (2013) aims to understand how firms manage their product and service offerings, integrating supply chain management (SCM) and demand chain management (DCM) strategies.

Madhani (2013) discusses the issues of the marketing led firms and the supply chain management (SCM) led firms. It aims to investigate between the renewed emphasis and interests in integration of marketing and SCM in the form of demand chain management (DCM).

Özcanl (2012) propose a framework for CRM on-demand system evaluation, especially for SMEs that need guidance in choosing a cost effective and reliable CRM on-demand solution among the various systems in the saturated CRM on-demand market.

Gattorna (2010) stresses that people and their behavior, and not technology, is driving the development of supply chains. Several areas of human activity along the supply chains must be examined and treated as social, economic and behavioral systems (Ericsson, 2011a).

The secret of designing superior supply chains is to start by re-segmenting customers along behavioral lines and then reverse engineer from there (Gattorna, 2010). The segmentation of customers together with product service and process differentiation to fit the segments are fundamental concepts in marketing. However, the use of marketing knowledge to guide the development of differentiated supply chains has not been overwhelming.

Juttner et al. (2010) discuss a strategic integration framework that captures the integration between marketing and supply chain strategies at the business unit level. It also supports the notion that marketing and supply chain strategy integration contributes to the effectiveness of business strategies in the whole network.

Frohlich & Westbrook (2002) introduce four web-based demand and supply integration strategies that describe the extent to which companies are using the Internet in integration with their suppliers or customers.

Taylor (2000) studied the effect of demand amplification in the supply chain and proposes a 7 step process approach to eliminate it.

The value driven operations model is the combination of business processes, management systems, organization structure and culture that makes it possible to deliver the value offer.

The operations model can be designed and developed in the way described by Ericsson(2011a).

Gartner comes very close to the DCM philosophy in the definition of a demand -driven value chain as "A system of technologies and processes that senses and responds to real-time demand signals across a supply network of customers, suppliers and employees" (Gartner, 2011).

Ericsson (2011a) creates a distinctive competence for the chain as a whole that helps to identify and satisfy customer needs and wishes. Ericsson (2011b) presents one practical approach to implement the theories put forth by (Ericsson,2011a)

Christopher (2000) discusses the concept of agility and identifies the four characteristics of an agile supply chain that includes market sensitivity as it relates to demand chain.

Georgiadis et al. (2001) describe the design and the implementation of a demand driven freight transport application, concentrating mainly on IT system architecture of the solution.

Childerhouse et al. (2002) proposed six steps methodological framework to develop focused demand chain strategy for each cluster of products commercialized by a company.

Ayers & Malmberg (2002) develop a four stages maturity model to show key enablers of supply chain improvement. Both for supply chain organization and demand chain supply chain.

Harrison (2003) proposes a framework to match supply chain strategies with product and industries. These strategies are Push-based, Pull-based and hybrid Push-Pull.

AMR research report (2005) introduces the concept of Demand-Driven Supply Network (DDSN) and propose 5 cross-functional strategies to become DDSN.

Godsell et al (2006) propose an approach including marketing that offers an integrated demand chain/supply chain with a number of activities.

Ayers (2006) advocates that the demand-driven supply chain changes many of the conditions that cause wasteful variation in supply chain production. He mentions that the foundation and the implementation of the "lean" chain helps establish the operating range for low-cost production supply chain.

This literature deals mainly with concepts and methodological frameworks for demand-driven supply chains. However, in this paper we are mainly interested in practical system level design for real estate online industry.

This emergence of the internet could change the planning and management of all activities involved in all logistics management activities. This also includes the coordination and collaboration with suppliers, intermediaries and third party services providers and customers.

The internet could also impact the demand chain activities; this includes the creation of a coordinated flows of demand. The type of the interaction between the different entities could also be impacted by the internet.

Customer relationship management (CRM) is a model for managing interactions between companies and their current and future customers. It involves using technology to organize, automate, and synchronize sales, technical support, customer service and marketing (CRM, wiki).

There are new CRM products called CRM on demand. On-demand, hosted delivery and cloud computing are the terms used to describe the shift in CRM and other business systems which now use the Web to deliver online access to hosted business software based on a subscription payment plan and managed by a third party organisation; as opposed to the former purchase, installation and maintenance of on-premise business systems.

This definition is different from CRM that supports on demand chain that will discuss later.

As the focus changes from supply chains to demand chains, strong customer relationships and the ability to harness customer insight continue to underline strong corporate performance.

CRM is about gaining customer insight and executing that insight through customer-centric processes to increase revenue and margin, and reduce costs, by focusing resources on the most profitable customers, and aligning processes and services to customer needs.

CRM supports Demand Management by implementing customer centric processes that enable customer management processes across all channels in order to effectively influence the customer.

Keith et al. (2008) identify a core group of expected CRM benefits and examine their ability to increase a firm's value equity, relationship equity and brand equity which are components of customer equity.

Hossein et al. (2012) explore and evaluate the important factors in CRM system design and implementation in the organizations. Their research methodology consists of studying and reviewing relevant literature related to the essential topics of CRM projects implementation.

In the last decade, packaged software solutions became very popular. These created "large information islands", where if common data had to change, it had to be updated manually. Long term scalable solutions were required. These solutions are called "Enterprise Application Integration" techniques.

There exist two types of integration architectures, Direct point-to-point (PTP) and Middleware-based.

Point-to-point is the basic traditional approach, used situations where we have few systems to integrate. The tight coupling, number of integration points, and dependence, are all major disadvantages.

Middleware-based provides layer to mediate between applications using generic interfaces. Once the logical architecture has been selected, There are three common integration methods:

Data-level integration, User interface (UI)-level integration, Application-level integration.

- **Data-Level Integration:** The backend data stores of the relevant application are integrated, and may be either pull or push based.
- **User Interface (UI)-Level Integration:** Ties integration logic to user interface code, and maybe either proxy or scripting based.
- **Application-Level Integration:** It uses APIs that allows invoking business logic to preserve data integrity.

After reviewing the real estate literature, almost all papers analyzing the Internet impact on the real estate industry in USA do not provide specifications details (Sawyer et al., 2005; Federal Trade Commission, 2007). Other work considers model specifications in different environments (Arvantis et al., 2004).

Sawyer et al, (2005) discuss three industry-level changes in the US residential real estate industry due to the uses of information and communication technologies (ICT) over a 10-year period of rapid computerization. They don't deal with model specifications.

We notice that the UML language (Unified Modeling Language) is used in the cadastral information system in term of functional, static and dynamics models (Mutambo, 2003; Eleni et al., 2003). A cadastre (also spelled cadaster), using a cadastral survey or cadastral map, is a comprehensive register of the metes-and-bounds real property of a country. In most countries, legal systems have developed around the original administrative systems and use the cadastre to define the dimensions and location of land parcels described in legal documentation. In USA, cadastres relate only to land parcels.

The work in the cadastrial information system has been made in Europe. However, in the USA real estate web services design there is no similar work using a formal language like UML.

The utilization of the UML language aim to better illustrate the evolution of the real estate transaction from traditional industry to online industry. (Booch et al., 2000)

The aim of our research in this paper is to study how the web is changing the value chain management in the residential real estate services. Address requirements analysis for the online real estate systems and to propose functional design of real estate web system integrating several services. This could be considered as a practical contribution in the context of demand-driven supply chains in the online real estate industry. The second aim is to propose a simplified implementation architecture for an integrated demand and supply chain management system for online real estate services. We chose API because it enables connections to a product or service and because it's a key growth driver for hundreds of companies across a wide range of industry sectors.

The knowledge gained from this work could help real estate companies in several ways. Understanding evolving requirements of real estate actors at the system level. Addressing integration issues of several complementary services. Creating added value in differentiating offered services compared to competitors in the value chain.

The paper has six sections. The first section examines the changes in the real estate industry after the introduction of the internet. The second section examines how the web is changing the value chain management and focus on the demand chain management considering as an example the residential real estate services.

The third section, discusses advantages of using CRM in demand-supply integration. Also, it discuss the evolution of the CRM to SaaS CRM and how mashup resolve some limitations of this evolution.

The fourth section discuss how Mashups enable integration via APIs, how API generate business value and how APIs are managed.

The fifth section address how the modules specified could be bundled together and implemented in practice. The sixth section specifies the different modules of the online real estate system.

CHANGES IN THE RESIDENTIAL REAL ESTATE INDUSTRY

Until recently, Realtors controlled the residential real estate sales process. Only Realtors had complete access to MLS listings and housing information. Even if a buyer saw a house in an advertisement, it usually never contained an address. This forced the buyer to call or visit a real estate office for more information and to interact with an agent.

After the introduction of the internet in the residential industry, home buyers have more information available to them than ever before. Because of this, Realtors no longer control the process, and it is possible today to link seller and buyer of a house without intermediaries. New forms of brokerage (e.g.

discounted brokerage) are evolving and modifying the real-estate industry structure. Besides, there seems to be a growing trend of unbundled services typically offered by real-estate agents.

There have been new development of internet services in real estate industry. Several real estate search engines have been developed providing advanced tools and information for the different actors of this industry.

This involves not only property search, but also other activities like mortgage search, title search, value analysis etc. In another work, we analyzed and compared several advanced real estate search engine services. These consist of several subsystems with many sets of activities or processes. As examples of these features we can list:

- The value analysis service,
- Mobile application,
- Home alert,
- Title company and
- Others.

These new services created new changes in the residential real estate structure.

One of the main and most useful tools is the mobile application. This application is downloaded and run by mobile devices. Users of the mobile application may search for properties on a map or locate properties based on their location using GPS (Global Positioning System) technology. GPS technology now gives brokers, agents, and developers even individual sellers the power to influence purchasing decisions, by delivering informative messages about properties for sale. Today there are GPS enabled self-guided sightseeing tours. The most impact GPS tours deliver the message when prospective buyers are in the area even when the sales office is closed.

Also as a result of the emergence of the internet, the supplier is no longer represented only by the seller but also represented by the third party provider. For example, the third party provider partner with real estate search engines to provide added value services to the customer.

Compared to the traditional real estate industry, the interaction between the different actors becomes electronic. For example, the interaction between the buyer and the real estate broker is no longer carried out by telephone or meeting but becomes carried out by email, teleconference, or file sharing.

In the traditional real estate industry, the interaction between the buyer and the real estate broker is carried out by telephone, fax and meeting.

In the advanced real estate scenarios, online companies have been providing real estate search engines with advanced tools and services for the different actors of this industry. These services change the type of the connection between the different real estate actors. (Cherif & Grant, 2014)

The interaction between the real estate agent and the buyer is now carried out by email, teleconference, file sharing. Also, we noticed that the role of the real estate agent played in the advanced real estate scenarios becomes less important compared to the traditional real estate industry. Using the real estate search engines, buyers and sellers can list and search for houses, potentially bypassing traditional real-estate agents.

We can consider that the change in residential real estate industry structure is illustrated in several dimensions.

- This industry is an information intensive and information driven. The change appears in the type, diversification and the degree of availability of this information.
- This industry is an intermediate market. The change appears in the connection between real estate actors. Previously, the agents and brokers connect buyers and sellers and now the system connect all these actors.
- This industry is based on agent-buyer-seller relationship. The change appears in the type of this relationship. The system becomes an important actor in this relationship.
- This industry is based with high value and asset specificity. The change appears in the decrease of the transaction cost enabled by the system.

The online real estate system becomes essential in the interaction between the different actors. The system interface handles the actors requests for the different real estate services.

INTERNET IMPACT ON VALUE CHAIN MANAGEMENT

We define the value chain as the chain of activities that an enterprise performs for the purpose of delivering valuable services or products (WikiValue). The value chain management consists of the demand chain management and the supply chain management.

We will examine in this section how the web is changing the value chain management. We focus on the demand chain management and we consider as an example the residential real estate services.

E-Demand Chain Management

A value chain is a chain of activities that a firm operating in a specific industry performs in order to provide valuable products and services for the market (WikiValue). Michael Porter (1985) has made a major contribution on related issues of business management.

The value-chain concept has been enlarged besides individual firms. It can apply to distribution networks and whole supply chains. The delivery of a mix of products and services to the end customer will mobilize different economic factors, each managing its own value chain.

The Supply chain management includes the methods, systems, and leadership that continuously improve an organization's integrated processes for product and service design, purchasing, inventory management, planning and scheduling, logistics, distribution, and customer satisfaction (Mentzer et al., 2001).

Demand chain management (DCM) is the same as supply chain management, but with emphasis on consumer pull vs. supplier push. The demand chain begins with customers, then funnels through any resellers, distributors, and other business partners who help sell the company's products and services. The available web-based technologies now permit strong customer and supplier integration for inventory planning, demand forecasting, order scheduling, targeted marketing and customer relationship management.

Frohlich and Westbrook (2002b) introduce four web-based demand and supply integration strategies (Figure 1) that describe the extent to which companies are using the Internet in integration with their suppliers or customers.

The resulting categories are web-based low integration (case A), web-based demand integration (case B), web-based supply integration (case C), and web-based demand chain management integration (case D)

The degree of internet web-based supply chain integration and the degree of internet based demand integration are low in the case A. Consequently, there is no electronic interaction between the suppliers and customers.

The degree of internet web-based supply chain integration is low and the degree of internet based demand integration is high in the case B. Consequently, there is electronic interaction between the company and customers. Company's strategies in this model involve web-based integration with their customers.

The degree of internet web-based supply chain integration is high and the degree of internet based demand integration is low in the case C. Consequently, there is an electronic interaction between the company and suppliers. Company's strategies in this model involve web-based integration with their suppliers.

The degree of internet web-based supply chain integration and the degree of internet based demand integration is high in the case D. Consequently, there is electronic interaction between the company, customers and suppliers

The DCM strategy (case D) should deliver the highest levels of performance. The higher the level of traditional integration with suppliers and customers the greater the benefits (Frohlich & Westbrook, 2001).

We will analyze in the next section the evolution of the interaction between the online residential real estate companies, customers and providers.

In this paper, we adopt the four web-based demand and supply chain integration strategies introduced by (Frohlich & Westbrook, 2002b) in the residential real estate industry. In this case, the suppliers are represented in fig1 by the sellers/third party provider, the customers are represented by the buyers and the companies are represented by the online real estate companies.

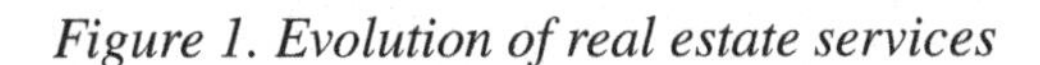

Figure 1. Evolution of real estate services

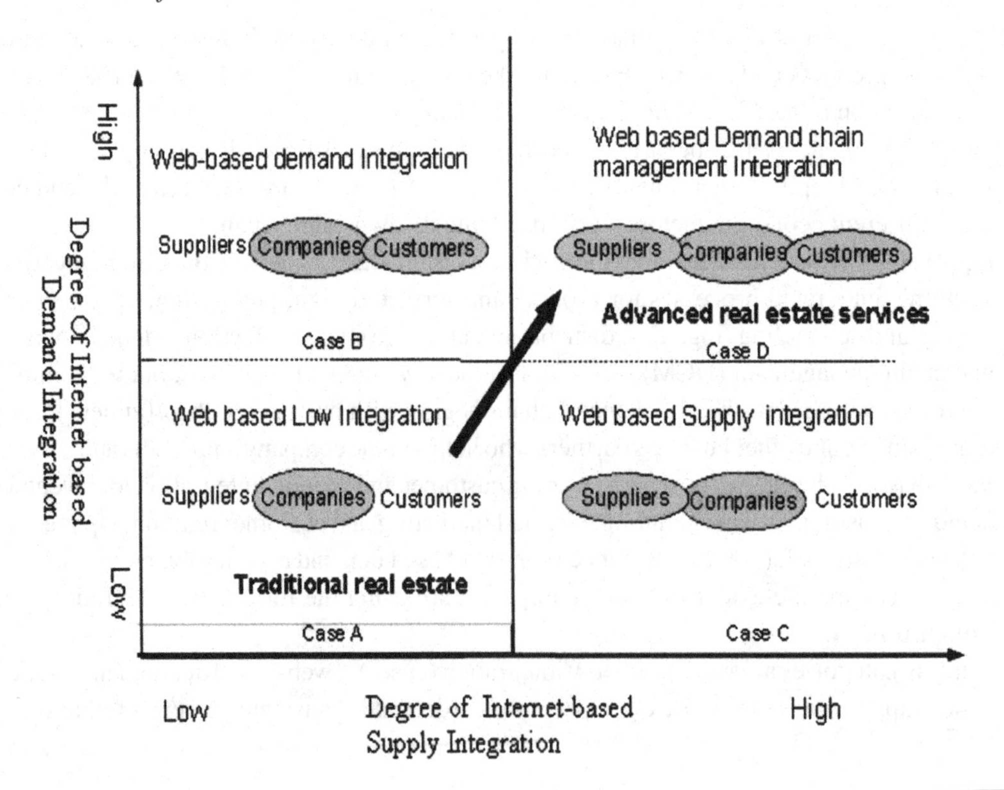

We noticed that the traditional real estate industry is represented in the case A and the advanced real estate services is represented in the case D.

SUPPLY-DEMAND INTEGRATION AND CRM

Figure 1 introduced four web-based demand and supply integration strategies describing the evolution of the interactions between the companies, suppliers and customers from the traditional to the online real estate industry.

In the case of advanced internet web based real estate, supply and demand chain integration is high as described in the case D. Consequently, there is an advanced electronic interaction between the company, customers and suppliers.

Major changes in supply chain management are taking place (IBM BCS, 2003). These have been driven by some common trends:

- Companies increased the use of e-business.
- Customers have become ever more demanding.
- Speed-to-market and successful product innovation have become critical to corporate success.
- Greater challenges in managing more global and complex supply and demand.
- Cost reduction has been a top priority.
- Extended number of players involved in delivering value to a customer, with global sourcing partners for cost and capability reasons.

By integrating the supply and demand chain activities, companies can create competitive advantage while positioning themselves to take full advantage of the potential of the Internet. Before they can successfully integrate the demand and supply functions, however, companies need to better understand the relationship between marketing and supply chain management. This understanding will allow them to begin to plan and implement an integrated demand and supply chain management system and begin to realize the competitive advantages.

New customer and distribution channels are being created, enhanced by new technological innovations and geographical expansion. Existing channels are under pressure and require constant change to retain market position. Customers are becoming more demanding, and their expectations are evolving toward greater levels of service and response with higher degrees of product and service customization. Empowered customers expect on-time delivery, self-service with real time order configuration and status information, and optimally priced product/service bundles.

Companies have to provide online and real time customer order configuration, updates and status throughout the order fulfillment pipeline. Doing so will help improve customer service levels and reduce operating costs. For example, in order management processes, a company that is static probably will not have any formal standards of order management.

Companies have to respond dynamically and rapidly to changes in customer demand, supply fluctuations, and market and environmental conditions. This capability will enable companies to be responsive to true demand requirements and help enhance profitability and will be customer pull-driven as opposed to push-driven.

Company infrastructure components (e.g., technology, process, organization, distribution network) have to be scalable to respond quickly to market changes. This capability will help reduce underutilized capital assets and process costs yet grow capacity as demand increases.

Companies have to dynamically configure and deliver product/service bundles based on actual demand and market conditions. Doing so will help optimize profitability and remove obsolete inventory from the pipeline.

In the case of advanced online real estate companies, the supply chain does not include any natural resources, raw materials and components, the suppliers use to develop physical products.

In our case, supply chain is abstracted in third-party providers that enter into partnerships with the online real estate companies. Supply chain integration is made using API facilities.

In the case of Demand chain integration for advanced real estate companies, we consider that the integration of an advanced CRM system could fulfill most of the demand chain requirements. CRM supports Demand Management by implementing customer centric processes that enable customer management processes across all channels in order to effectively influence the customer.

CRM is intended to improve the performance of the organization. If the objective is to increase the effectiveness of the Demand Management process, CRM represents an approach to harness customer insight to better match products and services to customer needs, identify areas of differentiation, and focus resources on the most valuable customers.

The CRM builds upon information on past demand, trends, and seasonal patterns to produce consumer and customer insight which can help forecast customer demand levels by identifying and anticipating requirements better. Better forecasts lead to more effective and efficient supply chains, meaning improved customer service and retention from the ability to set and meet delivery dates, and increased sales through the ability to confirm availability.

CRM can help the companies to create powerful value creating change in the following ways:

1. Companies need to build aligned and cooperative relationships. CRM is a way of building collaboration and relationships between different parts of the business. Successful CRM solutions connect information, functions and people from around the whole organization in the processes of customer service and value creation.
2. Companies need to build strategic alliances with partners. With the help of CRM systems it becomes easier to create structural bonds between companies that make it easy to do business together.
3. CRM knowledge management systems are ideally designed to collect knowledge and then distribute it to point of need.
4. CRM can help the organization become more aware of its most important customers, and can instill practices that improve personalized services to them.

For example, Cisco has gained some $450 million annually in cost savings by integrating supply and demand chains with Internet, making it feasible for its suppliers to access the company's enterprise resource planning system. Its partners have registered 50-60% decrease in order-processing time and 60% reduction in cycle time. (Cisco, 2007)

According to (Gartner, 2011), companies that succeed the most with supply demand product integration may register 60% better profit margins, 65% better EPS(Earning Per Share) and 2-3 times the ROA(Returns on assets).

The competitive global marketplace creates an imperative for improved service. The aim of the CRM strategy is therefore to add maximum value to customer, employees and organization as win-win-win set of outcomes. Any strategy that does not address these three-fold objectives with under perform as has been noticed by widespread research

Gartner in its (CRM Guide, 2014) has stated the rate at which CRM systems are expected to thrive within the next ten years. Gartner further anticipates SaaS deployments of CRM to reach a maximum of 80% to 85% by 2025.

Gartner forecasts the CRM software market to grow at low double digits, but the SaaS based CRM will grow higher then at least twice the rate of on premise CRM. This represents nearly a doubling of the market over the next six years.

With many on-premise applications, cases integration is across layers in a way not intended by the application's vendor but performed anyway as interfaces are unavailable, because companies do not have the necessary skill set or simply because it is faster and cheaper.

TheSaaS integration approach leverages a set ofstandard application programming interfaces (APIs) published by the SaaS solution provider. All data integration is executed though these APIs over the Internet, enabling SaaS solution providers to continuously provide upgrades functionality without breaking existing integrations. Complex company integration requirements challenge even the best SaaS applications there are still limitations and pitfalls that organizations must be wary of.

Some SaaS solution providers provideintegration service offering by providing an integration server with prebuilt connectors to common on-premise applications, which further reduces the integration effort and cost. Lastly, there are new emerging offerings dubbed integration as a service, which are analogous to SaaS applications in integration space. They could be used for Cloud-to-on-premise, Cloud-to-Cloud,, or on-premise to-on-premise integrations.

Once the fundamental integration requirements have been established, the process of designing the integration can begin. Given that SaaS integrations typically occur over the Internet, the integration architecture must consider the locations of the different on-premise source and target systems within the organization's network. Understanding the locations, connections, and protocols between these components and the other systems that must be traversed for Internet traffic will offer immediate insight into interoperability, security, scalability, and performance concerns.

Furthermore, defining performance metrics for each integration upfrontis important to the project success and could help define how the integration is designed and implemented.

In the area of SaaS integration, Web service integration and mashups are common, but they introduce factors that an organization has little control over such as the different service levels of the SaaS solution providers.

There are a some integration patterns that are usually applied to SaaS implementations.

The functionality offered by SaaS applications can be leveraged only if the relevant data is stored within the SaaS application's data tier.

This is essential to most SaaS applications and often leads to data replication and synchronization between the on-premise system of record and the SaaS application.

Most SaaS solution providers offer APIs that can facilitate batch synchronization of data through simple Create, Read, Update, and Delete (known as CRUD) statements. More sophisticate SaaS solution providers that may offer event-driven near-real time data synchronization capabilities.

Mashups are another common integration pattern used to support information sharing, information enrichment, and collaboration in SaaS applications.

In particular, mashups are utilized to enrich SaaS application data with realtime back-office data presented in concert seamlessly to the user. This is another possibility to the approach of replicating back-office data in the SaaS application. It is necessary to match the integration capabilities of a SaaS solution provider with the integration requirements and with the cons and pros of each.

Since all data integrations for the SaaS application take place via the API and many SaaS solution providers impose rate limits on the number of API calls that a company could perform within a certain period of time, it may be essential for the SaaS solution provider to raise those limits.

SaaS industry verticals tend to be hyper-competitive. As more organizations adopt SaaS applications with greater interoperability, an emerging integration-on-demand market calls for an integration service that provides all the benefits and architecture of SaaS. These services allow non-technical end users to customize and deploy integrations configuring data sources and targets, mappings, transformations, integration processes, and the scheduling of integration jobs.

API INTEGRATION

Mashup Platforms Based on APIs

With the rapid development of online Real Estate search engines, there is increasingly tremendous amount of information available on the Web, which is always distributed across different platforms. Thus, how to integrate the information to meet the end-users' need becomes a challenge. The rise of mashup provides a promising solution for this problem.

A mashup is a type of situational application that's composed by distinct components that have been linked to generate a new integrated experience. Mashups collect information, content or functionality from different sources and give the result in a Web interface where the source's owner has no participation in this process.

Mashups were initially conceived for the Web users to create their own applications starting from public programmable APIs, such as Google Maps Yahoo!Map, MapQuest APIs, or the TwitterAPI.

The three basic characteristics of all mashups are combination, visualization, and integration.

Mashups enables the online Real Estate search engines to use existing data resources and make customized data integrations for user-specific use cases. It implies easy, fast integration, generally made possible by access to open APIs and data sources to produce creative results.

Mashup online Real Estate search engines aggregate and visualize different web resources and allow users to create an ad-hoc composition of data outputs of existing services or APIs into a new representation and can be deployed on the Web.

Map mashups such as Google Maps, Yahoo!Map, MapQuest APIs, have been very successful especially in on online real estate search. But map mashups should not reply on these open data sources and services only. These could include data and data services provided by private companies, government agencies, together with other application-specific data and services.

A search on the Internet of some map mashups labeled as mapping show that several map mashups are produced for applications in transportation transit mapping (e.g., metro transit map), simple community services such as event mapping, real estate (e.g., resale home search), business locations (e.g., convenience stores), crime mapping, social networking (e.g., friends mapping), news incident locations, tourism, etc.

The development of adequate mashup process should reverse the innovation potential of mashups to compose an application responding to personal needs starting from functionality and given contents and to simply run it.

The development of modern Web applications has been characterized in the years by the prototype-centric and iterative approach is even more accentuated the composer, i.e., the mashup end user, just mashes up some services and runs the result to test if it works and respond to his demands. In case of unsatisfactory results, he fixes the problems and is immediately able to run the mashup again.

Mashup typically follow 3-tier architecture following a mix of client/server and web service model.

A general mashup architecture comprises three distinct participants that are physically and logically separate. Mashup client is on the top level and the data sources and bottom level. The middle tier is where the mashup logics endure.

The mashup logics for producing mashed content could executed within the web browser and also on the server. Mashups may create important competitive advantage by enabling for rapid innovation of business processes over the co-creation of systems which support the collective intelligence of an organization, additionally they can confirm very efficient and add value to enterprise with aspects and benefits.

Mashups help move Web 2.0 into the enterprise and improve time-to-market, increase productivity, development costs. In the center of a robust digital ecosystem, creating a mashup platform need a digital operating model, one that is suitably permeable to third parties that can co-generate new value from what a company and others have to offer.

It means taking profit of the interconnectedness and the increase of customers who will commit actively with a company if it permit them. More companies need to become like a software company within their habitat of the digital ecosystem.

A mashup platform approach positions legacy assets for the future by abstracting and combining them to augment their relevance to arising trends in social technologies, cloud, and mobile. Companies that have acted on the digital ecosystem in a big manner tend to be web-native enterprises, such as Facebook, Google, and various other companies offering social apps or mobile. Web native companies expand their reach and their capabilities by exhibiting their capacities via APIs to others. From the early days of software APIs have been utilized as a mechanism for connecting programs. Yet, API creation and design have significantly changed.

Before, methods were proprietary and established interdependent coupling between pieces of systems and code.

Over time, APIs matured to minimize the interdependency of tightly coupled interfaces, generally decreasing the complexity of integration.

The better created APIs are planned for a public audience, in spite of the most value in terms of consumption will be with strategic partners.

Previously, APIs regularly took a lot of time to use and make work. Actually, thanks to emerging practices with RESTful interfaces, utilize their time effectively.

When they easily exploit the company's assets, they concentrate more on creating value-added capability and bringing it to market quickly.

RESTful interfaces an architectural and programming model, create a level of simplicity which always accelerates things, making integrations cost-effective, the potential to minimize cost expands the opportunities to integrate.

RESTful interfaces deliver a scalable approach for both external and internal use. Now APIs, utilizing RESTful interfaces, enable to fluently serve 80 percent of the most common use cases. At the same time, ease of integration, reuse, the goals modularity, and flexibility apply to both approaches.

Many companies will begin by exposing services and datautilizing RESTful APIs to their external digital ecosystem of customers and partners.

However, a RESTful API approach for internal integration generates many of the same advantages of highly scalable coordinating and connecting of business processes at a low cost. Development time is reduced by 50 to75 percent using RESTful.

Actually, the time to integrate data needs only hours instead of six to eight months, combination of self-describing interfaces (RESTful APIs), standard access methods (HTTP) and identifiers (Uniform Resource Identifiers (URIs)), helps soften the long lead times for high costs created by proprietary integration methods, tightly coupled.

RESTful APIs are successful partially because developers are capable to develop modular capabilities with lightweight interfaces that don't require heavy integration

Regardless of increasing adoption, integration via RESTful APIs is better considered as a tool in the integration toolkit, and is not the appropriate solution in all use cases.

API Business Value

An aggressive road map to open new APIs across different service categories makes the network an intrinsic part of an innovation ecosystem and offers an opportunity for new monetization by serving business customers and consumers.

The API is an acknowledgment of the reality that there are many niches and many ways that customers require to be served.

They have digitized the value-added services they deliver. Being digital,these capabilities are simply to engage with and now function at a rapid pace with a large number of partners Exactly how companies make money with APIs depends on their business model and their product.

Some companies expose core features for consumption within complementary apps. Salesforce.com is a good example, as it provides CRM tools that complement a large variety of collaborative and line-of business applications.

On the other hand, Facebook and Twitter, count on APIs to drive much of the usage that makes their platforms valuable in the first place by extending engagement beyond their primary user interfaces, out to the edges via social applications, third-party Web, and mobile.

eBay, Netflix, and Amazon utilize APIs to share freemium content and commercial offers within third-party applications that drive commercial transactions and subscription growth.

Amazon decided that all IT assets were to be presented as APIs. That created anIT architecture that catalyzed and stocked the impressive AmazonWeb Services.

APIs are the vehicle that connects a product or service to these massive new communities, allowing developers, end-users to find innovative ways to incorporate your features and services into new social and mobile applications APIs are a key growth driver for hundreds of companies across a wide range of industry sectors. More than half of Salesforce.com revenue is generated through its APIs, not its user interfaces. Through its APIs, Twitter process a billion transactions a day. Google is around 5 billion transactions a day.

Amazon is closing in on a trillion transactions. APIs are considered by companies as products, inside developers are considered as strategic partners, and long tail developers are considered as customers.

So companies don't release an API; they deliver a product line of APIs with several methods, via its APIs, terms of use, access controls, service level agreements, and so on that addresses the varying demands of this customer base.

APIs can be viewed as a toolkit to co-generate value, so they have an effect the distribution of value in an industry ecosystem. All suppliers require new ways of thinking about their businesses APIs are becoming the basis for establishing digital value chains that reach and process information from traditional data stores humans, and a rising number of physical objects that include digital content, and containing digital indirect channels established before principally by purely web-based companies and software companies.

APIs are the building blocks of the digital economy. They make current capabilities compatible, thus it is possible to employ them in new ways easily and quickly, so spurring innovation and new value creation.

Likewise, to completely capitalize on current assets, other businesses must shift to platform-oriented business models that enable others to expand their capabilities in innovative ways by allowing new applications. When accessing these capabilities is costly, complex or time consuming.

Organizations have to make a view of the ecosystem that they will develop or be a part of and what role they would play. This perception is dependent on the current business model and assets that organizations can tap to generate new value. Organizations should also look for opportunities where they can digitize current processes, as those processes create the chances to expose APIs. In like manner any company that achieve with an API has a vibrant developer ecosystem.

Organizations that apply modern APIs presented digital operating model thinking have the chance to get competitive advantage via reduced friction in co-generating new value, building increased agility and persistent digital engagements.

Several third-parties are free to employ the API to enhance their own applications as they see fit, or third-party developers can use API as the foundation for a totally new application.

SaaS verticals are generally quite narrow and integration through API to other applications is necessary for SaaS start-up. Processing a suite of related APIs, and leaving the sales, marketing, and service to companies who are better adapted to that role.

Several potential business models exist in the API economy, none of which is more or less likely to succeed than the multitude of potential business models in SaaS.

In conclusion, therefore, is that it is crucial to identify your advantage early on and to choose the business model that most effectively leverages that competitive advantage.

Managing APIs

Previously, the interaction between customers and organizations always took place, at the website, in the context of the business, in the store, or in the service. Actually, the context is controlled by the customer, and the business must get into that context. In fact, customers are creating new context.

Even so RESTful APIs are simple to build, they still need management and maintenance. And despite the fact that it is fluent to manage a single API, all organizations will may have several APIs that strategic partners, internal developers, and public developers use to build applications through different platforms. This rise in APIs has conduct to the need for services and tools that help companies develop, publish, manage, operate and analyze APIs Analytics assist companies enhance and comprehend the value of their APIs.

Value-driven analytics scale API adoption by measuring purchases, traffic, and registrations.

Analytics may assist organizations to better understand who is using their APIs and through which channel they are accessing it, informing a suitable response.

For example, companies could divide audiences on applications and top developers, or they could analyze usage by API method.

Operational analytics offer visibility into the API platform to enhance efficiency. Such tools can be used by customers to troubleshoot problems, enhance service quality, analyze load statistics, measure latency monitor traffic flow and transaction data, or identify underlying API problems.

For companies that sustain their API platform internally, traffic control is valuable to protect back-end systems from surcharge. API traffic control tools may fix platform-wide rate limits, fix limits by other rules like IP (InternetProtocol) address or client, or create tiered systems to permit priority customers to consume more API data. Companies may define and enforce data consumption access levels using API traffic control tools.

API management can control scalability issues and fix lag time and latency when a wide number of devices applications, or developers concurrently use the APIs.

Companies can discharge the entire API management processes to external service providers using global API networks or cloud-based services They could also enable these solution providers to take over API management when traffic must remain internally.

SYSTEM IMPLEMENTATION ARCHITECTURE

We start by describing a real estate purchase scenario and the steps involved to select a real estate property. The first step concerns the construction of scenarios of interactions between the system and other entities outside the system boundaries. A normal scenario is just a sequence of events that causes an object to change state. An event occurs at any time information comes into the system or goes out from the system through programming interfaces. An abnormal scenario also called a scenario with exception includes error conditions, incorrect inputs by users, omitted inputs, data values outside the range of valid values, and where the time out will occur. A set of scenarios has been identified (Hawryszkiewycz, 2001)

Below are the steps involved in this scenario:

- The user selects the register module to subscribe with the system.
- The user selects the advanced search module to make an advanced property search. To do that, he enters convenient keywords in the search section, for example the location parameters (zip code, city), the property type (house, condo, townhouse) and others property criteria.
- He gets a property list matching to his search. He selects a property and may request its demographic information and its position on the map.
- The user selects the agent search module to choose an agent. To do that, he specifies the agent information(city/qualification). Then the system provides the user with the selected agent contact information.
- The user selects the E-shopping module to order for example the property title report.

- The user can use the mobile application module to perform for example GPS search and Map search.

The architecture of the system identifies major modules and interfaces (Figure 2). The modules provide both basic and value added services to the real estate buyer. The system provides facilities to handle:

- Control of process instances - creation, activation, suspension, termination, etc.
- Navigation between process activities, which may involve sequential or parallel operations, deadline scheduling, interpretation of relevant data.
- Sign-on and sign-off of specific users.
- Identification of process queue for user attention and an interface to support user interactions.
- Maintenance of control data, passing relevant data to/from applications or users.
- An interface to invoke external applications and link any relevant data.
- Supervisory actions for control, administration and audit purposes.

The product management module has special capabilities in the system. It illustrates how the administrator may interact with the system to create, delete, and add new modules/ functions/attributes. The administrator can manage customer interaction including, customer service and marketing technical support.

Figure 2. Interaction between the online real estate system and actors

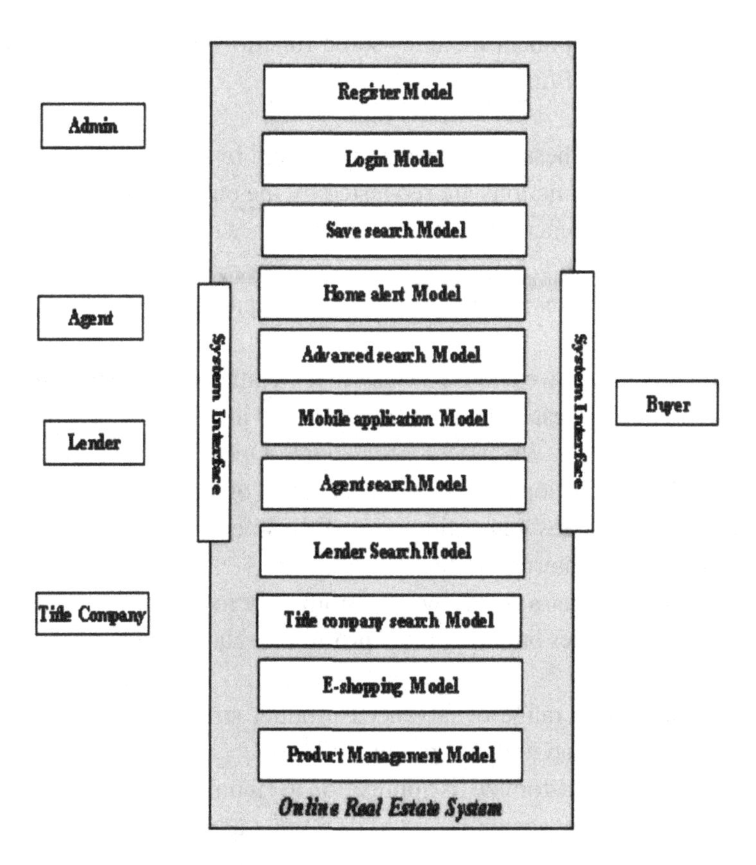

The architecture models are the Register Model, the Login Model, the Save Search Model and the Home Alert Model, the Lender Search Model, Agent Search Model, Advanced search, Mobile Application Model, Title Company Search Model, E-shopping Model and Product management Model.

We concentrate only in this paper on Register Model, Home alert Model, Advanced Search Model, Mobile application Model, Agent search Model, E-shopping and Product management Model.

In this paper we will propose the interaction model between the real estate and the other entities using UML design (Booch. et al., 2000). UML is a modeling language used to model the architecture of software system for several industry (Eriksson et al., 2000). We used an open source software (ModelSphereSoftware) for the design. This paper is concerned with design issues. Other issues related to testing and market evaluations of our design are addressed in other documents.

In the real estate system design, we consider that the internal computation steps are not events, except for decision points that interact with the external entities. Events include inputs, signals, transactions, and actions to or from entities. Each type of event must be allocated to the entities that send it and receive it.

An UML sequence diagram represents each model associated with a functional component. Each entity is assigned to a column in the sequence diagram.

We describe all the event traces established for each UML sequence diagram (SeqDiag). (Donald, 2004).

We also specify the functional components of the system; each functional component contains a set of related functions of the real estate web system. A functional component has a collection of characteristics:

Attributes: The attributes represent the information that is related to the object. These attributes do not represent a physical localization but the information needed to carry out the system functions that the component provides.

Functions: The functional component includes some functions to perform the functionality of the component. There are four types of functions:

(A) Administration Functions: These functions are requested by the administrator of the system.
(U) End-user Functions: These functions are requested by the end-user of the system.
(B) Back-end Functions: These functions process operations, which are automatically carried out by the system.
(T) Third Party Provider Functions: These functions are requested by the third party provider.

As an implementation prototype we choose a Customer Relationship Management (CRM) system as a platform for managing online real estate modules as described in Figure 2. This includes functionalities of the product management module. We choose open source OpenCRX system. (OpenCRX)

OpenCRX is an open CRM solution that meets the needs of organizations requiring multifunctional, enterprise-wide coordination of sales generation, sales fulfillment, marketing and service activities to customers, partners, suppliers or intermediaries.

Its account management provides a full view of customers across contracts, activities, products, and status. Account management enables building, more profitable relationships by understanding the status of each account.

OpenCRX supports the whole range of advanced product structuring, e.g. product bundling and design of product offerings based on multiple product bundles.

OpenCRX administrators can customize its application to fit unique business demands, from adding/removing attributes or changing the screen layout to designing advanced activity processes to enhance the information flow within your organization. Advanced access control allows you to share information or restrict access based on user profile, role or team.

The OpenCRX has a mobile user interface that is optimized for mobile devices, supporting most of features of the standard user interface. This includes viewing any object and searching for objects.

OpenCRX provides AirSync capability for over the air synchronization between mobile handsets and OpenCRX server.

OpenCRX features a Java API and a REST (Representational State Transfer) service that makes available the complete API for third-party applications. The openCRX REST adapter supports JSON and Swagger. Since January 2016 Swagger has been renamed to the Open Api Specification.

OpenCRX is ready for the cloud, supporting docker-compliant cloud services and Jelastic.

OpenCRX now offers an easy-to-use UI for web-based document management.

The application programming interface (API) is a popular protocol intended to be used as an interface by software components to communicate with each other. It may include specification for routines, data structures, object classes, and variables.

REST has emerged as a predominant web service design model, it facilitates the transaction between web servers by allowing loose coupling between different services. It uses low bandwidth.

The system provide a set of interfaces to users and applications. Each of these interfaces is a potential integration with other infrastructure application components.

These interfaces includes:

- Interfaces to support interaction with a different IT application types.
- Interfaces to support interaction with user interface desktop/mobile functions.
- Interfaces to support interoperability between different real estate systems.
- Interfaces to provide system monitoring and metric functions to facilitate the management of composite application environments.

Not all third party providers of value added modules may choose to expose every interface between the functional components within the model.

For each interface, it is expected that conformance will be classified at several levels. It provides a minimum level of interoperability at level 1, with the option for more complex products to achieve conformance against a higher level of functionality for richer interworking, where appropriate e.g. open interfaces (APIs) support multivendor integration.

APIs are a business development tool. They allow companies to create effective partnerships and expand their platform faster and more efficiently than ever before.

APIs have been around for a while, but in the past few years their popularity and usage have experienced exponential growth. Now APIs are a necessary business development tool for companies to scale, much as Twitter and Facebook used theirs to reach more users.

OpenCRX already supports functionalities in modules for user login, register, save search, home alert, mobile application, e-shopping and product management.

For modules not supported by OpenCRX, suitable products providing these services could be integrated using APIs.

As examples of APIs that are integrated with openCRX in the prototype, we mention the Zillow API Network (Zillow API), WalkScore API (WalkScore API), AgentRank API (AgentRank API), Peekacity API (Peekacity API) and PropertyShark API (PropertyShark API).

The Zillow API Network turns member sites into mini real estate portals by offering fresh and provocative real estate and mortgage content to keep people coming back.

It includes four categories of API: Home Valuation API, Property Details API, City and neighborhood market statistics and demographic data, and Mortgage rates and monthly payment estimates.

WalkScore API calculates the walkability of an address based on the distance from a house to nearby amenities. WalkScore API uses a RESTful (Representational State Transfer) interface and returns the Walk Score for any latitude and longitude in the U.S. in XML or JSON format.

AgentRank API accesses to real estate agent sales, forecast and reviews. This API uses REST interface.

Peekacity API has two types of APIs. The first is Embedded Amenity Map that locates an address on an interactive map and easily add in neighborhood amenities. The second is the Amenity Report that creates high quality PDF maps and reports of the neighborhood amenities.

PropertyShark API provides property title search capability. The user can choose the type of title report (building info, building photo, list of units for selling the building).

These APIs are not exclusive. But, we found these providing more functionalities and more complete than others.

These modules run as back office to process customer requests. The back office will keep a record of transactions, invoices, reports. It will also manage relationships with other partners providing value added modules via APIs.

The front office interface is a web page having good usability for the interaction with customers. An intuitive design with easy navigation proves to be most effective. We selected several features from successful online real estate websites (Zillow.com, Trulia.com etc.)

SYSTEM COMPONENTS SPECIFICATION

We would specify in this section different modules of the online real estate system. We use the term model to represent the specification of each module. Each model includes the UML sequence diagram, the module scenario, and its functional components.

Register Model

This model shows the different events between the different entities to enable the user to register with the system.

The system validates the user-name and the password selected by the user and creates an account.

UML Model

Presented in Figure 3.

Register Scenario

- User selects register section
- User chooses user-name & password
- System validates user-name& password

Figure 3. Register model sequence diagram

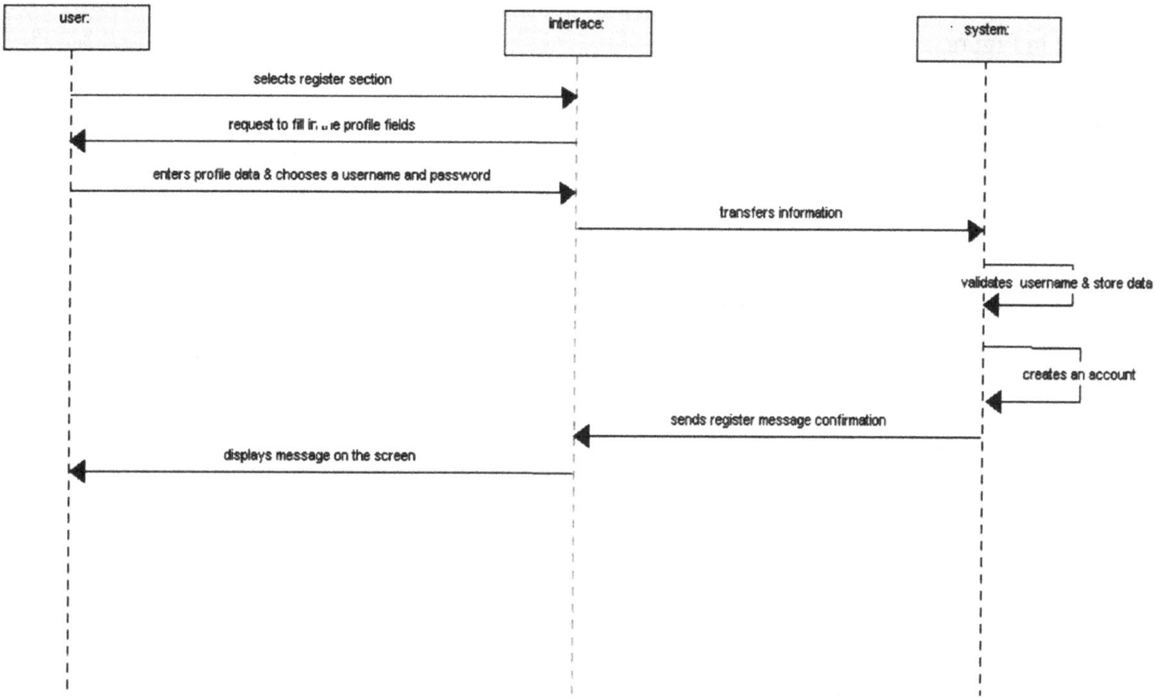

- System creates an account

Register Component

Functions:
U Selects-register-section()
U-Register-parameters()
B-Validates-register-parameters()
B-Creates-account()
Attributes:

- User-name
- Password
- Email address

Agent Search Model

This model illustrates how the user may interact with the system to select an agent.

The system executes the search according to the user specifications (agent city/qualification). After sorting the results, the user selects an agent. The system provides the user with the agent contact information.

UML Model

Presented in Figure 4.

Agent Search Scenario

- User selects real estate agent section
- User selects the agent city & qualification
- Interface transfers information to system
- System begins the search
- System sends an agent list
- Interface displays information on the screen
- User selects the sort options desired
- Interface displays sorted list

Figure 4. Agent search model sequence diagram

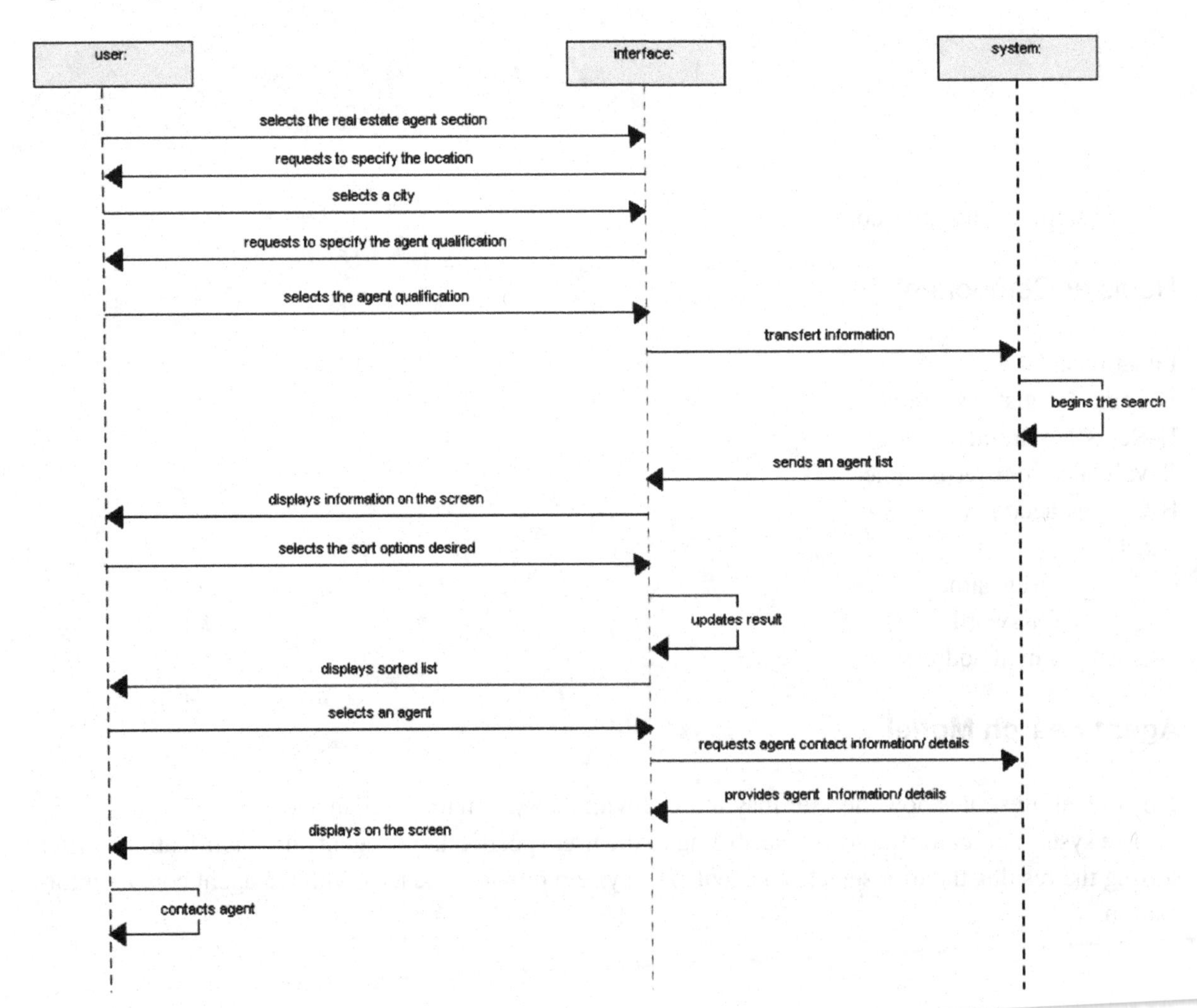

- User selects an agent
- System provides agent contact information
- User contacts agent

Agent Search Component

Functions:
U-Selects-real-estate-agent-section()
U-Selects-agent.Parameters()
U-Starts-search()
B-Executes-search()
U-Gets-agent-list()
U-Selects-sort-agent-list-option()
U-Selects-an-agent()
Attributes:
- User-ID
- Agent-location
- Agent-qualification
- Agent-list
- Agent-name/number
- Agent-email-address

Home Alert Model

This model shows how the user may interact with the system to receive the chosen listing update. The user saves his home alert preference after choosing the alert frequency, price change alert and how recent MLS listings are desired. The system confirms save alert preferences.

UML Model

Presented in Figure 5.

Home Alert Scenario

- User selects the home alert section
- User chooses alert frequency
- User saves alert frequency information
- System sends alert frequency confirmation
- User chooses price change alert
- System sends price change confirmation
- User chooses how recent MLS listing are wanted
- System sends confirmation
- User saves home alert preference
- System executes the saving and sends confirmation

Figure 5. Home alert model sequence diagram

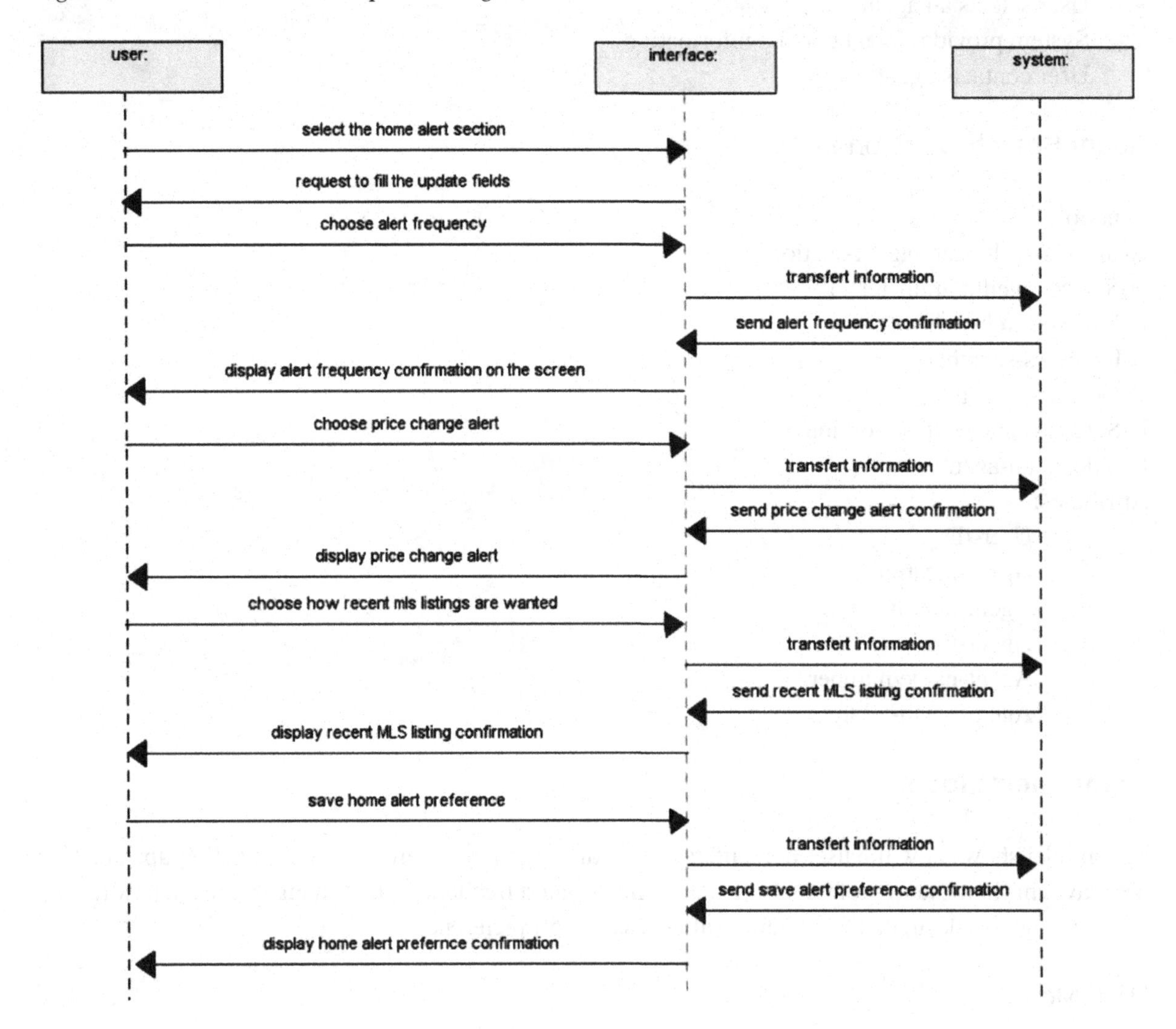

Home Alert Component

Functions:
U-Selects-home-alert-section()
U-Chooses-alert-frequency()
B-Confirm-record()
U-Chooses-price-changes-alert()
U-Chooses-how recent-MLSlisting-are-wanted()
U-Records-home-alert-preference()
Attributes:

- Alert-frequency
- Price
- MLS-listings-period
- User ID

Advanced Search Model

This model illustrates the different events and interactions between the system and the other entities to make a property advanced search. The user selects a property from the result list satisfying his search criteria provided by the system and requests more details, such as property position on the map, demographic information and value analysis.

UML Model

Presented in Figure 6.

Figure 6. Advanced search model sequence diagram

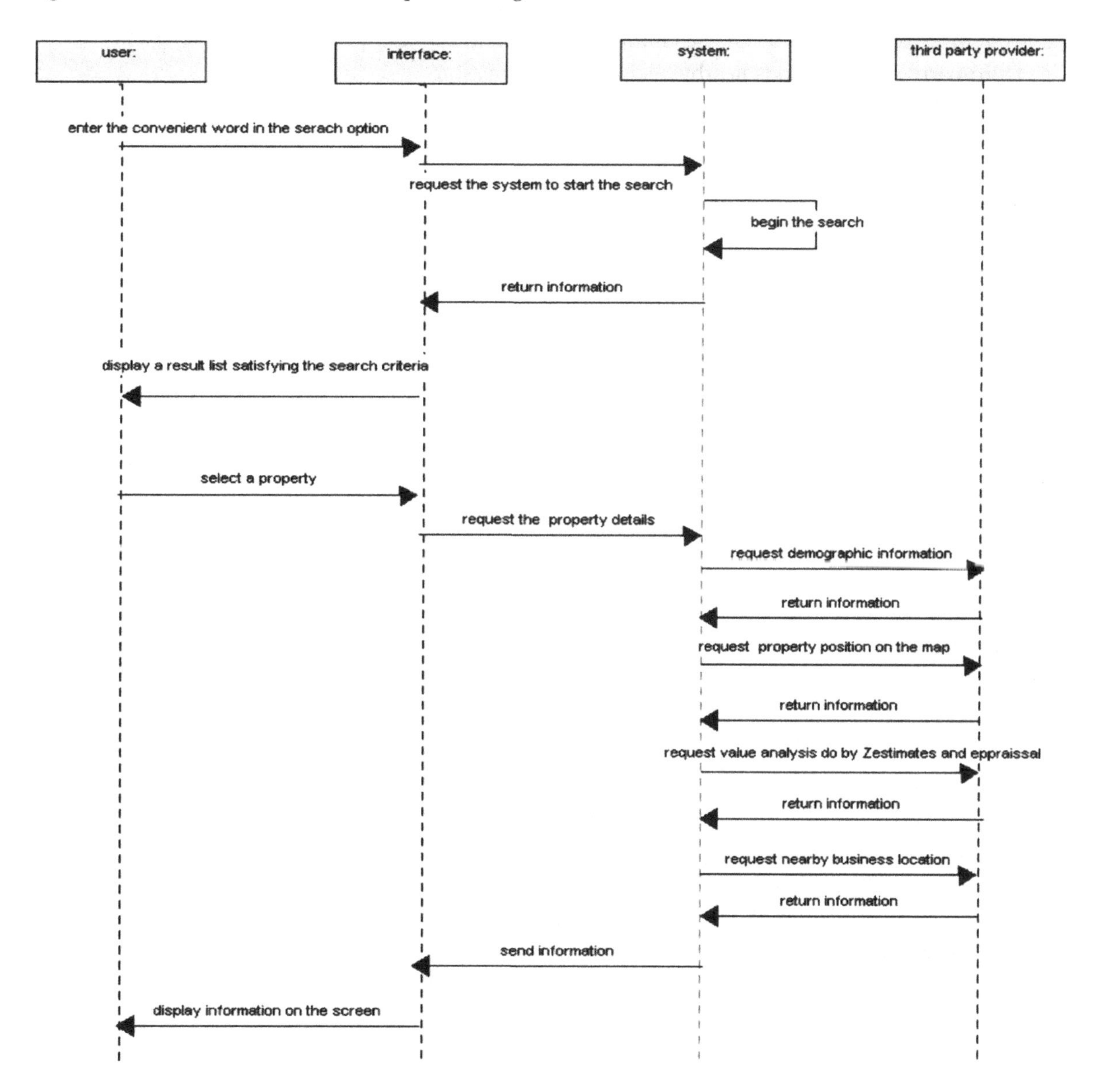

Advanced Search Scenario

- User enters convenient keywords in the search section
- User starts search
- System executes the search
- System sends search list
- User selects a property
- System requests demographics information from third-party provider
- Third-party provider sends demographics information
- System requests property position on the map from third-party provider
- Third-party provider Sends map information
- System requests value analysis from third-party provider
- Third-party provider sends value analysis information
- System requests nearby businesses information from third-party provider
- Third-party provider sends nearby businesses information
- System sends demographics/map/value analysis/nearby businesses information to the user interface

Advanced Search Component

Functions:
U-Selects-advanced-search()
U-Chooses-property-parameters()
B-Executes-the search()
U-Gets-property-list()
U-Selects-property()
B-Requests-property-details()
U-Gets-demographic-information()
U-Gets-map-property-position()
U-Gets-value-analysis-report()
U-Gets-nearby-business-location()
T-Sends-requested-information()
Attributes:

- User-ID
- Third-Party-ProviderID
- Property-parameters
- Property-address
- Property-list
- Demographics-details
- Value-analysis-report
- Nearby-business-location-details

Mobile Application Model

This model adapts the property search process to the cell phone. The user launches the real estate application on his cell phone. The application connects to the real estate server in order to make MLS search. User can also get the GPS information using his cell phone.

The search list result provided by the server will be displayed on the cell phone screen, and the user proceeds approximately the same steps to get more details concerning the property selected.

UML Model

Presented in Figure 7.

Mobile Application Scenario

- User launches the real estate mobile application
- System connects to the server
- User requests GPS information
- System requests GPS technology
- GPS party locates user position on the map
- System sends information
- User enters neighborhood city address in the search
- User starts the search
- System makes the search
- System requests demographics information from third-party provider
- Third-party provider sends demographics information
- System requests property position on the map from third-party provider
- Third-party provider Sends map information
- System requests value analysis from third-party provider
- Third party provider sends value analysis information
- System requests nearby businesses information from third-party provider
- Third-party provider sends nearby businesses information
- System sends demographics/map/value analysis/nearby businesses information to the user interface

Mobile Application Component

Functions:
U-Launches-mobile-application()
B-Server-connects-to the-mobile-application()
U-Asks-for-GPS information()
B-Requests-GPS localization()
T-Provides-GPS-information()
B-Sends-GPS information-to the user's-cellphone()
U-Enters-search-parameters()

Figure 7. Mobile application model sequence diagram

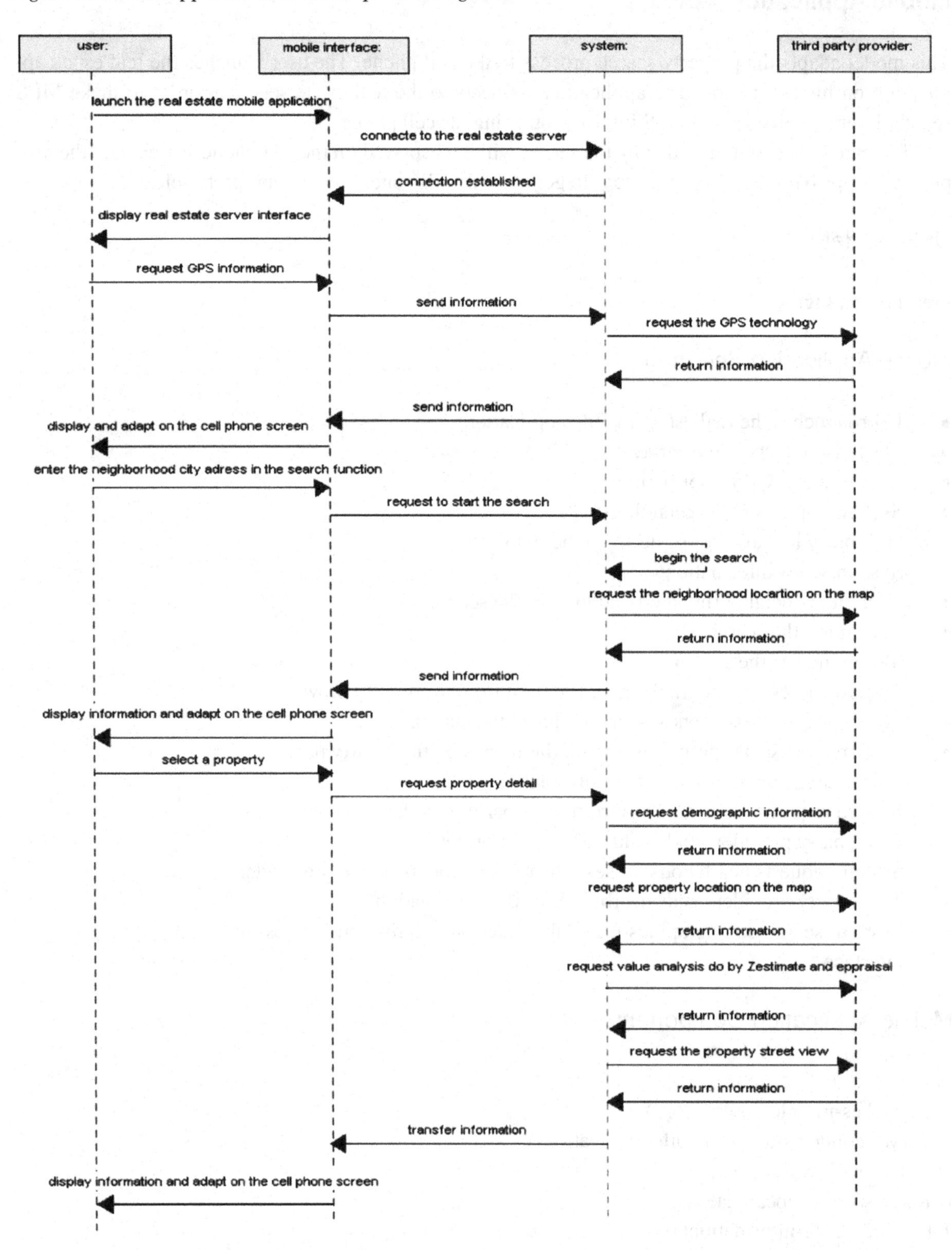

U-Starts-search-on-cellphone()
B-Executes-search()
U-Selects-property-on-cellphone()
B-Requests-neighborhood-map-location()
B-Requests-Demographics-information()
B-Requests-nearby-businesses-location()
B-Requests-value-analysis-report()
B-Processes/sends-received-information-to the user's-cellphone()
T-Provides-requested-information()
Attributes:

- User-ID
- Third-party-providerId
- Neighborhood-location
- Property-search-parameters
- Property-address
- Demographic-details
- Value-analysis-report
- Mobile-application-details
- Nearby-business-location-details

E-Shopping Model

This model illustrates how the user may interact with the system to buy products (e.g: title report). The user could place an order request by selecting the checkout section. The order is processed once all payments details are validated.

UML Model

Presented in Figure 8.

E-Shopping Scenario

- User selects a product name
- System requests new shopping cart
- Shopping cart provider creates a new process
- Shopping cart provider adds product to cart
- Shopping cart provider confirms add product
- System sends confirmation
- User selects checkout section
- Shopping cart provider adds tax & shipping cost
- Shopping cart provider updates payment amount
- User selects the payment type
- User selects the cart type
- User enters credit card number& validation date& address

Figure 8. E-Shopping model sequence diagram

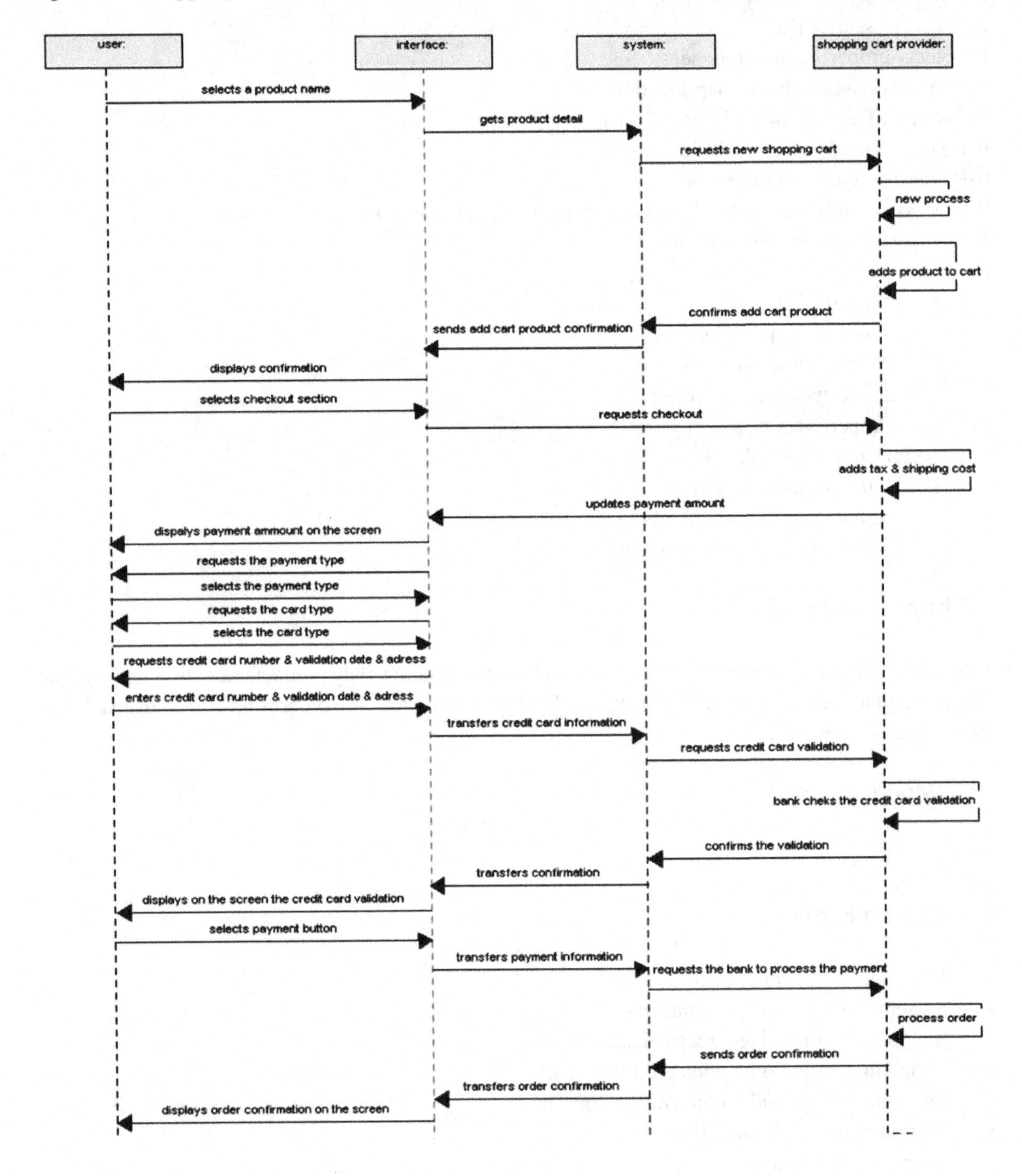

- System requests credit card validation
- Chopping cart provider checks credit card validation
- Chopping cart provider confirms the validation
- System transfers confirmation

- User selects payment button
- System requests the chopping cart provider to process the payment
- Chopping cart provider process the payment
- Chopping cart provider sends order confirmation
- System transfers order confirmation

E-Shopping Component

Function:
U- Selects-product-name()
B- Adds-cart-product()
T- Creates-new-process()
T- Adds-product-to cart()
T- Confirms-add-product()
T- Updates-payment-amount()
U- Selects-payment-type()
U- Selects-card-type()
U- Enters-credit-card parameters()
T- Checks-credit-card-validation()
T- Confirms-credit-card-validation()
U- Starts-payment()
T- Executes-payment-process()
T- Confirms-payment-process()
Attributes:

- ◦ Product
- ◦ Card-number
- ◦ Card-validation-date
- ◦ User-name
- ◦ User-address
- ◦ Tax-rate
- ◦ Shipping-cost
- ◦ Shopping-cart-providerId

Product Management Model

This model illustrates how the administrator may interact with the system to create, delete, and add new modules/ functions/attributes.

The system validates and stores administrator inputs and updates.

The administrator can also create, delete, and add new CRM (Customer Relationship Management) modules functions/attributes.

UML Model

Presented in Figure 9.

Figure 9. Product management model sequence diagram

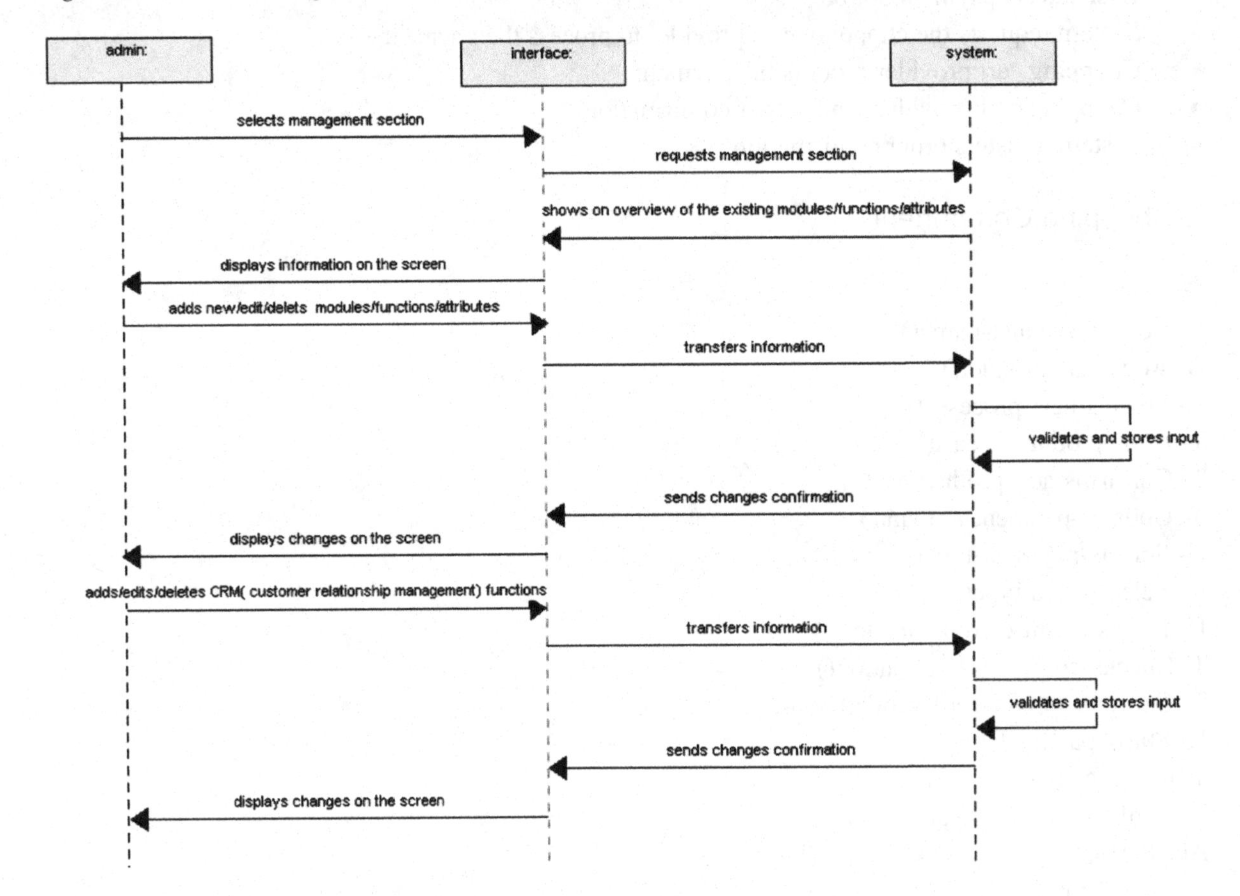

Product Management Scenario

- Administrator selects management section
- System delivers an overview of the existing modules/attributes/functions
- Administrator adds new/edit/deletes modules/functions/attributes
- System validates and stores input
- System confirms changes
- Administrator adds new/edit/deletes CRM modules/functions/attributes
- System validates and stores input

Product Management Components

Functions:
A- Selects management section()
B- Delivers overview()
A- Adds module/attribute/function()
A- Edits module/attribute/function()
A- Deletes module/attribute/function()

B- validates input()
Attributes:

- Admin-ID
- Module-ID
- Attribute-ID
- Function-ID

CONCLUSION

In this paper we examined how the web is changing the demand chain management. We Adopted the four web-based demand and supply chain integration strategies introduced by (Frohlich & Westbrook, 2002) and we apply it in the residential real estate industry.

Demand chain management requires extensive up and downstream integration between all business partners to succeed. And these types of connections have only recently become possible due to the web. The web allowed an efficient, reliable and rapid delivery of goods and services when and where they are needed. The web-based technologies are also increasing used for supply chain forecasting, planning, scheduling and execution.

We studied how the web is changing the value chain management in the residential real estate services and we proposed functional design of real estate web system integrating several services. This could be considered as a practical contribution in the context of demand-driven supply chains in the online real estate industry.

We choosed APIs because they enable to connect products or services and because they are a key growth driver for hundreds of companies across a wide range of industry sectors. Also, because APIs are the building blocks of the digital economy. They make current capabilities compatible, thus it is possible to employ them in new ways easily and quickly, so spurring innovation and new value creation. Organizations that apply modern APIs presented digital operating model thinking have the chance to get competitive advantage via reduced friction in co-generating new value, building increased agility and persistent digital engagements.

We proposed a simplified implementation architecture for an integrated demand and supply chain management system for online real estate services. We chosed an open source Customer Relationship Management system as a platform to manage some of the online real estate modules. The other modules are integrated from third-party providers using their APIs. As examples of APIs that are getting integrated with openCRX in the prototype, we mention the Zillow API Network, Walk Score API, AgentRank API, Peekacity API and PropertyShark API. This proof of concept helps demonstrating the feasibility of the supply and demand integration. Also, it helps establish the technical issues, and overall direction, as well as providing feedback for internal decision making processes. The Zillow APIs have been the most important part of our online real estate proof of concept as Zillow provides the main property data. This data is then augmented with results from other modules. Our choice is based on the fact Zillow is one of the most successful online real estate companies in the industry (Cherif & Grant, 2014). And Its APIs are the most complete ones available.

A benefit of this work is to present a practical design example for demand chain management for online real estate industry. A second benefit is to improve the transparency of real estate markets, to provide a stronger basis for reduction of costs of real estate transactions by preparing a set of formal models and assessing efficiency of these transactions. Other aspects and benefits include: ontological studies and semantic aspects of real estate transactions, effects of legislative, expert, public and administrative limitations.

As a conclusion, we consider that our proposal for a simplified supply and demand chain management integration is feasible. Online real estate services are information-based with light requirements on supply chain management capabilities. This helps reducing the complexity of the solution. In future work, we'll test different configurations for our proof of concepts prototype.

REFERENCES

Agrawal, D. K. (2012). Demand Chain Management: Factors Enhancing Market Responsiveness Capabilities. *Journal of Marketing Channels*, *19*(2), 101–119. doi:10.1080/1046669X.2012.667760

AMR Research Report. (2005). *The handbook for becoming demand driven*. Boston, MA: AMR Research. Retrieved from http://www.agentrank.com/api/

Arvantis, A., & Hamilou, E. (2004). *Modeling Cadastral Transaction in Greece Using UML.* Paper presented at The FIG Working Week, Athens, Greece.

Ayers, J., & James, B. (2006). *Handbook of supply chain management* (2nd ed.). Boca Raton, FL: Auerbach.

Ayers, J., & Malmberg, D. (2002). Supply Chain Systems: Are you Ready? *Information Strategy: The Executive's Journal*, *19*(1), 18–27.

Booch, G., Rumbaugh, J., & Jacobson, I. (2000). *The Unified Modelling Language User Guide*. Reading, MA: Addison Wesley Longman, Inc.

Bustinza, O. F., Parry, G. C., & Vendrell-Herrero, F. (2013). Supply and Demand Chain Management: The Effect of Adding Services to Product Offerings. *Supply Chain Management*, *18*(6), 618–629. doi:10.1108/SCM-05-2013-0149

Ceren, A. V. (2015). Sustainable Demand Chain Management: An Alternative Perspective for Sustainability in the Supply Chain. *Procedia: Social and Behavioral Sciences*, *207*, 262–273.

Cherif, E., & Grant, D. (2014). An Analysis of Online Real Estate Business Models, (To appear). *Electronic Commerce Research*, *14*(1). doi:10.1007/s10660-013-9126-z

Childerhouse, P., Aitken, J., & Towill, D. (2002). Analysis and design of focused demand chains. *Journal of Operations Management*, *20*(6), 675–689. doi:10.1016/S0272-6963(02)00034-7

Christopher, M. (2000). The agile supply chain-Competitive in volatile market. *Industrial Marketing Management*, *29*(1), 37–44. doi:10.1016/S0019-8501(99)00110-8

Christopher, M., & Holweg, M. (2011). Supply Chain 2.0: Managing supply chains in the era of turbulence. *International Journal of Physical Distribution & Logistics Management*, *41*(1), 63–82. doi:10.1108/09600031111101439

Donald, B. (2004). *UML basics: The sequence diagrams*. Retrieved from http://www.ibm.com/developerworks/rational/library/3101.html

Donovan, P. S., & Manuj, I. (2015). A Comprehensive Theoretical Model of the Complex Strategic Demand Management Process. *Transportation Journal*, *54*(2), 213–239. doi:10.5325/transportationj.54.2.0213

Ericsson, D. (2011a). Demand chain management: The evolution. *ORiON*, *27*(1), 45–81.

Ericsson, D. (2011b). Demand chain management: The implementation. *ORiON*, *27*(2), 119–145.

Eriksson, H. E., & Penker, M. (2000). *Business modeling with UML*. Wiley & Sons.

Federal Trade Commission. (2007). *Competition in the Real Estate Brokerage Industry Report*. Retrieved from http://www.ftc.gov/reports/realestate/V050015.pdf

Frohlich, M., & Westbrook, R. (2002b). Demand chain management in manufacturing and services: Web-based integration, drivers and performance. *Journal of Operations Management*, *20*(6), 729–745. doi:10.1016/S0272-6963(02)00037-2

Frohlich, M. T., & Westbrook, R. (2001). Arcs of integration: An international study of supply chain strategies. *Journal of Operations Management*, *19*(2), 185–200. doi:10.1016/S0272-6963(00)00055-3

Gartner. (2011). *The Gartner Supply Chain Top 25 for 2011*. Retrieved from http://www.gartner.com/id=1709016

Gartner CRM Vendor Guide. (2014). Retrieved from https://www.gartner.com/doc/2679218/gartner-crm-vendor-guide-Harrison

Gattorna, J. (2010). *Dynamic supply chains: delivering Value Through People* (2nd ed.). London: FT Prentice Hall, Harlow.

Georgiadis, D., Shinakis, M., & Tyrinopoulos, Y. (2001). The design and implementation of a demand driven freight transport application. In *Proceedings of the 7th World Congress on Intelligent Systems*.

Godsell, J., Harrison, A., Emberson, C., & Storey, J. (2006). Customer responsive supply chain strategy: An unnatural act? *International Journal of Logistics*, *9*(1), 47–56. doi:10.1080/13675560500534664

Hamilou. (2003). *Modelling Cadastral Transactions with the graphical object – oriented language UML*. Author. (in Greek)

Harrington, L. H., Boyson, S., & Corsi, T. M. (2011). *X-SCM: The new science of X-treme supply chain management*. New York: Routledge.

Harrison, Lee, & Neale. (2003). *The practice of supply chain management: Where theory and application converge*. New York: Springer.

Hawryszkiewycz, I. T. (2001). *Introduction to system analysis and design*. Frenchs Forest, Australia: Prentice Hall.

Hossein, V., Abbas, S., Mohammad, R. T. J., & Fataneh, S. S. (2012). Investigation Critical Success Factors of Customer Relationship Management Implementation. *World Applied Sciences Journal*, *18*(8), 1052–1064.

IBM BCS. (2003). *Transforming your supply chain to on demand: Competitive advantage or competitive necessity?*. Business Consulting Services Report (No. G510-3322-00).

Johnson, M. E., & Whang, S. (2002). E-business and supply chain management: An overview and framework. *Production and Operations Management, 11*(4), 413–423. doi:10.1111/j.1937-5956.2002.tb00469.x

Juttner, U., Christopher, M., & Godsell, J. (2010). A strategic framework for integrating marketing and supply chain strategies. *The International Journal of Logistics Management, 21*(1), 104–126. doi:10.1108/09574091011042205

Keith, A. R., & Eli, J. (2008). Customer relationship management: Finding value drivers. *Industrial Marketing Management, 37*(2), 120–130. doi:10.1016/j.indmarman.2006.08.005

Madhani, P. M. (2015). Demand Chain Management: Enhancing Customer Lifetime Value through Integration of Marketing and Supply Chain Management, *UP. The Journal of Business Strategy, 12*(3), Madhani, P. M. (2013). Marketing Firms vs. SCM-led Firms: DCM Comparatistics. *SCMS Journal of Indian Management, 10*(2), 5–19.

Mentzer, J. T., DeWitt, W., Keebler, J. S., Min, S., Smith, C. D., & Zacharia, Z. G. (2001a). What is supply chain management. In *Supply Chain Management*. Thousand Oaks, CA: Saga Publications.

Mutambo, L. S. (2003). *The Unified Modeling Language (UML) in Cadastral System Development* (Doctoral Dissertation). International Institute For Geo-information Science and Earth Observation(ITC), Enschede, The Netherlands. Retrieved from http://www.modelsphere.org

Özcanl, C. (2012). *A proposed Framework for CRM On-Demand System Evaluation* (Master of Science Thesis). Retrieved from http://www.opencrx.org/

Peekacity, A. P. I. (n.d.). Retrieved from http://www.peekacity.com/help/API.aspx

Porter, M. E. (1985). *Competitive advantage: Creating and sustaining superior performance*. New York: Collier Macmillan.

PropertyShark API. (n.d.). Retrieved from http://www.propertyshark.com/Real-Estate-Reports/2009/07/30/new-propertyshark-api-for-blogs-and-websites/

Report, C. (2007). *How Cisco Enables Electronic Interactions with Sales, Manufacturing, and Service Partners*. Cisco IT Case Study. Retrieved from http://www.cisco.com/web/about/ciscoitatwork/downloads/ciscoitatwork/pdf/Cisco_IT_Case_Study_B2B.pdf

Rigby, Reichheld, & Phil. (2002). Avoid the Four Perils of CRM.[PubMed]. *Harvard Business Review, 80*(2), 101–109.

Santos, J. B., & DAntone, S. (2014). Reinventing the wheel? A critical view of demand-chain management. *Industrial Marketing Management, 43*(6), 1012–1025. doi:10.1016/j.indmarman.2014.05.014

Sawyer, Rolf, & Wigand. (2005). Redefining access: Uses and roles of ICT in the US residential real estate industry from 1995 to 2005. *Journal of Information Technology, 20*(4), 213–223. doi:10.1057/palgrave.jit.2000049

SeqDiag. (n.d.). *Sequence Diagram*. Retrieved from http://www.visual-paradigm.com/VPGallery/diagrams/Sequence.html

Soosay, C. A., & Hyland, P. (2015). A decade of supply chain collaboration and directions for future research. *Supply Chain Management: An International Journal*, *20*(6), 613–630. doi:10.1108/SCM-06-2015-0217

Taylor, D. (2000). Demand amplification: Has it got us beat? *International Journal of Physical Distribution & Logistics Management*, *30*(6), 515–533. doi:10.1108/09600030010372630

WalkScore API. (n.d.). Retrieved from http://www.walkscore.com/professional/api.php

Wiki, C. R. M. (n.d.). Retrieved from http://en.wikipedia.org/wiki/Customer_relationship_management

WikiValue. (n.d.). *Value chain*. Retrieved from http://en.wikipedia.org/wiki/Value_chain

Zillow, A. P. I. (n.d.). Retrieved from http://www.zillow.com/howto/api/APIOverview.htm

Chapter 8
E-Business and Analytics Strategy in Franchising

Ye-Sho Chen
Louisiana State University, USA

Chuanlan Liu
Louisiana State University, USA & Central University of Finance and Economics, China

Qingfeng Zeng
Shanghai University of Finance and Economics, China

Renato F. L. Azevedo
University of Illinois at Urbana-Champaign, USA

ABSTRACT

Franchising as a global growth strategy, especially in emerging markets, is gaining its popularity. For example, the U.S. Commercial Service estimated that China, having over 2,600 brands with 200,000 franchised retail stores in over 80 sectors, is now the largest franchise market in the world. The popularity of franchising continues to increase, as we witness an emergence of a new e-business model, Netchising, which is the combination power of the Internet for global demand-and-supply processes and the international franchising arrangement for local responsiveness. The essence of franchising lies in managing the good relationship between the franchisor and the franchisee. In this paper, we showed how e-business and analytics strategy plays an important role in growing and nurturing such a good relationship. Specifically, we discussed: managing the franchisor/franchisee relationship, harnessing the e-business strategy with aligning the e-business strategy with application service providers, an attention-based framework for franchisee training and how big data and business analytics can be used to implement the attention-based framework.

INTRODUCTION

Franchising as a global growth strategy is gaining its popularity (Justis & Judd, 2002; Thomas & Seid, 2000; Chen & Justis, 2006). For example, the U.S. Commercial Service estimated that China, having over 2,600 brands with 200,000 franchised retail stores in over 80 sectors, is now the largest franchise market in the world (U.S. Commercial Service, 2008). By 2012, China has over 5,000 brands with the number of franchised stores exceeded 400,000 with an averaging 83 stores for a franchising brand. The total annual sales of CCFA (China chain store & franchise association) members reached nearly

DOI: 10.4018/978-1-5225-1680-4.ch008

US$300 billion in 2010 and Represented about 13% of total retail sales in China ("China Franchise: At a Glance"). The popularity of franchising continues to increase, as we witness an emergence of a new e-business model, Netchising, which is the combination power of the Internet for global demand-and-supply processes and the international franchising arrangement for local responsiveness (Chen, Justis, & Yang, 2004; Chen, Chen, & Wu, 2006).

Starting a new business is anything but easy, and taking in consideration emerging markets, choosing the franchising method can mitigate several risks, being the simplest and safest way to launch one's business in environments with volatility, uncertainty, complexity, and ambiguity (VUCA) (Wolf, 2007). Considering the ranking "Ease of Doing Business Index" by the World Bank, which ranks economies their ease of doing business, from 1–189 (World Bank, 2016), the variation is tremendous among countries. Brazil ranks 116 out of 189 countries in the ranking Ease of Doing Business Index by the World Bank. In Brazil, it takes up to 174 days to start a business and around 4 years to close it down mainly due to high levels of bureaucracy. In mainland China takes an average of 84 days. In India, 130 days, while in Russia, 51 days. By contrast, in the US, it takes only 7 days, and New Zealand just one day to open a business. (World Bank, 2016).

It is also known to be a challenge to consider the disparities of human capital development in emerging markets such as in Brazil, Russia, India and China (BRICs). (Ardichvili, Zavyalova & Minina, 2012; Azevedo et al., 2016) The e-business and analytics strategy in franchising offers an alternative to increase the easiness of doing business around the globe. For example, Entrepreneur magazine – well known for its Franchise 500 listing – in 2001 included Tech Businesses into its Franchise Zone that contains Internet Businesses, Tech Training, and Miscellaneous Tech Businesses. From then on, the listed companies have been increasing ("2012 franchise 500," 2012; "Franchise 500 directory 2014," 2014; "Franchise 500 ranking," 2015; "Franchise 500 directory 2013," 2013).

In his best seller, Business @ the Speed of Thought, Bill Gates (1999, p.6) wrote: "Information Technology and business are becoming inextricably interwoven. I don't think anybody can talk meaningfully about one without talking about the other." Gates' point is quite true when one talks about e-business strategy in franchising. Thus, to see how e-business can be "meaningfully" integrated into franchising, one needs to know how franchising really works. The success of networks, such as franchising, strategic alliances, joint ventures and clusters is highly dependent on the capability to create and transfer knowledge within the network (Gorovaia and Windsperger, 2010) and e-business strategy just can work if it combines the business model, business technology and value the network (Lin and Hsia, 2011).

FRANCHISING: DEVELOPING THE FRANCHISOR/ FRANCHISEE RELATIONSHIP

Franchising is "a business opportunity by which the owner (producer or distributor) of a service or a trademarked product grants exclusive rights to an individual for the local distribution and/or sale of the service or product, and in return receives a payment or royalty and conformance to quality standards. The individual or business granting the business rights is called the franchisor, and the individual or business granted the right to operate in accordance with the chosen method to produce or sell the product or service is called the franchisee." (Justis & Judd, 2002, pp. 1-3). Developing a good franchisor/franchisee relationship is the key for a successful franchise (Justis & Judd, 2002). Figure 1 describes how to develop a good franchisor/franchisee relationship in the dynamic environmental context including consumers and suppliers relationship development. The franchisor needs to learn continuously for the growth of the franchise. The learning process is developed through five stages (Justis & Judd, 2002):

1. **Beginner:** Learning how to do it;
2. **Novice:** Practicing doing it;
3. **Advanced:** Doing it;
4. **Master:** Teaching others to do it; and
5. **Professional:** Becoming the best that you can be.

Once reaching the Advanced stage, most preceding struggles have been overcome. However, further challenges will arise as the franchise continues growing, especially in the global markets. This is especially true once the system reaches the "Professional" stage, where various unpredicted and intricate problems could arise. Bud Hadfield (1995, 156), the founder of Kwik Kopy franchise and the International Center of Entrepreneurial Development, aptly stated: "The more the company grows, the more it will be tested." To capture the learning process, a counter-clockwise round dashed arrow surrounding the franchisor is used to depict the increasing intensity of learning as the franchisor continues to grow.

The franchisee also goes through five stages of franchisee life cycle (Schreuder, Krige, and Parker, 2000):

1. **Courting:** Both the franchisee and the franchisor are eager with the relationship;
2. **"We":** The relationship starts to deteriorate, but the franchisee still values the relationship;
3. **"Me":** The franchisee starts to question the franchisor that the success so far is purely of his/her own work;
4. **Rebel:** The franchisee starts to challenge the franchisor; and
5. **Renewal:** The franchisee realizes the "win-win" solution is to continue working with the franchisor to grow the system.

Figure 1. Understanding how to develop the franchisor/franchisee relationship

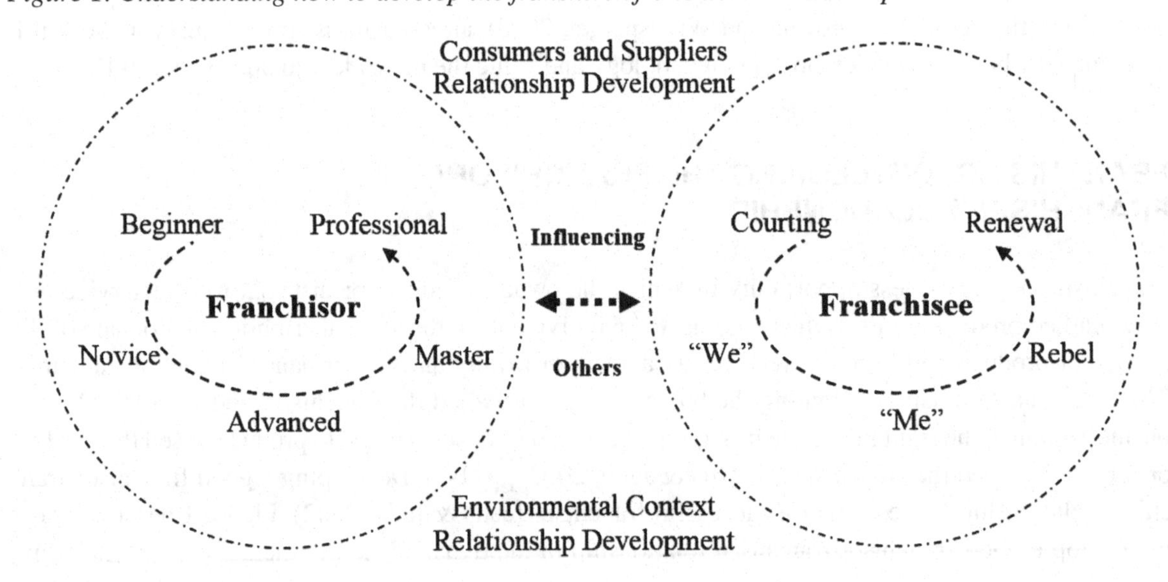

Similar to the franchisor, a counter-clockwise round arrow surrounding the franchisee is used in Figure 1 to depict the increasing intensity as the franchisee continues growing. As the franchisee progresses through the life cycle, the good relationship gradually develops an influencing process (Justis & Vincent, 2001), depicted in Figure 1 with a bi-directional arrow. By going through the processes of learning and influencing, both the franchisor and the franchisee gain the progressive working knowledge of relationship management with the consumers and suppliers. The franchisor, the franchisee, the consumers, and the suppliers in Figure 1 are surrounded with dashed lines, indicating that there is no limit to the learning process.

E-BUSINESS STRATEGY IN FRANCHISE RELATIONSHIP MANAGEMENT

With the advancement of Internet technology, franchise companies are adapting e-business strategies for perfecting the franchisor/franchisee relationship to grow their franchises globally. E-business strategy and activities include the sharing of business information, developing business models, and maintaining business relationships by means of inter-organizational information systems (Lin & Hsia, 2011). They emphasize that the success of franchising networks depend on the capability to create and transfer knowledge within the networks (Gorovaia & Windsperger, 2010) and it should combine the business model, business technology and continuous understanding of the value network (Lin & Hsia, 2011). This community of franchise companies, consumers, and suppliers can be virtually connected for relationship development and management as depicted in Figure 2 below:

- Intra-enterprise collaboration through Intranet, enabling the franchisor to build up relationships with the multi-unit franchisees, new franchisees, prospective franchisees, franchisor management, employees, and board of directors;
- Collaboration with consumers through Internet, enabling the franchisor and the franchisees to build up relationships with customers, prospective customers, investors, competitors, social media, blogs, advocacy groups, and government;
- Collaboration with suppliers through Extranet, enabling the franchisor and the franchisees to build up relationships with members and affiliates of international franchise association, law firms, co-branding partners, goods distributors, real estate agents, information systems consultants, accounting firms, and marketing agents.

HARNESSING THE E-BUSINESS STRATEGY AROUND THE CUSTOMER SERVICE LIFE CYCLE

Table 1 shows a customer-service-life-cycle (CSLC) (Ives & Mason, 1990) e-business strategy in franchising (Chen, Chong, & Justis, 2002) for relationship management depicted in Figure 2. Here we define the franchisee as the customer of the franchisor and the franchisee's customer as the customer's customer of the franchisor. The stages of CSLC are based on two well-known franchising books by Justis and Judd (2002) and Thomas and Seid (2000).

Figure 2. E-business strategy in franchise relationship management

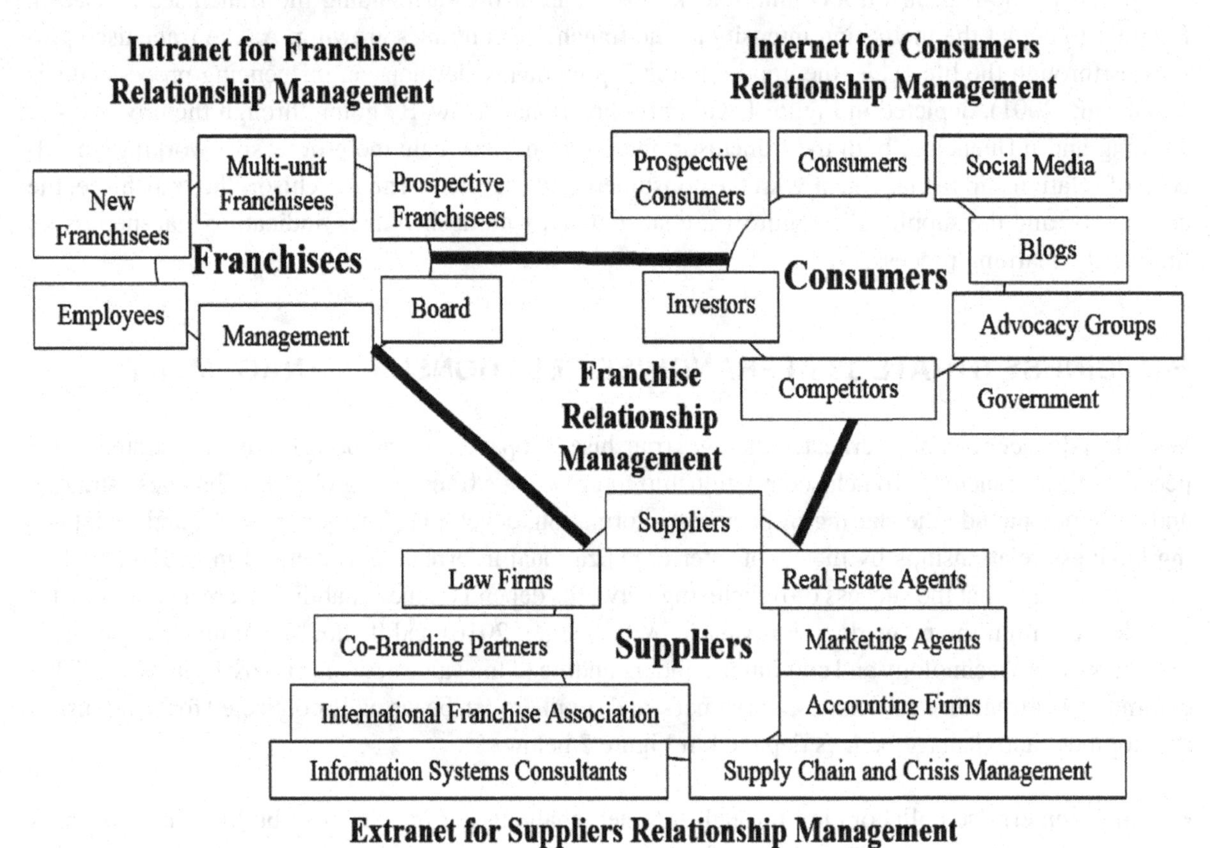

There are four major components in the e-business strategy:

1. Benchmarking the Requirements and Acquisition stages. The CSLC model shown in Table 1 is a comprehensive guide for a franchise to develop its web site, especially at the stages of Requirements and Acquisition. The model may be used to compare a franchise's e-business strategy with its competitors. As the industry progresses, best practices based on the CSLC model will evolve and become a standard for benchmarking and websites enhancements.
2. Helping the franchisees serve their customers in the Ownership stage without the Internet encroachment. There is a rich collection of studies in e-business in franchising (Chen, Chong, & Justis, 2002) showing how the Internet can help the franchisees serve their customers in the Ownership stage, including "Marketing & Promoting the Franchise Products/Services" and "Managing the Franchise System".
3. Cultivating the Ownership and Renewal/Retirement stages with effective knowledge management. As mentioned earlier, the greatest challenge in the Ownership stage is to build up the relationship between the franchisor and franchisee. To cultivate the Ownership stage so that "Professional" franchisee can advance to the Renewal stage instead of retiring, Chen, Chong, and Justis (2000) suggest building an Intranet-based Franchising Knowledge Repository. The Repository provides a framework based on which a franchise system may transform into a learning organization.

Table 1. The Customer-Service-Life-Cycle (CSLC) e-business strategy in franchising

CSLC	Sub-Stages	Intranet Strategy	Internet Strategy	Extranet Strategy
Requirements	Understanding How Franchising Works	Benchmarking and enhancing the web site continuously (Chen, Chong, and Justis, 2002; Chen, Justis, and Chong, 2008), e.g., identifying frequently the best practices of web design in the industry and improving the web site accordingly Using the search engine optimization technique to perfect the efficiency and effectiveness of the web searches	Using integrated marketing strategy and localized advertisement to execute synchronically Engaging in social media to do marketing and address public crises such as malicious slanders from customers or competitors Benchmarking and enhancing the web site continuously (Chen, Chong, and Justis, 2002; Chen, Justis, and Chong, 2008), e.g., identifying frequently the best practices of web design in the industry and improving the web site accordingly	Partnering with suppliers to enhance the various stages of CSLC continuously (Chen, Justis, and Wu, 2006), e.g., a franchise system may need to partner with banks to deliver good services at the stage of "Financing the Franchise Business". In addition, having easy-to-use and secure business transactions is of the first priority.
	Investigating Franchise Opportunities			
	Obtaining Franchisee Prospectus			
	Making the Choice			
Acquisition	Preparing Business Plan			
	Financing the Franchise Business			
	Signing the Contract			
Ownership	Marketing & Promoting the Franchise Products or Services	Helping the franchisees make sales and serve their customers with proper policies dealing with the Internet encroachment issues	Using the web site as the friendly customer relationship management tool to address customer concerns at various stages (Chen, Chong, and Justis, 2002), e.g., providing useful information on financing and showing how the franchise system may help finance the franchise investment	Aligning the Internet and Intranet Strategy with reputable Application Service Providers (ASP) having focused businesses reengineering around this stage of CSLC (Chen, Ford, Justis, and Chong, 2001)
	Managing the Franchise System	Transforming the organizational structure and corporate culture to fit the e-business operation pushed by the Intranet systems (Zeng, Chen, and Huang, 2008), e.g., designing an environment for more team work opportunities and establishing e-learning environment for the employees		Aligning the Internet and Intranet Strategy with reputable Application Service Providers (ASP) having focused businesses reengineering around this stage of CSLC (Chen, Ford, Justis, and Chong, 2001)
	Building the Relationship between the Franchisor and the Franchisee	Cultivating the franchisor/ franchisee relationship with effective knowledge management tools (Chen, Chong, Justis, 2000a,b; Chen, Hammerstein, and Justis, 2002; Chen, Seidman, and Justis, 2005), e.g., basic communications support, distance learning, and centralized franchise applications such as employee recruitment and online ordering		Aligning the Internet and Intranet Strategy with reputable Application Service Providers (ASP) having focused businesses reengineering around this stage of CSLC (Chen, Ford, Justis, and Chong, 2001)
Renewal or Retirement	Becoming a Professional Multi-unit Franchisee or Retiring from the Franchise System			

4. Partnering with the "disruptive technology" providers to enhance the CSLC stages. Innovative entrepreneurs will reengineer their franchise businesses around the CSLC model shown in Table 1. Their ability to track, analyze, and leverage the buying behaviors of their customers in the CSLC sub-stages is their real competitive advantage. For example, Statability.com is a "visionary Web-based Reporting" portal for the hospitality industry. It has the focused business reengineering around the stage of "Managing the Franchise System". Its focused service is being respected by franchise companies in the hospitality industry, as is evidenced from the ever-increasing list of its client base, including Hilton and Marriott. As discussed earlier, partnering with those "disruptive technology" providers will make the franchise system more competitive.

Although Internet technology can help deploy the franchise's e-business strategy, the immediate question is: at what cost? Because of the need for e-business processes to monitor the linkage of internal information technologies with external processing and services, the e-business investment could be very expensive and complicated. Many franchise companies, especially small ones, find it financially difficult to invest in the e-business technologies; however, a new type of service in e-business called Application Service Providers (ASP) promises to make e-business more economical and affordable to the franchise systems. The concept of subscribing information technologies through ASPs has special appeal in the franchising industry because an ASP can duplicate success for other similar franchises quickly and inexpensively (Chen, Ford, Justis, and Chong, 2001). When aligning the CSLC-based e-business strategy with ASPs, a franchise company should focus on (Chen, Ford, Justis, and Chong, 2001):

1. Develop an overall vision of the applications, including software and hardware, needed for the company.
2. Determine what applications and the specific services, e.g., to be available 24 hours a day and 7 days a week with 99.999% of reliability, you want an ASP to host, which have to be clearly defined in the Service Level Agreement.
3. Evaluate ASP providers, i.e., vendors who provide the applications services, using flexibility and trust relationship as the two primary factors.

AN ATTENTION-BASED FRAMEWORK FOR THE FRANCHISEE TRAINING

The third industrial revolution, combining information technology with globalization, produces an environment where everyone is facing the problem of information overload. Simon (1971) spoke for us all when he said that 'a wealth of information creates a poverty of attention." (p.41) Getting the franchisee's attention on training in an information rich world is a major challenge. Ocasio (1997) proposed an attention-based theory of the firm, which allows the firm to shield off irrelevant information and gain access to information relevant to what the firm focuses on. According to Ocasio (1997, p. 188), attention is defined to "encompass the noticing, encoding, interpreting, and focusing of time and effort by organizational decision-makers on both:

1. **Issues:** The available repertoire of categories for making sense of the environment: problems, opportunities, and threats; and

2. **Answers:** The available repertoire of action alternatives: proposals, routines, projects, programs, and procedures."

Ocasio (1997) further classifies attention into three principles:

1. Focus of attention, what decision makers do primarily depends on the selective issues and answers they focus attention on;
2. Situated attention, what decision makers focus on and do depends primarily on the particular contextual environment they are located in; and
3. Structural distribution of attention, how decision makers attend to the particular contextual environment they are in depends on how the firm's attention structure (including rules, resources, and relationships) channels and distributes various issues, answers, and decision makers into specific communications and procedures. It provides the attention structure connecting the needs of self-determination, self-efficacy and self-identity for entrepreneurial behavior in franchising.

Self-determination, accordingly to Kirkley (2016) is the first foundation component upon which entrepreneurial behavior is derived. It is the demonstration of conscientious efforts both physically and mentally in pursuing and identifying opportunities that are innovative and commercially viable. The attention-based framework for the franchisee offers key questions and points of consideration, as represented by the bullet points for each level on Table 2.

Self-efficacy comprises the knowledge, skill and experience (competence) to outwardly express self-determination (Bandura, 1977). The attention-based framework for the franchisee training "psychologically empowers" the stakeholders. It offers a model of entrepreneurial interaction of behaviors, as well, training that scaffold the appropriate requisite knowledge, skills and expertise associated with each level and stage of the franchisee life cycle.

Self-identity is the manner in which an individual describes themselves in certain roles, such as identifying as "being entrepreneurial". Kirkley (2016) exemplified this challenge, in which, there are some individuals whom others identify as "being entrepreneurial" and who appear to not see themselves as "entrepreneurs" neither behave accordingly. Or the contrasting view, in which individuals perceives themselves as entrepreneurs, but are not acknowledged in a wider social context, nor is it necessarily reflecting in their behavior. The attention-based framework bridges the communication, offering a focus of attention for each stage of the franchisee life cycle, considering the relationship touch-points.

It is keen to consider that the individual cannot claim to be entrepreneurial solely on the basis of an identity (Kirkley, 2016). As described by Giddens (1991) the emphasis on claiming a particular self-identity is inherently tied to their ability to convince those around them, through their behavior, that they are indeed entrepreneurial. It is a question of "keeping a particular narrative going". In the absence of the self-determination to be entrepreneurial, self-identity however has very little substance and the individual lacks a crucial element to sustain that narrative. Similarly, self-determination and self-identity are insufficient on their own to sustain the entrepreneurial identity unless it is supported with the requisite knowledge, skills, and expertise associated with entrepreneurial behavior. (Kirkley, 2016). The narrative of successful business and entrepreneurship would lack credibility and sustainability unless the individual can be seen to be practicing the competencies associated with entrepreneurial behaviour.

In the context of franchising, what do focus of attention, situated attention, and attention structures look like? How does a franchise design an attention-based training program for the franchisees? We propose an attention-based framework in Table 2 for the franchisee training. Such a framework has two dimensions. The first dimension is the franchisee life cycle, consisting of Beginner in the Courting Phase, Novice in the "We"-Phase, Advanced in the "Me"-Phase, Master in the Rebel Phase (since the rebel ones tend to be those who know the system well and are capable of influencing others to follow them), and Professional in the Renewal Phase. It is vital for relationship building to understand which stage the franchisee is situated and allocate appropriate resources at different touch-points to help them perform their focuses of attention. The second dimension is the demand-and-supply value networks (Chen, Justis, & Wu, 2006), the attention structures of the franchise, consisting of customers, franchisee outlet, franchisor headquarters, suppliers and partners, and franchise community. The main body of the framework is the focus of attention of the franchise of different levels.

Table 2. An attention-based framework for the franchisee training

<table>
<tr><th colspan="2" rowspan="2">Situated Attention: Relationship Touch-Points</th><th colspan="5">Attention Structures: Demand & Supply Value Networks</th></tr>
<tr><th>Customers</th><th>Franchisee Outlet</th><th>Franchisor Headquarters</th><th>Suppliers & Partners</th><th>Franchise Community</th></tr>
<tr><td rowspan="2">Franchisee Life Cycle</td><td>Beginner in the Courting Phase: Beginner Guide</td><td colspan="5">Focus of Attention: Learning how to become a franchisee:
• Understanding how franchising works
• Investigating franchise opportunities
• Obtaining franchisee prospectus
• Making the choice
• Preparing business plan
• Financing the franchised business
• Signing the contract</td></tr>
<tr><td>Novice in the "We"-Phase: Practicing</td><td colspan="5">Focus of Attention: Practicing how to do activities such as:
• How to get training and services from the headquarters
• How to find a good site
• How to find suppliers
• How to work with the franchisor
• How to work with fellow franchisees</td></tr>
<tr><td rowspan="2"></td><td>Advanced in the "Me"-Phase: Doing</td><td colspan="5">Focus of Attention: Doing activities such as:
• How to acquire and keep customers
• How to hire, train, and fire employees
• How to manage inventory
• How to manage the back office operations</td></tr>
<tr><td>Master in the Rebel Phase: Teaching Others</td><td colspan="5">Focus of Attention: Teaching others how to do activities such as:
• How to teach others
• How to work as team
• How to do the bulleted processes above for Beginner, Novice, and Advanced franchisees</td></tr>
<tr><td></td><td>Professional in the Renewal Stage: Creative Learning and Innovation</td><td colspan="5">Focus of Attention: Becoming the best he/she can be by:
Learning to creatively improve activities such as:
• How to cut the cost of the operations
• How to increase the profit of the operations
• How to acquire other franchises and brands
• How to continuously learn and propose new business solutions
Looking for opportunities for innovation such as:
• Are there new growth opportunities we can create based on our intangible assets of demand & supply value chains? How do we avoid the loss of this new venture?
• Are there any partnership opportunities with our customers and suppliers so that their customers could become ours and vice versa.
• What are the major concerns in the communities and how can we help to deal with them and build a good media relationship also?</td></tr>
</table>

Furthermore, we visualize our attention-based framework for the franchisee training in Figure 3. It illustrates the five focuses of attention starting from the Beginner until the Professional in the Renewal Stage (Focus of Learning, Focus on Practicing, Focus on Doing, Focus on Teaching and Focus on Becoming the best), in a spiraled move of continuous learning and development. Figure 3 calls for the attention that this process involves and engage all members of the supply chain interrelated (franchisee, franchisor, customers, suppliers and partners and the community).

BUSINESS ANALYTICS AND THE IMPLEMENTATION OF THE ATTENTION-BASED FRAMEWORK

In this section, we show how the attention-based framework for the franchisee training can be implemented through the following seven pillars of business analytics (Isson & Harriott, 2013): business challenges, data foundation, analytics implementation, insights, execution and measurements, distributed knowledge, and innovation. As was discussed earlier, developing a good "family" relationship between the franchisor and the franchisee is the key *business challenge* of a successful franchise. In addition, Figure 1 describes how such a "family" relationship is built in the franchise business community. Figure 2 shows that there are many "touchpoints" within the franchise business community where the franchisor and the franchisee can influence each other. Based on the CSLC model, Table 1 shows a comprehensive

Figure 3. A pictorial view of the attention-based framework for the franchisee training

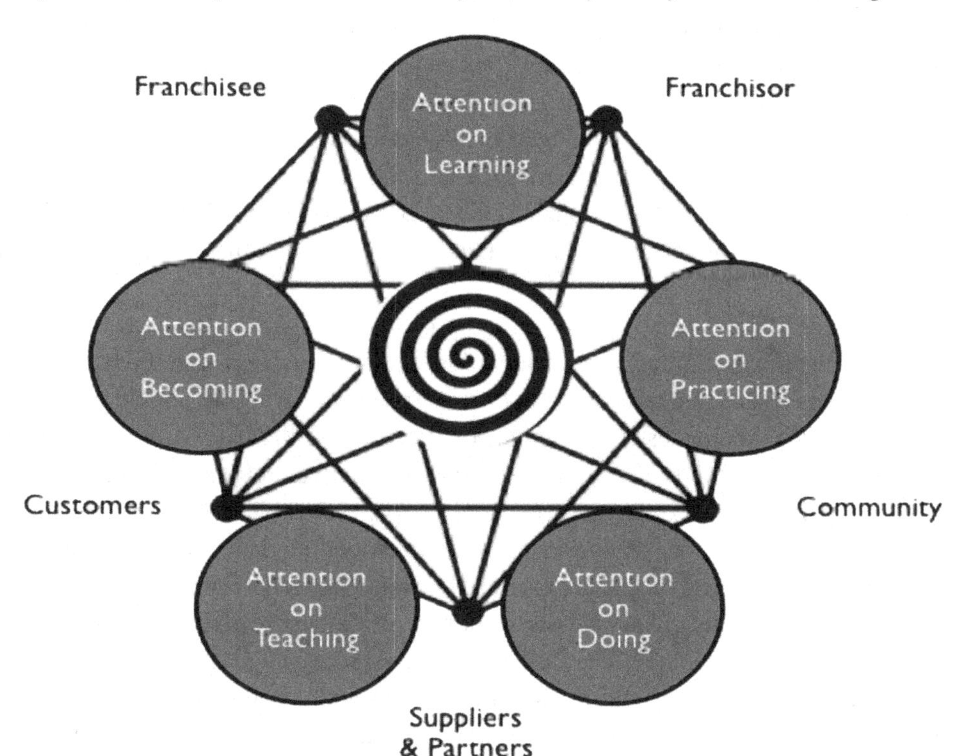

framework for a franchise to model the *data foundation* needed to serve its customers, i.e., franchisees and their customers. A well-designed Internet strategy, often enabled by Application Service Providers (ASP), shall empower the franchisor and the franchisees to collect, use, renew, store, retrieve, transmit, and share the organizational data needed to do the collaborative work in the various phases of the CSLC model, including unit operational data, external benchmarking data, and business legacy data.

An architecture of business *analytics implementation* in franchise organizations with respect to the franchisor/franchisee relationship management depicted in Figure 1 is shown in Figure 4. The architecture consists of four levels: data collection level, holding operational, external, and legacy data collected from the franchise business environment; reconciled data level, holding data warehouse data that are subject-oriented, integrated, time-variant, and non-volatile; derived data level, containing several data marts derived from the data warehouse based on various franchisee/customer-centred segmentations; and the analytical reporting level, producing various relationship performance reports for the decision makers using the decision support systems (DSS) with strong data visualization capabilities for their decision making. To move from the data collection level to the reconciled data level, data integration is needed. To move from the reconciled data level to the derived data level, data transformation is needed. To move from the derived data level to the analytical reporting level, data analysis is needed which involves two major activities online analytical processing (OLAP) and data mining (Chen, Justis, & Watson, 2000; Chen, Zhang, & Justis, 2005; Chen, Justis, & Chong, 2008). Since the data mining queries and related activities are not pre-defined, we call the supporting systems proactive DSS. In order to achieve higher success rate of data mining, we suggest (on the right side of Figure 4) that OLAP-based queries need to be conducted first. For example, one may find, through daily OLAP queries, that certain segments of customers buy certain products frequently. This pattern may lead to perform thorough and proactive analysis of the customer-product relationship and human resource analytics. The results may help the company provide legendary services to its clients and generate higher profits.

As mentioned in the discussions of Figure 1, the key for building the franchisor/franchisee "family" relationship is in the franchise organizational learning. In addition, there are five vital *insights* for a successful learning program: knowledge, attitude, motivation, individual behavior, and group behavior. Thus, working knowledge is the real foundation of a successful franchise "family" relationship. The working knowledge is structured in many forms of profiles that are embedded in the operational manuals of the franchise business processes. A working knowledge profile is developed when a certain task of the CSLC process is repeated several times with superior results. Consider the Site Profile as an example. The Site Profile is used to assist the new franchisee locate a high-quality business site. Typically it is the real estate department at the franchisor headquarters which is responsible for the profile development. The Site Profile is unremittingly being tested and enhanced. Various OLAP/Data Mining analytical reports, monitoring the performance of the sites, are generated at the Analytical Reports Level shown in Figure 3. Based on those reports, the real estate experts and their teams are able to fine-tune the attributes and the parameters within the Site Profile. Most often, the corresponding data collection procedures in the CSLC sub-stage also need to be revised and perfected so that better report scorecards can be generated.

This process of executing and enhancing the working knowledge profiles will achieve its high peak when both the franchisor and the franchisees are arriving at the Professional and Renewal stage of growth. A significant phenomenon of being a Professional franchisor and a Renewal franchisee are their ability to leverage the assets of the hard-earned working knowledge profiles into dynamic capabilities and high-business-value-creation completive-advantage strategies (Chen, Yuan, & Dai, 2004; Chen, Seidman, & Justis, 2005). The new products or services coming out of the process of leveraging the working

Figure 4. Analytics implementation: managing franchise organizational information

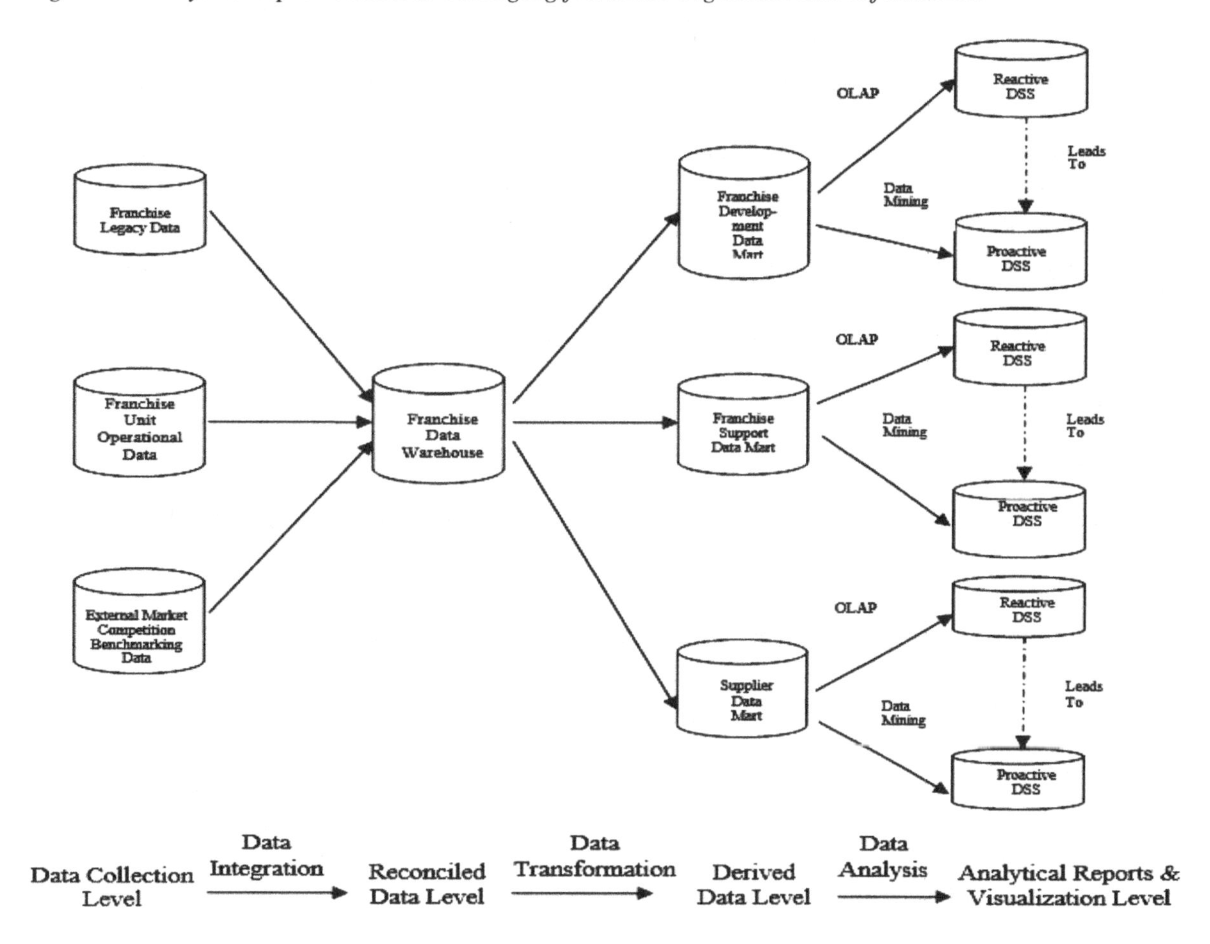

knowledge profiles may transform the franchise business into a more, sometimes surprisingly, profitable enterprise. The capability of leveraging the assets of franchise working knowledge into profitable products or services is at the heart of a successful franchise *execution and measurements*. For instance, consider the site selection working knowledge at McDonald's. The Franchise Realty Corporation real estate business, a result of site selection asset leveraging, is the real moneymaking engine at McDonald's. This as can be evidenced from the following speech of Ray Kroc, founder of McDonald's, to the MBA class at the University of Texas at Austin in 1974: "… I 'm not in the hamburger business. My business is real estate." (Kiyosaki, 2000, p. 85) In the book McDonald's: Behind the Arches (Love, 1995, p. 152), Ray Kroc commented further: "What converted McDonald's into a money machine had nothing to do with … the popularity of McDonald's hamburgers, French fries, and milk shakes. Rather, McDonald's made its money on real estate …." McDonald's makes money out of real estate by leasing properties from landlords and then subleasing the stores to the franchisees. The Professional franchisees, many of them are multiunit operators, can then focus on expending the business without worrying about finding good locations for the growth. This moneymaking real estate strategy is what separates McDonald's from other fast-food chains.

Knowledge repository systems, consisting of working knowledge profiles, can be linked into Table 2 for *distributed knowledge* management such as sharing, learning, and dissemination. Such a repository has two dimensions. First, there is a working knowledge level for the Attention Structures of Demand & Supply Value Networks: Customers, Franchisee Outlet, Franchisor Headquarters, Suppliers & Partners, and Franchise Community. Second, there are user skill levels, including Beginner in the Courting Phase, Novice in the "We"-Phase, Advanced in the "Me"-Phase, Master in the Rebel Phase (since the rebel ones tend to be those who know the system very well and are capable of influencing others to follow them), and Professional in the Renewal Stage of franchisee life cycle. The foundation of the framework is the working knowledge of the five crucial elements—Knowledge, Attitude, Motivation, Individual Behavior, and Group Behavior—used by the collaborative team, to effectively influence others in building the franchise "family" relationship. The working knowledge profiles at the franchisee outlet, the franchisor headquarters, and the franchise community can be modularized according to user's level. An Intranet-based curriculum of working knowledge modules can then be designed for the users to learn the working knowledge profiles effectively.

FUTURE TRENDS: BIG DATA AND THE ATTENTION-BASED FRAMEWORK

The emerging technologies in big data produce various new business analytics opportunities for *innovation* to grow the franchise system globally. There are three major characteristics of big data (Thomas & McSharry, 2015):

1. The volume of data is big;
2. There are many varieties of data formats such as numeric data, text data, image data, and video data; and
3. The velocity of data generation is very fast. To be useful, big data adopters must have value propositions to their businesses (Liebowitz, 2013).

In the context of the attention-based framework for the franchisee training depicted in Table 2, big data technologies need to have value propositions related to the Situated Attention of Relationship Touch-Point. For example, value network applications of big data, using business analytics techniques such as social network analysis, can be developed to connect Professional franchisees in the world. The goal is to facilitate the franchise system to successfully venture into new global emerging markets, e.g., China, through international franchising and develop innovative products/services through asset leveraging. During the recent few years, many established brands have been successfully venturing into China market through franchising (e.g., "Home Instead Senior Care opens 1,000th franchise Location and expands into China," 2013; "Mondaq.com: Franchising in China update - Australian franchisors moving Into China," 2009). However, to sustain and expand market through franchising has never been lack of challenges (e.g., "Yum Brands plans to spin off China business," 2015).

This could be done because franchise capabilities, structured in the working knowledge repository discussed above, enable the Professional franchisees to work with the franchisor to continuously improve and leverage the current franchise working knowledge. An example of value networks of Professional franchisees can be illustrated in Figure 5. There are six Professional franchisees (A - F) in the figure with three clusters (A-C, D-E, and F) of value networks. Each Professional franchisee (a dot) has his/her personal value network (arrows pointing out of the dot) tested and built over the years while doing day-to-day problems solving at the franchisee outlet. The value network may include the customers' likes

Figure 5. Value networks of professional franchisees

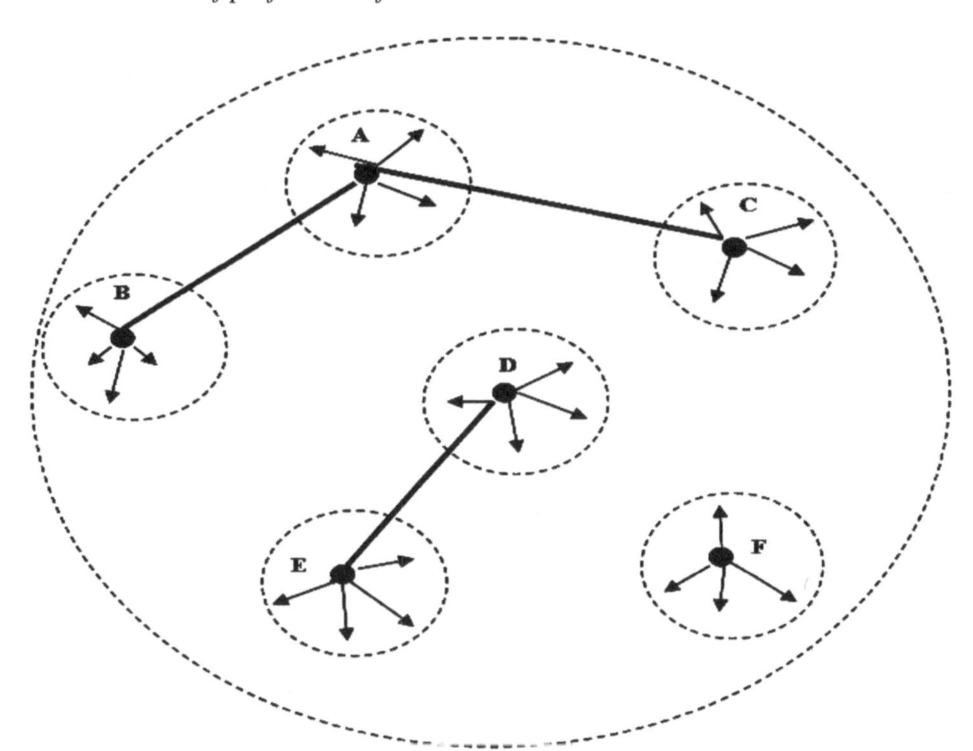

and dislikes, the kind of employees to hire, the competitors' and suppliers' pricing strategies, the social needs in the local community. Each Professional franchisee is surrounded with a circle with dashed lines, meaning there is no limit to the personal value network. In order to solve the problems more effectively, Professional franchisees may share with each other their approaches. Thus, clusters (connected dots) of value network are formed for solving various problems more effectively (Chen, Justis, & Wu, 2006).

CONCLUSION

Franchising has been popular as a growth strategy for businesses; it is even more so in today's global and e-commerce world (Chen, Chen, & Wu, 2005) and in times of increased volatility, uncertainty, complexity, and ambiguity (VUCA). The essence of franchising lies in managing the good relationship between the franchisor and the franchisee. In this paper we showed e-business strategy plays an important role in growing and nurturing such a good relationship. Specifically, we discussed:

1. Managing the franchisor/franchisee relationship through the CSLC approach, where organizational learning is believed to be the key to building the good relationship;
2. Harnessing the e-business strategy around the CSLC approach, where four major components are discussed: benchmarking the requirements and acquisition stages, helping the franchisees serve their customers in the ownership stage and avoiding Internet encroachment, cultivating the owner-

ship and renewal/retirement stages with effective knowledge management, and partnering with the "disruptive technology" providers to enhance the CSLC stages continuously; and

3. Aligning the CSLC-based e-business strategy with application service providers, where trust relationship and communication are the major issues.

With that in mind, a framework based on attention is suggested to enhance franchisee training and the awareness to involve and engage all members of the supply chain interrelated (franchisee, franchisor, customers, suppliers and partners and the community), considering the contextual environment depends on the firm's attention structure and scaffolding the appropriate needs of self-determination, self-identity and self-efficacy along the interrelated supply chain.

REFERENCES

Ardichvili, A., Zavyalova, E., & Minina, V. (2012). Human capital development: Comparative analysis of BRICs. *European Journal of Training and Development*, *36*(2/3), 213–233. doi:10.1108/03090591211204724

Azevedo, R. F. L., Ardichvili, A., Casa Nova, S., & Cornacchione Jr, E. B. (2016). Human Resource Development in Brazil. In T. Garavan (Ed.), *Global Human Resource Development* (pp. 250–265). New York: Routledge.

Bandura. (1997). Self-efficacy: Toward a unifying theory of behavioral change. *Psychological Review, 84*(2), 191-212.

Chen, Y., Chen, G., & Wu, S. (2006). A Simonian approach to e-business research: A study in Netchising. Advanced Topics in E-Business Research: E-Business Innovation and Process Management, 1.

Chen, Y., Chong, P., & Justis, R. T. (2000a). Information technology solutions to increase franchise efficiency and productivity.*Proceedings of the 2000 Franchise China Conference and Exhibition.*

Chen, Y., Chong, P., & Justis, R. T. (2000b). Franchising knowledge repository: A structure for learning organizations.*Proceedings of the 14th Annual International Society of Franchising Conference.*

Chen, Y., Chong, P., & Justis, R. T. (2002). E-business strategy in franchising: A customer-service-life-cycle approach.*Proceedings of the 16th Annual International Society of Franchising Conference.*

Chen, Y., Ford, C., Justis, R. T., & Chong, P. (2001). Application service providers (ASP) in franchising: Opportunities and issues.*Proceedings of the 15th Annual International Society of Franchising Conference.*

Chen, Y., Hammerstein, S., & Justis, R. T. (2002). Knowledge, learning, and capabilities in franchise organizations.*Proceedings of the 3rd European Conference on Organizational Knowledge, Learning, and Capabilities.*

Chen, Y., Justis, R., & Watson, E. (2000). Web-enabled data warehousing. In M. Shaw, R. Blanning, T. Strader, & A. Whinston (Eds.), *Handbook of electronic commerce* (pp. 501–520). Springer-Verlag. doi:10.1007/978-3-642-58327-8_24

Chen, Y., Justis, R., & Wu, S. (2006). Value networks in franchise organizations: A study in the senior care industry.*Proceedings of the 20th Annual International Society of Franchising Conference*.

Chen, Y., & Justis, R. T. (2006). Chinese franchise brands going globalization. *1st Annual China Franchise International Summit*. International Franchise Academy.

Chen, Y., Justis, R. T., & Chong, P. P. (2008). Data mining in franchise organizations. In J. Wang (Ed.), *Data Warehousing and Mining: Concepts, Methodologies, Tools, and Applications* (pp. 2722–2733). doi:10.4018/978-1-59904-951-9.ch169

Chen, Y., Justis, R. T., & Yang, H. L. (2004). Global e-business, international franchising, and theory of Netchising: A research alliance of east and west.*Proceedings of the 18th Annual International Society of Franchising Conference*.

Chen, Y., Seidman, W., & Justis, R. T. (2005). Strategy and docility in franchise organizations.*Proceedings of the 19th Annual International Society of Franchising Conference*.

Chen, Y., Yuan, W., & Dai, W. (2004). Strategy and nearly decomposable systems: A study in franchise organizations.*International Symposium on "IT/IS Issues in Asia-Pacific Region, Co-sponsored by ICIS-2004*.

Chen, Y., Zhang, B., & Justis, R. T. (2005). Data mining in franchise organizations. Encyclopaedia of Information Science and Technology, (pp. 714-722). Academic Press.

CN Franchise at a Glance. (n.d.). Retrieved from https://franchisemeets.com/report/asia/CN/

Franchise 500 Directory 2013. (2013). Entrepreneur.com, Inc.

Franchise 500 Directory 2014. (2014). Entrepreneur.com, Inc.

Franchise 500 Ranking. (2015). *Entrepreneur, 43*(1), 182-245.

Gates, B. (1999). *Business @ the Speed of Thought: Succeeding in the Digital Economy*. Warner Books.

Giddens, A. (1991). *Modernity and Self-identity: Self and Society in the Late Modern Age*. Cambridge, UK: Polity Press.

Gorovaia, N., & Windsperger, J. (2010). The use of knowledge transfer mechanisms in franchising. *Knowledge and Process Management, 17*(1), 12–21. doi:10.1002/kpm.337

Hadfield, B. (1995). *Wealth Within Reach*. Cypress Publishing.

Home Instead Senior Care opens 1,000th franchise Location and expands into China. (2013). Retrieved from http://libezp.lib.lsu.edu/login?url=http://search.ebscohost.com/login.aspx?direct=true&db=edsgbc&AN=edsgcl.351529234&site=eds-live&scope=site&profile=eds-main

Isson, J., & Harriott, J. (2013). *Win with advanced business analytics: Creating business value from your data*. Wiley and SAS Business Series.

Ives, B., & Mason, R. O. (1990). Can information technology revitalize your customer service? *The Academy of Management Executive, 4*(4), 52–69. doi:10.5465/AME.1990.4277208

Justis, R. T., & Judd, R. J. (2002). *Franchising*. DAME Publishing.

Justis, R. T., & Vincent, W. S. (2001). *Achieving wealth through franchising*. Adams Media Corporation.

Kirkley, W. W. (2016). Entrepreneurial behaviour: The role of values. *International Journal of Entrepreneurial Behavior & Research, 22*(3), 290–328. doi:10.1108/IJEBR-02-2015-0042

Kiyosaki, R. (2000). *Rich dad, poor dad*. Time Warner.

Liebowitz, J. (2013). *Big data and business analytics*. CRC Press. doi:10.1201/b14700

Lin, L. M., & Hsia, T. L. (2011). Core capabilities for practitioners in achieving e-business innovation. *Computer in Human Behavior Journal, 27*(5), 1844–1891. doi:10.1016/j.chb.2011.04.012

Love, J. (1995). *McDonald's: behind the arches*. Bantam Books.

Mondaq.com. (2009). *Franchising in China update - Australian franchisors moving Into China*. Retrieved from http://libezp.lib.lsu.edu/login?url=http://search.ebscohost.com/login.aspx?direct=true&db=edsnbk&AN=12B77223A134EA60&site=eds-live&scope=site&profile=eds-main

Ocasio, W. (1997). Towards an attention-based view of the firm. *Strategic Management Journal, 18*(S1), 187–206. doi:10.1002/(SICI)1097-0266(199707)18:1+<187::AID-SMJ936>3.3.CO;2-B

Perrigot, R., & Pénard, T. (2013). Determinants of e-Commerce strategy in franchising: A resource-based View. *International Journal of Electronic Commerce, 17*(3), 109–130. doi:10.2753/JEC1086-4415170305

Schreuder, A. N., Krige, L., & Parker, E. (2000). The franchisee lifecycle concept – A new paradigm in managing the franchisee-franchisor relationship. *Proceedings of the 14th annual International Society of Franchising Conference*.

Simon, H. A. (1971). Designing organizations for an information rich world. In Computers, Communications, and the Public Interest, (pp. 38-52). Baltimore, MD: The Johns Hopkins Press.

Thomas, D., & Seid, M. (2000). *Franchising for dummies*. IDG Books.

Thomas, R., & McSharry, P. (2015). *Big Data Revolution*. Wiley.

U.S. Commercial Service. (2008). *China franchising industry*. The JLJ Group.

Wolf, D. (2007). *Prepared and Resolved: The Strategic Agenda for Growth, Performance and Change*. DSB Publishing.

World Bank. (2016). *Doing Business: Measuring Business Regulations*. World Bank Group. Retrieved from http://www.doingbusiness.org/rankings

Yum Brands plans to spin off China business. (2015). Dolan Media.

Zeng, Q., Chen, W., & Huang, L. (2008). E-business transformation: An analysis framework based on critical organizational dimensions. *Journal of Tsinghua Science and Technology, 13*(3), 408–413. doi:10.1016/S1007-0214(08)70065-8

KEY TERMS AND DEFINITIONS

Customer Service Life Cycle: Serving customers based on a process of four stages: Requirements, Acquisition, Ownership, and Retirement. Many companies are using the approach to harness the Internet to serve the customers.

E-Business: Coined by IBM's marketing and Internet teams in 1996 it is defined as the application of information and communication technologies in support of all the business activities and processes in the entire value and supply chain.

E-Business Innovation: Innovation originating from innovative e-business applications that impact established business models and collaborations with stakeholders. (Lin and Hsia, 2011).

Franchisee: The individual or business who receives the business rights and pay the royalties for using the rights.

Franchisee Life Cycle: The stages a franchisee goes through in the franchise system: Courting, "We", "Me", Rebel, Renewal.

Franchising: A business opportunity based on granting the business rights and collecting royalties in return.

Franchisor: The individual or business who grants the business rights.

Franchisor/Franchisee Learning Process: The stages of learning, including Beginner, Novice, Advanced, Master, and Professional.

Franchisor/Franchisee Relationship Management: The vital factor for the success of a franchise, including: Knowledge, Attitude, Motivation, Individual Behavior, and Group Behavior.

Chapter 9
The Human Behavioral Response to Automated Trading

Roumen Vragov
EF International Academy, USA

ABSTRACT

The use of computer algorithms by human traders in markets has been steadily increasing. These electronic agents or proxies vary in terms of purpose and complexity, however, most of them first require some input on the part of the human trader and then perform the rest of the trading task autonomously. This paper proposes a theoretical model of human behavior that can be used to detect behavioral biases in commodity markets populated by humans and electronic proxies. The model's predictions are tested with the help of laboratory experiments with economically-motivated human subjects. Results suggests that the usefulness of automated trading is initially diminished by behavioral biases arising from attitudes towards technology. In some cases, the biases disappear with experience and in others they do not.

INTRODUCTION

During the last decade the number of E-commerce sites has exploded, and buying and selling of goods on the Internet has become a nontrivial task. Just looking at eBay's listings on 4/24/2016, 1:38 pm EST revealed 42,120 auctions for digital cameras going on simultaneously. The cameras come in a wide variety of type, resolution, quality, and they were represented by a variety of vendors, each with a different reputation score and history. The same digital cameras can be bought at other auction web sites or purchased directly from the sites of the camera makers or from the websites of a few big retailers. Additional units might be posted as available on sites that offer free ads as Craig's list. Each of these sites sells items in different ways. They require different user information and apply different restrictions. Navigating through this maze of information is still challenging. It is up to the user to choose which web site will better serve her purpose and what her optimal strategy will be given the different rules and requirements of the chosen sites. To deal with this issue programmers have started creating software applications to assist the user in her interactions on-line. These programs have been called robots, auctionbots, software agents, automated traders, proxies, etc. Such a feature is presently available on eBay, under the name of proxy bidding (Roth & Ockenfels, 2002). After a buyer has decided to participate in

DOI: 10.4018/978-1-5225-1680-4.ch009

an auction, she can give a limit price to her proxy. eBay keeps this information private. The proxy then bids in the auction. Every time the proxy is outbid but the current price remains below the limit price provided by the buyer, the proxy bids a minimum increment over the current bid. Meanwhile the buyer does not have to follow the auction. She can devote her time to more important activities. eBay's director for customer relations in Australia declared that the proxy-bidding service provided by his company's web-site was flexible enough to allow buyers and sellers to compensate for some inefficiencies due to eBay's auction design (Davidson, 2005). According to Hayne et al., (2003) 75% of all users on eBay use this feature. The remaining 25% usually participate directly or use more complicated proxies provided by vendors other than eBay. The usage of proxies for e-Commerce transactions is quickly becoming popular. The proxies can be used for searching for items to buy/sell; searching for the best web sites for buying/selling items; and devising different bidding or pricing strategies. Researchers at IBM report that "[trading] robots can make more cash than people when they trade commodities" (Graham-Row, 2001). Other studies (e.g. Miller, 2002) suggest that markets populated entirely of robots cannot attain efficient equilibria. At the same time agent research in E-commerce has flourished at different Universities in the US and abroad (Go to http://www.multiagent.com/Laboratories/Market-oriented/ for a comprehensive list of related initiatives). Most of the proxies currently used in practice or tested in research laboratories represent automated strategies characterized by different degrees of sophistication that first require some input on the part of the human trader and then perform the exchange task autonomously. Research efforts have been devoted to investigating agent communication protocols (Finin et al., 1995; Papastavrou et al.; 1999, Artikis et al., 2000) as well as to applying the principles of artificial intelligence to software agent design (Hryshko & Downs, 2004; Greenwald, 2003; Wooldridge, 2000).

Proxy trading has quickly become very popular in financial markets as well under the name of automated trading or high-frequency trading (Goldstein, 2013). The move to automation of trading was encouraged by the SEC especially on the NYSE by regulation NMS in 2005 (Jones, 2013). Computer algorithms are currently used to:

1. Break up a high-quantity order into smaller orders that can be executed without drastically affecting the market price;
2. Choose where orders should be routed (Avellaneda, 2011);
3. Serve as automated market makers in regular financial markets (Frankle, 2010) as well as in prediction markets (Othman, 2012);
4. Perform arbitrage and relative value trading;
5. Analyze news and try to quickly take advantage of the newly available information;
6. Minimize latency in trading (Jones, 2013).

There is disagreement in academic circles regarding the social and individual benefits of automated trading. Most empirical studies have shown automated trading to be beneficial but different theoretical models have generated different conclusions. Many traders still remember the flash crash on May 6, 2010 when an automated trading algorithm trading in E-Mini S&P500 futures supposedly caused a large drop in index and stock prices and trading had to be suspended for a short period of time. Another example was Knight Capital Group's $440 million loss on August 1st, 2012 due to a new trading algorithm (see Jones, 2013 for a review of many recent theoretical models and more details about the crash). With the advent of digital currencies and especially Bitcoin, automated trading has spread to markets where these currencies are exchanged as well. (Zbikowski, 2016; Bell, 2016).

Figure 1. The focus of the study is the relationship between the market participant and the trading agent

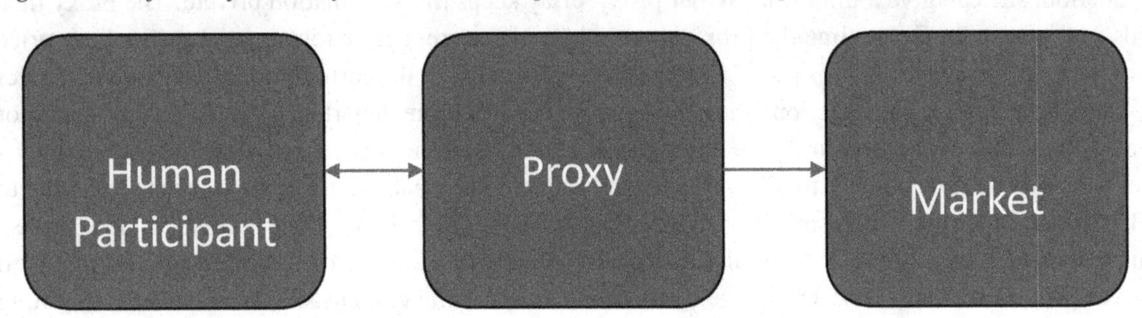

The practical contribution of this study is that it is one of the first studies to address the human behavioral response to the introduction of automated proxies in electronic markets (as shown in Figure 1) and to estimate the effect of this response on business profits.

The study also makes an important theoretical contribution. We can use previous research in two social sciences: economics and psychology to generate a model that links individual behavior in relation to proxies and market outcomes. The context in this paper is economic and psychological because we are specifically investigating behavior effects in a certain type of an electronic market. All decisions are made at the individual level, while outcomes are generated through interactions between humans and proxies in an auction market.

When looking at human behavior, it is often helpful to consider both rational and not so rational behavioral responses to stimuli. While we can use ideas from classical economics to shed some light on the human rational[1] response to the introduction of proxies, psychology is well placed to discuss other not strictly rational aspects of this response. This paper uses relatively current theoretical and experimental developments in psychology and economics to propose an interdisciplinary model of human behavior that takes into consideration the impact of strictly rational thought as well as some pre-conceived notions about computers in general on the human-proxy interaction in an auction setting and its results. The paper specifically focuses on mixed human-proxy auction environments and the usage of proxies who have limited autonomy as explained later.

My specific research question is whether and what kind of psychological biases we can detect in human market participants when they trade in mixed human-robot exchanges. To answer this question I use the methodology of Experimental economics. This research method is routinely used to study the validity of stylized theoretical models in terms of predicting the performance of real-world systems when considering the behavior and decision-making of real people in the research setting (Kagel, 1997). Based on induced value theory (Smith, 1976) and an extensive arsenal of experimental results, Smith has established and defended the external validity and usefulness of the experimental methodology in comparing alternative market designs and in testing underlying principles of human behavior (Smith, 1976, 1980, 2002, 2003). Experiments are also very common in the design sciences, where often a prototype system design must be tested and evaluated in the laboratory before it may be introduced in practice settings (Hevner et al., 2004, Goes, 2013). The need of laboratory experiments in e-commerce research has also been recognized and discussed in Kauffman and Wood (2008). Under this methodological framework, laboratory experiments allow the researcher to study relevant phenomena with complicating environmental context-related conditions removed. Such experiments enable precise measurements of relevant effects while necessarily sacrificing some generality and realism. Using this methodology I find that certain psychological biases are present and easy to detect in mixed human-proxy environments. Because of these biases humans under-report their valuations to their proxy-agents, which causes inefficiencies in trading.

The paper is organized in the following way:

- Section II describes theoretical developments in economics, game theory, and psychology pertinent to proxy usage;
- Section III describes in detail a theoretical model of human-proxy interaction;
- Section IV specifies the research hypotheses;
- Section V describes an experiment designed to test the hypotheses derived from the model;
- Section VI summarizes the experimental procedures;
- Section VII reports the results, Section VIII discusses the experimental findings;
- Section IX is devoted to the limitations of the study; and
- Section X concludes the paper.

THEORETICAL BACKGROUND

In the world of classical economics characterized by rational individuals, perfect information, and no transaction costs (Hollander, 1987) the introduction of software agents as proxies in a marketplace should have no enduring effect on market behavior. The trading proxy is only a technology that provides an interface to a market but does not change the market's underlying demand and supply conditions. Classical economics does not provide a concrete model for the behavior of the market participants except that they do everything in their power to maximize their utility from a market transaction. Neoclassical economics has recognized the existence of transaction costs and therefore accepted that the use of any kind of communication technology for trading should only influence transaction costs but not individual market behavior or other market characteristics (Domowitz, 2002). An individual will choose to use a proxy if the individual thinks that the use of proxy will result in transaction cost savings and not choose a proxy otherwise. At the aggregate level this should result in higher efficiency levels because all market participants should be more satisfied with the proxy option available than if the proxy option is not provided. The problem with using a model based solely on ideas from classical and neoclassical economics is that not fully rational behavior is not accounted for.

Current game theoretic models provide some guideline to the market behavior of rational individuals, and the possible effect of proxy usage in certain sterilized settings. Let us take as an example a theoretical model of a standard first price sealed bid auction as discussed in Elyakime (1994). In this auction a seller sets a secret reservation price that no one can observe. Next, all N buyers submit a sealed bid to buy the item for sale. After all bids are submitted, the bids are open and the buyer with the highest bid wins the auction. Unless the highest bidder's bid is lower than the seller's reservation price, the exchange occurs and the product is traded. It has been shown theoretically that in equilibrium, the seller has to set the reservation price equal to the seller's cost, and all buyers have to bid a fraction of their value, v or $\frac{N-1}{N}v$ when buyer values are distributed uniformly between 0 and 1.

Imagine that the seller and all buyers are given a proxy to use when they participate in a version of the first price sealed bid auction mentioned in the previous paragraph because they are not able to attend the auction personally or they would like to devote their attention to other activities. Suppose also that the seller's proxy is programmed to submit as reservation price the limit price reported to him by the seller, and the buyer's proxy is programmed to bid $\frac{N-1}{N}$ times the limit price that a buyer has provided. It is clear that in equilibrium the seller will report his cost to his proxy, and a buyer will report his value for the item to his proxy. If the buyer's and seller's proxy strategies are different than the ones described above, then the seller and the buyers will adjust their limit prices so as to have the proxies bid the cost and $\frac{N-1}{N}$ times the values respectively. The introduction of a proxy will not change the final allocation and auction price if the proxy strategy is known to the market participants.

Generally, game theory can be used successfully in static environments with a small number of participants and well defined information sets. In this sense naturally occurring trading environments are a source of many challenges that are hard to overcome by game theory. For example, it is difficult to predict what happens if the proxy strategy is not fully known or understood by the market participants. Many theorists will argue that there will be a learning period during which buyers and seller will discover the proxy strategy and adjust their limit prices accordingly (Camerer et al., 2003). During the initial periods individuals who use proxies will play randomly (Estes, 1994). With the flow of time, the variance will start decreasing and limit prices will start converging to the optimal prices. Eventually the same market allocation and price should be achieved. however, individuals will need to experience more than one auction. Again, this discussion is relevant only when individuals are rational decision-makers.

Past research in psychology is better positioned to give us a clue about the nature of the relationship between computerized proxies and their human partners and the non-rational biases involved in the decision-making process. For example, Turkle (1990) states that currently humans qualify computers as objects that are not alive but at the same time possess some kind of intelligence of their own. The only difference between a human and a computer that many adults currently cite is that human beings are emotional, unprogrammable and computers are extremely logical and rational. A similar attitude is represented by Miller (2004) although he claims that humans often ascribe social awareness qualities to agents. An experimental study by Bijou and Lester (2003) has demonstrated that human attitudes towards the Internet and e-Commerce are directly related to human attitudes towards computers in general. These attitudes find their cultural foundations in art, books, and movies and inevitably influence the relationship between humans and computers. Stafford & Stern (2002) show that these attitudes also determine consumer's willingness to participate in on-line auctions.

A basic psychological assumption is that human behavior is sometimes determined by preconceived notions about the way the world works that are not necessarily true or are based on genetic predispositions (Alexander, 1969). We would like to see if certain attitudes towards computers reported in psychological research can help us create a more realistic model of human behavior in a market environment with proxies. The relationship between humans and proxies is based on a market participant's view of the degree to which the task of buying and selling goods requires strictly computational skills or some emotional intelligence in addition. Buyers or sellers who choose to be represented by proxies think that trading is a computational task that could be done better by the automated proxy. Buyers or sellers who choose to participate themselves think that human intelligence is better fitted for the task. Using the theoretical developments mentioned in this section, we can create a model of human behavior that incorporates both rational and emotional elements in an attempt to paint a fuller picture of the interaction between human participants and proxies in an auction market. We will use the general approach of behavioral economics. Under that approach psychological insights about possible irrational behavior are included in a theoretical model as deviations from perfectly competitive equilibrium behavior (see Mullainathan & Thaler, 2002). Specific theoretical models of human-proxy interaction in auctions are currently absent form the literature.

There is considerable amount of research in economics, finance, psychology, and information systems that has looked at bidder behaviors in various auction markets. More recently, there has been some more research concentrating on bidder behavior in online auctions (e.g. Ariely & Simonson, 2003; Stafford & Stern, 2002; Oh, 2002, Roth & Ockenfels, 2002; Bapna et al., 2004; Vragov, 2005). However, these studies look at bidding behavior in general and do not isolate the effect of the automated proxy as a technological feature of some of these auctions on human bidding behavior and market outcomes. The reason is partially that "uncontaminated" data is not available. Proxies started being widely and openly used for the first time in C2C online auctions. The most popular of these web sites (e.g. eBay, Yahoo, Ubid, Amazon) have either not existed without offering some kind of a proxy feature or have forced users to use at least the default proxy feature provided by the site. Both of these factors obstruct the estimation of the proxy feature's pure effect on human behavior and market outcomes. An early attempt at discerning the effect of a specific proxy feature on auction success is reported in Bapna (2003). The author describes a natural experiment during which one unidentified eBay bidder participated in eBay auctions during three different phases (manual sniping, constrained manual sniping, and agent sniping) over a period of five years. The author reports that the use of a proxy sniping feature increased the percentage of auctions won. The present study is based on a reasonable sample size and goes further to estimate not only the increase in success rate due to proxy usage but also the more important effects on profits and overall market efficiency.

There are also some design studies (e.g. Ausubel, 2003; Bapna et al, 2004; Petchbordee & Sortrakul, 2005 among others) that analyze bidder behavior or specific auction mechanisms and then propose proxy designs that facilitate the different strategies that bidders are already using. A major implicit assumption of these studies is that auction participants will use the newly designed proxies only to further improve on the strategies that they have rationally chosen to play earlier before they adopted the proxies. The study here is the first to provide an empirical test of the validity of this assumption.

MODEL OF HUMAN-PROXY INTERACTION

The first part of the model is an extension of the classical economics model of perfect competition and the second part of the model is based on slight behavioral deviations from perfect competition. In the tradition of behavioral economics we will use the idea of competitive equilibrium to derive the strategies of the human traders when no proxies are available, and of modified competitive equilibrium when proxies are available. Under competitive equilibrium every trader is a price taker. The competitive equilibrium strategy for buyers and sellers is the equilibrium price at the intersection of the downward-sloping demand curve and upward-sloping supply curve. Notice that, according to the classical economics paradigm, the competitive strategy does not depend on the institutions (auctions) being used (Smith, 2003). The only slight departure that we make from the classical model is the introduction of transactions costs as explained in the next paragraph.

Let us suppose in our model that there is an auction environment characterized by an upward-sloping supply and downward-sloping demand curves that cross each other at a single point. The supply curve represents the costs of all items present at the auctions, and the demand curve represents the values that buyers place on all items at the auctions. The market environment is also characterized by transaction costs related to time, which represent the urgency of transactions, i.e. as time goes buy items become more costly to auction for the sellers and less valuable for the buyers. The auctions are conducted in the following way: any seller who wants to sell an item has to choose an auction type, start an auction, and specify his or her reservation price. Buyers can log in different auctions and submit bids. Let us assume that buyers and sellers are homogeneous in terms of item costs and values, and let us label with r_0 the optimal strategy (reservation price) for every seller and with b_0 the optimal strategy (bid) for every buyer in this environment. Since prices are determined by the bids, we can claim that $b_0 = p^e$, where p^e is the equilibrium price. We realize that in naturally occurring circumstances this result will be too strong. It will be more reasonable to expect that in equilibrium every buyer's bids will be somewhere in the neighborhood of the optimal strategies or $b_i = p^e + \varepsilon_i$ where ε_i is the error term distributed according to a symmetric distribution with a mean of 0. The sellers' reservation prices do not determine the transaction price; they only serve as a limit that the auction price has to cover if the transaction is to be completed. Therefore, a seller's optimal reservation price has to be lower than the equilibrium price or $r_i \leq p^e + \varepsilon_i$.

Suppose further that buyers and sellers are given an option to use an electronic proxy to participate in the auction environment. Note that the underlying demand and supply conditions as well as the competitive equilibrium price do not change. The buyers and sellers do not know the exact strategy of the proxy but are given a chance to experience it. In this part we also depart from the classical model of perfect competition because we will include some behavioral elements which might not be perfectly rational. We assume that after the introduction of the proxy the behavior of some of the market participants is influenced by non-rational biases. We define as biased the response which is motivated by preconceived (and often incorrect) notions about the way the proxy works and which changes slowly during trading. The biases appear when market participants are faced by uncertainty and/or complex tasks but might disappear after enough experiences is gathered (see Kahneman & Tversky, 1982). Using the results from the past research in psychology reviewed in the previous section we can argue that a biased seller, who chooses to use a proxy, is convinced that the proxy will be more profitable and will report to the proxy a higher reservation (or limit) price $r_i = p^e + \delta_i + \varepsilon_i$ where $\delta_i > 0$. A biased seller, who chooses not to use a proxy, believes that proxies are not fit for the trading task and will submit a reservation price of $r_i \leq p^e + \varepsilon_i$ as if the proxy is not there. Similarly, a biased buyer, who chooses a proxy, will submit lower bids $b_i = p^e + \lambda_i + \varepsilon_i$ where $\lambda_i < 0$, and a biased buyer, who chooses not to use a proxy, will submit the same bids $b_i = p^e + \varepsilon_i$ as if the proxy is not there (see Table 1).

Let us now discuss the response of a rational market participant to the introduction of an electronic proxy option at the beginning of a trading period. Following the discussion in section II we can say that rational market participants will choose proxies only in the presence of transaction costs but the resulting bids and reservation prices will be the same as when proxies are not available. This is because the underlying demand and supply conditions will not change and because every market participant will still be a price-taker. Therefore, we can still use the expression $r_i \leq p^e + \varepsilon_i$ to designate a rational seller's strategy. In this way the average reservation price for rational sellers with proxies will most likely be the same as if the proxy is not available. The same logic can be used to derive the expression for the strategy of rational buyers, who choose proxies, which is $b_i = p^e + \varepsilon_i$.

Looking at all the strategies displayed in Table 1, it is hard to say how economic efficiency will be affected with the introduction of the proxy. Clearly, the behavior of the biased market participants, who choose to be represented by a proxy, serves to lower efficiency. If market behavior is mostly biased, introducing a proxy will lower efficiency when there are no transaction costs. In this model transaction costs related to time are present. Since proxies are able to complete transactions much faster than humans, than we might expect that the use of proxies can have a positive effect of lowering transaction costs. The balance between the loss related to biases and the gain related to time-savings will determine the overall efficiency ranking of markets with proxies. This is why in our case the high levels of acceptance of the proxy technology does not automatically guarantee better market performance. The model also suggests that a high level of acceptance of the proxy technology does not necessarily result in higher individual performance. If acceptance is motivated by psychological biases then individual performance will be lower. Using the model in Figure 2, we can formulate several testable hypotheses described in the next section.

HYPOTHESES

Under naturally occurring circumstances we cannot observe the types of the market participants. We know whether a market participant is a buyer or a seller, and we can also observe whether a buyer or a seller chooses to use a proxy. The model described above can help us find out to what extent market

Figure 2. Types and strategies of market participants

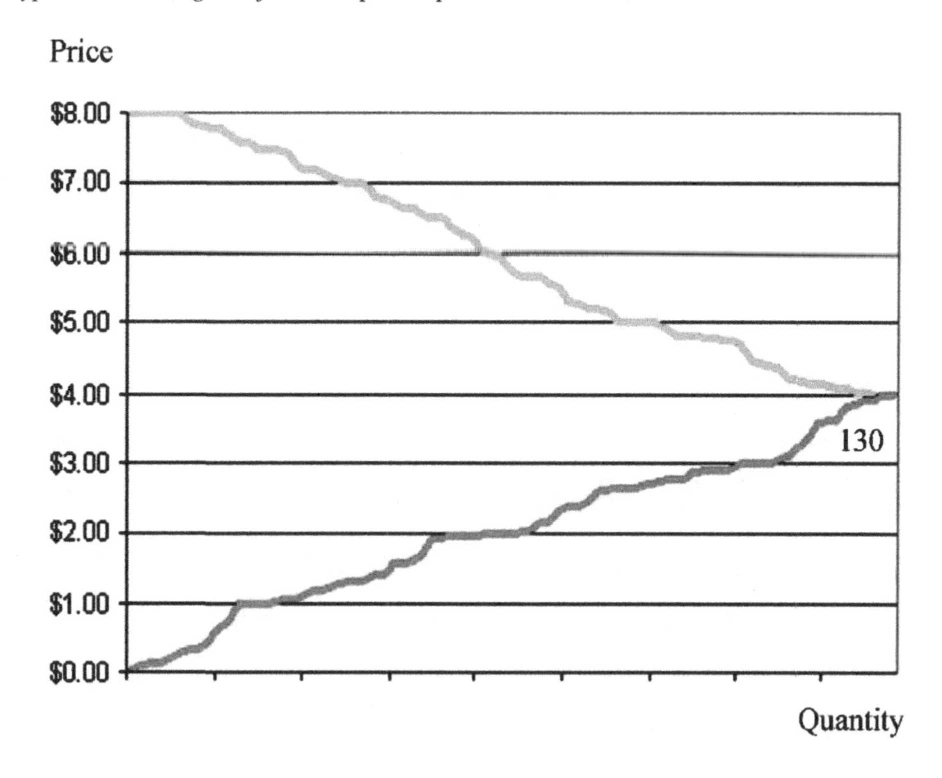

participants are influenced by biases when proxies are introduced. Two experimental treatments of the same market environment can be conducted. In the first baseline treatment human subjects can trade in an on-line auction environment by themselves (Baseline treatment), in the second treatment we can introduce proxies that buyers and sellers can opt to use (Proxy treatment). In order to test for the consistency of our model we first have to verify that the introduction of the proxy into a market with unchanged demand and supply conditions does not result in different transaction prices. This is the purpose of the first hypothesis.

H1: Price Equivalence Hypothesis

If we accept the notion of classical economics that, as long as humans participate in a market, equilibrium price is determined by the supply and demand conditions regardless of the proxy technology used as the foundation of this model, we can use the first hypothesis to verify the model's relevance. Transaction prices in the Baseline treatment should be equal to the transaction prices in the Proxy treatment or $p^B=p^P$. We can use a t-test based on the observed prices in the two treatments to verify this.

H2: Rational Versus Biased Human Response Hypothesis

Table 1 summarizes the four tests (one in each row) that we can perform in order to detect biased responses. The tests are based on comparisons between the bids and reservation prices in the Baseline treatment versus the Proxy treatment. We will show here the derivation of H2d). The remaining parts are derived in a similar manner. According to the model a buyer's bid in the baseline treatment will be $b_i=p^e+\varepsilon_i$. If buyers' response in the second treatment is mostly rational then the bids will be identical to the ones in the baseline treatment. If the buyers' response in the second treatment is mostly biased, then we have $b_i=p^e+\lambda_i+\varepsilon_i$ where $\lambda_i<0$. We would therefore expect that bids of the buyers with proxies in the proxy treatment to be lower.

According to our model, we can detect biases using the differences in bids and reservation prices demonstrated under hypotheses H2b) and H2d). We can accomplish this with a help of a t-test comparing the experimental bids and reservation prices. Under hypotheses H2a) and H2c) there is no difference between the rational and biased response. That is why, in addition to H2 we can use our model to detect biases by also looking at the influence of transaction costs on the choice of using a proxy.

Table 1. Human response hypotheses

	If Rational	If Biased
a) Sellers' reservation prices in the baseline treatment vs. reservation prices of the sellers without proxies in the Proxy treatment	$r_{HS}^B = r_{HS}^P$	$r_{HS}^B = r_{HS}^P$
b) Sellers' reservation prices in the baseline treatment vs. reservation prices of the sellers with proxies in the Proxy treatment	$r_{HS}^B = r_{PS}^P$	$r_{HS}^B \le r_{PS}^P$
c) Buyers' bids in the baseline treatment vs. bids of the buyers without proxies in the Proxy treatment	$b_{HB}^B = b_{HB}^P$	$b_{HB}^B = b_{HB}^P$
d) Buyers' bids in the baseline treatment vs. bids of the buyers with proxies in the Proxy treatment	$b_{HB}^B = b_{PB}^P$	$b_{HB}^B > b_{PB}^P$

H3: Transaction Costs Affect the Choice to Use or Not to Use a Proxy

We would expect that if market participants are rational then the probability of choosing a proxy will increase with the increase in transaction costs. If market participants have heterogeneous transaction costs, then we can use a standard probit model to detect the relationship between the level of transaction costs and the probability of choosing a proxy.

METHODOLOGY

Since 2002 (when Vernon Smith and Daniel Kahneman received a Nobel Prize in Economics for their work) using experiments with economically motivated human subjects has been accepted as a legitimate method to detect biases in human market behavior. One of the reasons is the problem with contaminated data already mentioned in section II. In addition reliable data about real costs and values is often unavailable (Smith, 2003). Exact surplus and profits are hard to measure in naturally occurring circumstances but are easy to measure in a well-controlled experimental setting. Research in auction theory suggests that the auction price is a function of the bids and offers, which are functions of the economic environment characterized by the sellers' real costs and buyers' real values (maximum willingness to pay) for the product that is being traded (Krishna, 2002; Klemperer, 2004; Milgrom, 2004). Sellers' real costs, buyers' real values, their transaction costs and the current market equilibrium price are not observable in naturally occurring markets. When scientist use data from real auctions to draw conclusions based on comparisons of outcomes they run into the problem of omitted variables. They usually have to make assumptions about these variables or assumptions about possible substitutes. Every assumption, however reasonable, weakens the results of the analysis. In this study these additional assumptions are not necessary because all of the above-mentioned variables are under the experimenter's control as mush as possible. In addition, Porter and Vragov (2006) show that results from market field experiments can be misleading unless they are calibrated with the help of laboratory experiments.

The main purpose of our experimental design is to find a good balance between satisfying the basic assumptions of the model described above without making the experimental environment too unrealistic. Human subjects have to be provided with proper incentives, so they are paid according to the profits that they make during the experiment as prescribed by induced value theory (Smith, 1976). Since the experimenter provides the subjects with their value and cost characteristics, he or she can see deviation from these specifications and thus directly observe efficiency and bidding strategies directly.

To satisfy the model's requirements the experimental environment possesses the following general characteristics:

1. There are 130 units of a homogeneous product to be traded;
2. The induced demand curve is downward-sloping, the induced supply curve is upward-sloping, and they cross at a single point;
3. Uncertainty is introduced by not fully disclosing the proxy strategy and by allowing the theoretical equilibrium price to vary within a 12 cent range throughout the experiment with the help of transaction costs related to time;

4. Complexity is introduced by allowing subjects to trade on four different auction web-sites with slightly different rules;
5. Heterogeneous time-related transactions costs are introduced for both buyers and sellers.

The specific design details are described in the following paragraphs.

The experiment consists of two basic treatments:

1. A baseline treatment; and
2. A Proxy treatment that will be described in detail below.

There are twenty-six subjects in each treatment (13 buyers and 13 sellers). None of the subjects participated in both treatments. Each buyer has values for ten units and each seller has costs for ten units. If all sellers start auctions for all of their items, the buyers can participate in as many as 130 auctions. Sellers' costs are independently drawn from a uniform distribution with support [$0.00, $4.00]; buyers' values are drawn independently from a uniform distribution with support [$4.00, $8.00]. This is done to ensure a high degree of buyer and seller homogeneity in terms of product costs. This also guarantees that all units present on the market might be exchanged without loss if time costs (described later) are disregarded.

Buyers can buy up to ten items. Buying more than ten items does not add value. Sellers can start up to ten auctions and can sell only up to ten items. A subject's profit from buying an item is v_i - p (value minus price) and from selling an item, p - c_i. Values are used in the following way: if Buyer 1 buys one unit for $4.00 and his value for the first unit is 8.00, his/her profit would be 8.00 – 4.00 = 4.00. If Buyer 1 buys three units for $4.00 each and his/her values for the first three units are 8.00, 7.41, and 6.22, then his profit is 8.00 + 7.41 + 6.22 – 3x4.00 = 9.63. Costs are used in the following way: if Seller 1 sells one unit at $4.00 and the cost of his/her first unit is 1.58, his/her profit would be 4.00 – 1.58 = 2.42. If Seller 1 sells three units at $5.00 and his/her costs are 1.58, 159, and 1.95, his/her profit would be 3x5.00 – 1.58 – 1.59 – 1.95 = 11.88 (see Figure 3).

Every minute during the experiment subjects incur two types of costs: The first is a monitoring cost that depends on the time they need to buy/sell 10 units. Every buyer is randomly assigned a monitoring

Figure 3. Induced demand and supply conditions at the start of each experimental session before subjects start incurring time costs

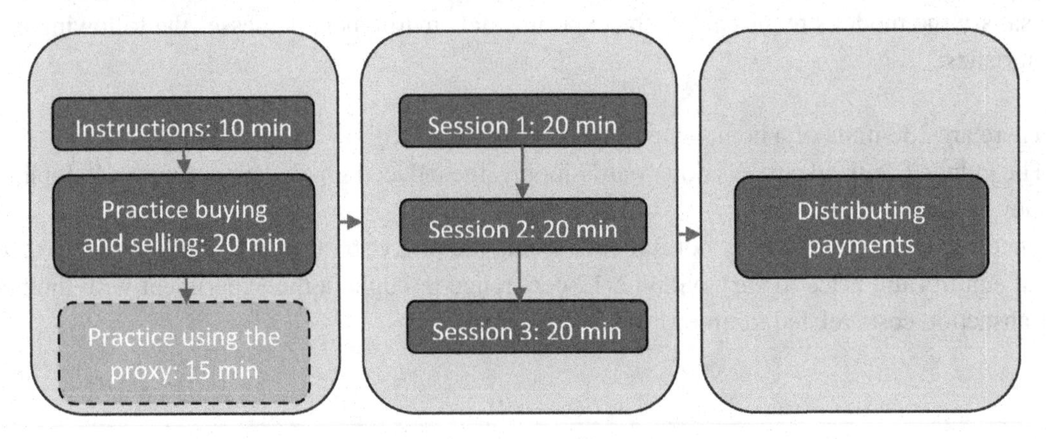

cost from the following set {0.00, 0.01, 0.02, 0.03, 0.04, 0.05, 0.06, 0.07, 0.08, 0.09, 0.1, 0.11, 0.12}. The same procedure is performed for the sellers. The second cost is an inventory cost per unsold item from the initial allocation. This charge is applied only to the sellers. For every seller a number is randomly chosen from the set {0.00, 0.01, 0.02, 0.03} to represent his/her inventory charge. These time costs are introduced in the experiment as a more direct way of measuring transactions costs. The intent is to create some level of urgency while still giving subjects the chance to earn a reasonable amount of money for their effort.

During the course of one experimental session a buyer could incur total time costs somewhere between \$0.00 and \$2.40, which is approximately between 0% and 13% of the possible attainable individual profit. For the sellers the corresponding figures are much larger. Their monitoring cost is in the same range as the buyers, but inventory costs can pile up quickly. They can be between \$0.00 and \$6.00, or approximately between 0% and 33% of the possible attainable individual profit per market participant. The maximum cost of \$6.00 is incurred only if a seller has not been able to sell anything throughout the duration of an experimental session.

Each treatment consists of three sessions, and each session is terminated at a specified time (20 minutes after start). Sellers can choose to start an auction at any time during the 20 minutes, and buyers can choose to participate in any of the active auctions. The timeline of the experiment in shown in Figure 4.

The induced demand and supply curves in the experiment cross at \$4.00. This price is the competitive equilibrium at the beginning of each session. The equilibrium quantity is 130, and the total surplus

Figure 4. Timeline of the experiment. The training session does not involve the last component during the baseline treatment.

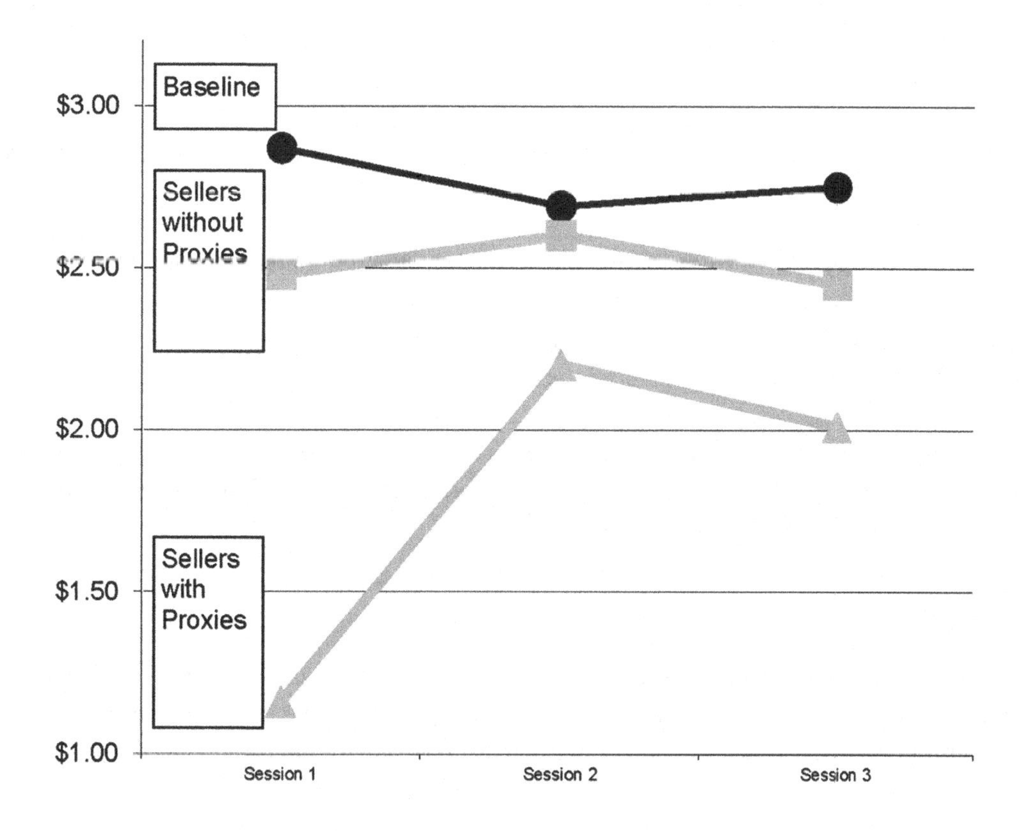

is $481.22. However, as the session goes on, buyers and sellers start incurring time costs. Since the sellers' time-related costs are higher than the buyers', the supply curve starts shifting up faster than the demand curve shifts down. Therefore, equilibrium quantity will be less than 130 and equilibrium price greater than $4.00. Given this situation, classical economic theory gives us no clues as to what an optimal strategy should look like.

The cost and value parameters are the same for all sessions and treatments. All subjects went through a training session that explained the rules of all trading institutions, described below, and gave the subjects the chance to participate in each one of them separately. Subjects also had a chance to participate in two short training sessions using agents as proxies. Subjects were paid $5.00 for showing up for the experiment on time, and they kept all profits ($18.00 on average) that they made from all sessions. The specific value and cost parameters cannot influence the results from the hypotheses because the hypotheses are used to compare the two treatments. Parameters in the two treatments are the same, the only difference is that buyers and sellers are given an option to use a proxy in the Proxy treatment.

Baseline Treatment

In the baseline treatment four different auctions are offered to the participants. Four auctions were chosen in order to make the market environment relatively complex. These four specific auction types have been chosen because of their popularity in theoretical and experimental literature. They are the standard First Price Sealed Bid Auction (see Cox et. al. 1988 for a description) with five required participants, the standard Second Price Sealed Bid Auction (see Vickrey, 1961; Coppinger et al., 1980) also with five required participants, the English Clock auction also with five required participants (see McCabe et al., 1991), and a simplified version of an eBay auction (see Vragov, 2005)

Proxy Strategies

The following three basic principles borrowed from previous research (see Greenwald, 2002) were used to design a proxy strategy:

1. **Partial Autonomy:** The proxies do not act completely autonomously. They require their users to provide them with limit prices at the beginning of each session in the experiment;
2. **Minimization of Losses:** The proxies strictly abide by the limit prices provided by the buyers and sellers. A proxy should never sell below a seller's reservation price and never buy above a buyer's limit price;
3. **Opportunity for Learning and Updating:** This is mostly concerning the buyer-proxy's strategy. Buyers should be trying to buy items at the lowest limit price first, and then go up to a higher limit price after a certain number of failed bids.

Proxy Treatment

In the Proxy treatment all experimental parameters are kept exactly the same as in the baseline treatment. The only difference is the fact that both buyers and sellers are given the option of choosing a proxy to represent them in the experimental market environment (this is like choosing proxy bidding on eBay although the automated strategy there is quite simple). Both the buyer and seller proxies implement a fixed sub-optimal strategy. They work according to the following algorithms.

Seller Proxy

At the beginning of every experiment the seller proxy starts an auction with every limit price provided by the seller as the reservation price. Auction types are chosen randomly with equal probability, and if eBay is chosen, auction lengths are chosen randomly with equal probability.

Buyer Proxy

The buyer proxy receives and processes information about all available auctions. Initially, it randomly chooses to participate in ten auctions comprised of Second price sealed bid-auctions, First price sealed bid-auctions and English clock auctions. It also stores information about the closing times of all eBay auctions. If an eBay auction reaches its end, the buyer-robot participates in it initially with the lowest limit price provided by the buyer. In case of success, the buyer proxy drops out of an EC auction. If there is no English clock auction available, the buyer proxy waits for a result from the other auctions before proceeding. In case of failure, the buyer proxy tries another eBay auction as soon as one is available. After a certain number of failures, the lowest limit price is raised to the second-lowest limit price. The buyer proxy makes sure that a certain ratio of active bids to units for which limit values are provided is kept constant throughout the experiment.

In order to follow the theoretical model specifications, subjects were not informed about these specifications. Instead, they were given a chance to experiment using their proxies in two 10-minute test-runs before the actual experiment started.

SUMMARY OF EXPERIMENTAL PROCEDURES

Fifty-two subjects were recruited randomly from the undergraduate student population at large state university and grouped into two sets of twenty-six participants. Then each participant was randomly assigned to one of the two treatments and to be a buyer or a seller. The subjects were paid a five dollar show up fee plus a performance-based payout that averaged about twenty-five dollars per person per experiment. Each experiment consisted of three sessions (see Figure 4). The subjects read a set of computerized instructions (see Appendix) and participated in a training session so that they can experience the rules of the market and the way to use the trading system that was developed for the experiment. Prior to the experiments, a number of pilots were run during the development of the electronic market design and the implementation of the trading system. The software was implemented as a real-time client/server application and programmed in Java.

RESULTS FROM HYPOTHESES TESTING

There were 164 completed auctions in the Baseline treatment with average price and its standard deviation of $\overline{p}^{B} = 4.05$ and s^{B}=1.09. During the Proxy treatment 249 auctions were completed with average price and standard deviation of $\bar{p}^P = 4.12$ and $s^P = 1.12$. A two sample t-test results in a $t = 0.63$, which supports our first hypothesis. This also solidifies our approach of using the classical competitive equilibrium idea as a foundation of our behavioral model.

Figures 5-6 and Tables 3-4 show the resulting average bids and reservation prices during the experiment with their standard deviations. Since the biased behavior will be most pronounced in the first session of the Proxy treatment we would like to first test hypothesis 2 by comparing the first sessions of the two treatments and then the last sessions of the two treatments to see if any changes have occurred. Table 5

Table 2. Results from the tests of the human response hypotheses throughout the three sessions of the experiment

Session	Hypothesis	Rational	Biased
1	2a)	Accept ($t = 1.23$, $df = 52$)	Accept
	2b)	Reject ($t = -5.20$, $df = 53$)	Reject
	2c)	Accept ($t = 1.83$, $df = 56$)	Accept
	2d)	Reject ($t = 2.92$, $df = 69$)	Accept
3	2a)	Accept ($t = 1.41$, $df = 89$)	Accept
	2b)	Reject ($t = -3.30$, $df = 112$)	Reject
	2c)	Accept ($t = -1.88$, $df = 106$)	Accept
	2d)	Accept ($t = 0.56$, $df = 100$)	Reject

Figure 5. Mean reservation prices of successfully completed auctions

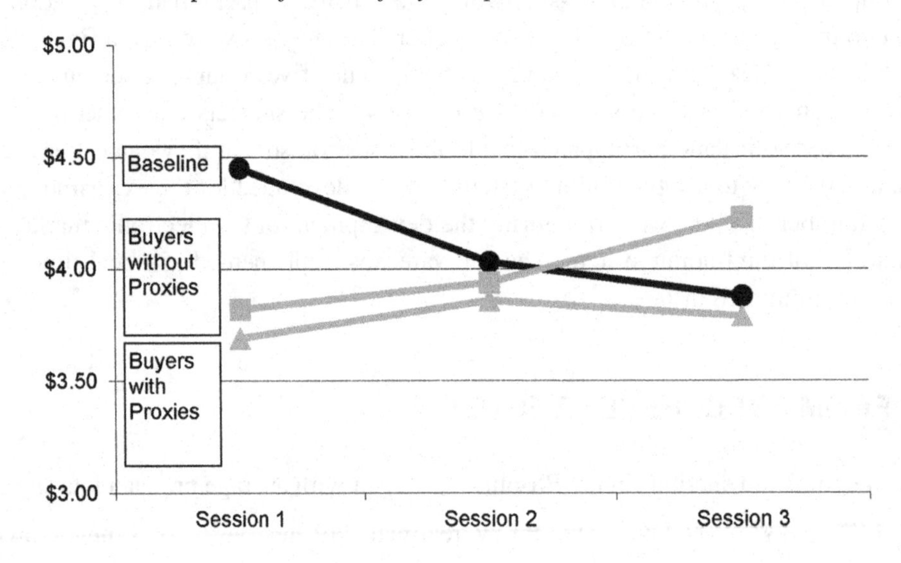

Table 3. Mean reservation prices with standard deviation and number of observations in parenthesis

Treatment		Session 1	Session 2	Session 3
Baseline		2.87 (1.08, 31)	2.69 (0.89, 66)	2.75 (1.02,66)
Proxy	Sellers without proxies	2.48 (1.20, 23)	2.60 (1.09, 18)	2.45 (0.86, 25)
	Sellers with proxies	1.16 (1.30, 24)	2.20 (1.26, 28)	2.01 (1.29, 48)

Figure 6. Mean winning bids in successfully completed auctions

Unit	Value	Price	Profit	Auction
1	8.00	0.00	0.00	
2	7.41	0.00	0.00	
3	6.22	0.00	0.00	
4	6.15	0.00	0.00	
5	5.74	0.00	0.00	
6	5.69	0.00	0.00	
7	5.58	0.00	0.00	
8	5.05	0.00	0.00	
9	4.04	0.00	0.00	
10	4.02	0.00	0.00	
		Trans Total	0.00	
Mon Cost	0.11		0.00	
Inv Cost	0.00		0.00	
Over cost	0.00	Total	0.00	
		Exch Rate	0.33	
		Exp Total	0.00	

Connect asen Timer

Table 4. Mean bids with standard deviation and number of observations in parenthesis

Treatment		Session 1	Session 2	Session 3
Baseline		4.45 (1.25, 31)	4.03 (1.03, 66)	3.88 (1.04, 66)
Proxy	Buyers without proxies	3.82 (1.36, 27)	3.94 (1.39, 21)	4.23 (0.87, 42)
	Buyers with proxies	3.69 (0.83, 40)	3.86 (0.52, 23)	3.79 (0.58, 36)

summarizes the results from testing the four different parts of H2 over the first and last sessions of the Proxy treatment. All tests are two-tailed and are based on a 5% confidence level.

The model seems to predict well the behavior of all buyers. Buyers acted in a biased manner at the beginning of the experiment but their bias dissipated towards the third session. We cannot say the same for sellers. The behavior of the sellers who chose not to use a proxy is in line with our predictions, however, the behavior of sellers who chose the proxy was unexpected. The latter chose to give unusually low reservation prices to their proxies consistently during all three sessions.

Table 5. Analysis of maximum likelihood estimates for the two probit models for binary choice β_1 is the coefficient of monitoring costs and η_1 is the coefficient of inventory costs

Parameter	DF	Estimate	Standard Error	Wald Chi-Square	P-Value
β_1	1	-5.1454	3.7352	1.8976	0.1683
η_1	1	3.1493	15.221	0.0428	0.8361

As mentioned earlier, the Proxy treatment involves 26 human subjects. Proxies were used by seven buyers and eight sellers in the first session, five buyers and seven sellers in the second session, and five buyers and eight sellers in the third session. The rate of proxy-usage is therefore 57.7%, 46.2%, and 50.0%. This gives us a chance to test the third hypothesis using a probit model for binary choice. Two separate tests are conducted. The first test investigates the influence of monitoring costs on the probability of buyers and sellers choosing a proxy. We fail to reject the null hypothesis that the effect of monitoring costs is significant at the 5% confidence level. The second test investigates the influence of inventory costs on the probability of sellers choosing a proxy. Again, we fail to reject the null hypothesis that the effect of inventory costs was significant. A more detailed output of the two probit models is shown in Table 6. From these tests we can conclude that the level of transaction costs did not overall influence the buyers' and sellers' choice of whether to choose a proxy.

ANALYSIS AND DISCUSSION

The results of the experiments suggest that subjects' acceptance decision is not necessarily motivated by rational thinking and that both buyers and sellers are influenced by psychological biases. This is confirmed by hypothesis 3 which shows that subjects' choice of proxy does not depend on the transaction costs and by some parts of hypotheses 2 that detect biased effects in bids and reservation prices. Once the acceptance choice is made, buyers and sellers respond differently to the introduction of the proxy. As indicated by hypothesis 2, at the beginning of the experiment buyers submit biased bids but towards the end of the experiment buyers bid as if proxies are not there. This means that buyers' biases are overcome by experience. The behavior of the sellers who chose not to use proxies is in line with our model predictions. The model, however, fails to predict the behavior of the sellers who choose to use a proxy. Contrary to our expectations these sellers submit much lower reservation prices. This might be an expression of another persistent psychological bias that we have not included in the model. Further experiments will be necessary to explain this phenomenon.

Table 6. Profit comparisons

Treatment		Mean Profits	St. Dev.	# of Observations
Baseline		3.184	2.56	78
Proxy	Used Proxy	4.034	2.63	40
	Did not use proxy	4.508	2.90	38
	All	4.252	2.76	78

These experimental results lead us to an important issue of the link between acceptance and usage of proxy technology in on-line auctions. Since the acceptance decision was mostly influenced by biases as shown by the results from testing hypotheses 2 and 3 we would expect that the acceptance decision had no significant effect on individual performance (see Table 6). A t-test between pay-offs of subjects who did not use a proxy and those who used a proxy in the Proxy treatment fails to reject the null hypothesis of no difference at the 5% confidence level ($t = 0.745$, $df = 76$). At the same time adding the proxy feature to the auction market significantly increased subjects' profitability ($t = 2.508$, $df = 154$) although the gains were distributed mostly to the subjects who decided not to use a proxy.

LIMITATIONS AND FUTURE RESEARCH

This study is one of the first to propose and test a model of human-proxy interaction in online auctions and as such it possesses several limitations that can be addressed in future studies. Let us first discuss the ones related to the theoretical model. The model described in this paper considers only one psychological bias towards computers. This bias was chosen because it is considered prevalent by previous studies. Many other cultural, social or psychological biases related to technology might exist and will need to be incorporated in a more general model of human-proxy interaction. A second important component is the modeling of human learning patterns and behaviors which needs to be added as well. Our model does not apply to market environments populated exclusively by proxies with very high levels of autonomy and not much human supervision. Efficiency and equilibrium prices in such markets will depend exclusively on the strategies used by the proxies and not on human behavioral characteristics. The model also does not apply to auctions with small number of participants (7 buyers and 7 sellers or less – see Smith, 1962). This is because the forces pushing prices to equilibrium levels in such environments depend to a large degree on the rules of the auctions chosen. That is why models of smaller auction environments need to incorporate possible strategic differences between auction types.

Generally, there are three common ways to generate data for hypothesis testing when probing human behavior. All of them have advantages and disadvantages. Data from naturally occurring online markets is messy and cannot provide good estimates of actual willingness to pay and therefore of actual economic efficiency and user performance, and data from computer-based simulations exclude any complex effects of human interaction. The third way to generate data involves conducting experiments. Experiments with human subjects partially solve some of the problems with the other two data generating procedures, however they have their own limitations. It is inevitable that some of the experimental parameters (especially the ones whose values are not suggested by the theory being tested) have to be chosen almost arbitrarily and subjectively by the experimenter. That is why experiments have to be repeated and extrapolated upon by other experimental scientists, and results from experiments have to be compared to outcomes from naturally occurring circumstances.

In the context of this specific experiment the amount of transaction costs is one of these arbitrarily chosen parameters. There are currently no studies that estimate these costs, and their reasonability is a matter of opinion and interpretation. There are subjects in the experiment that have no transaction costs, and there are subjects that have relatively high transaction costs. We can see the effect of the level of these costs on subject behavior, and we can also see that the loss related to the biases was not large enough to offset the gains related to time savings. This result is only relevant to the specific experimental setting.

Managers of online auctions should consider the amount of transaction costs and possible savings before they decide to provide a proxy feature to their web site.

Another limitation is the length of the conducted experiment. Using its results we are not able to predict subject long-term behavior. It will be interesting to see how the behavior changes past the third session of the Proxy treatment. Will prices converge completely to equilibrium levels, will the Proxy market achieve efficiency much closer to 100%, and will the sellers' psychological bias demonstrated in the beginning disappear completely? Unfortunately a longer experiment in a laboratory will be too draining for the subjects and it would require a substantial increase in subject payments to provide requisite material incentives. Field experiments conducted over the Internet might be able to offer us a way to reach a variety of audiences and observe human trading behavior for longer periods of time.

Given the current known usage of agents in practice it seems that subjects in the experiment did not have as much control over the agent strategy as they do in naturally occurring circumstances. We should keep in mind that the agents currently available on auction websites are only a very small fraction of all possible agent designs, some of which might be in use but are undetectable and some of which will be used in the very near future. Therefore the question of user control is interesting and definitely requires further work. The theoretical model in this paper does not address the impact of the level of user control over the agent. The model results should be applicable to all levels of control from the lowest possible to the highest possible. The experiment was also not designed with the specific purpose to test for the effect of different levels of control on the size of the psychological bias, however we can still use the results to make an interesting observation related to user control. Buyers with proxies could only choose the limit prices but not the actual proxy bids and the auctions for these bids, and sellers with proxies could not choose the auctions but could choose the reservation prices. This means that, from a certain point of view, sellers had more control over their proxies than buyers, yet sellers' bias was larger than the buyers'. This result suggests that the effect of increasing or decreasing the level of control over the proxy is complex. A new set of experiments will be necessary to investigate this effect after user control is incorporated into an updated model of behavior that can help us generate new hypotheses.

CONCLUSION

This paper investigates the human behavioral response to the introduction of electronic proxies in an auction market. The paper uses some ideas from economics and psychology to create a theoretical model of human behavior that takes into consideration human actions that are dictated by rational thought as well as ones dictated by pre-conceived notions about proxies and computers in general. The paper reports results from experiments specifically designed to test the model in a laboratory settings using humans as subjects. The experimental results generally confirm the presented model. The results also demonstrate that during initial trading periods humans respond in a biased rather than rational fashion to the introduction of proxies. In psychological terms this behavior could be considered a cultural bias. There are indications that the buyer bias might dissolve with experience, however, the behavior of sellers who are using proxies is not consistent with rational play during the entire experiment. This shows that the usage of proxies might not always improve further on the strategies that market participants are already using before the proxy is introduced. Sometimes the introduction of proxies triggers psychological biases in trading decisions that do not disappear with time.

The results from the study also suggest that the introduction of proxies to an auction market does not automatically lead to an increase in efficiency and profitability. Bapna (2003) discussed two main problems related to the use of proxy agents:

1. One is technical (clogging auction servers);
2. The other one is strategic (bidder collusion).

This study adds one more problem, which is psychological in nature. Managers need to estimate the possible loss related to biases towards the proxy before they decide to add such a feature to their auctions. At the same time online buyers and sellers should be aware that using a proxy does not guarantee higher pay-offs. Proxies should be used only after the market participant has enough information about the underlying demand and supply conditions of the items to be bought or sold. More research is necessary to understand the full nature of the bias towards the computerized proxies and the source of subject confusion when proxies are available. In addition to the above findings this research article is an example of the importance of collaboration between different scientific disciplines in developing a common theoretical understanding of consumer behavior.

REFERENCES

Alexander, T. (1969). *Children and Adolescents: A Biocultural Approach to Psychological Development*. New York: Atherton Press.

Ariely, D., & Simonson, I. (2003). Buying, Bidding, Playing, or Competing: Value Assessment and Decision Dynamics in Online Auctions. *Journal of Consumer Psychology, 13*(1-2), 113-123

Artikis, A., Pitt, J., & Stergiou, C. (2000). Agent Communication Transfer Protocol. *Proceedings of the 4th International Conference on Autonomous Agents*. doi:10.1145/336595.337577

Ausubel, L. (2003). Clock Auctions, Proxy Auctions, and Possible Hybrids. *Proceedings of the 3rd Combinatorial Bidding Conference*.

Avellaneda, M. (2011). *Algorithmic & High-Frequency Trading: An Overview*. Presentation, Quant Congress USA 2011.

Bapna, R. (2003). When Snipers Become Predators: Can Mechanism Design Save Online Auctions?. *Communications of the ACM, 46*(12), 152-158.

Bapna, R., Goes, P., Gupta, A., & Jin, Y. (2004). User Heterogeneity and Its Impact on Electronic Auction Market Design: An Empirical Exploration. MIS Quarterly, 28(1), 21 – 43.

Bell, T. (2016). *Bitcoin Trading Agents*. Working Paper. University of Southampton.

Bijou, Y., & Lester, D. (2003). Liaw's Scales to Measure Attitudes toward Computers and the Internet. *Perceptual & Motor Skills, 97*(2), 384.

Camerer, C., Ho, T., & Chong, K. (2003). Models of Thinking, Learning, and Teaching in Games. American Economic Review, 93(2), 192.

Coppinger, V., Smith, V., & Titus, J. (1980). Incentives and Behavior in English, Dutch, and Sealed-bid Auctions. *Economic Inquiry*, *18*, 1-22.

Cox, J. C., Smith, V. L., & Walker, J. M. (1988, March). Theory and Individual Behavior of First-Price Auctions. *Journal of Risk and Uncertainty*, *1*(1), 61–99. doi:10.1007/BF00055565

Davidson, J. (2005, June 4). eBay Rules 'stack cards against sellers'. Australian Financial Review, p. 12.

Domowitz, I. (2002). Liquidity, Transaction costs, and Reintermediation in Electronic Markets. *Journal of Financial Services Research*, *22*(1-2), 141-57.

Elyakime, B., Laffont, , Loisel, , & Vuong, . (1994, April-June). First-Price Sealed-Bid Auctions with Secret Reservation Prices. *Annales dEconomie et de Statistique*, (34), 115–141. doi:10.2307/20075949

Estes, W. (1994). Towards a Statistical Theory of Learning. *Psychological Review*, *101*(2), 282-290.

Finin, T., Labrou, Y., & Mayfield, J. (1995). KQML as an Agent Communication Language. In *Software Agents*. Cambridge, MA: MIT Press.

Frankle, J. (2010). *Theoretical & Practical Aspects of Algorithmic Trading* (Dissertation). Karlsruhe Institute of Technology.

Goes, P. B. (2013). Design science in top information systems research journals. *Management Information Systems Quarterly*, *38*(1), 3–8.

Goldstein, J. (2013, October 13). Trading Places. *The New York Times*, p. MM14.

Graham-Row, D. (2001). Robots Beat Human Commodity Traders. *New Scientist*, *14*(15).

Greenwald, A. (2003). The 2002 Trading Agent Competition: An Overview of Agent Strategies. *AI Magazine*, *24*(1), 83-92.

Hayne, S., Smith, C., & Vijayasarathy. (2003). Who Wins on eBay: An Analysis of Bidders and their Bid Behaviors. *Electronic Markets*, *13*(4), 262-293.

Hevner, A. R., March, S. T., Park, J., & Ram, S. (2004, March). Design Sciences in Information System Research. *Management Information Systems Quarterly*, *28*(1), 75–105.

Hollander, S. (1987). *Classical Economics, B*. New York: Blackwell.

Hryshko, A., & Downs, T. (2004). System for Foreign Exchange Trading Using Genetic Algorithms and Reenforcement Learning. *International Journal of Systems Sciences*, *35*(13-14), 763-774.

Jones, C. (2013). *What Do We Know about High-Frequency Trading?*. Working Paper. Columbia Business School.

Kagel, J. H. (1997). Auctions: A Survey of Experimental Research. In J. H. Kagel & A. E. Roth (Eds.), *The Handbook of Experimental Economics* (pp. 501–586). Princeton University Press.

Kauffman, R., & Wood, C. (2008). Research Strategies for E-Business: A Philosophy of Science View in the Age of the Internet. In R. Kauffman & P. Tallon (Eds.), *Economics, Information Systems, and Electronic Commerce: Empirical Research. M. E. Sharp, Inc.*

Klemperer, P. (2004). *Auctions: Theory and Practice*. Princeton, NJ: Princeton University Press.

Krishna, V. (2002). *Auction Theory*. San Diego, CA: Academic Press.

McCabe, K., Rassenti, S., & Smith, V. (1991). Testing Vickrey's and Other Simultaneous Multiple Unit Versions of the English Auction. Research in Experimental Economics, 4, 187.

Milgrom, P. (2004). *Putting Auction Theory to Work*. Boston, MA: Cambridge University Press. doi:10.1017/CBO9780511813825

Miller, C. (2004). Human-Computer Etiquette: Managing Expectations with Intentional Agents. *Communications of the ACM*, *47*(4), 31-34.

Miller, R. (2002). *Don't Let Your Robots Grow up to Be Traders: Artificial Intelligence, Human Intelligence, and Asset-market Bubbles*. Working Paper. Miller Risk Advisors.

Mullainathan, S., & Thaler, R. (2002). *International Encyclopedia of the Social and Behavioral Sciences*. Retrieved from www.iies.su.se/nobel/papers/Encyclopedia%202.0.pdf

Oh, W. (2002). C2C vs. B2C: A Comparison of the Winner's Curse in Two Types of Electronic Auctions. *International Journal of Electronic Commerce, 6*(4), 115-138.

Othman, A. (2012). *Automated Market-Making: Theory & Practise* (Thesis). Carnegie Melon University School of Computer science, CMU-CS-12-123.

Papastavrou, S., Samaras, G., & Pitoura, E. (1999). Mobile Agents for WWW Distributed Database Access. *Proceedings of the 5th International Conference on Data Engineering*. doi:10.1109/ICDE.1999.754928

Petchbordee, S., & Sortrakul, T. (2005). Online Auction Site: Proxy Bid Service with Time Awareness Engine. *Proceedings of the 4th International Conference on eBusiness.*

Porter, D., & Vragov, R. (2006). An Experimental Examination of Demand Reduction in Multi-unit Versions of the Uniform-price, Vickrey, and English Auctions. *Managerial and Decision Economics*, *27*(6), 445-458,

Roth, A., & Ockenfels, A. (2002, September). Last-Minute Bidding and the Rules for Ending Second-price Auctions: Evidence from eBay and Amazon Auctions on the Internet. *The American Economic Review*, *92*(4), 1093–1103. doi:10.1257/00028280260344632

Smith, V. L. (1962). An Experimental Study of Competitive Market Behavior. *The Journal of Political Economy*, *20*(2), 111-137.

Smith, V. L. (1976). Experimental Economics: Induced Value Theory. *American Economic Review*, *66*(2), 274-279.

Smith, V. L. (1980). Relevance of Laboratory Experiments to Testing Resource Allocation Theory. In J. Kmenta & J. Ramsey (Eds.), *Evaluation of Econometric Models* (pp. 345–377). San Diego, CA: Academic Press. doi:10.1016/B978-0-12-416550-2.50024-8

Smith, V. L. (2002, October). Method in Experiment: Rhetoric and Reality. *Experimental Economics*, *5*(2), 91–110. doi:10.1023/A:1020330820698

Smith, V. L. (2003). Constructivist and Ecological Rationality in Economics. *American Economic Review, 93*(3), 465-508.

Stafford, M., & Stern, B. (2002). Consumer Bidding Behavior in On-line Auction Sites. *International Journal of Electronic Commerce, 7*(1), 135-150.

Turkle, S. (1990). Growing Up in the Age of Intelligent Machines: Reconstructions of the Psychological and Reconsiderations of the Human. In R. Kurzweil (Ed.), *The Age of Intelligent Machines*. Boston, MA: MIT Press.

Tversky, A., & Kahneman, D. (1982). Subjective probability: A judgment of representativeness. In D. Kahneman, P. Slovic, & A. Tversky (Eds.), *Judgment under Uncertainty: Heuristics and Biases* (pp. 32–47). Cambridge, U.K.: Cambridge University Press. doi:10.1017/CBO9780511809477.007

Vickrey, W. (1961). Counterspeculation, Auctions, and Competitive Sealed Tenders. *The Journal of Finance*, (March), 16.

Vragov, R. (2005). Why is eBay the King of Internet Auctions? An Institutional Analysis Perspective. *eService Journal, 3*(3).

Wooldridge, M. (2000). On the Sources of Complexity in Agent Design. *Applied Artificial Intelligence, 14*(7), 623-644.

Zafirovsky, M. (2003). Human Rational Behavior and Economic Rationality. *Electronic Journal of Sociology, 7*(2).

Zbikowski, K. (2016). Application of Machine Learning Algorithms for Bitcoin Automated trading. In Machine Intelligence and Big Data in Industry (vol. 19, pp. 161-168). Springer International Publishing.

ENDNOTES

1. See Zafirovski (2003) for a definition of human rationality in economics, sociology, and psychology.
2. Item 6 and the image following it appear only in the instructions for the agent treatment.
3. Images for the sellers are similar to those of the buyers and are omitted for brevity.
4. Item 6 and the image below appear only in the instructions for the agent treatment.

APPENDIX

Experiment Instructions

This is an experiment in market decision making, and you will be paid for your participation in cash, at the end of the experiment. Different participants may earn different amounts. What you earn depends partly on your decisions and partly on the decisions of others. The experiment will take place through the computer terminals at which you are seated, and interaction among participants will take place primarily through these computers. It is important that you not talk or in any way try to communicate with other participants during the experiment. If you disobey the rules, we will have to ask you to leave the experiment. We will start with a detailed instruction period. During the instruction period, you will be given a complete description of the experiment and will be shown how to interact with the computers. If you have any questions during the instruction period, raise your hand and your question will be answered so everyone can hear. If any difficulties arise after the experiment has begun, raise your hand, and a monitor will come and assist you.

Buyers: In this experiment you will participate in several Internet auctions as a buyer. Buyers are given values for a fictitious good. As a buyer, your profit per unit is equal to your value for that unit minus the price paid. Your profit/unit = Value for that unit - Price for that unit Thus if you are a buyer, your total profit will be: Total profit = sum of the values of the items that you bought - sum of the prices of items that you bought. Remember that all values and costs in this experiment are between $0.00 and $8.00 per unit. In this experiment, you will also have a monitoring cost. Every minute in the experiment up to 1 hour after the start will cost you a certain amount of cents. This amount is shown to you in your balance sheet under the label Monitoring cost. Thus, your total experimental profit will be: Total profit = sum of the values of the items that you bought - sum of the prices of items that you bought - Monitoring cost In this experiment there is also an Exchange rate. Every experimental dollar is equal to 0.33 US dollars. Figure 7 shows an example of a buyer's balance sheet.

Figure 7. Example buyer's balance sheet

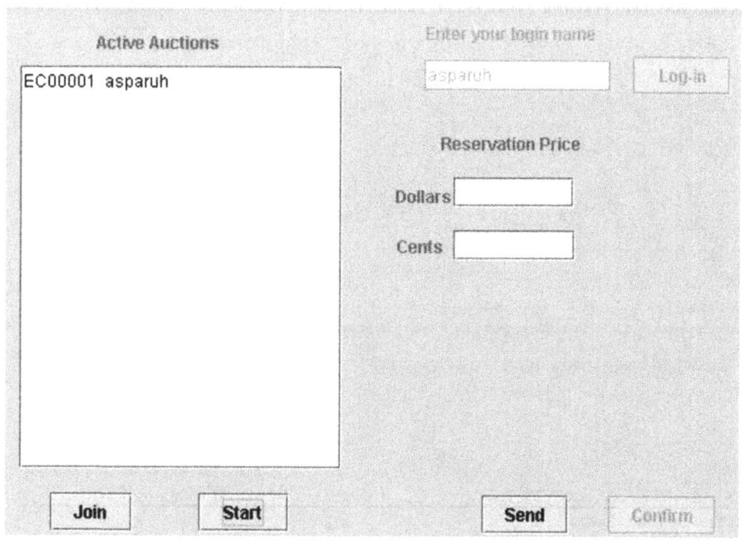

In this case, \$8.00 is the value to you of the first purchased unit and \$7.41 is the value to you of the second purchased unit. Your monitoring cost is \$0.11 per minute of the experiment. Your login name "asen" is shown at the bottom of the screen. If you buy an item, you will see the ID of the auction in which you bought the item in the column labeled "Auction" to the right. If you happen to buy an 11th, 12th, etc. items, you will NOT get value form them. However, you have to pay the price. This price will be called "Over cost" and it is also shown on your balance sheet. This cost will be subtracted from your Transactions Total. Remember that this is just an example. You will be given your values at the beginning of the experiment. You can choose to participate in auctions at 4 different web-sites. All 4 web-sites have different rules. This is the ECAuctions.com web site (see Figure 8).

To login, enter your password in the box and press the "Log - in" button. You will see a list of active auctions to the left. If you want to bid in an auction, you have to select one of the auctions on the list with your mouse and press the "Join" button. You will see the screen shown in Figure 9.

Every auction requires five participants. On the left side you see the owner of the item for sale. On the right side you see a list of all buyers who are participating in the auction. To bid in the auction: 1. Press Yes. You have to wait until five people press the Yes button. During that time you should not close this window. Closing the window means that you are no longer participating! 2. Every 20 seconds the price will rise with \$0.25 starting from \$2.00. You will be required to press the Yes button after every price increment to indicate that you still want the item at the current price. If you press No or if you miss to press Yes, your name will be removed from the list of active bidders and you will not be allowed to enter the auction again. The auction is over when there is only one bidder left in the auction. You do not have to wait for the auction result. You will be informed if you are the winner. The winner is the person who stayed in the auction until the end. If you win the auction, in which you participate, you have to pay the current price, shown on the screen. Your profit from the auction is equal to: Your

Figure 8. ECAuctions.com website

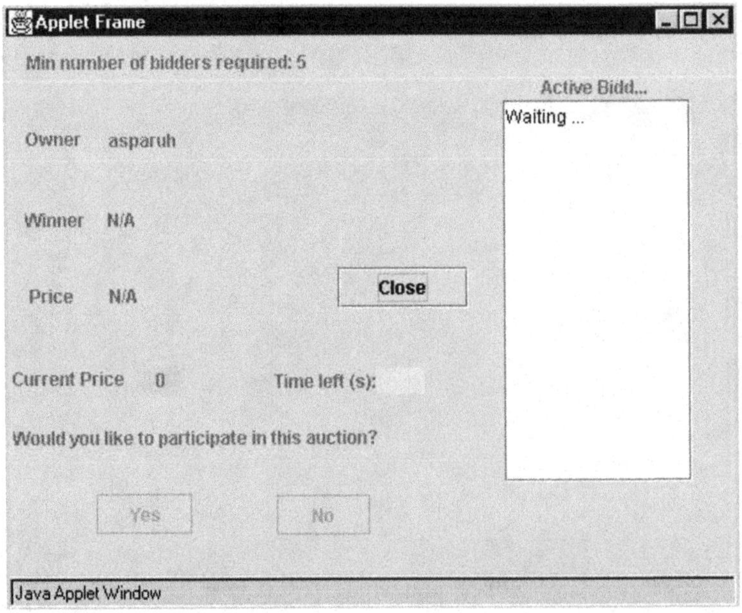

Figure 9. ECAuctions.com bidding screen

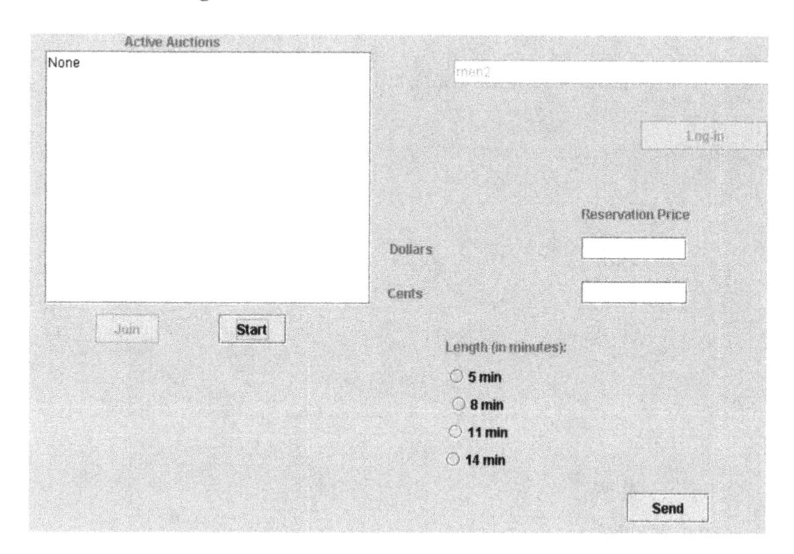

value for the item - The price of the item, which is equal to the current price. This is the BEAuctions.com web site (see Figure 10).

To login, enter your password in the box and press the "Log - in" button. You will see a list of active auctions to the left. If you want to bid in an auction, you have to select one of the auctions on the list with your mouse and press the "Join" button. You will see the screen shown in Figure 11.

Figure 10. BEAuctions website

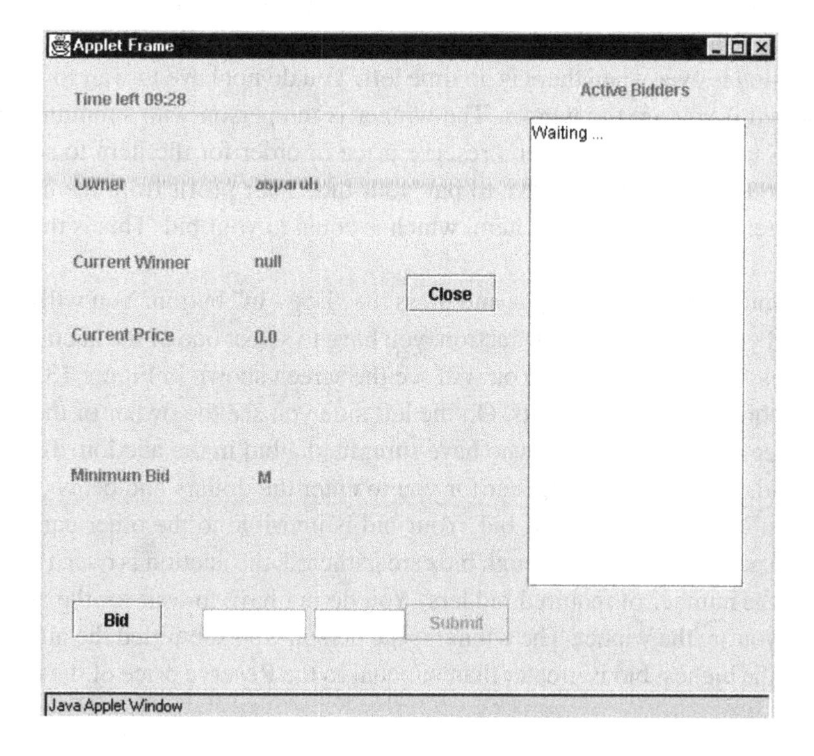

Figure 11. BEAuctions bidding screen

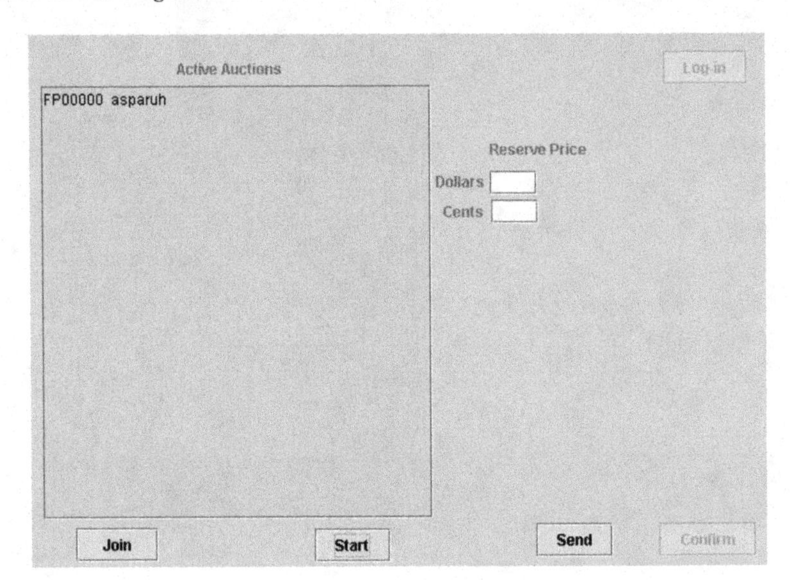

Every auction has a certain length chosen by the seller. You can see the time left in each auction in the top left corner of the screen. On the left side you see the owner of the item for sale. On the right side you see a list of all buyers who have submitted a bid in the auction together with their bids. To enter a bid in the auction: 1. Press Bid. Two boxes will appear for you to enter the dollars and cents (your bid price). Your bid has to be greater than or equal to the Minimum Bid shown on the screen. 2. Press Send and then Yes to confirm your bid. Your bid is visible to the other participants. You can submit many bids per auction as long as they are greater than the Minimum bid and there is still time left. 3. If the seller's Reserve price is reached during the auction a green upper case R will show up in the middle of the screen. The auction is over when there is no time left. You do not have to wait for the auction result. You will be informed if you are the winner. The winner is the person who submitted the highest bid. The highest bid has to be above the seller's reserve price in order for the item to sell. If you win the auction, in which you participate, you have to pay your bid. Your profit from the auction is equal to: Your value for the item - The price of the item, which is equal to your bid. This is the SPAuctions.com web site (see Figure 12).

To login, enter your password in the box and press the "Log - in" button. You will see a list of active auction to the left. If you want to bid in an auction, you have to select one of the auctions on the list with your mouse and press the "Join" button. You will see the screen shown in Figure 13.

Every auction requires five participants. On the left side you see the owner of the item for sale. On the right side you see a list of all buyers who have submitted a bid in the auction. To enter a bid in the auction: 1. Press Bid. Two boxes will appear for you to enter the dollars and cents (your bid price). 2. Press Send and then Yes to confirm your bid. Your bid is invisible to the other participants. You can submit only one bid per auction. Once enough bids are gathered, the auction is over. (the number of bids should be equal to the number of required bidders) You do not have to wait for the auction result. You will be informed if you are the winner. The winner is the person who submitted the highest bid. The item will be sold only if the highest bid is greater than or equal to the Reserve price of the seller, which is not

Figure 12. SPAuction.com website

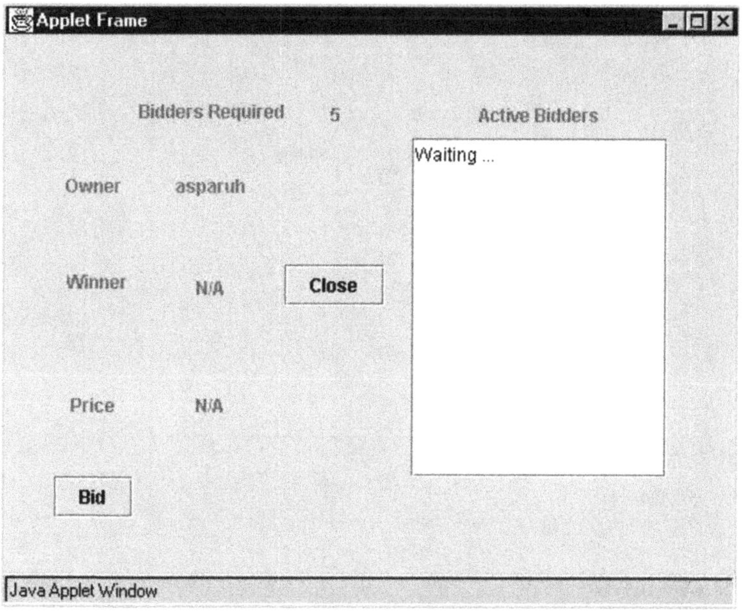

Figure 13. SPAuction.com bidding page

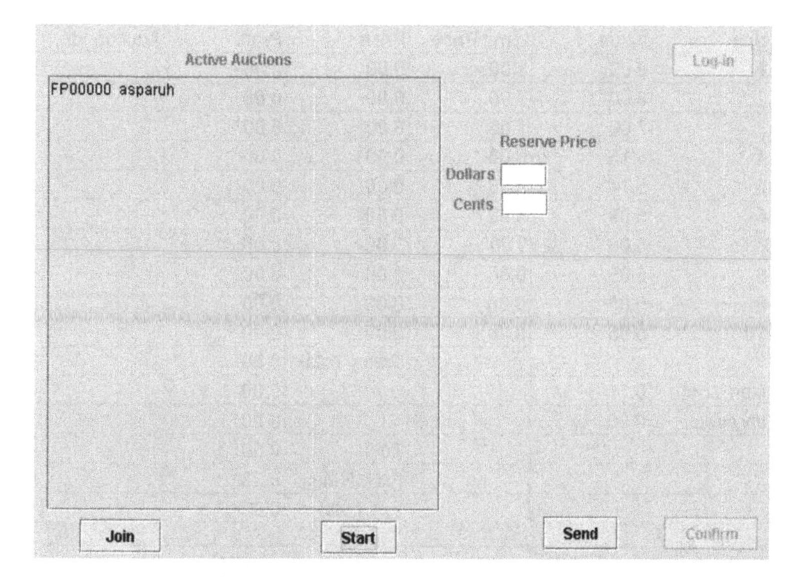

known to you. If you win the auction, in which you participate, you have to pay. Your profit from the auction is equal to: Your value for the item - The price of the item, which is equal to the second highest bid This is the FPAuctions.com web site (see Figure 14).

To login, enter your password in the box and press the "Log - in" button. You will see a list of active auction to the left. If you want to bid in an auction, you have to select one of the auctions on the list with your mouse and press the "Join" button. You will see the screen shown in Figure 15.

Figure 14. FPAuction.com website

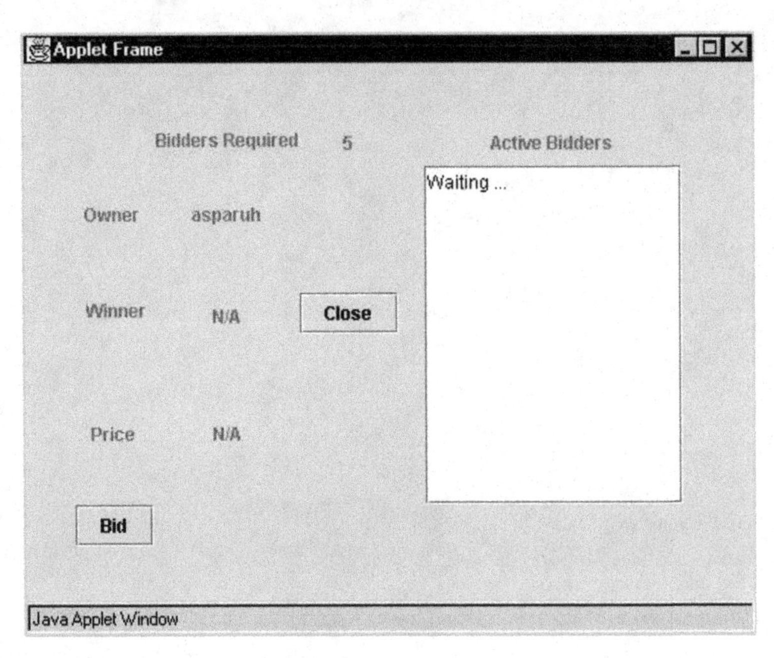

Figure 15. FPAuctions.com bidding page

Unit	Value	Limit Price	Price	Profit	Auction Id
1	8.00	8.00	0.00	0.00	
2	8.00	7.00	0.00	0.00	
3	7.00	7.00	0.00	0.00	
4	6.15	6.00	0.00	0.00	
5	5.74	6.00	0.00	0.00	
6	5.69	5.90	0.00	0.00	
7	5.05	0.00	0.00	0.00	
8	5.05	0.00	0.00	0.00	
9	5.05	0.00	0.00	0.00	
10	5.05	0.00	0.00	0.00	
			Trans Total	0.00	
Mon Cost	0.11			0.00	
Inv cost	0.00			0.00	
			Total	0.00	
			Exch Rate	0.33	
			Exp Total	0.00	

Connect asen Timer Start

Every auction requires five participants. On the left side you see the owner of the item for sale. On the right side you see a list of all buyers who have submitted a bid in the auction. To enter a bid in the auction: 1. Press Bid. Two boxes will appear for you to enter the dollars and cents (your bid price).2. Press Send and then Yes to confirm your bid. Your bid is invisible to the other participants. You can submit only one bid per auction. Once enough bids are gathered, the auction is over. (the number of bids should be equal to the number of required bidders) You do not have to wait for the auction result. You will be informed if you are the winner. The winner is the person who submitted the highest bid. The item will be sold only if the highest bid is greater than or equal to the Reserve price of the seller, which is not known to you. If you win the auction, in which you participate, you have to pay your own bid. Your profit from the auction is equal to: Your value for the item - The price of the item, which is equal to your bid

Summary: 1. Your total profit is equal to: the sum of the values of the items that you bought - the sum of the prices of the items that you bought - monitoring cost. 2. You can participate in auctions at 4 different web-sites that have different rules. 3. Make sure that you are monitoring your balance sheet. If you buy more than 10 items, you do not get a value but you have to pay for them. 4. The experiment will be three rounds with 20 minutes in each round. 5. If your screens do not act properly, close all open windows and try to login again. 6. You will be provided with robot assistants. You can choose to participate in the round yourself or to let a robot participate instead of you. The robot will automatically search all auction sites, trying to find the best deal for you, given the information available. Some of the robot actions are random, so different results might occur at different times. The only thing that you know for sure is that the robot will never buy above your limit prices. If you like to participate yourself press No when the round starts, otherwise press Yes and follow the instructions.[2] Here is an example of a buyer's balance sheet filled with limit prices. Only 6 limit prices are given. This means that the buyer wants to buy only 6 items. If you want to buy 10 items, you have to enter 10 limit prices

Sellers: In this experiment you will participate in several Internet auctions as a seller. Sellers have costs for selling a fictitious good. As a seller, your profit per unit is equal to the price received for that unit minus its cost. Your profit/unit = Price of that unit - Cost for that unit Your total profit will be: Total profit = The sum of the prices of the items that you sold - The sum of the costs of the items that you sold. Remember that all costs and values in this experiment are between $0.00 and $8.00 per unit. In this experiment you are also going to have two other types of cost. You will incur a Monitoring cost for each minute in the experiment. Your Monitoring cost is shown on your balance sheet. You will also incur an Inventory cost for each minute per every unsold item. Your Inventory cost per minute per unsold item is also shown on your balance sheet. Your total experiment profit will be: Total profit = The sum of the prices of the items that you sold - The sum of the costs of the items that you sold - Monitoring cost - Inventory cost In this experiments there is also an Exchange rate. Every experimental dollar is equal to 0.33 US dollars. Below you see an example of a seller's balance sheet.[3]

In this case, $0.13 is the cost to you of the first unit sold and $1.34 is the cost to you of the second unit sold. Your Monitoring cost is $0.04 per minute. Your Inventory cost is $0.03 per minute per unsold item. Your login name "boril" is shown at the bottom of the screen. If you sell an item, you will see the ID of the auction in which you sold the item in the column labeled "Auction" to the right. Remember that this is just an example. Your costs will be given to you at the beginning of the experiment. You can sell items at any of the 4 available auction web-sites. If you have values for 10 items, you can start only 10 auctions. This is the ECAuctions.com web site.

To login, enter your password in the box and press the "Log - in" button. You will see a list of active auction to the left. If you want to start an auction, press the "Start" button. Enter the minimum price at which you are willing to sell your item under the label "Reserve Price". Note that you have to enter the dollars and cents separately. Press "Send" and then "Yes" to start your auction. You will see an auction ID with your login name after it appear in the list of Active Auctions.

Every auction requires five participants. On the left side you will see your login name as the owner of the item for sale On the right side you see a list of all buyers who are active in the auction. The current price in the beginning of the auction will be $2.00. Every 20 seconds the price will rise with $0.25. All five buyers have to indicate if they want to stay in the auction at every new price. If a buyer does not press Yes for a price, he is out of the auction and cannot participate in it again. The auction ends when there is only one person left. The winner of the auction will be that last person. The current price at the end of the auction will be the amount of money that you will receive for your item. The current price has to be higher than your Reserve Price. If the item sold successfully, you will be informed about the winner and the price that he paid. Your profit form the auction is equal to: The price of the item sold, equal to the current price - The cost of the item to you.

To login, enter your password in the box and press the "Log - in" button. You will see a list of active auction to the left. If you want to start an auction, press the "Start" button. Enter the minimum price at which you are willing to sell your item under the label "Reserve Price". Note that you have to enter the dollars and cents separately. You have to choose the length of your auction. There are 4 options available: 5, 8, 11, and 14 minutes. Press "Send" and then "Yes" to start your auction. You will see an auction ID with your login name after it appear in the list of Active Auctions.

You will see the time left in the auction in the upper left corner of the screen. On the left side you will see your login name as the owner of the item for sale On the right side you see a list of all buyers who have submitted a bid in the auction, and their bids. The winner of the auction will be the person who has submitted the highest bid by the end of the auction. The highest bid has to be greater than or equal to your Reserve Price. The highest bid will be the amount of money that you will receive for your item. If the item sold successfully, you will be informed about the winner and the price that he paid. Your profit form the auction is equal to: The price of the item sold, which is the highest bid - The cost of the item to you. This is the SPAuctions.com web site.

To login, enter your password in the box and press the "Log - in" button. You will see a list of active auction to the left. If you want to start an auction, press the "Start" button. Enter the minimum price at which you are willing to sell your item under the label "Reserve Price". Note that you have to enter the dollars and cents separately. Press "Send" and then "Yes" to start your auction. You will see an auction ID with your login name after it appear in the list of Active Auctions. If you want to see the bidders participating in your auction, select your auction with the mouse button and press "Join".

Every auction requires five participants. On the left side you will see your login name as the owner of the item for sale. On the right side you see a list of all buyers who have submitted a bid in the auction. The winner of the auction will be the person who has submitted the highest bid by the end of the auction. The second highest bid is the price that he will pay. The second highest bid has to be greater than or equal to your Reserve Price. The second highest bid will be the amount of money that you will receive for your item. If the item sold successfully, you will be informed about the winner and the price that he paid. Your profit form the auction is equal to: The price of the item sold, which is the second highest bid - The cost of the item to you. This is the FPAuctions.com web site.

To login, enter your password in the box and press the "Log - in" button. You will see a list of active auction to the left. If you want to start an auction, press the "Start" button. Enter the minimum price at which you are willing to sell your item under the label "Reserve Price". Note that you have to enter the dollars and cents separately. Press "Send" and then "Yes" to start your auction. You will see an auction ID with your login name after it appear in the list of Active Auctions. If you want to see the bidders participating in your auction, select your auction with the mouse button and press "Join".

Figure 16. Example seller's balance sheet

Unit	Price	Limit Price	Cost	Profit	Auction Id
1	0.00	1.00	0.33	0.00	
2	0.00	1.00	0.34	0.00	
3	0.00	1.00	1.00	0.00	
4	0.00	2.00	1.00	0.00	
5	0.00	1.20	1.01	0.00	
6	0.00	0.00	1.56	0.00	
7	0.00	0.00	3.00	0.00	
8	0.00	0.00	3.00	0.00	
9	0.00	0.00	3.35	0.00	
10	0.00	0.00	3.61	0.00	
			Trans Total	0.00	
Mon Cost	0.08			0.00	
Inv cost	0.03			0.00	
			Total	0.00	
			Exch Rate	0.33	
			Exp Total	0.00	

Connect | ferdinand | Timer | Start

Every auction requires five participants. On the left side you will see your login name as the owner of the item for sale On the right side you see a list of all buyers who have submitted a bid in the auction. The winner of the auction will be the person who submitted the highest bid. The highest bid has to be greater than or equal to your Reserve Price. The highest bid will be the amount of money that you will receive for your item. If the item sold successfully, you will be informed about the winner and the price that he paid. Your profit form the auction is equal to: The price of the item sold - The cost of the item to you. 1. Your experiment profit is equal to: the sum of the prices of items sold - the sum of costs of items sold - Monitoring cost -Inventory cost 2. You can start auctions on any of the 4 web-sites. 3. You can start only as many auctions as the number of the items that you have values for. (10 in each round). 4. The experiments will have 3 rounds. Every round will last 20 minutes. 5. If your screens do not act properly, close all open windows and try to login again. 6. In this experiment you will be provided with robot assistants. You can choose to participate in the round yourself or to let a robot participate instead of you. The robot will automatically search all auction sites, trying to find the best deal for you, given the information available. Some of the robot actions are random, so different results might occur at different times. The only thing that you know for sure is that the robot will never sell below your limit prices. If you like to participate yourself press No when the round starts, otherwise press Yes and follow the instructions. Here is an example of a seller's balance sheet (see Figure 16) with some limit prices. You have to enter limit prices for all of your units[4].

Section 3

Strategic Information Technologies and Applications at the Societal Level:

Influences and Ecosystems

Chapter 10
ICT Strategy Development: From Design to Implementation – Case of Egypt

Sherif Kamel
The American University in Cairo, Egypt

Nagla Rizk
The American University in Cairo, Egypt

ABSTRACT

Information and communication technology (ICT) is continuously setting the pace for a changing, competitive and dynamic global marketplace and representing an enabling platform for business and socioeconomic development. The impact of ICT adoption, diffusion and adoption can go well beyond being a state-of the-art infrastructure; it can have concrete impact on development. ICT strategy development from start to finish, from design to implementation should cater to the different needs of the community whether it is societal, economic, business and political with an aim to realize universal access to optimize the impact in terms of scalability and sustainability. Building the ICT infrastructure and infostructure will not realize quantum leaps in the development process unless it is coupled with concrete projects and initiatives that engage the society at large with its multiple stakeholders from public, private, government and civil society organizations irrespective of their locations whether urban or remote, gender or background. This chapter describes the evolution of the ICT sector in Egypt with an emphasis on national ICT strategy development across its different design and implementation phases as an integral element of Egypt's overall development process within the context of an emerging economy.

INTRODUCTION

Developing nations when addressing their future development plans, they need to develop a formula that integrates the changes and developments that are taking place globally and adapt a methodology that addresses their local changing needs while optimally allocating their limited resources to serve their business and socioeconomic development requirements. For policymakers, promoting information and

DOI: 10.4018/978-1-5225-1680-4.ch010

communication technology (ICT) for development has taken center stage due to its impact on development and on democracy across different sectors with implications on governance, better management and transparency (Frasheri, 2002).

Within the context of ICT deployment in developing nations, it is worth noting that in the 1960s and 1970s the focus was more directed to the role played by the state and the public sector. This was followed in the 1980s and 1990s by diverting the attention to the role played by the private sector and ICT multinationals. In the early years of the 21st century, the attention was shifted to the role of non-governmental organizations (NGOs) and their vital involvement in diffusing ICT among different communities at urban and rural levels and especially underprivileged groups. Most recently, it is the small and medium-sized enterprises (SMEs) and startups who are taking center stage with the notion of entrepreneurship and innovation. Moreover, the role of the civil society was coupled with the growing attention being directed to corporate social responsibility (CSR) and the role of the community at large to integrate socially with the underprivileged segments in the community. The shifting role of ICT and the corresponding strategies have been consistently adapting to the dynamic changes taking place in global markets both developing and developed.

Developing nations should focus on various socioeconomic needs of the society and to the benefits that could be realized from the amalgamation of the experiences and resources of the state (government), private sector, public sector and the civil society through models of partnership and collaboration such as public-private partnership (PPP). In many cases, the national ICT strategy intends to deploy a multi stakeholders' approach to improve social inequality, economic development and the quality of life of the citizens. The objective is usually to contribute to the long-term national development plans by capitalizing on the opportunities enabled through ICT. These developments are changing, iterative and regularly adapting to market needs. Alternatively, in developing strategies, nations look at competition, investment, innovation and ICT as part of an overall integrated solution that needs to be formulated for ICT to have an effective impact on business and socioeconomic development and growth (Kamel, 2009). In Egypt, the primary objective of ICT adoption, diffusion and adaption is to support national development plans while engaging all stakeholders including the government, the private sector and the civil society. ICT is perceived as an enabler for socioeconomic development and a tool that can transform the society. The universal reach across different levels in the community is believed to be a key factor in realizing nationwide societal development.

ICT innovations are increasingly having important implications on business and socioeconomic development due to its role in introducing and diffusing the concepts of knowledge sharing, community development and equality. However, it is important to note that having an ICT infrastructure alone is not enough to solve all developmental problems; ICT should be looked at as a catalyst, a platform for development that needs the environmental and logistical setting to help the developmental process (Harris 1998; Kransberg 1991). The implications of ICT for development could be felt at the individual, organizational and societal levels. ICT advances have always changed the way human interact, learn, communicate, compete and strategize. While the basic needs of humankind have long been food, clothing and shelter, the time has come to add information to such invaluable list. Universal information access is becoming a primary need for everyone. Information and its technology platform is becoming an integral part of day-to-day lives around the world with implications on individuals, organizations and societies. This is manifested in the growing evolution of the information society, knowledge sharing, big data analytics and more.

The implications on developing nations could be remarkably effective if these technology innovations are properly introduced and managed in a world increasingly affected by access to timely, effective and accurate information. However, if the implementation process is not well supported and controlled, the result could be an increasing digital divide between developed and developing nations. It is important to avoid the fact that ICT could be marginalized in the development process. There is an urgent need to show that ICT generates the wealth of the enterprise, which in turn pays for socioeconomic development at large including but not limited to the effective role of SMEs. Moreover, it is ICT that is delivering the productivity gains that enable lives of material comfort for many around the world that would have been unthinkable only two centuries ago (Heeks, 2005).

ICT is not an end in itself but a means towards reaching broader policy objectives. ICT's main objective should be to improve the everyday lives of the community to fight poverty and to contribute towards the realization of the Millennium Development Goals (MDGs) (www.wsis-online.net). Moreover, WSIS emphasized the fact that ICT has the capability to provide developing nations with an unprecedented opportunity to meet vital development goals and thus empower them to leapfrog several stages of their development far more effectively than before (Ulrich & Chacko, 2005). However, there is a lot that still needs to be done within the context of developing nations for ICT to have the real anticipated impact. For example, it is widely diffused in the literature that the developing world's lack of universal access to ICT, often labelled the digital divide. Nevertheless, it is important to note that such divide is available between nations and within nations both developed and developing despite the fact that the impact of difference of rationalities exists between the developed and developing worlds (Avgerou, 2000). The digital divide is usually due to a number of reasons including, expensive personal computers for most citizens of developing nations, poor or limited telecommunications infrastructure especially in remote locations, and high illiteracy rates and poor educational systems (Radwan et al., 2009; Kamel & Tooma, 2005).

There are various factors that can help curb down the digital divide that relate to the legal and regulatory environment, awareness and capacity development among the community as well as the mechanisms in place for the collaboration between the different sectors in the economy. Moreover, the issue of electronic readiness (eReadiness) takes center stage in transforming the digital divide into a platform for social inclusion. Countries, sometimes, opt for massive national investments in rendering the population electronically ready to pave the way for electronic applications that could have implications on efficiency, transparency, rationalization of resources and social inclusion.

Since the early 1990s and with the diffusion of the Internet, millions of people around the world started relying on it for information interchange on a daily basis (Hashem, 1999). The Internet since its introduction has become the global medium for communication and is a major driving force of change in the global market place (Kamel, 1995). It is truly believed that ICT in general while neutralizing the time and distance barriers are the driving forces of globalization with great potentials for people to improve their lives (Colle & Roman, 2003). The reach of technology with the current and emerging communications platform makes the potentials without boundaries.

With the growing use of ICT, it is becoming a priority to deploy them effectively and efficiently to serve the socioeconomic and development objectives of the society. It is perceived that by combining emerging technology, appropriate organization, qualified human resources, capital formation techniques, and proper understanding of the needs of rural populations, this might pave the way for innovations that bring the Internet to underprivileged and rural areas in developing nations. Therefore, there is an urgent need to close the technology divide (gap) through a comprehensive plan for empowerment and social inclusion and by decentralizing the ICT infrastructure presence in developing nations beyond the nations' capitals and the major cities because the Internet connectivity in those areas is extremely poor and represents a compelling need to improve village life (Press, 1999a). This can only be realized through national ICT plans, strategies and policies that would characterize the needs of the community and set out initiatives and projects accordingly. It is important to note that improving ICT universal access has been one of the primary recommendations of the World Summit on the Information Society (WSIS) that was held in Geneva (Switzerland) in December 2003 and emphasized in the second summit in Tunis (Tunisia) in November 2005 (www.itu.int). Universal access through broadband initiatives is becoming an invaluable factor for engaging and empowering remote and underprivileged communities. Providing the community with access to the Internet and knowledge repositories in many ways contribute to societal development due to the knowledge sharing across different levels in the society.

According to the study conducted in 1995/1996 by the United Nations Commission on Science and Technology for Development (UNCSTD), it underlined the importance of coordination for the formulation of national ICT strategies (Mansell and When, 1998). Moreover, the study pointed out the complexity of strategies to attract and maintain support for installation and maintenance of national ICT infrastructure in relatively low-income developing nations. The need for resources mobilization, proper environment, legislations and regulations, amongst other elements is important for building and sustaining such infrastructure. It is important to note that to promote an efficient and equitable national information infrastructure, governments of developing nations must create a negotiating environment in which banks, local telecoms, as well as other concerned parties are willing to act in a developmentally responsible way (de Alcantara, 2001).

There are four aspects to the digital divide including people, information, knowledge, and technology and these critical aspects should be developed together for an effective implementation to take place. ICT, which is a vital element of the knowledge economy, can be both a unifying and a divisive force. Its divisive aspect has come to be known as the digital divide, referring to the differences between those who have digital access to knowledge and those who lack it (Arab Human Development Report, 2002). This notion has been revisited in every single report published since then as well. The digital divide also referred to as haves and have-nots, relates to the possession of ICT resources by individuals, schools and libraries to variables such as income level, age, ethnicity, education, gender and rural-urban residence (Kamel, 2005a). Reactions vary concerning the digital divide. In the final analysis, its existence is undeniable, but it is not a technological issue. Technology has always been, and will continue to be, a social product, an element that is greatly emphasized especially with the emergence of social networks and their impact on individuals and societies. It is important to note that the challenge has to do with the ecosystem at large with all logistics and operational details involved and not just the technological elements (Kamel, 2009).

For societies to develop, grow, and benefit from the ICT evolution, nationwide introduction, adoption, diffusion and adaptation of technology should take place, something that is hardly seen in developing nations where most of the technology implementations and infrastructure are focused in the capital and the major cities. All these elements demonstrate the importance of developing national ICT strategies. Respectively, based on WSIS recommendations, nations around the world since 2003 opted to develop national ICT strategy that is integral to their development process. These strategies were adapted to the continuous changes taking place in the local and global environments.

ICT developments and their contribution to socioeconomic development are often researched and studied to assess their effectiveness and benefits on individuals, organizations and societies especially in the context of developing nations. The objective of this chapter is to demonstrate the role of partnerships between different stakeholders in rendering ICT a platform for development and the implications on the economy. The evidence compiled from the literature is analysed to identify a set of lessons and recommendations for future implementations in similar environments. The focus is on showing how nations while developing their ICT strategies should also have the long-term vision and plans to move from the design to the execution phase. The research methodology utilized is mainly qualitative based on a set of interviews coupled with the researcher's impressions and interpretations of the implications of ICT diffusion within the community. In addition, a comprehensive analysis of the body of knowledge available coupled with an extensive literature survey of published reports, articles and documents on ICT deployment and diffusion in developing nations with a focus on Egypt was conducted. This chapter primarily focuses on the analysis of aggregate level information on ICT deployment in Egypt and its associated role on the economy at large given the identification of ICT as a driver for business and socioeconomic development.

EVOLUTION OF THE ICT SECTOR IN EGYPT

ICT in developing nations is becoming a necessity for socioeconomic development (Press, 1999b). ICT are increasingly being recognized as essential tools for development, tools that can empower people, enhance skills, increase productivity, and improve at all levels (Schware, 2005). However, this can only be realized through a two-tier approach where society will contribute in shaping the infrastructure, which will in-turn contribute in shaping the society. Egypt, as a developing country, has heavily invested in its technology and information infrastructure since 1985 to become the platform for the economy's development and growth (Kamel, 2005b). During the period 1985-1995, a government-private sector partnership had a remarkable impact on building Egypt's information (infostructure) infrastructure (Kamel, 1997, 1995). During that period, hundreds of informatics projects and centers were established in various government, public and private sector organizations targeting socioeconomic development (Kamel, 1998). These projects that included human, technology and financial infrastructure development had invaluable inputs in building a growing information technology literate society capable of leading Egypt into the 21st century from an information perspective (www.idsc.gov.eg). Such elements represented the major building blocks necessary to establish a full-fledged information infrastructure capable of keeping pace with the developments taking place globally.

In 1999, ICT was identified as a priority at the highest policy level and a new cabinet office was established namely the ministry of communications and information technology (MCIT) leading to more investments and infrastructure build-up (Kamel, 2005b). Respectively, the growth of the ICT industry took massive steps during the last decade in different aspects including human, information, legislation and infrastructure (American Chamber of Commerce in Egypt, 2007). The period 2005 and beyond witnessed a remarkable increase in the number of IT companies providing sales and technical support of hardware, software, and in the development of IT solutions, systems integration and consultation. This helped create employment opportunities for fresh graduates and unemployed candidates interested in the ICT sector within major cities. More importantly, it provided opportunities for those living in the remote and underprivileged communities directly contributing to improving their economic status. Moreover, it helped ICT multinationals coming to Egypt to expand their businesses and penetrate both local and regional markets that are growing in number as the potential for a large IT marketplace grows

(American Chamber of Commerce in Egypt, 2007). This was a period of constant growth due to the needs in the marketplace but also due to the growing size of the market.

During the period 2011 and beyond with the multiple economic and societal challenges that Egypt faced, the ICT sector was still expected to realize double digits' growth, far outpacing the economy at large. In many ways, the development of the ICT sector has the power and potential to become the platform for all the sectors of the economy to realize major transformations that can help realize socioeconomic development. With the development of Egypt's uprising in 2011, the ICT infrastructure including the growth in the use of social media was perceived as an effective enabler, a supporter and a facilitator for economic prosperity, freedom and social equity.

The ICT sector as a dynamic, growing and attractive sector succeeded to attract many talented human resources that used to work in a variety of diversified fields. Therefore, the number of ICT employees kept increasing in exponential terms with an annual growth ranging between 8-10% reaching around an additional 500K jobs by 2017-18. The ICT sector is a major building block of economic growth in Egypt contributing to real gross domestic product (GDP). The growth rate of the sector was 6% in 2011-12 and expected to grow to 10% by 2015-16. In terms of contribution to GDP expectation for it is to rise from 3.2% to 4.1% during the same period (MCIT, 2013). According to the minister of ICT, during the fiscal year 2017-18, ICT annual growth rates are expected to reach 20% and account to 6% of Egypt's GDP (Helmy, 2013). The ICT sector is one of the fastest growing sectors in Egypt. It has managed to transform itself from a sector that consumes resources in the infrastructure build-up phase into a sector that is generates revenues and provides employment opportunities and a platform for development and growth through its variety of value-added services. These figures could represent a major boost to a country that is ranked 16th in the world in 2008 terms of population with 76.8 million and expected to reach 150 million in 2050 becoming one of the most populous countries in the world (United Nations, 2015). The population is expected to hit 200 million by 2100 and judging by today's demographics whereas 60% of the population are under the age of 25, the youth opportunity is expected to grow demonstrating a massive marketspace for ICT adoption, diffusion and adaptation (World Population Prospects, 2015).

It is fair to say that 75% of Egypt's population are millennials (under the age of 40). They represent those born in the early 1980s through the early 2000. They have a different way to look at life and to things in general. They are predominantly tech/web savvy, they were born into an emerging world of technology and have grown-up connected to the Internet and are regularly surrounded by smart phones, laptops, tablets and other tech-based gadgets, tools, and applications. In brief, technology and smart devices are shaping their space. They are also passionate and ambitious when it comes to entrepreneurship and innovation, mostly are interested in tech-startups. Most of them are virtually connected via social networks and they value its impact on the community. They also believe in access rather than ownership giving regular and constant rise to the sharing economy. All these elements contribute to the development of increasing prospects of the role and impact that ICT can have on socioeconomic development in the society. Therefore, the formulation of strategies, especially digital strategies should cater to the evolving nature of the community in Egypt.

Respectively, multiple initiatives and projects were introduced in recent years all aiming at preparing the community for the information society such as Free-Internet model, PC for every home (PC2010), establishment of IT clubs, and the introduction of broadband services in addition to projects relating to key sectors such as education, health, banking, and public administration amongst others (MCIT, 2005a). These projects have helped improve the digital demographics of the community at large especially when the infrastructure was diffused to reach communities in the remote and unprivileged areas.

Table 1. Electronic readiness in Egypt

Indicators	Oct 1999	Dec 2002	Dec 2004	Dec 2006	Dec 2008	Dec 2011	Dec 2013	Dec 2015
Internet Subscribers	300,000	1.2 million	3.6 million	6 million	11.4 million	29.75 million	37.50 million	46.20 million
ADSL Subscribers (Broadband)	N/A	N/A	N/A	206,150	593,042	1.65 million	2.49 million	3.75 million
Internet Penetration per 100 Inhabitants	0.38%	2.53%	5.57%	8.25%	15.59%	34.83%	44.65%	51.34%
Mobile Phones	654,000	4.5 million	7.6 million	18 million	38.06 million	78.99 million	95.89 million	107.41 million
Mobile Phones Penetration per 100 Inhabitants	0.83%	5.76%	9.74%	23.07%	50.7%	97.93%	111.43%	118.89
Fixed Lines	4.9 million	7.7 million	9.5 million	10.8 million	11.4 million	8.96 million	7.47 million	6.06 million
Fixed Lines Penetration per 100 Inhabitants	6.2%	9.8%	12.1%	13.8%	15.2%	11.98%	8.22%	7.23%
Public Pay Phones	13,300	48,000	52,700	56,449	58,002	23,664	22,481	21,397
IT Clubs	30	427	1,055	1,442	1,751	2,163	2,163	2,163
ICT Companies	870	1,533	1,870	2,211	2,621	4,250	4,489	5,210
IT Companies	266	815	1,374	1,970	2,012	3,599	3,764	3,896
Communications Companies	59	75	152	244	265	295	310	328
Services Companies	88	121	148	211	242	356	490	578
Number of Employees in the ICT Sector[1]	48,090	85,983	115,956	147,822	174,478	212,260	256,400	280,415

Table 1 demonstrates the status of electronic readiness in Egypt showing the number of Internet users, PC penetration rates and the total number of IT clubs (Kamel, 2009; 2005b and 2004; MCIT, 2011).

One of the effective platforms that helped diffuse ICT in Egypt across different segments of the community during the last decade has been the models of IT clubs and Internet Cafés. They helped spread the usage of the technology among youth as well as other segments in the community. In addition, there were a variety of projects that were introduced that used a diversified scope of business and operational models for design and implementation as well as resource allocation; the most successful was the deployment of public-private partnership (PPP) models providing affordable Internet access throughout the nation's 27 provinces. The locations include youth centers, culture centers, non-governmental organizations, universities, schools, public libraries and information centers amongst other locations. The total number of clubs currently stands at 2,163 as compared to 30 in 1999 (MCIT, 2009). All IT clubs are equipped with computers with Internet connectivity (MCIT, 2007). Some facilities are remote and they move between towns and have wireless connectivity. They also have the facilities to invest in human resource capacities by offering training programs to help promote ICT awareness and utilization. Moreover, they offer seminars and orientation sessions on a variety of technology tools and applications. The model of IT clubs in Egypt reflects the typical telecenters available in many other developing nations (Kamel, 2004). In the case of Egypt, the objective of these telecentres goes beyond ICT diffusion with more focus on using the IT clubs as platforms supporting socioeconomic development of the local community especially in remote and unprivileged areas (Kamel, 2005a). In today's growing entrepreneurial environment, such platform is extremely useful for the proliferation of many tech-based startups that address different needs and requirements of the community.

An ideal ICT strategy should guide the development of a sound information environment in order to deliver convenient and universal access to information, improve communication, support collaboration and learning and ensure flexible, responsive and above all reliable systems. The strategic objective of the strategy should be able to develop and implement a business-driven institutional IT strategic plan that positions IT as a strategic asset and provides a context for institutional decisions regarding IT investments, governance and organizational structure. Being part of the global economy, Egypt has realized the importance of promoting the ICT sector and marked a new era for Egypt's ICT sector by the formation of MCIT in 1999, where the IT industry enjoyed a new and more liberalized regulatory framework. This was followed by the establishment of multiple organizations and institutions that support the development and continuous improvement of the ICT industry including but not limited to the Information Technology Industry Development Agency as well as the smart villages and many others.

Investment in the ICT sector grew from 8% to 15% annually out of the total investment compared to 3% in 2006. In 2008, 93% of total investments in the ICT sector were through private investments either local or based on foreign direct investments, which averaged around 1 billion US dollars in 2007, 2008 and beyond. The ICT market in Egypt generates around 2.9 billion US dollars of annual revenue with almost 2.5 billion US dollars (86%) derived from the telecommunications sector. The market in Egypt is one of the most advanced in the region due to service availability and the size of the market. Multiple developments and modernization is regularly taking place. For example, Telecom Egypt who holds the monopoly over landlines started to replace copper cables with fiber optic cables, a project that would cost around 5.6 billion US dollars (Egypt Economic Profile, 2016). This is just a sample of the amount of investment earmarked for the country's infrastructure. In addition, over the last decade, the investment in human capital has yielded dividends in the sense that Egypt is currently ranked 16th out of 55 countries according to A. T. Kearney's 2015 Global Service Location Index (GSLI) for outsourcing and offshoring businesses and is currently the region's industry leader and providing over 60K job opportunities.

During the period 2004-2008, as indicated in the seventh World Telecommunication ICT sector meeting held in Cairo in March 2009, the ICT sector witnessed an overall 20% growth with over 7.8 billion US dollars generated to the treasury; this was mainly due to the issuance of the third mobile operator in Egypt. Such investments are directed to the continuous development and improvement of the information infrastructure as well as for the investment in human resource capacities. The projections had indicated that continuous growth derived by increasing demand in response to bold trade and tax reforms would realize a stronger economic activity and increased disposable income for households (Kamel, 2006). However, following the 2011 uprising there has been a slowdown in the growth projections.

Reference Egypt's strategic vision, the government is sustaining its ongoing economic and institutional reforms, investment incentives, infrastructure development and global integration to enhance its competitiveness regionally and globally and to support investment in different fields especially in the ICT sector. Egypt planned to increase ICT exports to 1.1 billion US dollars by 2010 (MCIT, 2005b); which was realized coupled with a continuous growth in the local market. These projections were based on the increase in ICT investments due to the government efforts to improve the business climate, which led to foster economic growth since 2004. In terms of investment in human capacities, MCIT has made a commitment to invest in the future by working to ensure that today's students and employees receive the education and training that will prepare them to lead Egypt in the information society. MCIT in collaboration with its different partners is focusing on developing basic and professional ICT skills by collaborating with government ministries, agencies as well as multinationals and companies from the private sector to develop a variety of training programs designed to provide a wide range of ICT-related concepts and applications. Some of the initiatives and projects that contributed in the investments in human capacities included the smart schools network, the eLearning competence center as well as the support received from Egypt's ICT Trust Fund which was established in cooperation with UNDP in 2002 (ICT Trust Fund, 2007). These initiatives and many more were introduced in recent years targeting the remote locations and underprivileged communities.

FORMULATION OF EGYPT'S INFORMATION SOCIETY INITIATIVE

The evolution in the information society heralds a new socioeconomic order. This era is witnessing the emergence of information-based economies, with traditional economic, industrial and business activities moving towards more knowledge-driven processes and the progressive transformation of advanced economies into knowledge-based, technology-driven, services-dominated economies. These shifts are increasingly laying emphasis on economic activities with intellectual content and knowledge, enabled by the development and exploitation of emerging ICTs within all spheres of human endeavour. Against that background, Egypt is recognizing the need to develop rapidly its information and knowledge base through massive investments in ICT and human capacity development, improving and broadening universal access to higher and quality education and training with an emphasis on lifelong learning and creating digital content accessible to the society.

Egypt efforts for ICT development are government-led in collaboration with the private sector and civil society. In that respect, Egypt has developed a number of policies and strategies to facilitate socioeconomic development and accelerate the transformation of the nation's economy and society to become information-rich and knowledge-based. MCIT has formulated its 2007-2010 national ICT strategy with an objective to integrate different constituencies and to highlight its plans to use ICT as a platform and as an enabler to help socioeconomic development. The plan paved the way for the Egyptian Information Society Initiative (EISI), which is structured around seven major tracks, each designed to help bridge the digital divide and progress Egypt's evolution into an information society. The initiative has been constantly updated and amended to cater for the changing needs in the society and the changing dynamics in the marketplace.

EISI represented the vision of the ICT strategy translated into initiatives and programs that targets diffusing ICT connectivity. Table 2 demonstrates the different EISI building blocks. Egypt shares with other developing nations many of the challenges of building an information society, which could be rewarding to share with other countries with similar environments to learn from each other and capitalize on different lessons learned.

Table 2. Egypt information society initiative

eReadiness "Equal Access for All" • Enabling all citizens to have easy and affordable access to the opportunities offered by new technologies. • Developing a robust communication infrastructure is key.	**eLearning "Nurturing Human Capital"** • Promoting the use of ICT in education. • Developing a new generation of citizens who understand and are comfortable with the use of ICT in their daily lives.
eGovernment "Government Now Delivers" • Delivering high quality government services to the public in the format that suits them. • Reaching a new level of convenience in government services. • Offering citizens the opportunity to share in the decision making process and greatly improve efficiency and quality.	**eBusiness "A New Way of Doing Business"** • Creating new technology-based firms. • Improving workforce skills. • Using electronic documents. • Developing ePayment infrastructure. • Using ICT can be a significant catalyst to increase employment, creating new jobs and improving competitiveness.
eHealth "Increasing Health Services Availability" • Improving citizens' quality of life and healthcare workers work environment. • Adding value using ICT through reaching remote populations. • Providing continuous training for doctors, and offering the tools for building a national health network.	**eCulture "Promoting Egyptian Culture"** • Documenting Egyptian cultural identity through the use of tools to preserve. manuscripts, archives and index materials • Offering worldwide access to cultural and historical materials. • Generate and promote interest in Egyptian cultural life and heritage.
ICT Export Initiative "Industry Development" • Fostering the creation of an export-oriented ICT industry. • Developing an ICT industry can be a powerful engine for export growth and job creation.	

SWOT ANALYSIS OF THE ICT MARKET IN EGYPT

The ICT sector grew tremendously during the last 20 years going through a number of phases from introduction to adaptation to diffusion and adaptation. However, the analysis of the local and global markets showed a number of challenges that faced the growth of the sector. These challenges were augmented following the 2011 uprising given the changes in the economy. However, it is important to note that still the ICT sector has managed to maintain its competitive advantage and was one of the economic sectors that was least affected by the changes that took place. The following SWOT analysis has been developed based on studying the different factors related to the ICT sector and highlighting its relative and competitive advantages and its potentials for growth and contribution in overall development beyond the current capacities. The analysis served as a main platform for building Egypt national ICT strategy. Table 3 demonstrates the findings of the SWOT analysis.

FORMULATING EGYPT'S NATIONAL ICT STRATEGY

The government of Egypt since the late 1990s has embarked on a national effort to formulate a national ICT strategy that captures the national vision defining the introduction, use and diffusion of ICT for business and social economic development at large. The strategy that has been dynamically amended to reflect the changes in the global marketplace and catered for the transforming local needs was mainly related to infrastructure development, national information infrastructure build-up, investment in human resource capacities, market and environment development in the build-up to the formulation of the information society.

Table 3. SWOT analysis of the ICT sector in Egypt

Strengths	Weaknesses
• Number of university graduates. • Low employee turnover (labour laws). • Government vision and support to ICT. • Political stability. • Infostructure (national information infrastructure). • Telecommunication infrastructure. • Low ICT infrastructure cost. • Low cost of starting/doing business. • Skilled, qualified and multilingual fresh university graduates.	• Small market size (ICT companies and market). • Mainly hardware-dominated industry. • Limited services business opportunity. • Limited outsourcing projects (recently growing). • Most large bids are government-related. • Bureaucratic purchasing rules (red-tape). • Fierce competition and price-driven market. • Buyers market (service and quality value). • General business climate/environment (though progressing). • Import-based industry. • Limited industry expertise (need for critical mass). • Non-availability of enough capital investment.
Opportunities	**Threats**
• Growing economy with a focus on exports. • Potentials for an ICT service-oriented hub. • Possible Local market growth rate. • Human capacity building programs. • ICT to improve sectors competitiveness. • eGovernment services and applications. • Large number of private sector SMEs. • Growing role of the civil society. • Multinationals subcontracting national and local companies and vendors. • Price-sensitive markets/lines of business. • Outsourcing activities from US and EU. • Buyers' market created by competition. • Emerging technologies adopted to increase productivity and reduce costs. • Mobile technology advantages. • Role of government and NGOs in supporting and promoting the ICT sector.	• Availability of skills in required numbers. • Perception of ICT value and delivery of required quality. • Ability to cooperate between companies (legislative environment). • Competition between government and private sector companies. • Competition from other nations to Egyptian exports. • Minimal research and development efforts. • High local software and intellectual property piracy rate (recent improvements). • Inadequate legal and regulatory climate. • EU nations causing price pressures on ICT exporters to create low-cost, effective IT outsourcing to their markets.

The guiding principle of the comprehensive national ICT strategy was that it was integrated, embedded and clearly linked to the local national development priorities. In that sense, ICT as a sector was looked as a potential for a productive sector, contributing to GDP and a facilitator for overall development. The government gave a priority to the ICT sector as a driver of economic growth. According to the World Bank, Egypt's ICT expenditure on ICT has reached 5.95% of GDP in 2007 coming ahead of many developed and developing nations (World Bank, 2009). Moreover, the government is giving priority to the ICT sector within its policy development framework scoring 4.4 on a scale of (1-7) in 2006 (World Bank, 2008). This trend continued in the following years contributing to the treasury and helping create regular job opportunities in different sectors across different provinces. Developing national ICT strategies in recent years has been the culmination of efforts undertaken by many nations since the 1980s.

Strategies during that time were focusing on computerization of the government administrative and operational procedures, coordination of computer education and training as well as the development and promotion of a computer services industry. Highly articulated ICT policies were developed in the 1990s, inspired by the Unites States announcement of the development of a national information infrastructure (NII) plan with key focus on private investment, competition, access and universal services (UNECA, 2003a). Gradually, it was perceived that as part of their economic development strategy, governments should make substantial efforts to develop their national ICT strategies that can compete on a global scale (Neto et al., 2005). In that respect, developing nations followed two different approaches in defining their national ICT strategies.

Electronic readiness is important to place nations on the global ICT "digital" map, something that not all nations, especially developing, can afford missing. In that respect, ICT strategy, vision and policies must not only be suitable but should also be embedded in a holistic application and implementation scheme. The ICT strategy, vision and policies of a nation, cannot afford to keep the different building blocks of ICT separate. Their amalgamation must be done at a priority basis otherwise, ICT as a platform for development will not bring the desired results. Moreover, successful applications of ICT for development depend on macro drivers, availing the required ecosystem as well as the preconditions and building blocks of the required environment (Neto et al., 2005).

Egypt, as an African nation, was part of the framework of the African Information Society Initiative (AISI) that emerged from recommendations of the conference of African ministers of economic development and planning in 1996. Egypt among other nations strived to develop its national information and communication infrastructure (NICI) strategies and policies that articulate long-term policy, infrastructure, content and application as an integral part of overall national development (UNECA, 2003b). Egypt is considered among the nations that have advanced their national strategies from conceptualization to implementation. The advantage of the model is that all constituencies are involved, the government, the private sector and the civil society. The ICT strategy in Egypt was translated in the deployment of a two-tier approach, developing national strategies and harnessing ICT applications in key sectors such as education, health and commerce with an emphasis on promoting electronic commerce, attracting FDI to stimulate the knowledge-based economy and to create jobs for the youth and to harness the potential of ICT.

Egypt ICT strategy goes beyond telecom reaching a cross-sectoral approach to creating an enabling environment and mainstreaming ICT into national development policies by addressing all sectors such as trade, finance, investment, education, government, health, commerce and media amongst others. The target is to transform Egypt into becoming a vibrant and dynamic ICT hub in the Middle East with a thriving digital economy and IT-empowered citizens (MCIT, 2007). Figure 1 demonstrates the overall objectives of the national ICT strategy during the period 2000-2004 (MCIT, 2005a). As indicated earlier, it is important that ICT strategies are dynamic and iterative to match and realize the objective of the national strategies.

Figure 1. National ICT strategy building blocks (2000-2004)

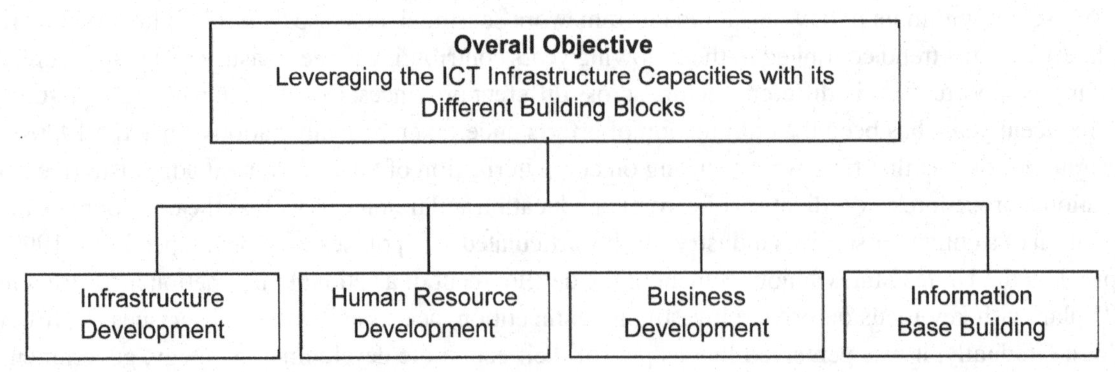

The national ICT strategy is a product of the collaboration of many stakeholders including the community, the government, private and public sector organizations as well as the civil society. The engagement model is a critical success factor in the realization of the objectives of the strategy. According to WSIS in 2003 and 2005, all nations were encouraged to develop their national ICT strategies including the necessary human capacity building taking into account national local conditions. In that respect, strategies should aim to maximize the social, economic and environmental benefits of the information society, which can only be realized if governments create a trustworthy, transparent and non-discriminatory legal, regulatory, and policy environment (www.wsis-online.net). Egypt national ICT strategy objectives were mainly formulated to promote the information society and to build an export-oriented ICT industry. Such objective by nature is dynamic and changing based on emerging ICTs and its relation to socioeconomic development.

The national ICT strategy was formulated to encourage social inclusion in the information age. The use of ICT to minimize the creation of communities of *haves* and *have-nots* was a key-targeted outcome. At the local level, the commitment to maximum social inclusion of its population required considerable pro-active support including financial investment to ensure that Egypt is given universal access to the Internet backbone and to NII. Moreover, the strategy addressed issues such as human resources capacity development and upgrading the physical infrastructure to be able to compete in global deregulated markets. At the global level, access became invaluable in shaping the role Egypt plays in global trade and markets. Respectively, convergence became vital. The emerging role of ICT and its integration in major sectors such as education, entertainment, health, and financial services became a prerequisite for developing nations to be able to integrate in the global information economy and Egypt factored that element in its national ICT strategy.

Egypt national ICT strategy has been dynamic and flexible adapting to the changing nature of the sector. In that respect, during the period 2004-2006 a revised strategy was formulated to include new elements such as providing an institutional support for developing electronic access (eAccess) and providing institutional development of electronic government (eGovernment) and electronic business (eBusiness). Figure 2 demonstrates the amendments that were introduced to the national ICT strategy for the period (2004-2006). The government of Egypt has made a strong commitment to advance the cause of human development in the context of an open economy. It is arguably believed that human capital represents Egypt's oil of the 21st century. The nation's main and most invaluable resource that could transform the economy and the society at large and the notion of information technology and innovation in general could play a pivotal role. Additionally, the structural adjustment program that began in the early 1990s has caused positive and profound changes in the competitiveness of the country. Something to capitalize on and to leverage moving forward. Three main elements could characterize the economy being more open and that includes strengthening of market mechanisms, privatization of government enterprises and an increasing role for the private sector and the civil society (Kamel, 2006).

The role of MCIT required the provision of a policy framework for the ICT sector to grow and become competitive both locally and globally. Table 4 demonstrates the main categories under which fall the changing projects affiliated and identified as part of the national ICT plan. The majority of the projects were implemented by the private sector with financial and technical support and guidance from MCIT (www.mcit.gov.eg). In 2006, and with the continuous development in the ICT sector in Egypt, a revisit to the strategy was conducted and a new ICT sector strategy was formulated for the period 2007-2010. The new strategy has been formulated to cater for three main components, ICT sector restructuring, ICT for reform and development and ICT industry development as demonstrated in Figure 3.

Figure 2. National ICT strategy building blocks (2004-2006)

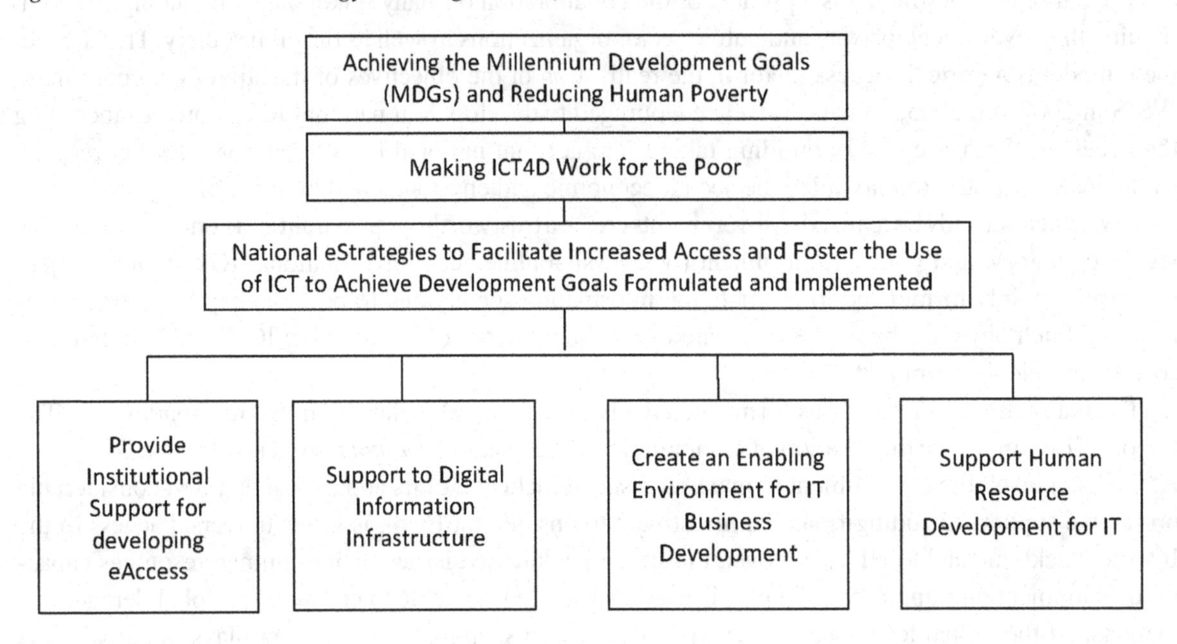

Table 4. National ICT plan projects categories

- Promoting national demand for ICT in collaboration with different stakeholders.
- Focusing on an export-oriented strategy with emphasis on software development through outsourcing.
- Investing in human resources as the primary building block in the ICT ecosystem.
- Forging international alliances and partnerships to increase diversity, encourage FDI and create job opportunities.
- Modernizing the ICT infrastructure to participate in the global ICT space.
- Availing the legislative environment allowing successful implementation and sustainability of projects.

Figure 3. National ICT strategy building blocks (2006-2010)

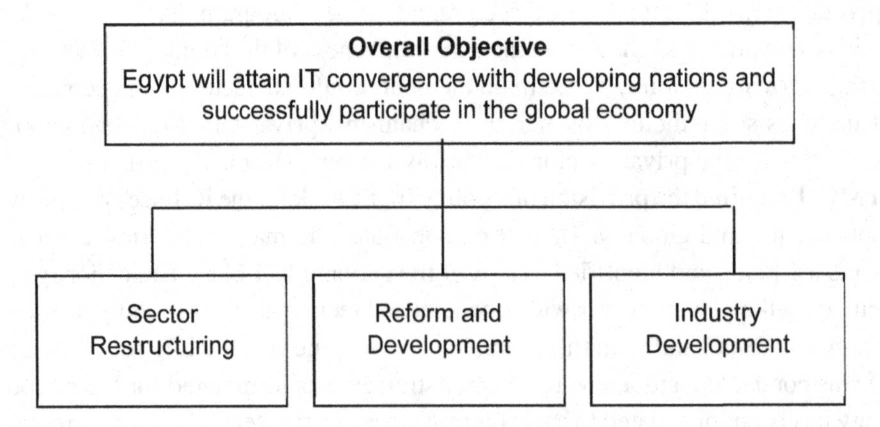

During the period 2007-2010, the focus of the amended national ICT strategy was on sector restructuring by increasing the state resources to reach 3.9 billion US dollars through restructuring the national postal service, initial public offering for Telecom Egypt (TE) and the provision of National Telecommunications Regulatory Authority (NTRA) licenses such as 3G and WIMAX services amongst others. Moreover, the government intended to exert maximum efforts to maintain the current level of investments in the ICT sector that is levelled at an annual growth rate of 20%. Finally, the government planned to help deploy state-of-the-art ICT tools and applications to serve the development in the society in different sectors. In terms of using ICT for reform and development, the strategy intended to follow three main paths. This included; deploying ICT tools through increasing the penetration rates to mobiles, PCs, Internet usage, broadband services and ICT clubs; developing the postal services network with its 4000+ branches; and finally completing the ICT infrastructure in different institutions. Moreover, the strategy focused on using ICT as a catalyst in reforming a number of sectors including:

- Education;
- Health; and
- Government institutions (ministries) amongst others.

In terms of industry development, the strategy intended to focus on innovation, research, and development in ICT through the formulation of partnership agreements with ICT multinational companies. This included the development of different technology incubators for small and medium-sized enterprises (SMEs) in the ICT sector, investing in human capital, media convergence, development of digital content and promoting ICT exports through outsourcing. The rationale was to look at ICT as a platform for empowering the community as a key element for socioeconomic development. In 2011 and post Egypt's uprising, a new amendment was introduced to the strategy by integrating a universal access modality that targets maximizing Internet access through broadband for the whole community. This is an attempt to support sectors such as industry, education and SMEs through capitalizing on what ICT can offer leapfrogging several sectors and contributing to the transformation of remove and underprivileged communities.

In 2012, post Egypt uprising a new strategy was developed to take the ICT platform from the planning to the execution phase. The emphasis at this stage was primarily on the digital economy. Institutional development was an integral element of the process. With a more challenging economy, the need for more FDI was important and ICT was perceived as one of the possible venues. The main building blocks of the new strategy included digital platforms, training and investing in human capital, technology parks, innovation clusters, reaching out to marginalized and underprivileged communities and more (MCIT, 2013). The vision that was known as digital economy 2020 was defined as "to realize the societal needs for all using simple, affordable access to knowledge and services through ICT anywhere and anytime". The overall objectives included attracting investment into the ICT sector, expanding ICT companies, creating job opportunities, providing public information access, availing most government services through online platforms and more.

The new strategy intended to realize a set of impacts that included improving efficiency, fighting corruption, enhancing transparency, ensuring social equality, reducing cost, decreasing time to service, supporting decision making at the centralized and decentralized levels and contributing to the nation's GDP. There were three strategic objectives for the strategy and that included:

- Developing a national integrated digital platform to contribute to achieving socioeconomic development and social equity;
- Supporting the ICT industry development through innovation and entrepreneurship attracting foreign direct investment and creating job opportunities;
- Building on Egypt's unique geographical location and optimum utilization of submarine cables to become a global Internet hub.

Table 5 demonstrates the main pillars of the strategy that reflect its primary directions being digital, industry-driven, development-oriented and targeting the positioning of Egypt in the global digital map as a focal hub. The strategy was launched with the national broadband initiative in December 2013 with a total investment of 40 million US dollars. The objective of the initiative was based on the fact that with 10% increase in broadband penetration, an additional 1.38% in GDP growth will be realized as 50K jobs will be created (Helmy, 2014). The overall strategy targets were identified as to move from 4% contribution to GDP in 2013-14 to around 7% in 2019-20 realizing a growth rate of the sector of about 17% as opposed to 10% in 2013-14. This would leave to creating around 400K job opportunities by 2020 (Helmy 2013).

CONCLUSION

Successful ICT strategies need a number of elements in order to be effective and to realize its targeted objectives. This includes, but is not limited to, leadership from top executives and policy makers, involving all stakeholders in implementation, deploying a holistic approach covering all sectors, having a clear vision, a set of realizable objectives and identified and agreed-upon set of key performance indicators, enabling a liberalized economy, monitoring ICT developments, tailoring towards the nation's requirements and mainstreaming ICT into national socioeconomic development plans. There is a need to emphasize the role of the government in creating the right atmosphere that encourages private sector investment in ICT related businesses. This role was maintained throughout the transition period that started in January 2011 and still in place with several governments in charge. However, all sharing the support to the ICT sector as an enabler for the targeted development process. The liberalization of the telecom sector is important to encourage competition and promote FDI. The creation of a universal access policy through broadband is invaluable to induce mass-market deployment of ICT leading to improving the service quality and speed. Moreover, instituting the necessary foreign investment laws and enforcing software piracy

Table 5. ICT strategy main pillars

Digital Strategy Pillars	
Basic infrastructure.	Information infrastructure and digital content.
Electronic, design and manufacturing.	Community development.
ICT industry programs and initiatives.	Cyber security and eSignature.
Legislative and policies framework.	

and copyright infringement laws, which encourage ICT multinationals to establish regional operations, thus providing work opportunities for skilled individuals and limiting the brain drain effect. Egypt has already shown over the last decade some headway on the ICT development path. However, it needs to strengthen its commitment and speed its process for a long-term sector development and growth. Such a strategy would invariably drive faster growth across all economic sectors, which will lead to a sustainable socioeconomic development that can be reflected at the individual and societal level.

REFERENCES

American Chamber of Commerce in Egypt. (2007). *Information Technology in Egypt*. Business Studies and Analysis Center.

American Chamber of Commerce in Egypt. (2016). *Egypt Economic Indicators*. Business Studies and Analysis Center.

Arab Human Development Report. (2002). *Creating Opportunities for Future Generations*. United Nations Development Programme and Arab Fund for Economic and Social Development.

Avgerou, C. (2000). Recognizing Alternative Rationalities in the Deployment of Information Systems. *Electronic Journal of Information Systems in Developing Countries*, *3*(7), 1–15.

Colle, R., & Roman, R. (2003). Challenges in the Telecentre Movement. In S. Marshall, W. Taylor, & X. Yu (Eds.), *Closing the Digital Divide: Transforming Regional Economics and Communities with Information Technology*. Westport, CT: Praeger.

De Alcantara, C. H. (2001). *The Development Divide in a Digital Age*. Issue Paper. United Nations Research Institute for Social Development, Technology, Business and Society Programme, No. 4.

Egypt I. C. T. Indicators. (n.d.). Retrieved from http://www.egyptictindicators.gov.eg

Frasheri, N. (2002). Critical View of e-Governance Challenges for Developing Countries. IFIP WG9.4 Work Conference ICT and Development, Bangalore, India.

Harris, R. (1998). Information Technology – The New Cargo Cult? Information Technology in Developing Countries. *Newsletter of the International Federation and Information Processing (IFIP) Working Group 9.4*, *8*(1).

Hashem, S. (1999). Technology Access Community Centers in Egypt: A Mission for Community Empowerment. *Proceedings of the Internet Society Conference*.

Heeks, R. (2005). *ICTs and the MDGs: on the Wrong Track*. Information for Development Magazine.

ICT Trust Fund. (n.d.). Retrieved from http://www.ictfund.org.eg

Information and Decision Support Center. (n.d.). Retrieved from http://www.idsc.gov.eg

International Telecommunication Union. (n.d.). Retrieved from http://www.itu.int

Kamel, S. (1995) Information Superhighways, a Potential for Socioeconomic and Cultural Development. In *Managing Information and Communications in a Changing Global Environment:Proceedings of the 6th Information Resources Management Association International Conference (IRMA)*.

Kamel, S. (1997). DSS for Strategic Decision-Making. In M. Khosrowpour & J. Liebowitz (Eds.), *Information Technology Management in Modern Organizations* (pp. 168–182). Hershey, PA: Idea Group Publishing.

Kamel, S. (1998). Decision Support Systems and Strategic Public Sector Decision Making. In *Egypt in Information Systems for Public Sector Management Working Paper Series*. Institute for Development Policy and Management, University of Manchester, Paper No. 3.

Kamel, S. (2004). Diffusing ICT Usage Through Technology Access Clubs: Closing the Digital Divide. *Proceedings of the Information Science, Technology and Management (CISTM) Conference on Improving Business Performance through Knowledge Management.*

Kamel, S. (2005a). Assessing the Impacts of Establishing an Internet Cafe in the Context of a Developing Nation.*Proceedings of the 16th International IRMA Conference on Managing Modern Organizations with Information Technology.*

Kamel, S. (2005b). The Evolution of Information and Communication Technology Infrastructure in Egypt. In G. Hunter & A. Wenn (Eds.), *Information Systems in an e-World* (pp. 117–135). The Information Institute.

Kamel, S. (2009). The Evolution of the ICT Sector in Egypt – Partnership4Development. *Proceedings of the 11th International Business Information Management Association (IBIMA) Conference on Innovation and Knowledge Management in Twin Track Economies: Challenges and Opportunities.*

Kamel, S., & Tooma, E. (2005). *Exchanging Debt for Development: Lessons from the Egyptian Debt-for-Development Swap Experience. Working Document.* World Summit on the Information Society.

Kamel, T. (2006). *Egypt Reforms: An update from the ICT Sector*. Academic Press.

Kransberg, M. (1991). IT as Revolution. In T. Forester (Ed.), *Computers in the Human Context*. MIT Press.

Mansell, R., & When, U. (1998). *Knowledge Societies: Information Technology for Sustainable Development.* Oxford, UK: Oxford University Press.

Ministry of Communications and Information Technology. (2005a). Egypt Information Society Initiative (4th ed.). Author.

Ministry of Communications and Information Technology. (2005b). *Building Digital Bridges*. Egypt's Vision of the Information Society.

Ministry of Communications and Information Technology. (2007). *Egypt's ICT Golden Book*. Author.

Ministry of Communications and Information Technology. (2009). *The Future of the Internet Economy in Egypt*. Statistical Profile.

Ministry of Communications and Information Technology. (2011). *ICT Indicators in Brief.* Retrieved 9 December from http://www.mcit.gov.eg/Publications

Ministry of Communications and Information Technology. (2013). *ICT Strategy*. Author.

Neto, I., Kenny, C., Janakiram, S., & Watt, C. (2005). Look before You Leap: The Bumpy Road to E-Development. In E-development from excitement to effectiveness. World Summit on the Information Society.

Press, L. (1999a, January-February). *Connecting Villages: The Grameen Bank Success Story. OnTheInternet.*

Press, L. (1999b, October-November). Developing Countries Networking Symposium. *OnTheInternet.*

Radwan, S., Kamel, S., & El Oraby, N. (2009). The Experience of the Italian-Egyptian Debt Swap Program (2001-2008). Partners for Development, Technical Support Unit, Embassy of Italy (Egypt) and Ministry of International Cooperation (Egypt).

Schware, R. (2005). Overview: E-Development: From Excitement to Effectiveness. In E-development from excitement to effectiveness. World Summit on the Information Society.

Ulrich, P., & Chacko, J. G. (2005). Overview of ICT Policies and e-Strategies: An Assessment on the Role of Governments. *Journal of Information Technology for Development*, *11*(2), 195–197. doi:10.1002/itdj.20011 PMID:16339190

United Nations Department of Economics and Social Affairs. (2015). Population Division. Author.

United Nations Economic Commission for Africa. (2003a). *Policies and Plans on the Information Society: Status and Impact*. Author.

United Nations Economic Commission for Africa. (2003b). *E-Strategies*. National, Sectoral and Regional ICT Policies, Plans and Strategies.

World Bank. (2008). *Little Data Book on ICT*. Author.

World Bank. (2009). *Little Data Book of ICT*. Author.

World Population Prospects. (2015). *Facts*. Author.

World Summit on the Information Society. (n.d.). Retrieved from http://www.wsis-online.net

ENDNOTES

1. There are over 54,000 indirect job opportunities associated with IT clubs and Internet cafés across Egypt.

Chapter 11
Gaining a Continuous Retaining Relationship with Customers in Mobile Sector

Irene Samanta
Technological Educational Institute of Piraeus (TEI), Greece

ABSTRACT

One of the main characteristics of the global economy is the creation of oligopolistic markets. The decisions of those industries are characterised by interactivity. The risk arising from the domination of the power of oligopoly is the previous stage of manipulation of the market. This situation is against the concept of competitiveness and causes an entirely new situation to the customer's disadvantage. Mobile industry which is a typical oligopolistic market in Europe leads us to examine this specific market in Greece. Therefore, the present study examines the factors that influence the relationship marketing strategy of the industry. The research was conducted using a sample of 806 users of mobile phones. The method used for the quantitative analysis is chi-square test, discriminant analysis, which is based on Multivariate Analysis of Variance (MANOVA). The study has indicated that intense competition between mobile phone firms in Greece leads to the manipulation of consumers' behaviour. Also, findings of the current research demonstrate that firms create a unified policy in order to restrain their customers' consuming behaviour to a state of inertia, the customer passively re-buys the same service provider without much thought.

INTRODUCTION

Globalization has created conditions of competition between countries as well as businesses. High competition between companies has presented its results, which are the creation of oligopoly markets, since only few firms can create a competitive advantage in order to survive, in a profitable way (Kyriazopoulos, 2001).

The mobile industry is one of the faster growing industries in the EU and worldwide (Anwar, 2003). During the last several years the adoption of new technology raises in Greece, which can also be seen at the mobile phone industry. The sector operate in a high competitive market, in reference to usage programs,

DOI: 10.4018/978-1-5225-1680-4.ch011

the prices, the width and the quality of the provided services, their consumers' point of view about the network and the quality of customer service. The new technologies market in Greece follows the global trends but through steadily increasing rhythms. Today the broadband services are used mostly for Internet access. The provision of such functions is the next step for the strengthening of the broadband services.

In this competitive market firms, in order to attract new customers, create a unified marketing strategy. This policy has the aim of manipulating the market at the expense of competition, in a way that customers will be restrained in this policy. This results to consumer's inertia in reference to their primary choice. In order to change that situation, drastic alterations should be made in the pricing policy, as well as in the innovation in both products and services and the customer service (Reinartz et al., 2000).

As a result, the market cannot be segmented and the firms apply an undifferentiated marketing strategy. The above situation appears to be applied to the mobile service sector in Greece. The vast majority of Greek users own a mobile phone while the sector is mainly driven by the network operators, who are looking not only to acquire new customers but also to increase and retain their proportion of higher-value subscribers and increase the revenue generated by each customer. The great extent, to which the mobile phone sector has promoted its products and services as well as established, maintained and enhanced the brand image over the past years, reflects the fast changing environment of the industry.

In order to examine the consequences invoked to the market because of high competition of the mobile sector, a primary research was conducted. The results of the research are presented in this paper in a way that covers both theoretical analysis of market competition concepts and aspects. Then it continues with some background information on the mobile sector in Greece. The study also includes applications and practices followed in the mobile service sector. Finally, the research analysis and methodology refers to the factors of relationship marketing and customer retention, as the business drivers of the mobile sector.

The aim of the research is to identify the general trends of the mobile sector in Greece and to examine how the relationship marketing strategy of the sector influences customer retention. Furthermore, the research determines the factors that have an important role concerning the final decision of the consumer, whether to remain with the same firm, or to move to another one.

BACKGROUND

Relationship Marketing Benefits

Relationship Marketing (RM) emphasizes on a long-term interactive relationship between the provider and the customer, leading to long-term profitability. It recognizes that both the customer and the seller can be active. They should see each other as partners in a win to win relationship (Gronroos, 1995). Both the marketing mix theory and RM are – in theory at least – based on the marketing concept, which focuses on customers and their needs. Although the marketing mix and its additions incorporate relationships and interaction to some extent, RM provides a more radical change, a paradigm shift. It seems though that the primary values of marketing mix concerning manipulation have not changed. Marketing techniques change to "trapping" customers, so as to restrain or even punish their escape (Rust et al., 2003). Nevertheless, if expressions like "customer retention" or "zero defection" are treated as referring to mere manipulation, the application of RM will not make a noteworthy contribution. Ideally, RM assumes good will from all parties (Bennet & Barkensjo, 2005). Relationships are seldom completely symmetrical; one party is often the stronger one. This is acceptable to a degree in an imperfect market, but from a welfare perspective it is unacceptable in the long term (Bendall & Powers, 2003). The main dimensions of relationship marketing include trust, commitment and satisfaction. Those three are established as measures of relationship quality.

Relationship attributes including the length or duration of the relationship; structural or social bonds, dependence and inertia relationship termination costs relationship switching costs cooperation commitment. Athanasopoulou (2009) try to observe the negative effects on RM and study the levels of uncertainty, distance and conflict and their effect on various dimensions of RQ.

Relationship marketing, defined as the degree of appropriateness of a relationship to fulfill the needs of the customer (Papassapa & Miller, 2007). It includes several key components reflecting the overall assessment of the strength of a relationship between the firms and consumers (Rust et al., 2003). Previous research conceptualized relationship marketing as a construct consisting of several distinct, though related, dimensions (Jeng & Bailey, 2012). While the exact dimensions making up relationship quality are still debatable, there is, however, a general agreement around the key components of: satisfaction with the service provider's performance, trust in the service provider, and commitment to the relationship with the mobile telecom networks (Dasgupta et al., 2008).

The construct of customer retention focuses on repeat patronage, and it is different from, while closely related to, purchasing behavior and brand loyalty, in that in retention the marketer is seen as having the more active role in the customer-firm relationship (White & Yanamandram, 2007). A number of factors may drive customer retention, such as satisfaction, quality, switching costs (Wolfl, 2005), marketing strategies (Kyriazopoulos, 2001), and customer acquisition (Cronin et al., 2000). This work focuses on the major motivators of cost, quality, and customer experience.

Factors Influence Relationship Marketing

The study took into consideration six elements, which determine the customer relationships and retention, which is the future propensity of a customer to stay with a service provider (White & Yanamandram, 2004). These elements are service quality, customer satisfaction, trust, inertia, indifference, switching barriers to customer retention.

Competition is the act of striving against another force for the purpose of achieving dominance or attaining goals. In order to examine this hypothesis in depth, we see into the factors leading to the state of inertia, in what concerns the consumers' behaviour to change firms, as a result of the manipulation circumstances of the market. The basic hypothesis examined in our study, is:

H1: The higher the level of competition, the higher the level of consumer's behaviour manipulation.

Service Quality

(Zeithmal et al., 1990) offer a conceptual model of service quality which affects particular behaviours that indicate, whether customers will remain loyal to or leave a firm. According to (Cronin, 2000) a research which involved six industries showed that quality service was closely related to the customers' behaviour. In Cronin study service quality did not appear to have a significant (positive) effect on repurchase intentions. Finally, it has been suggested by (Manoj & Sunil, 2011) that he majority of customers simply remains inactive and do not undertake any action following a negative service experience. In our study we define the customer's perception of the service quality point of view as an important factor of the inertia (White & Yanamandram, 2004a; White & Yanamandram, 2007).

H2: Quality service has a direct impact on customer's behavior.

Price Perceptions

Following (Chatura & Jaideep, 2003) barriers as constraints that prevent switching action. (Yanamandram & White, 2006) examines switching barriers as a determinant of customer switching behaviour. Subsequently, (Fraunholz & Kitchen, 2004) develop a model that includes switching costs as an antecedent of customer loyalty. Also they define switching costs as investment of time, money and effort that, in customers' perception, made it difficult to switch. In our study switching barriers are used in order to investigate the case, in which a homogenous pricing policy by the mobile industry results to the customer's behaviour manipulation in the Greek market. Alternatively, the price perceptions of the consumer confine customers in the same service provider, manipulating thus their behaviour (Kim et al., 2009).

H3: Price Perceptions has a direct impact on customer's behaviour.

Inertia

Inertia is the re-buy of the same service provider passively without much thought. The purchase may even be in spite of the consumer having negative perceptions (Seetharaman & Chintagunta, 1998) and reflects a non-conscious process. In this context, the consumer does not think of alternatives. The effect of inertia is to make re-buy respond to marketing variables. This happens because inertia leads the consumers to be more sensitive towards marketing variables, meaning price reductions or other promotional tools; suggested that the impact of inertia on retention would be determined by the competitive structure of the industry (Rust et al., 2003). In this study we define inertia, as an important factor that influences the customer in order to remain loyal in the same service provider (White & Yanamandram, 2004). As a result of this situation, mobile industry manipulates easier the customer's behaviour.

H4: The higher the level of inertia, the higher the probability of customer manipulation

Indifference

Zeelenberg and Pieters (2004) show that given a homogeneous supply and a heterogeneous demand, the satisfaction levels of the customer are reduced. In that way, customers could remain with a service provider for a long time. Furthermore, in the present research indifference can have a significant moderating effect, which linked with inertia can manipulate the customer's behaviour (Sharma et al., 2006).

H5: A customer's indifference switching to another company may increase the probability of retaining that customer.

Customer Satisfaction

Following (Cronin et al. 2000), we conceptualise customer satisfaction to be an evaluation of an emotion; reflecting the degree in which the customer believes the service provider evokes positive feelings (Lam et al., 2004). Numerous studies in the service sector have hypothesized and empirically validated the link between satisfaction and behaviours such as customer retention and word of mouth (Huang & Chiu, 2006). Indeed, this link is fundamental to the marketing concept, which indicates that satisfying customer needs and desires is the key to re-buy the service (Kim et al., 2009).

In the current study the customer's satisfaction constitutes the key factor in order to retain the customers.

H6: The higher the level of satisfaction, the more likely the retention of customer behaviour.

Trust

Following (Chatura & Jaideep, 2003) conceptualise trust based on interpretation of the construct of the commitment-trust theory of customer retention (Wong & Sohal, 2002). Trust could exist at the individual level or at the firm level (Rust et al., 2003). Furthermore, trust could also be thought of as trust in the service itself (Zeithmal et al., 1990). In our study, we look at a customer's trust in the service provider.

H7: The higher the level of trust, the more likely customer retention is.

Switching Barriers

According to (Yanamandram & White, 2004a), switching barriers are the factors which prevent a customer to change company. (Lam et al., 2004) was one of the first to have studied the barriers of change in relation to the customer behaviour. (Manoj and Sunil, 2011) define the costs of change by referring to time, money and the effort which the customer perceives in order to change firm. Since then, (Ramaseshan et al., 2006) among others have tested and confirmed the positive effect of switching barriers on customer retention. In the current study, we look switching barriers as the factitious constrains that a firm defines, in order to inert the customers' behaviour to change service provider (Athanasopoulou, 2009).

H8: The more a customer is becoming aware of switching barriers, the more likely it is to be retaining in a firm.

General Characteristics of the Mobile Sector

The Greek mobile sector is the fastest growing sector in the country, one of the most dynamic sectors of the economy. Currently there are four GSM mobile network operators, while three of them obtained a 3G license with the obligation to launch commercial UMTS (Universal Mobile Telecommunications System) network in year 2011 (Light et al., 2011). According to the announcements of Greek Mobile network operators in April 2011, there were 9.943.730 mobile subscribers. The distribution of mobile subscribers among the network operators as well as their segmentation based on the method of payment (prepay, post pay).

The distribution of mobile subscribers is performed mostly via specialized stores that the mobile firms mostly own, using their brand name. Nonetheless, other retailers are also involved, such as electrical stores. This day by day increasing distribution of mobile industry products from other retailers is justified, given the benefits offered by adding these sales to an existing range of products. Especially, since pre-paid packages come as a boxed solution, there is no necessity of a specialist's knowledge in order to sell it.

The mobile sector follows an advertising strategy in order to encourage existing mobile phone users to upgrade their telephone to newer ones. The use of the mobiles is also promoted not only for direct communication, but also as an information or multimedia tool for social interaction (Dagupta et al., 2008). On the other hand, advertisement focuses only on mobile handsets promotion and subscription upgrade by presenting the benefits of the enhanced mobile telephone and the new packages offered (Turkyilmaz & Ozkan, 2007). In response to a decline in new subscriptions demand, the falling prices and the intensifying competition, mobile network operators and retailers devote increasingly more resources to advertising as well as to other methods of promotion (Eagle & Kitchen, 2000). In the Greek market, advertisement strategies prefer television as medium of advertising. However, different marketing communication tools are used. Figure 1 presents direct advertising spending costs per medium in 2004 and 2011.

MAIN FOCUS OF THE CHAPTER

The present study investigates the extent to which relationship marketing strategy between mobile phone industries influence the consuming attitude of their customers. This leads to the testing of the hypothesis:

H1: The higher the level of relationship marketing strategy, the higher the level of customer retention.

Figure 1. Direct advertising spending cost per medium (Source: Media services media vest processing)

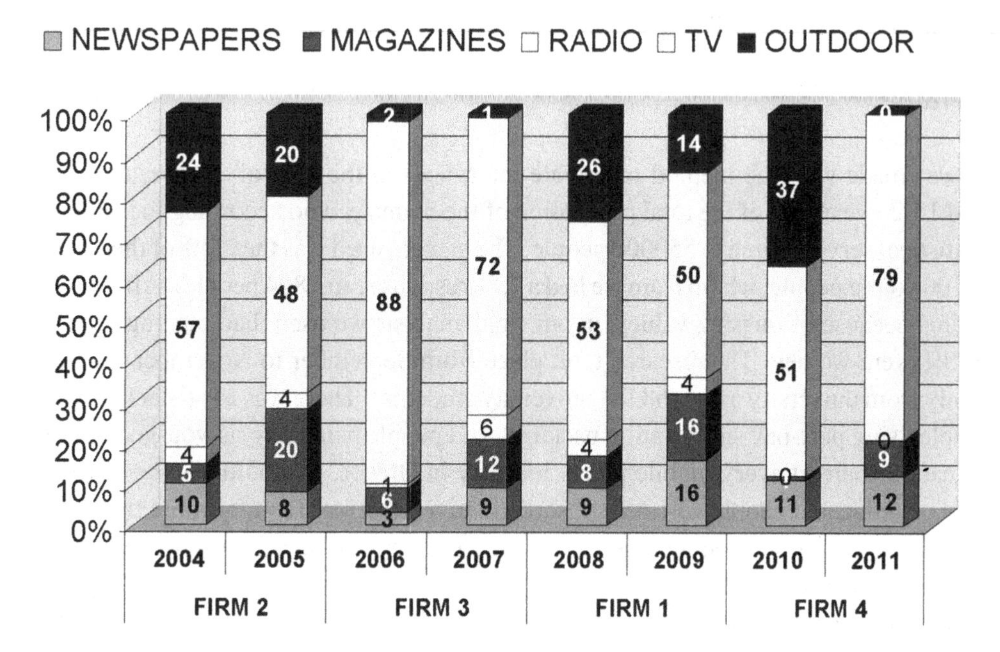

Firstly, we defined the factors that influence and strengthen the customer retention of the firm. Based on the literature review, we develop a framework linking service quality, customer satisfaction, trust, inertia, indifference, switching barriers to customer retention. According to Jeng and Bailey (2012) customer retention is the future propensity of a customer to stay with a service provider. On the other hand (Zeithaml et al., 1990) define the term "future behavioural intentions" in order to describe the construct with the above definition. In our work we follow (Cronin et al., 2000) who treat "behavioural intentions" and "customer retention" as synonymous constructs.

We examine the main effects of each of the independent variables and the simultaneous influence of the above variables on retention. The usage of each parameter related to the customer retention is also analysed. At the development and description of the factors that influence the consuming attitude of the customers the following criteria were taken in mind:

- Every factor examines the customers' attitude from a specific point of view;
- The factors express independently (as much as possible) the customers' attitude (the factors are mutually independent);
- The group of factors covers all the spectrum of the points of consideration that influence the customer retention.

Solutions and Recommendations

For the accomplishment of the research objectives, the questionnaire developed by Cronin, (2000), was used. Modifications were made to the instruments, taking into account the economic environment of Greece, including semantic changes, in order to suit the needs of this study. The questionnaire refers especially to the responders' experiences of the mobile industry. The questionnaire consisted on a variety of questions, concerning different areas of interest. The items of the questionnaire were in the form of statements based on the 5-point Likert – type scale, anchored on 1=totally agree, through 5=totally disagree. The applied questionnaire referred to issues, which are considered essential for the recording of the opinions of respondents. The topics included are (see Table 1).

Sample Frame

The study was made with the method of private interviews in the area of Greece, referring to young people aged 18-24 years old of the total population of the country, who according to the elements of the national statistical service come to 550000 people. The sample used was the 0.2% of the total population, meaning 1100 young people, whom from we had a 73% response rate (804 people). After excluding some questionnaires because of missing values, in our final analysis we used data coming from 707 people, of whom 73% were women. The research took place from September to November 2010. The sample comes mainly from university areas (68.9% university students). There was a satisfactory representation both of people using post-pay subscription packages and people using pay-as-you-go packages, according to the market share of every mobile phone industry in Greece. It should also be stated that 50% of the total sample concerns people who are subscribers to a particular firm for more than two years, fact that in combination with their young age, shows that probably it isn't the responders who define the relationship with the mobile industries, but their parents. There is a similar behaviour of the sample as far as their preferences are concerned (same percentage agree or disagree to the questions).

Table 1. The factors influence customer retention

Factors	Thematic Area
Customer satisfaction as a driver of customer retention	General customer satisfaction from the company Right choosing of the company from the customer
Price Perception as a driver of customer retention	How fix cost charges, seem to the customer How sms charges seem to the customer How variable charges seem to the customer How logical the charges seem to the customer
Switching barriers as a driver of customer retention	Technical difficulties to change firm Difficulty in changing one's number while changing firms Costs a lot to change firm Needs effort to change firm Not able to start a procedure of changing easily
Trust as a driver of customer retention	Company is reliable Company is a pioneer to the progresses
Service quality perceptions as a driver of customer retention	Information for a better use Personnel is helpful Correction measures to a probable problem Personal data security Economic offer packages
Inertia and Indifference as a driver of customer retention	Don't get in the process of changing firm There is no difference between firms There is little difference in the service between firms

The phase of the data processing includes a set of interactive procedures, in order to explore and mine the data and acquire knowledge concerning the behaviour of the customers. Two different approaches were applied.

Typical statistical analyses were used, such as descriptive frequency analysis and cross tabulation, in order to picture the customer behaviour concerning the main characteristics of the sample and the behaviour and preferences on the examined points of view. Also, chi-square test was used in order to determine differences and similarities among the different groups of customers, as well as to assess the attitudes of the customers related to their intention to change mobile phone firm. Figure 2 shown these simple and descriptive statistical techniques provide a medium that allows us to picture the general trends of the sample behaviour and discover or pose more complicated questions.

Figure 2. Data process and data mining

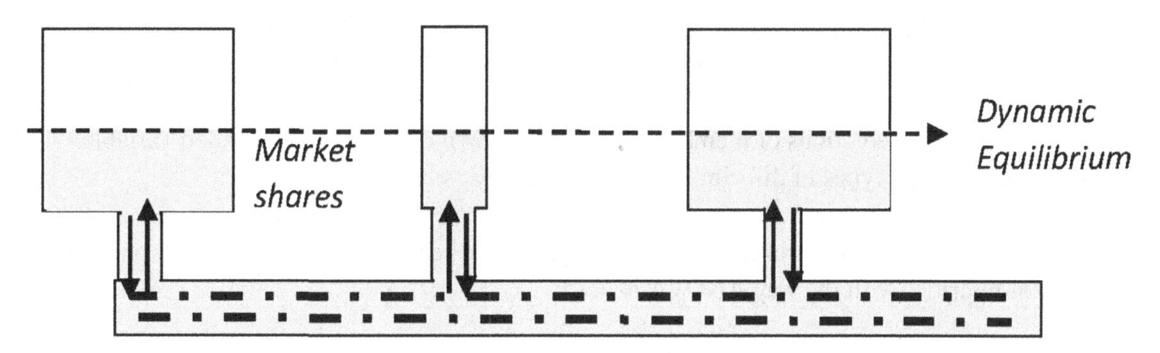

The second approach concerns discriminant analysis (Tabachmick & Fidel, (1989), an analytical technique from the field of the multivariate data analysis. Discriminant Analysis, which is based on Multivariate Analysis of Variance (MANOVA), provides a technique to construct a model (based on a set of known situations) that can discriminate the different behaviours expressed in a variable or question (called dependent variable) and explain this, taking into consideration a set of quantitative or categorical variables (called independent variables or predictors). The goal is to discover the dimension or dimensions along which the groups are different, and to construct functions able to support the classification of the cases and consequently to predict group membership. The significance and utility of discriminant analysis are:

- To determine which are the independent variables or predictors, reflecting the discrimination of the different groups as well as to assess their importance;
- To construct classification functions, which provide a mean to predict group membership of new cases from its values on the predictors.

The simplest form of classification functions (a classification function is estimated for every group) is:

$$C_j = c_{j0} + c_{j1}X_1 + c_{j2}X_2 + \dots + c_{jp}X_p$$

where $j=1,2,3,\dots,k$ are the different groups related to the depended variable and $X_1, X_2, \dots X_p$ the raw scores of a case on the predictors and c_{ji}, $i=1,2, \dots, p$ the classification coefficient. The classification coefficient is found from the mean of the p predictors and the pooled within-group variance-covariance matrix. In matrix form is represented as follow:

$$C_j = W^{-1} M_j$$

where W is the within-group covariance matrix and M_j is the matrix of the means of the p predictors for group j.

The constant for group j (c_{j0}) is calculated as follow:

$$c_{j0} = (-1/2)C_j M_j$$

A case is grouped according to its scores, coming from the classification functions. A new case is grouped in the group where the higher score was calculated or the score is close to the mean of the scores for this group of the known situations.

The adequacy of the assessed classification model can be examined through a set of indexes which is the same used in MANOVA. The most important used are the Wilks' Lamda and the approximate F ratio (Tabachmick & Fidel, 1989) while in practice the success of discriminant analysis is determined by the success rate of predictions of memberships of the known cases on the depended variable.

There are three main types of discriminant function analysis:

- The first is the Direct Discriminant Function Analysis where all predictors enter at once and has many similarities with the way ANOVA is used;

- The second is the Hierarchical Descriminant Analysis where the predictors enter to the analysis gradually in an order determined by the researchers;
- The third is the Stepwise Discriminant Function Analysis, also used in this research project, which includes techniques that allow the reducing of the number of predictors, selecting the ones that are significant for the examined case without reflecting population differences.

Descriptive Statistics

Descriptive statistics refer to seven areas of interest, analyzing each one of them. The following (Table 2) shows the frequencies of our variables.

The results given in Table 2 indicate that consumers, in a percentage of 66.8, show that they are satisfied of their company, showing in this way their trust towards their operator. Opinions of the responders concerning price perceptions seem to be similar, the ones who agree versus to the ones who disagree. They consider the charges of the SMS as well as the fixed charges to be high enough, though an important percentage (28.9%) seems to be indifferent to the pricing policy of the mobile industries. The barriers, which the consumer has to overcome while trying to change firm, consist mainly on technical difficulties and much less on the cost of this procedure (70.8%).

The perceptions of the responders related to the total of the services provided by the mobile phone industry seems to be of no importance for them. This means that the communicative policy of the industry hasn't succeeded in giving them attractive messages. The majority, however, acknowledges the facility with which thcy can turn to the industry's services when needed, though they don't feel that their company can always take correction measures in case of difficulties.

Nevertheless the 64% of the sample consider their firm to be reliable and pioneer of the sector. This combination of reliability and innovation affects their level of trust. Finally, a significant percentage shows that there is no difference between firms, having as a result a lower possibility for a customer to change firm. The fact that the answers of the sample are equally dispersed is also observed in the question of whether they would change firm in the next six months. This attitude indicates a dynamic equilibrium that has been achieved between the two greatest industries in Greece, in reference to the gaining or losing customers.

Discriminant Analysis

From the analysis of all the dependent variables concerning the behaviour of the consumers and their retention to a specific mobile phone industry, we were finally driven to a model of six significant parameters, which play a very important role and explain the desire and thus the final decision of the consumer, whether to remain at the same company or to change (Table 3), (Table 4), (Table 5). A 78,5% of original grouped cases are correctly classified.

Using the assessed discriminant model with the six predictors (Table 3) 78.5% of the cases were correctly classified according to their intention to change or not change mobile provider and the value of Wilks' Lamda is 0,808. These indexes present that the discriminant function can be accepted and use the assessed results for further analysis. The results shown indicate a unified relationship marketing strategy policy on behalf of mobile phone industries, which has as a target to manipulate the behaviour of consumers. The formcr lcads to the inactivation of the consumers, letting them encaged to a specific initial selection. In order to change firms, the consumer has to recognize the benefits from the new firm

Table 2. Descriptive statistics

Variables	Agree %	Neither Agree nor Disagree %	Disagree %
Customer Satisfaction			
- general customer satisfaction from the company	66,8	26,7	6,6
- company comes up to customer's expectations	53,6	37,4	9,1
- right choice of company from the customer	58,1	33,0	9,0
Price Perception			
- how fixed charges seem to the customer	21,1	52,1	26,8
- how sms charges seem to the customer	27,8	36,3	35,8
- how charges seem to the customer	28,9	45,6	25,5
- how logical the charges seem to the customer	21,1	45,5	33,4
Switching barriers			
- technical difficulties to change firm	70,8	12,2	16,9
- difficulty in changing one's number while changing firms	28,3	32,8	38,8
- costs a lot to change firm	31,7	28,5	39,8
- needs effort to change firm	35,2	28.3	36,5
- not able to start a procedure of changing easily	34,5	27,7	35,9
Service Quality Perception			
- information for better use	61,7	25,5	12,7
- the personnel is helpful	64,5	28,3	7,2
- better correspondence in the future	51,8	41,1	7,2
- trust for the future existence of the firm	73,0	21,2	5,1
- capable personnel	56,3	36,9	6,7
- polite personnel	75,2	18,5	6,2
- correction measures to a probable problem	43,5	36,4	20,1
- easy access	57,7	14,0	18,3
- understanding of needs	43,6	44,5	11,9
- Personal data security	52,0	36,1	11,8
- coming up to one's expectations	51,6	34,3	14,1
- economic offer packages	56,8	28,7	22,5
Trust			
- the firm is reliable	64,5	30,6	10,4
- the firm is a pioneer to the progresses	16,6	41,8	42,6
Indifference			
- there is no difference between firms	62,1	23,9	14,0
- there is little difference in the service between firms	45,7	23,2	31,1
Inertia			
- the don't in the procedure of changing firm	33	26,2	40.6

Table 3. Standardized canonical discriminant function coefficients

Factors		Function
Customer Satisfaction	Q15 Satisfaction from the selection of the given firm	.480
Customer Satisfaction	Q13 General satisfaction from the firm	.293
Prices Perceptions	Q22 The charges are reasonable (price perception)	.244
Prices Perceptions	Q20 SMS charges	.273
Inertia	Q25 Doesn't get in the procedure of changing (inertia)	.336
Indifference	Q23 There is no difference between them (indifference)	.244

Table 4. Classification results

		Predicted Group Membership		Total
	Intention	No Change	Change	
Count	No change	421	106	527
	Change	25	58	83
%	No change	79.9%	20.1%	100.0
	Change	30.1%	69.9%	100.0

Table 5. Function results

Test of Function(s)	Wilks' Lambda	Chi-Square	df	Sig.	
1	.808	129.300	6	.000	

both in the pricing policy and the innovation field. Consumer's perception of prices and innovation appear to be similar. This is a result of the intensity of the competition that exists between the industries of the sector. The intense competition concerns the similar offer packages that are promoted to the consumers through advertisement in the media. The policy of these mobile phone industries leads to inertia and lack of motive for the consumers, so as not to seek alternative solutions by changing service provider. As shown (Figure 3) the following model the present case of manipulation of the market.

The market behaviour presents the phenomenon of the communicating vessels, where a dynamic equilibrium exists. The disappointed customers of a mobile provider (a small proportion of the market share) move to another while the same happens to the second mobile provider. The total balance of the market shares for every enterprise remains the same with minor positive or negative variation. This is more intense in this case where the majority of the market shares are split in only two mobile providers. This conclusion comes as a result of the analysis of the customer with the intention to change enterprise for every operator. The findings (Table 6) emphasize that there were similar behaviours for customers' intentions for the two leader firms.

Figure 3. Market shares and the communicating vessels phenomenon

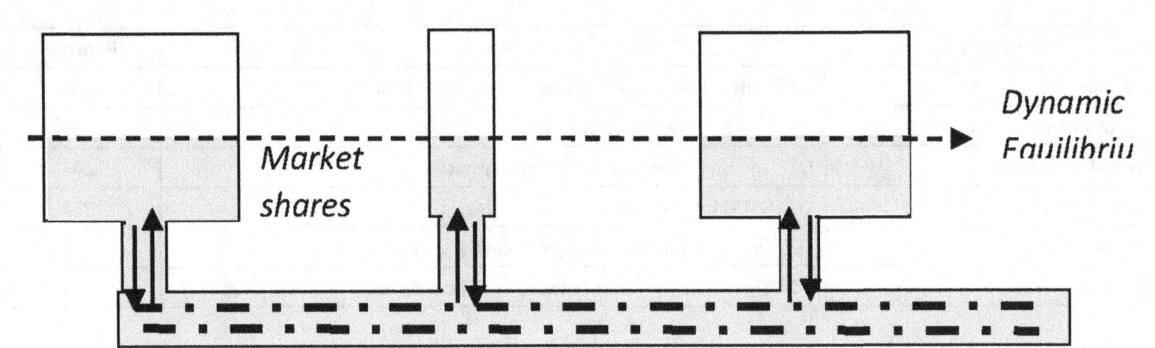

Table 6. Customers' intentions for the two firms

	FIRM 1		FIRM 2	
Intention	Count	Percentage	Count	Percentage
No Change	233	72,1%	212	65,4%
Doubt	59	18,3%	78	24,1%
Change	31	9,6%	34	10,5%
Total	323	100,0%	324	100,0%

Solutions and Recommendations

Examining the first results of globalisation we notice the creation of oligopolies in the market conditions of various economic sectors. The E.U. and the USA government have developed mechanisms in order to watch the newly developed market forces and identify cases of market manipulation with a view to prevent such phenomena (i.e. Microsoft's case in the USA and Siemens in Europe). The existing mechanisms though are watching the market through its results rather than having a pro-active approach. This means that consumers have already suffered the consequences of political intervention or monopolistic and oligopolistic market forces that work together in the form of cartels in an effort to forward their policies. In this article we examine the development of political manipulation of consumer behaviour through marketing strategies applied by companies, aiming to achieve public inactivity that will limit reaction.

The intense competition of the mobile industry with similar tools can lead to a state of consumers' inertia. As a result of this, a state of communicating vessels is created between the specific economic units, meaning that the amount of customers, who change firm driven to the competitive one, equals the amount of customers, who come from the second firm to the first one.

The manipulation of the market can also be seen on the market shares that the great companies possess, which consist of the 82% of the total market, divided almost equally into the two greater companies. Firms have to operate in a competitive market following rules in favour of the consumers; they should differentiate their strategy with drastic interventions. This creates the need to further utilize all marketing tools in an appropriate mix in order to promote new technologies and services that increase revenue per customer, as well as create the need for customers to upgrade their mobile phones and subscriptions

(Hackley & Kitchen, 1998). The drive for organizational integration contributes to greater influence over consumer perceptions.

Our research has shown that we can develop a model in order to present the situation of high competition among two firms. Through our findings elicited from the discriminant analysis, we saw that business firms using similar marketing tools, advertisement, package offers, pricing policy, try to manipulate the consumer's behaviour.

The main characteristic of the new economy is the great alterations in consumer purchase decisions; as a result it is increasingly difficult to develop long-term business programmes for two main reasons:

1. These days, consumer awareness levels are significantly higher than in the past; and
2. There are a big number of new and departing companies in the industry as life cycles are continuously reducing due to the increased scientific innovations in all fields.

In order to face the above phenomenon, companies must develop relationship marketing strategies that will crystallise consumer loyalty through bettering their relationships' conditions with the public i.e. trust, switching cost, barriers etc. This way, companies can create the basis upon which they can build their development strategies.

REFERENCES

Anwar, S. T. (2003). CASES Vodafone and the wireless industry: A case in market expansion and global strategy. *Journal of Business and Industrial Marketing*, *18*(3), 270–288. doi:10.1108/08858620310471331

Athanasopoulou, P. (2009). Relationship quality: A critical literature review and research agenda. *European Journal of Marketing*, *43*(5/6), 583–610. doi:10.1108/03090560910946945

Bendall-Lyon, D., & Powers, T. L. (2003). The influence of mass communication and time on satisfaction and loyalty. *Journal of Services Marketing*, *17*(6), 589–608. doi:10.1108/08876040310495627

Bennett, R., & Barkensjo, A. (2005). Relationship quality, relationship marketing, and client perceptions of the levels of service quality of charitable organisations. *International Journal of Service Industry Management*, *16*(1), 81–106. doi:10.1108/09564230510587168

Chatura, R., & Jaideep, P. (2003). The influence of satisfaction, trust and switching barriers on customer retention in a continuous purchasing setting. *International Journal of Service Industry Management*, *14*(Iss: 4), 374–395. doi:10.1108/09564230310489231

Cronin, J. J. Jr, Brady, M. K., & Hult, G. T. M. (2000). Assessing the effects of quality, value, and customer satisfaction on consumer behavioural intentions in service environments. *Journal of Retailing*, *76*(2), 193–218. doi:10.1016/S0022-4359(00)00028-2

Dasgupta, K., Singh, R., Viswanathan, B., Chakraborty, D., Mukherjea, S., & Nanavati, A. A. (2008). Social ties and their relevance to churn in mobile telecom networks. *Proceedings of the 11th International Conference on Extending Database Technology: Advances in Database Technology*. doi:10.1145/1353343.1353424

Eagle, L., & Kitchen, P. J. (2000). IMC, brand communications, and corporate cultures. *European Journal of Marketing*, *34*(5/6), 667–686. doi:10.1108/03090560010321983

Everrit, B. S., & Dunn, G. (2001). *Multivariate data analysis*. London: Arnold Publishers. doi:10.1002/9781118887486

Fraunholz, B., & Unnithan, C. (2004). Critical success factors in mobile communications: A comparative roadmap for Germany and India. *International Journal of Mobile Communications*, *2*(1), 87–101. doi:10.1504/IJMC.2004.004489

Hennig-Thurau, T., & Klee, A. (1997). The impact of customer satisfaction and relationship quality on customer retention: A critical reassessment and model development. *Psychology and Marketing*, *14*(8), 737–764. doi:10.1002/(SICI)1520-6793(199712)14:8<737::AID-MAR2>3.0.CO;2-F

Huang, H. H., & Chiu, C. K. (2006). Exploring customer satisfaction, trust and destination loyalty in tourism. *Journal of American Academy of Business*, *10*(1), 156–159.

Jeng, J., & Bailey, T. (2012). Assessing customer retention strategies in mobile telecommunications: Hybrid MCDM approach. *Management Decision*, *50*(9), 1570–1595. doi:10.1108/00251741211266697

Kim, K. Y., Yun, D. K., & Kim, D. Y. (2009). Expectations measurements in mobile data service: A case study. *International Journal of Mobile Communications*, *7*(1), 91–116. doi:10.1504/IJMC.2009.021674

Kyriazopoulos, P. (2000). The modern firm at the beginning of the 21st Century (A. S. Ekdotiki, Ed.). Academic Press.

Kyriazopoulos, P. (2001). *Apply Marketing*. Athens Sychroni Ekdotiki.

Lam, S. Y., Shankar, V., Erramilli, M. K., & Murthy, B. (2004). Customer value, satisfaction, loyalty, and switching costs: An illustration from a business-to-business service context. *Journal of the Academy of Marketing Science*, *32*(3), 293–311. doi:10.1177/0092070304263330

Light, C., Light, A., & Teulade, V. (2010). *A look at the future of mobile data*. Retrieved from www.pwc.com/en_GX/gx/communications/assets/Mobile_Content_final.pdf

Manoj, E., & Sunil, S. (2011). Role of switching costs in the service quality, perceived value, customer satisfaction and customer retention linkage. *Asia Pacific Journal of Marketing and Logistics*, *23*(3), 327–345. doi:10.1108/13555851111143240

Papassapa, R., & Miller, K. E. (2007). Relationship quality as a predictor of B2B customer loyalty. *Journal of Business Research*, *60*(1), 21–31. doi:10.1016/j.jbusres.2005.11.006

Ramaseshan, B., Yip, L. S., & Pae, J. H. (2006). Power, satisfaction and relationship commitment in Chinese store-tenant relationship and their impact on performance. *Journal of Retailing*, *82*(1), 63–70. doi:10.1016/j.jretai.2005.11.004

Reinartz, W., & Kumar, V. (2000). The Impact of Customer Relationship Characteristics on Profitable Lifetime Duration. *Journal of Marketing*, 67.

Rust, R., Katherine, T., Lemon, N., & Zeithaml, A. (2003). *Return on Marketing: Using Customer Equity to Focus Marketing Strategy*. *Journal of Marketing*.

Seetharaman, P. B., & Chintagunta, P. (1998). A model of inertia and variety-seeking with marketing variables. *International Journal of Research in Marketing*, *15*(1), 1–17. doi:10.1016/S0167-8116(97)00015-3

Sharma, N., Young, L., & Wilkinson, I. (2006). *The commitment mix: multi-aspect commitment in international trading relationships in India*. Unpublished Document.

Tabachmick & Fidell. (1989). *Using multivariate statistics*. New York: Harper Collins Publishers Inc.

Türkyilmaz, A., & Özkan, C. (2007). Development of a customer satisfaction index model: An application to the Turkish mobile phone sector. *Industrial Management & Data Systems*, *107*(5), 672–687. doi:10.1108/02635570710750426

White, L., & Yanamandram, V. (2004). Why customers stay: Reasons and consequences of inertia in financial services. *Managing Service Quality*, *14*(2/3), 183–194. doi:10.1108/09604520410528608

White, L., & Yanamandram, V. (2007). A model of customer retention of dissatisfied business services customers. *Managing Service Quality*, *17*(3), 298–316. doi:10.1108/09604520710744317

Wolfl, A. (2005). *The service economy in OECD countries*. STI working paper 2005/3. Statistical Analysis of Science, Technology and Industry, Paris Cedex.

Yanamandram, V. K., & White, L. (2006). Switching barriers in business-to-business services: A qualitative study. *International Journal of Service Industry Management*, *17*(2), 158–192. doi:10.1108/09564230610656980

Zeelenberg, M., & Pieters, R. (2004). Beyond valence in customer dissatisfaction: A review and new findings on behavioural responses to regret and disappointment in failed services. *Journal of Business Research*, *57*(4), 445–455. doi:10.1016/S0148-2963(02)00278-3

Zeithaml, V. A., Parasuraman, A., & Berry, L. L. (1990). *Delivering Quality Service: Balancing Customer Perceptions and Expectations*. New York, NY: The Free Press.

KEY TERMS AND DEFINITIONS

Customer Retention: The construct of customer retention focuses on repeat patronage, and it is different from, while closely related to, purchasing behavior and brand loyalty, in that in retention the marketer is seen as having the more active role in the customer-firm relationship.

Customer Satisfaction: Reflecting the degree in which the customer believes the service provider evokes positive feelings.

Indifference: Given a homogeneous supply and a heterogeneous demand, the satisfaction levels of the customer are reduced.

Inertia: Inertia is the re-buy of the same service provider passively without much thought.

Relationship Marketing: Emphasizes on a long-term interactive relationship between the provider and the customer, leading to long-term profitability.

Service Quality: Service quality of the product greatly affect consumer behavior.

Switching Barriers: Switching barriers are the factors which prevent a customer to change company.

Trust: Conceptualise trust based on interpretation of the construct of the commitment-trust theory of customer retention.

Chapter 12
Knowledge Management System from Individual Firm to National Scale

Mei-Tai Chu
La Trobe University, Australia

ABSTRACT

Knowledge management system (KMS) is capable of capturing explicit knowledge and tacit knowledge in a systematic manner. As any type of organization scales up, the issue in relation to, how to construct an effective knowledge sharing mechanism in KMS to covert individual knowledge into collective knowledge remains under surveyed. The rising concerns especially focus on the identification of individual knowledge worker, how firms facilitate knowledge sharing and the effectiveness of national knowledge management system. Communities of Practice (CoPs) are well known as effective mechanism to foster knowledge sharing theoretically and practically. This paper aims to explore the journey of CoPs driven KMS from the lens of individuals, firms' business strategies to the perspectives of national interest. On individual level, knowledge nodes are explored in the context of knowledge flow, which often transcend organizational boundaries and are distinct and different than workflow models. Thus, a CoPs centered knowledge flow model in a multinational organization is developed, implemented, and analyzed. On firm level, this model is underpinned in a CoPs framework built around four expected firms' major business strategies including four dimensions and sixteen criteria as a comprehensive mechanism to intensify knowledge sharing effect. Finally, a conceptual model of KMS embedded national innovation system is also addressed.

INTRODUCTION

Knowledge management system (KMS) implies a strategic information system and technology in knowledge intensive organizations, which can mine, store and disseminate organizational collective knowledge to improve knowledge sharing and lead to collaboration. Organizational collective knowledge in terms of expertise ability has to be leveraged as critical yet difficult to manage (Cham et al., 2016; Jan &

DOI: 10.4018/978-1-5225-1680-4.ch012

Contreras, 2016; Wayne et al., 2000; Parise & Henderson, 2001). Particularly organizations today exist in the knowledge era as against the information era of 1980 and 1990's. They compete with each other on the basis of knowledge and innovation (Wang & Libaers, 2015; OECD 1996, 1999). Thus organizational innovation through knowledge sharing and knowledge node identification is an important means of surviving as well as excelling in a highly competitive business environment, in pursuit of learning organizations of the future will not be constrained by traditional boundaries. Thus this research envisions organizations as a set of knowledge nodes to generate knowledge flow that can extend outside organizational boundaries as against conventional work flow networks. Unlike human nodes used in most of business processes, knowledge nodes can be quite different in the context of knowledge flow and knowledge sharing.

Knowledge node plays an important role known for the majority of professionals such as decision makers, technology developers, and knowledge workers in Communities of Practice (CoPs) in an organization (Huang et al., 2015; Lesser, 2001). CoPs have been proven as effective platform to facilitate knowledge sharing (Chu et al., 2014; McDermott, 1999; Grant, 1996). CoPs are identified as self-emerging groups initially but the strategic importance of CoPs has made organizations to look into the possibilities of identifying and creating CoPs. A number of organizations create communities with managed membership accordingly (John & Patricia, 2000). Resources in terms of technology, people and content (Grant, 1996) are then invested to develop CoPs and these resources have to be utilized optimally. Quite a few researches have suggested guidelines and models for creating CoPs (Wenger et al., 2002, Loyarte & Rivera, 2007, McDermott, 1999). However, a lack of comprehensive CoPs framework as powerful knowledge sharing mechanism drives a growing need to allocate appropriate resources. Therefore, the first objective of this paper is to develop an easy to understand CoPs hierarchy consisting of exhausting dimensions and criteria.

The importance of knowledge has made organizations to focus on knowledge sharing strategy (e.g. CoPs) and its alignment with how to identify the knowledge nodes effectively. Although several scholars have studied the incentives of knowledge sharing, most of them focus on situational characteristics and very limited study has involved the knowledge sharing and knowledge node. This study aims to bridge the gap by identifying knowledge node/knowledge worker in the context of CoPs. The alignment with the business goals and the objectives of the organization are necessary to achieve competitive advantage (Michael, 1999). The need for proper system to position where the knowledge nodes exist to connect with share knowledge in the context of CoPs has initiated the process of alignment. The realization of this alignment as a carrier to imitation (Kogut & Zander, 1992) has diverted the attention to tacit knowledge. CoPs have been identified as an important tool in managing the tacit knowledge and then the knowledge nodes can be identified the most intense knowledge sharing points which provides competitive advantage to the firm (Jeanne, 1999).

The previous work on knowledge node centered knowledge flow networks focus on linking people based on organization structure, tasks, and knowledge compatibility (Zhuge, 2006). In other works, these researches do not throw adequate light on the need that knowledge flow occurs between knowledge nodes outside traditional organizational structure, business functions and organizational boundaries. As the second aim in this paper, the authors propose to enhance in design of knowledge node embedded knowledge flow based on the survey in relation to CoPs perceptions in an organization.

A CoPs framework has been defined, which constitutes 16 criteria along four major dimensions in this research. These criteria and dimensions are used to identify common interaction factors (beliefs and attitudes) which link and facilitate effective knowledge sharing between knowledge workers/nodes in a knowledge flow. These factors and the CoPs model have been validated using a large multinational organization as a case study. Given that, knowledge flow is dynamic phenomena in an organization, a dynamic model for analyzing knowledge flow activities like knowledge sharing, knowledge discovery, and knowledge creation is also described.

Furthermore, both at firm and national level, particularly in the most developed economies, the increasing importance of knowledge have meant that the net stock of intangible capital has grown more rapidly than the tangible capital. This has unfortunately not yet happened in the developing economies (Mortensen et al., 1997). The world economy is becoming ever more dependent on creating, distributing, and using knowledge. Knowledge innovation activity penetrates the entire process including knowledge creation, transmission and application. Knowledge and information flow facilitates relationship and communication among the subsystems and various main bodies within the innovation system, which prompts the innovation system to be a more dynamic and more opening-up mutual promotion system. Information and knowledge resources' exchange, flowing and allocation are the prerequisite for safeguarding the innovation system's operation efficiency. Therefore, knowledge management construction for innovation system is the enterprise innovation guarantee factor as well as one essential part for superior National Innovation System (NIS). There is a need to a useful conceptual model of NIS to escalate the benefit of KMS in a larger scale.

This paper is thus followed by:

- Section 2 which reviews the existing studies including CoPs framework, knowledge flow architecture and NIS;
- Section 3 explains the research methodology via fuzzy AHP (Analytical Hierarchy Processing) and cluster analysis method to survey the chosen case;
- Section 4 demonstrates the research outcomes and conceptual model establishment of NIS;
- Section 5 concludes this paper.

RELATED WORK

The assumption of this research is that knowledge flow design is driven by the need to develop effective knowledge sharing and identify knowledge nodes in order to enable organizations to compete in a knowledge-based economy. In this context, the related knowledge sharing and CoPs literatures have been reviewed to establish an effective knowledge sharing mechanism. Then a CoPs framework is cited and adopted, which includes the key criteria and dimensions based on the business strategies or benefits in terms of expected performance. The next key component in this section is to build up the knowledge node embedded knowledge flow model. The last section reviews the NIS development.

How Communities of Practice Serves as Knowledge Sharing Mechanism

In terms of collective knowledge in organizations, knowledge has to be transferable from a more manageable perspective rather than natural behavior (Grant, 1996). Knowledge sharing impacts the sustainable development in most of the knowledge intensive institutions as the back bone of knowledge management system. Effective Knowledge sharing can be affected by a number of elements which has driven many researchers explore in this area. The major categories in relation to the motivation for knowledge sharing can be classified as extrinsic, intrinsic, personality traits, relationship factors, and organization culture (Chu, 2014). For example, the use of rewards and reciprocity can be regarded as extrinsic motivators (Cabrera & Cabrera, 2002; Zmud & Lee, 2005lBartol & Srivastava, 2002). The examples of intrinsic element are sense of self value (Zmud & Lee, 2005) and self-efficacy (Kankanhalli et al., 2005; Lu et al., 2006). In the group of personality traits include agreeableness (Todd et al., 2006; Namjae et al., 2007) and conscientiousness (Namjae et al., 2007). Trust (Politis, 2003; Levin et al., 2002; Levin & Cross, 2004) and identification (Cabrera & Cabrera, 2002) are commonly placed in the group of interrelationship. The elements of fairness, affiliation, and innovation (Zmud & Lee, 2005; McLure & Faraj, 2000; McDermott & O'dell, 2001) are tightly related to organization culture. The existing literatures have shown much of work on situational factors but little on knowledge node embedded knowledge flow.

It is envisaged that seventy percent of existing Knowledge Management (KM) tools have failed to achieve the anticipated business performance outcomes they had been designed for (Malhotra, 2004), regardless of the rise of technology-based KM tools, implementations often fail to realize their stated objectives (Ambrosio, 2000). One of the primary reasons identified for the failure of existing KM tools has been that existing KM tools and research have primarily been designed around technology push models as against strategy-pull models (Malhotra, 2004). The technology-push model which is based on application of information technologies on historical data largely produce pre-specified meanings/ knowledge and pre-specified outcomes which are useful in predictable and stable business environments. On the other hand, strategy-pull model turns the technology-push model on its head and drive the construction and creation of knowledge and related actions based on business strategy and performance driven outcome rather than find a suitable business strategy fit for the pre-determined knowledge and outcomes generated by technology-push approach.

While facing undergoing rapid, discontinuous and turbulent change for most organizations, it is imperative that KM systems and organizational entities like CoPs which facilitate KM and organizational transformation are more closely aligned with business strategies and goals of an organization. This would enable organizations to respond more quickly to changing business environments and business process and corresponding change in their KM needs continuously.

There is a rising need for information system design considering knowledge sharing other than technology development only. Particularly the realization of tacit knowledge sharing is a higher barrier to be imitated by competitors (Kogut & Zander, 1992) has drawn the attention to tacit knowledge. It is argued that the knowledge should belong and disseminate via well-designed communities and therefore CoPs facilitate a common platform and meaning for tacit knowledge transfer (McDermott, 1999; Grant, 1996). CoPs thus have been recognized as an important instrument to manage tacit knowledge and therefore provide competitive advantage to the firm (Jeanne, 1999). Wenger (1998) first proposed CoPs in the Harvard Business Review, who believes CoPs is an informal group sharing knowledge, points out CoPs is composed by three critical elements (mutual engagement, joint enterprise, shared repository). Allee (2000) further addressed knowledge should include and utilize CoPs to create organizational knowledge. Besides, CoPs are distinguishing from other organizational groups such as formal divisions, project teams and informal network (Cohendet & Meyer-Krahmer, 2001; Allee, 2000; Wenger et al., 2002). Knowledge workers are those people who constantly use their knowledge in accomplishing their tasks which require systematic training to upgrade skills and expertise (Drucker, 1969). Wenger (2002) defined CoPs is feathered that the knowledge workers can deepen the knowledge and expertise through interaction with other knowledge workers. CoPs also can be viewed from an organization perspective as a group of knowledge workers who undertake similar work (Brown & Duguid, 2000).

As the CoPs have been well positioned from several literatures, but the strategic challenge is how to identify and create suitable CoP's. Several studies have addressed the guidelines and models for creating suitable CoPs (Wenger et al., 2002; Loyarte & Rivera, 2007; McDermott, 1999). To organize and create communities with managed membership is also proposed (John & Patricia, 2000). More importantly, the resources in terms of technology, people and content have to be invested to develop CoPs to reach the optimal effect (Grant, 1996). The relevant theoretical studies have underpinned that CoPs can enable member interaction, knowledge sharing, organization learning, and open innovation simultaneously. It emphasizes more on facilitating, extracting and sharing tacit knowledge to maximize KM value. Many world class companies have taken CoPs as a new central role in the value chain (Chu et al., 2007). As cited from Chu et al. (2007) the expected performance of CoPs can be distinguished by organization performance and operation mode as the matrix shown in Figure 1. Mostly, some firms are likely to emphasize how to reduce costs or increase profits instead, while some companies tend to focus on group learning or reuse intellectual asset (IA) more. The first two factors (cost down and revenue up) can be categorized into organizational performance axle, and the latter two factors (group learning and reuse IA) can be grouped into operation mode axle in the matrix.

As CoPs emphasize competency and efficiency enhancement, their organization performance tends to cost down effectively, whereas when CoPs focus on innovation and responsiveness, which would aim at create new value or revenue up. Furthermore, this research points out that the operation mode residing in CoPs leads to behavioral changes, which in turn results in different preference on organizational performance. On one hand, when CoPs prefer explicit knowledge content, the operation mode may focus on reuse IA, and emphasize the storage, access, and reusing of knowledge. This sort of CoPs tends to pursue organizational performance on business strategies like Enhanced Working Efficiency and Promoted Responsiveness through getting warning through analysis and classification of knowledge. On the other hand, when CoPs prefer tacit knowledge, the operation mode may stress to create grouping learning, providing experts to exchange, interact, sharing best practices. This sort of CoPs tends to pursue knowledge flow and CoPs as organizational performance on business strategies like Increased Core Competency and Induced Innovation Learning through raising the capability via cross-domain knowledge sharing.

CoPs not only can link with organizational performance very well, but also essential to overcome the inherent problems of a slow-moving traditional hierarchy in a fast-moving knowledge economy. Therefore, this research uses the four CoPs expected performance, namely Induce Innovation Learning, Promote Responsiveness, Increase Core Competency, and Enhance Working Efficiency to develop the CoPs framework. These four CoPs expected performance need to be well defined and then pursued,

Figure 1. The Matrix of CoPs expected performance

		Organizational Performance	
		Cost Down	Revenue Up
Operation Mode	Group Learning	Increased Core Competency	Induced Innovation Learning
	Reuse IA	Enhanced Working Efficiency	Promoted Responsiveness

because they will influence the overall achievements and the community's resources allocation direction. The first expected performance is to Induce Innovation Learning. The specific characteristics include cross-domain sharing to support new idea and creation according to common interests through group learning. The CoPs under this strategy often provide a safe or low-cost infrastructure for try and error attempts freely to facilitate new thinking and innovation; the second expected performance is to Promote Responsiveness by collecting and classifying knowledge objects. CoPs can directly obtain the problem-oriented solution, because the colleagues with similar working experiences are easy to find. They can help other members who are facing same questions based on the common language and shared foundations which lead to promote responsiveness; the third expected performance is to Increase Core Competency. Members can promote skill by shifting the best knowledge practices. It will be efficient to figure out who are domain-experts, how to enable insight exchange between senior and junior members. The organization principals can be established and increase core competency; and the fourth expected performance is to Enhance Working Efficiency. CoPs members can reuse existing intellectual property invented by others in a well-structured database easily, access related documents and authors' information quickly. The entire productivity will be improved and working efficiency will be enhanced accordingly.

Key Dimensions and Criteria of CoPs Framework

With an attempt to realize the four expected performance outlined from above section, the CoPs framework is defined and evaluated along four expected performance with four dimensions and sixteen criteria (Chu et al., 2007). The hierarchy demonstrates four dimensions and sixteen criteria are shown in Table 1. The four dimensions are explained as follows respectively:

1. **Locus of Leadership:** Relates to enforcement or volunteer, wholly or partially adoption;
2. **Incentive Mechanism:** Relates to award or punishment;
3. **Member Interaction:** Relates to sharing or security; and
4. **Complementary Asset:** Relates to infrastructure and resource.

Additionally, the Locus of Leadership dimension contains four criteria:

1. Top-Down Assigning;
2. Bottom-Up Teaming;
3. Total Execution; and
4. Partial Pilot run.

The Incentive Mechanism dimension contains:

- Substantive Reward;
- Psychological Encourage;
- Achievements Appraisal Basis; and
- Peers Reputation.

Table 1. Dimension and criteria of CoPs framework

Dimension	Criteria
Locus of Leadership	Top-Down Assigning
	Bottom-Up Teaming
	Total Execution
	Partial Pilot run
Incentive Mechanisms	Substantive Reward
	Psychological Encouragement
	Achievements Appraisal Basis
	Peer Approval
Member Interaction	Homogeneity of members
	Differential members
	Emphasis on Security
	Emphasis on Cross-Domain Sharing
Complementary assets	Supplying Extra Resources
	Routine Daily Work
	Integrated IT Platform
	Independent IT platform

The Member Interaction contains: Homogeneity of members, Differential members, Emphasize security, and Emphasize cross-domain Sharing. The Complementary Asset dimension contains:

- Give Extra Resources;
- Just Daily Work;
- Integrated IT Platform; and
- Independent IT platform.

Knowledge Node Embedded Knowledge Flow Model

A knowledge node driven knowledge flow model based on CoPs is constructed in this section. In the preceding section the ground related to definition and construction of CoPs model has been outlined. In this section we use the CoPs centered parameters to define the components and terminologies of the knowledge flow model. The knowledge flow includes quantitative implications of the human and social factors like beliefs and attitudes for interaction between knowledge workers derived from the CoPs model (Thomas et al., 2001). These interaction beliefs and attitudes for knowledge sharing are based on the sixteen criteria used by the CoPs framework. Knowledge flow can also be considered as CoPs in an organization where people with a common goal come together to create, learn, process and share knowledge based on best practices. Organizations and research teams are held together by CoPs or knowledge flow.

It is vital to identify the knowledge node where they exist, reside and expand as people constantly wonder where knowledge lives and grows during knowledge sharing (Huggins & Johnston, 2010; Leistner, 2010; Zhuge, 2006; Zhuge et al., 2006; Fan & Lee, 2009; Stale et al., 2011). By the identification of knowledge node, it represents potential knowledge flow which can intensify richer communication or exchange. It then stimulates more active connections for continuous knowledge sharing which provides especially tacit knowledge deeper and meaningful flow between givers and receivers. A knowledge flow model is needed to embrace the knowledge sharing mechanism provided through CoPs associated with multi-dimensions (Zhuge, 2002).

Establishing a knowledge node embedded knowledge flow model is meant to develop actual knowledge node/human networks which can be used for creation, learning, processing and sharing of knowledge (Davenport et al., 2004; Malhotra, 2004; Ratcliffe et al., 2000; Nissen, 2002; Nonaka, 1994; Thomas et al., 2001; Zhuge, 2003; Desouza, 2003). Particularly the knowledge resulting from innovation needs is regarded as an organizational transformation initiative. The initiative involves transmission of explicit, tacit and embodied knowledge by means of knowledge flow iteratively. As seen in Figure 2, a knowledge flow model consists of knowledge nodes (human or knowledge portal or process), knowledge links and weight which help to specify the strength of the knowledge link. According to the definition of CoPs and existing research, knowledge workers share knowledge based on knowledge compatibility as well as a set of interaction principles and beliefs which define their underlying knowledge sharing philosophy (Thomas et al., 2001). Although these interaction principles are not a determining factor for knowledge sharing they do influence the effectiveness and efficiency of knowledge sharing between two knowledge workers. These interaction principles and beliefs are defined based on four dimensions and sixteen criteria adopted from CoPs framework as Table 1.

For example, an analogy is a recruitment scenario of sales candidate for selling laptops. The starting point is the recruitment panel will determine the knowledge compatibility of the sales candidate in the domain of laptops. Furthermore, they will also study or analyse (based on range of criteria) how this sales candidate will interact with a customer in an actual selling situation. Likewise, knowledge level and space of a knowledge worker or a researcher can be determined based on their previous experience and track record, etc. Nevertheless, the degree they actually engage in knowledge sharing, tacit knowledge particularly, may be impacted by the sixteen criteria for knowledge sharing and management. Other factors which can influence knowledge sharing can be trust and psychological profiles of the cooperating knowledge workers.

Figure 2. Knowledge node embedded knowledge flow model

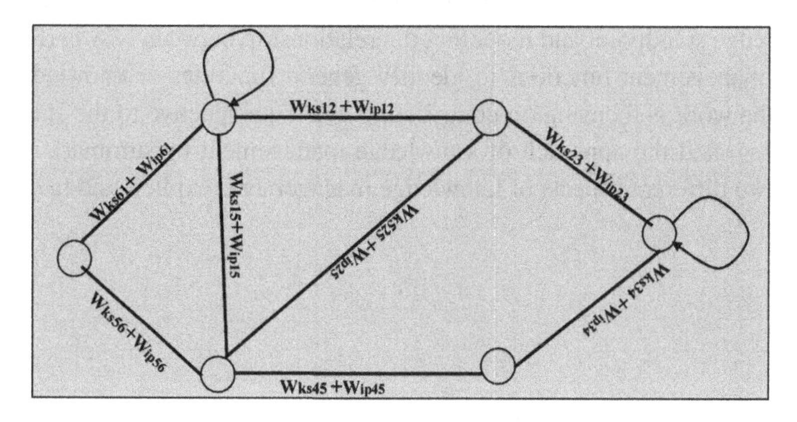

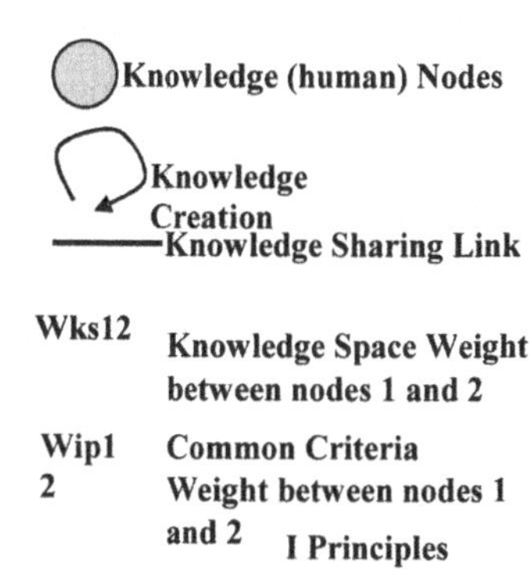

Two types of weights, knowledge space weight and interaction principles weight are considered in Figure 2. The knowledge space weight can vary between 0-1 and can be specified by the group or network leader based on knowledge and experience of the two knowledge workers, between discussions and consensus to calculate the impact of interaction principles on the overall effectiveness and efficiency of the knowledge link between two human nodes.

The established knowledge flow model not only helps to form and grow knowledge flow teams for knowledge intensive organizations, but also identifies high and low knowledge energy nodes. The human node in Figure 2 with the highest number of links is the node with highest knowledge energy as it represents knowledge sharing and interaction potential of the node. This pattern is quite different from traditional work flow, which may not follow the same pattern as knowledge flow.

Knowledge Management System and National Innovation System

The current industrialized countries have specific processes to focus on the creation of Knowledge-Based Economies (KBE) in their societies and industries (OECD, 1996; DTI, 1998). Hence the generation of new knowledge, technological progress and innovation are determining factors in economic growth. In this regard, the National Innovation Systems (NIS) acts through the introduction of knowledge in the economy. Nevertheless, this requires active learning both for individuals and organizations to participate in the innovation processes. Therefore, the concepts of knowledge and learning are important to contribute to the analysis of innovation systems (Lundvall, 1992; OECD, 1996). In 1987, Freeman proposed the concept of NIS. From then on, academic research on NIS has been flourishing along with studies about knowledge based economy and knowledge management in NIS.

Even quite a few existing work have focused on contributing a new perspective to the study of national innovation in the area of knowledge-based Economies using NIS approach (OECD, 1996; DTI, 1998; APEC Economic Committee, 2000; World Bank, 2002; Freeman, 1987; Lundvall, 1992; Nelson & Rosenberg, 1993; Patel and Pavitt, 1994; OECD, 1999), There is little research that compares approaches by discussing an effective KM framework as the central theme. Thus, one aim of this paper is to integrate systems of innovation studies and knowledge management functions to provide a better understanding of the NIS knowledge point of view. In this context, previous studies have been synthesized in this paper to develop a new model for illustrating how KM enables NIS.

Innovation system research emphasizes knowledge creation, transmission and application on region-level. It devotes to pull regional overall knowledge creation and innovative activities through innovation system's institutional arrangements within a region and the network architecture design to influence functional mechanism of the essential elements. According to this context, the paper also proposes the development of a NIS from a knowledge standpoint and modeling the relationship between NIS performance dimensions and knowledge management functions to identify general functions of knowledge management enables NIS. Hence, the work is focusing on contributing a new perspective to the study of national innovation, as it has integrated the approach of knowledge management by summarizing the results from research touching two different aspects of knowledge management (explicit and tacit).

RESEACH METHODOLOGY

The techniques used for construction of CoPs centered knowledge flow model in a large multinational organization are described in this section. The major research methods used in this paper include fuzzy AHP (Analytical Hierarchy Processing) and cluster analysis. Fuzzy AHP technique is used to calculate the importance, which is attributed to each dimension and criterion by the knowledge worker participating in the survey. Clustering analysis technique is used to connect knowledge workers/nodes with common criteria (attitudes and beliefs) in this model. Intuitively, common attitudes and beliefs between two knowledge workers/nodes imply that knowledge sharing among them is likely to be more effective than between knowledge workers/nodes with dissimilar attitudes and beliefs. These techniques include a CoPs questionnaire based survey of knowledge workers. The survey is used to evaluate the importance attributed by knowledge workers to sixteen CoPs criteria of knowledge workers along four expected performance.

Questionnaire Design

The CoPs framework consists of dimension and criteria in Table 1 is employed to design questionnaire. The first task is to examine participants' response in relation to the relative importance in terms of weights between the main four dimensions of Locus of Leadership, Incentive Mechanism, Member Interaction and Complementary Asset. The similar examination applies to the relative importance/weights at criteria level under each dimension. The results can reflect the true aspect of each opinion towards the relative importance of the evaluation dimension and criteria in the questionnaire. The fuzzy linguistic expression range is then defined to interpret their preference in a more precise way. The preference is meant for the four pre-determined expected CoPs performance, Induce Innovation Learning, Promote Responsiveness, Increase Core Competency, and Enhance Work Efficiency as seen in Figure 1.

There has been relatively little systematic and quantitative study on the linkage between community outcomes and the underlying functional structure, although many scholars assert that CoPs create organization value. The majority of paper focuses on individual and subjective viewpoints. This research attempts to determine these insufficiencies, and aims at debatable criteria for future analysis. The questionnaire is designed to reveal the perspectives of each researcher in five laboratories of our case. The questionnaire is also designed to weight their comparative importance of expected CoPs performance. The questionnaire is distributed to a broad sampling of researchers, to seek their views and calculate their final values. Thirty nine valid questionnaires out of seventy are collected with a response rate at 55.7 percent. The aim is to provide a valuable reference when choosing suitable CoPs expected performance.

RESEARCH FINDINGS

The research findings are described in two sections, which are the analysis outcomes from fuzzy AHP and cluster analysis respectively to understand the alignment of common beliefs between knowledge workers and their clusters. The final task is embarking the knowledge flow analysis.

Results from Fuzzy AHP

First of all the relative importance or priority of each dimension and criteria rated by participants from case study is discussed. The relative importance or priority is expressed in the form of weight. The total weight of four dimensions and sixteen criteria is normalized to 1. In particular, the priority result of all participants as shown in Table 2 displays the top weighting order in dimension as Member Interaction with a high score of 0.344. Nevertheless, Complementary Asset is the least highlighted dimension. As to the aspect of weight within criteria, the top ranked criteria is Bottom-Up Teaming in Locus of Leadership Dimension, Psychological Encourage in Incentive Mechanism Dimension, Emphasize Cross-Domain Sharing in Member Interaction Dimension, and Give Extra Resource in Complementary Asset Dimension. Meanwhile, the weight cross criteria reveal they focus on Emphasize Cross-Domain Sharing as the highest among 16 criteria, Independent IT Platform as the lowest rank instead.

In terms of the utility value matrix, each participant uses fuzzy language to express five types of effectiveness boundaries. These rankings are very high, high, fair, low, and very low. Table 3 demonstrates the example of fuzzy linguistic expression.

Table 2. Weight of dimension and criteria

Weight Dimension/Criteria	Weight of Each Dimension	Weight within Criteria	Weight Cross Criteria (Ranking)
Locus of Leadership	0.264		
Top-Down Assigning		0.271 (2)	0.071 (05)
Bottom-Up Teaming		0.305 (1)	0.080 (03)
Total Execution		0.164 (4)	0.043 (12)
Partial Pilot run		0.260 (3)	0.069 (06)
Incentive Mechanism	0.246		
Substantive Reward		0.177 (4)	0.044 (11)
Psychological Encourage		0.312 (1)	0.077 (04)
Achievements Appraisal Basis		0.252 (3)	0.062 (08)
Peers Reputation		0.259 (2)	0.064 (07)
Member Interaction	0.344		
Homogeneity member		0.135 (3)	0.046 (09)
Differential member		0.361 (2)	0.124 (02)
Emphasize Security		0.103 (4)	0.035 (15)
Emphasize Cross-Domain Sharing		0.401 (1)	0.138 (01)
Complementary Asset	0.147		
Give Extra Resource		0.303 (1)	0.045 (10)
Just Daily Work		0.256 (3)	0.038 (13)
Integrated IT Platform		0.260 (2)	0.038 (13)
Independent IT platform		0.181 (4)	0.027 (16)

Table 3. Fuzzy linguistic expression example

Participant Number	Very High	High	Fair	Low	Very Low
1	(0, 10, 20)	(20, 30, 40)	(40, 50, 60)	(60, 70, 80)	(80, 90, 100)
2	(0, 05, 10)	(15, 25, 40)	(35, 50, 65)	(60, 75, 90)	(90, 95, 100)
…	…	…	…	…	…
39	(0, 15, 25)	(20, 35, 45)	(40, 50, 65)	(55, 70, 85)	(75, 90, 100)

Each participant's utility value for four business strategies is derived. The averages of the all-participant utility values for four business strategy can be seen in Table 4. From this score, it is obvious that all researchers would rather Promote Responsiveness than others. Table 5 has the overview of average utility value and ranking comparison.

Results from Cluster Analysis

It is important to undertake the attribute analyses of knowledge flow Model for CoPs design which can determine the characteristic of each cluster and identify suggestions for effective linkage. This knowledge flow model adopts cluster analysis to be the basis of attribute analysis. Based on the differences of each participant, a hierarchical cluster diagram is generated.

The similarity degree increased gradually from top down; the lower the knowledge workers are on the hierarchy, the more unique they appear to be (Pellitteri, 2002; Akamatsu et al., 1998; OECD, 1996). The cluster analysis contains several steps. First, the factor scores are entered as the input to the model

Table 4. Average utility value

Four CoPs Expected Performance	Average Utility Values	Ranking
A. Induce Innovation Learning	60.38	2
B. Promote Responsiveness	61.21	1
C. Increase Core Competency	58.24	3
D. Enhance Work Efficiency	54.70	4

Table 5. Average utility values and ranking

Labs	Induce Innovation Learning	Promote Responsiveness	Increase Core Competency	Enhance Work Efficiency
1	58.98 (02)	60.75 (01)	58.88 (03)	57.76 (04)
2	58.21 (02)	60.10 (01)	55.72 (03)	54.17 (04)
3	62.73 (01)	59.27 (03)	60.43 (02)	51.84 (04)
4	62.26 (02)	63.07 (01)	59.34 (03)	54.13 (04)
5	64.93 (02)	66.04 (01)	58.33 (03)	54.88 (04)
All Labs	60.38 (02)	61.21 (01)	58.24 (03)	54.70 (04)

Table 6. Knowledge nodes in each knowledge flow

Knowledge Flow Number	No. of Knowledge Nodes
1	9
2	7
3	5
4	9
5	9

of cluster analysis. Second, five clusters are divided among all the participants. Third, the mean value and variable number of score of factor for each knowledge worker is calculated so as to explain their differences and characteristics. This research divides into five groups after the analysis results and actual discussions about the features towards CoPs beliefs in terms of their preference of four expected performance. The number of knowledge nodes in each knowledge flow is listed in Table 6.

Results from Knowledge Flow Analysis

The first research result in terms of knowledge flow analysis is shown in Figure 2. It helps to illustrate the application of knowledge link weights within a knowledge flow evident from the case study. The knowledge flow network has been constructed using the CoPs centered model designed in previous section. The CoPs framework is used to design a questionnaire involving four dimensions, sixteen criteria, and four expected performance preferences. The sixteen criteria represent among other aspects, represent beliefs and interaction principles of knowledge workers in the context of knowledge sharing. The responses from thirty- nine participants are used to compute the weight or relative importance assigned to each criterion by a participant. The weight values are than used to cluster the weighted responses from these participants. The purpose of clustering is to determine the similarities in relative importance of sixteen criteria among 39 participants. The clustering technique is derived from SPSS software (Zadeh, 1981). Five clusters or groups of researchers are identified. Each group or cluster in this research is considered to be eligible to form a knowledge flow network. The example of number 5 is regarded as a knowledge flow network as seen in Figure 3.

Clearly Table 7 has demonstrates the similar weight values for various criteria allocated by members of 5 knowledge flow. The weight values above 0.1 are highlighted in bold. These are used to calculate the Common Criteria Weight (CCW) between two members in a knowledge flow. As illustration knowledge flow for network number 5 is shown in Figure 3. The criteria weights for criteria differential member and cross-domain sharing are added up. The values based on experience of participants in a related knowledge domain.

As the extended research, a dynamic knowledge flow activity Model is also addressed in this section. In reality the knowledge flow and sharing in a project is a dynamic activity (Nissen, 2002; Zhuge 2003). A dynamic knowledge flow activity model is useful to visualize the knowledge flow activity in a given project and determine the bottlenecks for knowledge management, knowledge sharing and knowledge creation. The dynamic components and terms can be defined to model and analyze the dynamic flow of knowledge between two knowledge nodes. So far all the discussions in this paper centred around the individual and firm level KMS. Nest section, the larger scale in NIS connected with effective KMS framework is extended.

Figure 3. Example of knowledge flow network for number 5

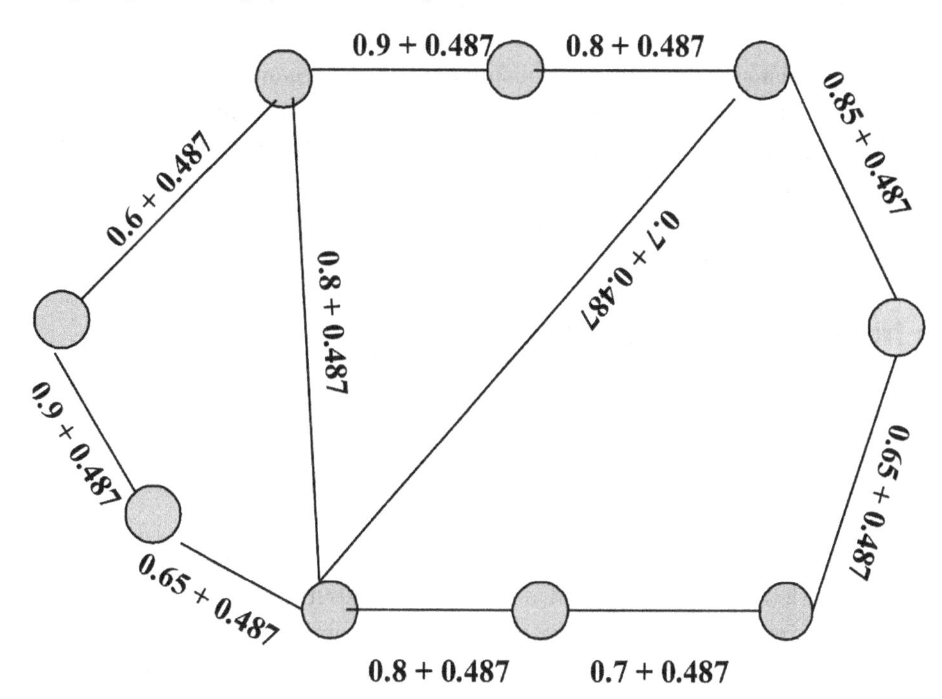

Table 7. Common criteria weight and knowledge flow network number

Variables	Cluster Group				
	1	2	3	4	5
Top-Down Assigning	**0.156**	0.060	0.022	0.052	0.043
Bottom-Up Teaming	**0.101**	**0.132**	0.063	0.044	0.066
Total Execution	0.085	0.043	0.021	0.038	0.020
Partial Pilot run	**0.126**	0.076	0.025	0.038	0.060
Substantive Reward	0.044	0.083	0.062	0.036	0.019
Psychological Encouragement	0.059	0.077	**0.214**	0.039	0.071
Achievements Appraisal Basis	0.051	**0.122**	0.094	0.045	0.038
Peer Approval	0.048	0.079	**0.182**	0.035	0.043
Homogeneity of members	0.031	0.054	0.027	0.047	0.062
Differential members	0.053	0.077	**0.121**	**0.142**	**0.207**
Emphasis on Security	0.028	0.034	0.023	0.049	0.035
Emphasis on Cross-Domain Sharing	0.080	0.068	0.087	**0.126**	**0.280**
Supplying Extra Resources	0.041	0.024	0.019	**0.101**	0.014
Routine Daily Work	0.031	0.024	0.012	0.077	0.023
Integrated IT Platform	0.034	0.019	0.013	0.092	0.011
Independent IT platform	0.031	0.030	0.014	0.040	0.009

NIS CONCEPTTUAL MODEL BUILDING

The ability to understand and exploit the relationship between KMS and innovation processes is highly desirable in today's competitive environments, where a dynamic capability to meet rapid change is an essential ingredient in achieving sustainable business success in volatile global and national marketplaces. The observation and analysis of KMS for innovation offers important fresh insights into the crucial relationship between knowledge management and innovation. This section summarizes the key indicators from KMS to construct a comprehensive NIS model.

Indicators from KMS to Facilitate NIS

This section aims to discuss which enablers from KMS can facilitate the operation of NIS. The first part outlines the concept of NIS from the viewpoint of KMS. The second part examines which KMS functions can impact on NIS performance. The main aim of this part is to reveal more clearly the research gap that assumes linking knowledge management issues to NIS discourse.

Knowledge management in the national innovation system is in fact, production and knowledge dissemination of knowledge, knowledge and intellectual creativity of the application of the network system and knowledge innovation through the production, dissemination and application of the whole process. On this basis, a state innovation system can be divided into four subsystems: knowledge innovation system, technological innovation system, knowledge dissemination of information systems and applications systems.

In the KMS and NIS field of study, a number of scholars have done several researches (Carayannis et al., 2000; Chuanqi, 2001; Cohen & Levintal, 1989; Cuiping, 2008; Debra, 1997; Foray, 1994; Helios & Hidalgo, 2008; Xiwei & Stößlein, 2010; Goh, 2004; Wang, 2002; Liu, 2005; Li, 2009; Leonard & Sensiper, 1998; Debra, 1997). As early as in 1998, Peng and Hu took charge of the State Natural Sciences Foundation project "information guarantee for scientific research and its development", which puts forward a systematic information guarantee theory (Peng & Hu, 1998).

In relational studies about information guarantee, knowledge innovation and innovation system, a common consent is that information guarantee system is one of sub-systems of innovation system, which is characterized by integrity, amalgamation, centrality, supportability and attribute of resources. At the same time, innovation system realizes the functions of information regulating, communicating, disseminating and information service (Wang & Kong, 2004; Zhao, 2003). It is an inevitable requirement of society development to construct an effective information guarantee system for knowledge creation in any innovation system. Meng (2005) and Wang (2002) propose an innovation-oriented information guarantee system conception and discuss its constitution frame as well as its essential factors. One scientific and reasonable information guarantee pattern should be created according to these rules of integrating region with system, all kinds of information institutions participating extensively and local characteristics driven, and so on (Xiao, 2004).

Other scholars raise the interaction between information users and brokers promoting knowledge flowing within certain regional Innovation System, and at the same time the interaction is one of the important fountainheads for knowledge creation in itself. Wang & Kong (2004) points out that to improve R&D broker service and to develop knowledge-intensive service are very important approaches to push forward Chinese innovation system and regional economy vigorously. From the other aspect, the scholars take their stands on technology brokers' significance for national innovation. Ma (2004) and Chen (2003) respectively study technology broker's function for regional Innovation System in some other countries, and analyzes their organizational performance, probes into their beneficial developing mechanism and proposes an overall framework of broking service. Helina and Vesa (2008) also emphasize information broking service as an essential factor for innovation system development in their study.

NSTL conducted a research named as "success & failure research on abroad and Taiwanese scientific & technological information organizations' services for industry innovation", in which the investigation and study covers science and technology information service in American, European Union, Japanese, South Korean, Indian and the Taiwan. It generalizes some successful experience for information organization serving innovation activities. Hu et al. (2008) put forwards their issue how to construct an integrated information service system for NIS, which provides basis for governance advancement.

At the end of this part, it is worth emphasizing that the investigations show KMS in NIS field of study, can be analysed from two angles. The study of the camera is based on knowledge production, dissemination and application of a logical picture innovation system and the establishment of the boundaries of innovation system. Another research in innovation is from the perspective of the specific purpose and requirement, to analyse and judge intellectual production, dissemination and application of the obstacles and bottlenecks, and improve the main body structure, and improve the main interaction between to improve the overall performance. On the other side, scholars emphatically summarized the relations between knowledge and information management with innovation by disclosing knowledge and information's function in Innovation System from theoretical empirical aspects.

NIS Model

The review of relationship between KMS and NIS clearly show that NIS performance dimensions can be enabled by KMS. The most important thing is the concept of KMS functions and explicit and implicit KMS and their relationship with NIS in an integrated and systematic approach, which has not been addressed in the literature. Hence, exploring the relationship between knowledge management and innovation system through the lens of KMS functions is studied in this paper.

Although much has been said, there are several questions still unanswered. The majority of the studies carried out on knowledge management processes and innovation have explored large rather than knowledge management functions in NIS. Much remains to be understood concerning the specific knowledge-management processes and NIS. Indeed, the way KMS enables NIS has not yet been fully understood by a comprehensive and systematic model (Carayannis et al., 2000; Chuanqi, 2001; Cohen & Levintal, 1989; Cuiping, 2008; Debra, 1997; Foray, 1994; Helios & Hidalgo, 2008; Xiwei & Stößlein, 2010; Goh, 2004; Liu, 2005; Li, 2009; Leonard & Sensiper, 1998).

Therefore, based on the mentioned findings, the author found some shortcomings that were not addressed in previous paper results. For example, there is no modeling to show how KMS functions enables NIS and influence on its performance in systematic approach. More over the studies suffer from complete knowledge management functions to improve NIS and on the other words how we can reach to the NIS enabled by KMS. As a result, the key dimensions and factors of NIS performance measurement are listed as follows:

- KMS and quantity of NIS;
- KMS and codification of knowledge in NIS;
- KMS and structure of NIS;

- KMS and efficiency of NIS;
- KMS and quality of NIS;
- KMS and knowledge internalization in NIS;
- KMS and expertise in NIS;
- KMS and effectiveness of NIS.

The conceptual model is thus composed of 8 paths as framework, which has been illustrated in Figure 4.

Considering how KMS supports NIS as illustrated in Figure 4, two dimensions are widely adopted to differentiate the focus and highlight. They are explicit knowledge and tacit knowledge. The former stresses on knowledge codification and specific knowledge object, while the latter emphasizes how knowledge workers share knowledge to facilitate tacit knowledge internalization. According to different nature of these two types knowledge, the key processes have been built up respectively. Explicit knowledge starts with building, and followed by gathering, distributing and reusing. There are particular key indicators to be reflected in each process as shown in the blue boxes on the top of Figure 4 (quantity, codification, structure and efficiency). It means that Explicit Knowledge building as a knowledge management function affects NIS by increasing the quantity of innovation knowledge in the system. Explicit Knowledge gathering as a knowledge management function affects NIS by increasing the codification of innovation knowledge. Explicit Knowledge distributing as a knowledge management function affects NIS by improving the structure of system, and Explicit Knowledge reusing as a knowledge management function affects NIS by increasing the efficiency of system.

Likewise, tacit knowledge starts with capturing, and followed by sharing, disseminating and innovating. There are particular key indicators to be reflected in each process as shown in the blue boxes on the bottom of Figure 4 (quality, internalization, expertise and effectiveness). That is, Tacit Knowledge capturing as a knowledge management function affects NIS by increasing the quality of innovation knowledge in the system; Tacit Knowledge sharing as a knowledge management function affects NIS by increasing

Figure 4. The conceptual model of NIS enabled by KMS

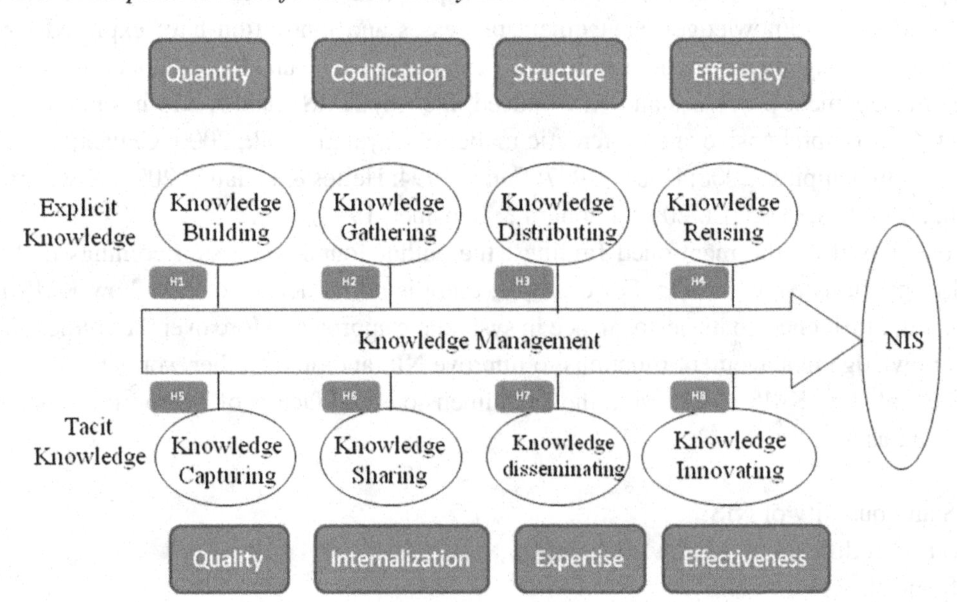

the internalization of innovation knowledge in the system; Tacit Knowledge disseminating as a knowledge management function affects NIS by increasing the expertise in the system; and Tacit Knowledge innovating as a knowledge management function affects NIS by increasing the effectiveness of system.

Hypotheses of NIS Model

In this activity, the existing literatures on NIS and KMS are surveyed to explore the implications for developing a conceptual model. The model integrates the main components of the aforementioned KMS process and functions base on (Newman & Conrod, 1999) and NIS performance dimensions into a comprehensive one composed of 8 paths which has been illustrated in Figure 4.

In this NIS model, the hypotheses have been defined base on the structural model. Hypotheses are based on the path analysis according to the relationship between the components (explored from literature) which the model has been built base on them. According to the related literature, for relationship between components of the model the following hypotheses have been built:

H1: Explicit Knowledge building has positive effect on NIS by increasing the quantity of innovation knowledge in the system.
H2: Explicit Knowledge gathering has positive effect on NIS by increasing the codification of innovation knowledge.
H3: Explicit Knowledge distributing has positive effect on NIS by improving the structure of system.
H4: Explicit Knowledge reusing has positive effect on NIS by increasing the efficiency of system.
H5: Tacit Knowledge capturing has positive effect on NIS by increasing the quality of innovation knowledge in the system.
H6: Tacit Knowledge sharing has positive effect on NIS by increasing the internalization of innovation knowledge in the system.
H7: Tacit Knowledge disseminating has positive effect on NIS by increasing the expertise in the system.
H8: Tacit Knowledge innovating has positive effect on NIS by increasing the effectiveness of system.

CONCLUSION

Knowledge sharing and knowledge flow heavily involve in knowledge creation and innovation context. Existing studies have shown the effective knowledge sharing activity can occur depending upon the mechanism facilitated by Communities of Practice (CoPs). Any significance result identified by means of this research could be of great importance to organizations implementing CoP's. Communities of Practice is an emerging field and therefore the benefits of CoP's and its performance measurement is not clearly laid out, however identifying suitable knowledge worker/knowledge node for CoP's will have huge implication in terms of resource utilization. Right set of knowledge workers for CoP's will enable CoP's success and thereby achieving competitive advantage. By contrasting conventional view that organization consist primarily of workflow networks, knowledge flow consist of knowledge nodes, knowledge links and knowledge link weight respectively. The knowledge nodes are primarily human nodes but also can be resource nodes. The need for developing comprehensive CoPs centered knowledge sharing framework align with knowledge node embedded knowledge flow model is increasingly important both in theory and practice.

This paper aims to achieve a significant goal to explore how CoPs can help to synergize the knowledge sharing collaboration and construction of knowledge flow by identifying knowledge node in an open innovation infrastructure. The knowledge flow is constructed based on actual study of CoPs in one large multinational R&D organization. The knowledge link weight between two human nodes consists of Knowledge Space (or compatibility) Weight (KSW) and Common Criteria Weight (CCW). KSW between two human nodes is determined by a manger or group leader based on CV, experience of the two human nodes and their knowledge compatibility. The 16 criteria along four CoPs expected performance is established (Locus of leadership, Member interaction, Incentive mechanism and Complementary asset) in the questionnaire design. It is further to collect information on the interaction attitude and beliefs of researchers for cooperation and knowledge sharing. These interaction principles although, not a determining factor for knowledge sharing, can improve or enhance the effectiveness of knowledge sharing, creation and innovation. The feedback on the CoPs questionnaire, among other aspects, is used for clustering the researchers in knowledge flow network group. In this research 39 participants have been clustered into five knowledge flow. Fuzzy MCDM techniques and tools have been used to compute the data from questionnaire feedback.

As creating a beneficial and valuable infrastructure to connect knowledge nodes in a knowledge flow is crucial, the results in the study show concentration on Member Interaction the most compared to the other three dimensions. Overall, the opinions from five laboratories surveyed are similar, even though there is slight difference in some criteria and dimensions. Among the sixteen criteria, they emphasize Bottom-Up Teaming, Psychological Encourage, Emphasize Cross-Domain Sharing and Give Extra Resource in each dimension respectively. In particular, Emphasize Cross-Domain Sharing receives the highest rank among 16 criteria. As to the preferred CoPs expected performance, the case study shows the tendency to view Promote Responsiveness as the first priority relatively. It is likely researchers' expectations are considering to promote responsiveness as a business strategy seriously, and solve problems to enable open innovation rapidly, so that they can justify strategy by getting more support from top management to deal with conflicts between current and expected situation. For example, organization can implement CoPs as a major approach to outline the future roadmap by frequent member interaction. During the development, psychological encouragement could be the best reward for knowledge sharing between researchers to respond to changing customer needs. Thus findings of this research can promote performance and can facilitate allocation of organizational resources for knowledge sharing and innovation among the knowledge nodes in knowledge flow networks.

The results obtained from the review of the different the general KMS model and NIS approaches allow the development of the new NIS approach from a systemic point of view. Since a large part of the previously analysed approaches generally use similar indicators (i.e. capacity, effectiveness, efficiency, etc.), the main issue of the proposed approach (to stand out) is that it takes into account those indicators that allow the NIS performance with regard to explicit and implicit KM activities. Therefore, the scope of the proposal covers the KMS processes and activities of those dimensions of NIS performance.

To sum up, knowledge management system represents the decisive basis for intelligent, competent behavior at the individual, firm, and national level. Managing knowledge requires an organizing principle, such as the approach to identify knowledge node to share knowledge, a framework to allocate resources to facilitate knowledge sharing, and extend knowledge to innovation at national scale for best benefit. The research regarding the mechanisms of knowledge production and propagation, information disposition and knowledge sharing within these three levels is still deficiency. This paper can contribute to the theory and practice to differentiate knowledge management system at three major levels by linking the management and innovation of knowledge and also to such a relationship for innovative performance impact.

REFERENCES

Allee, V. (2000). Knowledge Networks and Communities of Practice. *OD Practitioner Online, 32*(4).

Ambrosio, J. (2000). *Knowledge Management Mistakes*. Retrieved from http://www.computerworld.com/industrytopics/energy/story/0,10801,46693,00.html

Bartol, K., & Srivastava, A. (2002). Encouraging knowledge sharing: The role of organizational reward systems. *Journal of Leadership & Organizational Studies, 9*(1), 64–76. doi:10.1177/107179190200900105

Brown, J. S., & Duguid, P. (2000). Balancing act: How to capture knowledge without killing it. *Harvard Business Review*, (May-June). PMID:11183980

Buckley, J. J. (1985). *Ranking* Alternatives Using Fuzzy Number. *Fuzzy Sets and Systems, 15*(1), 21–31. doi:10.1016/0165-0114(85)90013-2

Cabrera, A., & Cabrera, E. (2002). Knowledge-sharing dilemmas. *Organization Studies, 23*(5), 687–710. doi:10.1177/0170840602235001

Carayannis, E., Alexander, J., & Ioannidis, A. (2000). Leveraging knowledge, learning, and innovation in forming strategic government–university–industry (GUI) R&D partnerships in the US, Germany and France. *Journal of Technovation*, (20), 477–488.

Cham, T. H., Lim, Y. M., Cheng, B. L., & Lee, T. H. (2016). Determinants of knowledge management systems success in the banking industry. *VINE Journal of Information and Knowledge Management Systems, 46*(1), 2–20. doi:10.1108/VJIKMS-03-2014-0021

Chen, H. (2003). Study on Technological Intermediaries, Development in Innovation System. *Industrial Technology & Economy*, (3), 15-16.

Chu, M-T., KrishnaKumar, P., & Khosla, R. (2014). *Mapping knowledge sharing traits to business*. Academic Press.

Chu, M. T., Shyu, J. Z., Tzeng, G. H., & Khosla, R. (2007). Comparison among Three Analytical Methods for Knowledge Communities Group-Decision Analysis. *Expert Systems with Applications, 33*(4), 1011–1024. doi:10.1016/j.eswa.2006.08.026

Chu, M. T., Shyu, J. Z., Tzeng, G. H., & Khosla, R. (2007). Using Non-Additive Fuzzy Integral to Assess Performance of Organization Transformation via Communities of Practice. *IEEE Transactions on Engineering Management, 54*(2), 1–13. doi:10.1109/TEM.2007.893987

Chuanqi, H. (2001). *Knowledge Innovation: New Focus of Competition: Front of Second Modernization*. Economic Management Press.

Clatworthy, J., Buick, D., Hankins, M., Weinman, J., & Horne, R. (2005). The use and reporting of cluster analysis in health psychology: A review. *British Journal of Health Psychology*, *10*(3), 329–358. doi:10.1348/135910705X25697 PMID:16238852

Cohen, W. M., & Levintal, D. A. (1989). Innovation and learning: The two faces of R&D. *The Economic Journal*, *99*(49), 569–596. doi:10.2307/2233763

Cohendet, P., & Meyer-Krahmer, F. (2001). The Theoretical and Policy Implications of Knowledge Codification. *Research Policy*, *30*(9), 1563–1591. doi:10.1016/S0048-7333(01)00168-8

Cuiping, W. (2008). A Review of Research in Knowledge Management and Information Guarantee of National Innovation System. *Library and Information Service*, (2), 203-205.

Davenport, T. H., Jarvenpaa, S. I., & Beer, M. C. (2004). Improving Knowledge Work Process. *Sloan Management Review*, *34*(4), 53–65.

Debra, M. (1997). *Innovation Strategy for the Knowledge Economy: The Ken Awakening*. Newton, MA: Butterworth Heinmann.

Desouza, K. C. (2003). Facilitating Tacit Knowledge Exchange. *Communications of the ACM*, *46*(6), 85–86. doi:10.1145/777313.777317

Drucker, P. F. (1969). *The age of discontinuity: Guidelines to our changing society*. New York: Harper & Row.

DTI. (1998). *Our competitive future: Building the knowledge driven economy. Technical report*. Department of Trade and Industry London.

Fan, I., & Lee, R. (2009). A Complexity Framework on the Study of Knowledge Flow, Relational Capital and Innovation Capacity. *Proceedings of the International Conference on Intellectual Capital, Knowledge Management & Organizational Learning*, (pp. 115 - 123).

Foray, D. (1994). Production and distribution of knowledge in the new systems of innovations: The role of intellectual property rights. *STI Review, 14*, 119-52.

Fowlkes, E. B., & Mallows, C. L. (1983). A Method for Comparing Two Hierarchical Clusterings. *Journal of the American Statistical Association*, *78*(383), 553–584. doi:10.1080/01621459.1983.10478008

Freeman, C. (1987). *Technology and Economic Performance: Lessons from Japan*. London: Pinter.

Genrich, A., & Lautenbach, K. (1981). System Modelling with High Level Petri Nets. *Theoretical Computer Science*, *35*, 1–41.

Goh, A. (2004, October). University of South Australia‘, Enhancing Organizational Performance Through Knowledge Innovation: A Proposed Strategic Management Framework. *Journal of Knowledge Management Practice*.

Grant, R. M. (1996). Toward a Knowledge-Based Theory of the Firm. *Strategic Management Journal, 17*(S2), 109–122. doi:10.1002/smj.4250171110

Helina, M., & Vesa, H. (2008). Data, Information and Knowledge in Regional Innovation Networks. *European Journal of Innovation*.

Helios, V., & Hidalgo, A. (2008). Towards a National Innovation System in México Based on Knowledge. *The International Journal of Technology. Knowledge in Society*, *4*(1), 1832–366.

Hu, C., Cao, N., & Zhang, M. (2008). *The Transformation of Information Service and its Development Strategy for Innovative Nation. Journal of Shanxi University:Philosophy and Social Sciences Edition.*

Huang, Y., Jiang, Z., Liu, L., Song, B., & Han, L. (2015). Building a knowledge map model situated in product design. *International Journal of Information Technology and Management*, *14*(1), 76. doi:10.1504/IJITM.2015.066059

Huang, Z. (1998). Extensions to the K-means Algorithm for Clustering Large Datasets with Categorical Values. *Data Mining and Knowledge Discovery*, *2*(3), 283–304. doi:10.1023/A:1009769707641

Huggins, R., & Johnston, A. (2010). Knowledge Flow and Inter-firm Networks: The Influence of Networks Resources, Spatial Proximity and Firm Size. *Entrepreneurship & Regional Development*, *22*(5), 457–484. doi:10.1080/08985620903171350

Hwang, C. L., & Yoon, K. (1981). *Multiple Attribute Decision Making: Methods and Applications, A State-of-Art Survey*. New York: Springer-Verlag. doi:10.1007/978-3-642-48318-9

Jan, A. U., & Contreras, V. (2016). Success model for knowledge management systems used by doctoral researchers. *Computers in Human Behavior*, *59*, 258–264. doi:10.1016/j.chb.2016.02.011

Jeanne, L. (1999). Linking competitive advantage with communities of practice. *Journal of Management Inquiry*, *8*(1), 5–16. doi:10.1177/105649269981002

Jensen, K. (1981). Colored Petri Nets and the Invariant Method. *Theoretical Computer Science*, *14*(3), 317–336. doi:10.1016/0304-3975(81)90049-9

John, S., & Patricia, A. H. (2000). Knowledge Diffusion through Strategic Communities. *Sloan Management Review*, *41*(2), 63.

Kerzner, H. (1989). *A System Approach to Planning Scheduling and Controlling*. New York: Project Management.

Kogut, B., & Zander, U. (1992). Knowledge of the Firm, Combinative Capabilities, and the Replication of Technology. *Organization Science*, *3*(3), 383–397. doi:10.1287/orsc.3.3.383

Leistner, F. (2010), Mastering Organizational Knowledge Flow, how to Make Knowledge Sharing Work. SAS Institute, 183.

Leonard, D., & Sensiper, D. (1998). The role of tacit knowledge in group innovation. *California Management Review*, *40*(3), 112–131. doi:10.2307/41165946

Lesser, E. L., & Storck, J. (2001). Communities of Practice and Organizational Performance. *IBM Systems Journal*, *40*(4), 831–841. doi:10.1147/sj.404.0831

Levin, D., & Cross, R. (2004). The strength of weak ties you can trust: The mediating role of trust in effective knowledge transfer. *Management Science*, *50*(11), 1477–1490. doi:10.1287/mnsc.1030.0136

Levin, D., Cross, R., Abrams, L., & Lesser, E. (2002). *Trust and knowledge sharing: A critical combination.* IBM Institute for Knowledge-Based Organizations.

Li, W. (2009). *A Review of Literature on Knowledge Information Service for Regional Innovation System.* IEEE. doi:10.1109/ICMSS.2009.5301524

Liu, S. (2005). Study on Knowledge Intensive Services in Innovation System. *Science of Science and Management of S & T,* (3), 61-65.

Loyarte, E., & Rivera, O. (2007). Communities of practice: A model for their cultivation. *Journal of Knowledge Management*, *11*(3), 67–77. doi:10.1108/13673270710752117

Lu, L., Leung, K., Koch, P., & Tong, K. (2006). Managerial knowledge sharing: The role of individual, interpersonal, and organizational factors. *Management and Organization Review*, *2*(1), 15–41. doi:10.1111/j.1740-8784.2006.00029.x

Lundvall, B. (1992). *National Systems of Innovation: towards a theory of innovation and interactive learning*. London: Pinter Publishers.

Lutters, Ackerman, Boster, & McDonald. (2000). Mapping Knowledge Networks in Organizations: Creating a Knowledge Mapping Instrument. *Proceedings of the Americas Conference on Information Systems* (AMCIS), (pp. 2014-18).

Lyons, M., Akamatsu, S., Kamachi, M., & Gyoba, J. (1998). Coding facial expressions with Gabor wavelets Automatic Face and Gesture Recognition. *Third IEEE International Conference*, (pp. 200-205).

Ma, S. (2004). A Research on the Functions of Intermediary Service of Science and Technology in National Innovation System and the Construction of the Organization System. *China Soft Science*, (1), 109-113.

MacKay, D. J. C. (2003). *Information Theory, Inference, and Learning Algorithms*. Cambridge University Press.

Malhotra, Y. (2004), Why Knowledge Management Systems Fail? Enablers and Constraints of Knowledge Management in Human Enterprises. American Society for Information Science and Technology Monograph Series.

McDermott, R. (1999). Learning across teams. *Knowledge Management Review*, *8*(3), 32–36.

McLure Wasko, M., & Faraj, S. (2000). It is what one does: Why people participate and help others in electronic communities of practice. *The Journal of Strategic Information Systems*, *9*(2-3), 155–173. doi:10.1016/S0963-8687(00)00045-7

Meng, X. (2005). Information Guarantee System Construction Supporting Knowledge Creation. Information and Documentation Services, (3), 15-19.

Michael, H. Z. (1999). Developing a knowledge strategy. *California Management Review*, *41*(3), 125–145. doi:10.2307/41166000

Mon, D. L., Cheng, C. H., & Lin, J. C. (1994). Evaluating Weapon System Using Fuzzy Analytic Hierarchy Process Based on Entropy Weigh. *Fuzzy Sets and Systems*, *61*, 1–8.

Mortensen, J., Eustace, C., & Lannoo, K. (1997). *Intangibles in the European economy*. CEPS Workshop on intangibles in the European economy, Brussels, Belgium.

Namjae, C., Guo Zheng, L., & Che-Jen, S. (2007). An Empirical study on the effect of individual factors on Knowledge Sharing by Knowledge type. *Journal of Global Business and Technology*, *3*, 1.

Nelson, R. R., & Rosenberg, N. (1993). Technical Innovation and National Systems. In R. R. Nelson (Ed.), *National Innovation Systems. A Comparative Analysis*. New York: Oxford University Press.

Newman, B., & Conrod, K. W. (1999). *A frame work for characterizing knowledge management method, practices and technologies*. Retrieved from http://www.3-cities.com/~bonewman/newman_conrad%20 PAKM2000-16.pdf

Nissen, M. E. (2002). An Extended Model of Knowledge flow Dynamics. *Communications of the ACM*, *8*, 251–266.

Nonaka, I. (1994). A Dynamic Theory of Organizational Knowledge Creation. *Organization Science*, *5*(1), 14–37. doi:10.1287/orsc.5.1.14

OECD. (1996). *The Knowledge Based Economy*. Paris: Science, Technology and Industry Outlook.

OECD. (1999). *Measuring Knowledge in Learning Economies and Societies*. Draft Report on Washington Forum.

Parise, S., & Henderson, J. C. (2001). Knowledge resource exchange in strategic alliances. *IBM Systems Journal*, *40*(4), 908–924. doi:10.1147/sj.404.0908

Patel, P., & Pavitt, K. (1994). The nature and economic importance of national innovation systems. *STI Review*, (14), 9-32.

Pellitteri, J. (2002). The Relationship between Emotional Intelligence and Ego Defense Mechanisms. *The Journal of Psychology*, *136*(2), 182–194. doi:10.1080/00223980209604149 PMID:12081093

Peng, F., & Hu, C. (1998). *Information Guarantee for Scientific Research*. Wuhan, China: Wuhan University Press.

Petri, C. (1966). *Communication in Automata*. Technical Report RADC-TR-65-377. Rome Air Development Center.

Politis, J. (2003). The connection between trust and knowledge management: What are its implications for team performance. *Journal of Knowledge Management*, *7*(5), 55–66. doi:10.1108/13673270310505386

Ratcliffe-Martin, V., Coakes, E., & Sugden, G. (2000). Knowledge Management Issues in Universities. *Vine Journal*, *121*, 14-19.

Saaty, T. L. (1977). A Scaling Method for Priorities in Hierarchical Structures. *Journal of Mathematical Psychology*, *15*(2), 234–281. doi:10.1016/0022-2496(77)90033-5

Saaty, T. L. (1980). *The Analytic Hierarchy Process*. New York: McGraw-Hill.

Stale, G., Cakula, S., & Kapenieks, A. (2011). *Application of a Modelling Method for Knowledge Flow Analysis in an Educational IT Ecosystem*. Virtual and Augmented Reality in Education (VARE 2011), Valmiera, Latvija.

Tang, M. T., & Tzeng, G. H. (1999). A Hierarchy Fuzzy MCDM Method for Studying Electronic Marketing Strategies in the Information Service Industry. *Journal of International Information Management*, *8*(1), 1–22.

Thomas, J. C., Kellog, W. A., & Erickson, T. (2001). The Knowledge Management Puzzle: Human and Social factors in Knowledge Management. *IBM Systems Journal*, *40*(4), 863–884. doi:10.1147/sj.404.0863

Todd, M., Birgit, R., & Kurt, M. (2006). Who Trusts? Personality, Trust and Knowledge Sharing. *Management Learning*, *37*(4), 523–540. doi:10.1177/1350507606073424

Tsaur, S. H., Tzeng, G. H., & Wang, K. C. (1997). Evaluating Tourist Risks From Fuzzy Perspectives. *Annals of Tourism Research*, *24*(4), 796–812. doi:10.1016/S0160-7383(97)00059-5

Tzeng, G. H. (1977). A Study on the PATTERN Method for the Decision Process in the Public System. *Japan Journal of Behavior Metrics*, *4*(2), 29–44. doi:10.2333/jbhmk.4.2_29

Tzeng, G. H., Shian, T. A., & Lin, C. Y. (1992). Application of Multicriteria Decision Making to the Evaluation of New Energy-System Development in Taiwan. *Energy*, *17*(10), 983–992. doi:10.1016/0360-5442(92)90047-4

Tzeng, G. H., & Shiau, T. A. (1987). Energy Conservation Strategies in Urban Transportation: Application of Multiple Criteria Decision-Making. *Energy Systems and Policy*, *11*(1), 1–19.

Tzeng, G. H., & Teng, J. Y. (1994). Multicriteria Evaluation for Strategies of Improving and Controlling Air-Quality in the Super City: A case of Taipei city. *Journal of Environmental Management*, *40*(3), 213–229. doi:10.1006/jema.1994.1016

U.S. Department of Commerce. (1965). *National Technical Information Service*. NASA.

Wang, B., & Kong, J. (2004). Information Needs and Information Guarantee in National Innovation System. *Information Science*, (6), 657–659, 663.

Wang, C. (2002). Information Guarantee Construction of National Innovation System. Information and Documentation Services, (2), 12-15.

Wang, T., & Libaers, D. (2015). Nonmimetic Knowledge and Innovation Performance: Empirical Evidence from Developing Countries. *Journal of Product Innovation Management*. doi:10.1111/jpim.12306

Wenger, E. (1998). *Communities of Practice*. Cambridge University Press. doi:10.1017/CBO9780511803932

Wenger, E., McDermott, R. A., & Snyder, W. (2002). *Cultivating Communities of Practice*. Boston: Harvard Business School Press.

Xiao, X. (2004). Information Guarantee Model and Operation Mechanism of Knowledge Innovation. *Journal of Foshan University (Social Science Edition),* (1), 90-93.

Xiwei, W., & Stößlein, M. (2010). Designing knowledge chain networks in China - A proposal for a risk management system using linguistic decision making. *Technological Forecasting and Social Change*, *77*(6), 902–915. doi:10.1016/j.techfore.2010.01.002

Zadeh, L. A. (1981). *A Definition of Soft Computing*. Retrieved from http://www.soft-computing.de/def.html

Zhao, B. (2003). On the Information Guarantee of Intellectual Innovation Systems. *Information Science*, (1), 10–14.

Zhuge, H. (2003). Component-based Workflow Systems Design. *Decision Support Systems*, *35*(4), 517–536. doi:10.1016/S0167-9236(02)00127-6

Zhuge, H. (2006). Discovery of Knowledge Flow in Science. *Communications of the ACM*, *49*(5), 101–107. doi:10.1145/1125944.1125948

Zhuge, H. (2006). Knowledge flow Network Planning and Simulation. *Decision Support Systems*, *42*(2), 571–592. doi:10.1016/j.dss.2005.03.007

Zhuge, H., Guo, W., Li, X., & Ding, L. (2006). Knowledge Energy in Knowledge Flow Networks. *Proceedings of the First International Conference on Semantics, Knowledge, and Grid*. IEEE Computer Society.

Zmud, R., & Lee, J. (2005). Behavioral intention formation in knowledge sharing: Examining the roles of extrinsic motivators, social-psychological forces, and organizational climate. *Management Information Systems Quarterly*, *29*(1), 87–111.

Chapter 13
Information Technologies and Analytical Models for Strategic Design of Transportation Infrastructure

L. Douglas Smith
University of Missouri – St. Louis, USA

Robert M. Nauss
University of Missouri – St. Louis, USA

Liang Xu
University of Missouri – St. Louis, USA

Juan Zhang
University of Missouri – St. Louis, USA

Jan Fabian Ehmke
Freie Universität Berlin, Germany

Laura Hellmann
Freie Universität Berlin, Germany

ABSTRACT

Statistical modeling, deterministic optimization, heuristic scheduling procedures, and computer simulation enable the strategic design of service systems while considering complex interdependencies in system operations. Performance on multiple dimensions may be investigated under alternative physical configurations and operating procedures while accommodating time-varying mixes of traffic and demands for service. This paper discusses how analytical tools and a conceptual framework developed for inland waterway transportation were extended and applied to the more complex operating environment of commercial airports. Networks of staged queues constitute the conceptual framework and discrete-event simulation provides the integrating modeling platform. Within the simulation model, statistical models represent time-varying behavior, traffic intensity is adjusted, resources are allocated to system users, traffic is controlled according to prevailing conditions, and decision rules are tested in pursuit of optimal performance.

DOI: 10.4018/978-1-5225-1680-4.ch013

INTRODUCTION

Strategic analysis and design of service systems require solid conceptual frameworks, supporting data, analytical models, solution engines, interpretive tools, and creative insight in the application of analytical results. This is especially the case where the strategic choices involve direct impacts on operational processes. In their 2012 article in the *Journal of Strategic Information Technology and Applications*, Smith et al. described how the concept of staged queues, computer simulation and analytical models were used to investigate how changes in infrastructure and operating procedures could alleviate seasonal bottlenecks for barge traffic in the Upper Mississippi River (UMR) Transportation System. They mentioned how the concept of staged queues and discrete-event simulation can be applied to other transportation services, traffic intersections, port facilities, distribution centers, and production operations. In each of these environments, resources serve arrivals from different streams and need to be allocated dynamically to achieve efficiency and equity in traffic or work flow. Airport operations were suggested as a particularly suitable (and more complex) application of this concept and for the use of similar analytical tools. In this chapter, we review information systems and technologies employed for strategic analysis in the waterway and airport settings. We also illustrate the application of discrete-event simulation with staged queues to airport capacity planning.

BACKGROUND: PREVALENCE OF STAGED QUEUEING SYSTEMS

The strategic design of service systems requires a conceptual framework and an effective information infrastructure. Queueing systems or waiting lines are the means by which we organize activity involving shared resources. Fast-food restaurants, roadways, airport check-in stations, call-service centers, supermarket checkouts, and myriads of other common service systems require the management of queueing systems. In a Wall Street Journal article, Bialik (2012) reported how Alfred Blumstein suggested the queuing structure for UK passport control might be changed to reduce queuing times in anticipation of a flood of visitors to the Olympic Games. By staging individuals next in line more closely to individual passport control officers, one may eliminate the delays that occur as individuals walk from the head of a single queue to the next available agent. Doing so, however, exposes the travelers to a risk of being stuck behind a person who requires an unduly long processing time while individuals who arrived later proceed through another channel.

In cross-docking facilities, tractor-trailers are positioned for loading and unloading with different mixes of cargo. Manpower and equipment are allocated to unload incoming shipments and load outgoing shipments (Bartholdi & Gue, 2000; Gue & Kang, 2001). In production and maintenance facilities, there is often a preparatory step before an operation whereby the next entity to be processed receives a necessary pre-treatment (Guo et al., 2012; Hung & Chang, 2002). Port facilities require vessels to be positioned for loading and unloading with land-based resources (Shabayek & Yeung, 2002). In busy urban environments, signaling is used to grant priority to buses and regulate flows of other traffic through intersections (Wu & Hounsell, 1998). Medical facilities perform triage and assign patients to examination rooms, surgical theatres and diagnostic equipment (Oredsson et al., 2011). When queued entities have identifiable characteristics that affect the expected time to service them, efficiencies can be achieved by altering queueing structures and the sequences in which entities are served.

Blends of statistical modeling, deterministic optimization, heuristic scheduling procedures, and computer simulation can be employed to study the behavior of and improve system performance. Allahverdi et al. (1999, 2008) surveyed 300+ papers on the scheduling of work in job shops where, as in lockage operations, the setup times between jobs depend on the sequence of operations performed. They noted that, in this research, stochastic aspects of job-shop scheduling problems were usually ignored to make them analytically tractable. Various integer programming (IP) models and heuristic solution procedures have been employed for scheduling problems when setup times depend on job sequences (Balas et al., 2008; Carroll & Bronzini, 1973; Dai & Schonfeld, 1998; Gagné et al., 2002; Gendreau et al., 2001; Gupta & Smith, 2006). These discrete optimization models contain foundational elements for scheduling activities with sequence-dependent processing times, but they fail to take into consideration the constraints imposed by the staged queuing structure. Nor, of course, do they reveal the effects of variation in processing times or the effects of random impairments or failures of system components.

The challenge in our application settings is to represent system behavior with sufficient granularity, consider random behavior (uncertainty), keep things computationally tractable and communicate results in a meaningful way for strategic decisions. With this backdrop, we shall discuss the melding of the aforementioned methods in our two transportation settings and outline the information infrastructure needed to support the work.

STRATEGIC PLANNING FOR INLAND WATERWAYS

For decades, researchers on inland waterway operations suggested that improvements in system performance in busy periods could be achieved with innovative scheduling procedures. Using discrete-event simulation models with simplified representations of traffic movements and lockage operations, Dai and Schonfeld (1998), Kim and Schonfeld (1995), Martinelli and Schonfeld (1995), Ramanathan and Schonfeld (1994), Ting and Schonfeld (1998, 2001a, 2001b), Wei et al. (1992), and Zhu et al. (1999) illustrated how some form of priority scheduling might improve the efficiency of inland waterway navigation systems. They recognized, however, that more refined models would be needed to estimate the prospective benefits of specific changes in operational procedures. Nauss (2008) formulated two integer programming models that addressed the scheduling of tows/barges with sequence dependent setup times through a river lock. A special purpose implicit enumeration algorithm was designed and computational experiments were presented. Recently, Passchyn et al. (2016a) formulated a similar model using dynamic programming and Verstichel et al. (2011, 2014a, 2014b, 2015) extended the problem to consider parallel locks with positioning a set of ships into as few lock chambers as possible. They formulate part of the problem as a mixed integer linear program utilizing Benders' decomposition. An efficient heuristic is also employed to place ships in particular positions within a lock. Yuan et al (2016) devised a novel heuristic to schedule lock and water/land transshipment options that first determine whether ship cargo should be off-loaded to land or should continue through a lock. For ships traveling through the lock a heuristic is used to balance the efficiency of lock operations and fairness to each ship in terms of waiting time. Passchyn et al. (2016b) extended lock scheduling analysis to multiple contiguous locks and considered an environmental emissions objective as well. Caris et al. (2014) present a research taxonomy for the integration of inland waterway transport in an intermodal supply chain.

Modeling the Upper Mississippi Navigation System

Our inland waterway application involved a section of the UMR Navigation System where a series of five 600-foot locks create a seasonal bottleneck between two 1200-foot locks with greater throughput capacity. Figure 1 shows the actual physical configuration of a 600-foot lock on the UMR navigation system with a towboat and 15 barges departing the lock and two tows upstream awaiting lockage. For these large tows, a "double" lockage operation is required which involves decoupling the barge tow, winching part of the tow through the lock, and re-coupling the tow after the tow boat emerges at the new water level. This takes almost two hours to complete. Each of the smaller tows behind, however, may be accommodated in a "single" lockage where the towboat enters the lock with its barges under power and leaves under power at the new water level. That typically requires less than half an hour. There is a limited maneuvering area in the vicinity of the lock so that the vessel positioned to be locked next in each direction must be processed before any vessel behind it. We thus have a staged queuing system.

To relieve the seasonal congestion, the US Army Corps of Engineers (USACE) proposed to expand each of the five locks to match the capacity of the 1200-foot locks immediately downstream and upstream. This, however, would require a capital investment of several billion dollars. Before undertaking such an investment, the USACE required an assessment of how system performance would be affected by major changes in physical infrastructure, adding supporting resources to increase throughput with existing resources, or simply using alternative scheduling procedures. They also needed to assess how the changes would affect different classes of users that constitute waterway traffic.

Figure 1. Barge tows undergoing lockage on the UMR Navigation System (Source: photo courtesy of the U.S. Army Corps of Engineers)

Supporting Data

To support the analysis of current operations and provide detailed data for planning purposes, the USACE designed and implemented its OMNI database system which provides necessary detail for analyzing the system "as is". For each lockage operation, there is an identifier of the powered vessel, the number of barges in tow, direction of travel, time at which the vessel presented itself for lockage, the time at which the vessel was signaled to enter the lock, the time of passage of the lock thresholds on entry and departure, and the time at which it cleared the area for vessels approaching in the opposite direction. These data revealed the intensity and mix of traffic throughout the waterway system over the shipping season – including information about the length of queues and waiting times for individual vessels at each lock. In addition, the USACE maintains parallel data regarding the operational status of each lock. When locking operations are impaired, the cause of impairment (e.g., severe weather, ice, accident or mechanical failure) is noted along with the degree to which operations are impaired. The OMNI database thus provides essential information for constructing and validating the analytical models for strategic inquiry.

The UMR Simulation Model

To investigate the impact of these alternatives, which differ dramatically in their fixed costs and operational costs, an ARENA simulation model (Smith et al., 2009) was constructed to represent the operation of the system under different traffic scenarios. The simulation model was designed to:

- Accommodate multiple classes of traffic with different arrival patterns, itineraries and service characteristics which vary throughout the shipping season;
- Capture the physical realities of upstream and downstream traffic movements and the staged queuing restrictions at each lock;
- Incorporate the effects of impairments to operations that occur randomly;
- Allow the tracking of each simulated operation and produce detailed measures of system performance for small time intervals at each lock;
- Facilitate tests of statistical significance of observed effects on system performance.

Nonstationary exponential distributions with complementary intensification and thinning mechanisms are used to create the proper mix of random arrivals at each lock according to month of year, day of week and time of day. Vessel itineraries are generated dynamically with logistic models that determined the likelihoods that an individual tow would continue to the next lock, rather than terminating its voyage in the next section (pool) of the river. Lognormal distributions are used for activity times at each lock. The parameters are adjusted with regression models that consider tow characteristics and prevailing river conditions (which vary by month of the year). Severe impairments are imposed randomly at each lock using exponential distributions for times between impairments and duration of impairments, with means that reflected historical experience in respective months of the year at each lock. Activities at a lock are interrupted and suspended for the duration of any simulated impairment. The model was validated by comparing detailed simulated performance with actual performance (including seasonal variation in lengths of queues, waiting times at locks and lock utilization) under the range of traffic levels experienced over the previous 20 years. The validated model was then applied to study the potential effects of the alternative scheduling rules and infrastructure changes.

Simulation results revealed how the different scheduling rules would affect various classes of users of the UMR navigation system. A priority-dispatching scheme was devised and shown to foster equity among user classes without a terribly deleterious effect on overall efficiency. The simulation results showed how the benefits of alternative scheduling mechanisms depend on traffic levels, and they revealed the traffic intensities at which the infrastructure changes would be required to avoid unacceptably long delays in seasonal peaks (Campbell et al., 2009).

The possibility of achieving further improvements in throughput was revealed by a mixed integer programming (MIP) model that imposes the staged queueing queue discipline while limiting the wait for each vessel to its wait under a first-in first-out (FIFO) solution plus a stipulated amount. Solutions from the MIP model resulted in queue-clearance times that were about 9% lower than solutions from the job-shop scheduling rules (Smith et al., 2011). Generation of the MIP solution for a single queue-clearing problem with 20 vessels required about 30 seconds of processing time – sufficiently quickly for actual operations in this particular application, because the processing time for each lockage is much longer.

To simulate 100 annual shipping seasons of operating activity, the 30-second solution time for the MIP becomes impracticable, as hundreds of thousands of calls would be made to the MIP solver in the process. For simulation, the researchers turned to a 25-step heuristic procedure that was tested and validated with the MIP model on randomly generated test problems and embedded into the simulation model as the schedule "optimizer" (Smith et al., 2012).

Enhanced Analytics for the Waterway Simulation Model

Strategic design of a service system requires an understanding of the dynamic system behavior at critical points of time and control. To provide this, a detailed event log is created by the Arena model for every lockage operation similarly to the USACE OMNI database. The Statistical Analysis System (SAS) is used to create detailed reports of system performance from the perspectives of users and operators of the navigation system. SAS reports for a single simulation run contain summary statistics (means, medians, percentiles, etc.) for waiting times and processing times for each type of vessel processed at each lock in each direction. They show queue sizes through time and how the processing times and waiting times compared for vessels (and tows) of each type. For model validation, the reports show the percentage of vessels processed at each lock that arrived after constituting their tows in the current section of the river, as opposed to continuing from the previous lock in the same direction. They also show the percentage of lockages that involved recycling the lock to accept vessels travelling in the opposite direction with a concomitant delay, the percentage that involved a turnback of the lock to process a vessel travelling in the same direction with a concomitant delay, and the percentage that involved no delay because there were no vessels being processed when the vessel arrived.

Beyond reporting for specific scenarios, it is helpful to be able to perform meta-analysis of the hundreds of millions of lockage operations across decision rules, traffic levels, or physical infrastructure employed required. Exploratory analysis of the detailed simulation results along many dimensions was further facilitated by online analytic processing (OLAP) tools. A Pentaho Data Warehouse was constructed on a MySQL database to allow inquiries on many dimensions and to explore the interactions of factors affecting system performance (Ehmke et al., 2010).

AIRPORT CAPACITY PLANNING

In recent years, major U.S. airlines have altered their route structures and schedules to concentrate their flight activity at a few mega-hubs. Consolidation of this sort and additional flights of express freight carriers strain some airports while others find themselves with unplanned excess capacity. Airport planners thus seek ways of better utilizing existing assets in some environments, intelligently expanding them in others, and selectively removing assets from service to reduce operating costs where precipitous drops in traffic have occurred.

Highly sophisticated simulation models have been used for decades to aid in the design of airports and simulate air traffic with remarkable realism (Atkin et al., 2009, 2010; Bazargan et al., 2002; Bertino & Boyajian, 2011; Brentnall & Cheng, 2009; Bubalo & Daduna, 2011; Capozi et al., 2013; FAA, 1989; Fishburn et al., 1995; Gilbo, 1993; Gotteland et al., 1991; Herrero et al., 2005). These engineering models are excellent for studying system behavior in microscopic detail, but they carry enormous overhead for studies that are more strategic in nature. Traditional operational research models, in contrast, have been used for optimizing aspects of airport activity such as timing pushbacks, sequencing arrivals or departures, performing regular gate services, or performing special services such as de-icing aircraft (Horstmeier & Haan, 2001; Ravizza et al., 2013; Sherali et al., 1992; Yan et al., 2002). The OR models, however, tend to ignore stochastic aspects of system behavior or necessary interactions with other parts of the system. In developing our models, we strive to capture the essential interactions of key system components, represent the system with sufficient granularity, and facilitate the efficient conduct of experiments with multiple replications of a wide range of planning scenarios and operating rules. As mentioned earlier, the integrative conceptual framework is the representation and control of the system as a network of staged queues (Gue & Kang, 2001; Smith et al., 2011, 2014).

Factors Affecting Airport Activity

We began our modeling of airport operations with detailed statistical analyses of a complete year of activity at Lambert St. Louis International Airport in the USA and at Frankfurt Airport in Germany. Hourly patterns of airport activity (arrival and departure delays, numbers of aircraft at terminal gates, aircraft taxiing inbound and outbound, and aircraft queued for departure) were summarized for validation of the simulation model. Statistical models were constructed to identify key determinants of system performance at each site. Table 1, for example, shows coefficients for a pair of logistics models constructed from individual departure records over an entire year to compute the likelihood of departure delays at the respective airports. Airlines at the two airports similarly experience departure delays that depend on the time of day (as traffic intensity varies), time of year (as weather changes), departing airspace sector (reflecting flight destination), size of aircraft, and runway used (affected by wind direction). Specific impacts of factors differed between the two settings. At Frankfurt, for example, delays were most likely to occur mid-day. At St. Louis, the likelihoods of delay kept increasing over the course of the day until late evening. We attributed the difference in these patterns to the cascading effects of departure delays at major hub airports for flights into St. Louis and to higher risk of thunderstorms later in the day in the American Midwest. Further analysis of data for St. Louis revealed significant differences among airlines. Separate parameters were therefore developed for flights of individual airlines in the simulation model.

Table 1. Logistic models for probabilities of delay for Frankfurt (left) and St. Louis (right)

Parameters	Estimate	Standard Error	Chi-Square	Pr > ChiSq
intercept	0.1539	0.053	8.4424	0.0037
hourbef6	-0.5819	0.0769	57.2675	<.0001
hour6to8	-0.3812	0.0496	59.0603	<.0001
hour8to10	-0.3974	0.0441	81.3722	<.0001
hour10to12	-0.1997	0.0442	20.4488	<.0001
hour16to18	0.3932	0.0418	88.2823	<.0001
hour18to20	-0.2153	0.0431	25.0046	<.0001
houraft22	-0.9344	0.1522	37.7022	<.0001
may	-0.1383	0.0481	8.2894	0.004
july	-0.1235	0.0476	6.7405	0.0094
august	-0.2084	0.0483	18.6217	<.0001
september	0.1576	0.0471	11.2001	0.0008
october	0.1038	0.0465	4.9762	0.0257
november	-0.3171	0.0496	40.9015	<.0001
rwy07C	-0.4891	0.1045	21.9196	<.0001
rwy25L	-0.2696	0.0342	62.0043	<.0001
rwy25C	-0.8032	0.0634	160.6153	<.0001
rwy25R	0.1324	0.0322	16.9391	<.0001
NW	0.1568	0.0376	17.4344	<.0001
SW	0.2621	0.0327	64.4297	<.0001
classM	-0.2618	0.0421	38.6954	<.0001
classL	-0.6304	0.0766	67.7005	<.0001

Parameters	Estimate	Standard Error	Chi-Square	Pr > ChiSq
Intercept	-2.5905	0.0673	1480.3474	<.0001
hourbef6	-1.0051	0.4241	5.6167	0.0178
hour6to8	-1.0904	0.1225	79.259	<.0001
hour10to12	0.3371	0.0748	20.3374	<.0001
hour12to14	0.841	0.0668	158.5462	<.0001
hour14to16	1.3742	0.0651	445.5213	<.0001
hour16to18	1.5742	0.0657	573.6536	<.0001
hour18to20	1.8975	0.0616	949.3157	<.0001
hour20to22	2.3613	0.0647	1331.2957	<.0001
houraft22	2.2326	0.7162	9.718	0.0018
january	0.2136	0.0625	11.69	0.0006
march	0.4805	0.0587	67.108	<.0001
april	0.3558	0.0646	30.3237	<.0001
may	0.7305	0.0628	135.4951	<.0001
june	0.7807	0.0641	148.5153	<.0001
july	0.6103	0.0649	88.5107	<.0001
august	0.7671	0.0656	136.7958	<.0001
december	0.5861	0.0579	102.311	<.0001
rwy12L	-0.1837	0.0503	13.3522	0.0003
rwy29	0.2785	0.0912	9.3373	0.0022
rwy30L	0.1902	0.0517	13.5531	0.0002

The Airport Simulation Model

In contrast to barge traffic, arrivals and departures of commercial aircraft occur according to published schedules. Aircraft arrivals are therefore generated according to daily schedules of individual airlines, but with random deviations appropriate for the scenario being simulated. For St. Louis, arriving aircraft are placed in conceptual queues at the final approach fix (FAF) for an active runway (Figure 2 left side). At Frankfurt (Figure 2 right side) the flight data contain the time at which flights enter the terminal environment "10 minutes out" for vectoring to the final approach. For Frankfurt, therefore, we impute a FAF for the runway with an appropriate offset of time to reach the imputed FAF. Movements of aircraft are simulated from the FAF until the designated flight's activity at the airport is completed (with termination at the gate, or if continuing to another destination, after turnaround and departure (Figure 3)).

Figure 4 illustrates the physical layout of runways, taxiways and ramp areas with key intersections that aircraft traverse from the points of touchdown to the gates and from the gates to the points of liftoff. Both Frankfurt and St. Louis have three parallel runways and a cross runway.

Figure 2. Final approach fixes for St. Louis, USA (left) and Frankfurt, Germany (right)

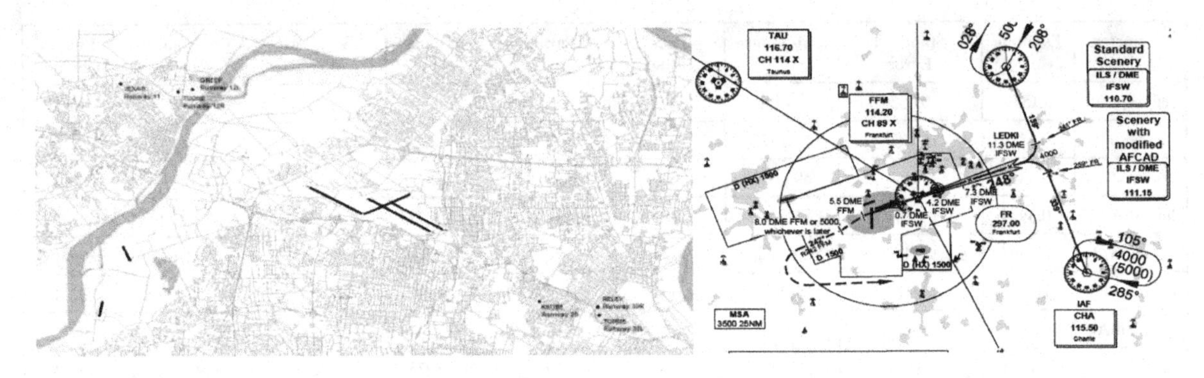

Figure 3. Domain of airside activity simulated

Figure 4. Airport layouts at St. Louis, USA (left) and Frankfurt, Germany (right)

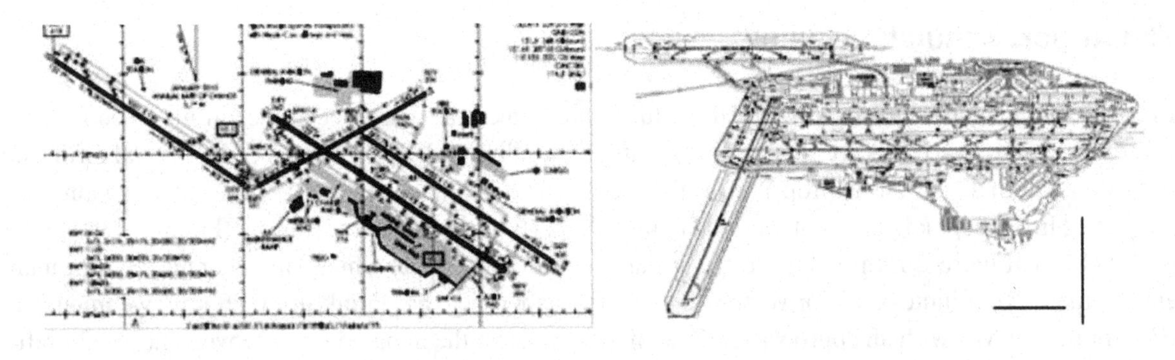

We identify points on the airport surface where aircraft may be staged as they progress from runways to gates and vice versa. Routes between staging points across ramps and along taxiways are mapped and aircraft are directed to the next staging point depending on which runways are in use for landings and takeoffs and which staging points between their current position and airport destination (gate or runway) can accommodate them.

Aircraft may be held at a staging point until the next segment of its route is available to traffic in the desired direction. They cannot enter a segment of a taxiway, for example, earlier than when it would be vacated by aircraft currently traversing it in the opposite direction. Some staging points may have sufficient maneuvering space to allow re-sequencing of queued aircraft for the next segment of their taxi routes; others may require the aircraft to be processed in order of their arrivals. Unlike SIMMOD and other highly realistic simulators for real-time simulation of ground operations, we do not indicate the specific physical locations of each aircraft waiting at staging points; nor do we regulate the speed of aircraft to maintain realistic physical separation while they are in motion.

To accommodate airlines' independent behavior in managing their own resources on the ground and dispatching their flights, we designate separate staging areas on the ramp for each airline's arrivals and departures. Arriving aircraft are staged in queues in one area of the ramp pending the availability of a gate (and clear path to it). Departing aircraft (which may be held on the ground by ATC for weather or traffic control) are staged at another area if they must clear a gate to accommodate arriving aircraft. Figure 5 shows the gate staging areas and taxiing routes to the gates for four major airlines at St. Louis Lambert Airport Terminal 1. Areas on the airfield may be designated for spillover when physical capacity is reached at the primary ramp locations for staging the airlines' arrivals and departures.

Other areas on the airfield may be designated as staging points for departing aircraft when there is a backlog for takeoffs, traffic holds due to weather conditions in departure sectors, or holds due to weather or congestion at hub destinations. In addition to queues that are associated with physical positions on the airport property, aircraft are placed in conceptual queues to control the sequences of operations. Aircraft whose routes involve sectors of airspace temporarily restricted by severe weather, for example, may be held in a common queue and released in sequences determined by the simulated scheduling regime in effect.

Figure 5. Staging areas for arriving and departing aircraft in the vicinity of their gates

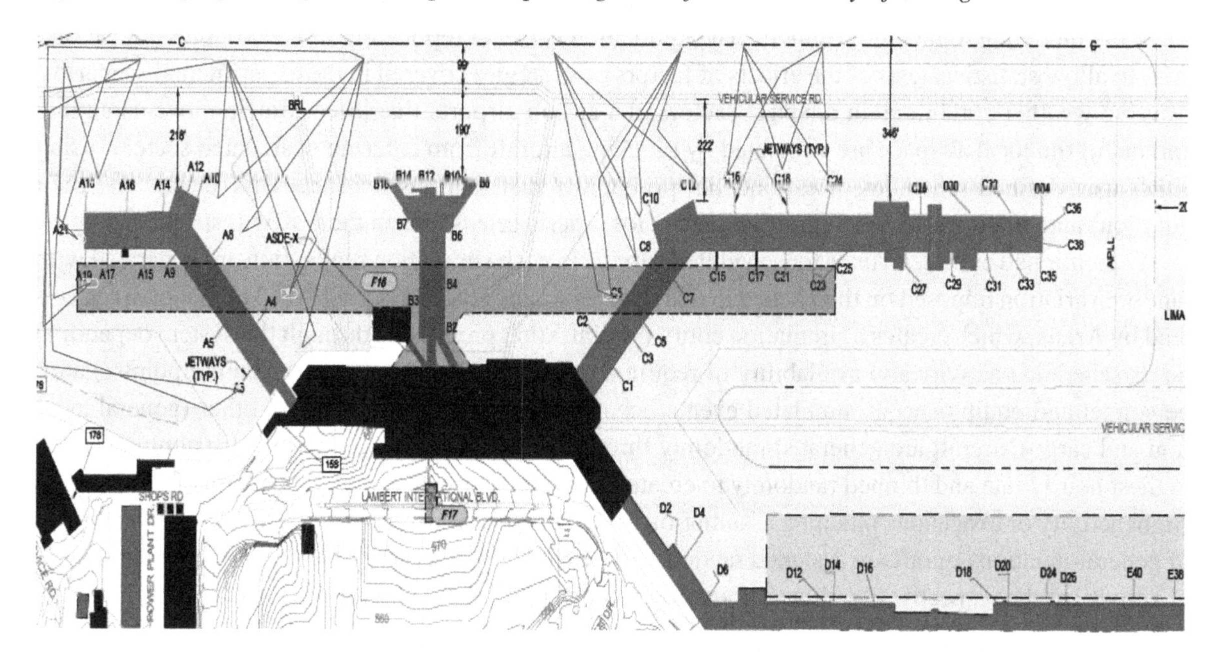

Model Calibration and Validation

Calibration and validation of the model require integration of gate data maintained by individual airlines and flight data that are maintained by air traffic control (ATC) systems for aircraft that operate under instrument flight rules (IFR). From airline data we acquire information about aircraft type, origin and destination for the flight leg, and the scheduled and actual times of arrival or departure (pushback) at the gate. From ATC data, we obtain the time when an arriving flight reached the FAF and when it landed (touched down) on the runway. For departing flights, ATC data indicate the takeoff (liftoff) time. Merging these data, we are able to determine the itineraries of flights that arrive at the airport with continuing legs and generate the files used to activate arrivals and originating flights in the simulation model. Routings along taxiways and staging of aircraft to coordinate traffic on the airport surface occur at the discretion of ATC ground controllers who are located in the airport control tower alongside controllers of traffic in the local airspace. Direct observation and interviews with ATC controllers are required to understand the combinations of runways, taxiways and staging points used for arrivals and departures under different wind and weather conditions. Separation standards (used to space arrivals at the FAF and provide appropriate time intervals between successive takeoffs from the same runway) are derived from operating policy manuals. Airports at the point of origin for inbound flights and airports at the destination of outbound flights are grouped according to ATC sectors. This enables deviations from schedule to contain systematic elements related to wind and weather – which affect arrival itineraries and runways in use.

Modeling Tools

For the discrete-event simulation, we again use ARENA 14.7 on a Windows platform. Heuristic scheduling and sequencing procedures are able to be written in C++ or Visual Basic and called by "event" blocks when the modeling logic requires them. The simulation is run in replicating mode (suppressing animation) to allow statistical tests of the effects of factors or strategies covered in the experimental scenarios. Adverse weather conditions in airspace sectors and at hub airports that affect traffic movements into and out of the local airspace are simulated by blocking aircraft from entering designated sectors (using either user-defined schedules or exponential probability distributions for successive events and their duration) and placing affected aircraft in queues for orderly release when the traffic restrictions expire.

As mentioned earlier, arrivals for scheduled service in each simulation replication are generated with random variation imposed on their scheduled arrival times and stacked at the FAF. The file of arrivals is read by Arena, which creates a simulation entity (aircraft) that progresses through the system depending on its scheduled activity and availability of required resources (taxiways, ramps, staging points, gates, personnel and equipment) as simulated events occur. Arrivals and departures for other (general aviation and cargo) aircraft are generated randomly through the day (using exponential distributions at the highest hourly rate and thinned randomly to create hourly intensity determined by historical patterns of flight activity or exogenous planning assumptions). Airport locations (gates) for arrivals and departures of general-aviation aircraft are assigned randomly (as each flight is generated) in conformity with levels of activity at the respective fixed-base operations.

A subroutine assigns the aircraft to one of the active runways and the route to be followed from the point of landing to an available gate for the airline. Taxi-route segments are defined so that they have associated resources with capacity to hold a designated number of aircraft. Originating flights (as opposed to continuing flights) are placed at an available gate for the airline at the later of its scheduled departure time or the time at which a gate and an aircraft become available for it (i.e., from the morning pool of available aircraft or an aircraft freed by a terminating flight). The model, in its present form, does not force a reconciliation of inbound and outbound aircraft for each carrier. This could be done by artificially defining every arrival and departure as a continuing flight with a unique flight number (perhaps a combination of the inbound and outbound number).

Parameters for the simulation model are estimated using logistic and regression models which are developed and maintained by the Statistical Analysis System (SAS). Likelihood (and length of) of an arrival delay for an airline's flight might, for example, be stated as a function of scheduled hour of day, total duration of the flight, whether the flight originated at a major hub, and an interaction term for arrival sector and runways in use. SAS is also used to generate the files of arrivals for individual airlines (with some flights terminating and others continuing after turnaround at the gate) in conformity with historical airline schedules. SAS is used similarly to generate the file of originating flights for the simulated scenario. Scheduled flight activity may be intensified or thinned by inserting new flights (indicating airline, flight number, origin, destination, aircraft type and scheduled time) or removing existing flights. Randomness in arrivals and departures of scheduled flights is imposed with daily and hourly time-varying means and standard deviations determined from historical airline gate data. Flows inbound from a sector or hub airport may be adjusted to simulate the effects of unusual conditions or events. Flows outbound from the airport may also be regulated to reflect flight restrictions in departure sectors or into destination airports.

For reporting of simulation results, we create detailed logs of simulated activity (written to flat files) and perform the analysis with SAS. Table 2 illustrates information that is saved for individual aircraft. Separating the simulation and analysis in this fashion, we can use data from multiple replications to investigate thoroughly how system performance varies through time. We can also assess the differential

Table 2. Excerpt from the simulation event log for aircraft movements

Obs	Replic.No.	Event Time	Event	Airline	Flight Number	Lambert Gate	City	Continuing	Next City	Next Departure Time
139	1	0746	3: Originate	AA	1141	C6	DFW	No	000	0000
140	1	0746	4: Pushback	AA	1141	C6	DFW	No	000	0000
141	1	0746	5: Liftoff	US	595	C18	SJC	No	000	0000
142	1	0746	2: Arrival	WN	6281	E10	DAL	No	XXX	0000
143	1	0747	1: Touchdown	AA	1380		ORD	Yes	ORD	0900
144	1	0748	2: Arrival	WN	2103	E6	HOU	Yes	DTW	0845
145	1	0748	2: Arrival	WN	452	E12	LGA	Yes	SNA	0810

effects that physical or operational changes have on individual airlines or types of aircraft and estimate the extent to which variation is attributable to systematic versus random effects. With similar recording of information as planes leave or arrive at key queuing points, we can retrospectively deduce the state of the system at any point in simulated time (e.g., gates in use, queues at various stages for arriving and departing flights, simulated aircraft in motion on the ground, aircraft holding on a ramp or taxiway, and aircraft in the simulated airspace).

Strategies for dealing with weather interruptions are employed by both airline operations and ATC. Our modeling framework readily allows an exploration of alternative actions from individual airlines, on one hand, and from ATC ground control on the other hand, if flights to some destinations need to be held. Aircraft may be held at the gate or directed it to a staging position elsewhere on the field if its departure would be delayed by weather or traffic on its planned route. Since delays are calculated as deviations from scheduled pushback rather than liftoff, the staged queuing strategy to cope with traffic holds have a significant impact on actual and reported performance for an airline. Moving an aircraft to free a gate may make it possible for an airline to accommodate incoming traffic without interruption and enable an "on-time" departure, but it may also create congestion elsewhere on the ground that interferes with other departures.

To investigate how the effects of different operating conditions and practices would be revealed in practice, multiple replications are required with stochastic times for activities and random generation of interfering events (equipment failure, weather). For 100 replications of a day's schedule with 900 flights using simple scheduling rules (e.g., FCFS except for aircraft subject to gate and ramp holds) and with pre-designated taxiing routes for active runways, less than 8 minutes of CPU time is required on a laptop computer with an Intel® Core™2DuoCPU E8400 processor @ 3.0GHZ and 3.5GB of RAM.

Data Required for Model Calibration and Validation

Calibration and validation of the model require integration of gate data maintained by individual airlines and flight data that are maintained by ATC systems for aircraft that operate under instrument flight rules (IFR). From airline data we acquire information about aircraft type, origin and destination for the flight leg, and the scheduled and actual times of arrival or departure (pushback) at the gate. From ATC data, we obtain the time when an arriving flight reached the FAF and when it landed (touched down) on the runway. For departing flights, ATC data indicate the takeoff (liftoff) time. Merging these data, we are able to determine the itineraries of flights that arrive at the airport with continuing legs and generate the files used to activate arrivals and originating flights in the simulation model. Routings along taxiways and staging of aircraft to coordinate traffic on the airport surface occur at the discretion of ATC ground controllers who are located in the airport control tower alongside controllers of traffic in the local airspace. Direct observation and interviews with ATC controllers are required to understand the combinations of runways, taxiways and staging points used for arrivals and departures under different wind and weather conditions. Separation standards (used to space arrivals at the FAF and provide appropriate time intervals between successive takeoffs from the same runway) are derived from operating policy manuals. Airports at the point of origin for inbound flights and airports at the destination of outbound flights are grouped according to ATC sectors. This enables deviations from schedule to contain systematic elements related to wind and weather – which affect arrival itineraries and runways in use.

Aviation is particularly prone to the effects of severe weather and airport operations can be affected by conditions or events outside the immediate vicinity. Historical data of weather reports at the airport, at connected hubs and at airports in adjacent ATC sectors through which flights occur allow us to determine the conditions under which the operations took place and to design simulation scenarios accordingly.

Performance Metrics and Sample Scenarios

Performance statistics of airport activity include:

- Number of arrivals and departures for each hour of the day;
- Distributions of delays (differences between actual and scheduled times for arrivals at the gate and departures (pushbacks) from the gate);
- Percentage of delays that constitute a significantly late arrival or departure (e.g., delays in excess of 15 minutes);
- Distributions of time required to taxi from touchdown on the runway to the designated arrival gate;

Table 3. Delays in 100 days of simulated activity of September 2013 schedule with dominant runway configuration

Airline	Event	Delays (Av. Min. Delay)		Flights with Delay > 15 Min.		Ramp and Taxi Time
		Flights	Av. Delay	Number over 15 Min.	P (>15 min.)	Av. Minutes
American	2: Arrival	2,598	1.2	709	0.273	6.1
	4: Departure	2,600	5.8	269	0.103	12.3
CG	2: Arrival	0	.	0	0.000	9.3
	4: Departure	0	.	0	0.000	4.0
Cape Air	2: Arrival	2,500	6.7	62	0.025	6.4
	4: Departure	2,500	3.5	193	0.077	7.9
Delta	2: Arrival	1,944	5.8	312	0.160	6.0
	4: Departure	1,600	4.0	107	0.067	14.5
GA	2: Arrival	0	.	0	0.000	11.8
	4: Departure	0	.	0	0.000	4.0
United	2: Arrival	3,277	8.3	1,258	0.384	6.1
	4: Departure	3,400	6.8	468	0.138	14.8
US Air	2: Arrival	1,400	0.1	359	0.256	6.0
	4: Departure	1,400	2.8	80	0.057	13.3
Southwest	2: Arrival	9,494	0.6	2,256	0.238	7.3
	4: Departure	9,500	10.1	1,269	0.134	11.6
Overall		42,213	3.8	7,342	0.130	9.0

- Numbers of aircraft at gates, taxing inbound, being held on a ramp or pad, taxiing outbound, approaching the airport from adjoining airspace and departing the airport into adjoining airspace;
- Distributions of time from pushback at the gate to liftoff;
- Frequencies with which different runways are used for landings and departures;
- Frequency, duration and timing of ramp and gate holds for weather events;
- Frequency, duration and timing of ramp and gate holds for traffic congestion at destination hubs.

Table 3 illustrates a report of delays and taxiing times in 100 days of simulated activity for the dominant runway configuration at Lambert Airport without adverse weather conditions. Arrival delays are minimal (indeed, some flights arrive early, on average) and relatively few departure delays occur.

This is unsurprising, as airline traffic dropped precipitously from the peak levels in year 2000 after American Airlines acquired TWA and stopped using the airport as a major hub. The airport, like other former hub airports in the American Midwest, now has excess capacity. This is particularly ironic because, in April, 2006, the new runway (RWY 11-29) at the west end of the airport increased airport capacity by roughly 60% in IFR conditions. To illustrate how the simulation model may be used to assess airport capacity and test the possible consequences of changing operating procedures, we provide, in Table 4,

Table 4. Delays in 100 days of simulated activity with dominant runway configuration and 80% traffic increase

Airline	Event	Delays (Av. Min. Delay)		Flights with Delay > 15 Min.		Ramp and Taxi Time
		Flights	Av. Delay	Number over 15 Min.	P (>15 Min.)	Av. Minutes
American	2: Arrival	4,695	3.1	1,425	0.304	6.7
	4: Departure	4,700	5.2	456	0.097	116.0
CG	2: Arrival	0	.	0	0.000	10.7
	4: Departure	0	.	0	0.000	4.1
Cape Air	2: Arrival	4,500	-5.9	137	0.030	7.7
	4: Departure	4,499	4.4	417	0.093	131.5
Delta	2: Arrival	3,552	-6.2	562	0.158	6.6
	4: Departure	3,199	4.0	202	0.063	115.4
GA	2: Arrival	0	.	0	0.000	12.2
	4: Departure	0	.	0	0.000	5.2
United	2: Arrival	5,878	13.9	2,564	0.436	11.7
	4: Departure	6,000	11.0	1,440	0.240	119.8
US Air	2: Arrival	2,500	0.4	626	0.250	6.6
	4: Departure	2,500	2.6	115	0.046	110.0
Southwest	2: Arrival	17,098	0.8	4,186	0.245	9.4
	4: Departure	17,100	10.7	2,338	0.137	119.9
Overall		76,221	4.9	14469	0.160	55.5

the results of simulating activity with an 80% intensification of traffic and same runway usage as in Table 3. Note the extreme delays on outbound taxi times (including time queued for takeoff) that result. Arrivals on RWY 30R are given priority to cross RWY 30L after clearing RWY 30R. This ties up RWY 30L for takeoffs. In Table 5, we show the effects of handling the 80% increase in traffic by using RWY 29 for takeoffs of three airlines operating out of Terminal 1. The outbound ramp and taxiing times for the simulated flights drop dramatically.

CONCLUSION

The research philosophy and analytic techniques employed in the UMR studies provided a solid foundation for the analysis and strategic design of service systems. They have since been applied successfully in the airport environment. In both settings, statistical models embedded in a discrete-event simulation model allow multiple factors to affect the dynamics of system behavior and allow the adjustment of probability distributions to reflect prevailing conditions. The recording of detailed simulated events and

Table 5. Delays in 100 days of simulated activity with 80% traffic increase and use of new runway for three airlines

Airline	Event	Delays (Av. Min. Delay)		Flights with Delay > 15 Min.		Ramp and Taxi Time
		Flights	Av. Delay	Number over 15 Min.	P (>15 Min.)	Av. Minutes
American	2: Arrival	4,695	2.9	1,400	0.298	6.5
	4: Departure	4,700	5.2	448	0.095	9.9
CG	2: Arrival	0	.	0	0.000	9.9
	4: Departure	0	.	0	0.000	4.1
Cape Air	2: Arrival	4,500	-6.4	107	0.024	7.2
	4: Departure	4,500	3.7	357	0.079	11.2
Delta	2: Arrival	3,552	-6.3	558	0.157	6.5
	4: Departure	3,200	4.3	226	0.071	11.2
GA	2: Arrival	0	.	0	0.000	12.2
	4: Departure	0	.	0	0.000	4.7
United	2: Arrival	5,878	13.8	2,557	0.435	11.5
	4: Departure	6,000	11.2	1,436	0.239	11.1
US Air	2: Arrival	2,500	0.3	622	0.249	6.4
	4: Departure	2,500	2.5	113	0.045	18.3
Southwest	2: Arrival	17,098	0.7	4,152	0.243	9.2
	4: Departure	17,099	10.6	2,326	0.136	14.8
Overall		76,222	4.8	14302	0.158	10.4

use of separate tools for multidimensional presentation and analysis ensure that important aspects of system performance are not overlooked. Statistical modeling of results helps to distinguish systematic and random variation in performance measures. The general conceptual framework of staged queues provided a unifying structure for modeling transportation infrastructure in these seemingly disparate environments. The conceptual framework and modeling techniques discussed in this chapter are readily adaptable for strategic information systems in many other business settings.

REFERENCES

Allahverdi, A., Gupta, J. N. D., & Aldowaisan, T. (1999). A review of scheduling research involving setup considerations. *Omega*, *27*(2), 219–239. doi:10.1016/S0305-0483(98)00042-5

Allahverdi, A., Ng, C. T., Cheng, T. C. E., & Kovalyov, M. Y. (2008). A Survey of Scheduling Problems with Setup Times or Costs. *European Journal of Operational Research*, *187*(3), 985–1032. doi:10.1016/j.ejor.2006.06.060

Atkin, J. A. D., Burke, E. K., Greenwood, J. S., & Reeson, D. (2009). An examination of take-off scheduling constraints at London Heathrow airport. *Public Transport*, *1*(1), 169–187. doi:10.1007/s12469-009-0011-z

Atkin, J. A. D., Burke, E. K., & Ravizza, S. (2010). *The airport ground movement problem: past and current research and future directions.* 4th International Conference on Research in Air Transportation, Budapest, Hungary.

Balas, E., Simonetti, N., & Vazacopoulas, A. (2008). Job shop scheduling with setup times, deadlines and precedence constraints. *Journal of Scheduling*, *11*(4), 253–262. doi:10.1007/s10951-008-0067-7

Bartholdi, J. J. III, & Gue, K. R. (2000). Reducing Labor Costs in an LTL Crossdocking Terminal. *Operations Research*, *48*(6), 823–832. doi:10.1287/opre.48.6.823.12397

Bazargan, M., Fleming, K., & Subramanian, P. (2002). A simulation study to investigate runway capacity using TAAM.*Proceedings of the 2002 Winter Simulation Conference*, (pp. 1235-1242). doi:10.1109/WSC.2002.1166383

Bertino, J. & Boyajian, E. (2011, May-June). 21st Century Fast-time Airport and Airspace Modeling Analysis with Simmod. *Managing the Skies*, 21-23.

Bialik, C. (2012, May 4). Border delay data leave fliers up in the air. *Wall Street Journal*, p. A4.

Brentnall, A. R., & Cheng, R. C. H. (2009). Some Effects of Aircraft Arrival Sequence Algorithms. *The Journal of the Operational Research Society*, *60*(7), 962–972. doi:10.1057/palgrave.jors.2602636

Bubalo, B., & Daduna, J. R. (2011). Airport capacity and demand calculations by simulation – the case of Berlin-Brandenburg International Airport. *NETNOMICS: Economic Research and Electronic Networking*, *12*(3), 161–181. doi:10.1007/s11066-011-9065-6

Campbell, J. F., Smith, L. D., & Sweeney, D. C. II. (2009). A robust strategy for managing congestion at locks on the Upper Mississippi River. In *Proceedings of the 42nd Hawaii International Conference on Systems Sciences* (pp. 1-10). Washington, DC: IEEE Computer Society.

Capozzi, B., Brinton, M., Churchill, A., & Atkins, S. (2013). The Metroplex Simulation Environment. In *Digital Avionics Systems Conference (DASC), 2013 IEEE/AIAA 32nd* (pp. 1E5-1). doi:10.1109/DASC.2013.6712528

Caris, A., Limbourg, S., Macharis, C., & Cools, M., (2014) Integration of Inland Waterway Transport in the Intermodal Supply Chain: a Taxonomy of Research Challenges. *Journal of Transport Geography, 41,* 126-136.

Carroll, J. L., & Bronzini, M. S. (1973). Waterway transportation simulation models: Development and application. *Water Resources Research, 9*(1), 51–63. doi:10.1029/WR009i001p00051

Dai, M. D. M., & Schonfeld, P. (1998). Metamodels for estimating waterway delays through series of queues. *Transportation Research Part B: Methodological, 32*(1), 1–19. doi:10.1016/S0191-2615(97)00003-9

Ehmke, J. F., Großhans, D., Mattfeld, D. C., & Smith, L. D. (2011). Interactive Analysis of Discrete Event Logistics Systems with Support of a Data Warehouse. *Computers in Industry, 62*(6), 578–586. doi:10.1016/j.compind.2011.04.007

Federal Aviation Administration. (1989). *SIMMOD Reference Manual AOR-200.* Office of Operations Research, Federal Aviation Administration. Retrieved from http://www.tc.faa.gov/acb300/how_simmod_works.pdf

Fishburn, P. T., Golkar, J., & Taafe, K. (1995). Simulation of Transportation Systems.*Proceedings of the 1995 Winter Simulation Conference,* (pp. 51-54).

Gagné, C., Price, W. L., & Gravel, M. (2002). Comparing an ACO algorithm with other heuristics for the single machine scheduling problem with sequence-dependent setup times. *The Journal of the Operational Research Society, 53*(8), 895–906. doi:10.1057/palgrave.jors.2601390

Gendreau, M., Laporte, G., & Guimaraes, E. M. (2001). A divide and merge heuristic for the multiprocessor scheduling problem with sequence dependent setup times. *European Journal of Operational Research, 133*(1), 183–189. doi:10.1016/S0377-2217(00)00197-1

Gilbo, E. P. (1993). Airport capacity – representation, estimation, optimization. *IEEE Transactions on Control Systems Technology, 1*(3), 144–154. doi:10.1109/87.251882

Gotteland, J. B., Durand, N., Alliot, J. M., & Page, E. (2001). Aircraft ground traffic optimization. In *4th USA/Europe Air Traffic Management Seminar* (pp. 04-07).

Gue, K. R., & Kang, K. (2001). Staging Queues in Material Handling and Transportation Systems. In *Proceedings of the 2001 Winter Simulation Conference* (pp. 1104-1108). doi:10.1109/WSC.2001.977421

Guo, C., Zhibin, J., Zhang, H., & Li, N. (2012). Decomposition-based classified ant colony optimization algorithm for scheduling semiconductor wafer fabrication system. *Computers & Industrial Engineering*, *62*(1), 141–151. doi:10.1016/j.cie.2011.09.002

Gupta, S. R., & Smith, J. S. (2006). Algorithms for single machine total tardiness scheduling with sequence dependent setups. *European Journal of Operational Research*, *175*(2), 722–739. doi:10.1016/j.ejor.2005.05.018

Herrero, J. G., Berlanga, A., Molina, J. M., & Casar, J. R. (2005). Methods for operations planning in airport decision support systems. *Applied Intelligence*, *22*(3), 183–206. doi:10.1007/s10791-005-6618-z

Horstmeier, T., & de Haan, F. (2001). Influence of ground handling on turn round time of new large aircraft. *Aircraft Engineering and Aerospace Technology*, *73*(3), 266–270. doi:10.1108/00022660110390677

Hung, Y. F., & Chang, C. B. (2002). Dispatching Rules Using Flow-Time Predictions for Semiconductor Wafer Fabrications. *Journal of the Chinese Institute of Industrial Engineers*, *19*(1), 67–75. doi:10.1080/10170660209509184

Khadilkar, H., & Balakrishnan, H. (2013). *Network congestion control of airport surface operations. Journal of Guidance, Control and Dynamics.*

Kim, Y. M., & Schonfeld, P. (1995). Neural network estimation of waterway lock service times. *Transportation Research Record*, *1497*, 36–43.

Martinelli, D., & Schonfeld, P. (1995). Approximating delays at interdependent locks. *Journal of Waterway, Port, Coastal, and Ocean Engineering*, *121*(6), 300–307. doi:10.1061/(ASCE)0733-950X(1995)121:6(300)

Nauss, R. M. (2008). Optimal sequencing in the presence of setup times for tow/barge traffic through a river lock. *European Journal of Operational Research*, *187*(3), 1268–1281. doi:10.1016/j.ejor.2006.06.071

Norin, A., Granberg, T. A., Varbrand, P., & Yuan, D. (2009). *Integrating optimization and simulation to gain more efficient airport logistics*. Eighth USA/Europe Air Traffic Management Research and Development Seminar.

Odoni, A. R., Bowman, J., Delahaye, D., Deyst, J. J., Feron, E., Hansman, R. J., & Simpson, R. W. et al. (1997). *Existing and required modeling capabilities for evaluating ATM systems and concepts*. International Center for Air Transportation, Massachusetts Institute of Technology.

Offerman, H. (2001). Simulation to Support the Airport Stakeholder Decision-Making Process. *Air & Space Europe*, *3*(1/2), 60–67. doi:10.1016/S1290-0958(01)90017-6

Oredsson, S., Jonsson, H., Rognes, J., Lind, L., Göransson, K. E., Ehrenberg, A., & Farrohknia, N. et al. (2011). A systematic review of triage-related interventions to improve patient flow in emergency departments. *Scandinavian Journal of Trauma, Resuscitation and Emergency Medicine*, *19*(1), 43. doi:10.1186/1757-7241-19-43

Passchyn, W., Briskorn, D., & Spieksma, F. (2016b). Mathematical Programming Models for Lock Scheduling with an Emission Objective. *European Journal of Operational Research*, *248*(3), 802–814. doi:10.1016/j.ejor.2015.09.012

Passchyn, W., Coene, S., Briskorn, D., Hurink, J., Spieksma, F., & Vanden Berghe, G. (2016a). The lockmasters problem. *European Journal of Operational Research*, *251*(2), 432–441. doi:10.1016/j.ejor.2015.12.007

Ramanathan, V., & Schonfeld, P. (1994). Approximate delays caused by lock service interruptions. *Transportation Research Record*, *1430*, 41–49.

Ravizza, S., Chen, J., Atkin, J. A. D., Burke, E. K., & Stewart, P. (2013). The trade-off between taxi time and fuel consumption in airport ground movement. *Public Transport*, *4*(1-2), 25–40. doi:10.1007/s12469-013-0060-1

Shabayek, A. A., & Yeung, W. W. (2002). A Simulation Model for the Kwai Chung Container Terminals in Hong Kong. *European Journal of Operational Research*, *140*(1), 1–11. doi:10.1016/S0377-2217(01)00216-8

Sherali, H. D., Hobeika, A. G., Trani, A. A., & Kim, B. J. (1992). An integrated simulation and dynamic programming approach for determining optimal runway exit locations. *Management Science*, *38*(7), 1049–1049. doi:10.1287/mnsc.38.7.1049

Smith, L. D., Ehmke, J. F., Mattfeld, D. C., Waning, R., & Hellman, L. (2014). Strategic Decision Support for Airside Operations at Commercial Airports. In Computational Logistics (LNCS), (vol. 8760, pp. 132–150). Springer. doi:10.1007/978-3-319-11421-7_9

Smith, L. D., & Nauss, R. M. (2010). Investigating strategic alternatives for improving service in an inland waterway transportation system. *International Journal of Strategic Decision Sciences*, *1*(2), 62–81. doi:10.4018/jsds.2010040103

Smith, L. D., Nauss, R. M., Mattfeld, D. C., Ehmke, J. F., & Bahr, F. (2012). Scheduling logistics activities in staged queues with sequence-dependent changeover and processing times. In *Proceedings of the 2012 45th Hawaii International Conference on System Sciences* (pp. 1296-1305). Washington, DC: IEEE Computer Society. doi:10.1109/HICSS.2012.511

Smith, L. D., Nauss, R. M., Mattfeld, D. C., Li, J., & Ehmke, J. F. (2011). Scheduling Operations at System Choke Points with Sequence-dependent Delays and Processing Times. *Transportation Research Part E, Logistics and Transportation Review*, *47*(5), 669–691. doi:10.1016/j.tre.2011.02.005

Smith, L. D., Sweeney, D. C. II, & Campbell, J. F. (2009). Simulation of alternative approaches to relieving congestion at locks in a river transportation system. *The Journal of the Operational Research Society*, *60*(4), 519–533. doi:10.1057/palgrave.jors.2602587

Snowdon, J. L., MacNair, E., Montevecchi, M., Callery, C. A., El-Taji, S., & Miller, S. (2000). IBM journey management library: An arena system for airport simulations. *The Journal of the Operational Research Society*, *51*(4), 449–456. doi:10.2307/254172

Ting, C. J., & Schonfeld, P. (1998). Optimization through simulation of waterway transportation investments. *Transportation Research Record*, *1620*, 11–16. doi:10.3141/1620-03

Ting, C. J., & Schonfeld, P. (2001a). Efficiency versus fairness in priority control: Waterway lock case. *Journal of Waterway, Port, Coastal, and Ocean Engineering*, *127*(2), 82–88. doi:10.1061/(ASCE)0733-950X(2001)127:2(82)

Ting, C. J., & Schonfeld, P. (2001b). Control alternatives at a waterway lock. *Journal of Waterway, Port, Coastal, and Ocean Engineering*, *127*(2), 89–96. doi:10.1061/(ASCE)0733-950X(2001)127:2(89)

Verstichel, J., De Causmaecker, P., Spieksma, F., & Vanden Berghe, G. (2014). The generalized lock scheduling problem: An exact approach. *Transportation Research E. Logistics and Transportation Review*, *65*, 16–34. doi:10.1016/j.tre.2013.12.010

Verstichel, J., De Causmaecker, P., Spieksma, F., & Vanden Berghe, G. (2014). Exact and heuristic methods for placing ships in locks. *European Journal of Operational Research*, *235*(2), 387–398. doi:10.1016/j.ejor.2013.06.045

Verstichel, J., De Causmaecker, P., & Vanden Berghea, G. (2011). Scheduling algorithms for the lock scheduling problem. *Procedia: Social and Behavioral Sciences*, *20*, 806–815. doi:10.1016/j.sbspro.2011.08.089

Verstichel, J., Kinable, J., De Causmaecker, P., & Vanden Berghe, G. (2015). A Combinatorial Benders decomposition for the lock scheduling problem. *Computers & Operations Research*, *54*, 117–128. doi:10.1016/j.cor.2014.09.007

Wei, C. H., Dai, M. D. M., & Schonfeld, P. (1992). Computational characteristics of a numerical model for series of waterway queues. *Transportation Research Record*, *1333*, 45–54.

Wei, G., & Siyuan, J. (2010). Simulation study on closely spaced parallel runway analysis using SIMMOD Plus. 2010.*International Conference on Intelligent Computation Technology and Automation*. IEEE. doi:10.1109/ICICTA.2010.223

Wu, J., & Hounsell, N. (1998). Bus Priority Using Pre-Signals. *Transportation Research Part A, Policy and Practice*, *32*(8), 563–583. doi:10.1016/S0965-8564(98)00008-1

Yan, S., Shieh, C., & Chen, M. (2002). A simulation framework for evaluating airport gate assignments. *Transportation Research Part A, Policy and Practice*, *36*(10), 885–898. doi:10.1016/S0965-8564(01)00045-3

Yuan, X., Ji, B., Yuan, Y., & Zhang, X. (2016). Co-scheduling of lock and water–land transshipment for ships passing the dam. *Applied Soft Computing*, *45*, 150–162. doi:10.1016/j.asoc.2016.04.019

Zhu, L., Schonfeld, P., Kim, Y. M., Flood, I., & Ting, C. J. (1999). Queuing network analysis for waterways with artificial neural networks. *Artificial Intelligence for Engineering Design, Analysis and Manufacturing*, *13*(5), 365–375. doi:10.1017/S0890060499135017

Zografos, K. G., & Madas, M. A. (2006). Development and demonstration for an integrated decision support system for airport performance analysis. *Transportation Research Part C, Emerging Technologies*, *14*(1), 1–17. doi:10.1016/j.trc.2006.04.001

Compilation of References

Agrawal, D. K. (2012). Demand Chain Management: Factors Enhancing Market Responsiveness Capabilities. *Journal of Marketing Channels, 19*(2), 101–119. doi:10.1080/1046669X.2012.667760

Alavi, M., & Leidner, D. (2001). Knowledge management and knowledge management systems: Conceptual foundations and research issues. *Management Information Systems Quarterly, 25*(1), 107–136. doi:10.2307/3250961

Alavi, M., & Tiwana, A. (2003). Knowledge management: The information technology dimension. In M. Easterby-Smith & M. A. Lyles (Eds.), *Organizational learning and knowledge management* (pp. 104–121). London: Blackwell Publishing.

Alexander, T. (1969). *Children and Adolescents: A Biocultural Approach to Psychological Development.* New York: Atherton Press.

Allahverdi, A., Gupta, J. N. D., & Aldowaisan, T. (1999). A review of scheduling research involving setup considerations. *Omega, 27*(2), 219–239. doi:10.1016/S0305-0483(98)00042-5

Allahverdi, A., Ng, C. T., Cheng, T. C. E., & Kovalyov, M. Y. (2008). A Survey of Scheduling Problems with Setup Times or Costs. *European Journal of Operational Research, 187*(3), 985–1032. doi:10.1016/j.ejor.2006.06.060

Allee, V. (2000). Knowledge Networks and Communities of Practice. *OD Practitioner Online, 32*(4).

Ambrosio, J. (2000). *Knowledge Management Mistakes.* Retrieved from http://www.computerworld.com/industrytopics/energy/story/0,10801,46693,00.html

American Chamber of Commerce in Egypt. (2007). *Information Technology in Egypt.* Business Studies and Analysis Center.

American Chamber of Commerce in Egypt. (2016). *Egypt Economic Indicators.* Business Studies and Analysis Center.

AMR Research Report. (2005). *The handbook for becoming demand driven.* Boston, MA: AMR Research. Retrieved from http://www.agentrank.com/api/

Anthony, R. N. (1965). *Planning and Control Systems: A Framework for Analysis.* Cambridge, MA: Harvard University Press.

Anthony, R. N., Dearden, J., & Vancil, R. F. (1972). *Management Control Systems.* Homewood, IL: Irwin.

Anwar, S. T. (2003). CASES Vodafone and the wireless industry: A case in market expansion and global strategy. *Journal of Business and Industrial Marketing, 18*(3), 270–288. doi:10.1108/08858620310471331

Arab Human Development Report. (2002). *Creating Opportunities for Future Generations.* United Nations Development Programme and Arab Fund for Economic and Social Development.

Arce, E., & Flynn, D. (1997). A CASE Tool to Support Critical Success Factors Analysis in IT Planning and Requirements Determination. *Information and Software Technology, 39*(5), 311–321. doi:10.1016/S0950-5849(96)01150-0

Ardichvili, A., Zavyalova, E., & Minina, V. (2012). Human capital development: Comparative analysis of BRICs. *European Journal of Training and Development, 36*(2/3), 213–233. doi:10.1108/03090591211204724

Arend, R. J., Patel, P. C., & Park, H. D. (2014). Explaining post-IPO venture performance through a knowledge-based view typology. *Strategic Management Journal, 35*(3), 376–397. doi:10.1002/smj.2095

Ariely, D., & Simonson, I. (2003). Buying, Bidding, Playing, or Competing: Value Assessment and Decision Dynamics in Online Auctions. *Journal of Consumer Psychology, 13*(1-2), 113-123

Artikis, A., Pitt, J., & Stergiou, C. (2000). Agent Communication Transfer Protocol. *Proceedings of the 4th International Conference on Autonomous Agents*. doi:10.1145/336595.337577

Arvantis, A., & Hamilou, E. (2004). *Modeling Cadastral Transaction in Greece Using UML.* Paper presented at The FIG Working Week, Athens, Greece.

Ashford, J. B., & LeCroy, C. W. (2010). *Human behavior in the social environment: A multidimensional perspective* (4th ed.). Belmont, CA: Wadsworth, Cengage Learning.

Athanasopoulou, P. (2009). Relationship quality: A critical literature review and research agenda. *European Journal of Marketing, 43*(5/6), 583–610. doi:10.1108/03090560910946945

Atkin, J. A. D., Burke, E. K., & Ravizza, S. (2010). *The airport ground movement problem: past and current research and future directions.* 4th International Conference on Research in Air Transportation, Budapest, Hungary.

Atkin, J. A. D., Burke, E. K., Greenwood, J. S., & Reeson, D. (2009). An examination of take-off scheduling constraints at London Heathrow airport. *Public Transport, 1*(1), 169–187. doi:10.1007/s12469-009-0011-z

Atthirawong, W., & McCarthy, B. (2001). *Critical Factors in International Location Decisions: A Delphi Study.* Paper presented at the Twelfth Annual Conference of the Production and Operations Management Society, Orlando, FL.

Ausubel, L. (2003). Clock Auctions, Proxy Auctions, and Possible Hybrids. *Proceedings of the 3rd Combinatorial Bidding Conference.*

Avellaneda, M. (2011). *Algorithmic & High-Frequency Trading: An Overview.* Presentation, Quant Congress USA 2011.

Avgerou, C. (2000). Recognizing Alternative Rationalities in the Deployment of Information Systems. *Electronic Journal of Information Systems in Developing Countries, 3*(7), 1–15.

Ayers, J., & James, B. (2006). *Handbook of supply chain management* (2nd ed.). Boca Raton, FL: Auerbach.

Ayers, J., & Malmberg, D. (2002). Supply Chain Systems: Are you Ready? *Information Strategy: The Executive's Journal, 19*(1), 18–27.

Azevedo, R. F. L., Ardichvili, A., Casa Nova, S., & Cornacchione Jr, E. B. (2016). Human Resource Development in Brazil. In T. Garavan (Ed.), *Global Human Resource Development* (pp. 250–265). New York: Routledge.

Balas, E., Simonetti, N., & Vazacopoulas, A. (2008). Job shop scheduling with setup times, deadlines and precedence constraints. *Journal of Scheduling, 11*(4), 253–262. doi:10.1007/s10951-008-0067-7

Bandura, A. (1989a). Social cognitive theory. In R. Vasta (Ed.), Annals of child development. Vol.6. Six theories of child development (pp. 1-60). Greenwich, CT: JAI Press.

Bandura, A. (2008). Toward an agentic theory of the self. In H. Marsh, R. G. Craven, & D. M. McInerney (Eds.), Advances in Self Research: Self-processes, learning, and enabling human potential (vol. 3, pp. 15-49). Charlotte, NC: Information Age Publishing.

Bandura. (1997). Self-efficacy: Toward a unifying theory of behavioral change. *Psychological Review, 84*(2), 191-212.

Bandura, A. (1977). *Social learning theory*. Englewood Cliffs, NJ: Prentice-Hall.

Bandura, A. (1989b). Human agency in social cognitive theory. *The American Psychologist, 44*(9), 1175–1184. doi:10.1037/0003-066X.44.9.1175 PMID:2782727

Bandura, A. (2001). Social cognitive theory: An agentic perspective. *Annual Review of Psychology, 52*(1), 1–26. doi:10.1146/annurev.psych.52.1.1 PMID:11148297

Bandura, A. (2002). Social cognitive theory in cultural context. *Applied Psychology, 51*(2), 269–290. doi:10.1111/1464-0597.00092

Bandura, A. (2005). Evolution of social cognitive theory. In K. G. Smith & M. A. Hitt (Eds.), *Great minds in management* (pp. 9–35). Oxford, UK: Oxford University Press.

Bandura, A. (2006). Adolescent development from an agentic perspective. In F. Pajares & T. Urdan (Eds.), *Self-efficacy beliefs of adolescents* (Vol. 5, pp. 1–43). Greenwich, CT: Information Age Publishing.

Bandura, A. (2006a). Toward a psychology of human agency. *Perspectives on Psychological Science, 1*(2), 164–180. doi:10.1111/j.1745-6916.2006.00011.x PMID:26151469

Bandura, A. (2009). Social cognitive theory of mass communications. In J. Bryant & M. B. Oliver (Eds.), *Media effects: Advances in theory and research* (2nd ed.; pp. 94–124). Mahwah, NJ: Lawrence Erlbaum.

Bapna, R. (2003). When Snipers Become Predators: Can Mechanism Design Save Online Auctions?. *Communications of the ACM, 46*(12), 152-158.

Bapna, R., Goes, P., Gupta, A., & Jin, Y. (2004). User Heterogeneity and Its Impact on Electronic Auction Market Design: An Empirical Exploration. MIS Quarterly, 28(1), 21 – 43.

Baporikar, N. (2015a). Information Strategy as Enabler of Competitive Advantage. In Economics: Concepts, Methodologies, Tools, and Applications (pp. 599-610). Hershey, PA: Business Science Reference. doi:10.4018/978-1-4666-8468-3.ch032

Baporikar, N. (2013). CSF Approach for IT Strategic Planning. *International Journal of Strategic Information Technology and Applications, 4*(2), 35–47. doi:10.4018/jsita.2013040103

Baporikar, N. (2014a). Strategic Management Overview and SME in Globalized World. In K. Todorov & D. Smallbone (Eds.), *Handbook of Research on Strategic Management in Small and Medium Enterprises* (pp. 22–39). Hershey, PA: Business Science Reference; doi:10.4018/978-1-4666-5962-9.ch002

Baporikar, N. (2014b). Information Strategy as Enabler of Competitive Advantage. *International Journal of Strategic Information Technology and Applications, 5*(1), 30–41. doi:10.4018/ijsita.2014010103

Baporikar, N. (2015b). Holistic Framework for Evolving Effective Information Systems Strategy. *International Journal of Strategic Information Technology and Applications, 6*(4), 30–43. doi:10.4018/IJSITA.2015100103

Barat, J. (1992). Scenario Playing for Critical Success Factor Analysis. *Journal of Information Technology, 7*(1), 12–19. doi:10.1057/jit.1992.3

Bartholdi, J. J. III, & Gue, K. R. (2000). Reducing Labor Costs in an LTL Crossdocking Terminal. *Operations Research, 48*(6), 823–832. doi:10.1287/opre.48.6.823.12397

Bartol, K., & Srivastava, A. (2002). Encouraging knowledge sharing: The role of organizational reward systems. *Journal of Leadership & Organizational Studies, 9*(1), 64–76. doi:10.1177/107179190200900105

Bazargan, M., Fleming, K., & Subramanian, P. (2002). A simulation study to investigate runway capacity using TAAM. *Proceedings of the 2002 Winter Simulation Conference*, (pp. 1235-1242). doi:10.1109/WSC.2002.1166383

Bell, T. (2016). *Bitcoin Trading Agents*. Working Paper. University of Southampton.

Bendall-Lyon, D., & Powers, T. L. (2003). The influence of mass communication and time on satisfaction and loyalty. *Journal of Services Marketing*, *17*(6), 589–608. doi:10.1108/08876040310495627

Bennett, R., & Barkensjo, A. (2005). Relationship quality, relationship marketing, and client perceptions of the levels of service quality of charitable organisations. *International Journal of Service Industry Management*, *16*(1), 81–106. doi:10.1108/09564230510587168

Bernard, S. A. (2005). *An Introduction to Enterprise Architecture* (2nd ed.). Bloomington, IN: Author-House.

Bertino, J. & Boyajian, E. (2011, May-June). 21st Century Fast-time Airport and Airspace Modeling Analysis with Simmod. *Managing the Skies*, 21-23.

Bhagat, R. S., Kedia, B. L., Harveston, P. D., & Triandis, H. C. (2002). Cultural variations in the cross-border transfer of organizational knowledge: An integrative framework. *Academy of Management Review*, *27*, 204–221.

Bhatt, C., Koshti, A., Agrawal, H., Malek, Z., & Trivedi, B. (2011). Architecture for intrusion detection system with fault tolerance using mobile agent. *International Journal of Network Security & Its Applications*, *3*(5), 167–175. doi:10.5121/ijnsa.2011.3513

Bialik, C. (2012, May 4). Border delay data leave fliers up in the air. *Wall Street Journal*, p. A4.

Bijou, Y., & Lester, D. (2003). Liaw's Scales to Measure Attitudes toward Computers and the Internet. *Perceptual & Motor Skills*, *97*(2), 384.

Binde, B. E., McRee, R., & O'Connor, T. J. (2011). *Assessing outbound traffic to uncover advanced persistent threat*. Retrieved May 1, 2016, from http://www.sans.edu/student-files/projects/JWP-Binde-McRee-OConnor.pdf

Blau, S.K. (2003). The Force Need Not Be With You: Curvature Begets Motion.

Blough, D. R. (2003). Integrating GIS into the Survey Research Process:Using Geographic Information Systems in Institutional Research. Jossey-Bass.

Bogdan, R. C., & Biklen, S. K. (2007). *Qualitative research for education* (5th ed.). Boston: Pearson.

Booch, G., Rumbaugh, J., & Jacobson, I. (2000). *The Unified Modelling Language User Guide*. Reading, MA: Addison Wesley Longman, Inc.

Brancheau, J., Janz, B., & Wetherbe, J. (1996). Key Issues in Information Systems Management: 199495 SIM Delphi Result. *Management Information Systems Quarterly*, *20*(2), 225–242. doi:10.2307/249479

Brancik, K., & Ghinita, G. G. (2011, February). *The optimization of situational awareness for insider threat detection*. Presented at the First ACM Conference on Data and Application Security and Privacy, San Antonio, TX. doi:10.1145/1943513.1943544

Brentnall, A. R., & Cheng, R. C. H. (2009). Some Effects of Aircraft Arrival Sequence Algorithms. *The Journal of the Operational Research Society*, *60*(7), 962–972. doi:10.1057/palgrave.jors.2602636

Brill, A. E. (2010). From hit and run to invade and stay: How cyberterrorists could be living inside your systems. *Defense Against Terrorism Review*, *3*(2), 23–36.

Brown, J. (2002). Training needs assessment: A must for developing an effective training program. *Public Personnel Management, 31*(4), 569–578. doi:10.1177/009102600203100412

Brown, J. S., & Duguid, P. (2000). Balancing act: How to capture knowledge without killing it. *Harvard Business Review*, (May-June). PMID:11183980

Bruning, R. H., Schraw, G. J., Norby, M. M., & Ronning, R. R. (2004). *Cognitive psychology and instruction*. Upper Saddle River, NJ: Prentice Hall.

Bruno, A., & Leidecker, J. (1984). Identifying and Using Critical Success Factors. *Long Range Planning, 17*(1), 23–32. doi:10.1016/0024-6301(84)90163-8

Bubalo, B., & Daduna, J. R. (2011). Airport capacity and demand calculations by simulation – the case of Berlin-Brandenburg International Airport. *NETNOMICS: Economic Research and Electronic Networking, 12*(3), 161–181. doi:10.1007/s11066-011-9065-6

Buckley, J. J. (1985). *Ranking* Alternatives Using Fuzzy Number. *Fuzzy Sets and Systems, 15*(1), 21–31. doi:10.1016/0165-0114(85)90013-2

Bustinza, O. F., Parry, G. C., & Vendrell-Herrero, F. (2013). Supply and Demand Chain Management: The Effect of Adding Services to Product Offerings. *Supply Chain Management, 18*(6), 618–629. doi:10.1108/SCM-05-2013-0149

Cabrera, A., & Cabrera, E. (2002). Knowledge-sharing dilemmas. *Organization Studies, 23*(5), 687–710. doi:10.1177/0170840602235001

Camerer, C., Ho, T., & Chong, K. (2003). Models of Thinking, Learning, and Teaching in Games. American Economic Review, 93(2), 192.

Campbell, J. F., Smith, L. D., & Sweeney, D. C. II. (2009). A robust strategy for managing congestion at locks on the Upper Mississippi River. In *Proceedings of the 42nd Hawaii International Conference on Systems Sciences* (pp. 1-10). Washington, DC: IEEE Computer Society.

Capellini, V., Constantinides, A.G., & Emiliani, P. (1978). Digital filters and their applications. London: Academic Press.

Capozzi, B., Brinton, M., Churchill, A., & Atkins, S. (2013). The Metroplex Simulation Environment. In *Digital Avionics Systems Conference (DASC), 2013 IEEE/AIAA 32nd* (pp. 1E5-1). doi:10.1109/DASC.2013.6712528

Caralli, R. A. (2004). *The Critical Success Factor Method: Establishing a Foundation for Enterprise Security Management (CMU/SEI-2004-TR-010).*Software Engineering Institute, Carnegie Mellon University.

Carayannis, E., Alexander, J., & Ioannidis, A. (2000). Leveraging knowledge, learning, and innovation in forming strategic government–university–industry (GUI) R&D partnerships in the US, Germany and France. *Journal of Technovation*, (20), 477–488.

Caris, A., Limbourg, S., Macharis, C., & Cools, M., (2014) Integration of Inland Waterway Transport in the Intermodal Supply Chain: a Taxonomy of Research Challenges. *Journal of Transport Geography, 41,* 126-136.

Carroll, J. L., & Bronzini, M. S. (1973). Waterway transportation simulation models: Development and application. *Water Resources Research, 9*(1), 51–63. doi:10.1029/WR009i001p00051

Casenove, M., & Kowalczewska, K. (2015). APT – The new cyberforce? *The Polish Quarterly of International Affairs, 3*, 719.

Cassidy, A. (2006). *A Practical Guide to Information Systems Strategic Planning* (2nd ed.). Boca Raton, FL: Auerbach Publications.

Ceren, A. V. (2015). Sustainable Demand Chain Management: An Alternative Perspective for Sustainability in the Supply Chain. *Procedia: Social and Behavioral Sciences*, *207*, 262–273.

Chabat, B. (1959). *Introduction à l'analyse complexe* (Tome 2: fonctions de plusieurs variables). Moscou: MIR.

Cham, T. H., Lim, Y. M., Cheng, B. L., & Lee, T. H. (2016). Determinants of knowledge management systems success in the banking industry. *VINE Journal of Information and Knowledge Management Systems*, *46*(1), 2–20. doi:10.1108/VJIKMS-03-2014-0021

Chan, K., & Liebowitz, J. (2006). The synergy of social network analysis and knowledge mapping: A case study. *Int. J. Management and Decision Making*, *7*(1), 19–35. doi:10.1504/IJMDM.2006.008169

Chari, S., Habeck, T., Molloy, I., Park, Y., & Teiken, W. (2013, June). *A bigdata platform for analytics on access control policies and logs*. Presented at the SACMAT 2013, Amsterdam, The Netherlands. doi:10.1145/2462410.2462433

Chatura, R., & Jaideep, P. (2003). The influence of satisfaction, trust and switching barriers on customer retention in a continuous purchasing setting. *International Journal of Service Industry Management*, *14*(Iss: 4), 374–395. doi:10.1108/09564230310489231

Chen, H. (2003). Study on Technological Intermediaries, Development in Innovation System. *Industrial Technology & Economy*, (3), 15-16.

Chen, P., Desmet, L., & Huyens, C. (2014, September). *A study on advanced persistent threats*. Presented at the 15th Conference in Communications and Multimedia Security, Aveiro, Portugal.

Chen, Y., & Justis, R. T. (2006). Chinese franchise brands going globalization. *1st Annual China Franchise International Summit.* International Franchise Academy.

Chen, Y., Chen, G., & Wu, S. (2006). A Simonian approach to e-business research: A study in Netchising. Advanced Topics in E-Business Research: E-Business Innovation and Process Management, 1.

Chen, Y., Zhang, B., & Justis, R. T. (2005). Data mining in franchise organizations. Encyclopaedia of Information Science and Technology, (pp. 714-722). Academic Press.

Chen, Y., Chong, P., & Justis, R. T. (2000a). Information technology solutions to increase franchise efficiency and productivity.*Proceedings of the 2000 Franchise China Conference and Exhibition.*

Chen, Y., Chong, P., & Justis, R. T. (2000b). Franchising knowledge repository: A structure for learning organizations. *Proceedings of the 14th Annual International Society of Franchising Conference.*

Chen, Y., Chong, P., & Justis, R. T. (2002). E-business strategy in franchising: A customer-service-life-cycle approach. *Proceedings of the 16th Annual International Society of Franchising Conference.*

Chen, Y., Ford, C., Justis, R. T., & Chong, P. (2001). Application service providers (ASP) in franchising: Opportunities and issues.*Proceedings of the 15th Annual International Society of Franchising Conference.*

Chen, Y., Hammerstein, S., & Justis, R. T. (2002). Knowledge, learning, and capabilities in franchise organizations. *Proceedings of the 3rd European Conference on Organizational Knowledge, Learning, and Capabilities.*

Chen, Y., Justis, R. T., & Chong, P. P. (2008). Data mining in franchise organizations. In J. Wang (Ed.), *Data Warehousing and Mining: Concepts, Methodologies, Tools, and Applications* (pp. 2722–2733). doi:10.4018/978-1-59904-951-9.ch169

Chen, Y., Justis, R. T., & Yang, H. L. (2004). Global e-business, international franchising, and theory of Netchising: A research alliance of east and west.*Proceedings of the 18th Annual International Society of Franchising Conference.*

Chen, Y., Justis, R., & Watson, E. (2000). Web-enabled data warehousing. In M. Shaw, R. Blanning, T. Strader, & A. Whinston (Eds.), *Handbook of electronic commerce* (pp. 501–520). Springer-Verlag. doi:10.1007/978-3-642-58327-8_24

Chen, Y., Justis, R., & Wu, S. (2006). Value networks in franchise organizations: A study in the senior care industry. *Proceedings of the 20th Annual International Society of Franchising Conference.*

Chen, Y., Seidman, W., & Justis, R. T. (2005). Strategy and docility in franchise organizations.*Proceedings of the 19th Annual International Society of Franchising Conference.*

Chen, Y., Yuan, W., & Dai, W. (2004). Strategy and nearly decomposable systems: A study in franchise organizations. *International Symposium on "IT/IS Issues in Asia-Pacific Region, Co-sponsored by ICIS-2004.*

Cherif, E., & Grant, D. (2014). An Analysis of Online Real Estate Business Models, (To appear). *Electronic Commerce Research, 14*(1). doi:10.1007/s10660-013-9126-z

Childerhouse, P., Aitken, J., & Towill, D. (2002). Analysis and design of focused demand chains. *Journal of Operations Management, 20*(6), 675–689. doi:10.1016/S0272-6963(02)00034-7

Choi, B., & Lee, H. (2003). An empirical investigation of knowledge management styles and their effect on corporate performance. *Information & Management, 40*, 403–417. doi:10.1016/S0378-7206(02)00060-5

Choi, C., Choi, J., & Kim, P. (2014). Ontology-based access control model for security policy reasoning in cloud computing. *The Journal of Supercomputing, 67*(3), 711–722. doi:10.1007/s11227-013-0980-1

Chougule, A., Mukhopadhyay, D., & Randhe, V. (2013). *Reverse Proxy Framework using Sanitization Technique for Intrusion Prevention in Database.* CoRR, abs/1311.6578

Christopher, M. (2000). The agile supply chain-Competitive in volatile market. *Industrial Marketing Management, 29*(1), 37–44. doi:10.1016/S0019-8501(99)00110-8

Christopher, M., & Holweg, M. (2011). Supply Chain 2.0: Managing supply chains in the era of turbulence. *International Journal of Physical Distribution & Logistics Management, 41*(1), 63–82. doi:10.1108/09600031111101439

Chu, M-T., KrishnaKumar, P., & Khosla, R. (2014). *Mapping knowledge sharing traits to business.* Academic Press.

Chuanqi, H. (2001). *Knowledge Innovation: New Focus of Competition: Front of Second Modernization.* Economic Management Press.

Chu, M. T., Shyu, J. Z., Tzeng, G. H., & Khosla, R. (2007). Comparison among Three Analytical Methods for Knowledge Communities Group-Decision Analysis. *Expert Systems with Applications, 33*(4), 1011–1024. doi:10.1016/j.eswa.2006.08.026

Chu, M. T., Shyu, J. Z., Tzeng, G. H., & Khosla, R. (2007). Using Non-Additive Fuzzy Integral to Assess Performance of Organization Transformation via Communities of Practice. *IEEE Transactions on Engineering Management, 54*(2), 1–13. doi:10.1109/TEM.2007.893987

Ciulin, D. (1979, July). Statistical accumulation in time for distribution of noise in L2. *Proceedings of theInternational Symposium on Circuits and Systems*, Tokyo, Japan.

Ciulin, D. (2007, December 3-12). About Sign function and some extensions. *Proceedings of the CISSE '07 Online E-Conference.*

Ciulin, D. (2007a). Motor that assures space displacements of a vehicle by means of inertial forces. Idea for European Project Proposal, Proceedings of ERIMA07' symposium, Biarritz.

Ciulin, D. (2008). System to produce mechanical inertial force and/or torque. *Proceedings of the International Joint Conference on Computer, Information and System Science and engineering (CIS²E '08).*

Ciulin, D. (2010a). Loops and extensions to meromorphic signals. *Proceedings of theInternational Conference on Advances in Recent Technologies in Communication&Computing, ARTCom '10*, Kottayam, Kerala, India.

Ciulin, D. (2010b, December 3-12). Models for some smart toys and extensions. *Proceedings of CISSE '10 Online E-Conference.*

Ciulin, D. (2011). A Nearly One-to-One Method to Convert Analogue Signals into a Small Volume of Data. Second Part - 2-D Signals and More. *International Journal of Strategic Information Technology and Applications*, *2*(4).

Ciulin, D., & Longchamp, J.-F. (1995). Verfahren und Vorrichtung zur Reduzierung der Nutzbandbreite eines bandbegrenzten Signals durch Kodieren desselben und Verfahren und Vorrichtung zum Dekodieren des bandbegrenzten Signals-Verfahren und Vorrichtung zur Reduzierung der Nutzbandbreite ein..." European patent: DE58908835D - 1995-02-09.

Ciulin, D., (2010). A Nearly One-to-One Method to Convert Analog Signals into a Small Volume of Data. First Part: 1-D Signals. *International Journal of Strategic Information Technology and Applications*, *1*(4).

Ciulin, D., (2013). Contribution to a future inertial motor and more. *International Journal of Strategic Information Technology and Applications*, *4*(1).

Ciulin, D., (2013a). About space-time and more. *International Journal of Strategic Information Technology and Applications*, *4*(3).

Ciulin, D. (2006, November 26–December 1). Inverse Problem for a Car Headlight Reflector. *Proceedings of Virtual Concept '06*, Playa Del Carmen, Mexico.

Ciulin, D. (2009). *System to produce mechanical inertial force and/or torque. In Technological Developments in Education and Automation.* London: Springer.

Clatworthy, J., Buick, D., Hankins, M., Weinman, J., & Horne, R. (2005). The use and reporting of cluster analysis in health psychology: A review. *British Journal of Health Psychology*, *10*(3), 329–358. doi:10.1348/135910705X25697 PMID:16238852

Clemons, E. K., & Row, M. C. (1992). Information technology and industrial cooperation: The changing economics of coordination and ownership. *Journal of Management Information Systems*, *9*(2), 9–28. doi:10.1080/07421222.1992.11517956

CN Franchise at a Glance. (n.d.). Retrieved from https://franchisemeets.com/report/asia/CN/

Cohendet, P., & Meyer-Krahmer, F. (2001). The Theoretical and Policy Implications of Knowledge Codification. *Research Policy*, *30*(9), 1563–1591. doi:10.1016/S0048-7333(01)00168-8

Cohen, W. M., & Levintal, D. A. (1989). Innovation and learning: The two faces of R&D. *The Economic Journal*, *99*(49), 569–596. doi:10.2307/2233763

Cohen, W. M., & Levinthal, D. A. (1990). Absorptive capacity: A new perspective on learning and innovation. *Administrative Science Quarterly*, *35*(1), 28–152. doi:10.2307/2393553

Colle, R., & Roman, R. (2003). Challenges in the Telecentre Movement. In S. Marshall, W. Taylor, & X. Yu (Eds.), *Closing the Digital Divide: Transforming Regional Economics and Communities with Information Technology*. Westport, CT: Praeger.

Conner, M., & Norman, P. (Eds.). (2005). Predicting health behaviour (2nd ed. rev.). Buckingham, UK: Open University Press.

Coppinger, V., Smith, V., & Titus, J. (1980). Incentives and Behavior in English, Dutch, and Sealed-bid Auctions. *Economic Inquiry*, *18*, 1-22.

Coutinho, S. (2008). Self-efficacy, metacognition, and performance. *North American Journal of Psychology*, *10*(1), 165–172.

Cox, J. C., Smith, V. L., & Walker, J. M. (1988, March). Theory and Individual Behavior of First-Price Auctions. *Journal of Risk and Uncertainty*, *1*(1), 61–99. doi:10.1007/BF00055565

Creswell, J. W. (2008). *Educational research* (3rd ed.). Upper Saddle River, NJ: Pearson.

Cronin, J. J. Jr, Brady, M. K., & Hult, G. T. M. (2000). Assessing the effects of quality, value, and customer satisfaction on consumer behavioural intentions in service environments. *Journal of Retailing*, *76*(2), 193–218. doi:10.1016/S0022-4359(00)00028-2

Crosier, S. (2009). *John Snow: The London Cholera Epidemic of 1854*. Center for Spatially Integrated Social Science, Regents of University of California, Santa Barbara. Retrieved on October 14, 2010. http://www.csiss.org/classics/content/8

Cuiping, W. (2008). A Review of Research in Knowledge Management and Information Guarantee of National Innovation System. *Library and Information Service*, (2), 203-205.

Dai, M. D. M., & Schonfeld, P. (1998). Metamodels for estimating waterway delays through series of queues. *Transportation Research Part B: Methodological*, *32*(1), 1–19. doi:10.1016/S0191-2615(97)00003-9

Daniel, D. E. (2008). *Executive Summary: Thoughts on Creating More Tier One Universities in Texas*. The University of Texas at Dallas. Retrieved on May 28, 2010. http://www.utdallas.edu/president/documents/executive-summary.pdf

Daniel, D. R. (1961). Management Information Crisis. *Harvard Business Review*, *39*(5), 111–116.

Dasgupta, K., Singh, R., Viswanathan, B., Chakraborty, D., Mukherjea, S., & Nanavati, A. A. (2008). Social ties and their relevance to churn in mobile telecom networks. *Proceedings of the 11th International Conference on Extending Database Technology: Advances in Database Technology*. doi:10.1145/1353343.1353424

Davenport, T. H., Jarvenpaa, S. I., & Beer, M. C. (2004). Improving Knowledge Work Process. *Sloan Management Review*, *34*(4), 53–65.

Davenport, T., DeLong, D., & Beers, M. (1998). Successful knowledge management projects. *Sloan Management Review*, *39*(2), 43–57.

Davidson, J. (2005, June 4). eBay Rules 'stack cards against sellers'. Australian Financial Review, p. 12.

Davis-Kean, P. E., Huesmann, L. R., Jager, J., Collins, W. E., Bates, J. E., & Lansford, J. E. (2008). Changes in the relation of self-efficacy beliefs and behaviors across development. *Child Development*, *79*(5), 1257–1269. doi:10.1111/j.1467-8624.2008.01187.x PMID:18826524

Davis, R. H., Alexander, L. T., & Yelon, S. L. (1974). *Learning system design: an approach to the improvement of instruction*. New York: McGraw-Hill.

Day, J. D., & Wendler, J. C. (1998). Best practices and beyond: Knowledge strategies. *The McKinsey Quarterly*, *1*, 19–25.

De Alcantara, C. H. (2001). *The Development Divide in a Digital Age*. Issue Paper. United Nations Research Institute for Social Development, Technology, Business and Society Programme, No. 4.

Debra, M. (1997). *Innovation Strategy for the Knowledge Economy: The Ken Awakening*. Newton, MA: Butterworth Heinmann.

Desouza, K. C. (2003). Facilitating Tacit Knowledge Exchange. *Communications of the ACM*, *46*(6), 85–86. doi:10.1145/777313.777317

Dess, G., & Robinson, R. (1984). Measuring Organizational Performance in the Absence of Objective Measures. *Strategic Management Journal*, *5*(3), 265–285. doi:10.1002/smj.4250050306

Devlin, K. (1998). Mathematics: The new golden age (in Romanian). Fundatia Theta, Arta grafica, Bucuresti: Romania.

Dick, W., Carey, L., & Carey, J. O. (2008). *The Systematic Design of Instruction* (7th ed.). Boston, MA: Allyn & Bacon.

Domowitz, I. (2002). Liquidity, Transaction costs, and Reintermediation in Electronic Markets. *Journal of Financial Services Research*, *22*(1-2), 141-57.

Donald, B. (2004). *UML basics: The sequence diagrams*. Retrieved from http://www.ibm.com/developerworks/rational/library/3101.html

Donate, M. J., & Canales, J. I. (2012). A new approach to the concept of knowledge strategy. *Journal of Knowledge Management*, *16*(1), 22–44. doi:10.1108/13673271211198927

Donate, M. J., & Guadamillas, F. (2007). The relationship between innovation and knowledge strategies: Its impacts on business performance. *International Journal of Knowledge Management Studies*, *1*(3/4), 388–422. doi:10.1504/IJKMS.2007.012532

Donovan, P. S., & Manuj, I. (2015). A Comprehensive Theoretical Model of the Complex Strategic Demand Management Process. *Transportation Journal*, *54*(2), 213–239. doi:10.5325/transportationj.54.2.0213

Drucker, P. F. (1969). *The age of discontinuity: Guidelines to our changing society*. New York: Harper & Row.

DTI. (1998). *Our competitive future: Building the knowledge driven economy. Technical report*. Department of Trade and Industry London.

Du Val, P. (1973). *Elliptic Functions and Elliptic Curves*. Cambridge: University Press.

Dvir, D., Lipovetsky, S., Shenhar, A., & Tishler, A. (1996). Identifying Critical Success Factors in Defense Development Projects: A Multivariate Analysis. *Technological Forecasting and Social Change*, *51*(2), 151–171. doi:10.1016/0040-1625(95)00197-2

Dyer, J. H. (1997). Effective interfirm collaboration: How transactors minimize transaction costs and maximize transaction value. *Strategic Management Journal*, *18*(7), 535–556. doi:10.1002/(SICI)1097-0266(199708)18:7<535::AID-SMJ885>3.0.CO;2-Z

Dyer, J. H., & Singh, H. (1998). The relational view: Cooperative strategies and sources of interorganizational competitive advantage. *Academy of Management Review*, *23*(4), 660–679.

Eagle, L., & Kitchen, P. J. (2000). IMC, brand communications, and corporate cultures. *European Journal of Marketing*, *34*(5/6), 667–686. doi:10.1108/03090560010321983

Earl, M. (2001). Knowledge management strategies: Toward a taxonomy. *Journal of Management Information Systems*, *18*(1), 215–233.

Earnshaw, E. (1842a). On the nature of the molecular forces which regulate the constitution of the luminiferous ether. *Transaction Cambridge Philosophical Society*, *7*, 87–112.

Egypt I. C. T. Indicators. (n.d.). Retrieved from http://www.egyptictindicators.gov.eg

Ehmke, J. F., Großhans, D., Mattfeld, D. C., & Smith, L. D. (2011). Interactive Analysis of Discrete Event Logistics Systems with Support of a Data Warehouse. *Computers in Industry*, *62*(6), 578–586. doi:10.1016/j.compind.2011.04.007

Eilbeck, J.C., Enolskii, V.Z., Previato, E. (2016). On A Generalized Frobenius - Stickelberger Addition Formula. *Letters in Mathematical Physics*, *63*(1), 5-17.

Ellegard, C., & Grunert, K. (1993). The Concept of Key Success Factors: Theory and Method. In M. Baker (Ed.), *Perspectives on Marketing Management* (pp. 245–274). Chichester, UK: Wiley.

Elyakime, B., Laffont, , Loisel, , & Vuong, . (1994, April-June). First-Price Sealed-Bid Auctions with Secret Reservation Prices. *Annales dEconomie et de Statistique*, (34), 115–141. doi:10.2307/20075949

Ericsson, D. (2011a). Demand chain management: The evolution. *ORiON*, *27*(1), 45–81.

Ericsson, D. (2011b). Demand chain management: The implementation. *ORiON*, *27*(2), 119–145.

Eriksson, H. E., & Penker, M. (2000). *Business modeling with UML.* Wiley & Sons.

ESRI. (2010). *ESRI Info: Company History.* Retrieved on May 6, 2010. http://www.esri.com/about-esri/about/history.html

Estes, W. (1994). Towards a Statistical Theory of Learning. *Psychological Review*, *101*(2), 282-290.

Esteves, J. (2004). *Definition and Analysis of Critical Success Factors for ERP Implementation Projects* (Doctoral thesis). Universitat Politècnica de Catalunya, Barcelona, Spain.

Esteves, J., & Pastor, J. (1999). *An ERP Lifecycle-based Research Agenda.* Paper presented at the First International Workshop on Enterprise Management Resource and Planning Systems EMRPS, Venice, Italy.

EuroPhotonics. (2012). Euro Photonics Autumn 2012, "Atoms signal their entanglement. *Science*, *2012*. doi:10.1126/science.1221856

Evangelista, F., & Hau, L. N. (2009). Organizational context and knowledge acquisition in IJVs: An empirical study. *Journal of World Business*, *44*(1), 63–73. doi:10.1016/j.jwb.2008.03.016

Everrit, B. S., & Dunn, G. (2001). *Multivariate data analysis.* London: Arnold Publishers. doi:10.1002/9781118887486

Fan, I., & Lee, R. (2009). A Complexity Framework on the Study of Knowledge Flow, Relational Capital and Innovation Capacity. *Proceedings of the International Conference on Intellectual Capital, Knowledge Management & Organizational Learning*, (pp. 115 - 123).

Federal Aviation Administration. (1989). *SIMMOD Reference Manual AOR-200.* Office of Operations Research, Federal Aviation Administration. Retrieved from http://www.tc.faa.gov/acb300/how_simmod_works.pdf

Federal Trade Commission. (2007). *Competition in the Real Estate Brokerage Industry Report.* Retrieved from http://www.ftc.gov/reports/realestate/V050015.pdf

Ferguson, J., & Khandewal, V. (1999). *Critical Success Factors (CSF) and the Growth of IT in Selected Geographic Regions.* Paper presented at the Hawaii International Conference on System Sciences, Hawaii, HI.

Finin, T., Labrou, Y., & Mayfield, J. (1995). KQML as an Agent Communication Language. In *Software Agents.* Cambridge, MA: MIT Press.

Fishburn, P. T., Golkar, J., & Taafe, K. (1995). Simulation of Transportation Systems.*Proceedings of the 1995 Winter Simulation Conference*, (pp. 51-54).

Fogg, D. C. (1994). *Team-Based Strategic Planning: A Complete Guide to Structuring, Facilitating, and Implementing the Process*. New York: AMACOM/American Management Association.

Foray, D. (1994). Production and distribution of knowledge in the new systems of innovations: The role of intellectual property rights. *STI Review, 14*, 119-52.

Fowlkes, E. B., & Mallows, C. L. (1983). A Method for Comparing Two Hierarchical Clusterings. *Journal of the American Statistical Association, 78*(383), 553–584. doi:10.1080/01621459.1983.10478008

Franchise 500 Directory 2013. (2013). Entrepreneur.com, Inc.

Franchise 500 Directory 2014. (2014). Entrepreneur.com, Inc.

Franchise 500 Ranking. (2015). *Entrepreneur, 43*(1), 182-245.

Frankle, J. (2010). *Theoretical & Practical Aspects of Algorithmic Trading* (Dissertation). Karlsruhe Institute of Technology.

Frasheri, N. (2002). Critical View of e-Governance Challenges for Developing Countries. IFIP WG9.4 Work Conference ICT and Development, Bangalore, India.

Fraunholz, B., & Unnithan, C. (2004). Critical success factors in mobile communications: A comparative roadmap for Germany and India. *International Journal of Mobile Communications, 2*(1), 87–101. doi:10.1504/IJMC.2004.004489

Freeman, C. (1987). *Technology and Economic Performance: Lessons from Japan*. London: Pinter.

Frohlich, M. T., & Westbrook, R. (2001). Arcs of integration: An international study of supply chain strategies. *Journal of Operations Management, 19*(2), 185–200. doi:10.1016/S0272-6963(00)00055-3

Frohlich, M., & Westbrook, R. (2002b). Demand chain management in manufacturing and services: Web-based integration, drivers and performance. *Journal of Operations Management, 20*(6), 729–745. doi:10.1016/S0272-6963(02)00037-2

Fronimos, D., Magkos, E., & Chrissikopoulous, V. (2014, October). *Evaluating low interaction honeypots and on their use against advanced persistent threats*. Presented at the 18th Panhellenic Conference on informatics, Athens, Greece. doi:10.1145/2645791.2645850

Gagné, C., Price, W. L., & Gravel, M. (2002). Comparing an ACO algorithm with other heuristics for the single machine scheduling problem with sequence-dependent setup times. *The Journal of the Operational Research Society, 53*(8), 895–906. doi:10.1057/palgrave.jors.2601390

Garavelli, C., Gorgoglione, M., & Scozzi, B. (2004). Knowledge management strategy and organization: A perspective of analysis. *Knowledge and Process Management, 11*(4), 273–282. doi:10.1002/kpm.209

Gardner, H. (2004). The Theory of Multiple Intelligences (20th anniversary ed.). New York, NY: Basic Books.

Gardner, R. III, Nobel, M., Hessler, T., Yawn, C. D., & Heron, T. (2007). Tutoring system innovations: Past practice to future prototypes. *Intervention in School and Clinic, 43*(2), 71–81. doi:10.1177/10534512070430020701

Gartner CRM Vendor Guide. (2014). Retrieved from https://www.gartner.com/doc/2679218/gartner-crm-vendor-guide-Harrison

Gartner. (2011). *The Gartner Supply Chain Top 25 for 2011*. Retrieved from http://www.gartner.com/id=1709016

Gates, B. (1999). *Business @ the Speed of Thought: Succeeding in the Digital Economy*. Warner Books.

Gattorna, J. (2010). *Dynamic supply chains: delivering Value Through People* (2nd ed.). London: FT Prentice Hall, Harlow.

Gell-Mann, M. (1994). *The quark and the jaguar*. New York: W.H. Freeman and Company.

Gelo, O., Braakman, D., & Benetka, G. (2008). Quantitative and qualitative research: Beyond the debate. *Integrative Psychological & Behavioral Science*, *42*(3), 266–290. doi:10.1007/s12124-008-9078-3 PMID:18795385

Gendreau, M., Laporte, G., & Guimaraes, E. M. (2001). A divide and merge heuristic for the multiprocessor scheduling problem with sequence dependent setup times. *European Journal of Operational Research*, *133*(1), 183–189. doi:10.1016/S0377-2217(00)00197-1

Genrich, A., & Lautenbach, K. (1981). System Modelling with High Level Petri Nets. *Theoretical Computer Science*, *35*, 1–41.

Georgiadis, D., Shinakis, M., & Tyrinopoulos, Y. (2001). The design and implementation of a demand driven freight transport application. In *Proceedings of the 7th World Congress on Intelligent Systems*.

Gerlach, V. S., & Ely, D. P. (1980). *Teaching & media: a systematic approach* (2nd ed.). Englewood Cliffs, NJ: Prentice-Hall.

Ghazinour, K., & Ghayoumi, M. (2015, November). *A dynamic trust model enforcing security policies*. Presented at the International Conference on Intelligent Information processing, Security and Advanced Communication, Batna, Algeria. doi:10.1145/2816839.2816909

Gibson, N., Holland, C., & Light, B. (1999). *A Critical Success Factors Model for Enterprise Resource Planning Implementation*. Paper presented at the European Conference on Information Systems, Copenhagen, Denmark.

Giddens, A. (1991). *Modernity and Self-identity: Self and Society in the Late Modern Age*. Cambridge, UK: Polity Press.

Gilbo, E. P. (1993). Airport capacity – representation, estimation, optimization. *IEEE Transactions on Control Systems Technology*, *1*(3), 144–154. doi:10.1109/87.251882

Goddard, R. D., LoGerfo, L., & Hoy, W. K. (2004). High school accountability: The role perceived collective efficacy. *Educational Policy*, *18*(3), 403–425. doi:10.1177/0895904804265066

Godsell, J., Harrison, A., Emberson, C., & Storey, J. (2006). Customer responsive supply chain strategy: An unnatural act? *International Journal of Logistics*, *9*(1), 47–56. doi:10.1080/13675560500534664

Goes, P. B. (2013). Design science in top information systems research journals. *Management Information Systems Quarterly*, *38*(1), 3–8.

Goh, A. (2004, October). University of South Australia‘, Enhancing Organizational Performance Through Knowledge Innovation: A Proposed Strategic Management Framework. *Journal of Knowledge Management Practice*.

Goldstein, J. (2013, October 13). Trading Places. *The New York Times*, p. MM14.

Gorovaia, N., & Windsperger, J. (2010). The use of knowledge transfer mechanisms in franchising. *Knowledge and Process Management*, *17*(1), 12–21. doi:10.1002/kpm.337

Gotteland, J. B., Durand, N., Alliot, J. M., & Page, E. (2001). Aircraft ground traffic optimization. In *4th USA/Europe Air Traffic Management Seminar* (pp. 04-07).

Goursat, E. (1949). *Cours d'Analyse Mathématique* (Vol. II). Paris: Gauthier Villard.

Graham-Row, D. (2001). Robots Beat Human Commodity Traders. *New Scientist*, *14*(15).

Graham, S. (2011). Self-efficacy and academic listening. *Journal of English for Academic Purposes*, *10*(2), 113–117. doi:10.1016/j.jeap.2011.04.001

Granados, M. (2003). Mapping Data on Enrolled Students. In D. Teodorescu (Ed.), Using Geographic Information Systems in Institutional Research. Jossey-Bass. doi:10.1002/ir.90

Granger. A.R. (1995). Fluid Mechanics. (1995). New York: Dover Publications, INC.

Grant, R. M. (1996). Toward a Knowledge-Based Theory of the Firm. *Strategic Management Journal*, *17*(S2), 109–122. doi:10.1002/smj.4250171110

Grant, R. M. (2002). *Contemporary strategy analysis. Concepts, techniques, and applications* (4th ed.). Boston: Blackwell Publishers.

Grant, R. M., & Baden-Fuller, C. (2004). A knowledge accessing theory of cooperation agreements. *Journal of Management Studies*, *41*(1), 61–79. doi:10.1111/j.1467-6486.2004.00421.x

Greenwald, A. (2003). The 2002 Trading Agent Competition: An Overview of Agent Strategies. *AI Magazine*, *24*(1), 83-92.

Guadamillas, F., Donate, M. J., & Sánchez de Pablo, J. D. (2006). Sharing knowledge in cooperation agreements to build collaborative advantage. In S. Martínez-Fierro, J. A. Medina-Garrido, & J. Ruiz-Navarro (Eds.), *Utilizing information technology in developing cooperation agreements among organizations* (pp. 99–122). Hershey, PA: IGI Global.

Guarniere, M., Marinovoc, S. & Basin, D. (2016). *Strong and provably secure database access control.* CoRR, abs/1512.01479

Gue, K. R., & Kang, K. (2001). Staging Queues in Material Handling and Transportation Systems. In *Proceedings of the 2001 Winter Simulation Conference* (pp. 1104-1108). doi:10.1109/WSC.2001.977421

Gulati, R., Nohria, N., & Zaheer, L. (2000). Strategic networks. *Strategic Management Journal*, *21*(3), 203–215. doi:10.1002/(SICI)1097-0266(200003)21:3<203::AID-SMJ102>3.0.CO;2-K

Gunasekaran, S., & Garets, D. (2004). Managing the IT Strategic Planning Process. In Healthcare Information Management Systems Cases, Strategies, and Solutions. Springer. doi:10.1007/978-1-4757-4041-7_2

Guo, C., Zhibin, J., Zhang, H., & Li, N. (2012). Decomposition-based classified ant colony optimization algorithm for scheduling semiconductor wafer fabrication system. *Computers & Industrial Engineering*, *62*(1), 141–151. doi:10.1016/j.cie.2011.09.002

Gupta, K., Sleezer, C., & Russ-Eft, D. F. (2006). *A practical guide to needs assessment* (2nd ed.). San Francisco, CA: John Wiley and Sons.

Gupta, S. R., & Smith, J. S. (2006). Algorithms for single machine total tardiness scheduling with sequence dependent setups. *European Journal of Operational Research*, *175*(2), 722–739. doi:10.1016/j.ejor.2005.05.018

Hadfield, B. (1995). *Wealth Within Reach.* Cypress Publishing.

Hamel, G. (1991). Competition for competence and interpartner learning within international cooperation agreements. *Strategic Management Journal*, *12*, 83–103. doi:10.1002/smj.4250120908

Hamilou. (2003). *Modelling Cadastral Transactions with the graphical object–oriented language UML.* Author. (in Greek)

Harrington, L. H., Boyson, S., & Corsi, T. M. (2011). *X-SCM: The new science of X-treme supply chain management.* New York: Routledge.

Harris, R. (1998). Information Technology – The New Cargo Cult? Information Technology in Developing Countries. *Newsletter of the International Federation and Information Processing (IFIP) Working Group 9.4*, *8*(1).

Harrison, Lee, & Neale. (2003). *The practice of supply chain management: Where theory and application converge.* New York: Springer.

Hashem, S. (1999). Technology Access Community Centers in Egypt: A Mission for Community Empowerment. *Proceedings of the Internet Society Conference.*

Havnes, A. (2008). Peer-mediated learning beyond the curriculum. *Studies in Higher Education, 33*(2), 193–204. doi:10.1080/03075070801916344

Hawryszkiewycz, I. T. (2001). *Introduction to system analysis and design.* Frenchs Forest, Australia: Prentice Hall.

Hayne, S., Smith, C., & Vijayasarathy. (2003). Who Wins on eBay: An Analysis of Bidders and their Bid Behaviors. *Electronic Markets, 13*(4), 262-293.

Heeks, R. (2005). *ICTs and the MDGs: on the Wrong Track.* Information for Development Magazine.

Helina, M., & Vesa, H. (2008). Data, Information and Knowledge in Regional Innovation Networks. *European Journal of Innovation.*

Helios, V., & Hidalgo, A. (2008). Towards a National Innovation System in México Based on Knowledge. *The International Journal of Technology. Knowledge in Society, 4*(1), 1832–366.

Hennig-Thurau, T., & Klee, A. (1997). The impact of customer satisfaction and relationship quality on customer retention: A critical reassessment and model development. *Psychology and Marketing, 14*(8), 737–764. doi:10.1002/(SICI)1520-6793(199712)14:8<737::AID-MAR2>3.0.CO;2-F

Heracleous, L. (1998). Strategic Thinking or Strategic Planning. *Long Range Planning, 31*(3), 481–487. doi:10.1016/S0024-6301(98)80015-0

Herrero, J. G., Berlanga, A., Molina, J. M., & Casar, J. R. (2005). Methods for operations planning in airport decision support systems. *Applied Intelligence, 22*(3), 183–206. doi:10.1007/s10791-005-6618-z

Hevner, A. R., March, S. T., Park, J., & Ram, S. (2004, March). Design Sciences in Information System Research. *Management Information Systems Quarterly, 28*(1), 75–105.

Hitt, M. A., Ireland, R. D., & Santoro, M. D. (2004). Developing and managing cooperation agreements, building social capital and creating value. In A. Ghobadian et al. (Eds.), *Strategy and performance: Achieving competitive advantage in the global marketplace.* New York: Palgrave. doi:10.1057/9780230523135_2

Hofstede, G. (1991). *Cultures and organizations: Software of the mind.* New York: McGraw-Hill.

Hollander, S. (1987). *Classical Economics, B.* New York: Blackwell.

Home Instead Senior Care opens 1,000th franchise Location and expands into China. (2013). Retrieved from http://libezp.lib.lsu.edu/login?url=http://search.ebscohost.com/login.aspx?direct=true&db=edsgbc&AN=edsgcl.351529234&site=eds-live&scope=site&profile=eds-main

Horstmeier, T., & de Haan, F. (2001). Influence of ground handling on turn round time of new large aircraft. *Aircraft Engineering and Aerospace Technology, 73*(3), 266–270. doi:10.1108/00022660110390677

Hossein, V., Abbas, S., Mohammad, R. T. J., & Fataneh, S. S. (2012). Investigation Critical Success Factors of Customer Relationship Management Implementation. *World Applied Sciences Journal, 18*(8), 1052–1064.

Hryshko, A., & Downs, T. (2004). System for Foreign Exchange Trading Using Genetic Algorithms and Reenforcement Learning. *International Journal of Systems Sciences, 35*(13-14), 763-774.

Hsiao, Y. P., Brouns, F., Kester, L., & Sloep, P. B. (2009). *Using Peer Tutoring to Optimize Knowledge Sharing in Learning Networks: A Cognitive Load Perspective*. Retrieved March 6, 2011 from http://celstec.org/printpdf/1210

Huang, H. H., & Chiu, C. K. (2006). Exploring customer satisfaction, trust and destination loyalty in tourism. *Journal of American Academy of Business*, *10*(1), 156–159.

Huang, Y., Jiang, Z., Liu, L., Song, B., & Han, L. (2015). Building a knowledge map model situated in product design. *International Journal of Information Technology and Management*, *14*(1), 76. doi:10.1504/IJITM.2015.066059

Huang, Z. (1998). Extensions to the K-means Algorithm for Clustering Large Datasets with Categorical Values. *Data Mining and Knowledge Discovery*, *2*(3), 283–304. doi:10.1023/A:1009769707641

Hu, C., Cao, N., & Zhang, M. (2008). *The Transformation of Information Service and its Development Strategy for Innovative Nation. Journal of Shanxi University:Philosophy and Social Sciences Edition.*

Huggins, R., & Johnston, A. (2010). Knowledge Flow and Inter-firm Networks: The Influence of Networks Resources, Spatial Proximity and Firm Size. *Entrepreneurship & Regional Development*, *22*(5), 457–484. doi:10.1080/08985620903171350

Hung, Y. F., & Chang, C. B. (2002). Dispatching Rules Using Flow-Time Predictions for Semiconductor Wafer Fabrications. *Journal of the Chinese Institute of Industrial Engineers*, *19*(1), 67–75. doi:10.1080/10170660209509184

Huplic, V., Pouloudi, A., & Rzevski, G. (2002). Towards an integrated approach to knowledge management: Hard, soft, and abstract issues. *Knowledge and Process Management*, *9*(2), 90–102. doi:10.1002/kpm.134

Hwang, C. L., & Yoon, K. (1981). *Multiple Attribute Decision Making: Methods and Applications, A State-of-Art Survey*. New York: Springer-Verlag. doi:10.1007/978-3-642-48318-9

IBM BCS. (2003). *Transforming your supply chain to on demand: Competitive advantage or competitive necessity?*. Business Consulting Services Report (No. G510-3322-00).

ICT Trust Fund. (n.d.). Retrieved from http://www.ictfund.org.eg

IFAC. (2012). IFAC Keyword List of Control Terminology.

Information and Decision Support Center. (n.d.). Retrieved from http://www.idsc.gov.eg

Inkpen, A. C. (1998). Learning, knowledge acquisitions, and cooperation agreements. *European Management Journal*, *16*(2), 223–229. doi:10.1016/S0263-2373(97)00090-X

Inkpen, A. C. (2000). A note on the dynamics of learning alliances: Competition, cooperation, and relative scope. *Strategic Management Journal*, *21*(7), 775–779. doi:10.1002/1097-0266(200007)21:7<775::AID-SMJ111>3.0.CO;2-F

Inkpen, A. C., & Beamish, P. W. (1997). Knowledge, bargaining power, and the instability of international. *Joint Ventures Academy of Management Review*, *22*(1), 177–202.

International Telecommunication Union. (n.d.). Retrieved from http://www.itu.int

Ireland, R. D., Hitt, M. A., & Vaidyanath, D. (2002). Alliance management as a source of competitive advantage. *Journal of Management*, *28*(3), 413–446. doi:10.1177/014920630202800308

Ishlinsky, A. (1984). *Orientation, gyroscopes et navigation par inertie* (Vol. 1 & 2). Moscou: MIR.

Isson, J., & Harriott, J. (2013). *Win with advanced business analytics: Creating business value from your data*. Wiley and SAS Business Series.

Ives, B., & Mason, R. O. (1990). Can information technology revitalize your customer service? *The Academy of Management Executive*, *4*(4), 52–69. doi:10.5465/AME.1990.4277208

Jaidi, F., & Ayachi, F. L. (2015, January). *The problem of integrity in rbac-based policies within relational databases: Synthesis and problem study*. Presented at the 9th International Conference on Ubiquitous Information Management and Communication, Bali, Indonesia. doi:10.1145/2701126.2701196

Jan, A. U., & Contreras, V. (2016). Success model for knowledge management systems used by doctoral researchers. *Computers in Human Behavior*, *59*, 258–264. doi:10.1016/j.chb.2016.02.011

Jardine, D. D. (2003). Using GIS in Alumni Giving and Institutional Advancement. In D. Teodorescu (Ed.), Using Geographic Information Systems in Institutional Research. Jossey-Bass. doi:10.1002/ir.94

Jeanne, L. (1999). Linking competitive advantage with communities of practice. *Journal of Management Inquiry*, *8*(1), 5–16. doi:10.1177/105649269981002

Jeng, J., & Bailey, T. (2012). Assessing customer retention strategies in mobile telecommunications: Hybrid MCDM approach. *Management Decision*, *50*(9), 1570–1595. doi:10.1108/00251741211266697

Jenkins, A., Kock, N., & Wellington, R. (1999). A Field Study of Success and Failure Factors in Asynchronous Groupware Supported Process Improvement Groups. *Business Process Management Journal*, *5*(3), 238–253. doi:10.1108/14637159910283010

Jensen, K. (1981). Colored Petri Nets and the Invariant Method. *Theoretical Computer Science*, *14*(3), 317–336. doi:10.1016/0304-3975(81)90049-9

John, S., & Patricia, A. H. (2000). Knowledge Diffusion through Strategic Communities. *Sloan Management Review*, *41*(2), 63.

Johnson, M. E., & Whang, S. (2002). E-business and supply chain management: An overview and framework. *Production and Operations Management*, *11*(4), 413–423. doi:10.1111/j.1937-5956.2002.tb00469.x

Jonassen, D. H., & Land, S. M. (2000). *Theoretical foundations of learning environments*. Mahwah, NJ: Lawrence Erlbaum.

Jones, C. (2013). *What Do We Know about High-Frequency Trading?*. Working Paper. Columbia Business School.

Judge, T. A., Erez, A., Bono, J. E., & Thoresen, J. (2002). Are measures of self-esteem, neuroticism, locus of control, and generalized self-efficacy indicators of a common core construct? *Journal of Personality and Social Psychology*, *83*(3), 693–710. doi:10.1037/0022-3514.83.3.693 PMID:12219863

Justis, R. T., & Judd, R. J. (2002). *Franchising*. DAME Publishing.

Justis, R. T., & Vincent, W. S. (2001). *Achieving wealth through franchising*. Adams Media Corporation.

Juttner, U., Christopher, M., & Godsell, J. (2010). A strategic framework for integrating marketing and supply chain strategies. *The International Journal of Logistics Management*, *21*(1), 104–126. doi:10.1108/09574091011042205

Kagel, J. H. (1997). Auctions: A Survey of Experimental Research. In J. H. Kagel & A. E. Roth (Eds.), *The Handbook of Experimental Economics* (pp. 501–586). Princeton University Press.

Kale, P., Singh, H., & Perlmutter, H. (2000). Learning and protection of proprietary assets in cooperation agreements: Building relational capital. *Strategic Management Journal*, *21*, 217–237. doi:10.1002/(SICI)1097-0266(200003)21:3<217::AID-SMJ95>3.0.CO;2-Y

Kambow, N., & Passi, L. K. (2014). Honeypots: The need of network security. *International Journal of Computer Science and Information Technologies*, *5*(5), 60986101.

Kamel, S. (1995) Information Superhighways, a Potential for Socioeconomic and Cultural Development. In *Managing Information and Communications in a Changing Global Environment:Proceedings of the 6th Information Resources Management Association International Conference (IRMA).*

Kamel, S. (1998). Decision Support Systems and Strategic Public Sector Decision Making. In *Egypt in Information Systems for Public Sector Management Working Paper Series*. Institute for Development Policy and Management, University of Manchester, Paper No. 3.

Kamel, T. (2006). *Egypt Reforms: An update from the ICT Sector*. Academic Press.

Kamel, S. (1997). DSS for Strategic Decision-Making. In M. Khosrowpour & J. Liebowitz (Eds.), *Information Technology Management in Modern Organizations* (pp. 168–182). Hershey, PA: Idea Group Publishing.

Kamel, S. (2004). Diffusing ICT Usage Through Technology Access Clubs: Closing the Digital Divide. *Proceedings of the Information Science, Technology and Management (CISTM)Conference on Improving Business Performance through Knowledge Management.*

Kamel, S. (2005a). Assessing the Impacts of Establishing an Internet Cafe in the Context of a Developing Nation.*Proceedings of the 16th International IRMA Conference on Managing Modern Organizations with Information Technology.*

Kamel, S. (2005b). The Evolution of Information and Communication Technology Infrastructure in Egypt. In G. Hunter & A. Wenn (Eds.), *Information Systems in an e-World* (pp. 117–135). The Information Institute.

Kamel, S. (2009). The Evolution of the ICT Sector in Egypt – Partnership4Development. *Proceedings of the 11th International Business Information Management Association (IBIMA) Conference on Innovation and Knowledge Management in Twin Track Economies: Challenges and Opportunities.*

Kamel, S., & Tooma, E. (2005). *Exchanging Debt for Development: Lessons from the Egyptian Debt-for-Development Swap Experience. Working Document.* World Summit on the Information Society.

Kamra, A., Bertino, E., & Lebanon, G. (2008, June). *Mechanisms for database intrusion detection and response*. Presented at the Second SIGMOD PhD Workshop on Innovative Database Research, Vancouver, Canada. doi:10.1145/1410308.1410318

Kamra, A., Terzi, E., & Bertina, E. (2008). Detecting anomalous access patterns in relational databases. *The VLDB Journal*, *17*(5), 1063–1077. doi:10.1007/s00778-007-0051-4

Kauffman, R., & Wood, C. (2008). Research Strategies for E-Business: A Philosophy of Science View in the Age of the Internet. In R. Kauffman & P. Tallon (Eds.), *Economics, Information Systems, and Electronic Commerce: Empirical Research. M. E. Sharp, Inc.*

Kearsley, G. (2004). *Online education: Learning and teaching in cyberspace*. Belmont, CA: Thompson.

Keith, A. R., & Eli, J. (2008). Customer relationship management: Finding value drivers. *Industrial Marketing Management*, *37*(2), 120–130. doi:10.1016/j.indmarman.2006.08.005

Kerzner, H. (1989). *A System Approach to Planning Scheduling and Controlling*. New York: Project Management.

Khadilkar, H., & Balakrishnan, H. (2013). *Network congestion control of airport surface operations. Journal of Guidance, Control and Dynamics.*

Khandewal, V., & Miller, J. (1992). Information System Study. In *Opportunity Management Program*. New York: IBM Corporation.

Khanna, T., Gulati, R., & Nohria, N. (1998). The dynamics of learning alliances: Competition, cooperation, and relative scope. *Strategic Management Journal*, *19*(3), 193–210. doi:10.1002/(SICI)1097-0266(199803)19:3<193::AID-SMJ949>3.0.CO;2-C

Kharche, S., Patil, J., Gohad, K., & Ambetkar. (2015). *Preventing sql injection attack using pattern matching algorithm.* CoRR, abs/1504.06920

Kim, K. Y., Yun, D. K., & Kim, D. Y. (2009). Expectations measurements in mobile data service: A case study. *International Journal of Mobile Communications*, *7*(1), 91–116. doi:10.1504/IJMC.2009.021674

Kim, S. J., Cho, D. E., & Yeo, S. S. (2014). Secure model against apt in m-connected scada network. *International Journal of Distributed Sensor Networks.*

Kim, S., Cho, N. W., Lee, Y. J., Kang, S., Kim, T., Hwang, H., & Mun, D. (2013). Application of density-based outlier detection to database activity monitoring. *Information Systems Frontiers*, *15*(1), 55–65. doi:10.1007/s10796-010-9266-9

Kim, Y. M., & Schonfeld, P. (1995). Neural network estimation of waterway lock service times. *Transportation Research Record*, *1497*, 36–43.

Kim, Y., & Baylor, A. L. (2006). A social-cognitive framework for pedagogical agents as learning companions. *ETR&D*, *54*(6), 569–596. doi:10.1007/s11423-006-0637-3

King-Sears, M. E. (2001). Institutionalizing peer-mediated instruction and interventions in school: Beyond Train and Hope. *Remedial and Special Education*, *22*(2), 89–101. doi:10.1177/074193250102200203

Kirkley, W. W. (2016). Entrepreneurial behaviour: The role of values. *International Journal of Entrepreneurial Behavior & Research*, *22*(3), 290–328. doi:10.1108/IJEBR-02-2015-0042

Kiyosaki, R. (2000). *Rich dad, poor dad.* Time Warner.

Kleinsasser, J. (2012, September 21). Physicist explains significance of Higgs boson discovery. *Phys.org*. Retrieved from http://phys.org/news/2012-09-physicist-significance-higgs-boson-discovery.html#_methods=onPlusOne%2C_ready%2C_close%2C_open%2C_resizeMe%2C_renderstart%2Concircled%2Conauth%2Conload&id=I0_1350801851796&parent=http%3A%2F%2Fphys.org

Klemperer, P. (2004). *Auctions: Theory and Practice*. Princeton, NJ: Princeton University Press.

Kogut, B., & Zander, U. (1992). Knowledge of the firms, combinative capabilities, and the replication of technology. *Organization Science*, *3*(3), 383–397. doi:10.1287/orsc.3.3.383

Kransberg, M. (1991). IT as Revolution. In T. Forester (Ed.), *Computers in the Human Context*. MIT Press.

Krishna, V. (2002). *Auction Theory*. San Diego, CA: Academic Press.

Kuang, J. L., & Leung, A. Y. T. (2005). Homoclinic orbits of the Kovalevskaya top with perturbations. *Journal of Applied Mathematics and Mechanics*, *85*(4).

Kul, G., Luong, D., Xie, T., & Coonan, P. (2016, April). *Ettu: Analyzing query intents in corporate databases*. Presented at 2016 World Wide Conference, Montreal, Canada.

Kundu, A., Sural, S., & Majumdar, A. K. (2010). Database intrusion detection using sequence alignment. *International Journal of Information Security*, *9*(3), 179–191. doi:10.1007/s10207-010-0102-5

Kyriazopoulos, P. (2000). The modern firm at the beginning of the 21st Century (A. S. Ekdotiki, Ed.). Academic Press.

Kyriazopoulos, P. (2001). *Apply Marketing*. Athens Sychroni Ekdotiki.

Ladon, I. F. (1949). Les bases du calcul vectorielle (Vol. 1 & 2). Romania.

Lam, S. Y., Shankar, V., Erramilli, M. K., & Murthy, B. (2004). Customer value, satisfaction, loyalty, and switching costs: An illustration from a business-to-business service context. *Journal of the Academy of Marketing Science*, *32*(3), 293–311. doi:10.1177/0092070304263330

Lane, P. J., & Lubatkin, M. (1998). Relative absorptive capacity and interorganizational learning. *Strategic Management Journal*, *19*(5), 461–477. doi:10.1002/(SICI)1097-0266(199805)19:5<461::AID-SMJ953>3.0.CO;2-L

Leistner, F. (2010), Mastering Organizational Knowledge Flow, how to Make Knowledge Sharing Work. SAS Institute, 183.

Leonard, D., & Sensiper, D. (1998). The role of tacit knowledge in group innovation. *California Management Review*, *40*(3), 112–131. doi:10.2307/41165946

Les, C. B. (2012). Laser swarm could swat asteroids away. *Photonics Spectra*, June.

Lesser, E. L., & Storck, J. (2001). Communities of Practice and Organizational Performance. *IBM Systems Journal*, *40*(4), 831–841. doi:10.1147/sj.404.0831

Levin, D., Cross, R., Abrams, L., & Lesser, E. (2002). *Trust and knowledge sharing: A critical combination.* IBM Institute for Knowledge-Based Organizations.

Levin, D., & Cross, R. (2004). The strength of weak ties you can trust: The mediating role of trust in effective knowledge transfer. *Management Science*, *50*(11), 1477–1490. doi:10.1287/mnsc.1030.0136

Li, Y., Yang, D., Ren, J., & Hu, C. (2009, August). *An approach for database intrusion detection based on the event sequence clustering*. Presented at the Fifth International Joint Conference on INC, IMS and IDC, Seoul, South Korea. doi:10.1109/NCM.2009.30

Lian, K.-Y., Wang, L.-S., Fu, L.-C. (1994). Controllability of Spacecraft Systems in a Central Gravitational Field. *IEEE Transaction on Automatic Control, 39*(12).

Liebowitz, J. (2007). Developing knowledge and learning strategies in mobile organisations. *International Journal Mobile Learning and Organizations*, *1*(1), 5–14. doi:10.1504/IJMLO.2007.011186

Liebowitz, J. (2013). *Big data and business analytics*. CRC Press. doi:10.1201/b14700

Light, C., Light, A., & Teulade, V. (2010). *A look at the future of mobile data*. Retrieved from www.pwc.com/en GX/gx/communications/assets/Mobile_Content_final.pdf

Ligorio, M. B., Talamo, A., & Simmons, R. (2002). Synchronic tutoring of a virtual community. *Mentoring & Tutoring*, *10*(2), 137–152. doi:10.1080/1361126022000002455

Lindsay, R.B. (1961). Physical mechanics. London: D.Van Nostrand Company, Inc.

Lin, L. M., & Hsia, T. L. (2011). Core capabilities for practitioners in achieving e-business innovation. *Computer in Human Behavior Journal*, *27*(5), 1844–1891. doi:10.1016/j.chb.2011.04.012

Lin, S. Y., & Overbaugh, R. C. (2009). Computer-mediated discussion, self-efficacy and gender. *British Journal of Educational Technology*, *40*(6), 999–1013. doi:10.1111/j.1467-8535.2008.00889.x

Liu, S. (2005). Study on Knowledge Intensive Services in Innovation System. *Science of Science and Management of S & T*, (3), 61-65.

Liu, S. T., Chen, Y. M., & Hung, H. C. (2012, August). *N-victims: An approach to determine N victims for APT investigations*. Presented at the 13th International Workshop on information Security Applications, Jeju Island, South Korea. doi:10.1007/978-3-642-35416-8_16

Li, W. (2009). *A Review of Literature on Knowledge Information Service for Regional Innovation System*. IEEE. doi:10.1109/ICMSS.2009.5301524

Lizarraga, A., Lysecky, R. & Lysecky, S. (2013). Dynamic profiling and fuzzy-logic-based optimizing of sensor network platforms. *ACM Transactions on Embedded Computing Systems, 13*(3).

Love, J. (1995). *McDonald's: behind the arches*. Bantam Books.

Loyarte, E., & Rivera, O. (2007). Communities of practice: A model for their cultivation. *Journal of Knowledge Management, 11*(3), 67–77. doi:10.1108/13673270710752117

Lu, L., Leung, K., Koch, P., & Tong, K. (2006). Managerial knowledge sharing: The role of individual, interpersonal, and organizational factors. *Management and Organization Review, 2*(1), 15–41. doi:10.1111/j.1740-8784.2006.00029.x

Lundvall, B. (1992). *National Systems of Innovation: towards a theory of innovation and interactive learning*. London: Pinter Publishers.

Luo, Y. (2008). Structuring interorganizational cooperation: The role of economic integration in cooperation agreements. *Strategic Management Journal, 29*(6), 617–637. doi:10.1002/smj.677

Luszczynska, A., Scholz, U., & Schwarzer, R. (2005). The general self-efficacy scale: Multicultural validation studies. *The Journal of Psychology, 139*(5), 439–457. doi:10.3200/JRLP.139.5.439-457 PMID:16285214

Luszczynska, A., & Schwarzer, R. (2005). Social cognitive theory. In M. Conner & P. Norman (Eds.), *Predicting health behavior* (2nd ed.; pp. 127–169). Buckingham, UK: Open University Press.

Lutters, Ackerman, Boster, & McDonald. (2000). Mapping Knowledge Networks in Organizations: Creating a Knowledge Mapping Instrument. *Proceedings of the Americas Conference on Information Systems* (AMCIS), (pp. 2014-18).

Lyons, M., Akamatsu, S., Kamachi, M., & Gyoba, J. (1998). Coding facial expressions with Gabor wavelets Automatic Face and Gesture Recognition. *Third IEEE International Conference*, (pp. 200-205).

MacKay, D. J. C. (2003). *Information Theory, Inference, and Learning Algorithms*. Cambridge University Press.

Madhani, P. M. (2015). Demand Chain Management: Enhancing Customer Lifetime Value through Integration of Marketing and Supply Chain Management, *UP. The Journal of Business Strategy, 12*(3), Madhani, P. M. (2013). Marketing Firms vs. SCM-led Firms: DCM Comparatistics. *SCMS Journal of Indian Management, 10*(2), 5–19.

Maier, R., & Remus, U. (2002). Defining process-oriented knowledge management strategies. *Knowledge and Process Management, 9*(2), 103–118. doi:10.1002/kpm.136

Malhotra, Y. (2004), Why Knowledge Management Systems Fail? Enablers and Constraints of Knowledge Management in Human Enterprises. American Society for Information Science and Technology Monograph Series.

Mali, Y. M., Raj, R. M. J. V., & Gaykar, A. T. (2014, April). Honeypot: A tool to track hackers. *Engineering Science and Technology: An International Journal, 4*(2), 52–55.

Mandiant. (2010). *M Trends:The advanced persistent threat*. Retrieved May 1, 2016, from www.princeton.edu/~yctwo/files/readings/M-Trends.pdf

Manoj, E., & Sunil, S. (2011). Role of switching costs in the service quality, perceived value, customer satisfaction and customer retention linkage. *Asia Pacific Journal of Marketing and Logistics*, *23*(3), 327–345. doi:10.1108/13555851111143240

Mansell, R., & When, U. (1998). *Knowledge Societies: Information Technology for Sustainable Development*. Oxford, UK: Oxford University Press.

Margolis, H. (2005). Increasing struggling learners self-efficacy: What tutors can do and say. *Mentoring & Tutoring*, *13*(2), 221–238. doi:10.1080/13611260500105675

Martinelli, D., & Schonfeld, P. (1995). Approximating delays at interdependent locks. *Journal of Waterway, Port, Coastal, and Ocean Engineering*, *121*(6), 300–307. doi:10.1061/(ASCE)0733-950X(1995)121:6(300)

Ma, S. (2004). A Research on the Functions of Intermediary Service of Science and Technology in National Innovation System and the Construction of the Organization System. *China Soft Science*, (1), 109-113.

Matsushima, R., & Shiomi, K. (2003). Social self-efficacy and interpersonal stress in adolescence. *Social Behavior and Personality*, *31*(4), 323–332. doi:10.2224/sbp.2003.31.4.323

Matthews, R., & Sample, I. (1996). Breakthrough as scientists beat gravity. *The Journal of ideas*, 4.

McCabe, K., Rassenti, S., & Smith, V. (1991). Testing Vickrey's and Other Simultaneous Multiple Unit Versions of the English Auction. Research in Experimental Economics, 4, 187.

McCormick, B. G. (2003). Developing Enterprise GIS for University Administration: Organizational and Strategic Considerations. In D. Teodorescu (Ed.), Using Geographic Information Systems in Institutional Research. Jossey-Bass.

McDermott, R. (1999). Learning across teams. *Knowledge Management Review*, *8*(3), 32–36.

McLure Wasko, M., & Faraj, S. (2000). It is what one does: Why people participate and help others in electronic communities of practice. *The Journal of Strategic Information Systems*, *9*(2-3), 155–173. doi:10.1016/S0963-8687(00)00045-7

Meier, M. (2011). Knowledge management in cooperation agreements: A review of empirical evidence. *International Journal of Management Reviews*, *13*, 1–23. doi:10.1111/j.1468-2370.2010.00287.x

Meng, X. (2005). Information Guarantee System Construction Supporting Knowledge Creation. Information and Documentation Services, (3), 15-19.

Mentzer, J. T., DeWitt, W., Keebler, J. S., Min, S., Smith, C. D., & Zacharia, Z. G. (2001a). What is supply chain management. In *Supply Chain Management*. Thousand Oaks, CA: Saga Publications.

Mesquita, L. F., Anand, J., & Brush, T. H. (2008). Comparing the resource-based and relational views: Knowledge transfer and spillover in vertical alliances. *Strategic Management Journal*, *29*(9), 913–941. doi:10.1002/smj.699

Milgrom, P. (2004). *Putting Auction Theory to Work*. Boston, MA: Cambridge University Press. doi:10.1017/CBO9780511813825

Miller, C. (2004). Human-Computer Etiquette: Managing Expectations with Intentional Agents. *Communications of the ACM*, *47*(4), 31-34.

Miller, R. (2002). *Don't Let Your Robots Grow up to Be Traders: Artificial Intelligence, Human Intelligence, and Asset-market Bubbles*. Working Paper. Miller Risk Advisors.

Ministry of Communications and Information Technology. (2005a). Egypt Information Society Initiative (4th ed.). Author.

Ministry of Communications and Information Technology. (2005b). *Building Digital Bridges*. Egypt's Vision of the Information Society.

Ministry of Communications and Information Technology. (2007). *Egypt's ICT Golden Book*. Author.

Ministry of Communications and Information Technology. (2009). *The Future of the Internet Economy in Egypt*. Statistical Profile.

Ministry of Communications and Information Technology. (2011). *ICT Indicators in Brief*. Retrieved 9 December from http://www.mcit.gov.eg/Publications

Ministry of Communications and Information Technology. (2013). *ICT Strategy*. Author.

Misner, C.W. & Thorne, K. (1988). *Gravitation*. W. H. Freeman and Company.

Mon, D. L., Cheng, C. H., & Lin, J. C. (1994). Evaluating Weapon System Using Fuzzy Analytic Hierarchy Process Based on Entropy Weigh. *Fuzzy Sets and Systems*, *61*, 1–8.

Mondaq.com. (2009). *Franchising in China update - Australian franchisors moving Into China*. Retrieved from http://libezp.lib.lsu.edu/login?url=http://search.ebscohost.com/login.aspx?direct=true&db=edsnbk&AN=12B77223A134EA60&site=eds-live&scope=site&profile=eds-main

Moon, D., Im, H., Lee, J. D., & Park, J. H. (2014). MLDS: Multi-layer defense system for preventing advanced persistent threats. *Symmetry*, *6*(4), 997–1010. doi:10.3390/sym6040997

Mora, V. J. (2003). Applications of GIS in Admissions and Targeting Recruiting Efforts. In D. Teodorescu (Ed.), Using Geographic Information Systems in Institutional Research. Jossey-Bass. doi:10.1002/ir.89

Mortensen, J., Eustace, C., & Lannoo, K. (1997). *Intangibles in the European economy*. CEPS Workshop on intangibles in the European economy, Brussels, Belgium.

Mowery, D. C., Oxley, J. E., & Silverman, B. S. (1998). Technological overlap and interfirm cooperation: Implications for the resource-based view of the firm. *Research Policy*, *27*(5), 507–523. doi:10.1016/S0048-7333(98)00066-3

Mullainathan, S., & Thaler, R. (2002). *International Encyclopedia of the Social and Behavioral Sciences*. Retrieved from www.iies.su.se/nobel/papers/Encyclopedia%202.0.pdf

Murchison, S. B. (2010). Uses of GIS for Homeland Security and Emergency Management at Higher Education Institutions. In N. Valcik (Ed.), *Institutional Research: Homeland Security*. Hoboken, NJ: John Wiley and Sons, Inc. doi:10.1002/ir.344

Muris, P. (2001). A Brief Questionnaire for Measuring Self-Efficacy in Youths. *Journal of Psychopathology and Behavioral Assessment*, *23*(3), 145–149. doi:10.1023/A:1010961119608

Musashi, M. (2009). *The Book of Five Rings: Classic Treaty on Military Strategy*. Wildside Press.

Mutambo, L. S. (2003). *The Unified Modeling Language (UML) in Cadastral System Development* (Doctoral Dissertation). International Institute For Geo-information Science and Earth Observation(ITC), Enschede, The Netherlands. Retrieved from http://www.modelsphere.org

Myalapalli, V. K. (2014, March). An appraisal to overhaul database security configurations. *International Journal of Scientific and Research Publications*, *4*(3), 1–4.

Namjae, C., Guo Zheng, L., & Che-Jen, S. (2007). An Empirical study on the effect of individual factors on Knowledge Sharing by Knowledge type. *Journal of Global Business and Technology*, *3*, 1.

NASA.gov. (2012). NASA. Retrieved from http://www.nasa.gov/mission_pages/station/main/index.html

Nauss, R. M. (2008). Optimal sequencing in the presence of setup times for tow/barge traffic through a river lock. *European Journal of Operational Research*, *187*(3), 1268–1281. doi:10.1016/j.ejor.2006.06.071

Nelson, R. R., & Rosenberg, N. (1993). Technical Innovation and National Systems. In R. R. Nelson (Ed.), *National Innovation Systems. A Comparative Analysis*. New York: Oxford University Press.

Neto, I., Kenny, C., Janakiram, S., & Watt, C. (2005). Look before You Leap: The Bumpy Road to E-Development. In E-development from excitement to effectiveness. World Summit on the Information Society.

Newman, B., & Conrod, K. W. (1999). *A frame work for characterizing knowledge management method, practices and technologies*. Retrieved from http://www.3-cities.com/~bonewman/newman_conrad%20PAKM2000-16.pdf

Nissen, M. E. (2002). An Extended Model of Knowledge flow Dynamics. *Communications of the ACM*, *8*, 251–266.

Nonaka, I. (1994). A dynamic theory of organizational knowledge creation. *Organization Science*, *5*(1), 14–37. doi:10.1287/orsc.5.1.14

Nonaka, I., & Takeuchi, H. (1995). *The knowledge-creating company*. New York: Oxford University Press.

Norin, A., Granberg, T. A., Varbrand, P., & Yuan, D. (2009). *Integrating optimization and simulation to gain more efficient airport logistics*. Eighth USA/Europe Air Traffic Management Research and Development Seminar.

O'Brien, E., & Hall, T. (2004). Training Needs Analysis: the first step in authoring e-learning content. *Proceedings of the 2004 ACM Symposium on Applied Computing*. Retrieved August 16, 2009 from http://delivery.acm.org.library.capella.edu/10.1145/970000/968090/p935-obrien.pdf?key1=968090&key2=3210411521&coll=portal&dl=ACM&CFID=824734&CFTOKEN=52522302

Ocasio, W. (1997). Towards an attention-based view of the firm. *Strategic Management Journal*, *18*(S1), 187–206. doi:10.1002/(SICI)1097-0266(199707)18:1+<187::AID-SMJ936>3.3.CO;2-B

Odoni, A. R., Bowman, J., Delahaye, D., Deyst, J. J., Feron, E., Hansman, R. J., & Simpson, R. W. et al. (1997). *Existing and required modeling capabilities for evaluating ATM systems and concepts*. International Center for Air Transportation, Massachusetts Institute of Technology.

OECD. (1996). *The Knowledge Based Economy*. Paris: Science, Technology and Industry Outlook.

OECD. (1999). *Measuring Knowledge in Learning Economies and Societies*. Draft Report on Washington Forum.

Offerman, H. (2001). Simulation to Support the Airport Stakeholder Decision-Making Process. *Air & Space Europe*, *3*(1/2), 60–67. doi:10.1016/S1290-0958(01)90017-6

Oh, W. (2002). C2C vs. B2C: A Comparison of the Winner's Curse in Two Types of Electronic Auctions. *International Journal of Electronic Commerce, 6*(4), 115-138.

Oliveira, M. (1999). Core competencies and the knowledge of the firm. In M. A. Hitt, (Eds.), *Dynamic strategic resources: Development, diffusion, and integration* (pp. 17–41). New York: John Wiley and Sons.

Oracle (2012). *DISA oracle 11 database security technical implementation guide Version 8 Release 1.9*. Retrieved May 1, 2016, from http://iase.disa.mil/stigs/app_security/database/

Oracle (2016b). *DISA oracle 12c database security technical implementation guide Version 1 Release 3*. Retrieved May 1, 2016, from http://iase.disa.mil/stigs/app_security/database/

Oracle. (2011). *Oracle Database Security Guide 11g Release 1 (11.1)*. Retrieved May 1, 2016, from http://docs.oracle.com/cd/B28359_01/network.111/b28531.pdf

Oracle. (2016a). *Oracle Database Security Guide 12c Release 1 (12.1)*. Retrieved May 1, 2016, from http://docs.oracle.com/database/121/DBSEG/toc.htm

Oredsson, S., Jonsson, H., Rognes, J., Lind, L., Göransson, K. E., Ehrenberg, A., & Farrohknia, N. et al. (2011). A systematic review of triage-related interventions to improve patient flow in emergency departments. *Scandinavian Journal of Trauma, Resuscitation and Emergency Medicine*, *19*(1), 43. doi:10.1186/1757-7241-19-43

Ormrod, J. E. (2006). *Educational psychology: Developing learners* (5th ed.). Upper Saddle River, NJ: Pearson/Merrill Prentice Hall.

Ormsby, T., Napoleon, E., Burke, R., Grossl, C., & Bowden, L. (2008). *Getting to Know ArcGIS Desktop*. Redlands, CA: ESRI Press.

Othman, A. (2012). *Automated Market-Making: Theory & Practise* (Thesis). Carnegie Melon University School of Computer science, CMU-CS-12-123.

Oxley, J. E., & Sampson, R. C. (2004). The scope and gobernance of international R&D alliances. *Strategic Management Journal*, *25*(89), 723–749. doi:10.1002/smj.391

Özcanl, C. (2012). *A proposed Framework for CRM On-Demand System Evaluation* (Master of Science Thesis). Retrieved from http://www.opencrx.org/

Paci, H., Mece, E. K., & Xhuvani, A. (2012). Protecting Oracle PLP/SQL source code from a DBA user. *International Journal of Database Management Systems*, *4*(4), 43–52. doi:10.5121/ijdms.2012.4404

Pajares, F. (2009). Toward a positive psychology of academic motivation: The role of self-efficacy beliefs. In R. Gilman, E. S. Huebner, & M. J. Furlong (Eds.), *Handbook of positive psychology in schools* (pp. 149–160). New York: Taylor & Francis.

Palca, B.P. (1991). An introduction to complex function theory. Berlin: Springer Verlag.

Palloff, R. M., & Pratt, K. (2005). *Collaborating Online: learning together in community*. San Francisco, CA: Jossey-Bass.

Panigrahi, S., Sural, S., & Majumdar, A. K. (2013). Two-stage database intrusion detection by combining multiple evidence and belief update. *Information Systems Frontiers*, *15*(1), 35–53. doi:10.1007/s10796-010-9252-2

Papassapa, R., & Miller, K. E. (2007). Relationship quality as a predictor of B2B customer loyalty. *Journal of Business Research*, *60*(1), 21–31. doi:10.1016/j.jbusres.2005.11.006

Papastavrou, S., Samaras, G., & Pitoura, E. (1999). Mobile Agents for WWW Distributed Database Access. *Proceedings of the 5th International Conference on Data Engineering*. doi:10.1109/ICDE.1999.754928

Parise, S., & Henderson, J. C. (2001). Knowledge resource exchange in strategic alliances. *IBM Systems Journal*, *40*(4), 908–924. doi:10.1147/sj.404.0908

Parunak, H.V.D., Nickels, A. & Frederiksen, R. (2014, May). *An agent-based framework for dynamical understanding of dns events (DUDE)*. ACySe, Paris, France.

Passchyn, W., Briskorn, D., & Spieksma, F. (2016b). Mathematical Programming Models for Lock Scheduling with an Emission Objective. *European Journal of Operational Research*, *248*(3), 802–814. doi:10.1016/j.ejor.2015.09.012

Passchyn, W., Coene, S., Briskorn, D., Hurink, J., Spieksma, F., & Vanden Berghe, G. (2016a). The lockmasters problem. *European Journal of Operational Research*, *251*(2), 432–441. doi:10.1016/j.ejor.2015.12.007

Patel, P., & Pavitt, K. (1994). The nature and economic importance of national innovation systems. *STI Review*, (14), 9-32.

Paunonen, S. V., & Hong, R. Y. (2010). Self-efficacy and the prediction of domain-specific cognitive abilities. *Journal of Personality*, *78*(1), 339–360. doi:10.1111/j.1467-6494.2009.00618.x PMID:20433622

Peekacity, A. P. I. (n.d.). Retrieved from http://www.peekacity.com/help/API.aspx

Pellitteri, J. (2002). The Relationship between Emotional Intelligence and Ego Defense Mechanisms. *The Journal of Psychology*, *136*(2), 182–194. doi:10.1080/00223980209604149 PMID:12081093

Peng, F., & Hu, C. (1998). *Information Guarantee for Scientific Research*. Wuhan, China: Wuhan University Press.

Penrose, R. (2005). *The road to reality*. Vintage books.

Pérez-Nordtvedt, L., Kedia, B. L., Datta, D. K., & Rasheed, A. A. (2008). Effectiveness and efficiency of cross-border knowledge transfer: An empirical examination. *Journal of Management Studies*, *45*(4), 714–744. doi:10.1111/j.1467-6486.2008.00767.x

Perrigot, R., & Pénard, T. (2013). Determinants of e-Commerce strategy in franchising: A resource-based View. *International Journal of Electronic Commerce*, *17*(3), 109–130. doi:10.2753/JEC1086-4415170305

Petchbordee, S., & Sortrakul, T. (2005). Online Auction Site: Proxy Bid Service with Time Awareness Engine. *Proceedings of the 4th International Conference on eBusiness*.

Petri, C. (1966). *Communication in Automata*. Technical Report RADC-TR-65-377. Rome Air Development Center.

Phillips, J. J. (2000). *Performance analysis and consulting*. Alexandria, VA: ASTD.

Photonics Media. (2014). Photon state teleported at 25 km. Retrieved from http://www.photonics.com/Article.aspx?PID=6&AID=56699&refer=weeklyNewsletter&utm_source=weeklyNewsletter_2014_09_25&utm_medium=email&utm_campaign=weeklyNewsletter

Photonics.com. (2012), Knots in light! Retrieved from http://www.photonics.com/Article.aspx?AID=52196&refer=weeklyNewsletter&utm_source=weeklyNewsletter_2012_11_01&utm_medium=email&utm_campaign=weeklyNewsletter

Pinto, J., & Prescott, J. (1988). Variations in Critical Success Factors over the Stages in the Project Lifecycle. *Journal of Management*, *14*(1), 5–18. doi:10.1177/014920638801400102

Pinto, J., & Slevin, D. (1987). Critical Factors in Successful Project Implementation. *IEEE Transactions on Engineering Management*, *34*(1), 22–27. doi:10.1109/TEM.1987.6498856

Poellhuber, B., Chomienne, M., & Karsenti, T. (2008). The effect of peer collaboration and collaborative learning on self-efficacy and persistence in a learner-paced continuous intake model. *Journal of Distance Education*, *22*(3), 41–62.

Poggenpoel, M., & Myburgh, C. P. H. (2005). Obstacles in Qualitative Research: Possible Solutions. *Education*, *126*(2), 304–311.

Politis, J. (2003). The connection between trust and knowledge management: What are its implications for team performance. *Journal of Knowledge Management*, *7*(5), 55–66. doi:10.1108/13673270310505386

Poole, C.P., Jr. (1967). Electron spin resonance. A comprehensive treatise on experimental techniques. London: Interscience Publishers.

Porter, D., & Vragov, R. (2006). An Experimental Examination of Demand Reduction in Multi-unit Versions of the Uniform-price, Vickrey, and English Auctions. *Managerial and Decision Economics*, *27*(6), 445-458,

Porter, M. E. (1985). *Competitive advantage: Creating and sustaining superior performance*. New York: Collier Macmillan.

Porter, M. E. (1996). What is Strategy? *Harvard Business Review*, (November-December), 61–78.

Prat-Sala, M., & Redford, P. (2010). The interplay between motivation, self-efficacy, and approaches to studying. *The British Journal of Educational Psychology*, *80*(2), 283–305. doi:10.1348/000709909X480563 PMID:20021729

Press, L. (1999b, October-November). Developing Countries Networking Symposium. *OnTheInternet*.

Press, L. (1999a, January-February). *Connecting Villages: The Grameen Bank Success Story. OnTheInternet.*

PropertyShark API. (n.d.). Retrieved from http://www.propertyshark.com/Real-Estate-Reports/2009/07/30/new-propertyshark-api-for-blogs-and-websites/

Radwan, S., Kamel, S., & El Oraby, N. (2009). The Experience of the Italian-Egyptian Debt Swap Program (2001-2008). Partners for Development, Technical Support Unit, Embassy of Italy (Egypt) and Ministry of International Cooperation (Egypt).

Ramanathan, V., & Schonfeld, P. (1994). Approximate delays caused by lock service interruptions. *Transportation Research Record*, *1430*, 41–49.

Ramaprasad, A., & Williams, J. (1998). *The Utilization of Critical Success Factors: A Profile*. Paper presented at the 29th Annual Meeting of the Decision Sciences Institute, Las Vegas, NV.

Ramaseshan, B., Yip, L. S., & Pae, J. H. (2006). Power, satisfaction and relationship commitment in Chinese store-tenant relationship and their impact on performance. *Journal of Retailing*, *82*(1), 63–70. doi:10.1016/j.jretai.2005.11.004

Ratcliffe-Martin, V., Coakes, E., & Sugden, G. (2000). Knowledge Management Issues in Universities. *Vine Journal*, *121*, 14-19.

Ravizza, S., Chen, J., Atkin, J. A. D., Burke, E. K., & Stewart, P. (2013). The trade-off between taxi time and fuel consumption in airport ground movement. *Public Transport*, *4*(1-2), 25–40. doi:10.1007/s12469-013-0060-1

Raynor, M. E. (2007). *The Strategy Paradox: Why Committing to Success Leads to Failure (and What to Do About It)*. New York: Doubleday.

Reinartz, W., & Kumar, V. (2000). The Impact of Customer Relationship Characteristics on Profitable Lifetime Duration. *Journal of Marketing*, 67.

Report, C. (2007). *How Cisco Enables Electronic Interactions with Sales, Manufacturing, and Service Partners*. Cisco IT Case Study. Retrieved from http://www.cisco.com/web/about/ciscoitatwork/downloads/ciscoitatwork/pdf/Cisco_IT_Case_Study_B2B.pdf

Rigby, Reichheld, & Phil. (2002). Avoid the Four Perils of CRM.[PubMed]. *Harvard Business Review*, *80*(2), 101–109.

Rockart, J. (1979, March-April). Chief Executives Define Their Own Information Needs. *Harvard Business Review*, 81–92.

Rockart, J. (1982). The Changing Role of the Information Systems Executive: A Critical Success Factors Perspective. *Sloan Management Review*, *23*(1), 3–13.

Rockart, J., & Van Bullen, C. (1986). A Primer on Critical Success Factors. In J. Rockart & C. Van Bullen (Eds.), *The Rise of Management Computing*. Homewood, IL: Irwin.

Rodríguez, C. M., & Wilson, D. T. (2002). Relationship bonding and trust as a foundation for commitment in U.S.-Mexican cooperation agreements: A structural equation modeling approach. *Journal of International Marketing*, *10*(4), 53–76. doi:10.1509/jimk.10.4.53.19553

Roth, A., & Ockenfels, A. (2002, September). Last-Minute Bidding and the Rules for Ending Second-price Auctions: Evidence from eBay and Amazon Auctions on the Internet. *The American Economic Review*, *92*(4), 1093–1103. doi:10.1257/00028280260344632

Rust, R., Katherine, T., Lemon, N., & Zeithaml, A. (2003). *Return on Marketing: Using Customer Equity to Focus Marketing Strategy. Journal of Marketing.*

Saaty, T. L. (1977). A Scaling Method for Priorities in Hierarchical Structures. *Journal of Mathematical Psychology*, *15*(2), 234–281. doi:10.1016/0022-2496(77)90033-5

Saaty, T. L. (1980). *The Analytic Hierarchy Process*. New York: McGraw-Hill.

Sampson, R. C. (2005). Experience effects and collaborative returns in R&D alliances. *Strategic Management Journal*, *26*(11), 1009–1031. doi:10.1002/smj.483

Sánchez de Pablo, J. D. (2009). Influencia de la estrategia genérica de la empresa en la estrategia empresarial. *Revista Europea de Dirección y Economía de la Empresa*, *18*(4), 155–174.

Sánchez de Pablo, J. D., Guadamillas, F., Dimovski, V., & Škerlavaj, M. (2008). Exploratory study of organizational learning network within a Spanish high-tech company. *Proceedings of Rijeka Faculty of Economics Journal of Economics and Business*, *26*(2), 257–277.

Sanchez, R., & Mahoney, J. T. (1996). Modularity, flexibility, and knowledge management in product and organization design. *Strategic Management Journal*, *17*(S2), 63–76. doi:10.1002/smj.4250171107

Santos, J. B., & DAntone, S. (2014). Reinventing the wheel? A critical view of demand-chain management. *Industrial Marketing Management*, *43*(6), 1012–1025. doi:10.1016/j.indmarman.2014.05.014

Saud, Z., & Islam, M. H. (2015, September). *Towards proactive detection of advanced persistent threat (apt) attacks using honeypots*. Presented at the 8th International Conference on Security of Information and networks, Sochi, Russian Federation. doi:10.1145/2799979.2800042

Sawyer, Rolf, & Wigand. (2005). Redefining access: Uses and roles of ICT in the US residential real estate industry from 1995 to 2005. *Journal of Information Technology*, *20*(4), 213–223. doi:10.1057/palgrave.jit.2000049

Saxton, T. (1997). The effects of partner and relationship characteristics on alliances outcomes. *Academy of Management Journal*, *40*(2), 443–461. doi:10.2307/256890

Schmaltz, R., Hagenhoff, S., & Kaspar, C. (2004). *Information technology support for knowledge management in cooperation.* Paper presented at the Fifth European Conference on Organizational Knowledge, Learning, and Capabilities, Innsbruck, Austria.

Schmidt, A. M., & DeShon, R. P. (2010). The moderating effects of performance ambiguity on the relationship between self-efficacy and performance. *The Journal of Applied Psychology*, *95*(3), 572–581. doi:10.1037/a0018289 PMID:20476834

Scholz, U., Gutiérrez-Doña, B., Sud, S., & Schwarzer, R. (2002). Is general self-efficacy a universal construct? Psychometric findings from 25 countries. *European Journal of Psychological Assessment*, *18*(3), 242–251. doi:10.1027//1015-5759.18.3.242

Schreuder, A. N., Krige, L., & Parker, E. (2000). The franchisee lifecycle concept – A new paradigm in managing the franchisee-franchisor relationship.*Proceedings of the 14th annual International Society of Franchising Conference.*

Schware, R. (2005). Overview: E-Development: From Excitement to Effectiveness. In E-development from excitement to effectiveness. World Summit on the Information Society.

Schwartz, P. (1991). *The Art of the Long View: Planning for the Future in an Uncertain World.* Currency Doubleday.

Seetharaman, P. B., & Chintagunta, P. (1998). A model of inertia and variety-seeking with marketing variables. *International Journal of Research in Marketing*, *15*(1), 1–17. doi:10.1016/S0167-8116(97)00015-3

SeqDiag. (n.d.). *Sequence Diagram.* Retrieved from http://www.visual-paradigm.com/VPGallery/diagrams/Sequence.html

Shabayek, A. A., & Yeung, W. W. (2002). A Simulation Model for the Kwai Chung Container Terminals in Hong Kong. *European Journal of Operational Research*, *140*(1), 1–11. doi:10.1016/S0377-2217(01)00216-8

Shabtai, A., Bercovitch, M., Rokach, L., Gal, Y., Elovici, Y. & Shmueli, E. (2016). Behavioral study of users when interacting with active honeytokens. *ACM Transactions on Information and Systems Security, 18*(9).

Shannon, C. E. (1949). Communication in the Presence of Noise. *Proceedings of the IRE*, 37.

Sharma, N., Young, L., & Wilkinson, I. (2006). *The commitment mix: multi-aspect commitment in international trading relationships in India.* Unpublished Document.

Sherali, H. D., Hobeika, A. G., Trani, A. A., & Kim, B. J. (1992). An integrated simulation and dynamic programming approach for determining optimal runway exit locations. *Management Science*, *38*(7), 1049–1049. doi:10.1287/mnsc.38.7.1049

Simon, H. A. (1971). Designing organizations for an information rich world. In Computers, Communications, and the Public Interest, (pp. 38-52). Baltimore, MD: The Johns Hopkins Press.

Simon, M. D., Heflinger, L. O., & Ridgway, S. L. (1997, April). Spin stabilized magnetic levitation. *American Journal of Physics*, *65*(4).

Sivoukhine, D. (1982). *Cours de physique générale, Mécanique*. Moscou: MIR.

Smirnov, V. I. (1955). *Cours de Mathématiques supérieures* (R. Technica, ed., Vol. 3).

Smith, L. D., Ehmke, J. F., Mattfeld, D. C., Waning, R., & Hellman, L. (2014). Strategic Decision Support for Airside Operations at Commercial Airports. In Computational Logistics (LNCS), (vol. 8760, pp. 132–150). Springer. doi:10.1007/978-3-319-11421-7_9

Smith, V. L. (1962). An Experimental Study of Competitive Market Behavior. *The Journal of Political Economy*, *20*(2), 111-137.

Smith, V. L. (1976). Experimental Economics: Induced Value Theory. *American Economic Review*, *66*(2), 274-279.

Smith, V. L. (2003). Constructivist and Ecological Rationality in Economics. *American Economic Review*, *93*(3), 465-508.

Smith, H. M., & Betz, N. E. (2000). Development and validation of a scale of perceived social self-efficacy. *Journal of Career Assessment*, *8*(3), 286. doi:10.1177/106907270000800306

Smith, L. D., & Nauss, R. M. (2010). Investigating strategic alternatives for improving service in an inland waterway transportation system. *International Journal of Strategic Decision Sciences*, *1*(2), 62–81. doi:10.4018/jsds.2010040103

Smith, L. D., Nauss, R. M., Mattfeld, D. C., Ehmke, J. F., & Bahr, F. (2012). Scheduling logistics activities in staged queues with sequence-dependent changeover and processing times. In *Proceedings of the 2012 45th Hawaii International Conference on System Sciences* (pp. 1296-1305). Washington, DC: IEEE Computer Society. doi:10.1109/HICSS.2012.511

Smith, L. D., Nauss, R. M., Mattfeld, D. C., Li, J., & Ehmke, J. F. (2011). Scheduling Operations at System Choke Points with Sequence-dependent Delays and Processing Times. *Transportation Research Part E, Logistics and Transportation Review*, *47*(5), 669–691. doi:10.1016/j.tre.2011.02.005

Smith, L. D., Sweeney, D. C. II, & Campbell, J. F. (2009). Simulation of alternative approaches to relieving congestion at locks in a river transportation system. *The Journal of the Operational Research Society*, *60*(4), 519–533. doi:10.1057/palgrave.jors.2602587

Smith, P. L., & Ragan, T. J. (2005). *Instructional Design* (3rd ed.). Hoboken, NJ: Wiley.

Smith, V. L. (1980). Relevance of Laboratory Experiments to Testing Resource Allocation Theory. In J. Kmenta & J. Ramsey (Eds.), *Evaluation of Econometric Models* (pp. 345–377). San Diego, CA: Academic Press. doi:10.1016/B978-0-12-416550-2.50024-8

Smith, V. L. (2002, October). Method in Experiment: Rhetoric and Reality. *Experimental Economics*, *5*(2), 91–110. doi:10.1023/A:1020330820698

Snowdon, J. L., MacNair, E., Montevecchi, M., Callery, C. A., El-Taji, S., & Miller, S. (2000). IBM journey management library: An arena system for airport simulations. *The Journal of the Operational Research Society*, *51*(4), 449–456. doi:10.2307/254172

Sohrabi, M., Javisi, M. M., & Hashemi, S. (2014, June). Detecting intrusion transactions in database systems: A novel approach. *Journal of Intelligent Information Systems*, *42*(3), 619–644. doi:10.1007/s10844-013-0286-z

Sood, A. K. & Enbody, R. J. (2012). Targeted cyber attacks: A superset of advanced persistent threats. *IEEE Security & Privacy Magazine, 99.*

Soosay, C. A., & Hyland, P. (2015). A decade of supply chain collaboration and directions for future research. *Supply Chain Management: An International Journal*, *20*(6), 613–630. doi:10.1108/SCM-06-2015-0217

Spender, J. C. (1996). Making knowledge the basis of a dynamic theory of the firm. *Strategic Management Journal*, *17*(S2), 45–62. doi:10.1002/smj.4250171106

Stafford, M., & Stern, B. (2002). Consumer Bidding Behavior in On-line Auction Sites. *International Journal of Electronic Commerce*, *7*(1), 135-150.

Stale, G., Cakula, S., & Kapenieks, A. (2011). *Application of a Modelling Method for Knowledge Flow Analysis in an Educational IT Ecosystem.* Virtual and Augmented Reality in Education (VARE 2011), Valmiera, Latvija.

Stuart, T. E. (2000). Interorganizational alliances and the performance of firms: A study of growth and innovation rates in a high-technology industry. *Strategic Management Journal*, *21*(8), 791–811. doi:10.1002/1097-0266(200008)21:8<791::AID-SMJ121>3.0.CO;2-K

Sumner, M. (1999). *Critical Success Factors in Enterprise Wide Information Management Systems Projects.* Paper presented at the Americas Conference on Information Systems, Milwaukee, WI. doi:10.1145/299513.299722

Szymczyk, M. (2009, June). *Detecting botnets in computer networks using multi-agent technology.* Presented at the Fourth International Conference on Dependability of Computer Systems, Brunow, Poland. doi:10.1109/DepCoS-RELCOMEX.2009.46

Tabachmick & Fidell. (1989). *Using multivariate statistics.* New York: Harper Collins Publishers Inc.

Tang, M. T., & Tzeng, G. H. (1999). A Hierarchy Fuzzy MCDM Method for Studying Electronic Marketing Strategies in the Information Service Industry. *Journal of International Information Management*, *8*(1), 1–22.

Tankard, C. (2011). Persistent threats and how to monitor and deter them. *Network Security*, *8*(8), 16–19. doi:10.1016/S1353-4858(11)70086-1

Taylor, D. (2000). Demand amplification: Has it got us beat? *International Journal of Physical Distribution & Logistics Management, 30*(6), 515–533. doi:10.1108/09600030010372630

Technologies, C. A. (2012). *Advanced persistent threats: Defending from the inside out.* Retrieved May 1, 2016, from http://www.ca.com/us/collateral/white-papers/na/Advanced-Persistent-Threats-Defending-From-The-Inside-Out.aspx

The University of Texas at Dallas Office of the Registrar. (2012). *Student Information Systems and Logistical Tracking System.* Author.

The University of Texas at Dallas. (2010). *Enrollment.* Office of Strategic Planning and Analysis. Retrieved on May 17, 2010, from http://www.utdallas.edu/ospa/stats/Enrollment.html

The University of Texas at Dallas. (2012). Student Information Systems. Author.

Thomas, D., & Seid, M. (2000). *Franchising for dummies.* IDG Books.

Thomas, J. C., Kellog, W. A., & Erickson, T. (2001). The Knowledge Management Puzzle: Human and Social factors in Knowledge Management. *IBM Systems Journal, 40*(4), 863–884. doi:10.1147/sj.404.0863

Thomas, R., & McSharry, P. (2015). *Big Data Revolution.* Wiley.

Thorne, K. S. (1994). *Black holes & time warp.* London: W.W. Norton & Company.

Ting, C. J., & Schonfeld, P. (1998). Optimization through simulation of waterway transportation investments. *Transportation Research Record, 1620*, 11–16. doi:10.3141/1620-03

Ting, C. J., & Schonfeld, P. (2001a). Efficiency versus fairness in priority control: Waterway lock case. *Journal of Waterway, Port, Coastal, and Ocean Engineering, 127*(2), 82–88. doi:10.1061/(ASCE)0733-950X(2001)127:2(82)

Ting, C. J., & Schonfeld, P. (2001b). Control alternatives at a waterway lock. *Journal of Waterway, Port, Coastal, and Ocean Engineering, 127*(2), 89–96. doi:10.1061/(ASCE)0733-950X(2001)127:2(89)

Todd, M., Birgit, R., & Kurt, M. (2006). Who Trusts? Personality, Trust and Knowledge Sharing. *Management Learning, 37*(4), 523–540. doi:10.1177/1350507606073424

Topping, K. J. (2005). Trends in peer learning. *Educational Psychology, 25*(6), 631–645. doi:10.1080/01443410500345172

Tsaur, S. H., Tzeng, G. H., & Wang, K. C. (1997). Evaluating Tourist Risks From Fuzzy Perspectives. *Annals of Tourism Research, 24*(4), 796–812. doi:10.1016/S0160-7383(97)00039-5

Turkle, S. (1990). Growing Up in the Age of Intelligent Machines: Reconstructions of the Psychological and Reconsiderations of the Human. In R. Kurzweil (Ed.), *The Age of Intelligent Machines.* Boston, MA: MIT Press.

Türkyilmaz, A., & Özkan, C. (2007). Development of a customer satisfaction index model: An application to the Turkish mobile phone sector. *Industrial Management & Data Systems, 107*(5), 672–687. doi:10.1108/02635570710750426

Tversky, A., & Kahneman, D. (1982). Subjective probability: A judgment of representativeness. In D. Kahneman, P. Slovic, & A. Tversky (Eds.), *Judgment under Uncertainty: Heuristics and Biases* (pp. 32–47). Cambridge, U.K.: Cambridge University Press. doi:10.1017/CBO9780511809477.007

Tzeng, G. H. (1977). A Study on the PATTERN Method for the Decision Process in the Public System. *Japan Journal of Behavior Metrics, 4*(2), 29–44. doi:10.2333/jbhmk.4.2_29

Tzeng, G. H., Shian, T. A., & Lin, C. Y. (1992). Application of Multicriteria Decision Making to the Evaluation of New Energy-System Development in Taiwan. *Energy, 17*(10), 983–992. doi:10.1016/0360-5442(92)90047-4

Tzeng, G. H., & Shiau, T. A. (1987). Energy Conservation Strategies in Urban Transportation: Application of Multiple Criteria Decision-Making. *Energy Systems and Policy*, *11*(1), 1–19.

Tzeng, G. H., & Teng, J. Y. (1994). Multicriteria Evaluation for Strategies of Improving and Controlling Air-Quality in the Super City: A case of Taipei city. *Journal of Environmental Management*, *40*(3), 213–229. doi:10.1006/jema.1994.1016

U.S. Commercial Service. (2008). *China franchising industry*. The JLJ Group.

U.S. Department of Commerce. (1965). *National Technical Information Service*. NASA.

Ulrich, P., & Chacko, J. G. (2005). Overview of ICT Policies and e-Strategies: An Assessment on the Role of Governments. *Journal of Information Technology for Development*, *11*(2), 195–197. doi:10.1002/itdj.20011 PMID:16339190

Umble, E., & Umble, M. (2001). *Enterprise Resource Planning Systems: A Review of Implementation Issues and Critical Success Factors*. Paper presented at the 32nd Decision Sciences Institute Annual Meeting, San Francisco, CA.

United Nations Department of Economics and Social Affairs. (2015). Population Division. Author.

United Nations Economic Commission for Africa. (2003a). *Policies and Plans on the Information Society: Status and Impact*. Author.

United Nations Economic Commission for Africa. (2003b). *E-Strategies*. National, Sectoral and Regional ICT Policies, Plans and Strategies.

Valcik, N. (2003). Building a Space Management System. Midwestern Review of Business and Economics,32, 16-21.

Valcik, N. (2007). The Logistical Tracking System (LTS) Five Years Later: What have we Learned?. In N. Valcik (Ed.), Space: The Final Frontier for Institutional Research. John Wiley and Sons, Inc.

Valcik, N. (2009a). University Enhances Its Logistical Tracking System with GIS. *ESRI ArcNews, 31*(1). Retrieved from http://www.esri.com/news/arcnews/spring09articles/university-enhances.html

Valcik, N. (2009b). *New Homeland Security Concerns Regarding Higher Education Institutions and Chemical Hazardous Materials*. The CIP Report, George Mason University School of Law. Retrieved on May 6, 2010, from http://cip.gmu.edu/archive/cip_report_8.4.pdf

Valcik, N., & Huesca-Dorantes, P. (2003). Building a GIS Database for Space and Facilities Management. In D. Teodorescu (Ed.), Using Geographic Information Systems in Institutional Research. Jossey-Bass.

Valcik, N. (2006). *Regulating the Use of Biological Hazardous Materials in Universities: Complying with the New Federal Guidelines*. Lewiston, NY: Edwin Mellen Press.

Valcik, N. (2010). New Hazardous Materials (HAZMAT) Federal Regulations for Higher Education Institutions. In N. Valcik (Ed.), *Institutional Research: Homeland Security. New Directions for Institutional Research*. Hoboken, NJ: John Wiley and Sons, Inc.

Valcik, N., Aiken, C. L. V., Xu, X., & Al Farhan, M. S. (2009). Homeland Security in the United States: An analysis of the utilization of novel information and virtual technologies for Homeland Security. In K. Jaishankar (Ed.), *International Perspectives on Criminology and Criminal Justice*. New Castle, UK: Cambridge Scholars Publishing.

van der Heijden. (1996). *Kees. Scenarios: The Art of Strategic Conversation*. John Wiley & Sons Limited.

Verstichel, J., De Causmaecker, P., Spieksma, F., & Vanden Berghe, G. (2014). Exact and heuristic methods for placing ships in locks. *European Journal of Operational Research*, *235*(2), 387–398. doi:10.1016/j.ejor.2013.06.045

Verstichel, J., De Causmaecker, P., Spieksma, F., & Vanden Berghe, G. (2014). The generalized lock scheduling problem: An exact approach. *Transportation Research E. Logistics and Transportation Review*, *65*, 16–34. doi:10.1016/j.tre.2013.12.010

Verstichel, J., De Causmaecker, P., & Vanden Berghea, G. (2011). Scheduling algorithms for the lock scheduling problem. *Procedia: Social and Behavioral Sciences*, *20*, 806–815. doi:10.1016/j.sbspro.2011.08.089

Verstichel, J., Kinable, J., De Causmaecker, P., & Vanden Berghe, G. (2015). A Combinatorial Benders decomposition for the lock scheduling problem. *Computers & Operations Research*, *54*, 117–128. doi:10.1016/j.cor.2014.09.007

Vickrey, W. (1961). Counterspeculation, Auctions, and Competitive Sealed Tenders. *The Journal of Finance*, (March), 16.

Vragov, R. (2005). Why is eBay the King of Internet Auctions? An Institutional Analysis Perspective. *eService Journal, 3*(3).

WalkScore API. (n.d.). Retrieved from http://www.walkscore.com/professional/api.php

Wang, C. (2002). Information Guarantee Construction of National Innovation System. Information and Documentation Services, (2), 12-15.

Wang, B., & Kong, J. (2004). Information Needs and Information Guarantee in National Innovation System. *Information Science*, (6), 657–659, 663.

Wang, T., & Libaers, D. (2015). Nonmimetic Knowledge and Innovation Performance: Empirical Evidence from Developing Countries. *Journal of Product Innovation Management*. doi:10.1111/jpim.12306

Wang, Y., Peng, H., Huang, R., Hou, Y., & Wang, J. (2008). Characteristics of distance learners: Research on relationships of learning motivation, learning strategy, self-efficacy, attribution and learning results. *Open Learning*, *23*(1), 17–28. doi:10.1080/02680510701815277

Ward, B. (1990). Planning for Profit. In T. J. Lincoln (Ed.), *Managing Information Systems for Profit* (pp. 103–146). Chichester, UK: John Wiley & Sons.

Webb, T. L., & Sheeran, P. (2008). Mechanisms of implementation intention effects: The role of goal intentions, self-efficacy, and accessibility of plan components. *The British Journal of Social Psychology*, *47*(3), 373–395. doi:10.1348/014466607X267010 PMID:18096108

Wei, C. H., Dai, M. D. M., & Schonfeld, P. (1992). Computational characteristics of a numerical model for series of waterway queues. *Transportation Research Record, 1333*, 45–54.

Wei, G., & Siyuan, J. (2010). Simulation study on closely spaced parallel runway analysis using SIMMOD Plus. 2010. *International Conference on Intelligent Computation Technology and Automation*. IEEE. doi:10.1109/ICICTA.2010.223

Wenger, E. (1998). *Communities of Practice*. Cambridge University Press. doi:10.1017/CBO9780511803932

Wenger, E., McDermott, R. A., & Snyder, W. (2002). *Cultivating Communities of Practice*. Boston: Harvard Business School Press.

White, L., & Yanamandram, V. (2004). Why customers stay: Reasons and consequences of inertia in financial services. *Managing Service Quality*, *14*(2/3), 183–194. doi:10.1108/09604520410528608

White, L., & Yanamandram, V. (2007). A model of customer retention of dissatisfied business services customers. *Managing Service Quality*, *17*(3), 298–316. doi:10.1108/09604520710744317

Whitman, M., & Mattord, H. (2015, October). *Ongoing threats to information protection*. Presented at the Information Security Curriculum Development Conference, Kennesaw, GA.

Wiki, C. R. M. (n.d.). Retrieved from http://en.wikipedia.org/wiki/Customer_relationship_management

Wikipedia. (2012). Carnot cycle. Retrieved from https://en.wikipedia.org/wiki/Carnot_cycle

Wikipedia. (2012). electrostatics. Retrieved from http://en.wikipedia.org/wiki/Electrostatics

Wikipedia. (2012). elliptic functions. Retrieved from http://en.wikipedia.org/wiki/Elliptic_function

Wikipedia. (2012). force. Retrieved from http://fr.wikipedia.org/wiki/Force_(physique)

Wikipedia. (2012). Haar wavelet. Retrieved from http://en.wikipedia.org/wiki/Haar_waveletHaar

Wikipedia. (2012). hysteresis. Retrieved from http://fr.wikipedia.org/wiki/Hyst%C3%A9r%C3%A9sis

Wikipedia. (2012). Kaluza-Klein. Retrieved from http://fr.wikipedia.org/wiki/Th%C3%A9orie_de_Kaluza-Klein

Wikipedia. (2012). Maxwell's equations. Retrieved from http://en.wikipedia.org/wiki/Maxwell's_equations

Wikipedia. (2012). M-theory. Retrieved from http://en.wikipedia.org/wiki/M-theory

Wikipedia. (2012). Nuclear magnetic resonance. Retrieved from http://en.wikipedia.org/wiki/Nuclear_magnetic_resonance

Wikipedia. (2012). Rotation. Retrieved from http://fr.wikipedia.org/wiki/Rotation#En_math.C3.A9matiques

Wikipedia. (2012). Spin. Retrieved from http://en.wikipedia.org/wiki/Spin_(physics)

Wikipedia. (2012). String theory. Retrieved from http://en.wikipedia.org/wiki/String_theory

Wikipedia. (2013). Atom. Retrieved from http://en.wikipedia.org/wiki/Atom

Wikipedia. (2013). Atomic Nucleus. Retrieved from http://en.wikipedia.org/wiki/Atomic_nucleus

Wikipedia. (2013). Causality. Retrieved from https://en.wikipedia.org/wiki/Causality

Wikipedia. (2013). Electron. Retrieved from http://en.wikipedia.org/wiki/Electron

Wikipedia. (2013). Magnetic field. Retrieved from http://en.wikipedia.org/wiki/Magnetic_field

Wikipedia. (2013). Magnetic Moment. Retrieved from http://en.wikipedia.org/wiki/Magnetic_moment

Wikipedia. (2013). Neural network. Retrieved from http://en.wikipedia.org/wiki/Neural_network

Wikipedia. (2013). neuron. Retrieved from http://www.scholarpedia.org/article/Neuron

Wikipedia. (2013). Total order. Retrieved from http://en.wikipedia.org/wiki/Total_order

Wikipedia. (2013). Transducer. Retrieved from http://en.wikipedia.org/wiki/Transducer

Wikipedia. (2013). Visible Spectrum. Retrieved from http://en.wikipedia.org/wiki/Visible_spectrum

Wikipedia. (2013). Wave. Retrieved from http://en.wikipedia.org/wiki/Wave

Wikipedia. (2013). Work function. Retrieved from http://en.wikipedia.org/wiki/Work_function

Wikipedia. (2014). Gyroscope. Retrieved from http://en.wikipedia.org/wiki/Gyroscope

Wikipedia. (2014). Soliton. Retrieved from http://fr.wikipedia.org/wiki/Soliton

Wikipedia. (2014). Soundcloud. Retrieved from https://soundcloud.com/esaops/a-singing-comet

Wikipedia. (2014). Standing Wave. Retrieved from http://en.wikipedia.org/wiki/Standing_wave

Wikipedia. (2014). Telecommunications. Retrieved from http://en.wikipedia.org/wiki/Telecommunication

Wikipedia. (2015). Saser. Retrieved from https://en.wikipedia.org/wiki/Sound_amplification_by_stimulated_emission_of_radiation

Wikipedia. (2016). Curie temperature. Retrieved from https://en.wikipedia.org/wiki/Curie_temperature

Wikipedia. (2016). Electron paramagnetic resonance. Retrieved from https://en.wikipedia.org/wiki/Electron_paramagnetic_resonance

Wikipedia. (2016). gravitational waves. Retrieved from http://www.sciencemag.org/news/2016/02/gravitational-waves-einstein-s-ripples-spacetime-spotted-first-time

Wikipedia. (2016). Levitron. Retrieved from https://en.wikipedia.org/wiki/Levitron

Wikipedia. (2016). Noether's theorem. Retrieved from https://en.wikipedia.org/wiki/Noether%27s_theorem

Wikipedia. (2016). Polaron. Retrieved from https://en.wikipedia.org/wiki/Polaron

Wikipedia. (2016). Reactionless drive. Retrieved from https://en.wikipedia.org/wiki/Reactionless_drive

Wikipedia. (2016). Smaglev. Retrieved from https://en.wikipedia.org/wiki/smaglev

WikiValue. (n.d.). *Value chain*. Retrieved from http://en.wikipedia.org/wiki/Value_chain

Wiklund, J., & Shepherd, D. A. (2009). The Effectiveness of Alliances and Acquisitions: The Role of Resource Combination Activities. *Entrepreneurship Theory and Practice*, *33*(1), 193–212. doi:10.1111/j.1540-6520.2008.00286.x

Wittmann, C. M., Hunt, S. D., & Arnett, D. B. (2009). Explaining alliance success: Competences, resources, relational factors, and resource-advantage theory. *Industrial Marketing Management*, *38*(7), 743–756. doi:10.1016/j.indmarman.2008.02.007

Wolf, D. (2007). *Prepared and Resolved: The Strategic Agenda for Growth, Performance and Change*. DSB Publishing.

Wolfl, A. (2005). *The service economy in OECD countries*. STI working paper 2005/3. Statistical Analysis of Science, Technology and Industry, Paris Cedex.

Wong, W. K., Kao, B., Cheung, D. W. L., Li, R., & Yiu, S. M. (2014, June). *Secure query processing with data interoperability in a cloud database environment*. Presented at the ACM SIGMOD International Conference on Management of Data, Snowbird, UT. doi:10.1145/2588555.2588572

Wood, C. L., Mackiewicz, S. M., Van Norman, R. K., & Cooke, N. L. (2007). Tutoring with technology. *Intervention in School and Clinic*, *43*(2), 108–115. doi:10.1177/10534512070430020201

Wooldridge, M. (2000). On the Sources of Complexity in Agent Design. *Applied Artificial Intelligence*, *14*(7), 623-644.

World Bank. (2008). *Little Data Book on ICT*. Author.

World Bank. (2009). *Little Data Book of ICT*. Author.

World Bank. (2016). *Doing Business: Measuring Business Regulations*. World Bank Group. Retrieved from http://www.doingbusiness.org/rankings

World Population Prospects. (2015). *Facts*. Author.

World Summit on the Information Society. (n.d.). Retrieved from http://www.wsis-online.net

Wu, G., & Huang, Y. (2009, May). *Design of a new intrusion detection system based on database*. Presented at the 2009 International Conference on Signal Processing Systems, Singapore.

Wu, J., & Hounsell, N. (1998). Bus Priority Using Pre-Signals. *Transportation Research Part A, Policy and Practice*, *32*(8), 563–583. doi:10.1016/S0965-8564(98)00008-1

Wu, X., Zhu, X., Wu, G., & Ding, W. (2013). Data mining with big data. *IEEE Transactions on Knowledge and Data Engineering*, *26*(1), 97–107.

Xiao, X. (2004). Information Guarantee Model and Operation Mechanism of Knowledge Innovation. *Journal of Foshan University (Social Science Edition)*, (1), 90-93.

Xiwei, W., & Stößlein, M. (2010). Designing knowledge chain networks in China - A proposal for a risk management system using linguistic decision making. *Technological Forecasting and Social Change*, *77*(6), 902–915. doi:10.1016/j.techfore.2010.01.002

Xu, Y., Gelfer, J. I., Sileo, N., Filler, J., & Perkins, P. G. (2008). Effects of peer tutoring on young childrens social interactions. *Early Child Development and Care*, *178*(6), 617–635. doi:10.1080/03004430600857485

Yanamandram, V. K., & White, L. (2006). Switching barriers in business-to-business services: A qualitative study. *International Journal of Service Industry Management*, *17*(2), 158–192. doi:10.1108/09564230610656980

Yang, H., Zheng, Y., & Zhao, X. (2014). Exploration or exploitation? Small firms alliance strategies with large firms. *Strategic Management Journal*, *35*(1), 146–157. doi:10.1002/smj.2082

Yan, S., Shieh, C., & Chen, M. (2002). A simulation framework for evaluating airport gate assignments. *Transportation Research Part A, Policy and Practice*, *36*(10), 885–898. doi:10.1016/S0965-8564(01)00045-3

Yazdani, N. M., Panahi, M. S., & Poor, E. S. (2013). Intelligent detection of intrusion into database using extended classier system. *Iranian Journal of Electrical and Computer Engineering*, *3*(5), 708–712.

Yuan, X., Ji, B., Yuan, Y., & Zhang, X. (2016). Co-scheduling of lock and water–land transshipment for ships passing the dam. *Applied Soft Computing*, *45*, 150–162. doi:10.1016/j.asoc.2016.04.019

Yum Brands plans to spin off China business. (2015). Dolan Media.

Zack, M. (1999). Developing a knowledge strategy. *California Management Review*, *41*(3), 125–145. doi:10.2307/41166000

Zadeh, L. A. (1981). *A Definition of Soft Computing*. Retrieved from http://www.soft-computing.de/def.html

Zafirovsky, M. (2003). Human Rational Behavior and Economic Rationality. *Electronic Journal of Sociology*, *7*(2).

Zahedi, F. (1987). Reliability of Information Systems Based on Critical Success Factors Formulation. *Management Information Systems Quarterly*, *11*(2), 187–203. doi:10.2307/249362

Zander, U., & Kogut, B. (1995). Knowledge and the speed of transfer and imitation of organizational capabilities: An empirical test. *Organization Science*, *6*(1), 76–92. doi:10.1287/orsc.6.1.76

Zbikowski, K. (2016). Application of Machine Learning Algorithms for Bitcoin Automated trading. In Machine Intelligence and Big Data in Industry (vol. 19, pp. 161-168). Springer International Publishing.

Zeelenberg, M., & Pieters, R. (2004). Beyond valence in customer dissatisfaction: A review and new findings on behavioural responses to regret and disappointment in failed services. *Journal of Business Research*, *57*(4), 445–455. doi:10.1016/S0148-2963(02)00278-3

Zeithaml, V. A., Parasuraman, A., & Berry, L. L. (1990). *Delivering Quality Service: Balancing Customer Perceptions and Expectations*. New York, NY: The Free Press.

Zeng, Q., Chen, W., & Huang, L. (2008). E-business transformation: An analysis framework based on critical organizational dimensions. *Journal of Tsinghua Science and Technology*, *13*(3), 408–413. doi:10.1016/S1007-0214(08)70065-8

Zhao, B. (2003). On the Information Guarantee of Intellectual Innovation Systems. *Information Science*, (1), 10–14.

Zhuge, H., Guo, W., Li, X., & Ding, L. (2006). Knowledge Energy in Knowledge Flow Networks. *Proceedings of the First International Conference on Semantics, Knowledge, and Grid.* IEEE Computer Society.

Zhuge, H. (2003). Component-based Workflow Systems Design. *Decision Support Systems*, *35*(4), 517–536. doi:10.1016/S0167-9236(02)00127-6

Zhuge, H. (2006). Discovery of Knowledge Flow in Science. *Communications of the ACM*, *49*(5), 101–107. doi:10.1145/1125944.1125948

Zhuge, H. (2006). Knowledge flow Network Planning and Simulation. *Decision Support Systems*, *42*(2), 571–592. doi:10.1016/j.dss.2005.03.007

Zhu, L., Schonfeld, P., Kim, Y. M., Flood, I., & Ting, C. J. (1999). Queuing network analysis for waterways with artificial neural networks. *Artificial Intelligence for Engineering Design, Analysis and Manufacturing*, *13*(5), 365–375. doi:10.1017/S0890060499135017

Zillow, A. P. I. (n.d.). Retrieved from http://www.zillow.com/howto/api/APIOverview.htm

Zmud, R., & Lee, J. (2005). Behavioral intention formation in knowledge sharing: Examining the roles of extrinsic motivators, social-psychological forces, and organizational climate. *Management Information Systems Quarterly*, *29*(1), 87–111.

Zografos, K. G., & Madas, M. A. (2006). Development and demonstration for an integrated decision support system for airport performance analysis. *Transportation Research Part C, Emerging Technologies*, *14*(1), 1–17. doi:10.1016/j.trc.2006.04.001

Zulkosky, K. (2009). Self-Efficacy: A Concept Analysis. *Nursing Forum*, *44*(2), 93–102. doi:10.1111/j.1744-6198.2009.00132.x

About the Contributors

Neeta Baporikar is a Professor in the area of Strategic Management and Entrepreneurship, is currently on an academic assignment with Ministry of Higher Education, Sultanate of Oman, as Head, Scientific Research Department, College of Applied Sciences, Salalah. She holds PhD in Management, MBA (Distinction) and Law (Hons.) degrees. With more than a decade of experience in industry, consultancy and training, she made a lateral switch to research and academics in 1993. Apart from this, she is an Accredited Management Teacher, Qualified Trainer, Doctoral Guide and Board Member of Academics and Selection Committee in accredited B-Schools. At University of Pune, she supervises a number of doctoral research students and currently collaborates with colleagues and outside on multidisciplinary research projects in the area strategy, entrepreneurship and management education. Dr. Baporikar is widely traveled across India and abroad on professional and academic assignments to Bhutan, Japan, Bangkok, UAE, Oman etc. Since 1998, her research and writing activities have mainly focused on Strategy, Entrepreneurship and Management Education. Reviewer for international journals, she has to her credit more than 100 research papers, published invited chapters, articles and chaired technical sessions both at national and international conferences. She has authored books in the area of Entrepreneurship, Strategy and Management Education, which are widely read and recommended by leading universities/ institutes in India. Dr. Baporikar has been honoured with "Doctor of Science in Management Studies" by the International University of Contemporary Studies, USA in 2009 and Listed in Marquis Who'sWho in the World 2010.

Ye-Sho Chen received his Ph.D. degree in Operations Research from Purdue University in 1985. He is a Professor of Management Information Systems in the Department of Information Systems and Decision Sciences, E. J. Ourso College of Business, Louisiana State University. He is the Director of Globalization in the College. He also holds the James C. & Cherie H. Flores Professor of MBA Studies #2. He received The Tiger Athletic Foundation Tenured Faculty Teaching Award in 2011 & 2016, Tenured Faculty Teaching Award in 2007, and The Erich Sternberg Foundation Excellence in Teaching Award in 1992. He has published more than 120 papers in journals and conference proceedings. Dr. Chen's major interest of teaching, research, and consulting is to help companies grow globally through the "Flying High, Landing Soft" platform of global entrepreneurship.

Emna Cherif has been a Visiting Research Scholar at Depaul University in the School of Accountancy and MIS. She has been visiting research scholar at University of Illinois at Chicago. She has been a system analyst at Station Electronic Service company. She has a master degree in logistics and e-logistics at National Institute of Industrial Management, Sfax-Tunisia. Her research interest includes e-commerce, logistics, system design, innovation strategies.

Mei-Tai Chu is currently Research Manager at RECCSI, Program Director of Master of Business Information Management and Systems, and Senior Lecturer in the La Trobe Business School at La Trobe University. She has multi-disciplinary background and has over 10 year's industry experience globally. For example, she has been a visiting scholar at NEC Corporation Japan and invited speaker at National University of Singapore. She has worked as a knowledge management consultant for several organizations including public and private sectors such as International Technology Research Institute where she has coached and coordinated 40 Communities of Practices. She has published many good quality journals (e.g. IEEE Transactions in Engineering Management, Expert Systems with Applications and Journal of International Manufacturing) and conference papers in diverse areas such as Knowledge Management, Communities of Practice, Multi-agent Systems, Computational Intelligence, Expert Systems, Technology Management and Human Resource Management.

Dan Ciulin was born in Bucharest, Romania on 4 July 1934. He studied to the Polytechnic School of Bucharest the section radio and telecommunication and obtained his degree in 1959. Then, he worked as researcher at the Institute of Biology and Radiobiology and also as lecturer at the Polytechnic School of Bucharest. In 1980, after 2 years passed as lecturer at Institute of Telecommunication Oran, Algeria, he moved as researcher to the Research Institute Robert Bosch in Lonay, Switzerland. Here he worked in telecommunication, optics and gravitation. Now he is professor at E-I-A (Ecole d'ingénierie Appliquée) in Lausanne. He had published many research papers on electronics, sound and image processing and gravitation and has also a number of patents. His main fields of interest are electronics, sound and image processing, electromagnetic and gravitational fields and time.

Mario J. Donate is Associate Professor of Business Administration at the University of Castilla-La Mancha. He teaches courses on Strategic Management, Entrepreneurship and Knowledge Management at the Faculty of Law and Social Sciences in Ciudad Real, Spain. He obtained his PhD from the University of Castilla-La Mancha in 2006. His research mainly focuses on knowledge management, technological innovation, and corporate social responsibility and he has published a number of papers in specialised journals about these subjects in the last few years.

Jan Fabian Ehmke is an Assistant Professor of Advanced Business Analytics at Freie Universität Berlin, Germany. He received his PhD from the University of Braunschweig in 2011. His research interests include intelligent data analysis and optimization for dynamic and stochastics problems of transportation. Jan Ehmke has published more than 20 scientific articles in international journals such as European Journal of Operational Research, Transportation Research – Part C, Computers & Operations Research and Business Information Systems Engineering.

Renato Ferreira Leitão Azevedo is a PhD Student in Educational Psychology at the University of Illinois at Urbana-Champaign (UIUC). He holds a M.S. in Applied Statistics from UIUC, a M.Sc. in Accounting Education & Research from University of Sao Paulo (USP), Brazil, and B.S. in Information Systems and B.S. in Accounting. He has been a MBA FIPECAFI Instructor for Management Accounting Cases and Business Strategy Games Courses. He was a Visiting Graduate Student at UCLA and Visiting Scholar at Mercer University. He has published scholarly papers and lectured at universities in many countries. He is the author of Accountants: career development, perceptions and their social role" (in Portuguese).

María Isabel González-Ramos is Assistant Professor of Business Administration at the University of Castilla-La Mancha. He teaches courses on Business Administration and Human Resource Management at the Faculty of Law and Social Sciences in Toledo, Spain. He obtained his PhD from the University of Castilla-La Mancha in 2013. His research mainly focuses on the relationship between corporate social responsibility and technological innovation, and knowledge management.

Fátima Guadamillas-Gómez is Professor of Business Administration at the Faculty of Law and Social Sciences in Toledo, Spain. She has a degree in Economics and obtained her PhD from the University of Castilla-La Mancha. She teaches courses at the degree level on strategic and general management and on knowledge management, innovation and strategic management at the MBA and PhD levels. Her research focuses on innovation, knowledge management strategies and factors related to resource sharing and knowledge transfer. Her works have mainly been published in specialised journals and books.

Laura Hellman is a consultant for Altran Deutschland S.A.S. & Co. KG in the field of big data and analytics. In 2015, she received a Master of Science in Business Informatics at Freie Universität Berlin, Germany. Her research interests include intelligent data analytics, supply chain risk management, computational logistics, and predictive asset maintenance.

Sherif Kamel is vice president for information management and professor of management at the American University in Cairo. He was founding dean of the school of business (2009-2014). He led a major repositioning of the school by focusing on entrepreneurship, innovation, leadership and responsible business. During his tenure as dean, he initiated and achieved the EQUIS, AMBA and ACCET accreditations and got the school reaccredited by AACSB joining 70 business school in the world that are known as triple-crowned accredited. He established the Center for Entrepreneurship and Innovation and the university's Venture Lab becoming Egypt's primary university-based incubator. He was associate dean for executive education (2008-2009); director of the Management Center (2002-2008) and director of the Institute of Management Development (2002-2006). Before joining the university, he was director of the Regional IT Institute (1992-2001), and helped establish and manage the training department of the Cabinet of Egypt Information and Decision Support Center (1989-1992). Kamel is an Eisenhower Fellow (2005). He is a board member of the Egyptian American Enterprise Fund (2012-present), a member of the Egypt-US Business Council (2013-present) and a member of the AACSB International Middle East Advisory Council (2015-present). He was a member in the World Bank Knowledge Advisory Commission (2012-2014). He is a founding member of the Internet Society of Egypt and chairs the education committee at AmCham Egypt.

Chuanlan Liu is an associate professor of merchandising in Louisiana State University, and adjunct professor in Central University of Finance and Economics, China. Her research focuses on consumer behavior, brand extension, entrepreneurship, and e-commerce. She published research in peer-reviewed journals including Journal of Business Research, and Journal of Interactive Marketing.

Robert M. Nauss, Founder's Professor of Management Science at the University of Missouri-St. Louis, received his Ph.D. in Operations Research from UCLA (1974). His research interests include algorithmic development for solution of large-scale integer programs. Application areas include bus dispatching, sequencing tow/barges through river locks, municipal bond bidding, and structured design of bond issues for purchase of pools of government guaranteed mortgage-backed securities He has published articles in journals such as Management Science, INFORMS Journal on Computing, European Journal of Operations Research, Journal of the Operational Research Society, Decision Sciences, Interfaces, Computers and Operations Research, Transportation Research, Journal of Banking and Finance, and Financial Management.

Nagla Rizk is Professor of Economics and Founding Director of the Access to Knowledge for Development Center (A2K4D) at the American University in Cairo's School of Business. Her research area is the economics of knowledge, technology and human development with focus on digital platforms, entrepreneurship, intellectual property and business models in the digital economy. She is Faculty Associate at Harvard's Berkman Klein Center for Internet and Society, Affiliated Fellow of Yale Law School's Information Society Project and Affiliated Faculty at Harvard Law School's Copyrightx course. She is also member of the Executive Committee of the prestigious International Economic Association, and the Steering Committee of the Open African Innovation Research Network. At AUC she served as Associate Dean for Graduate Studies and Research at the School of Business and Chair of the Economics Department. She taught at Columbia University, Yale Law School and the University of Toronto.

Jesús David Sánchez de Pablo is Associate Professor of Business Administration at the University of Castilla-La Mancha. He teaches courses on Strategic Management, and Operations Management at the Faculty of Law and Social Sciences in Ciudad Real, Spain. He obtained his PhD from the University of Castilla-La Mancha in 2008. His research mainly focuses on strategic alliances, cooperative agreements, knowledge management, and organizational learning and he has published a number of papers in specialised journals and books about these subjects in the last few years.

L. Douglas Smith is Professor of Management Science and Director of the Center for Business and Industrial Studies (CBIS) at the University of Missouri-St. Louis. He received his Ph.D. in Management Sciences from the University of Minnesota (1972). Smith's articles have appeared in leading journals for decision sciences, finance, and information systems including Decision Sciences, Transportation Research, European Journal of Operational Research, International Journal of Production Research, Naval Research Logistics, Computers and Operations Research, Journal of Banking and Finance, Financial Management, OMEGA, INFOR, Interfaces, MIS Quarterly, Journal of Management Information Systems, and Information and Management. Smith is a former Associate Editor of Decision Sciences and is currently an Associate Editor of The International Journal of Strategic Decision Sciences and the International Journal of Revenue Management.

Ivan Tirado-Cordero, PhD, is an instructional designer, artist, and part-time faculty of inquiry based learning at Quinnipiac University in Hamden, CT. His research focuses on Social Cognitive Theory. Dr. Tirado's interest is to understand how self-efficacy beliefs are formed and modified based on antecedents and former learning experiences and interpretations. This interest emerged from his teaching experience with children, special education students, teenagers, adults, and senior citizens. His teaching experience includes art instruction (drawing, sculpting, and painting), computer instruction, corporate training, and academic advising. Future research interests include the inclusion of the affective and spiritual domains, as well as a broader view of the physical domain beyond psychomotor skills in triadic reciprocal determinism, and the use of art and creativity as a tool to increase and improve self-efficacy beliefs in patients with traumatic experiences.

Nicolas A. Valcik is currently the Director of Institutional Research for West Virginia University. Dr. Valcik was previously an Associate Director for the Office of Strategic Planning and Analysis at UTD. Dr. Valcik has previously worked municipalities as well as NORTEL Networks. Dr. Valcik has earned an Associate's Degree in Political Science from Collin County Community College (1994), a Bachelor's Degree in Interdisciplinary Studies from UTD (1994), a Master's Degree in Public Affairs from UTD (1996) and a Ph.D. in Public Affairs from UTD (2005). He has authored and edited ten books in regard to institutional research for higher education, homeland security, and is currently co-authoring a Non-Profit Organization case study book with Ted Benavides and Kim Scruton for the ASPA series through Taylor and Francis – CRC Press. In addition Dr. Valcik has authored 19 articles and chapters as well as obtaining three software copyrights and a provisional patent.

Roumen Vragov specializes in the study of digital economic systems: auctions, exchanges, negotiation & prediction markets. He received his PhD in Economic Systems Design with minor in Management of Information Systems at the University of Arizona. Prof. Vragov has published articles in scientific journals and has presented his research at national and international conferences. He has participated in several consulting projects for businesses and government agencies including FCC, Microsoft, and Epic Technologies, and has received several research grants in support of his studies. His current research interests are Sponsored search advertising and digital asset exchanges. Dr. Vragov has taught at several public and private Universities in the United States for 15 years with an emphasis on interactive learning. He is also the founder of "The Right Incentive LLC", a business consulting company.

Liang Xu is a doctoral candidate in Logistics and Supply Chain Management at University of Missouri – St. Louis. He has more than seven years of working experiences at NR Electric, a leading solution provider for electric generation, transmission, and distribution. He is a student member of Council of Supply Chain Management Professionals and Decision Science Institute. Liang Xu's research interests include supply chain risk management, computational logistics, business process simulation, management sciences, and data analytics.

Qingfeng Zeng is currently an associate professor at Shanghai University of Finance & Economics (SUFE) in Shanghai, China. He earned his PhD degree in Information Systems from Fudan University in China in 2005, and M.S. in Information Systems from Yunnan University in 2002, and B.S. in Applied Mathematics from Xiangtan University in 1999. His current research interests focus on E-business transformation of tradition enterprises, online brand management and franchising, he has already published more than 20 papers in conferences and journals in recent years. He has also been actively involved in management consulting projects for Shanghai municipal government and a variety of companies.

Juan Zhang is a PH.D. student in Logistics and Supply Chain Management at University of Missouri - St. Louis. Currently, she is focusing on developing strategic models for the design of truck - drone hybrid delivery systems. Her research interests include mathematical modeling and simulation in logistics and transportation systems.

Index

K

L

M

N

O

P

R

S

T

Printed in the United States
By Bookmasters